The Beginner's Guide

to the

C4 Engine

James Brady

A. A. Cruz

James Huntsman

David Vasquez

Terathon Software LLC

Roseville, CA

The Beginner's Guide to the C4 Engine
Second Edition

Published by Terathon Software LLC
ISBN-13: 978-0-9858117-1-6

http://www.terathon.com/

To Heidi, Seana, and Patrick.
—James Brady

To Sheryll,
for supporting my every endeavor and being
eternally patient with my plans for world domination.
—A.A.Cruz

To Aiza, Chris, and Monica.
—David Vasquez

Foreword

At the time of this writing, it has been just over one year since the C4 Engine was made available to independent game developers. When the engine was first released in May 2005, there was literally no community to speak of, but a decent-sized group of recurring visitors to our online forums quickly sprang from the internet. It was not long before an active community developed, and I was happy to see that users of C4 tended to be very professional and were frequently willing to exert a surprising amount of effort to help others. Among those users were the authors of this book.

The four names on the title page are those of people who have shown true dedication to sharing their knowledge of the C4 Engine by taking the time to write this book. They have been long-time members of the C4 community and have made significant contributions in the form of documentation and add-on tools. These authors have independently assembled this book with the goal of providing a reference that makes learning C4 easier, and I'm confident that the experience they have consolidated herein will prove useful to beginners and advanced users alike.

Eric Lengyel, Ph.D.
Creator of the C4 Engine

Contents

Introduction

It's easy when you know how.

As a newcomer making your first game with the C4 Engine, the task can appear daunting. Without a guide to show the way, it is easy to get lost and become frustrated. The purpose of the Guide is to provide a helping hand, by highlighting essential information, and outlining a sequence of steps that will help you get started with your first simple game projects using the C4 Engine.

Who Should Read the Guide?

The *Guide* is intended for newcomers to the C4 Engine, who are ready to get started with their first games. It is not primarily intended for people who have already made significant progress with the engine, nor does it pretend to be a guide to designing and programming 3D games in general. And while we do provide information on textures and materials, the *Guide* is not going to turn you into a game artist!

Our focus is on how to use the C4 Engine tool set, and how to begin writing applications and games using the C4 Engine Application Programming Interface (API), at a beginner's level. Having said all that, there are nuggets of information within the *Guide* that even the experienced user may find of use.

To get started with the C4 Engine, you will need the following:

1 A computer that has either an Nvidia graphics card (GeForce 6600 or better), an AMD graphics card (Radeon HD 2600 or better), or an Intel onboard video card (Sandy Bridge or better).

2 Visual C++ 2010 Express Edition for Windows [MSFT10]. Although the *Guide* focuses on using the C4 Engine on Windows, a Mac OS X version of the C4 Engine is available that can be built using Xcode 4 [APPL12], and a Linux version of the C4 Engine is also available.

3 C++ know-how. The C4 Engine is written in C++, and your C4 Engine-based applications and games will also be written in C++, so you'll at least need to know basic C++. You don't need to be an expert C++ programmer—the C4 Engine is a great tool to use if you want to improve your C++ skills. Beginning C++ programmers can refer to Appendix A, "Learning C++ with the C4 Engine" to better understand some of the C++ constructs that are used in the context of C4 Engine applications.

4 Mathematics know-how. Basic linear algebra, including vectors and matrices. See Chapter 10, "Essential Mathematics" for a refresher.

5 A license for the C4 Engine is highly recommended. In order to write and compile your own games—and to get the most out of Part IV • The Games—you'll need access to the C4 Engine source code.

About the C4 Engine Wiki

As we mentioned in the preface and the acknowledgments, we are not the first authors to lend a helping hand to other users of the C4 Engine. The C4 Engine Wiki has been a long-time source of detailed reference information about many aspects of the C4 Engine, and it is regularly updated with late-breaking details about the most recent build of the C4 Engine.

The *Guide* is not a replacement for the C4 Engine Wiki, and we encourage you to use both resources as you learn more about the C4 Engine. Please see "Overview of the C4 Engine Wiki" in Chapter 1, "What is the C4 Engine?", for a more detailed overview of the C4 Engine Wiki.

How much math do I need to know?

You may be thinking, "Hey, I'm here to write games, not to learn mathematics. Why do I need to know so much math to write a game using C4?"

To write games and applications with the C4 Engine, you don't need to learn all that much mathematics. If you were going to write the game engine itself, then you would need a whole lot more! Or, if you wanted to understand in depth how the C4 Engine itself works, then you would also need to learn all that math. Eric Lengyel has written a book, *Mathematics for 3D Game Programming and*

Computer Graphics [LENG11], that contains that level of detail, and we recommend it for further reading (see the References section at the back of the *Guide* for more useful books).

In this book, we will only scratch the surface, and describe a very small subset of 3D mathematics that covers the essential basics needed by a writer of applications based on the C4 Engine. For example, we think you'll need to have at least a basic understanding of vectors and matrices for many of the tasks you'll want to accomplish with the C4 Engine. Once you are comfortable with at least these basic mathematical topics, you will have much greater proficiency in the proper use of the the C4 Engine.

As you become more proficient as a user of the C4 Engine, you will begin to use parts of the API which will probably inspire you to delve deeper into the mathematics behind the C4 Engine, and we encourage you to do so.

How the Guide Is Organized

Part I • Getting Started introduces the C4 Engine and explains how to install the engine and demo game source code, configure your IDE, and run the various tutorials and demos. It also provides an overview of the C4 Engine Wiki.

Part II • Designing Worlds guides the reader through the **World Editor** tool, starting with the creation of a simple world, and then showing how to create worlds filled with terrain and water. It then goes on to present more world editor features, and a detailed presentation of materials and textures.

Part III • Under the Hood delves into basic game programming theory and the essential mathematics you will need to understand to work with quantities such as vectors and matrices.

Part IV • The Games presents a series of simple game tutorials, with explanations of how each game is implemented. It then presents a chapter with an RTS game constructed completely from scratch.

The appendices cover topics such as learning C++ with the C4 Engine, using Blender to prepare artwork for use with the C4 Engine, and a FAQ containing a collection of questions that are commonly asked on the C4 Engine forum. We have also included a detailed diagram of the C4 Engine architecture, suitable for printing and hanging on your wall.

About Keyboard Shortcuts

When referring to menu commands, the *Guide* gives the name of the pull-down menu, followed by an angle bracket separator (>), and then the name of the menu command. The keyboard shortcut is often given in parenthesis, and it is valid on Windows and Linux. On Mac OS X, the control key in any shortcut should be replaced by the command key. For example, the **Open World** menu command in the **Tools** pull-down menu, which has the keyboard shortcut of Control-O on Windows or Linux and Command-O on Mac OS X, is shown as **Tools > Open World (Ctrl-O)**.

Keywords

Throughout the text, the *Guide* uses distinct typographic styles to highlight certain types of keywords.

User-typed text, type and variable names, names of specific files, and source code listings, all appear in a mono-spaced typeface like this:

`score += 10;`   `MyFirstMaterial`   `SimpleCar.cpp`   `Vector3D`

Links to web sites and other parts of the *Guide*, such as glossary entries, appear as lightly underlined, blue hyperlinks, in bold sans-serif type:

http://www.terathon.com/   ambient occlusion

Names for resource data, such as source images, textures, and sounds, as well as directory paths to those resources, appear in dark green, bold, sans-serif type:

MyWorld   **<C4>/Data/Tutorials/**

The title of a third-party publication and other emphasized text appears in italicized type:

Defining a Custom Controller   an *emphasized* word

The name of a user interface element, such as a window, dialog, or control setting, appears in black, bold sans-serif type:

The **Command Console** window. The **Node Info** dialog.

Part I

Getting Started

1

What is the C4 Engine?

The C4 Engine is a 3D game engine that can be used to create next-generation, visually rich, real-time, interactive computer applications. Compared to other independent game engines currently on the market, the C4 Engine has one of the most comprehensive feature sets available.

The Big Picture

The C4 Engine is rapidly evolving. Terathon Software frequently releases builds with new features that keep the C4 Engine on the cutting edge of the most advanced technology available to the game industry.

> **LATEST FEATURE LIST**
> Check out C4 Engine Features[1] for the full, up-to-date feature list.

To enable the creation of games or other interactive applications, the C4 Engine provides several layers of functionality. Here's a quick, general look at what the C4 Engine has to offer across a broad range of levels and disciplines, from programmer, to designer, to artist:

1 On the surface, the C4 Engine has a **World Editor** tool which allows you to build your own levels, a visual scripting tool that allows you to create your

[1] http://www.terathon.com/c4engine/features.php

own behaviors, and tools for importing your own resources, such as models, animations, textures, sounds, and text.

2. Digging a little deeper, the C4 Engine API allows you to create your own games without having to dive into the details of how the underlying system works. At this level, programmers can create custom behaviors, properties, and scripts that can then be used in the **World Editor** tool for easy drag-and-drop game building.
3. Programmers can easily extend the features of the **World Editor** tool, with custom plug-ins for making development more efficient and more specific to your own projects.
4. At the lowest level, standard and professional C4 Engine licensees have access to the full source code for the engine and its tools, allowing you to make custom modifications, and making it easier to test and debug your game by letting you know what's going on behind the scenes.

> **HEAD-TO-HEAD COMPARISONS**
> If you'd like to compare the C4 Engine feature set against some other leading independent game engines out there, check out the engines database at devmaster.net.[2]

The C4 Engine Does Not Do Your Laundry

"It looks like C4 is quite the all-around game engine for what I need to get my project done." Before we convince you that the C4 Engine can also make you toast, wash your dishes, and do your laundry, let's put the C4 Engine into perspective with other game development methods:

1. The C4 Engine is not a game that is intended to be modified. "What? I can't modify anything?" No, that's not what we mean. We mean that the C4 Engine is not a mod tool for an existing game. However, nobody is stopping you from taking the demo game and turning it into your own game. But if you want to do more than simply swapping out graphics and sound and creating scripts for different game play mechanics, you'll have to do some programming in C++.
2. The C4 Engine is not a point-and-click game authoring system. Most game authoring systems make it easy to import graphics and sound, and to build

[2] http://devmaster.net/devdb/engines

game logic—usually through drag-and-drop graphical user interfaces and simple scripts—but with a minimal amount of control. The C4 Engine goes beyond point-and-click to provide absolute control, with full source code, and the tools that were built from that source code are straightforward and extremely flexible.

3 On the opposite end of the spectrum, the C4 Engine is not a group of independent code libraries. The many components of the C4 Engine are cleanly separated so you can clearly understand the various systems it provides, but all of these components are integrated. Also, although the C4 Engine systems are integrated, application developers are never forced into using all of them. If you decide that you do not need multi- player support in your game, don't include it. If you decide that you want your application to focus on audio-only, then that's possible too. Do you want your game to be two-dimensional? That's possible too! You can even add a third-party physics or sound system.

Overview of the C4 Engine Wiki

You may be asking—what about the C4 Engine Wiki?[3] Can't I learn all of this by reading the Wiki? The answer to that is yes, the C4 Engine Wiki is an extremely useful resource when it comes to learning what the C4 Engine is and how to begin using it. It has an "official" section, which contains information which has been written, or at least carefully reviewed for accuracy, by Terathon Software. The Official Documentation section is split into several subsections including:

1 *General Reference*

This is the place to go when you first start out with the C4 Engine. There are clear instructions here on how to install and build the C4 Engine , as well as information on third-party tools and other resources that will be useful for anyone using the C4 Engine.

2 *Programming Topics*

When you are ready to write your first applications with the C4 Engine, read the topics in this section first. Key C4 Engine programming concepts—including the scene graph, nodes, models, objects, controllers, and proper-

[3] http://www.terathon.com/wiki/index.php/Main_Page

ties—are all clearly explained here, at a high level. There are also topics on how the C4 Engine helps you to detect memory leaks, how to use the Command Console window, string tables, and sound.

Of particular significance, a tutorial is provided that explains how to define a custom Controller. Controllers are needed for any game object whose behavior (or motion) changes over time. For the player or your NPCs (Non-Player Characters) to move, they will need a controller. To fire bullets, rockets and other projectiles, again, you will need a controller. Understanding controllers is key to working with the C4 Engine, so this tutorial is a must.

Finally, there are two heavily commented simple application examples called *SimpleBall* and *SimpleChar*, that provide essential reading for the C4 Engine beginner.

3 *World Editor*

Here you will find descriptions for each of the tools shipped with the C4 Engine, including the all important World Editor. Each of the menus and other interactive items within the World Editor is described here.

4 *Engine Concepts*

Here you will find more details on some key C4 Engine concepts including the various passes in The C4 Rendering Pipeline, Geometry Internals, Lights and Shadows, Fog Spaces, Motion Blur, Creating a GUI Skin, and Shaders.

The Official Documentation section also includes subsections on Shaders, Scripting, Terrain, Panels, Models, Materials, Fonts and Pack Files. Below the Official Documentation section, there is a section called User-Contributed References and Tutorials which contains information contributed and maintained by the C4 Engine community. There are some real gems in here, and the authors of the Guide have also contributed to some of this material. This section is also divided into several sub-sections including:

1 *Coding and Games*

There are simple programming examples here, such as Introduction—Hello World, but there are also examples of how to work with User Input as well as a section of useful code snippets. In the Games subsection, there is an RTS tutorial, which is one of the more in-depth user-contributed tutorials and it explains how to create a C4 Engine game from scratch. This tutorial has been included in the Guide in a slightly modified and extended form in Part IV •

The Games. There is also a series of tutorials called the "Pong Series" as well as a set of "Beginner Game Tutorials".

2 *Game Editing*

We have included a modified and extended version of the Creating a Basic World tutorial in Chapter 4, "Creating a Simple World".

3 *Art*

Here you'll find examples on how to use various tools to create and improve your artwork. Hey, it might even help programmers finally make some decent art for a change!

4 *Advanced Programming and Networking*

These sections discuss some more advanced topics, such as networking, serialization, and Pathfinding.

As a recommended "path" through the C4 Engine Wiki to those just starting with the C4 Engine, begin with the installation and building instructions, and then read the Programming Introduction to the C4 Engine article to get a feel for the C4 Engine concepts.

Next, have a look at the article Models, Controllers, Properties, since you may be used to these terms from other engines. It's important to understand that the use of those terms within the C4 Engine may be quite different from what you might be used if you have worked with other engines. Both the Guide and the C4 Engine Wiki provide a full glossary of terms for this reason.

To create some content for your games, we recommend you use our modified and extended version of the Creating a Basic World tutorial, in Chapter 4, "Creating a Simple World". It will help you get started with using the **World Editor** tool to produce your first results.

When you're ready to program your own applications, start with the Hello World tutorial and then read the comments in the *SimpleBall* and *SimpleChar* tutorials. The next must-read article for programmers to cover is the Defining a Custom Controller tutorial in the Official Documentation section.

On the homepage,[4] you'll find links to News, Features, Screenshots, a high-level FAQ (which in turn links to a more technical FAQ), Licensing, and Download.

The homepage and main C4 Engine Wiki page also both provide a link to the Support Forums, where many C4 Engine licensees are happy to take the time to

---

[4] http://www.terathon.com/c4engine/index.php

answer your questions. It can save a lot of time to read what is on the C4 Engine Wiki (and the *Guide*) first, before asking the first questions that pop into your head. You can also search through the forums to see if your question has already been asked and answered. The chances are high that the Wiki or previous forum topics will be able to help you out most of the time. But if not, then go ahead and ask in the Beginners section.

Besides providing links to Release Notes and a Bug Tracker, the main C4 Engine Wiki page also links to the API Documentation. You can search there for details on the C4 Engine classes, members and methods. We find it particularly useful to look at the class hierarchies. Click on the link to the API Documentation, and then go ahead and type `hierarchy` into the search box. You'll see that most class hierarchies are covered. As an example, click on the `Controller` hierarchy, and you will find a very helpful graphic, demonstrating how the various Controller classes and subclasses relate to one another.

Finally, note also that there is even more useful information tucked away in a section of the C4 Engine Wiki called the Sandbox. You can access that area through a link in the "navigation" box on the left side of any Wiki page. There you will find tutorials which are very much a work in progress, and which haven't yet reached a level of completeness to warrant promotion to the main C4 Engine Wiki page. They nonetheless do contain some gems, and it is worth checking that section out from time to time for a preview of things to come.

"OK, well why didn't you tell me all this before I bought this book?," we hear you say, "It sounds like the wiki has all that I need to start writing applications with C4! Why do I need this book then?"

As mentioned in the opening paragraphs, our personal experiences with learning to use the C4 Engine was that, while the C4 Engine Wiki and the forums were immensely helpful and informative, we still found it very difficult to make progress on our own first games. Something was missing. We created the Guide to help fill that gap, by providing a path through the most relevant information, and by providing explained set of game tutorials developed for the C4 Engine.

2

Installation

Unzipping

After downloading the three zip files, `Code.zip`, `Data.zip`, and `Binaries.zip`, from the C4 Engine Licensed Account[1] page, we recommend that beginners unzip the contents of all three zip files into the same target directory. This works out well for new users, because for programming, the Visual Studio project files that are included in `Data.zip` file contain references to relative paths for libraries and header files in `Code.zip` that are conveniently set up for you if you unzip them like this. Also, keep in mind that it is not necessary to unzip the pre-built binary files contained in `Binaries.zip` if you are planning to compile all the source code yourself. However, it's a good idea to at least try out the prebuilt binaries, just to make sure that you can run `C4Engine.exe` on your machine.

WHAT'S THE DIFFERENCE BETWEEN CODE AND BINARIES?

Non-programmers may not be familiar with the term "binaries", which is programmer's jargon for the executable files and the files that the executable needs to run. They're referred to as "binaries" because they are generated by compiling source code to create files that are formatted in binary (zeros and ones).

[1] https://www.terathon.com/c4engine/reg/index.php

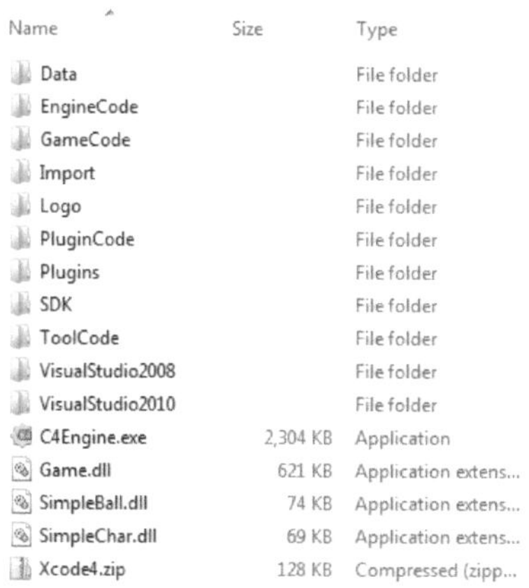

Figure 2-1. The C4 Engine directory structure.

The C4 Engine Directory Structure

Now that the C4 Engine is installed, let's take a look at its directory structure. Open the C4 Engine root directory (the Guide will also refer to the C4 Engine root directory as <C4>). The root directory should appear as shown in Figure 2-1.

The C4 root directory contains the executable file (`C4Engine.exe`), three dynamic link libraries (`Game.dll`, `SimpleBall.dll`, and `SimpleChar.dll`), and several subdirectories, as shown in Figure 2-2. By default, launching `C4Engine.exe` starts up the demo game. You can try it now by double-clicking on `C4Engine.exe`. The DLL files are applications that are run by `C4Engine.exe`. All the logic in the demo game is contained in `Game.dll`. Similarly, `SimpleBall.dll` and `SimpleChar.dll` are applications launched via `C4Engine.exe`, but are not launched by default. `Xcode4.zip` and `C4.app.zip` contain the necessary files for Mac development, but Mac setup is not covered in this guide.

So, what's in the subdirectories?

The Code and Project Directories

The EngineCode, GameCode, PluginCode, and ToolCode subdirectories are shown in Figure 2-3, and they contain, you guessed it, source code!

- EngineCode contains all of the source code used to compile `C4Engine.exe`.

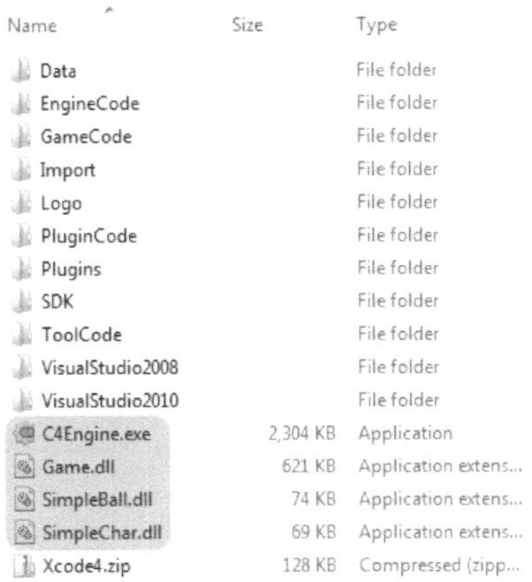

Figure 2-2. The C4 executable and game extensions.

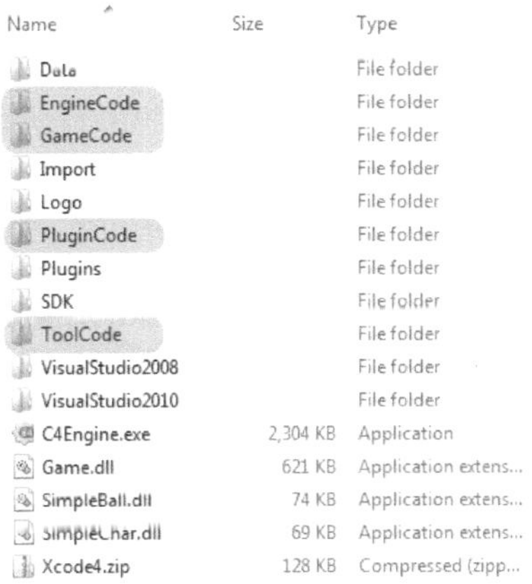

Figure 2-3. The Code and Project directories.

- GameCode contains all of the source code used to compile `Game.dll`, `SimpleBall.dll`, and `SimpleChar.dll`.
- PluginCode contains all source code used for the plugins in the Plugins directory (the Plugins directory contains more DLLs that are loaded by the executable).

Table 2-1. C4 source code directories and the resulting binaries.

Source Code Directory	Binary Output
EngineCode	`C4Engine.exe`
GameCode	`Game.dll`, `SimpleBall.dll`, and `SimpleChar.dll`
ToolCode	`Plugins\Tools\*.dll`
PluginCode	`Plugins\*.dll`

- ToolCode contains the source code for tools like the **World Editor**, **Movie Player**, and the resource importers, which are also DLLs contained in the Plugins directory.

Table 2-1 shows the relationship between the directories that contain source code and the binary files that result from compiling them.

You will notice two Visual Studio directories: VisualStudio2008 and VisualStudio2010. Depending on which version of the Visual Studio IDE you are using, you will use either one or the other. Both of these directories contain the Solution file `C4.sln` that organizes and links to all of the Project files that reside in each of the project subdirectories below it, as shown in Figure 2-4. Custom project directories can be added by programmers during development of their own games and add-ons.

That's a lot of directories and files to keep track of, but as a programmer, you'll usually only be working in just a few directories at a time.

The Data and Import Directories

The Data directory is where all game resources (images, movies, sounds, geometry, animation, text, etc.) are contained. The Import directory goes hand in hand with the Data directory, in that files from the Import directory are meant to be converted into the C4 Engine-equivalent file types in the Data directory. These directories will be covered in greater detail in the next section. These are the directories that the artists and designers would work with.

The Other Directories

The remaining directories are Logo and SDK. The Logo directory contains image files for the C4 Engine logo and the SDK directory contains libraries required by the C4 Engine during compile time and do not ever need to be modified.

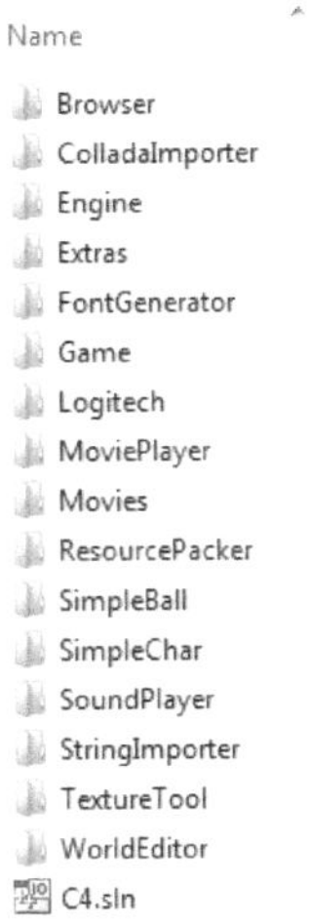

Figure 2-4. The project directories in the VisualStudio2010/C4/ directory.

Table 2-2 surveys all of the directories in the C4 root directory and their contents. You will notice a trend that generally, programmers will be working with the files contained in the Code directories and artists will generally be working with the Import and Data directories.

Understanding the C4 Virtual File System

Working with the Import and Data Directories

The C4 Engine uses a virtual file system which adds a lot of flexibility and freedom with setting up directories for your own project files. However, it has also become a subtle challenge to learn for newcomers so we will spend some time describing it here.

At the Top

The term *virtual file system* is used to describe the contents of the <C4>/Data/ directory. The top-level sub-directories that are contained immediately in the Data directory are considered as a single *virtual directory*, any part of which can be processed by the **Resource Packer** tool into a single pack file. Pack files can be accessed as if their contents are still in an open directory, but they make it much

Table 2-2. Summary of the C4 Engine directory structure.

Discipline	Directory	Contents
Engineering	EngineCode	All source code used to compile `C4Engine.exe`.
	GameCode	All source code for `Game.dll`.
	PluginCode	All source code for the plugins in the Plugins directory.
	ToolCode	All source code for tools like the **World Editor**, **Movie Player**, and the resource importers, which are also DLLs contained in the Plugins directory.
	TutorialCode	Source code for SimpleBall and SimpleChar tutorial projects.
	Plugins	All the DLL plugins compiled from PluginCode and ToolCode. Custom plugins would also go into this directory.
	VisualStudio2008 or VisualStudio2010	The solution file `C4.sln` that contains all of the Project files that reside in each of the subdirectories below it.
	SDK	Compile-time libraries.
Art & Design	Data	All content loaded from C4 applications.
	Import	All resources that are to be imported into the Data directory.
Splash / Marketing	Logo	C4 Engine logo Photoshop files.

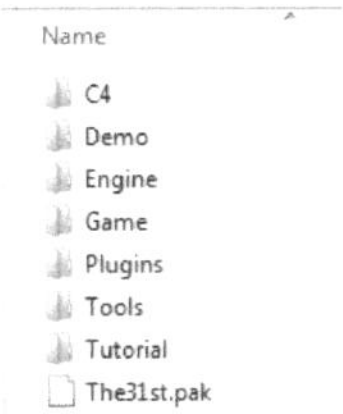

Figure 2-5. Contents of the <C4>/Data/ directory.

easier to manage and deliver any number of assets as a single file, while providing a method of concealment to prevent external tampering with your contents.

Take a look at the contents of the Data directory that comes with the build, as shown in Figure 2-5.

This directory structure keeps C4 Engine data separate from Demo game data. You can add your own subdirectories to this directory structure to keep your work separate from the C4 Engine build content, and to organize data for multiple projects. You can also add a subdirectory for textures and models that are shared between projects. Also notice the `The31st.pak` file. This was pregenerated by using the previously-mentioned **Resource Packer** tool, which is available through the console.

Example Directory Structure

Each top-level subdirectory can contain any number of directories and files in any directory hierarchy you require for your projects. Figure 2-6 shows an example structure that you could use.

In this example, the subdirectories Common, MyProject, and Prototype1 are each treated as if they are actually top-level directories, or as a "package". Notice that each of these top-level directories contains subdirectories for holding custom models and textures. Just keep in mind that there is no hard and fast rule for how your directory structure should be laid out. You can set up your directory hierarchy in any way you like, with two exceptions:

Do Not Put Files Directly in the Data Directory

Do not put any files directly into the Data directory! If you do, the files will not be usable by the C4 Engine. Instead, be sure that all of your data files reside in at least one subdirectory below the Data directory. Only top-level directories and pack files are contained directly underneath the Data directory.

Figure 2-6. Example directory structure.

Path and File Name Collision

The other exception is that since the top level subdirectories are considered part of the same virtual file system, it is possible that two different directories can each contain a file with the same file name. For example, consider the two files:

```
<C4>/Data/MyProject/Textures/stucco.tex
<C4>/Data/Prototype1/Textures/stucco.tex
```

A file with the name `stucco.tex` (which may or may not have the same image) exists in two locations, with the only difference being the top-level directories, MyProject or Prototype1. This will result in a name collision and will result in possibly unexpected behavior. Just make sure that your directories and file names have no file path and file name collisions, and everything should be cool.

Setting Up Your Import Directory

If you plan on importing your own resources to use with the C4 Engine (which we imagine you will), there is no doubt that you will be working with the <C4>/Import/ directory. This is the directory in which you will put your raw texture map files, 3D geometry and animation files, sound files, etc., that need to be converted to their corresponding C4 Engine-specific file formats. To make your development life with the C4 Engine easier, it is best to set up your Import directory structure identically to your Data directory structure.

We'll see the reason for this logic later on when we import textures, geometry, and animation into the C4 Engine. Again, this is not a hard and fast rule. It's merely a recommendation for saving you from some headaches down the road when development gets more involved.

Configuration Files

There is one more thing that needs mentioning before we close out the chapter. There is a configuration file contained in the <C4>/Data/Engine/ directory named `input.cfg`.

The release notes of C4 version 2.0 state:

> Files that are written by the engine, such as configuration files, the log, and saved games, are now stored in special directories designated by the operating system as places where these kinds of files should be stored. Under Windows, the configuration files `engine.cfg` and `input.cfg` are stored in the user's roaming application data directory, and the `C4Log.html` file is stored in the user's non-roaming application data directory. Saved games and screenshots are stored in the user's documents directory. In all cases, the files are stored in a subdirectory having the name of the application. Under Mac OS X, all of these files are stored in the `~/Library/Application Support/<application name>/` directory.

This means that if your game (or the demo game, for instance) changes any settings (e.g., video or audio settings), they will be saved to your operating system's data directory as specified above. Thus, the `input.cfg` file contained in <C4>/Data/Engine/ is simply a default file, in the case that the file has not yet been created in the operating system's data directory. So, if you notice that your changes in `engine.cfg` or `input.cfg` in <C4>/Data/Engine/ are not making a difference, check in your operating system's special data directories to see if they have been overridden.

Next Steps

We've taken a quick look at what a C4 Engine build contains, and where files relevant to programmers, artists, and level designers reside in the build. Familiarizing yourself with the directory structure of the C4 Engine build will help you to understand how all the files work together and how your changes affect other parts of your project.

Let's move on to compiling the C4 Engine and running games and tools from that compiled code.

3

First Steps with the C4 Engine

Your first steps with the C4 Engine will be in exploring what the engine has to offer. To do this, we will build the engine and the existing game applications that use the engine, and then we will run them to make sure everything works. This chapter will also explain what is going on when you compile and link the C4 Engine, and why the project properties are set the way they are.

Setting Up the IDE

On Windows, building the C4 Engine and your game requires the Visual C++ 2008 or Visual C++ 2010 IDE (Integrated Development Environment). Here, we'll cover the setup for Visual C++ 2010 Express. Once you have downloaded and installed the IDE, open up `C4.sln` in the <C4>/VisualStudio2010/ directory. The C4 Engine projects refer to your most current installation of DirectX. You can verify this by right-clicking the Engine project in the **Solution Explorer** panel and choosing **Properties**. In the **Engine Property Pages** dialog, under the **Configuration Properties** group, the **VC++ Directories** subgroup will show the Include and Library Directories using the `$(DXSDK_DIR)` macro, as seen in Figure 3-1.

Next, simply choose **Build > Build Solution** to build the `C4Engine.exe` executable, which will also build the supporting dynamic libraries (DLLs) that are shipped together with the C4 Engine.

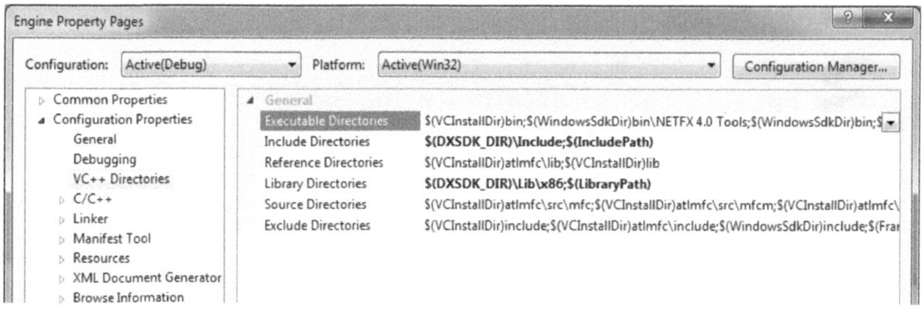

Figure 3-1. The C4 Engine projects use the `$(DXSDK_DIR)` macro to refer to your most current installation of DirectX.

Building the solution may take a while if you haven't previously compiled any of the projects before, so you may have to be a little patient. The Engine project typically only needs to be compiled once, so after building all of the projects for the first time, subsequent compile times will be significantly shorter.

Don't Forget to Set the Working Directory!

Before you run the debugger on your project for the first time within Visual C++, set the **Working Directory** as follows:

1. Right-click the Engine project in the **Solution Explorer** panel and choose **Properties**.
2. In the **Engine Property Pages** dialog, under the **Configuration Properties** group, select the **Debugging** subgroup.
3. As shown in Figure 3-2, set the **Working Directory** value to "`..\..\..`".

Taking the Engine for a Spin

After successfully completing the build, Visual Studio will show a console indicating that there are no errors or warnings. You are then ready to start up C4, and explore the demos delivered with the C4 Engine. You can either start from within Visual Studio by choosing **Debug > Start Debugging (F5)**, or in Windows Explorer, you can navigate to the `C4Engine.exe` file and run it from there.

Once the C4 Engine starts up, you will be greeted by a menu of options. Click **Start New Game** and you will be presented with a selection of demo worlds, as shown in Figure 3-3. Go ahead and try out each of the demo worlds.

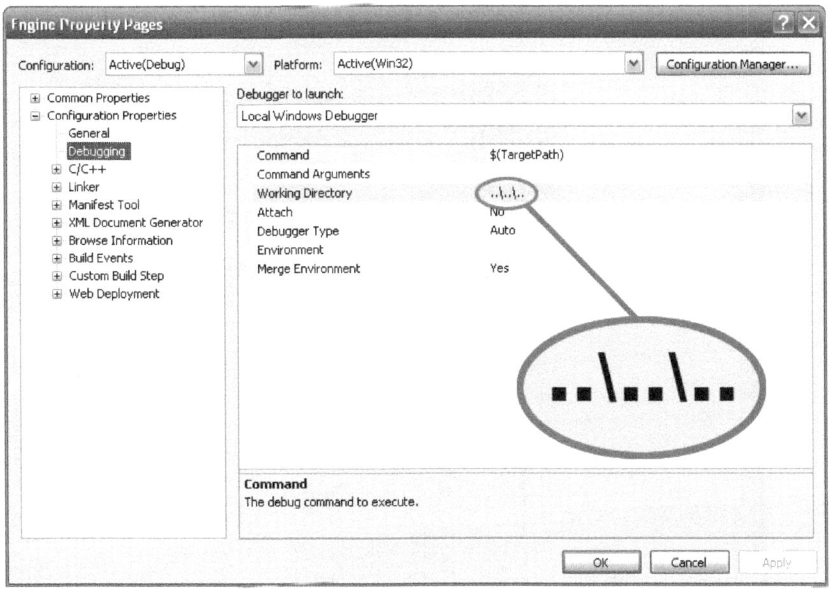

Figure 3-2. The **Working Directory** setting allows the debugger to find the files to debug, which are located three directories above the Engine.vcxproj Visual Studio project file.

> **LOCALIZED KEYBOARD SHORTCUTS**
> For non English keyboards, you will need to edit the player controls. For example, the German keyboard does not recognize the key name space, which is the preset shortcut for jumping. On the German keyboard, the key is named `LEER`, and in Spanish it is named `ESPACE`. In the **Control Settings** window, click the **Up / Jump** action and press the space key to set the shortcut. Key bindings are saved in the input.cfg text file, located in the user's roaming application files directory (<User>/AppData/Roaming/C4 Engine).

SimpleBall

Once you have experimented with the demo game, quit C4 and navigate to the directory <C4>/Data/Game/. There you will find a file called `game.cfg`. Edit that file with any text editor (Notepad or WordPad will do), change the value of the variable called `$gameModuleName` from `"Game"` to `"SimpleBall"` as follows, and save the file.

Figure 3-3. The **Start New Game** window shows the demo worlds that ship with the C4 Engine.

```
$gameModuleName = "SimpleBall";
```

This variable tells the engine which application to load. It must be the name of a DLL which is in the same directory as the `C4Engine.exe` file. You will notice that there are three DLLs in that directory after you compile the C4 solution, namely `Game.dll`, `SimpleBall.dll`, and `SimpleChar.dll`. The `Game.dll` file contains the compiled code for the demo application, whereas `SimpleBall.dll` and `SimpleChar.dll` contain the compiled code for the tutorial applications, that show how to start building your own projects from scratch.

GAME DLLS VS WORLDS

Each of the "games" listed in the **Start New Game** window (Lost Cemetery, Haunted Arena, etc.,) uses the same code in the DLL named Game. The code and the behavior of the game objects is the same, but the game world is different in each case. Other DLLs, such as SimpleBall, provide different game behaviors, even if you use the same world file.

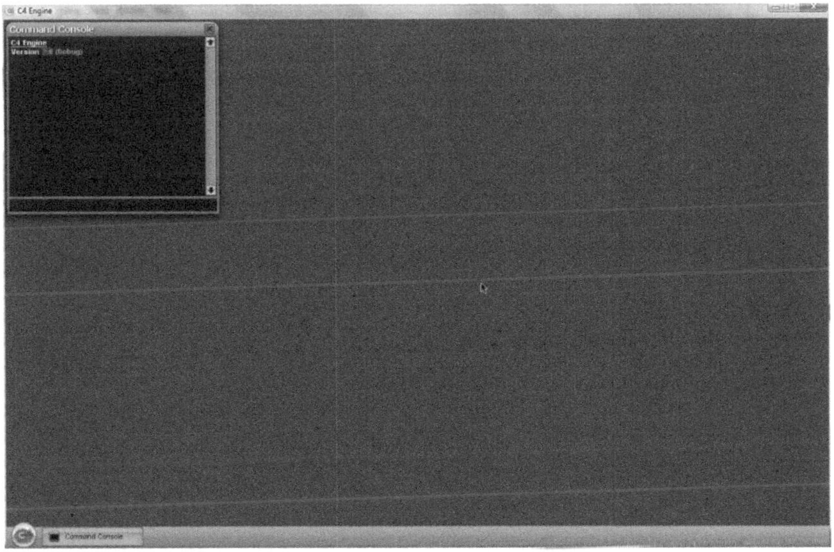

Figure 3-4. The **Command Console** window.

To test the *SimpleBall* application, launch C4 again, now that `$gameModuleName` has been changed to the value `SimpleBall`. This time you will be greeted with a simple dialog. The menu we saw above was part of the `Game.dll` application, so it is not available to the *SimpleBall* application. Simply click on the Start button to try it out.

To stop the application, do the following:

1. Find and press the **tilde/grave** key, the one just above the tab key. It is ‘`’ on an English keyboard, and ‘^’ on a German keyboard.

2. You should now see the **Tools** menu and the **Command Console** window as shown in Figure 3-4. Type `unload` into the **Console** window to tell the engine to unload the *SimpleBall* application.

3. Next, to open a tutorial world, choose **C4 Button > Open World (Ctrl-O)**. The tutorial worlds are located in the directory Tutorial/world/. The world that is designed for the *SimpleBall* application is named, you guessed it, SimpleBall, and it is shown in Figure 3-5.

The **World Editor** will be explained in Part II • Designing Worlds. For now, just be aware that the editor allows you to construct a “world” for your application, including lights, cameras, effects, geometry, and much more. The circled

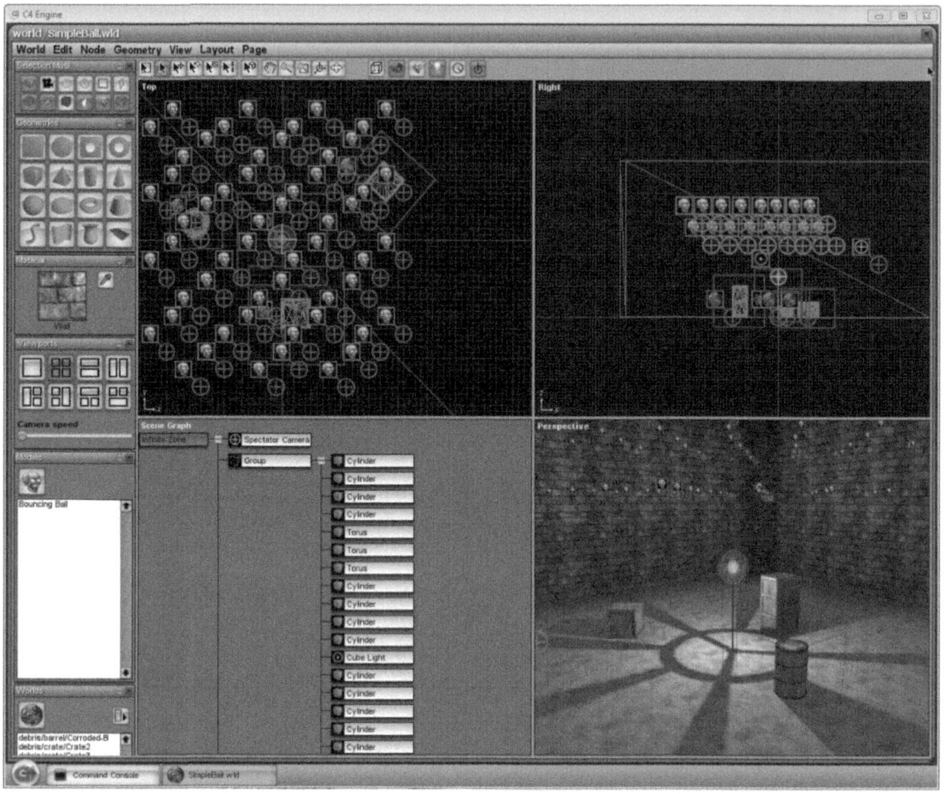

Figure 3-5. The SimpleBall world in the **World Editor** window.

crosses with the skull icons in the world represent models, in this case little balls, which are created and controlled in code.

To test the application again, choose **World > Save and Play World (Ctrl-P)**. This will launch the SimpleBall demo again, as shown in Figure 3-6. Use the mouse to move the camera and press the W, A, S, and D keys (forward, left, right, and back) to move around.

To stop the application again, press the '`' (grave) key again to open the **Command Console** window, as in Step 1 above. Then type `unload` to stop the demo again.

You can then open the SimpleBall world again as before. You can experiment with the world, but before doing so, it is a good practice to save the world under a different name—such as "`mySimpleBall`"—to ensure that the original world is left unchanged.

Figure 3-6. The SimpleBall game in action.

SimpleChar

You can test the *SimpleChar* demo similarly. First, quit C4 by pressing the `` ` `` (grave) key to open the **Command Console**, and type `quit`. Now re-edit the game.cfg file and change the `$gameModuleName` variable from `"SimpleBall"` to `"SimpleChar"` and save the file again:

```
$gameModuleName = "SimpleChar";
```

Launch C4 again and press the `` ` `` (grave) key. **C4 Button > Open World (Ctrl-O)** to open the Water.wld tutorial world, which is located in the Tutorial/world/ directory. Choose **World > Save and Play World (Ctrl-P)** to test the application using the Water world.

This time you will spawn into the Water world as a soldier model. You can move the soldier around the world by pressing the W, A, S, and D keys (forward, left, right, and back), and can change the camera direction using the mouse.

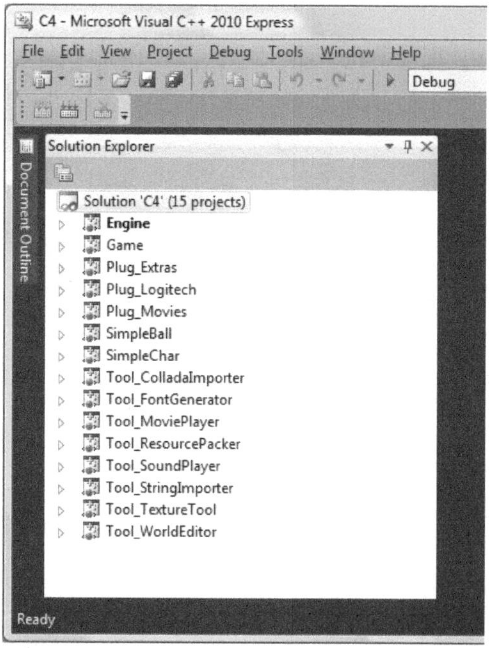

Figure 3-7. The C4 Engine (Standard Edition) solution in Visual C++ 2010 Express Edition.

Another Look at the C4 Solution in Visual C++ 2010 Express Edition

The Visual Studio solution file is called `C4.sln`. After a standard installation, you will find it in the <C4>/VisualStudio2010/C4/ directory. If you open the `C4.sln` file, the solution explorer in Visual C++ should appear as shown in Figure 3-7.

What you see here is the Solution, named "C4", as well as the projects that are part of that solution. All Visual C++ solutions contain at least one project. Think of the solution as a sort of container for projects which are in some way related to one another. Each project `.vcxproj` file is loaded using a link stored in the solution `.sln` file, and in turn, contains links to the C++ source and header files for that project.

If you return to the directory where `C4.sln` is located, you will notice that there are directories there for each of the projects that ship with the engine. If you look inside for example the Engine/Debug/ directory, you will find all of the object and other files that were generated during the compilation process for that project. The object files were linked together with other library files by the link-

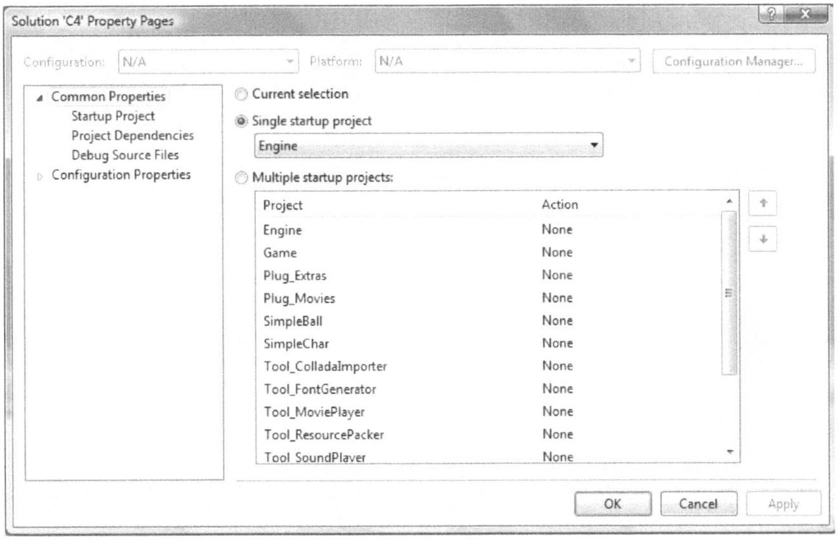

Figure 3-8. The C4 Engine Solution Property Pages.

er, to create the executable (or DLL, as you will find in the Game/Debug/, SimpleBall/Debug/, or SimpleChar/Debug/ directories). Other files in that directory include the "Incremental Linker" `.ilk` file, which is used by the linker to allow incremental linking when you rebuild your projects and the "Program Debug Database" `.pdb` file, which contains information that is used when you run the application in debug mode.

Notice in Figure 3-7 that the Engine project is marked in bold type. This indicates that Engine is the "startup" project, and it is in fact the only start up project in the C4 solution. To see how this setting has been configured, right-click the **Solution** item and choose **Properties** from the contextual menu.

As shown in Figure 3-8, we see again that the C4 solution has a single startup project. Now select the **Project Dependencies** panel, as shown in Figure 3-9.

You can select any project from the project drop-down list, to see what other projects it depends on. For the Standard Edition, we see that the Game project depends on the Engine and the Plug_Extras projects. You will see that all projects depend on at least the Engine project. The Engine project itself however does not depend on any other projects.

If you now select the **Configuration Properties** panel, as shown in Figure 3-10, you will see that for this solution, all projects should be built in the "Debug Configuration" for the Win32 platform. **Debug** is the active configura-

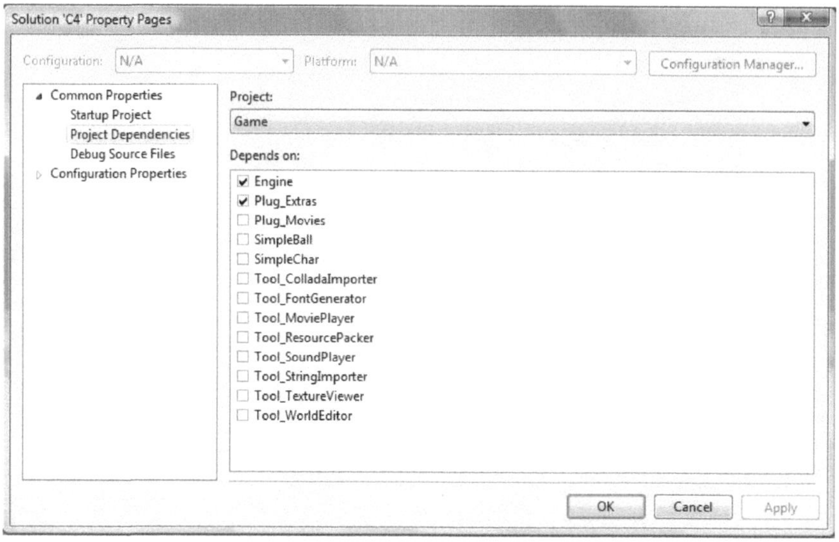

Figure 3-9. The C4 Engine project dependencies.

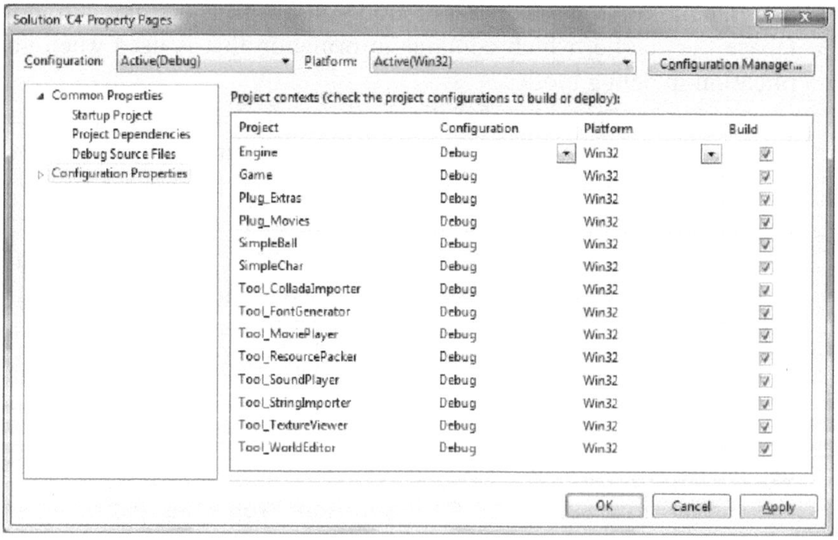

Figure 3-10. The configuration properties for this solution.

tion so that when you build, the code will not be optimized as it will include additional information needed by the debugger.

The other main type of configuration is called the "Optimized configuration". You would make that the active configuration as soon as you have finished debugging and testing—i.e., when you are ready to release your application, choosing **Optimized** from the **Configuration** menu.

Optimized Builds

Although optimized builds are intended for performance profiling or for the release of your C4 Engine-based application (i.e., when you're ready to ship your product, or release it for public evaluation, demo, etc.), it's a good practice to occasionally compile and test an optimized build after major software changes. This can be helpful if by chance the optimized build did not work when the debug build did work. It can also help in catching early bugs that are related to directory setup, security issues, memory handling issues, and other headaches.

DON'T MIX DEBUG AND OPTIMIZED BUILDS!
If by chance you end up mixing libraries from **Debug** and **Optimized** builds, a linker error will be thrown when you attempt to launch C4. Be sure to cleanly build your entire solution under a single configuration.

Project Properties

Right-click the Engine project item, and choose **Properties** from the contextual menu. Once the **Engine Property Pages** dialog opens, select the **General** panel (the first panel in the **Configuration Properties** panel group), as shown in Figure 3-11.

Notice here that for the Engine project, the **Configuration Type** is set to **Application (.exe)**. Engine is the only project which is built as an executable. You can verify that all other projects within the C4 solution have **Configuration Type** set to **Dynamic Library (.dll)**

Some libraries, called *static* libraries with the extension `.lib`, are linked into the executable at compile time. They increase the size of the executable and each program which uses that static library will have its own copy of the functions in memory when that program runs. A DLL, or dynamic linked library, is loaded by any executable which requires it at run time. Only one copy of the functions in the DLL is loaded into memory and that copy is shared among the various applications using it. Windows removes the DLL from memory as soon as the last program using it has terminated.

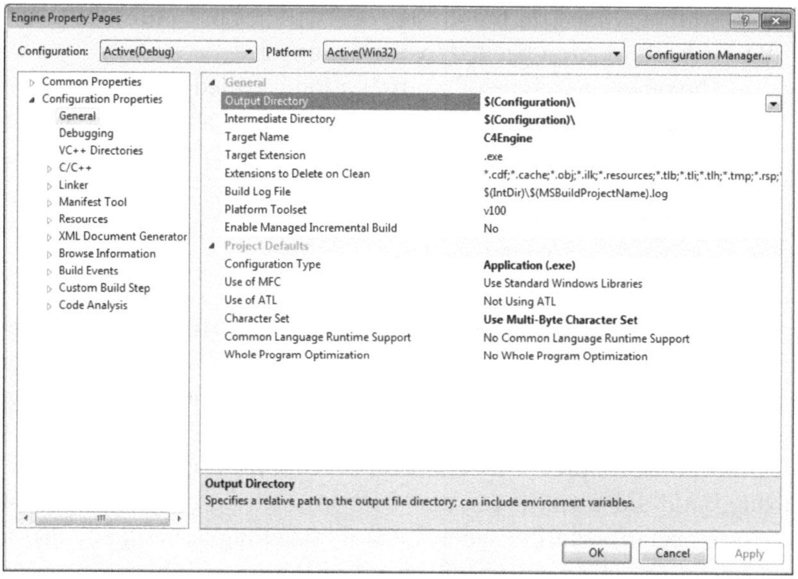

Figure 3-11. The Engine property pages.

Switching Between Modules

When working with the C4 Engine, we can use the variable called `$gameModuleName`, which is defined in the configuration file game.cfg under Data/Game/, to tell the C4 Engine which application (i.e., DLL) it should try to load. Code within the `C4Engine.exe` file then calls the `ConstructApplication()` function, which you define (as `extern` so it can be accessed externally) in your application DLL as follows:

```
extern "C"
{
    C4MODULEEXPORT C4::Application
        *ConstructApplication(void);
}
```

The `ConstructApplication()` function is called by the C4 Engine once the DLL has been loaded successfully. We create an instance of our game in the `ConstructApplication()` function of our application using code like this:

```
Application *ConstructApplication(void)
{
   return (new MyApplication);
}
```

Don't worry if you can't follow this code just yet. We will be using code like this again in the tutorial games, in Part IV • The Games.

Next, right-click on the SimpleBall (or on any other) project, and choose **Properties** from the contextual menu. Although there are many configurable properties here, we'll draw your attention to the three areas you will most likely need to be aware of when adding your own DLL projects. The first area is the **General** panel under the C/C++ panel group, as shown in Figure 3-12. Here, you let the compiler know the location of any additional header files that your code needs to include.

Next, select the **General** panel in the **Linker** panel group, as shown in Figure 3-13. Here you can indicate where the DLL should be placed once it has been successfully linked.

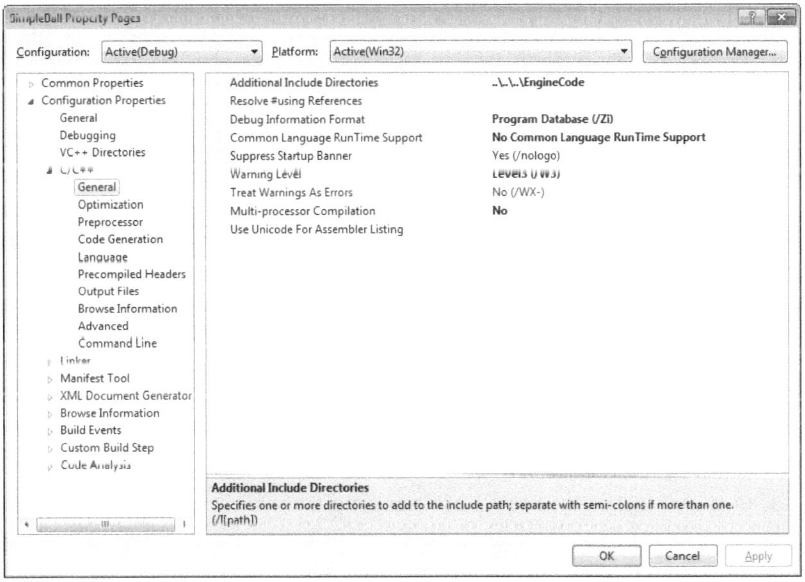

Figure 3-12. The SimpleBall property pages.

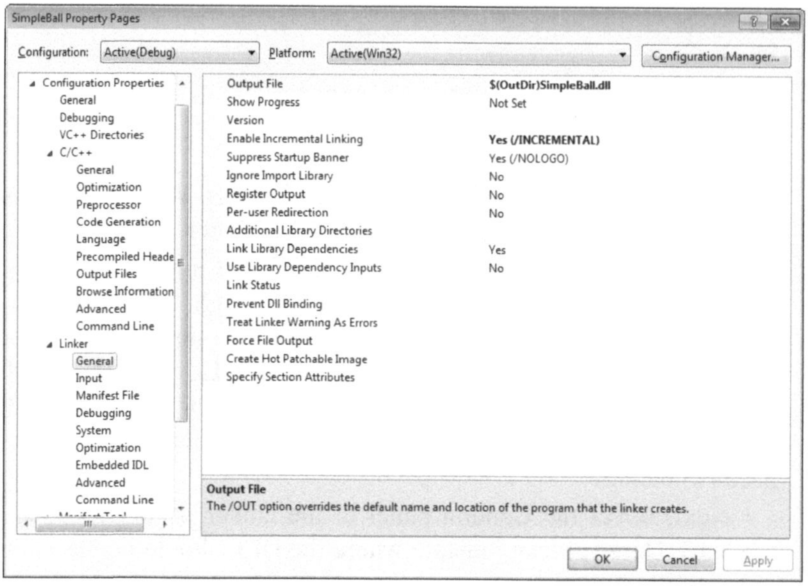

Figure 3-13. The **Linker > General** panel in the SimpleBall property pages dialog.

Now, select the **Linker > Input** panel, as shown in Figure 3-14. Here you specify to the linker the location of any additional libraries needed. Make sure that `C4Engine.lib` is included in this list. If you are having trouble at link time, it may be that the location of `C4Engine.lib` is incorrect. Note that `C4Engine.lib` won't exist if you have not yet successfully compiled the Engine project.

Finally, select the **Custom Build Step** panel, as shown in Figure 3-15. This command copies the output file generated by the build process into the appropriate directory where it can be used by the main engine executable. Every project has a **Custom Build Step** to serve this purpose. If all the output files were not copied to a common relative location, they would not know about each other. This is also the reason why setting the working directory to `..\..\..` in the **Debugging** panel is necessary.

Automatically Setting $gameModuleName

If you end up getting tired of changing `$gameModuleName` in the game.cfg every time you want to test a project, there is a way to set up your projects to automatically change the target application when launching the debugger in Visual Studio.

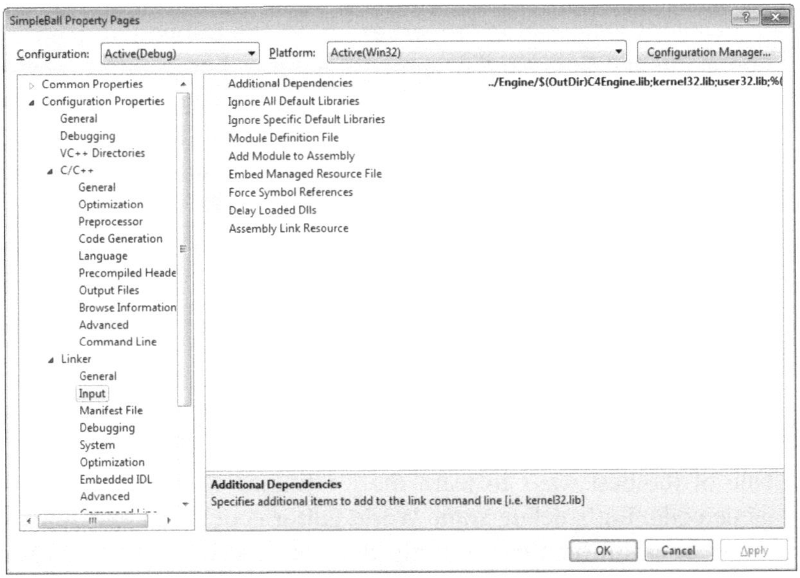

Figure 3-14. The **Linker > Input** panel in the SimpleBall property pages dialog.

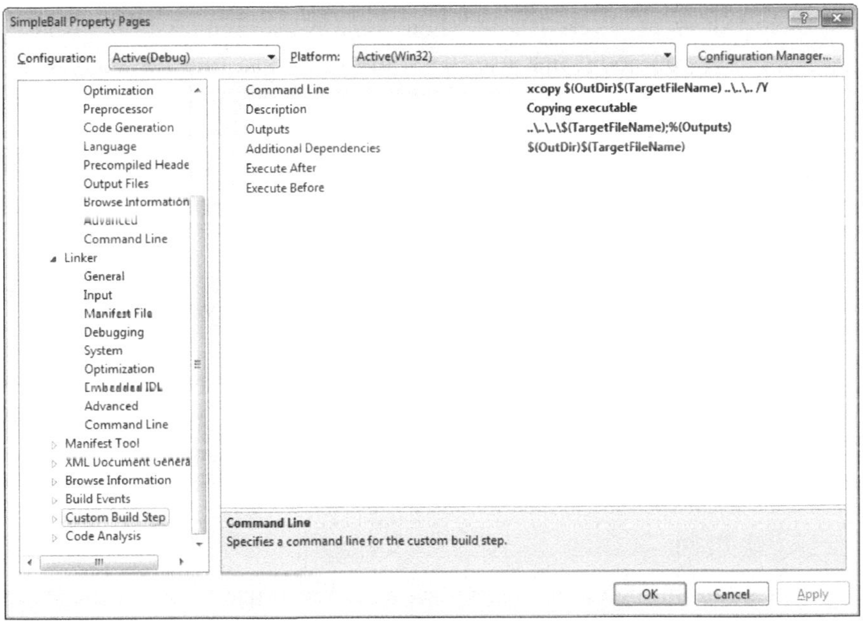

Figure 3-15. The **Custom Build Step** panel in the SimpleBall property pages dialog.

Under **Configuration Properties**, select the **Debugging** panel, and look at the **Command** and **Command Arguments** settings. For example, if you have the SimpleChar project set as your startup project, you can change the **Command** field to `C4Engine.exe` and the **Command Arguments** field to `$gameModuleName = "SimpleChar"`. If you have SimpleBall set as your startup project, you can set up the **Command Arguments** field to `$gameModuleName = "SimpleBall"`. This parameter will override whatever you have `$gameModuleName` set to in your game.cfg file, and you will only ever have to change this configuration value for your Visual Studio project once.

Debugging the C4 Engine within Visual C++ 2010 Express Edition

One of the best ways to learn the C4 Engine is to debug the engine, tool, and game code. Let's debug some **World Editor** code as an example. With the C4 solution open in the Visual Studio development environment, choose **Edit > Find and Replace > Find in Files (Ctrl-Shift-F)** to open the **Find and Replace** dialog in **Find in Files** mode. Enter the text `TransformPage::HandleRotationTextEvent` into the **Find what** text box, choose **Entire Solution** from the popup menu under the **Look in** text box, and then click **Find All**. The **Ctrl-Shift-F** keyboard shortcut is very useful when you are searching within Visual Studio. Alternatively, you could just use the solution tree to find the method within the file `C4EditorPages.cpp`, which is part of the Tool_WorldEditor project.

Once you have found `TransformPage::HandleRotationTextEvent`, set a breakpoint on that function by left-clicking in the shaded margin area to the left of the first line in the method. You can also right-click on a line of source code and choose **Breakpoint > Insert Breakpoint** from the contextual menu.

PLEASE DON'T FORGET TO SET THE WORKING DIRECTORY!

We mentioned this earlier, but novices forget so often that it bears repeating: Before you run the debugger on your project for the first time within Visual C++, set the **Working Directory**. See the section Don't Forget to Set the Working Directory! for more details about how to configure this setting.

A Debugging Session

Let's run through a debugging session. We'll use a few of the **World Editor** features here, but for a full introduction to the **World Editor** and its capabilities, please see Part II • Designing Worlds.

1. Start debugging by choosing **Debug > Start Debugging (F5)**. Once the C4 Engine is running, open up a new world by choosing **C4 Button > New World (Ctrl-N)**.
2. Add a cube using the **Geometries** page.
3. With the cube still selected in a viewport, open up the **Transform** page by choosing **Page > Transform**. To trigger the breakpoint, highlight the text in the **Rotation X** field and type the number `9`.
4. You should now be back in the debugger. Step through the code in this function by pressing the **F10** key.
5. When you get to the line which begins with `float x =`, hover your mouse over the `x` and it will show you the value of `x`.
6. Right-click the `x` and choose **Add watch** from the contextual menu. A new window will open which allows you to monitor the value of this local variable.
7. Left-click on the line below the `x` variable in the **Watch1** panel, so that the cursor starts blinking on that line. Type the word `this` and press Enter. `this` refers to the `TransformPage`. You can open up the data structure by clicking on the "+" sign to the left of this. Open it up until you see `textStorage` (under `rotationTextWidget[0], C4::TextWidget`), which contains the string value stored in the field **Rotation X**. Note that the variable `x` is in radians, whereas the value you type is in degrees.
8. Once you have stepped over that line beginning with `float x =`, continue running the C4 Engine by pressing the **F5** key, which tells the debugger to continue program execution.
9. Add a `0` behind the `9` you previously entered into the **Rotation X** value. Again, you will be taken back to the `HandleRotationTextEvent()` function, and you can once again step down to the line whose values you are watching.

Notice what the `HandleRotationTextEvent()` function does. It converts the string values, which are typed by the user into the **Transform** page, into floating-point values, then converts them to radians. The results are then used to set the node's transform by calling the `SetNodeMatrix3D()` function, with some help from the `SetEulerAngles()` function:

```
node->SetNodeMatrix3D(Matrix3D().SetEulerAngles(x, y, z));
```

We will learn more about manipulating a node's transform later in the *Guide*.

Experiment with some of the other debugging features by opening up each of the various windows under **Debug > Windows**. The **Call Stack** view is useful, particularly if the program crashes, to see the sequence of function calls that have led up to the current function.

Next Steps

We don't have much of a game to debug yet, so let's create some interesting worlds for our games, in Part II • Designing Worlds.

Part II

Designing Worlds

4

Creating a Simple World

This chapter shows how to create a simple world using the **World Editor** tool. In this basic world, you can run around, fire weapons, and collect ammo.

The Simple World

This tutorial shows you how to:

- Set up the virtual file system.
- Create a new world and add a skybox.
- Add geometry and lighting.
- Add a player or spectator spawn point marker.
- Register your world to show up in the Start New Game window.
- Add physics interactions

The tutorial describes new concepts for the first time in detail when possible. However, this chapter does not provide an in depth discussion about every aspect of creating a world; the focus is on a simple process for creating a world for the first time.

> **About the Screen Shots**
> The world created in this chapter uses geometry that is smaller than it should be, so that the screen shots can display as much information as possible. The final world file that is made available for download will be larger.

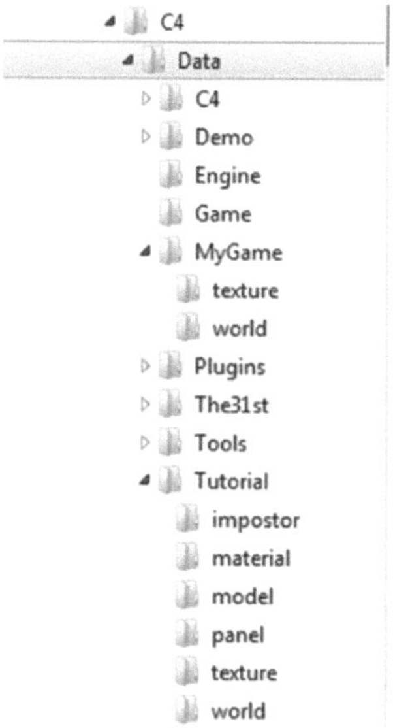

Figure 4-1. A sample Data directory structure.

Set Up the Virtual File System

We described the virtual file system in Part I • Getting Started, but now we'll put that knowledge into action. The C4 Engine implements a virtual file system, which means that the directories directly underneath <C4>/Data/ are treated as a single directory. For example, consider the directory structure shown in Figure 4-1.

A file residing in Data/Tutorial/world/ is considered to be in the same directory as a file in the directory Data/MyGame/world/, and they are referenced by omitting Data and the name of the first-level directory from the file path. For example, the texture Data/Game/texture/tex01.tex is referenced as texture/tex01.tex. There is one possible problem though—if two files have the same name, and reside in different subdirectories in the Data directory, only the first texture found will be returned, so we recommend using unique file names to avoid this possible conflict.

To set up our own virtual file system, we'll start by creating a directory structure similar to the one shown in Figure 4-1.

1. In the C4 root directory, navigate to the Data directory and create a subdirectory named MyGame.

Figure 4-2. The directory structure used in this tutorial.

2 Create two more subdirectories in the MyGame directory, one named texture and the other named world.

When importing textures and models for use with the C4 Engine, they need to be in a similar directory structure within the Import directory. For example, the source image file Import/MyGame/texture/texture01.tga will be imported as the texture file Data/MyGame/texture/texture01.tex.

3 For this tutorial, create a directory structure similar to the one shown in Figure 4-2.

Using this approach, project resources can be cleanly split into multiple directories within the Data directory. Then, using the **Resource Packer** tool, the contents of each directory can be packed into individual `.pak` files containing multiple resources. For example, the contents of the MyGame directory would be packed into `MyGame.pak` and then the MyGame directory could be deleted. The C4 Engine would then access the resources through the single `.pak` file. The C4 Engine demo game employs this technique. The only downside is that the resources will not show up in any of the C4 Engine file pickers, but the paths can be manually typed in.

Create a New World

Let's create a new world to explore some more features.

1 Start C4, and when the main menu is displayed, press the ESC key to close it, as shown in Figure 4-3.

2 Click the C4 button at the bottom left of the screen and then choose **New World (Ctrl-N)**, as shown in Figure 4-4. A new world file is displayed in the **World Editor** window, as shown in Figure 4-5.

3 Choose **World > Save World As**, as shown in Figure 4-6.

Figure 4-3. Starting from the main menu bar.

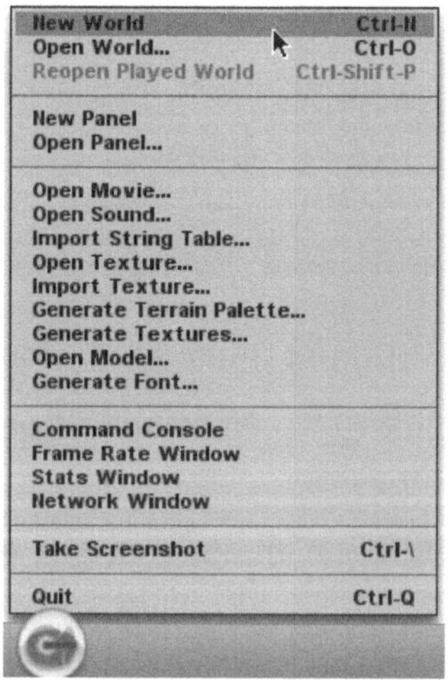

Figure 4-4. Creating a new world.

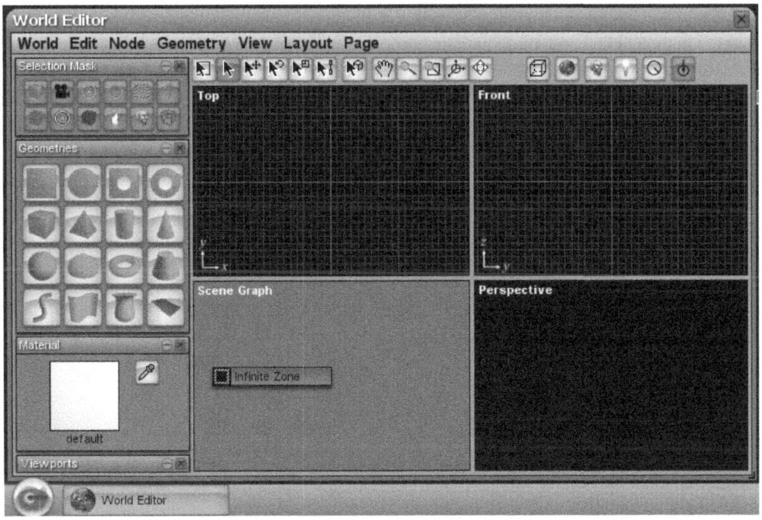

Figure 4-5. A new world in the **World Editor** window.

4 Save the world as Base in the directory Data/MyGame/world/, as shown in Figure 4-7.

The name and path to the Data directory are then displayed in the title bar of thc **World Editor** window, as shown in Figure 4-8.

To minimize the potential for loss of data, save worlds on a regular basis. When making major changes, add a version number suffix to the end of the file name, so if the world file is corrupted at any point, it is easy to use the previous version. For example, the next time the file needs saving, choose **World > Save World As** and change the name to Base-01. After the next change, save with the name Base-02, and so forth.

Figure 4-6. Saving the initial world file.

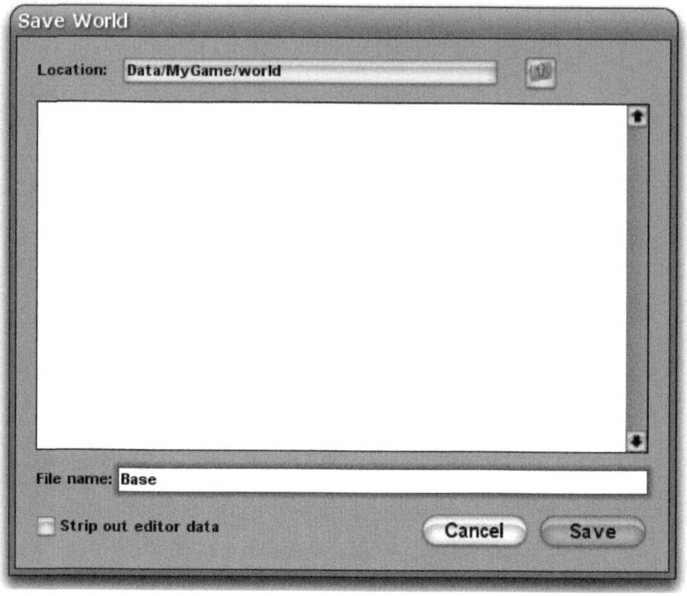

Figure 4-7. Saving our Base world using the **Save World** dialog.

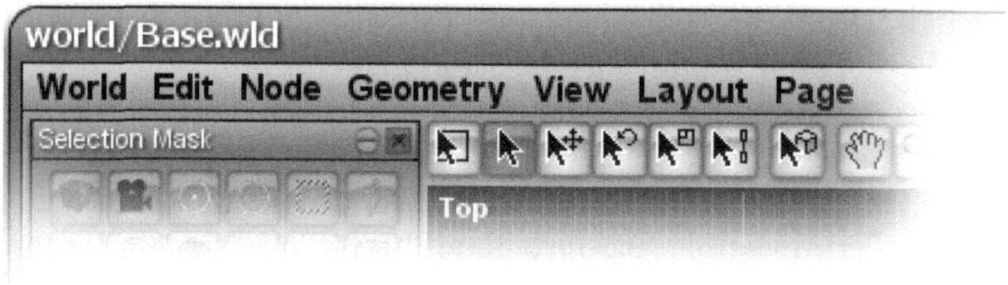

Figure 4-8. The title bar of the **World Editor** window shows the file name of the world.

Navigating around the New World and Creating a Skybox

The **World Editor** window is preset to display four viewports. Each viewport can be maximized by pressing Ctrl-1 through to Ctrl-4. Each viewport also has the current view in Yellow in the top right and the axis it represents in the bottom left, as shown in Figure 4-9.

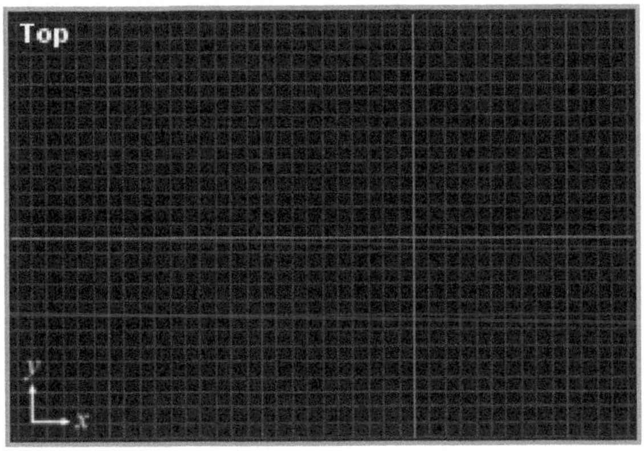

Figure 4-9. Showing the viewport descriptions.

To pan around the viewport, press and drag the mouse while pressing the middle mouse button, or press Alt and drag the mouse while holding down the left mouse button.

You can change the viewport by right-clicking in a viewport and choosing a new view from the contextual menu, as shown in Figure 4-10. For example, changing the scene graph to the **Right (–y)** view.

Change the viewport back to display the scene graph. The scene graph displays all of the world's nodes in a hierarchical tree structure, with the infinite zone at the root, which is also called the root node. As this is a new world file, no nodes have been added to the scene graph yet, but a world always starts with an **Infinite Zone** node, as shown in Figure 4-11.

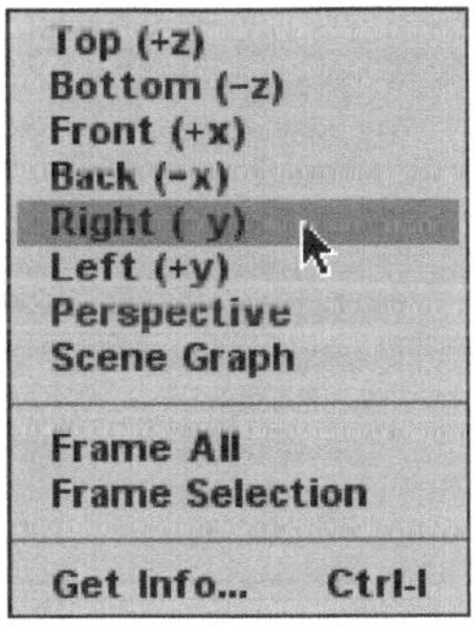

Figure 4-10. Showing the **Right** viewport.

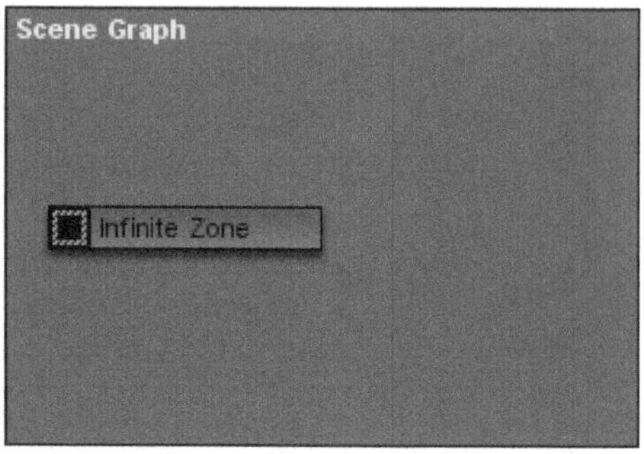

Figure 4-11. In a world file, the infinite zone is always there.

1 In the viewport that is displaying the scene graph, select the **Infinite Zone** node. To select the node, either click on the node **Select** tool (Figure 4-18), or press 1 to enter node selection mode. The selected node is highlighted in green, as shown in Figure 4-12. You can also see that the zone, a small box, has been highlighted in the other viewports as well.

2 Once highlighted, choose **Node > Get Info (Ctrl-I)**, double click the node or right-click on the node and choose **Get Info** from the contextual menu, as shown in Figure 4-13.

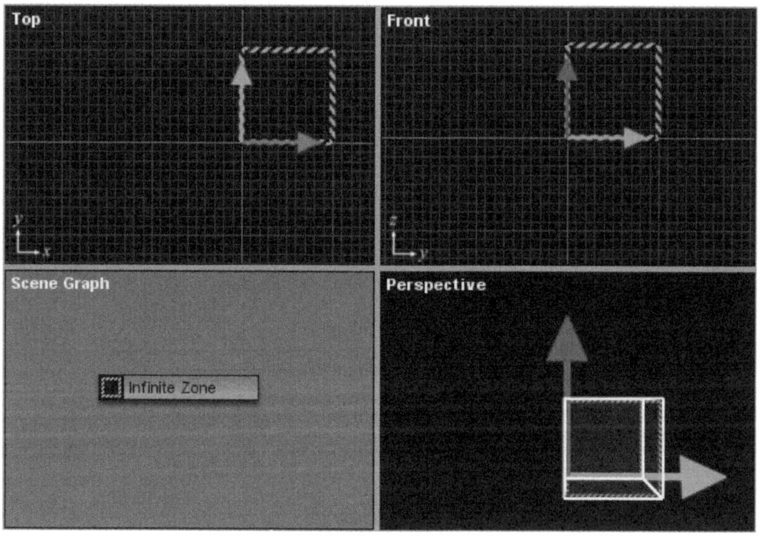

Figure 4-12. A selected **Infinite Zone** node.

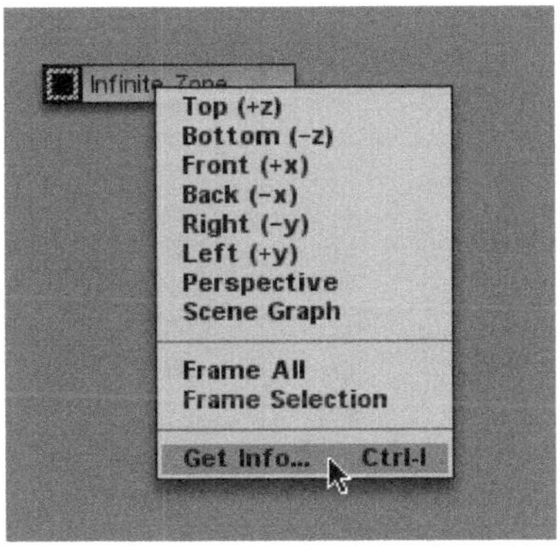

Figure 4-13. The viewport contextual menu.

When using the context menu, always make sure that the node is highlighted, because the contextual menu will always be displayed even if a node is not selected.

The **Node Info** dialog is displayed for the infinite zone, with the **Zone** tab panel selected.

3 We'll be adding a skybox to the infinite zone, so select the **Render skybox in this zone** option, as shown in Figure 4-14.

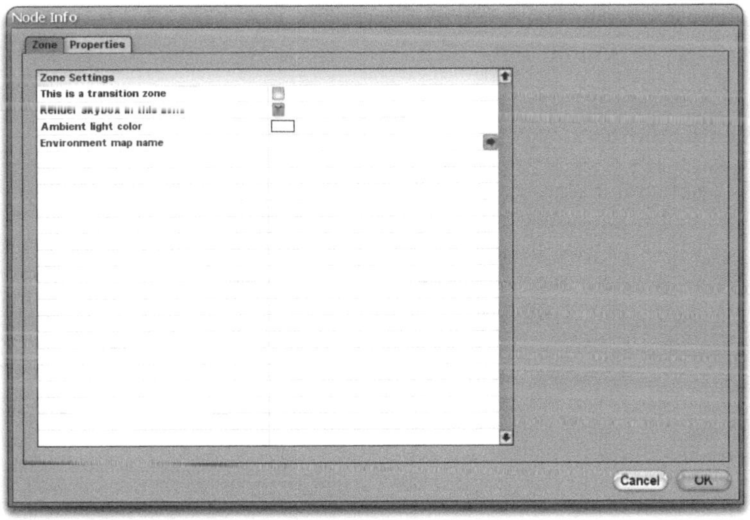

Figure 4-14. Selecting the **Render skybox in this zone** option in the **Node Info** dialog.

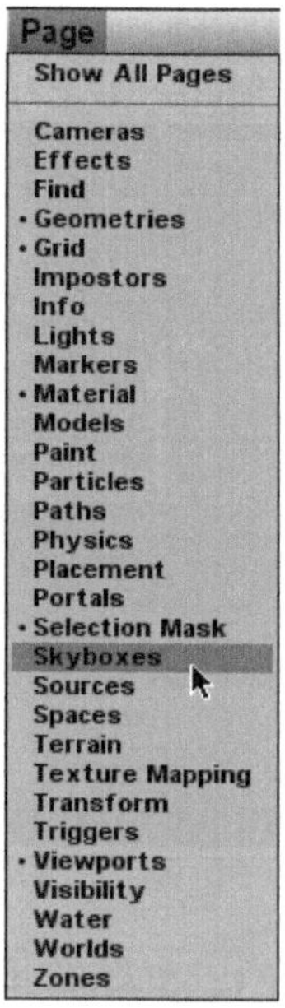

Figure 4-15. Opening the **Skyboxes** page panel.

4 Click **OK** to save your changes and close the **Node Info** dialog.

5 Choose **Page > Skyboxes** to display the **Skyboxes** page panel in the editor, as shown in Figure 4-15.

By default, the **Skyboxes** page panel is displayed in the left column of the **World Editor** window, as shown in Figure 4-16.

6 Select the **Skybox** tool. The cursor changes into a small crosshair.

7 Click on the infinite zone node in the scene graph viewport. The skybox node is now attached to the infinite zone node. The scene graph should appear as shown in Figure 4-17. The new node is highlighted in green once it is added.

Figure 4-16. The **Skyboxes** page.

Figure 4-17. A selected skybox node.

Figure 4-18. The **Select Nodes** tool.

8 Press the 1 key or click the tool button, to select the **Select Nodes** tool, as shown in Figure 4-18.

9 Choose **Node > Get Info (Ctrl-I or Right-Click > Get Info)** to open the **Node Info** dialog, as shown in Figure 4-19.

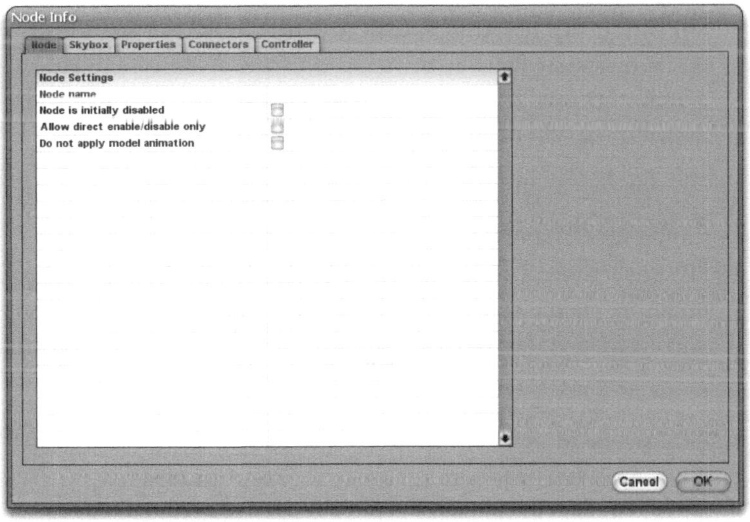

Figure 4-19. The **Node Info** dialog displaying a skybox node.

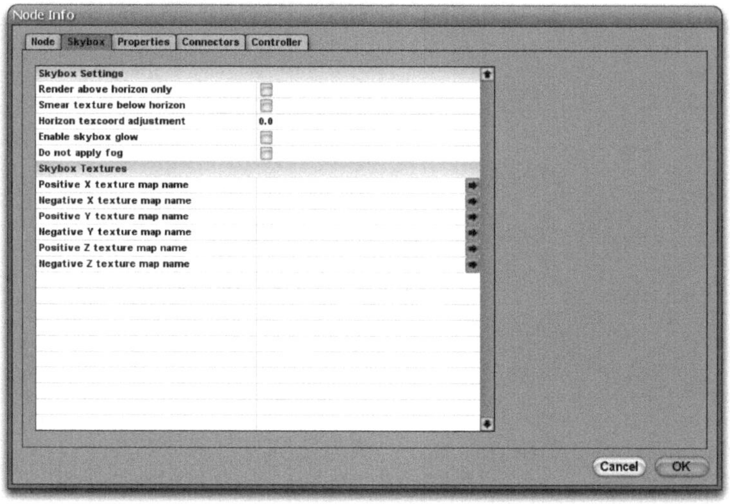

Figure 4-20. The **Skybox** tab panel in the **Node Info** dialog.

10 Select the **Skybox** tab panel, as shown in Figure 4-20.

11 Select the **Enable skybox glow** option.

12 To add a texture, click the arrow icon to the right of the **Positive X texture map name** text box, to open the **Texture Map** selection dialog. Unfortunately all of the sky textures that ship with C4 are not for use by licensees. And as such reside in the `Pack.pak` file. To use these textures in our example, we cannot browse to the virtual folder in the .pak file using the texture map dialog. So we will have to manually enter the texture names.

13 To add the texture names manually, type `sky/Cloudy1` in the **Positive X texture map name** setting as shown in Figure 4-21.

14 To save time, you can copy the first texture name and paste it into the remaining fields, changing the final number as you go. After all of the textures have been set, the **Node Info** dialog should appear as shown in Figure 4-22.

Figure 4-21. The **Skybox Textures** settings.

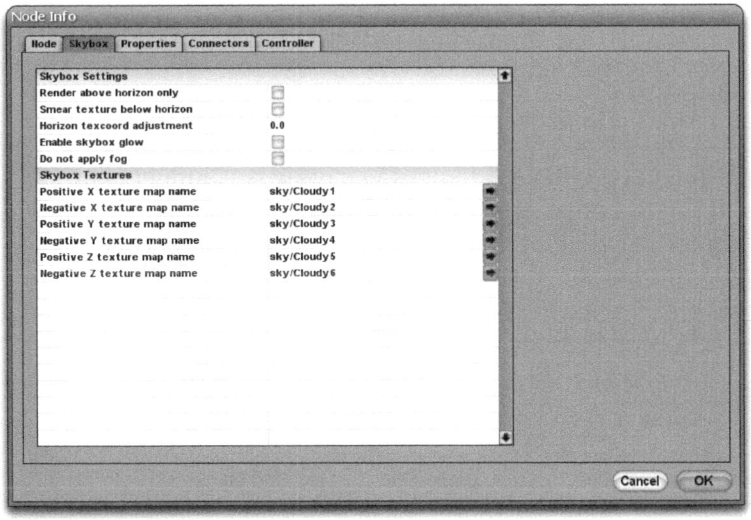

Figure 4-22. The **Skybox Textures** settings with all textures set.

15 Click **OK** to save your changes and close the **Node Info** dialog. At this moment, there isn't very much visible in the perspective viewport.

16 To show real-time lighting in the perspective viewport, click the **Toggle Lighting** button.

17 The clouds can occasionally be created upside-down. If you need to flip the clouds right-side up, select the skybox node and choose **Node > Reset Transform to Identity**.

18 Save the world file as Base-01.

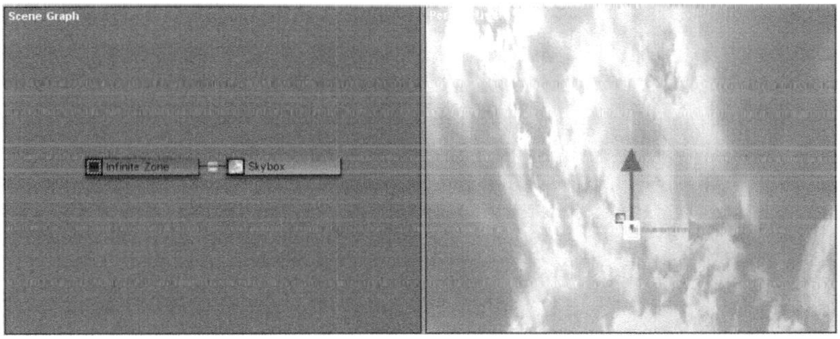

Figure 4-23. Clouds in the perspective viewport.

Add Geometry and Lighting

Geometry

To create a basic world in which a player can run around, fire weapons, and pick up ammo, we will need to put some basic structure in place. The building process will involve creating a floor to run on, and barriers at the edges of the floor to stop the player from falling off into 'space'—the barriers should also be invisible and not stop any of the weapon projectiles, only the character.

1. If you haven't done so already, open the Base-01 world file.
2. Change the bottom-left viewport back to the **Right** viewport by right-clicking inside it and choosing **Right (–y)** from the contextual menu, as shown in Figure 4-24.
3. Disable the **Toggle Lighting** option at this time.
4. On the **Geometries** page panel, select the **Box** tool (the first icon from the left on the second row, as shown in Figure 4-25).

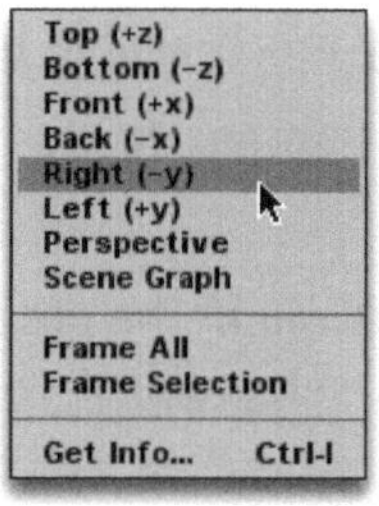

Figure 4-24. Choosing the **Right** viewport.

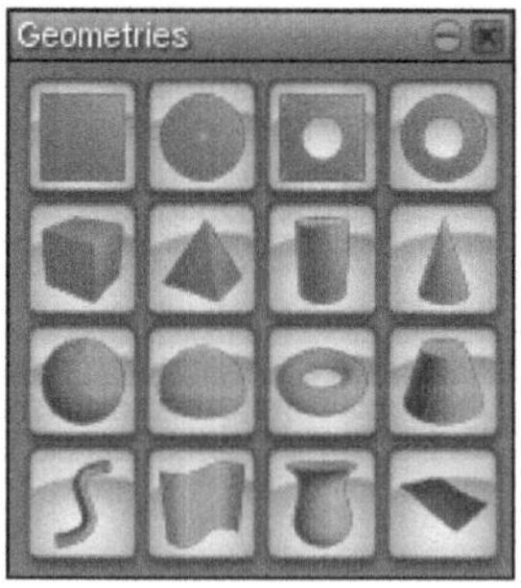

Figure 4-25. Selecting the **Box** tool from the **Geometries** page.

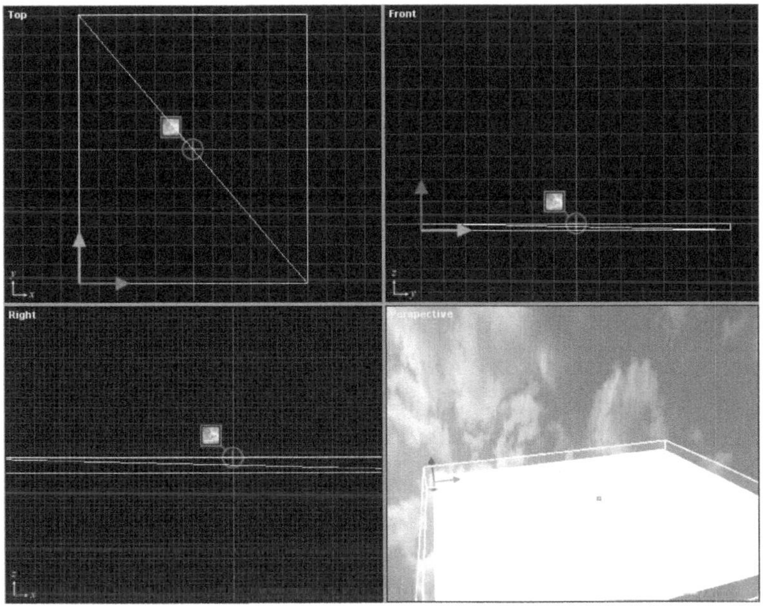

Figure 4-26. Drawing the floor area.

5 Moving back to the first (**Top**) viewport, draw a floor area, as shown in Figure 4-26.

6 Once the floor wall has been created, notice that the dimensions may not be correct in the other viewports. Press 4 to select the **Scale Nodes** tool.

7 Resize the floor in the top right (*y-z*) viewport using the green manipulation handles displayed on the corners of the box.

At the moment, the box has the default texture. This is because the **World Editor** applied the currently selected material when the primitive geometry was drawn out. In this case, since we are working with a new world file, a default material is provided.

The material can be changed in a couple of ways. You could change the texture that the default material uses, which would automatically update the box with the new texture. Or, you could create a new material and apply it to the box. Let's use the second approach.

8 Double-click the current material thumbnail in the **Material** page panel, on the left-hand side of the **World Editor** window, as shown in Figure 4-27. The **Material Manager** window is displayed, as shown in Figure 4-28.

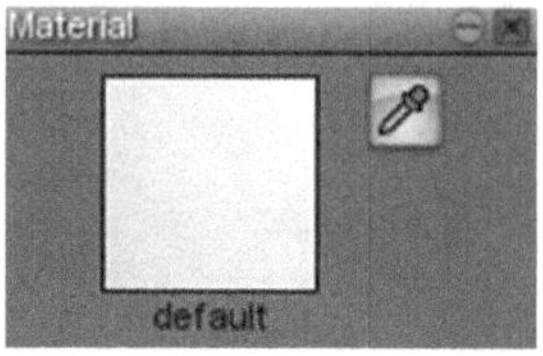

Figure 4-27. The **Material** page.

For the Base world, three new materials need to be created; Floor, Barrier, and Marble, using the default textures that come with the C4 Engine. If the demo game is being used, it will not be possible to use the texture selection dialog box to find the correct textures, so the texture names will have to be manually entered into the respective text boxes.

9 For the first material, click **New**, to create a new material.

10 Populate the texture fields with the values shown in Figure 4-29.

11 Set the **Material name** to floor.

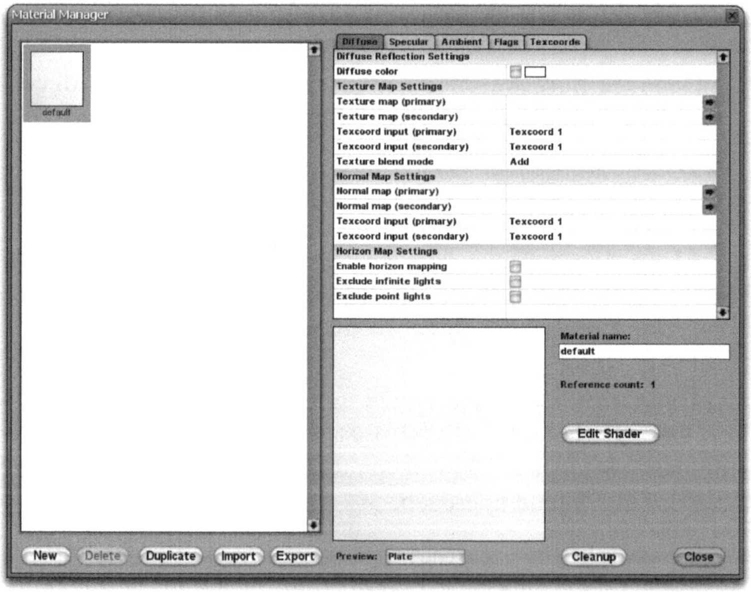

Figure 4-28. The **Material Manager** window with a default material.

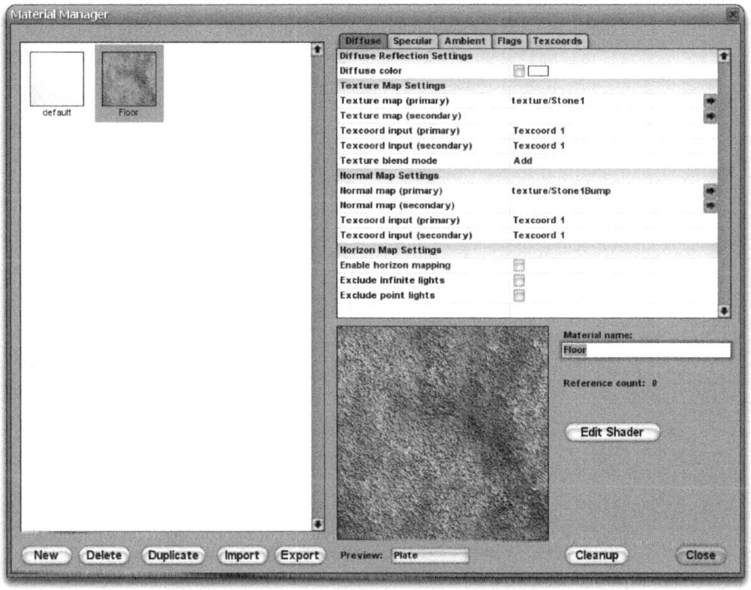

Figure 4-29. Setting up the floor material.

Note that if you are typing in the values manually, they are only case sensitive if you are using Linux. Therefore, you may run into problems if you are sharing worlds between operating systems. We recommend that you make a practice of using the correct case from the start.

12 Click **New** to create the second material as seen in Figure 4-30.

13 Change the **Material name** to Barrier.

Finally, we'll add a third marble-like material. This material needs textures along with a specular value.

14 Make sure the **Diffuse** tab panel is still selected, and set the values to match the settings shown in Figure 4-31.

15 Name the material Marble.

16 Select the **Specular** tab and then select the **Specular color** option, as shown in Figure 4-32. The specular color defaults to white.

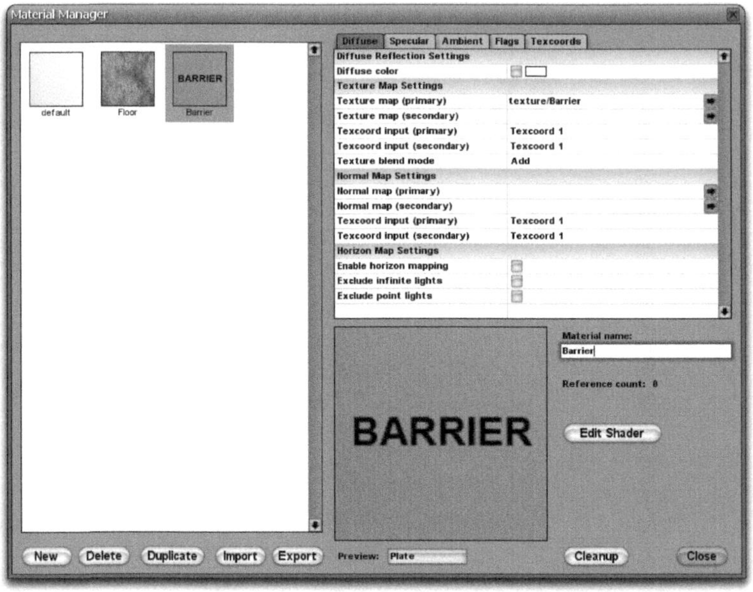

Figure 4-30. Setting up the Barrier material.

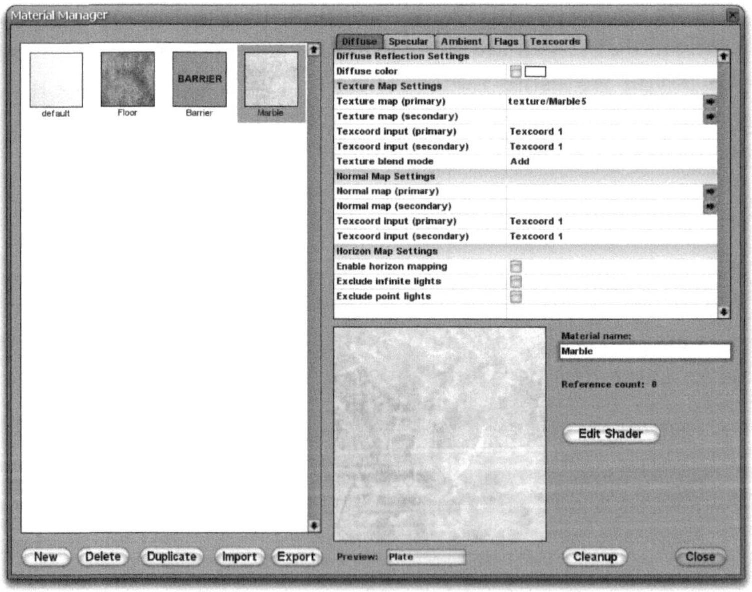

Figure 4-31. Setting up the Marble material.

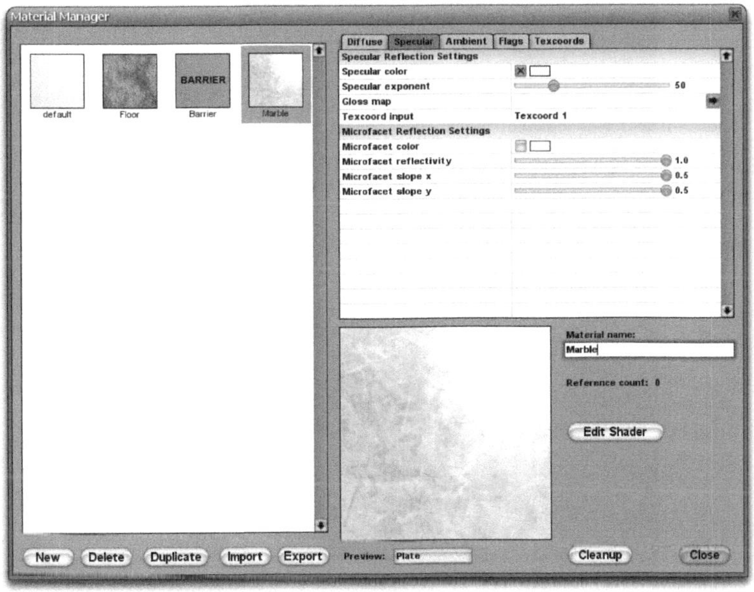

Figure 4-32. The **Specular** attribute settings for the Marble material.

17 Slide the **Specular exponent** slider above 80, to sharpen the shininess.

18 Select the floor material in the material catalog view, since we will now apply that material to the floor geometry.

19 Click **Close** to close the **Material Manager** window. Notice that the selected material has updated to the floor material, but the box primitive is still textured in the default texture.

20 To apply the current material to the box primitive, select the floor box primitive, and choose **Geometry > Set Material (Ctrl-M)** to apply the current material to the geometry.

21 The texture should now be visible, as shown in Figure 4-33.

22 Press Ctrl-4 to maximize the perspective viewport and press the 9 key to switch to the **Free Camera Move** tool, and move around the scene by pressing the W, S, A, and D keys while dragging the left mouse button to aim the camera.

23 Press Ctrl-4 to switch back to the perspective viewport.

24 Open the **Material Manager** window again, and select the Barrier material.

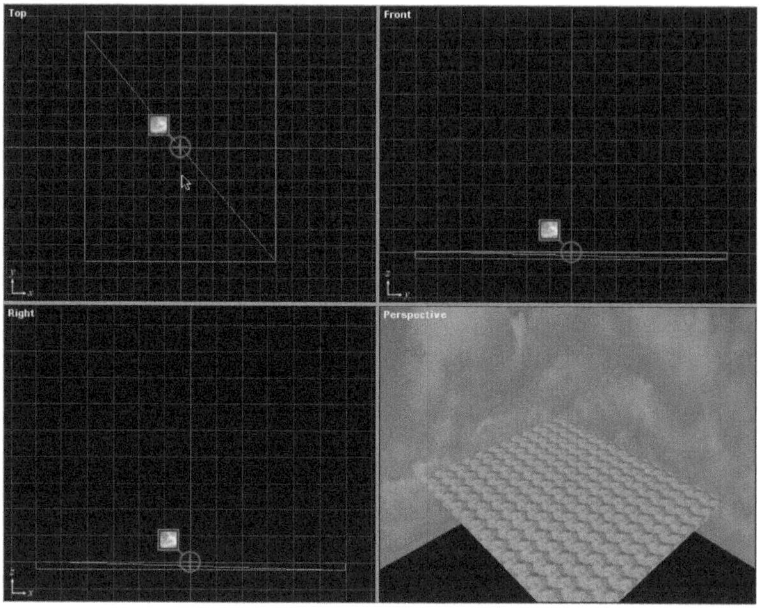

Figure 4-33. A box node with the Floor material applied.

25 Close the **Material Manager** window.

26 In the **World Editor** window, create a new box for the barrier wall. Start out in the top-left viewport and draw it out. Note that the current material is applied when the geometry primitive is created.

27 Once the barrier wall has been created, notice again that the dimensions may not be correct in the other viewports. Press 4 to select the **Scale Nodes** tool.

28 Resize the barrier using the green manipulation handles displayed on the corners of the box, as shown in Figure 4-34.

29 Using the manipulation handles, adjust the scale so that the barrier's shape looks like the one shown in Figure 4-35.

30 Once the initial barrier wall has been created, create three more barrier walls, and position them so that the floor is surrounded, as shown in Figure 4-35.

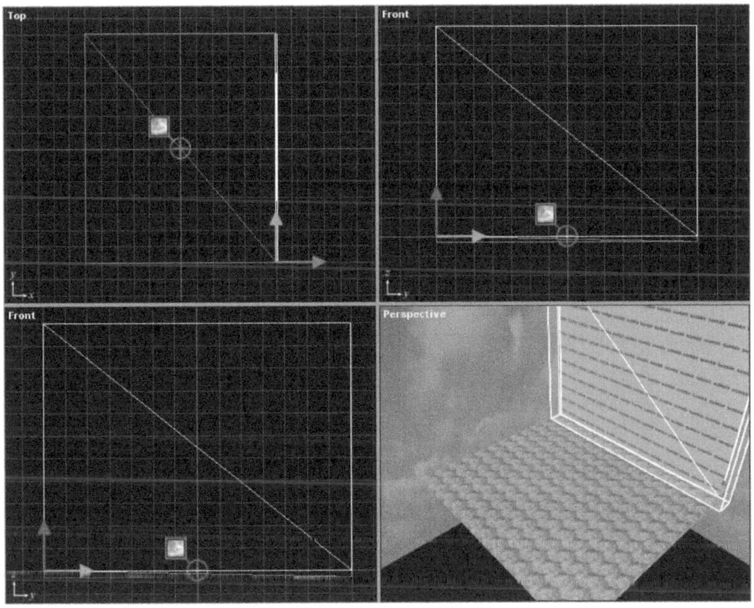

Figure 4-34. Using the resize manipulation handles.

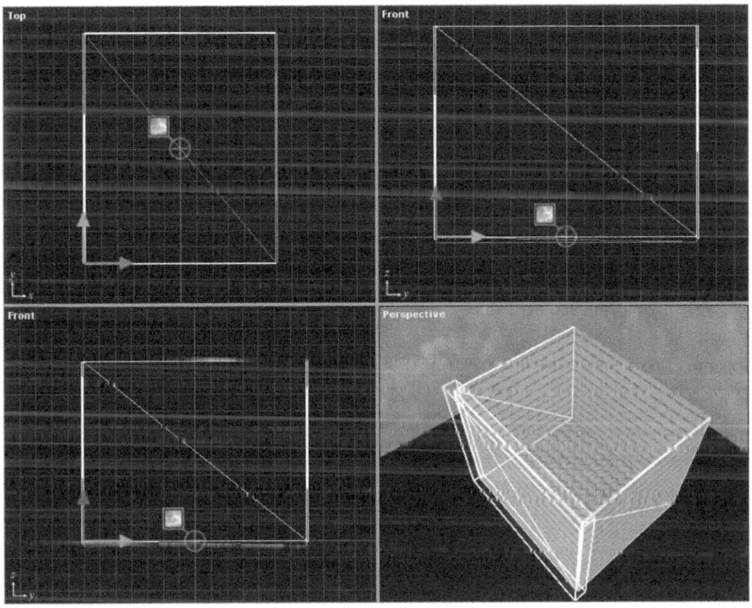

Figure 4-35. Building the four barrier walls.

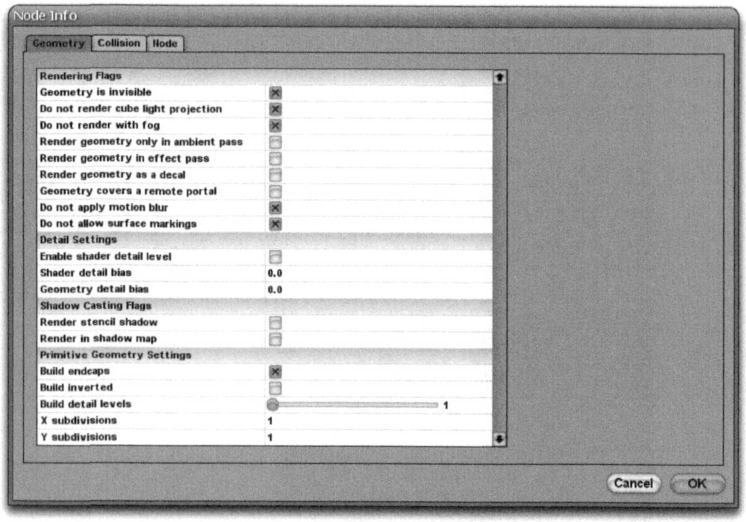

Figure 4-36. The **Node Info** settings for the barriers.

31 Use the shift key while you left click to select all four new walls and choose **Node > Get Info (Ctrl-I)** to open the **Node Info** dialog for the selected nodes. We will update the data for all four primitives at once.

32 Select the **Geometry** tab panel and make sure that the **Geometry is invisible** option is selected and that the **Render stencil shadow** option is not selected and make sure that surface markings and motion blur are not enabled as well as not rendering with fog or a cube light projection, as shown in Figure 4-36. Once you click **OK**, the four walls will be invisible.

33 Select the **Collision** tab panel, and then select the various options as shown in Figure 4-37.

34 Click **OK** to save your changes.

35 Open the **Material Manager** window and select the Marble texture.

36 Now create a pillar, by using two boxes and a cylinder geometry that is quite high and rests on the floor, as shown in Figure 4-38. Once you have the three pieces of geometry in place, select them all and either select **Node > Group Nodes (Ctrl-G)**. You may find it difficult to select the nodes when they are behind the walls. In the scene graph, select the walls and then select **View > Hide Selected (Ctrl-H)**, and the hidden nodes will now be dark gray in the scene graph.

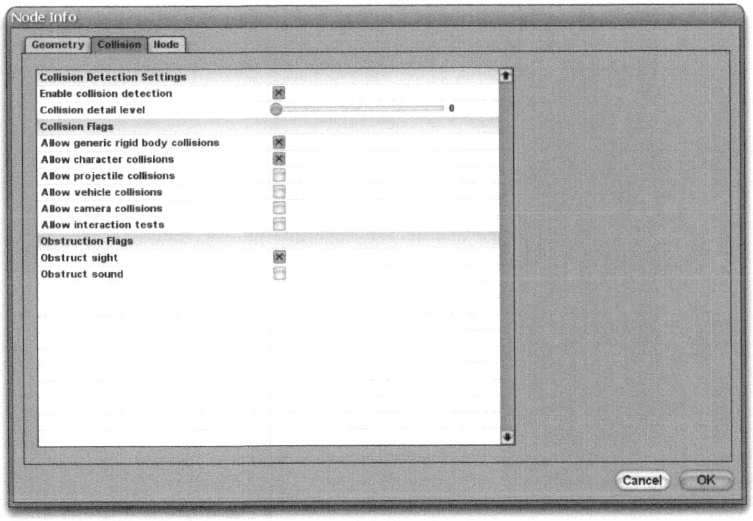

Figure 4-37. The **Collision** tab panel settings.

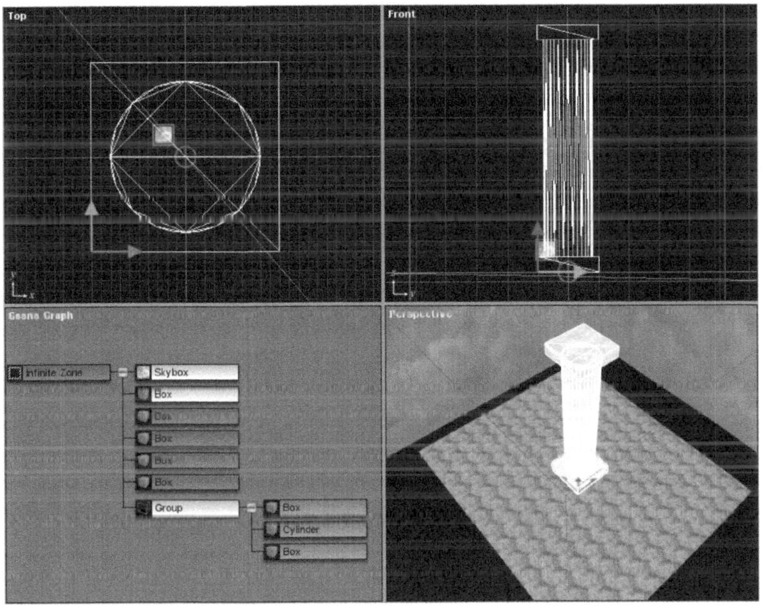

Figure 4-38. Creating a marble column.

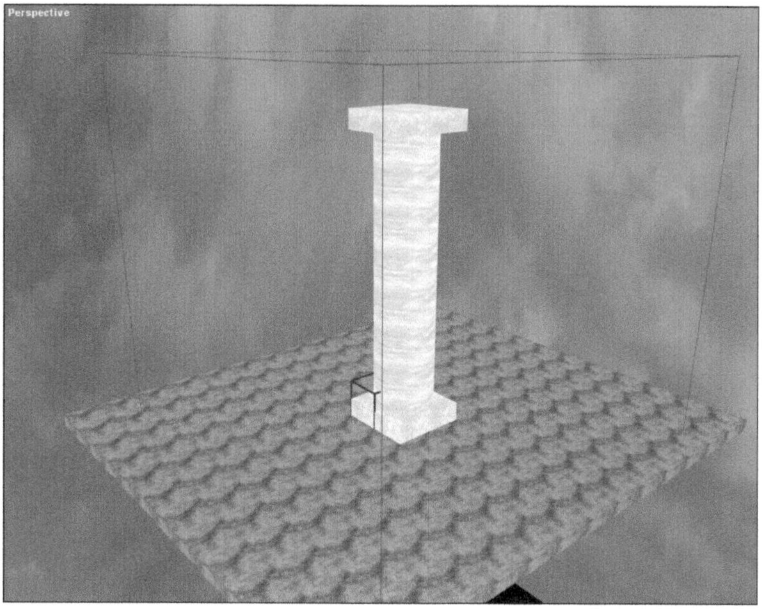

Figure 4-39. Unlit geometries with no scene lighting.

Lighting

Let's add some lighting. If you click the **Toggle Lighting** button, you will see that although there is a skybox, the scene looks a bit dull especially with no visible shadows. And when the button is toggled, nothing happens As shown in Figure 4-39.

1. Choose **Page > Lights** to open the **Lights** page panel, as shown in Figure 4-40.
2. Select the **Infinite Light** tool.

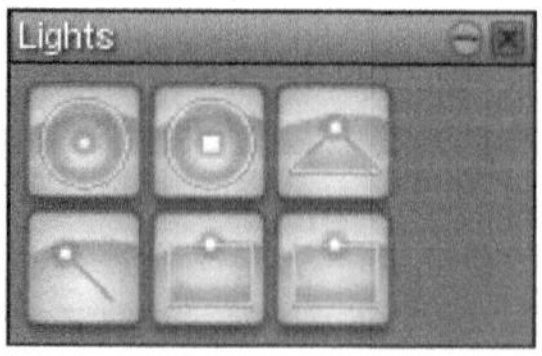

Figure 4-40. The **Lights** page.

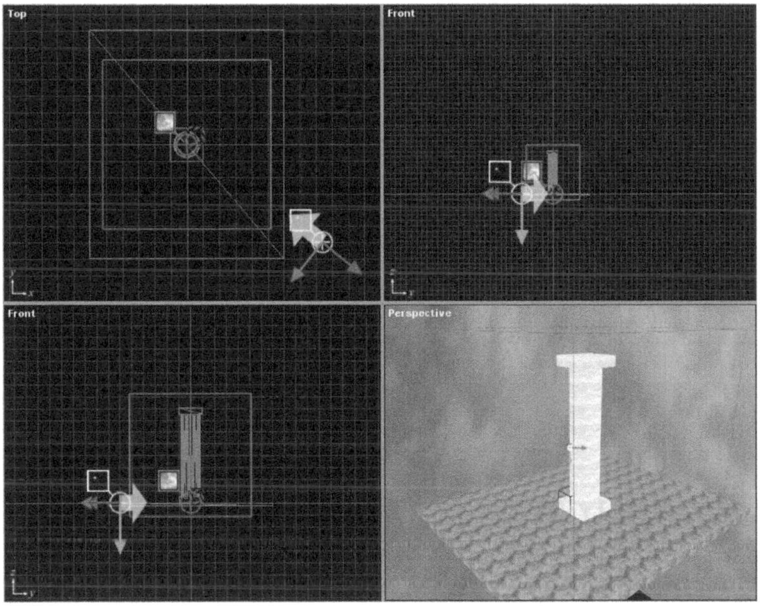

Figure 4-41. Adding an infinite light.

3 In the top-left viewport, click somewhere in the bottom-right to add an infinite light as shown in Figure 4-41. Once the node has been added it is made active.

4 Press 1 on the keypad to make sure the **Select Nodes** tool is selected.

5 Select the **Move Nodes (2)** tool.

6 Press Ctrl-2 to maximize viewport 2, as shown in Figure 4-42.

7 We'll next raise the height of the light so that it will shine down and light the scene. To move the light in the *z* direction, click on the green gizmo arrow and move the light upwards so that it is higher than the top of the scene, as shown in Figure 4-43.

8 Press Ctrl-2 again to return to the default four viewports.

Looking closer at the light, notice that apart from the usual three axis manipulators there is an extra one, a large yellow arrow, this is the light direction. At the moment it may be pointing away from the column.

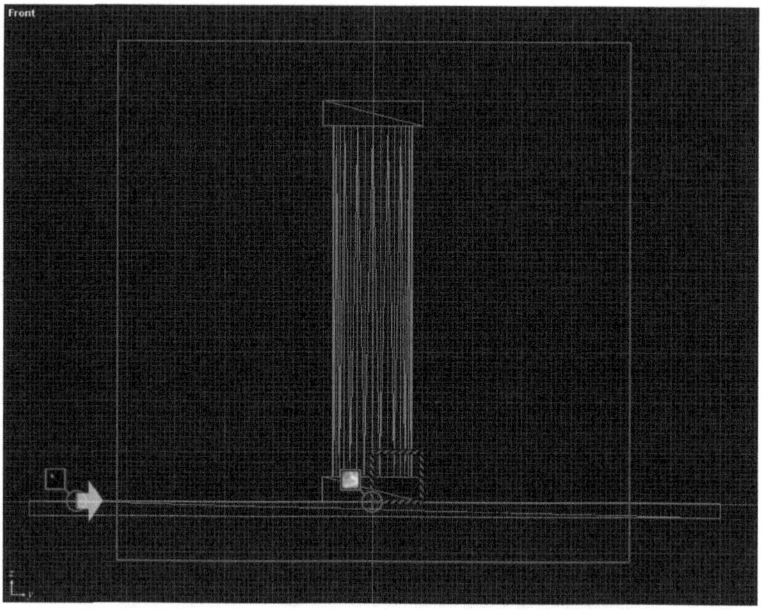

Figure 4-42. Adjusting the position of the infinite light.

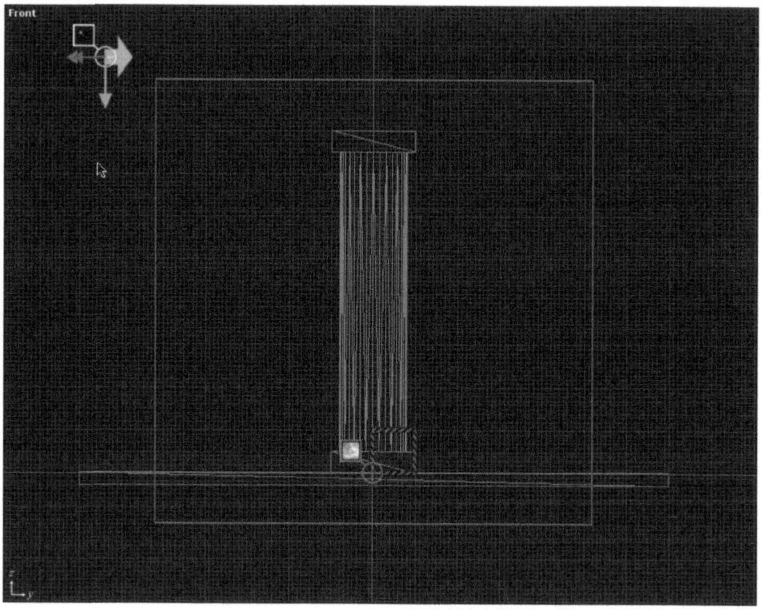

Figure 4-43. Elevating the infinite light.

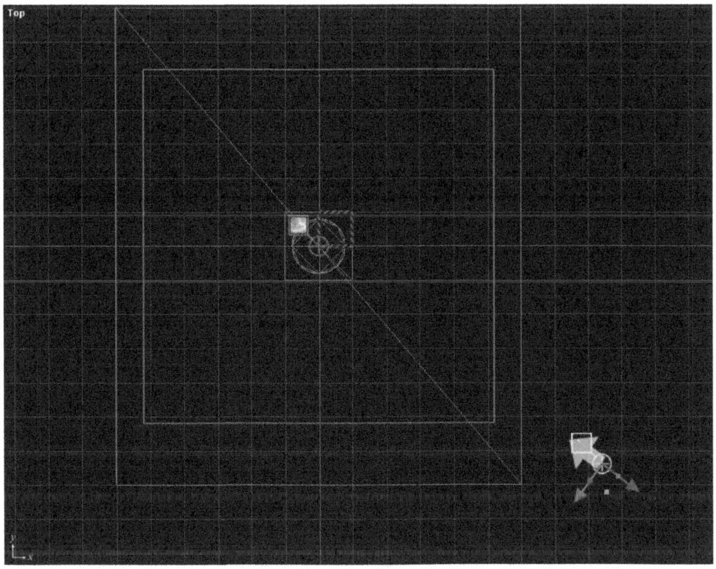

Figure 4-44. Rotating the infinite light.

9 Choose **Layout > Show Viewport 1 (Ctrl-1)** to maximize the **Top (+z)** viewport, and zoom right in to the light, remembering where the column is in relation to the light. It is important to zoom in close to the light as it makes selecting the light direction easier.

10 Press 3 on the keypad to select the **Rotate Nodes** tool, and click on the small green square. Now you can rotate the light direction so that it points towards the column, if it isn't already, as shown in Figure 4-44.

11 Choose **Layout > Show Viewport 1 (Ctrl-1)** once again, to return to the four viewport layout.

Although the light is now pointing towards the column, it is not yet casting a shadow. The light needs to be angled down slightly.

12 Without maximizing a viewport (in order to see the dynamic shadows added in the perspective viewport) zoom into the light and select the small red square in viewport 2, as shown in Figure 4-45.

13 Slightly angle the light direction downwards, as shown in Figure 4-46. This will cause the shadows to be dynamically cast behind the column in the perspective viewport. The perspective viewport should appear as shown in Figure 4-47.

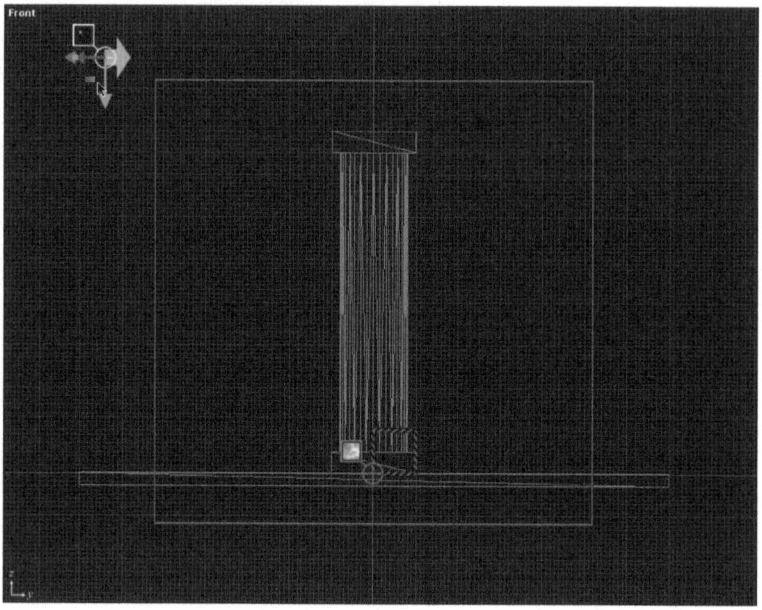

Figure 4-45. Selecting the direction arrow on the infinite light manipulation gizmo.

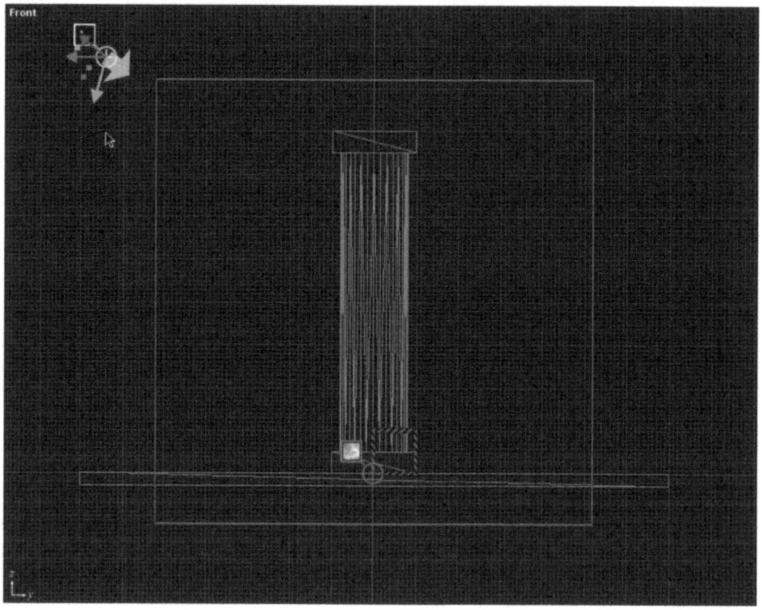

Figure 4-46. Angling the infinite light to face slightly downwards.

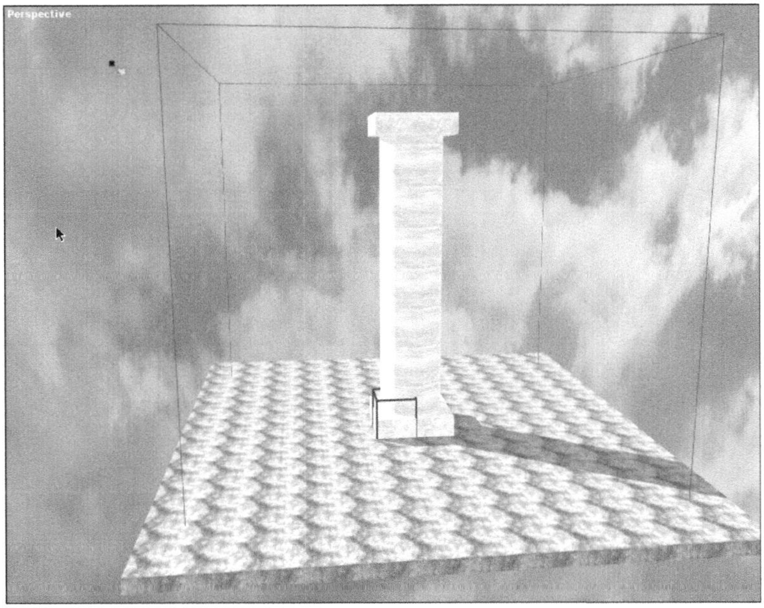

Figure 4-47. The perspective viewport showing the infinite light illuminating the scene.

Add a Player or Spectator Spawn Marker

The world now contains geometry and lights. To enable us to run the world and enter it, we need to add a spawn or spectator marker.

1 Choose **Page > Markers** to open the **Markers** page panel, as shown in Figure 4-48. Note that the named markers in the list are defined by the game code and not by the C4 Engine.

2 Add a **Spawn** marker to the scene using the top-left viewport. Add the marker on top of the floor, in the bottom-left, as shown in Figure 4-49. Use the move tool to elevate the marker slightly off the floor.

3 Rotate the marker around so that the red arrow points towards the column, as shown in Figure 4-50. The red arrow is the direction the player will point when spawning.

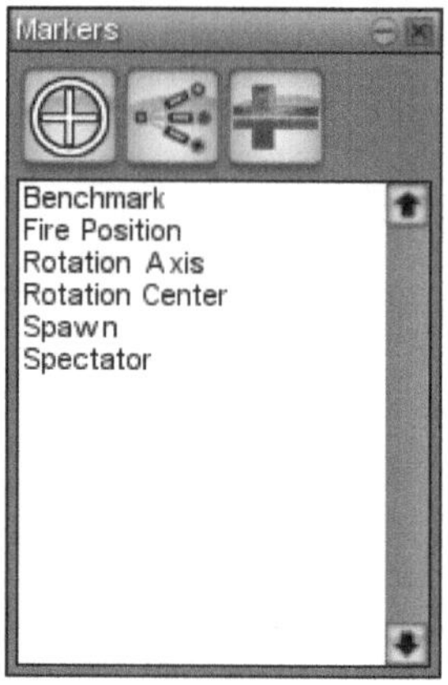

Figure 4-48. The **Markers** page.

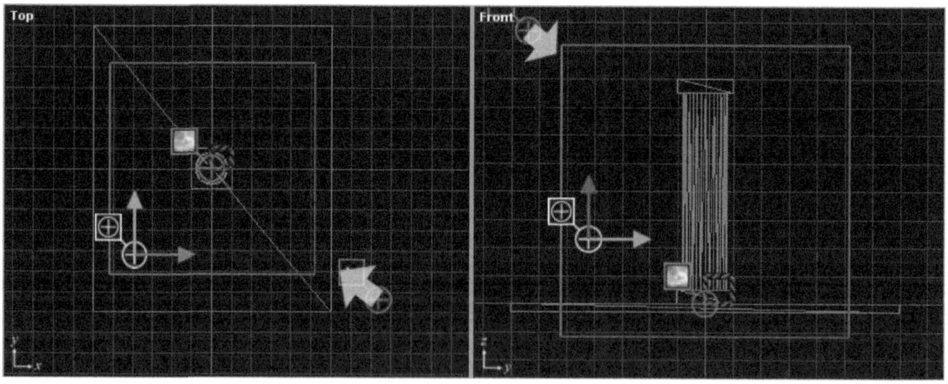

Figure 4-49. Adding the spawn marker node.

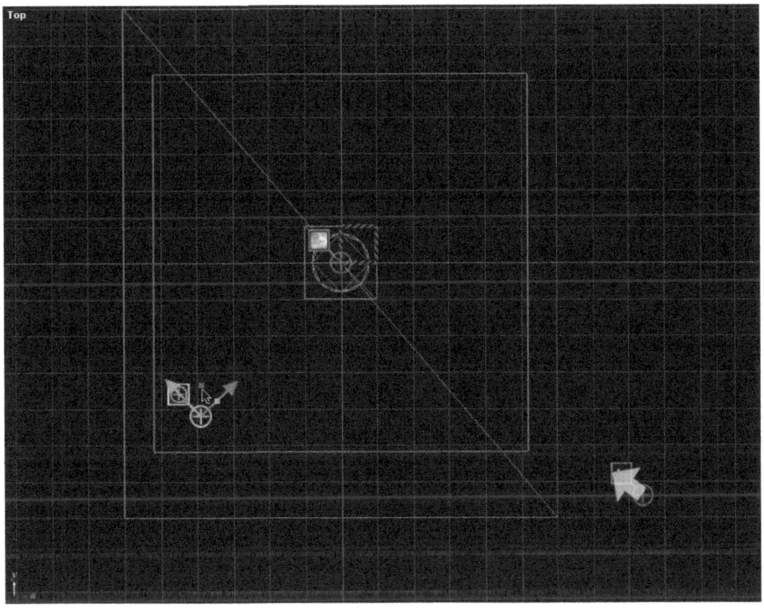

Figure 4-50. Adjusting the heading of the spawn marker node.

As a final step before trying out our newly created world, we need to add a **Physics** node to simulate gravity, because otherwise the player will just hang in the air when the world loads.

4 Choose **Page > Physics** to display the **Physics** page panel in the editor, as shown in Figure 4-51.

5 Switch to the scene graph view and select the **Infinite Zone, click on the Physics Node** and place it in the world by left clicking the **Infinite Zone** and it is added to the scene. So that the scene graph looks like Figure 4-52.

6 Now, resize the infinite zone to encompass all of the world. This can be done using the resize too, so that world looks like Figure 4-53.

6 Save the world file as Base-02.

7 Choose **World > Save and Play World (Ctrl-P)**, as shown in Figure 4-54. You can now move around the world as a character and shoot at the column.

8 To exit the game and return to the **World Editor**, press ESC and then press **Exit Current Game**.

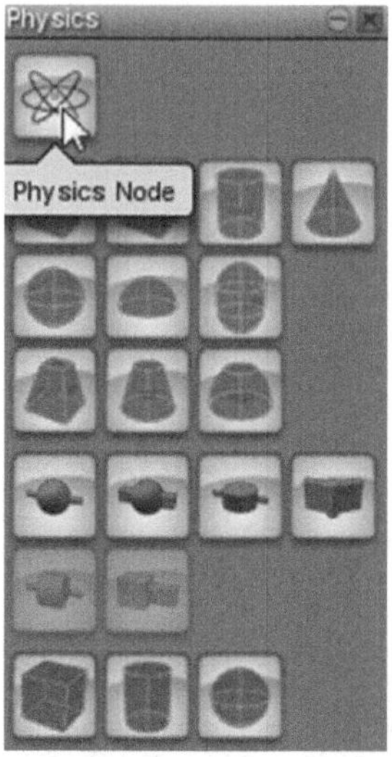

Figure 4-51. The **Physics** page.

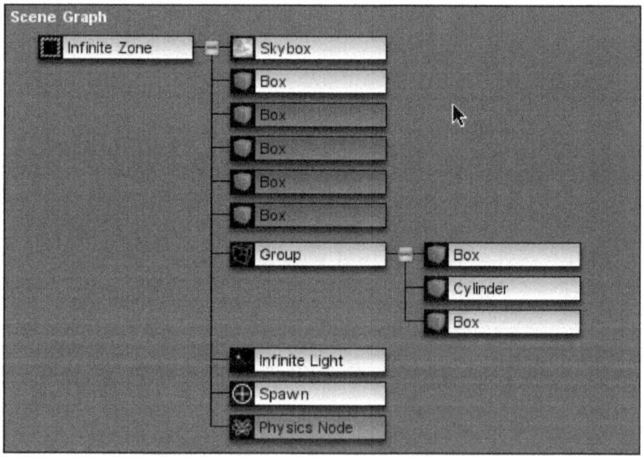

Figure 4-52. The scene graph.

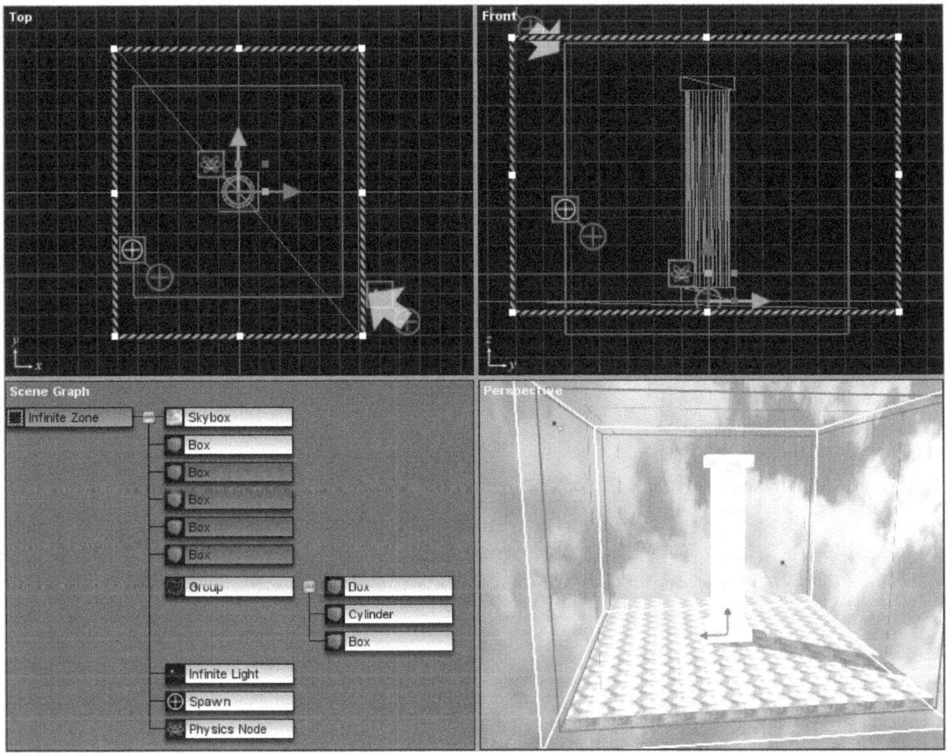

Figure 4-53. The infinite zone resized.

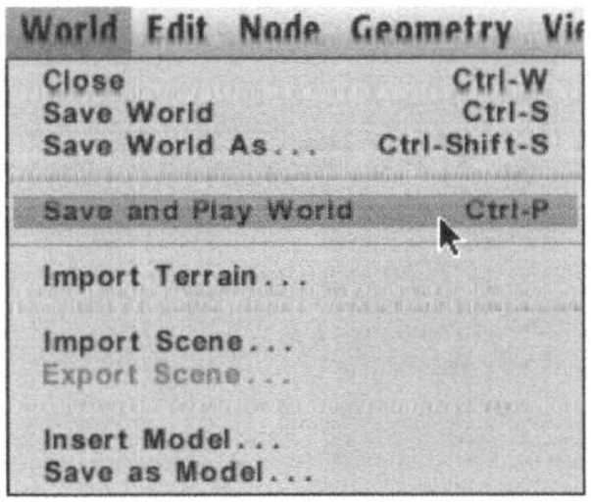

Figure 4-54. Choosing **Save and Play World**.

Register Your World to Show up in the Start New Game window

The C4 Engine demo game is provided with a list of world file names to present in the **Start New Game** window. These world file names are provided in the file `Worlds.txt`, which is located in **Import/Demo/game/**. The file currently has several entries, such as the following:

```
'GRAV' "world/Cem/Cemetery"
{
    'TITL' "Lost Cemetery"
    'AUTH' "Gameplay Demo"
}
'AREN' "world/Arena/Arena"
{
    'TITL' "Haunted Arena"
    'AUTH' "Gameplay Demo"
}
'LAND' "world/Island/Island"
{
    'TITL' "Island"
    'AUTH' "Tree and Water Demo"
}
'HELL' "world/Hellsmouth/Hellsmouth"
{
    'TITL' "Hell's Mouth"
    'AUTH' "Multiplayer Map"
}
'DUNG' "world/Dungeon/Dungeon"
{
    'TITL' "Dungeon"
    'AUTH' ""
}
'PHYS' "world/Physics/Physics"
{
    'TITL' "Physics"
    'AUTH' "Rigid Body Demo"
}
'POND' "world/Pond/Pond"
{
```

```
    'TITL' "Pond"
    'AUTH' "Wave Demo"
}
```

1 Add an entry to the bottom of the file that creates a unique identifier followed by the virtual path where the world file is located. For example:

```
'BASE' "world/Base-02"
```

This basic entry is acceptable if you only wish to display the world name in the **Start New Game** dialog. It is a nice touch to display a title for the world and your name as the author, but these strings are not mandatory:

```
{
    'TITL' "My First World"
    'AUTH' "Me"
}
```

2 Save the text file and open C4.

3 Choose **Tools > Import String Table**, as shown in Figure 4-55.

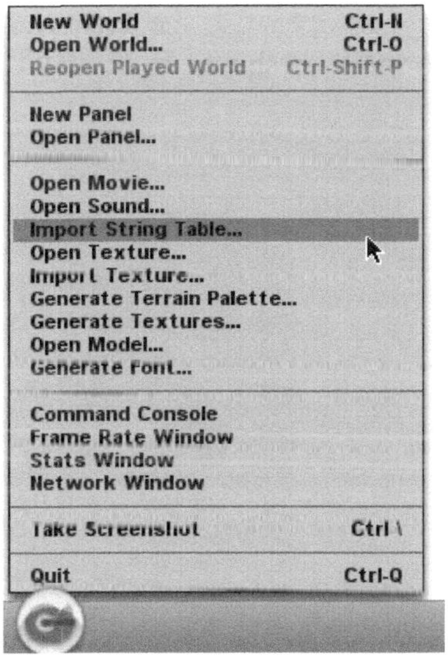

Figure 4-55. Starting the **String Importer** tool.

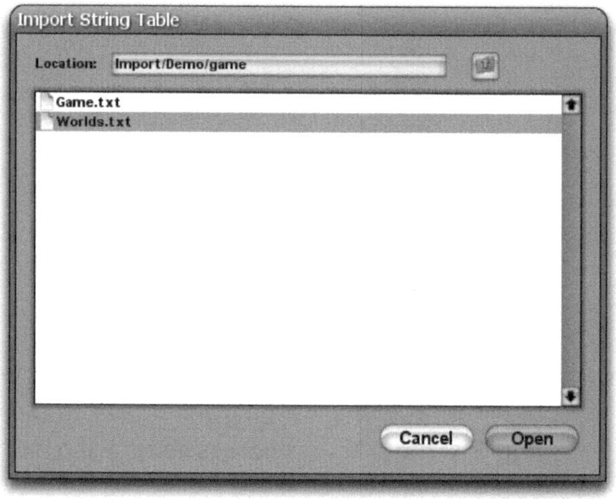

Figure 4-56. Importing the `Worlds.txt` file.

4 Navigate to the Import/Demo/game/ directory and select `Worlds.txt`, as shown in Figure 4-56.

5 Click **OK** to confirm your selection.

6 Exit C4.

The next time you open C4, the **Start New Game** window will display the Base world file to load, as shown in Figure 4-57. A preview image is not displayed for now.

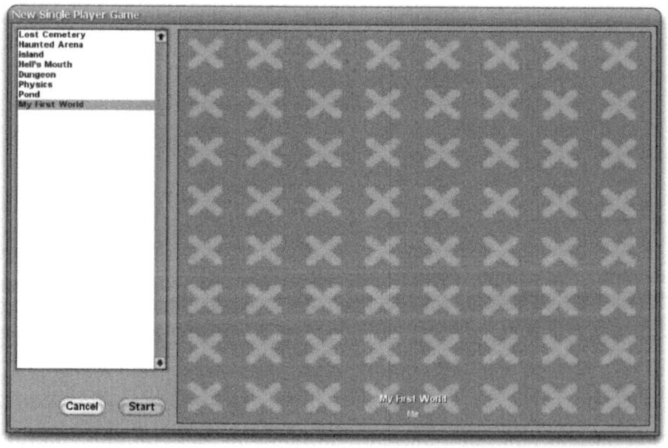

Figure 4-57. The **Start New Game** dialog.

Add Physics Interactions

In this section we are going to add some rigid bodies that will react to being shot with the pistol and will move when the player runs into them. In order for this to happen, we will need to add some geometry, exactly like we added the pillar earlier. But if you remember when walking around the world we created, nothing happened when the pillar was shot or we ran into it.

We need to take the geometry that is currently static and make it dynamic (i.e., make it into a rigid body). We achieve this by adding a controller to geometry, called a *rigid body controller*. But first we must add a physics shape to the geometry in question, in this case a sphere shape. The reason we have to do this is that we can have a very complicated geometry, but we want to use a simple collision shape, so we just draw one out for the rigid body controller to use.

With Base-02 open, select a sphere geometry from the **Geometries** page and draw out a sphere in the top left viewport. If you click on the shift key as you do this, the sphere will be drawn as an exact sphere. Move the sphere away from the floor and away from the player's spawn point, so it looks like Figure 4-58. Now, select the sphere shape from the **Physics** page, as shown in Figure 4-59. And drag out the sphere shape as you did for the geometry in the top left viewport. Again press shift to get a sphere and match the size of the geometry, as shown in Figure 4-60.

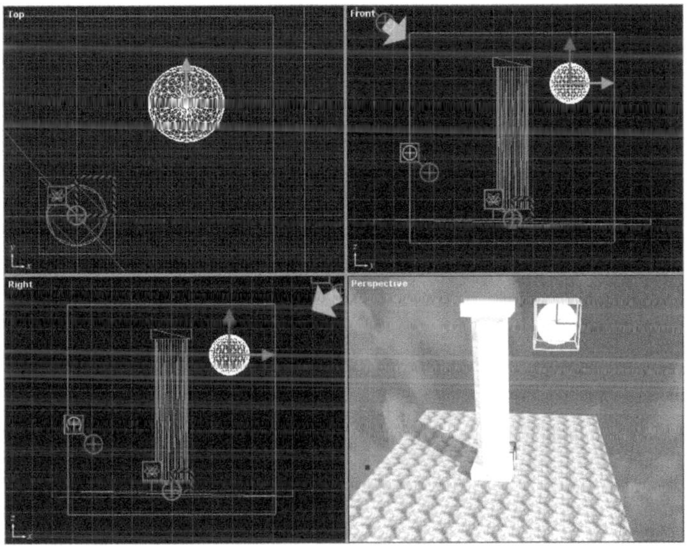

Figure 4-58. Adding a sphere geometry.

Figure 4-59. Selecting the sphere shape.

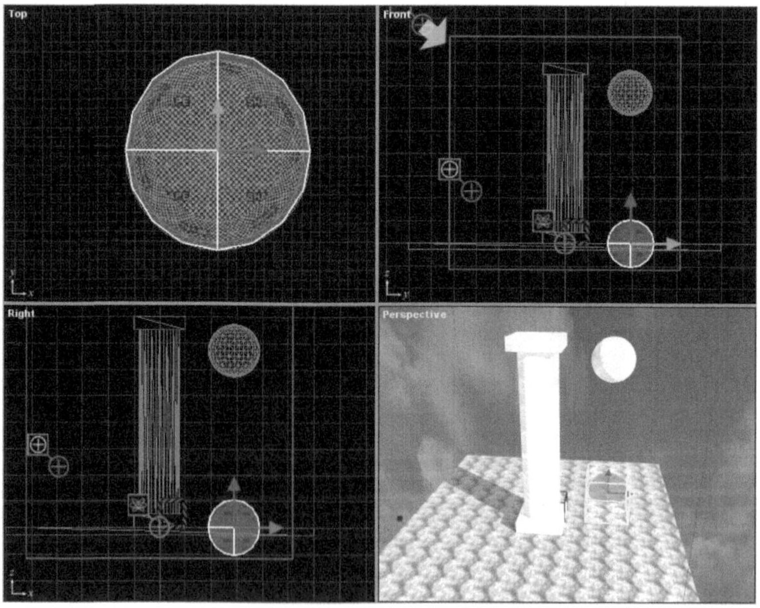

Figure 4-60. Drawing the sphere shape.

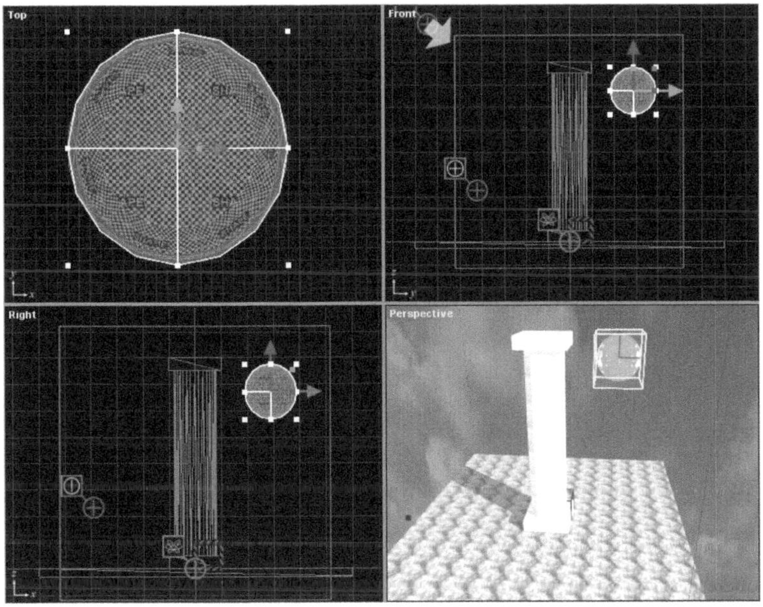

Figure 4-61. Correcting the position of the sphere shape.

You can see from the previous figure that although the shape has been drawn to the correct size, it currently is in the wrong position. Move the shape so that it is covering the geometry in all of the viewports, as shown in Figure 4-61.

If we look at the scene graph, we can see that although the shape is in the scene, it is on the same level as the geometry. That is, it is a child of the root node, as shown in Figure 4-62. We need the shape to be a child of the geometry. Using the move tool, move the shape and drop it onto the geometry, as shown in Figure 4-63. And now the shape is a child of the geometry, as shown in Figure 4-64. We can now add a rigid body controller to the geometry. Open the node info for the geometry, and click on the **Controller** tab. Select **Rigid Body** from the list of controllers. Leave the settings as they are, as shown in Figure 4-65. Save the world as Base-03 and play the world, you now have a physics shape that you can run into and shoot.

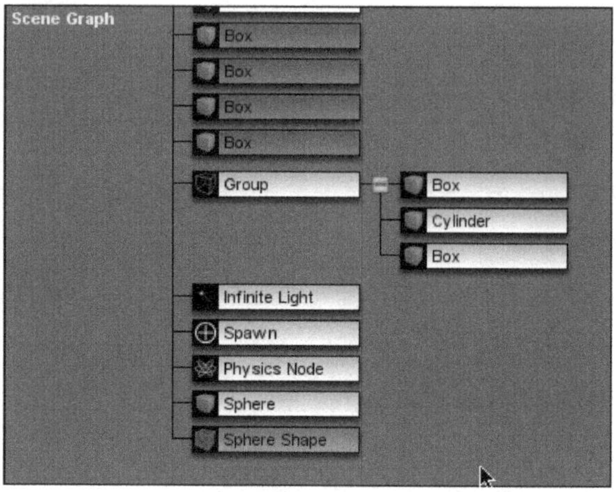

Figure 4-62. Sphere shape in the scene graph.

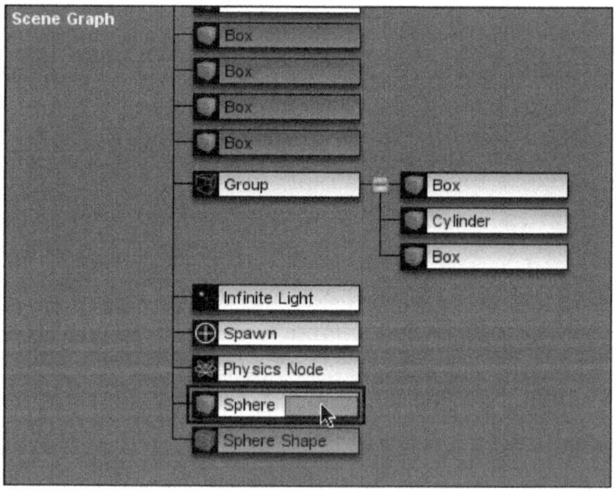

Figure 4-63. Dragging the sphere shape.

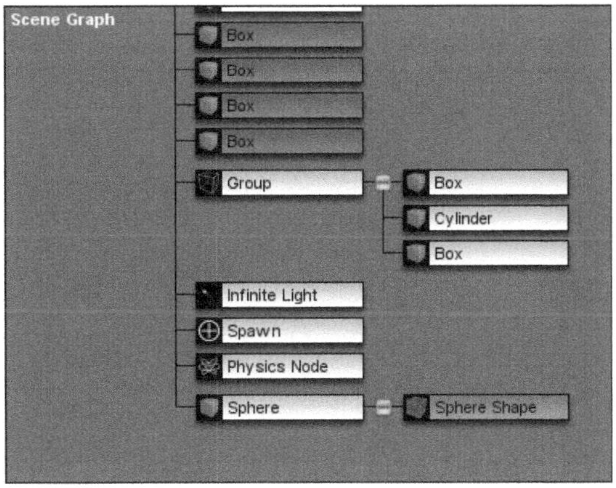

Figure 4-64. Dropping the sphere shape into its correct position.

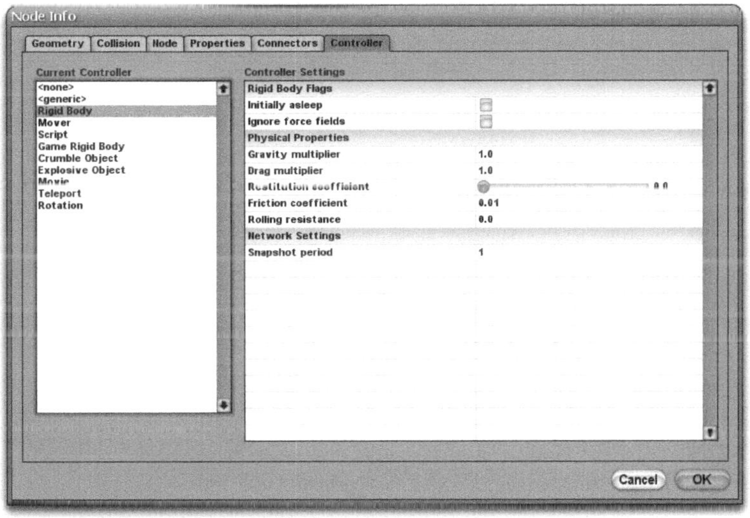

Figure 4-65. The **Rigid Body** controller.

Next Steps

Now that we have learned the basic world creation process, let's move on to adding terrain and water to a world, in Chapter 5, "Terrain and Water".

5

Terrain and Water

This chapter shows how to create terrain from a height map and then add water to the world.

Prerequisites

We recommend that you first run through Chapter 4, Creating a Simple World, prior to working through this chapter, and that you are comfortable with the basic operation of the **World Editor** window. Download the zipped texture files from the resources for this chapter to your root C4 directory. Extract the files to the root directory and they will be copied to their respective locations.

Create the Terrain

Let's create a terrain.

1. Start up the C4 Engine and choose **Tools > Import** texture. The **Import Texture** dialog opens, as shown in Figure 5-1.
2. Import Lake01.tga and Lake01Heightmap.tga, one at a time, as shown in Figure 5-2.
3. Leave the settings in the **Import Texture** dialog at the default values, as shown in Figure 5-3.
4. Create a new subdirectory within the Data/Lake/ directory named world.
5. Create a new world by choosing **Tools > New World (Ctrl-N)**.
6. Save the new world as Lake01 in the Data/Lake/world/ directory.

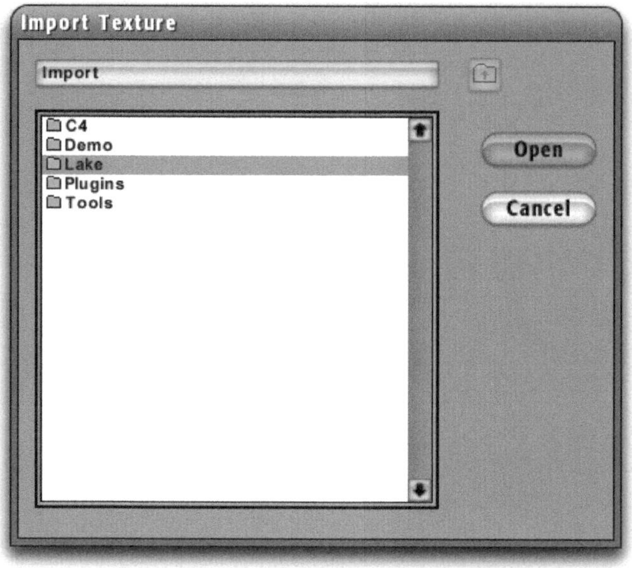

Figure 5-1. The **Import Texture** dialog.

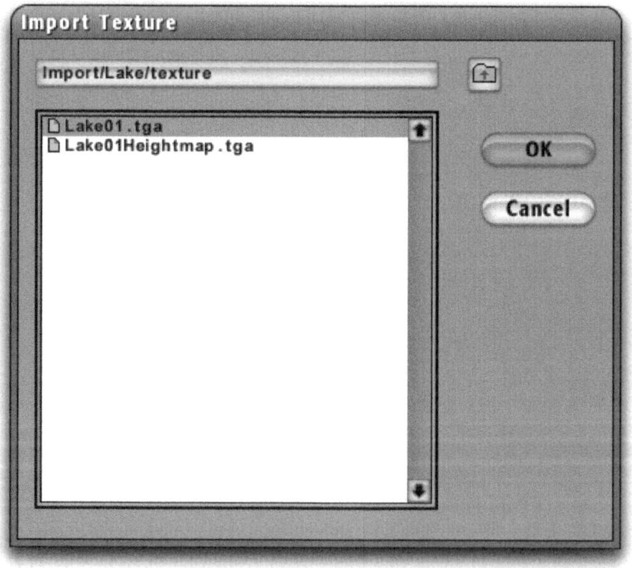

Figure 5-2. Importing the Lake TGA files.

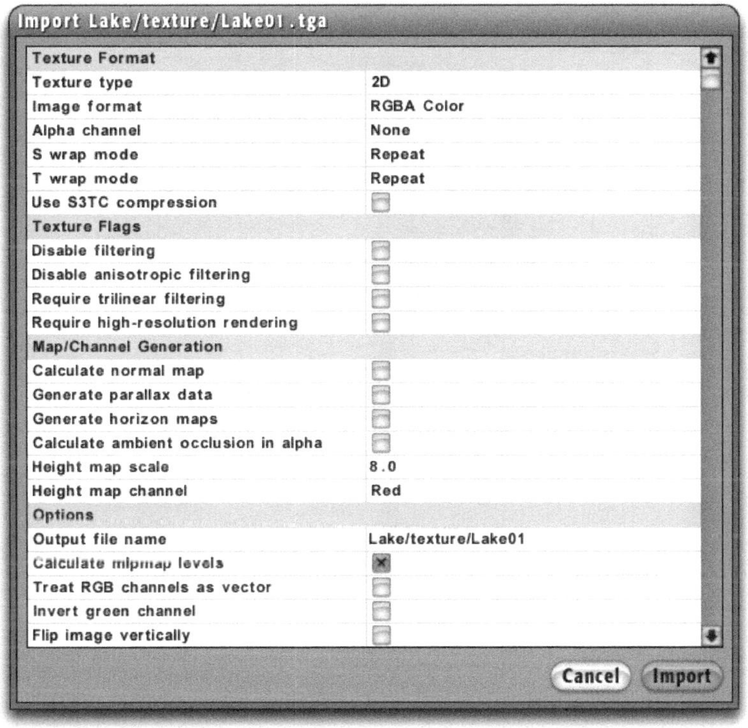

Figure 5-3. The Lake01 texture import settings.

7 Choose **Page > Skyboxes** to open the **Skybox** page panel.

8 Select the **Skybox** tool and create a skybox node in the world by clicking in one of the viewports.

9 Open the **Node Info** dialog (Ctrl-I), select the **Skybox** tab panel, and then choose the textures for the **Skybox Textures** settings group. For this tutorial, the textures sky/Cloudy1 through sky/Cloudy5 were used for the skybox. Select also the **Render above horizon only** option. See Figure 5-4.

10 Select the infinite zone node and open the **Node Info** dialog (Ctrl-I). Select the **Render Skybox in this Zone** option and click **OK**.

11 Next, open the **Material Manager** window and click **New** to create a new material.

12 Set the name of the new material to Lake.

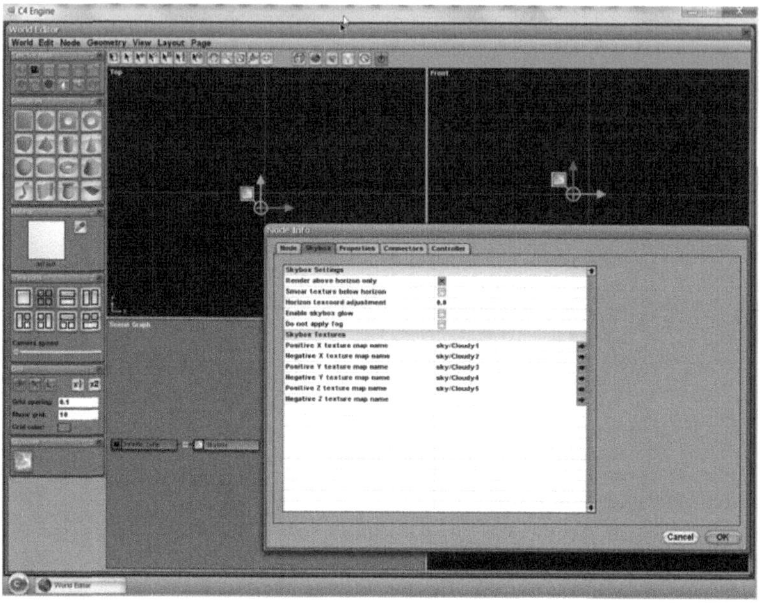

Figure 5-4. Setting up the skybox.

13 Choose the new texture Lake01.tex for the **Texture Map (Primary)** material setting, as shown in Figure 5-5.

14 The **Material Manager** window should appear as shown in Figure 5-6.

15 On the **Grid** page, set the grid spacing to 10 m. This means that each small grid spacing is 10 m and therefore each large grid spacing is 100 m.

16 Choose **Page > Terrain** to open the **Terrain** page.[1] Click the **Terrain Block** tool and then drag out a square in the top viewport (the upper-left viewport) of about 4 large grid squares on each side. When you release the mouse button, a dialog box appears as shown in Figure 5-7.

17 Select **Import TGA Height Field** from the **Terrain Builders** list. We are going to initialize the terrain block with height data from the TGA file we imported above. For the **Height field image file** setting, select the file Lake01Heightmap.tga. To set the vertical scale, enter 20.0 in the **Height scale (distance)** setting. Click **Build**, and after a couple seconds, the scene should appear as in Figure 5-8.

---

[1] See also http://www.terathon.com/wiki/index.php/Terrain.

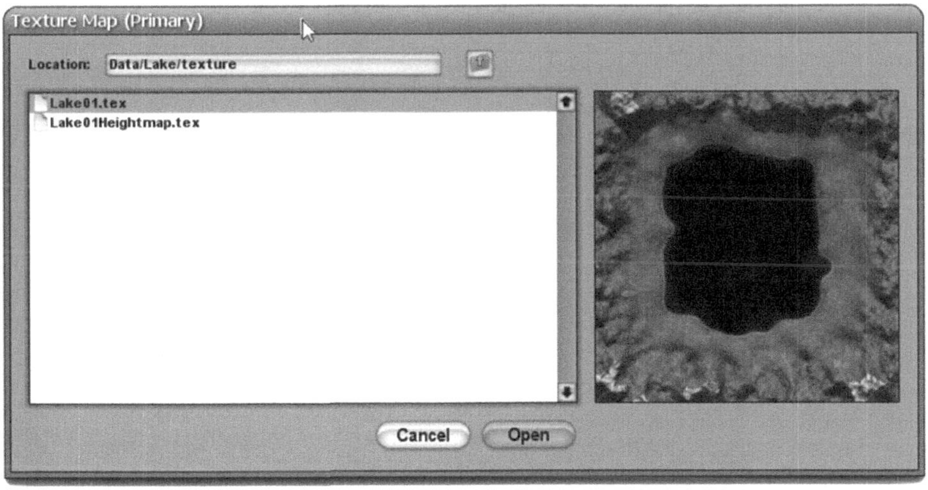

Figure 5-5. Choosing the Lake01 texture.

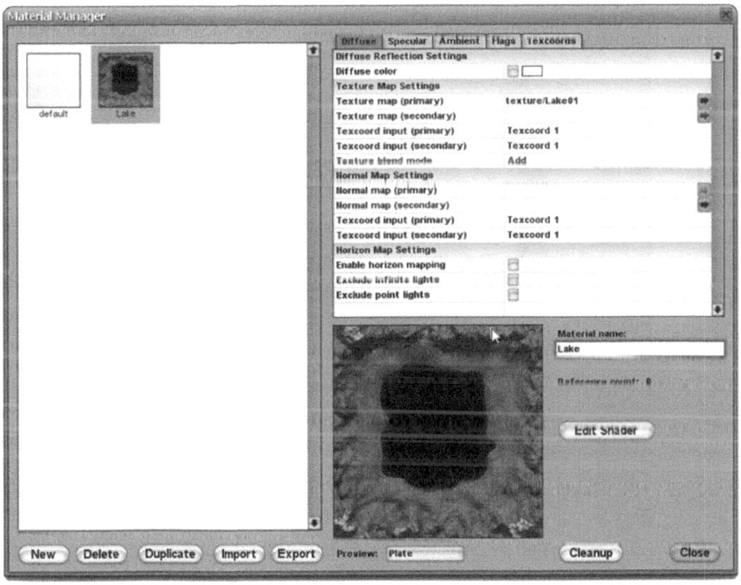

Figure 5-6. The **Material Manager** window.

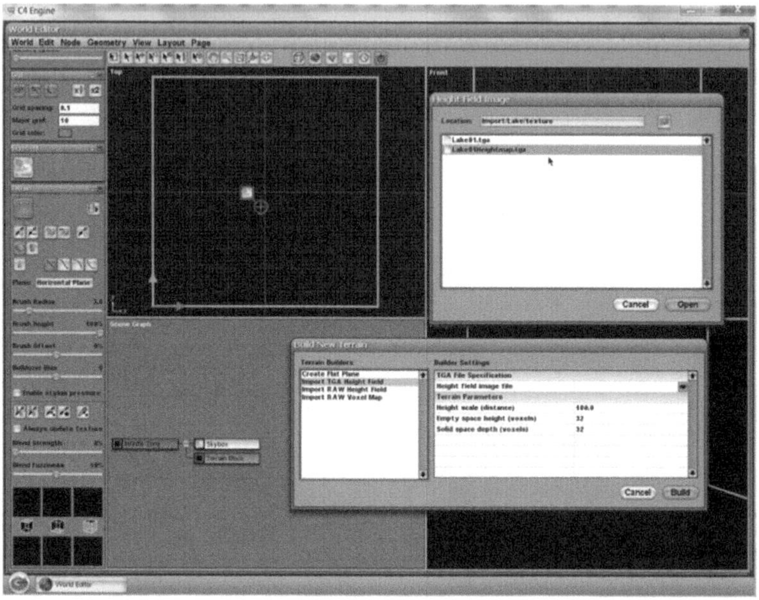

Figure 5-7. Creating a terrain block.

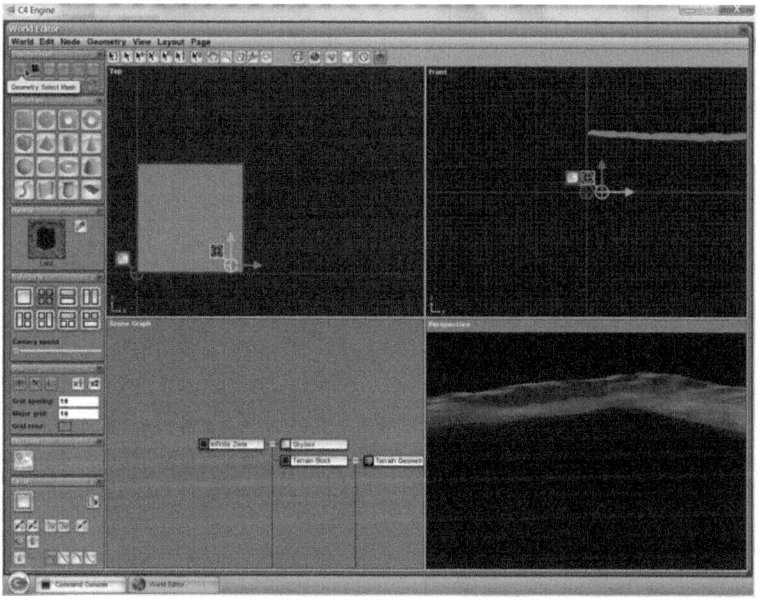

Figure 5-8. The imported terrain in the **World Editor**.

Add a Spawn Point and a Light

In this next series of steps, we'll add the spawn point for where the player first appears as well as a light to illuminate the world.

1. Open the **Markers** page in the **World Editor** by choosing **Page > Markers**.
2. Add a **Spawn** marker to the bottom-right of the world using the top-left viewport.

Since the next few steps only involve a marker, light, and skybox, the geometry nodes can be temporarily hidden, using the **Selection Mask** feature.

3. Click the geometry mask to toggle it off, as shown in Figure 5-9.
4. You can use the scene graph, which is by default in viewport three, to easily re-select the marker if it is accidentally deselected.
5. Collapse the terrain nodes underneath the first node, to make the scene graph more manageable.
6. The spawn marker is added pointing in the wrong direction, so rotate it round such that the red arrow points into the world.

It may be necessary to zoom in quite close to manipulate the rotation handles on the marker. Remember to use the scene graph viewport to re-select the spawn marker if you accidentally miss clicking on the rotation handle.

7. In the top-right viewport, elevate the spawn point marker above the terrain, as shown in Figure 5-10. This step gives the player character some room to fall from a short height into place, when it spawns into the game world.
8. Open the **Lights** page in the **World Editor** by choosing **Page > Lights**.
9. Select the **Infinite Light** tool.
10. Click in one of the viewports to add an infinite light to the world.

Figure 5-9. Masking off geometry node types.

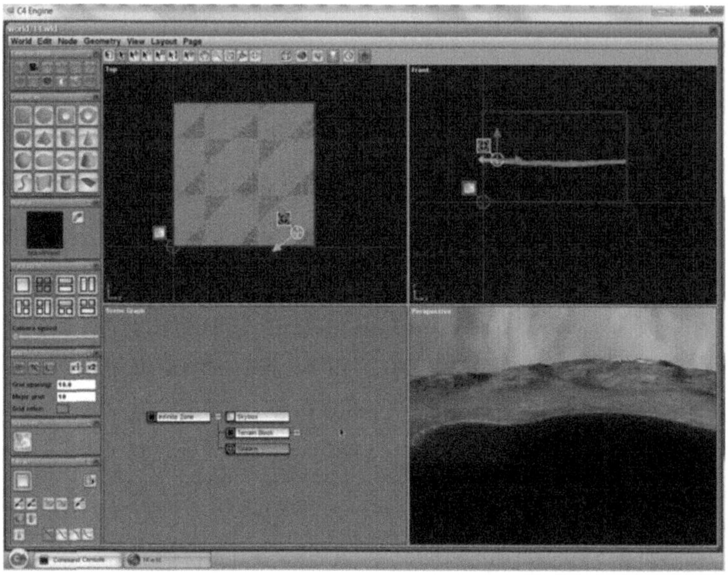

Figure 5-10. Elevating the spawn point marker above the terrain.

11 Drag the infinite light to a position that is to the left side of the world, rotating it so that it appears as shown in Figure 5-11.

12 Click the **Toggle Lighting** button to turn on the dynamic lights for the world. The perspective viewport should appear to be rendered with a real-time display of the world as it would appear in-game.

Create the Water

The easiest way to create a water material for your world is to export one from an existing demo or tutorial world and then to import it into your own world. We like the water in the island demo world, so let's use that one.

1 Open the Island demo world which is under Data/Demo/world/Island.

2 Double click on the **Material** page to open the **Material Manager**.

3 Left click on the Water material and then select **Export**. Type IslandWater for the file name and press **Save**.

4 Press Ctrl-3 to display the scene graph viewport. Shift-left click the two gog space and single remote portal nodes to select them, as shown in Figure 5-12.

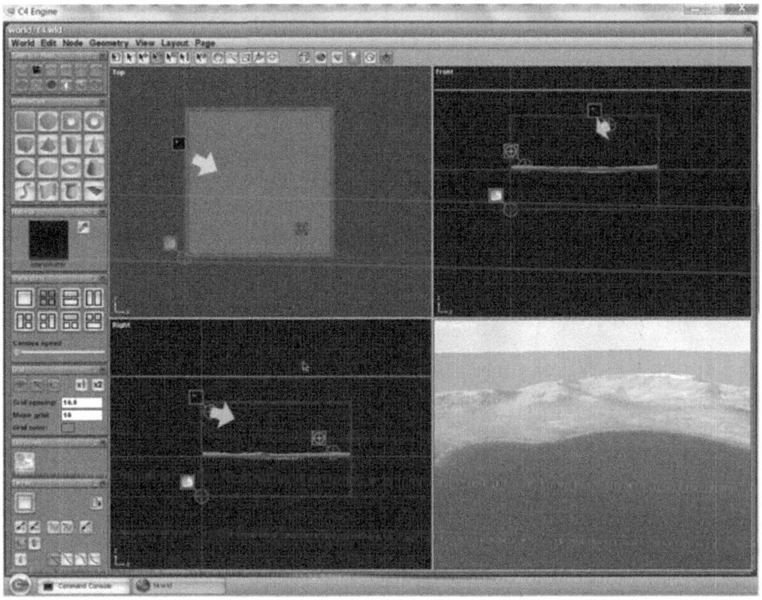

Figure 5-11. Positioning the infinite light.

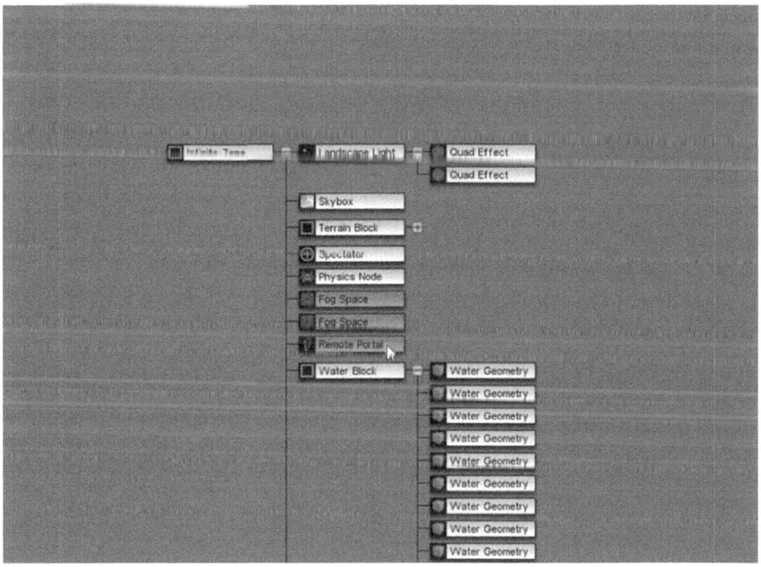

Figure 5-12. Fog and remote portal nodes selected in the Island world.

5 Now press Ctrl-C to copy the three selected nodes. We will paste them into the scene graph of our own world next.

6 Close the Island world without saving and back in our own world, press Ctrl-V to paste the three nodes that we just copied from the Island world. We will place them later on.

7 Double click on the **Material** page to open the **Material Manager**.

8 Click on the **Import** button to import the IslandWater material that you just exported from the Island demo world. Close the **Material Manager**.

9 Open the **Water** page[2] panel by choosing **Page > Water**.

10 Left click on the **Water Block** tool and then drag out an area almost the size of your terrain block in the top-left viewport. A **Build Water** dialog will appear. Accept the default values and click **Build** to create the water.

11 Open the **Transform** page panel and use it to raise the height of the water block to $z = 108.5$. In the perspective viewport, you should now see the water.

12 Use the **Transform** page to also set the height of the remote portal, as well as the first of the fog spaces to the same z value ($z = 108.5$). Leave the z value of the other fog space as is. See Figure 5-13.

13 The last thing we need to do is to add a physics node. To do so, open the **Physics** page panel using **Page > Physics** and select the **Physics** tool. Click anywhere in the top viewport to create the physics node. This ensures that the world has gravity switched on and that the physics engine will calculate physical interactions for us.

14 Choose **World > Save and Play World (Ctrl-P)** to try it out. Your world should now appear as in Figure 5-14.

Next Steps

We have only used a small number of the **World Editor** features in this chapter. Chapter 6, "More World Editor Features", introduces more of the tools and options that are available as you create your own worlds.

---

[2] See also http://www.terathon.com/wiki/index.php/Water_Page.

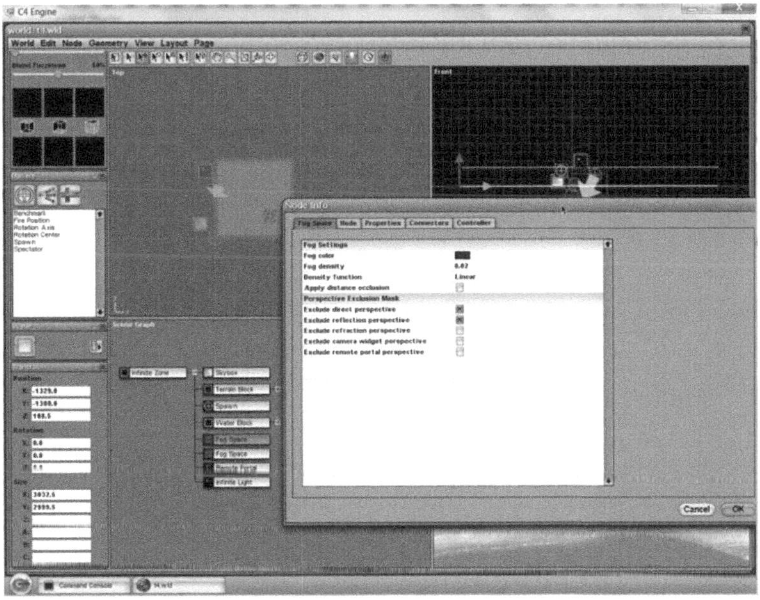

Figure 5-13. Using the **Transform** page to set the height of one of the fog spaces.

Figure 5-14. The completed terrain and water world.

6

More World Editor Features

Going beyond the water world.

Beyond the Basics

Chapter 4, "Creating a Simple World", and Chapter 5, "Terrain and Water", covered many of the basic **World Editor** tools. We covered the use of geometries, lights, markers, materials, the selection mask, and skyboxes. We also used the **World Editor** tools to move, scale, and rotate world objects.

This next tutorial uses the **Water** tutorial world as a setting, and will cover many additional features, such as:

- Cameras
- Effects
- Info
- Particle Systems
- Paths
- Sources
- Transform
- Triggers
- Viewports
- Visibility

Setting the Current Game Variable

For this tutorial, use the demo game application that ships with the C4 Engine, by setting the variable `$gameModuleName`, in the file <C4>/Data/Game/game.cfg, to the value `"Game"`:

```
$gameModuleName = "Game";
```

Panels, Transforms, Cameras, and Rain

Let's start by adding a panel effect node, which we will use to see what a camera can see. Later on, we will also add buttons to switch other effects on and off, such as sound.

1. Start up the C4 Engine and choose **Tools > Open World (Ctrl-O)** to open the Water world, located in the Tutorial/world/ directory. Use Ctrl-4 to display 4 viewports as shown in Figure 6-1.

2. Before you make any changes, choose **World > Save World As (Ctrl-Shift-S)**, and save the world file as EditorFeatures, or some other name of your choice.

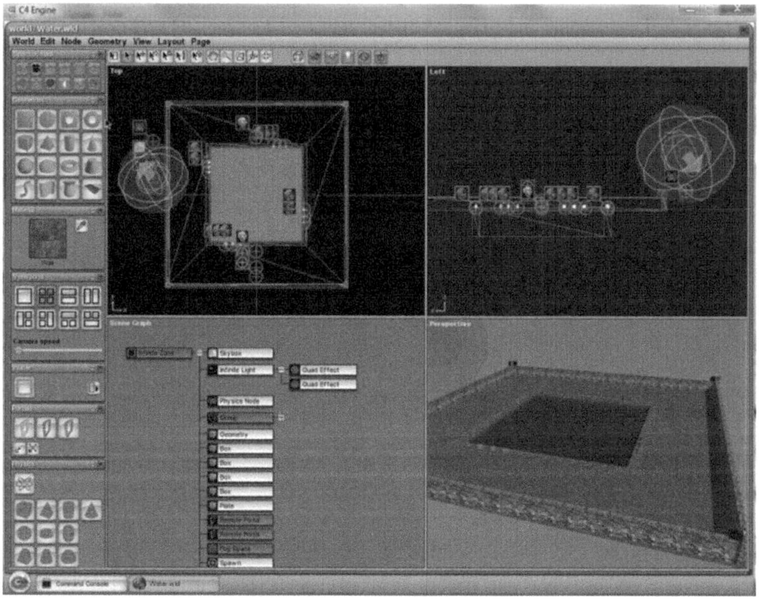

Figure 6-1. The Water world.

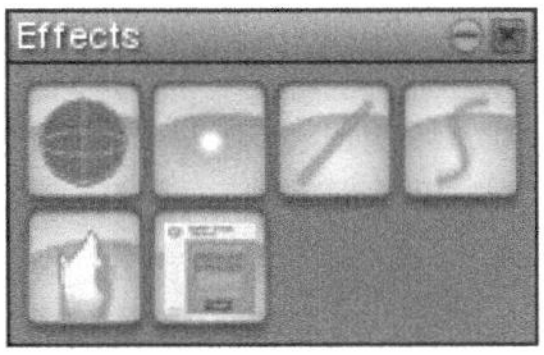

Figure 6-2. The **Effects** page.

3 Open the **Effects** page panel by choosing **Page > Effects**, if that page panel is not already open. Minimize some of the other page panels if you can't see the **Effects** page panel in the **World Editor** window.

4 Select the **Panel Effect** tool, as shown in Figure 6-2.

5 Drag out a panel effect of any size in the viewport that is marked with the x-z symbol, as shown in Figure 6-3.

6 If the **Transform** page panel isn't open already, open it by choosing **Page > Transform**. Minimize some of the other page panels if you can't see the **Transform** page panel in the **World Editor** window, as shown in Figure 6-4.

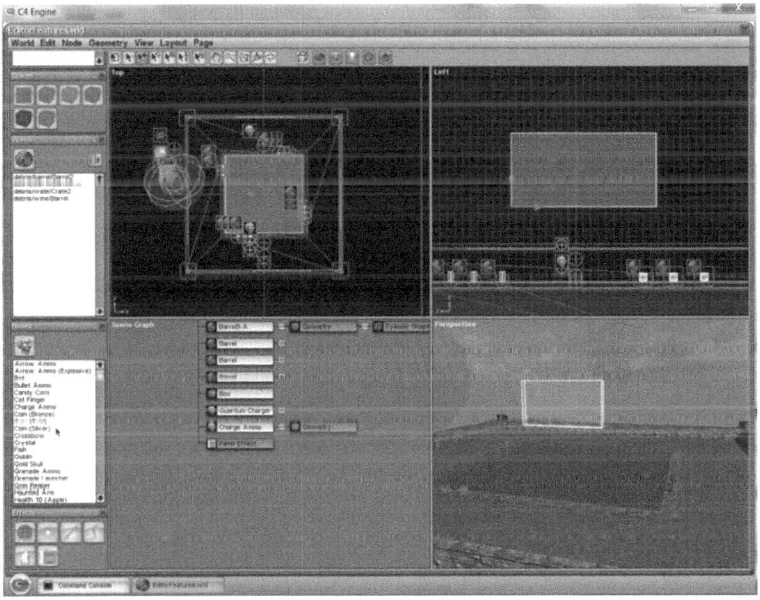

Figure 6-3. Creating the panel effect.

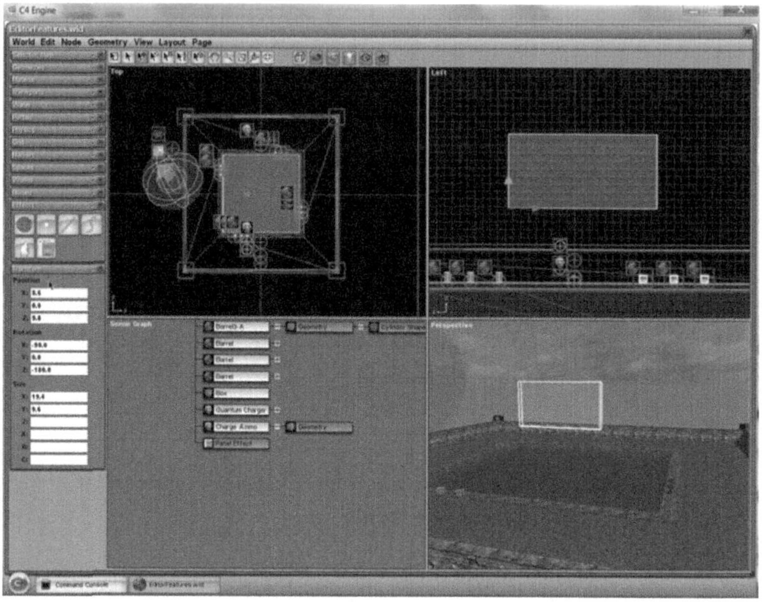

Figure 6-4. Making room for the **Transform** page.

7 Set the size of the panel effect node to 5 units in the *x* and *y* directions. The *z* position should be set to 1.0, the *x* position to 0.0, and the *y* position should be set to –30.0.

8 Set the *z* rotation to 0.0, the *y* rotation to 0.0, and the *x* rotation to 90.0, as shown in Figure 6-5.

9 Open the **Cameras** page panel by choosing **Page > Cameras**, and select the **Frustum Camera** tool, if it's not already open, as shown in Figure 6-6.

10 Click in one of the viewports to add a frustum camera node to your world.

11 Use the **Transform** page panel to set the size of the camera to 5 units in the *x* direction and to 1 in the *y* direction. The *x* position should be set to 0.0, the *y* position should be set to –30.0 and the *z* position should be set to 10.0. The *x* rotation should be set to –90.0 and the *y* and *z* rotations can be left at 0.0, as shown in Figure 6-7.

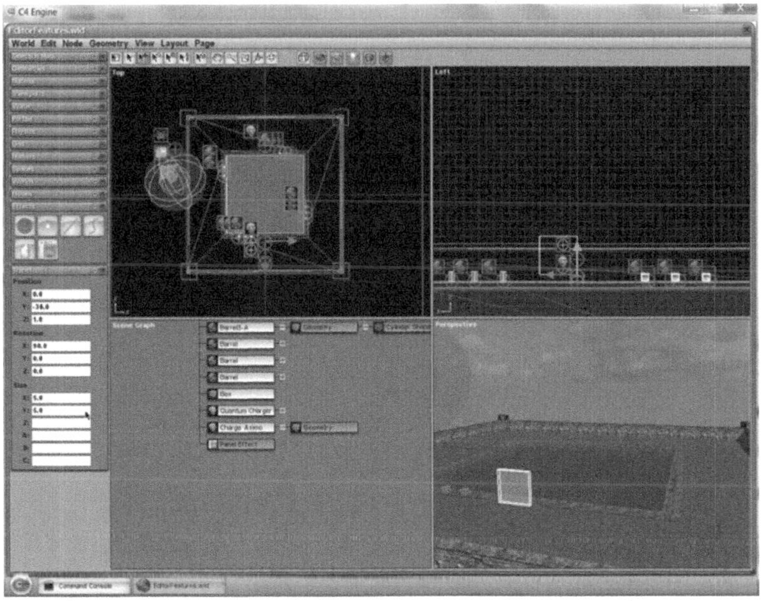

Figure 6-5. The **Transform** page settings for the panel effect.

12 Select the panel effect and choose **Node > Get Info (Ctrl-I)** to open the **Node Info** dialog.

13 Select the **Properties** tab panel, as shown in Figure 6-8.

14 In the **Available Properties** list box, select **Interaction**.

15 Click the **Assign** button.

The **Interaction** property appears in the **Assigned Properties** list, as shown in Figure 6-9. The **Interaction** property makes the panel interactive.

Figure 6-6. The **Frustum Camera** tool in the **Cameras** page.

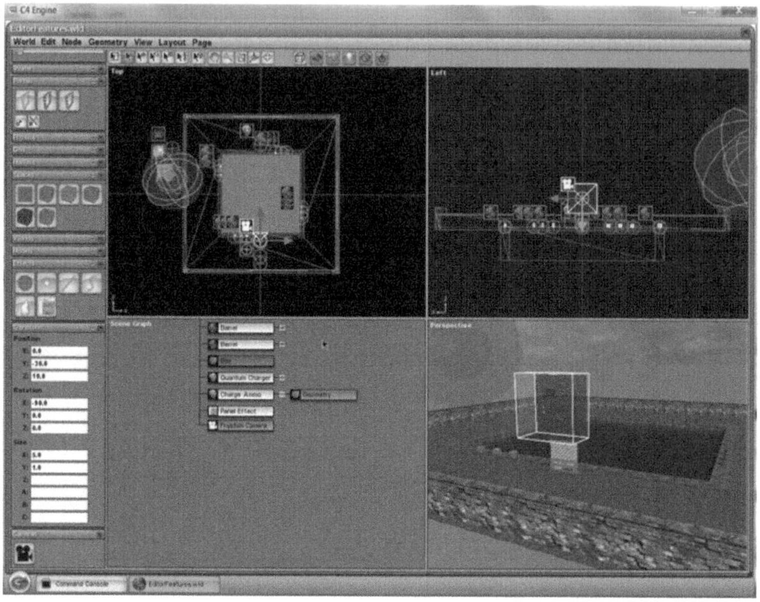

Figure 6-7. The transformed frustum camera in the **World Editor** window.

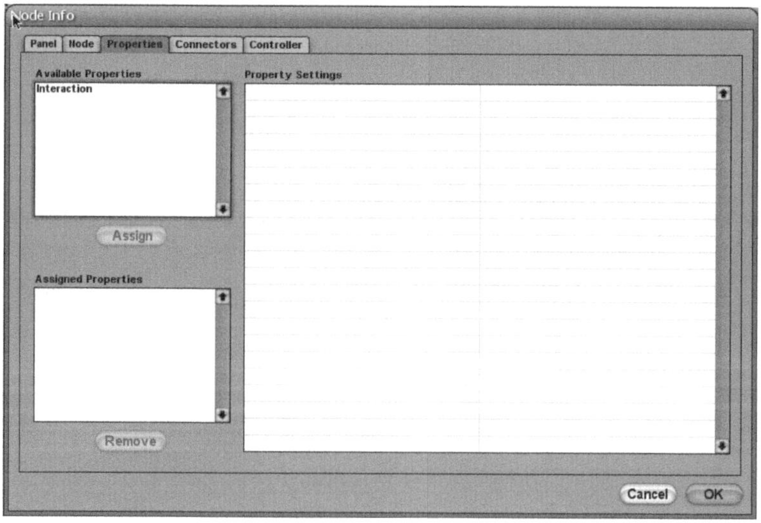

Figure 6-8. The **Properties** tab panel in the **Node Info** dialog.

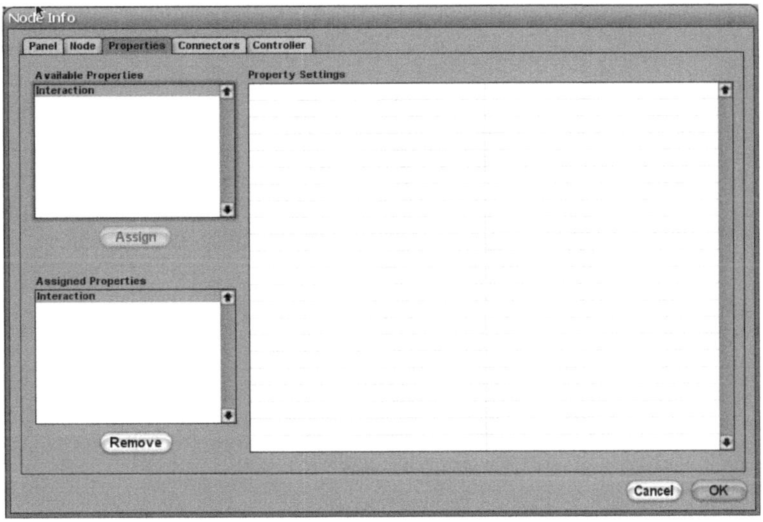

Figure 6-9. The assigned **Interaction** property.

16 Select the **Connectors** tab panel, as shown in Figure 6-10.

17 Click the **New** button to add a new connector.

18 Names the connector `CAM0`, as shown in Figure 6-11. We will connect this connector to our camera so that the camera's view can be shown on a window in our panel.

19 Select the **Controller** tab panel. In the **Current Controller** panel, the **Panel** controller type is selected by default, as shown in Figure 6-12.

20 Click **Edit Panel** to open the **Panel Editor** dialog, as shown in Figure 6-13.

21 Select the **Camera** widget from the list of tools in the upper-left corner of the **Panel Editor** dialog, as shown in Figure 6-14.

22 Drag out a rectangle for the camera view as shown in Figure 6-15.

As shown in Figure 6-16, you can select movement, rotation, and scaling tools in **Panel Editor** dialog, just as you can in the **World Editor** window.

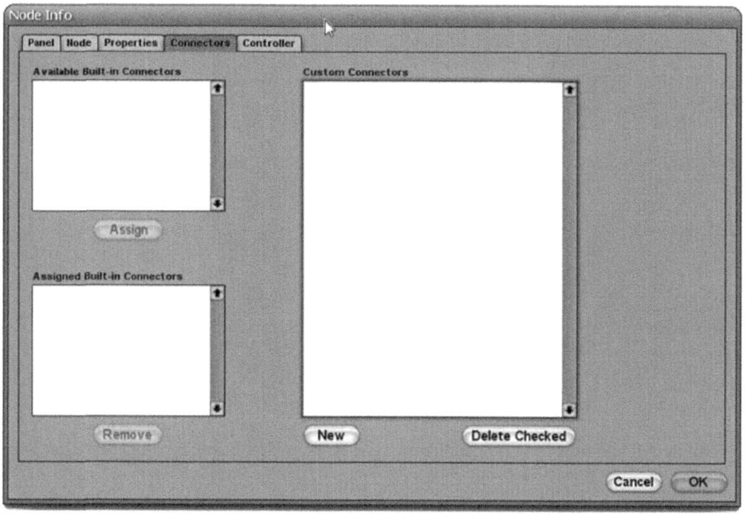

Figure 6-10. The **Connectors** tab panel in the **Node Info** dialog.

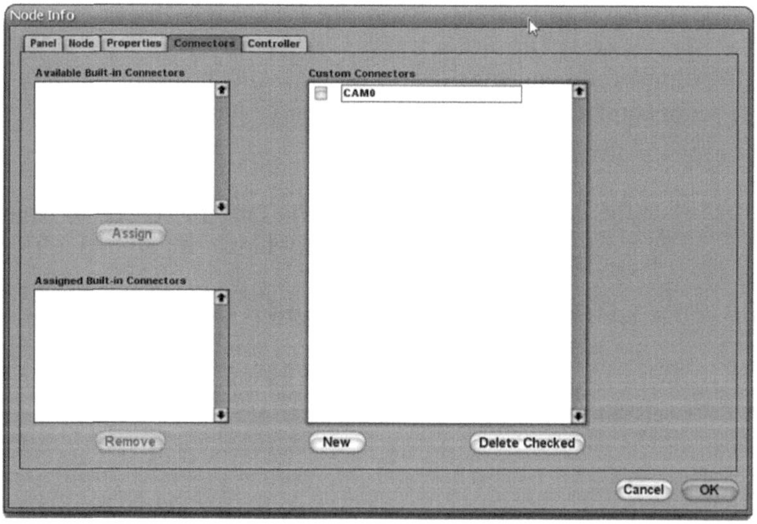

Figure 6-11. Setting the **Key** value for the `CAM0` connector.

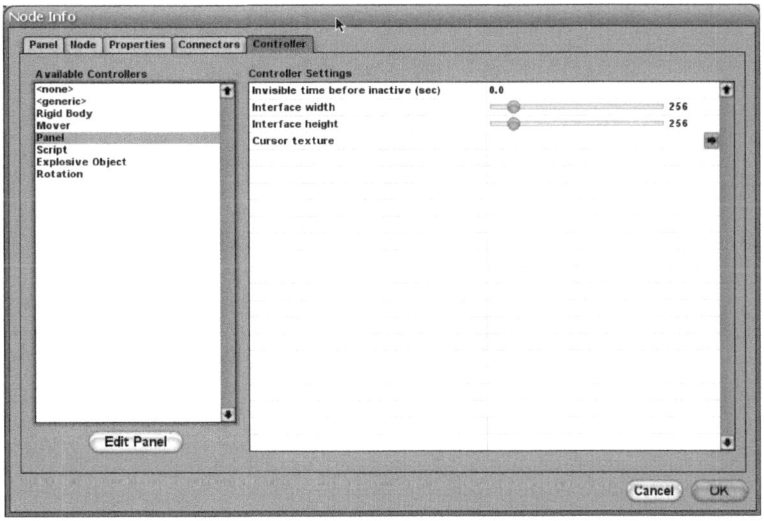

Figure 6-12. The **Controller** tab panel in the **Node Info** dialog.

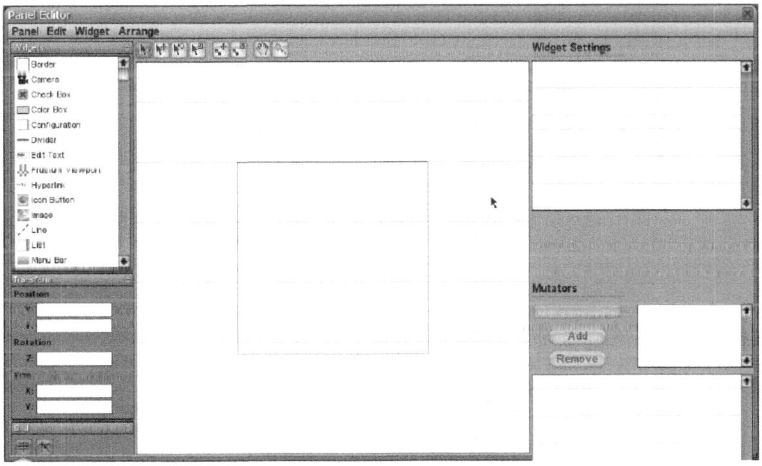

Figure 6-13. The **Panel Editor** dialog.

Figure 6-14. Selecting the **Camera** widget in the **Panel Editor** dialog.

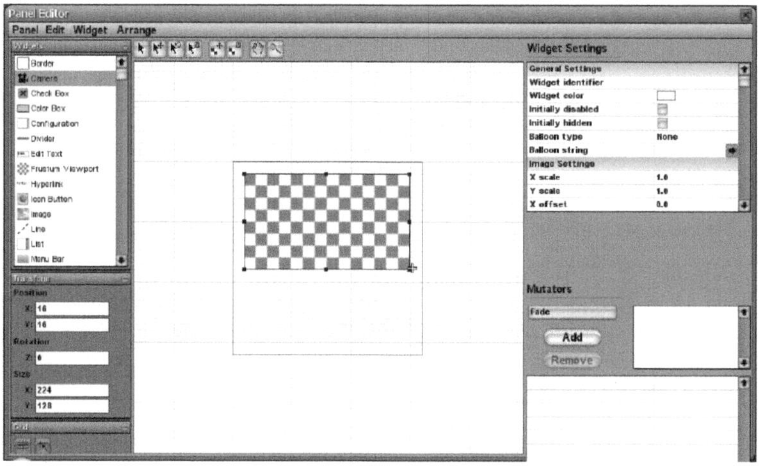

Figure 6-15. Creating a **Camera** widget in the **Panel Editor** dialog.

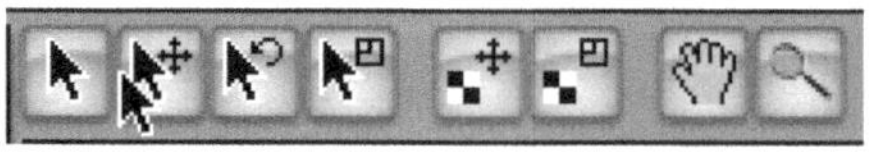

Figure 6-16. The transform tools in the **Panel Editor** dialog.

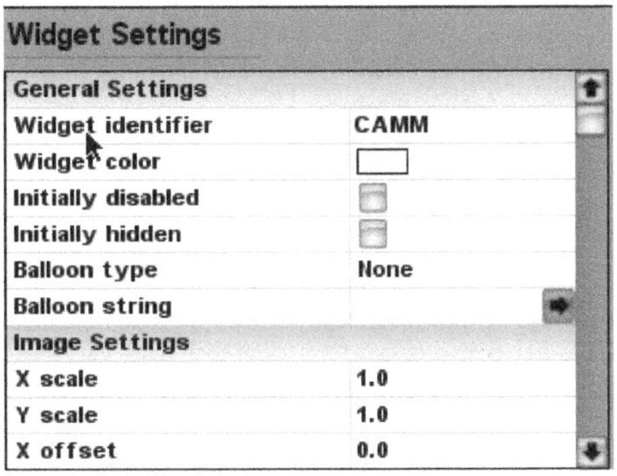

Figure 6-17. Setting the **Widget Settings** for the camera widget in the **Panel Editor** dialog.

23 In the **Widget Settings** group, set the **Widget identifier** value to `CAMM` and the **Camera connector** value to `CAM0`, as shown in Figure 6-17. Note that you may have to scroll down to find the **Camera connector key** value setting.

24 From the menu at the top of the **Panel Editor**, select **Panel > Save Panel (Ctrl-S)** to save your changes. Then select **Panel > Close (Ctrl-W)** to close the **Panel Editor**. Then click **OK** to confirm the **Node Info** dialog changes.

25 Back in the **World Editor** window, select the **Connect Nodes (5)** tool, as shown in Figure 6-18.

The `CAM0` connector appears in each of the orthographic viewports, as shown in Figure 6-19. You may need to pan or zoom in our out of the various viewports to see the panel and the camera.

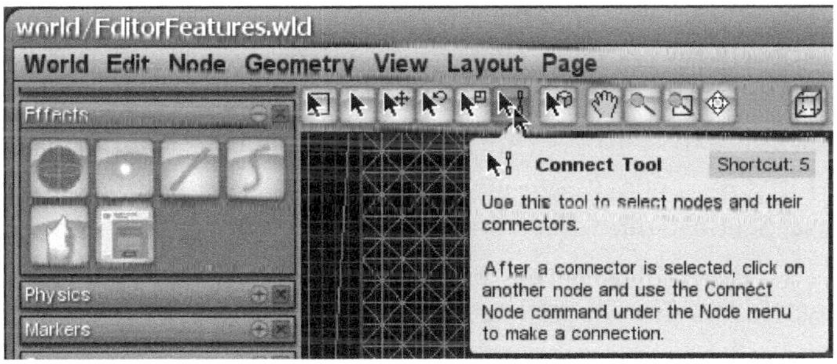

Figure 6-18. Selecting the **Connect Nodes** tool in the **World Editor** window.

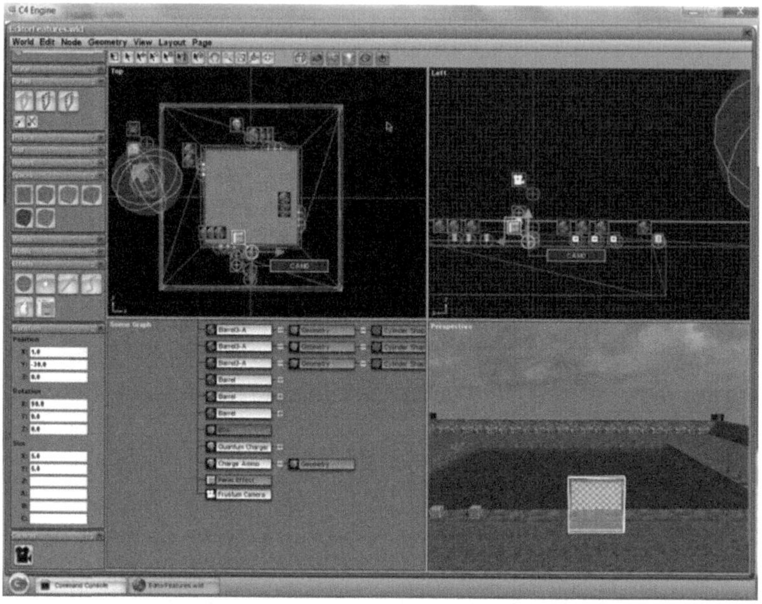

Figure 6-19. The `CAM0` connector, ready to be linked.

26 To make the next step easier, while hovering the mouse over the center of the *x-y* **Top (+z)** viewport, use the scroll wheel to zoom in on the panel and camera nodes, as shown in Figure 6-20. You can pan the view by holding the scroll wheel and dragging.

27 Select the `CAM0` connector, and then select the camera, as shown in Figure 6-21.

When a connector is selected by the **Connect Nodes** tool, selecting another node acts as a secondary selection, leaving the connector selected as a potential source link.

Using the Scene Graph for Faster Selection

As an alternative to zooming in, node selections can be made more quickly by viewing the scene graph in one of the viewports. Right-click a viewport and choose **Scene Graph** from the contextual menu to switch that viewport into the scene graph display mode. The scene graph presents a tree view of each node in the world, as shown in Figure 6-22. You can quickly pan the scene graph by dragging the mouse while pressing the Alt key or by dragging the mouse while holding the scroll button. In the scene graph view, you first left-click to select the

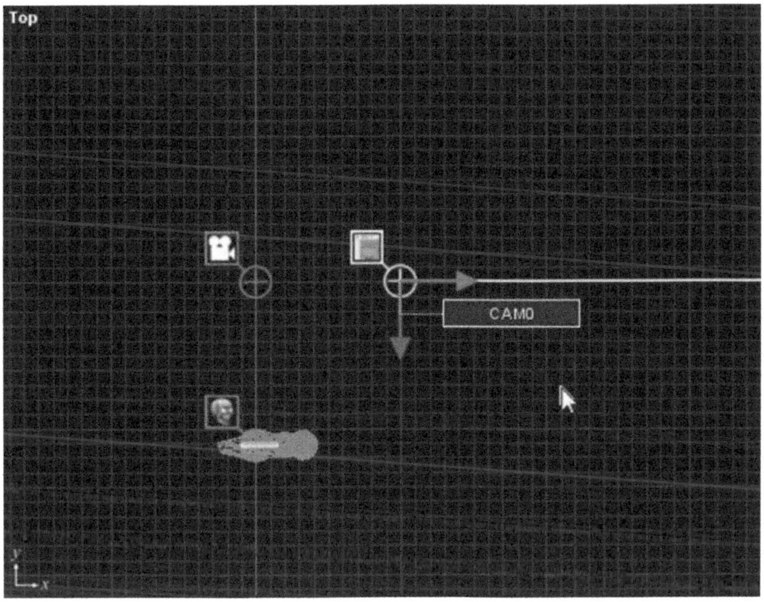

Figure 6-20. Zooming in to get a closer look.

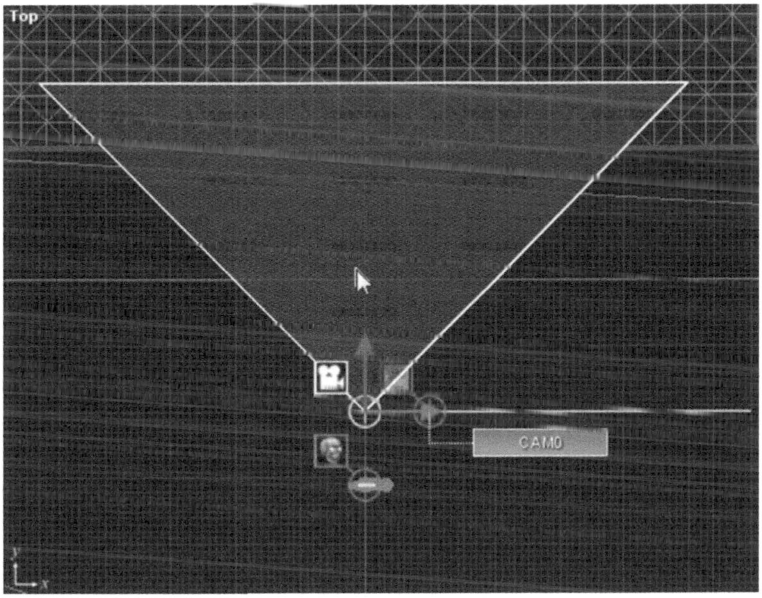

Figure 6-21. Selecting the `CAM0` connector and the camera node.

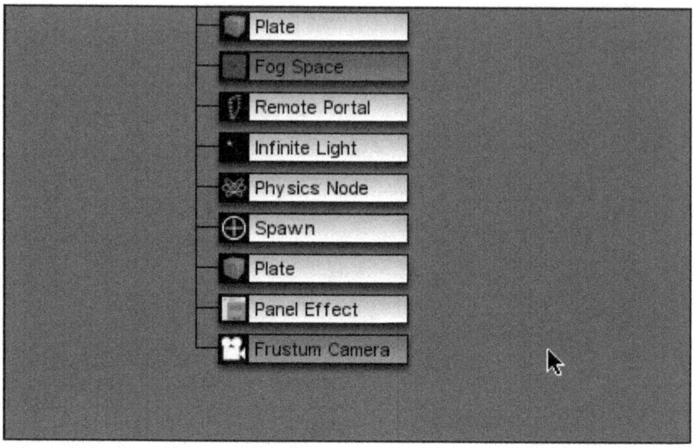

Figure 6-22. Using the scene graph to quickly make a node selection.

Panel Effect node and then left-click to select the **Frustum Camera** node. At this point, only the **Frustum Camera** node will be high- lighted as selected in the scene graph.

28 Choose **Node > Connect Node (Ctrl-L)** to link the panel to the camera using your `CAM0` connector. A link graphic should appear as shown in Figure 6-23. If you need to disconnect the nodes later on, you can choose **Node > Unconnect Node (Ctrl-U)**.

29 Choose **World > Save and Play World (Ctrl-P)** to save and play your world. You should see the panel showing the image that is seen by the camera, as shown in Figure 6-24. The effect is a bit like a portal, and can be used to implement monitors showing what is happening elsewhere in the game world. You could also add a rotation controller to the camera, to continuously rotate the image shown by the camera.

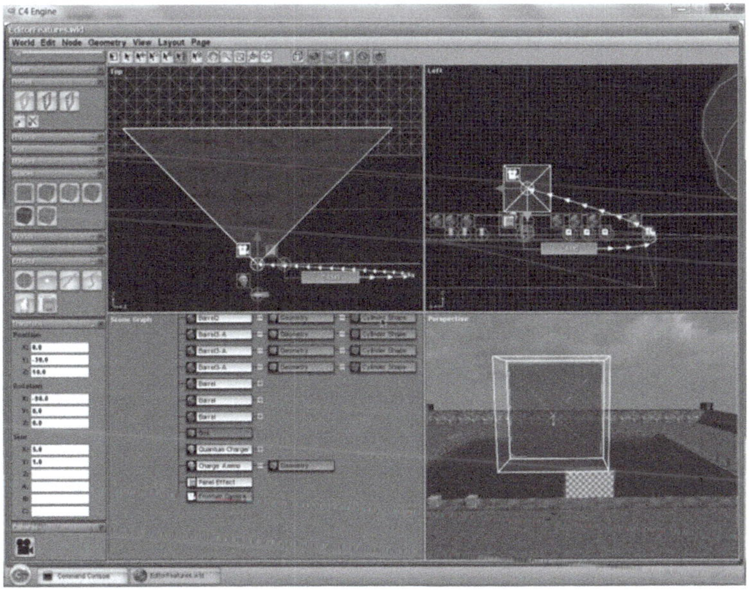

Figure 6-23. The panel effect linked to the camera using the CAM0 connector.

Figure 6-24. The panel effect provides the view as seen by a camera placed elsewhere in the world.

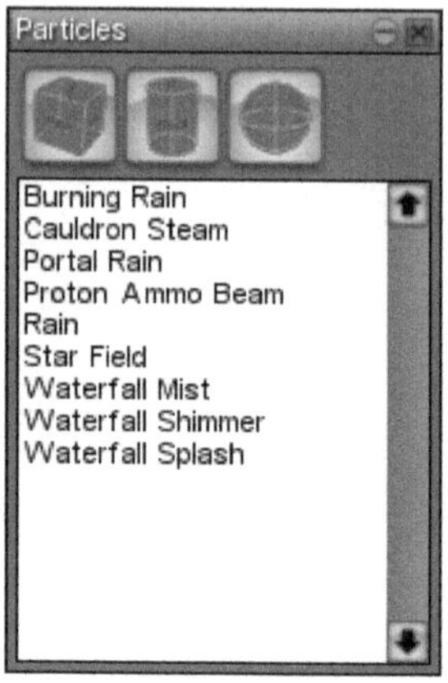

Figure 6-25. The **Particles** page.

Adding Rain

Let's add some rain. It's really easy—when you know how!

1. Choose **Tools > Open World (Ctrl-O)** and open your EditorFeatures world in the **World Editor**.
2. Choose **Page > Particles** to open the **Particles** page panel, as shown in Figure 6-25.
3. Select the **Box Emitter** tool, as shown in Figure 6-26.
4. Drag out a box emitter in the *x-y* **Top (+z)** viewport, such that it covers the entire world, as shown in Figure 6-27.
5. Using the **Transform** page panel, reduce the height of the box emitter, by setting its *z* size to 72 meters, as shown in Figure 6-28.

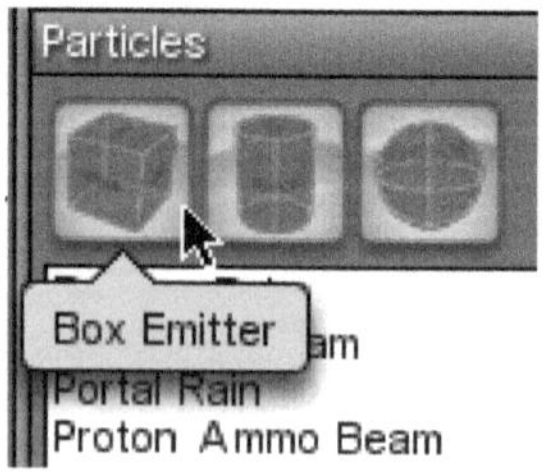

Figure 6-26. Selecting the **Box Emitter** tool in the **Particles** page.

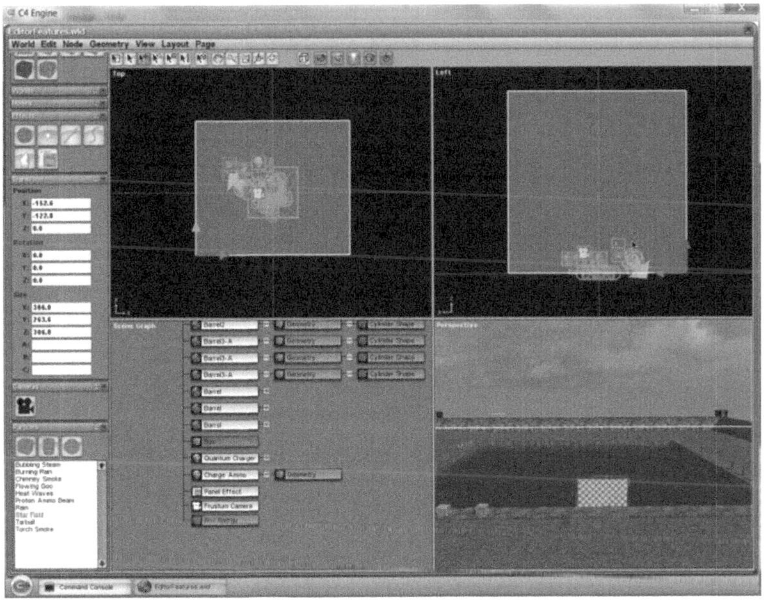

Figure 6-27. Creating a box emitter to cover the entire world.

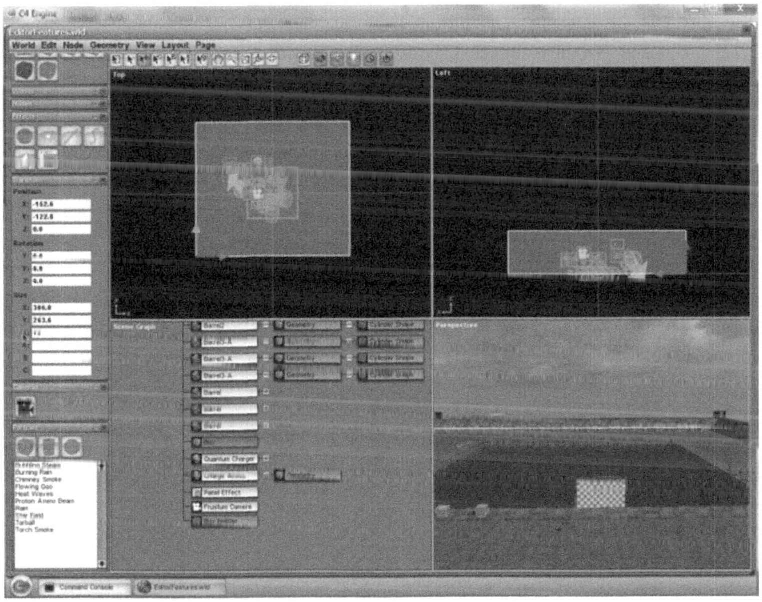

Figure 6-28. Reducing the height of the box emitter.

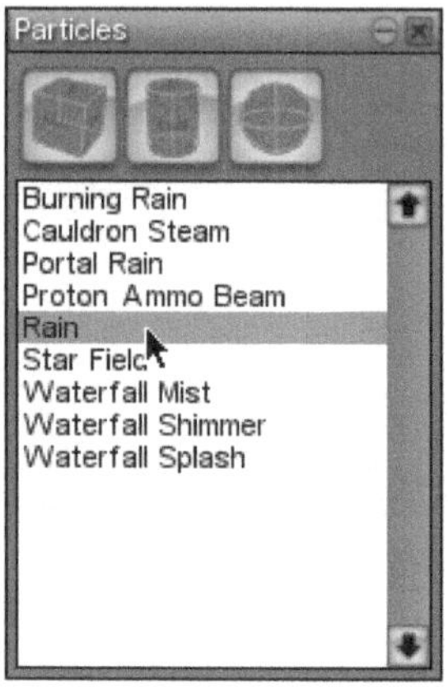

Figure 6-29. Selecting the **Rain** particle system.

6 In the **Particles** page, select the **Rain** particle system, as shown in Figure 6-29.

7 In the *x-z* **Left (+y)** viewport, click the mouse to place the rain particle system above the box emitter, as shown in Figure 6-30.

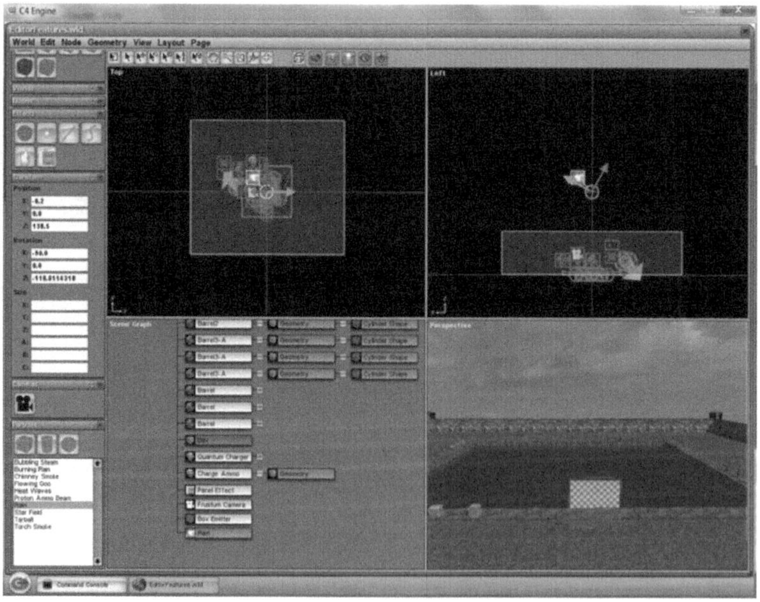

Figure 6-30. Placing the rain particle system.

8 With the rain node still selected, choose **Node > Get Info (Ctrl-I)** to open the **Node Info** dialog. In the **Connectors** tab panel, click on Emitter and then click Assign. Press **OK** to confirm the changes. Now, with the rain node still selected, select the **Connect Nodes (5)** tool. The rain node displays connector named `%Emitter`.

9 Select the `%Emitter` connector.

10 Select the box emitter. The selection should appear as shown in Figure 6-31.

11 Choose **Node > Connect Node (Ctrl-L)** to connect the rain to the box emitter. The selection should appear as shown in Figure 6-32.

We're ready to make it rain in our world!

12 Choose **World > Save and Play World (Ctrl-P)** again to save your work and test the world. As shown in Figure 6-33, it's raining!

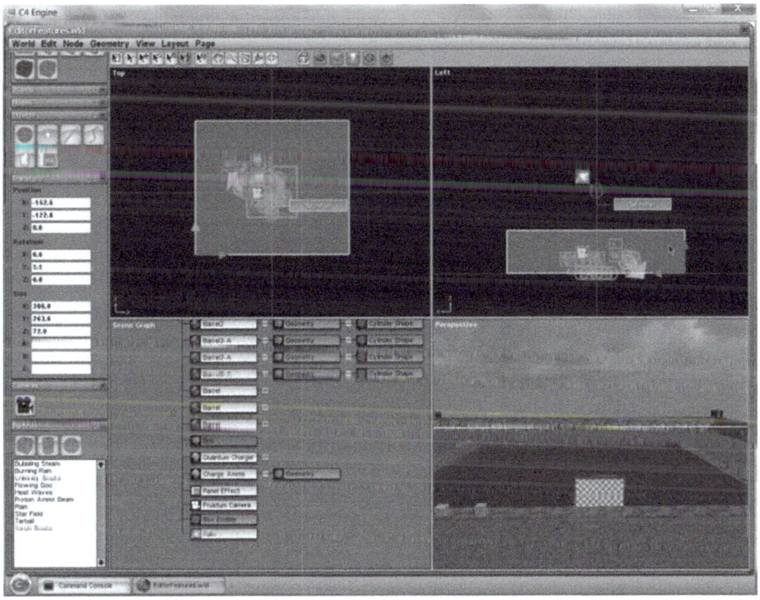

Figure 6-31. Ready to link the box emitter and the rain particle system.

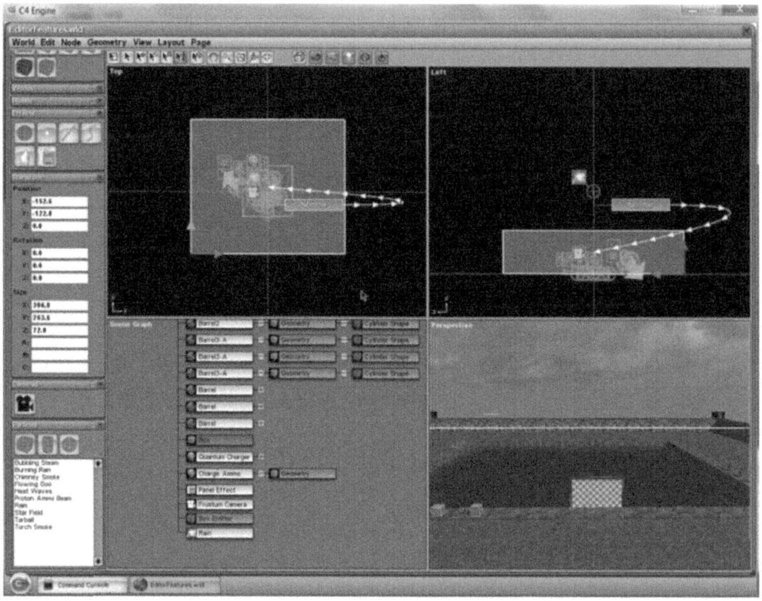

Figure 6-32. The rain node connected to the box emitter.

Figure 6-33. It's raining!

Triggers and Scripts

For those of us who don't enjoy rainy days, let's see if we can control the weather! Let's add a trigger to turn the rain off when we walk into a specific spot in the world.

1. Choose **Tools > Open World (Ctrl-O)** and open your EditorFeatures world in the **World Editor**.

2. Choose **Page > Triggers** to open the **Triggers** page panel, as shown in Figure 6-34.

3. Select the **Box Trigger** tool, as shown in Figure 6-35.

4. Drag out a box trigger in the *x-y* **Top (+z)** viewport, in the lower-left corner of the world, as shown in Figure 6-36.

Figure 6-34. The **Triggers** page.

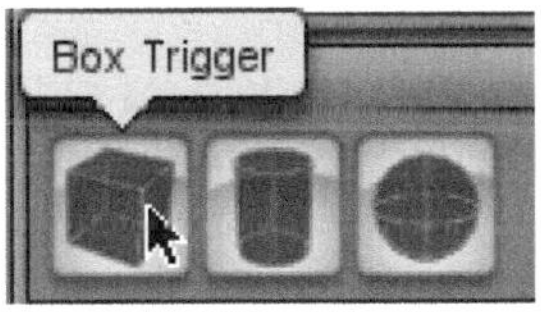

Figure 6-35. Selecting the **Box Trigger** tool.

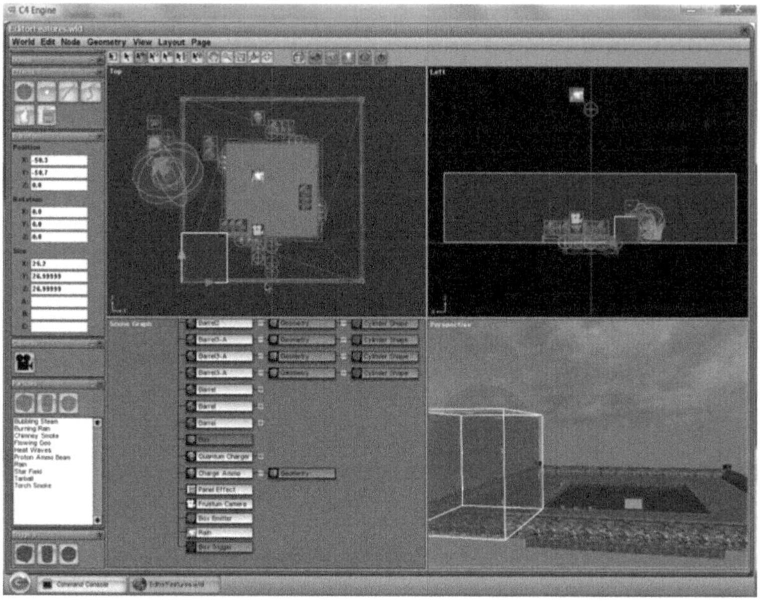

Figure 6-36. Adding a box trigger to turn off the rain.

5 With the box trigger node still selected, choose **Node** > **Get Info (Ctrl-I)** to open the **Node Info** dialog. In the **Connectors** tab panel, click New to create a new connector. Call it `TARG`. Press OK to confirm the changes. Now select the **Connect Nodes (5)** tool and check that the `TARG` connector is visible, as shown in Figure 6-37.

6 Select the `TARG` connector.

7 In the scene graph, select the rain particle system. The selection should appear as shown in Figure 6-38.

8 Choose **Node** > **Connect Node (Ctrl-L)** to link the box trigger to the rain particle system. The selection should appear as shown in Figure 6-39.

Now that all of our nodes are properly connected, we can create a script with a method to disable the rain particle system when the player enters the box trigger.

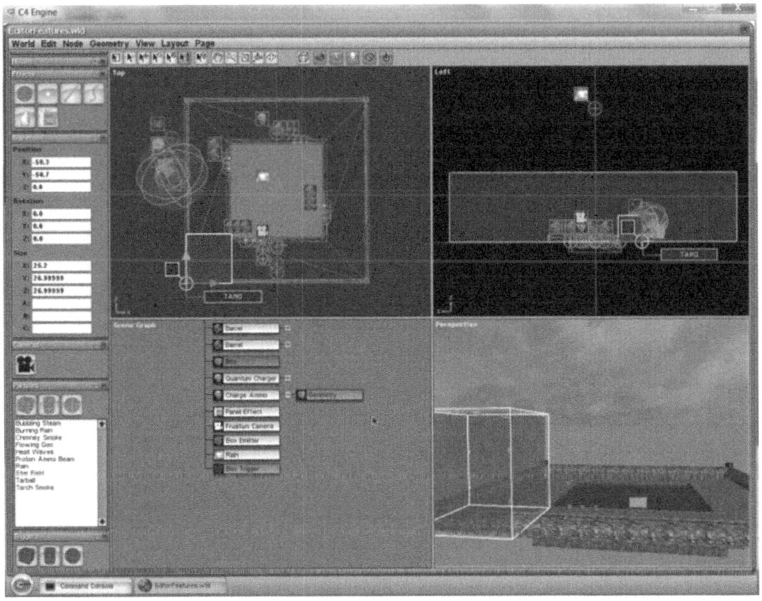

Figure 6-37. Preparing to connect the box trigger to the rain particle system.

Figure 6-38. Selecting the TARG connector and the rain particle system.

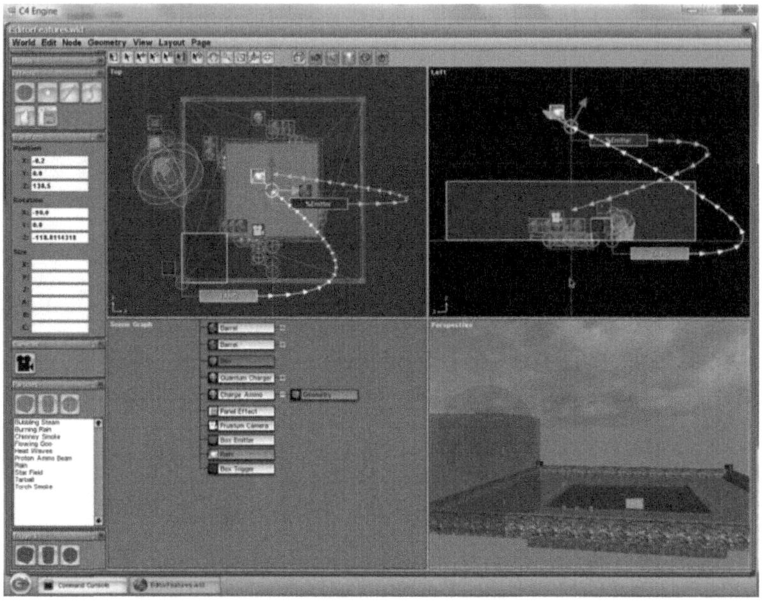

Figure 6-39. The connected box trigger and rain particle system.

9 Select the box trigger.

10 Choose **Node > Get Info (Ctrl-I)** to open the **Node Info** dialog, as shown in Figure 6-40.

11 Select the **Controller** tab panel.

12 In the **Controller type** list, select the **Script** controller, as shown in Figure 6-41.

13 Click **Edit Script** to open the **Script Editor** dialog, as shown in Figure 6-42.

14 Select the **Standard** methods tab panel, as shown in Figure 6-43.

15 Select the **Disable Node** method, as shown in Figure 6-44.

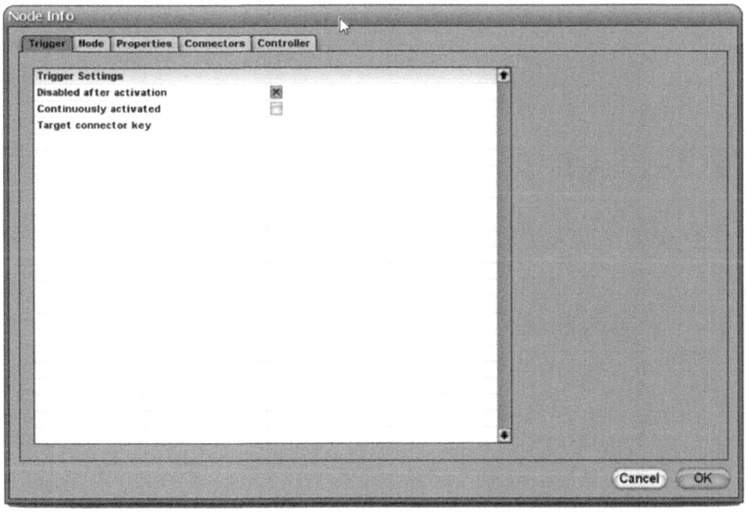

Figure 6-40. Editing a box trigger node with the **Node Info** dialog.

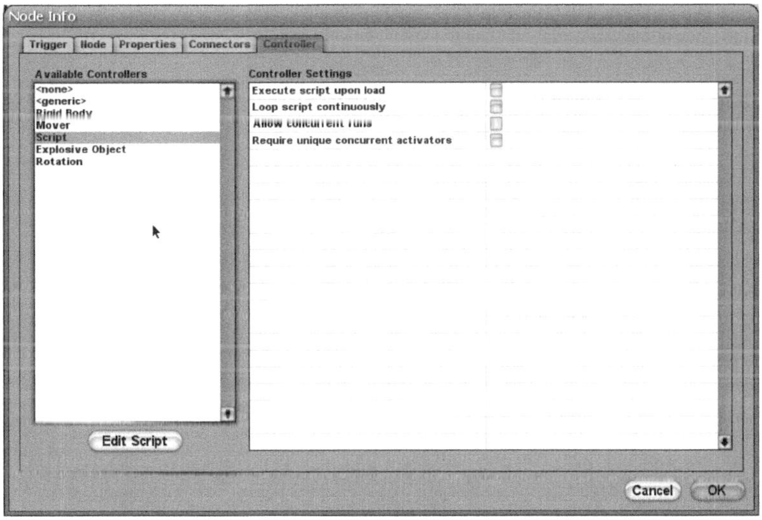

Figure 6-41. Selecting the **Script** controller.

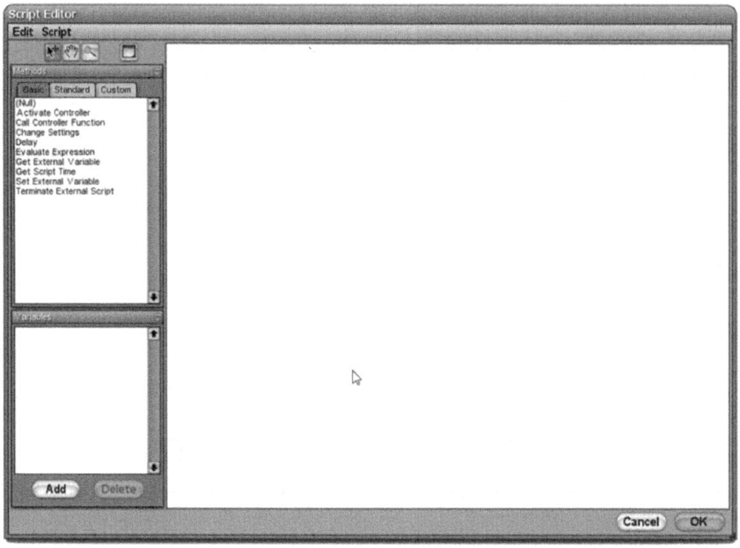

Figure 6-42. The **Script Editor** dialog.

Figure 6-43. Selecting the **Standard** methods tab panel in the **Script Editor** dialog.

Figure 6-44. Selecting the **Disable Node** method in the **Standard** methods list.

16 Click in the center of the work area of the **Script Editor** dialog to place the **Disable Node** method, as shown in Figure 6-45.

17 Select the **Select / Move Tool** at the top of the **Script Editor** window, as shown in Figure 6-46.

18 Double-click the **Disable Node** method. The **Method Info** dialog opens, as shown in Figure 6-47.

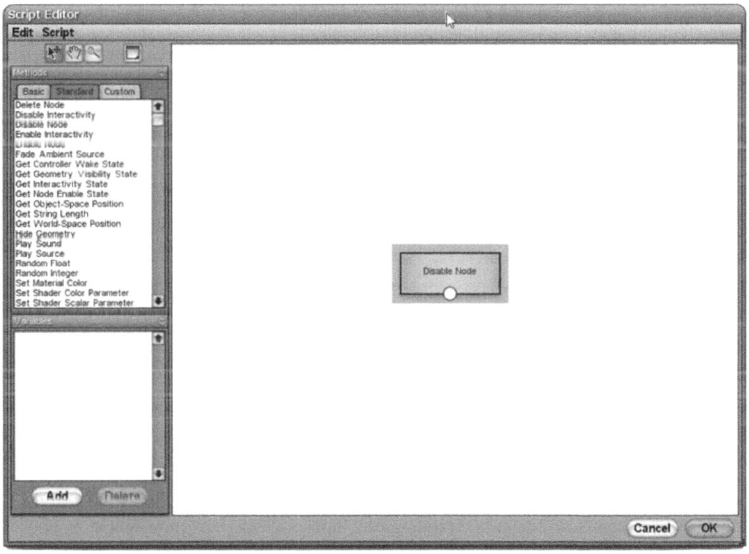

Figure 6-45. Placing the **Disable Node** method.

Figure 6-46. Selecting the **Select / Move Tool** in the **Script Editor**.

19 In the **Target Node** list, select **Connector TARG**, as shown in Figure 6-48. `TARG` is the default connector for a trigger node.

20 Click **OK** to save your method changes.

21 Click **OK** two more times, once to confirm your **Script Editor** changes, and again to confirm your **Node Info** dialog changes.

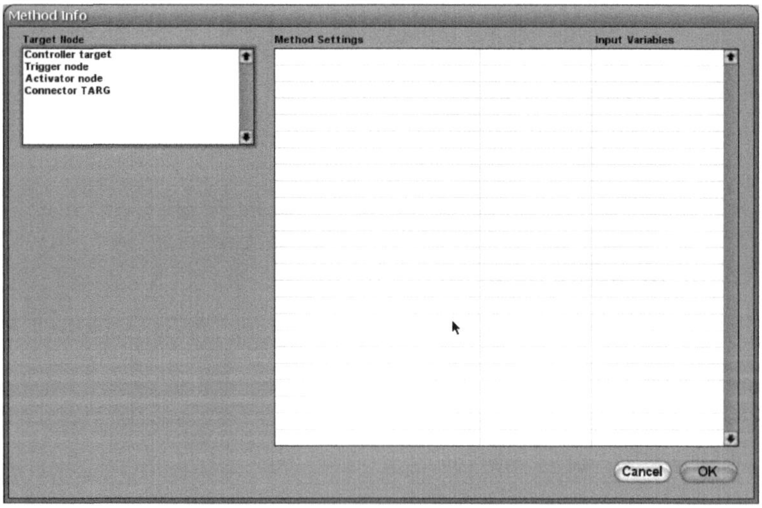

Figure 6-47. The **Method Info** dialog.

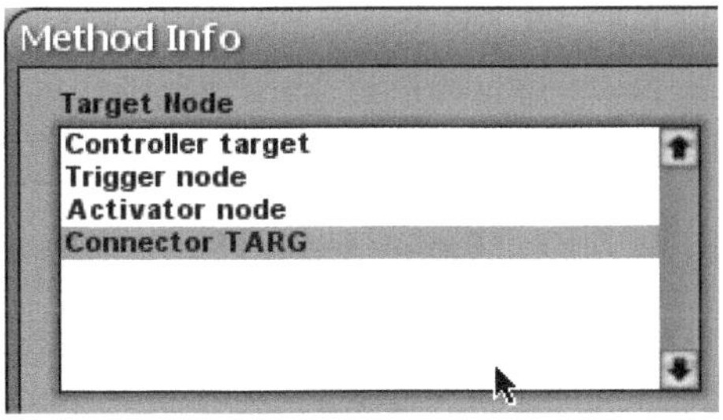

Figure 6-48. Setting the target node to **Connector TARG**.

Note that if the **Spawn** node for the player is inside the trigger area, the rain will stop as soon as the player spawns. If this is the case, use the **Move Nodes (2)** tool in the **World Editor** to move the **Spawn** node to a location outside the trigger area and try again. You can find the **Spawn** node by selecting it in the scene graph and it will become easily visible in any of the other viewports.

22 Test the behavior of the box trigger by choosing **World > Save and Play World (Ctrl-P)**. Walk into the area enclosed by the trigger, and the rain stops!

It's easy to add other items besides the camera to your panel. You can experiment by adding images with rotating or fading pictures, or by adding scrolling text or the pseudo-code texture.

Adding Buttons to Control Sound, Rain, and Cameras

In this next series of steps, we'll add two buttons to control various aspects of our world—sound, rain, and cameras.

Controlling a Sound Source

1 Choose **Tools > Open World (Ctrl-O)** and open your EditorFeatures world in the **World Editor**.

2 Choose **Page > Sources** to open the **Sources** page panel, as shown in Figure 6-49.

3 Select the **Omnidirectional Source** tool, as shown in Figure 6-50.

4 Click in a viewport to create an omnidirectional source node, as shown in Figure 6-51.

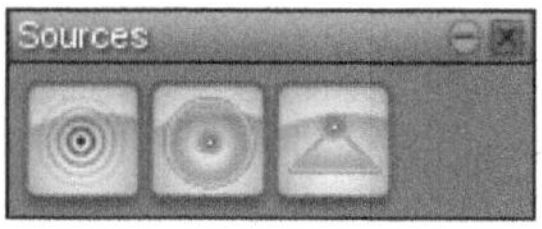

Figure 6-49. The **Sources** page.

Figure 6-50. Selecting the **Omnidirectional Source** tool.

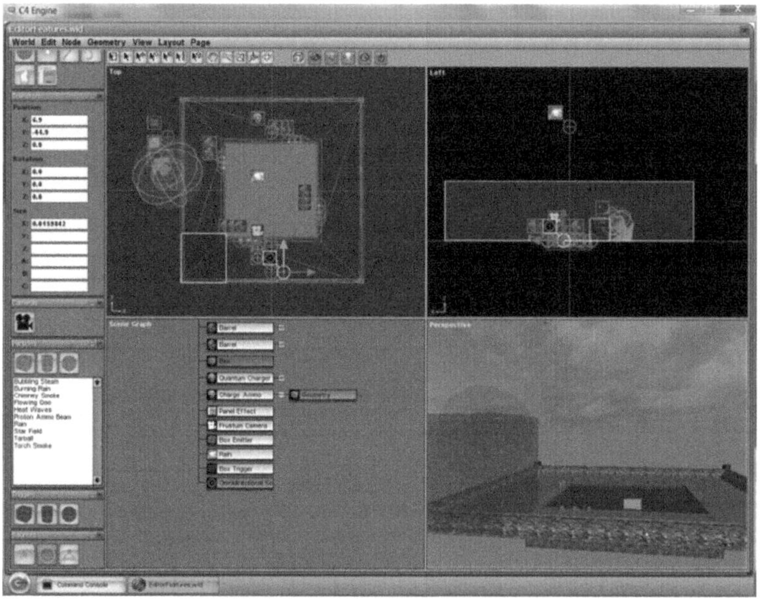

Figure 6-51. Creating the omnidirectional source node.

5 To make it easier to move the omnidirectional source into place, mask off selection of geometry, trigger, and effect nodes, by toggling off the **Geometry Select Mask**, **Trigger Select Mask**, and **Effect Select Mask**, as shown in Figure 6-52.

Figure 6-52. Masking off selection of geometry and effect nodes.

6 Select the **Move Nodes (2)** tool, and position the omnidirectional source near the location where the player will spawn into the game, as shown in Figure 6-53.

7 Choose **Node > Get Info (Ctrl-I)** to open the **Node Info** dialog, as shown in Figure 6-54.

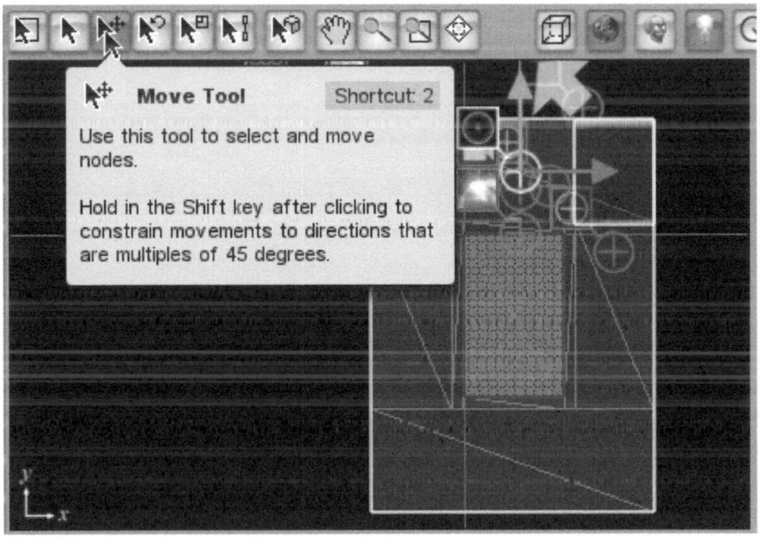

Figure 6-53. Positioning the omnidirectional source node.

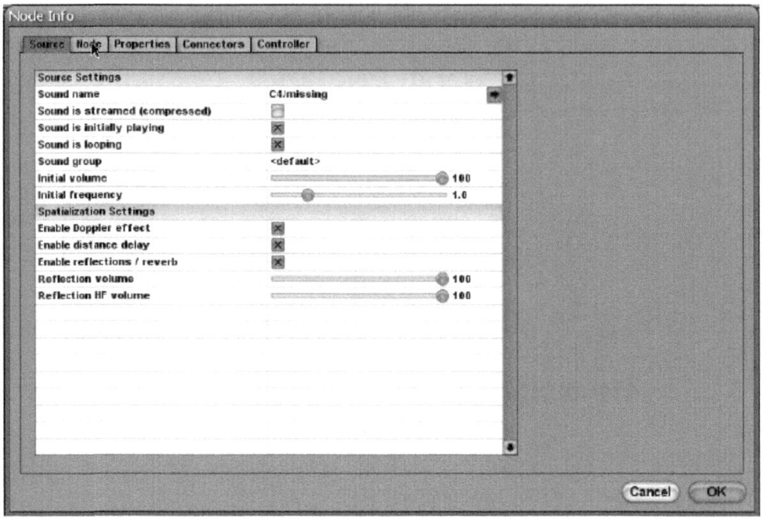

Figure 6-54. Editing the settings for an omnidirectional source node in the **Node Info** dialog.

8 In the **Source Settings** group, click the arrow-shaped icon to the right of the **Sound name** setting, to open the sound selection dialog, as shown in Figure 6-55.

9 For this tutorial, select any of the sound files located in the Data/Demo/sound/ directory, and then click **OK** to confirm your selection.

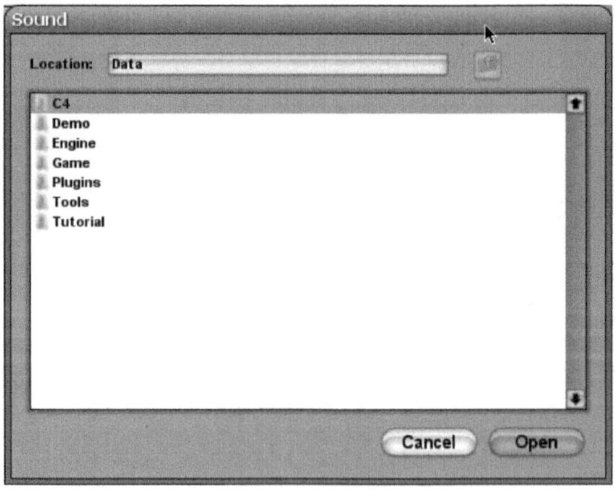

Figure 6-55. The sound selection dialog.

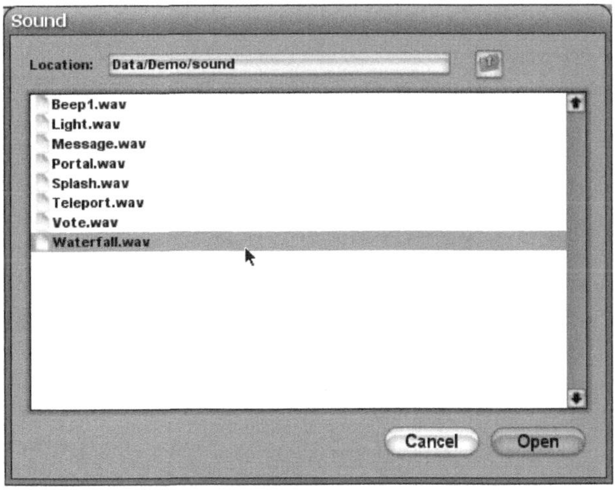

Figure 6-56. Selecting a sound file.

10 Select the **Sound is streamed (compressed)** option, as shown in Figure 6-57,for longer music files. Short sound effects, such as explosions, rapid weapon firing, or switching effects, don't need to be streamed.

11 Confirm that the **Sound is looping** and **Sound is initially playing** options are both selected.

12 Click **OK** to save your changes.

13 In the **Transform** page panel, set the *x* size of the omnidirectional source to 50.0 meters. The omnidirectional source should appear similar to the source shown in Figure 6-58.

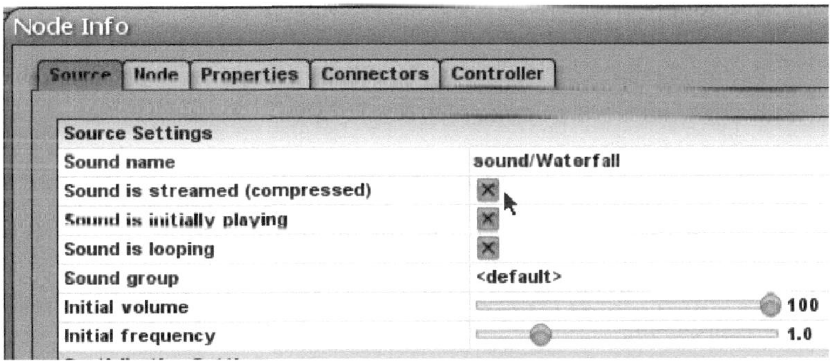

Figure 6-57. Selecting the **Sound is streamed (compressed)** option.

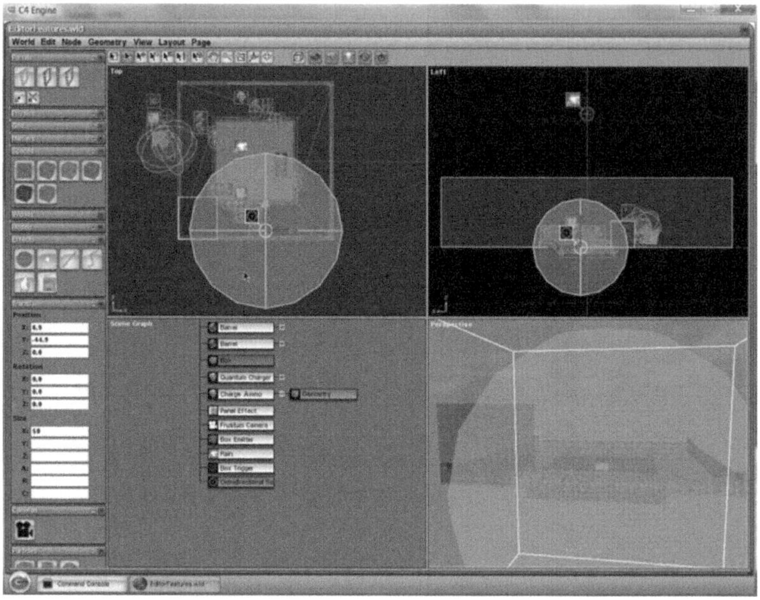

Figure 6-58. Setting the size of the omnidirectional sound source.

14 Choose **Save and Play World (Ctrl-P)** to run the world and verify that the omnidirectional sound plays as expected. The volume of the sound source should decrease as the player walks away from its node position.

15 Back in the **World Editor** window, select the panel effect, as shown in Figure 6-59.

16 Choose **Node > Get Info (Ctrl-I)** to open the **Node Info** dialog, and select the **Connectors** tab panel.

17 Click **New** to add a new connector, and set its **Key** value to `SON0`, as shown in Figure 6-60.

18 Click **OK** to save your settings changes.

Figure 6-59. Selecting the panel effect.

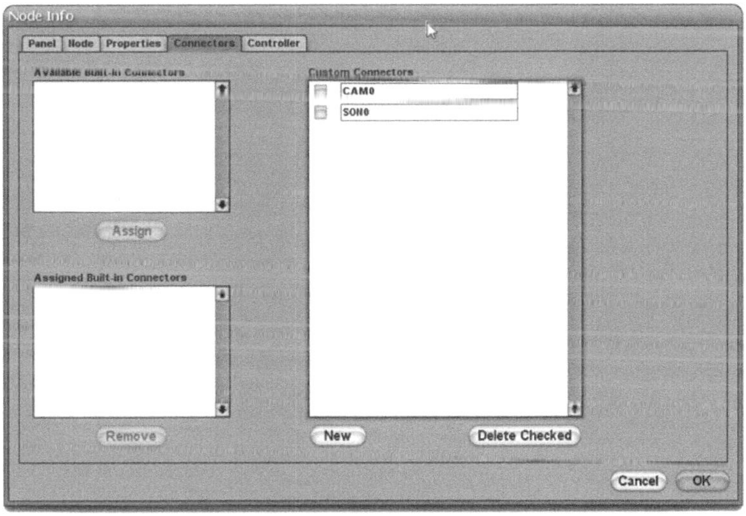

Figure 6-60. Adding the `SON0` connector.

Linking the Panel Effect to the Sound Source

Next, we'll link the panel effect connector with the key value `SONO` with the omnidirectional sound source.

19 Select the **Connect Node (5)** tool.

20 Select the panel effect node. The selection should appear as shown in Figure 6-61.

21 Select the connector with the key value `SONO` in one of the orthographic viewports.

22 Select the omnidirectional source node to add it to the selection. The selection should now appear as shown in Figure 6-62.

23 Choose **Node > Connect Node (Ctrl-L)** to connect the panel effect node to the omnidirectional source node. The selection should now appear as shown in Figure 6-63.

Figure 6-61. Preparing to connect the panel effect to the omnidirectional source.

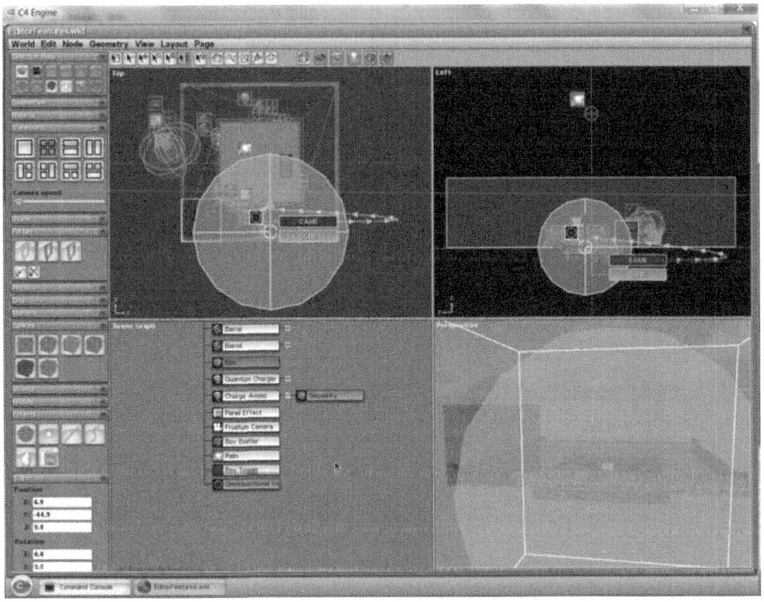

Figure 6-62. The selected omnidirectional source and SONO connector.

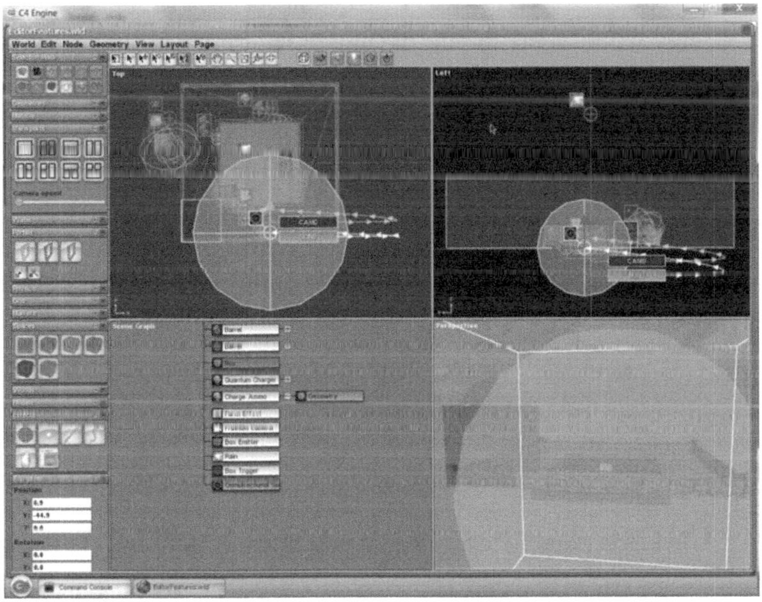

Figure 6-63. The connected panel effect and omnidirectional source nodes.

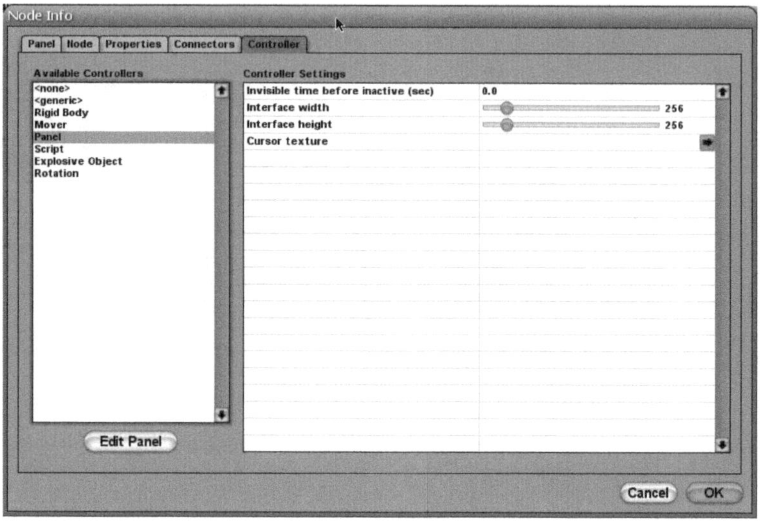

Figure 6-64. The **Controller** tab panel for the panel effect.

24 Select the panel effect.

25 Now we're ready to edit the contents of the panel effect. Choose **Node > Get Info (Ctrl-I)** to open the **Node Info** dialog.

26 Select the **Controller** tab panel, as shown in Figure 6-64.

Setting the Cursor Texture

27 Click the arrow-shaped icon to the right of the **Cursor texture** setting, to open the cursor texture selection dialog.

28 Select the `arrow.tex` texture, located in the Data/C4/C4/ directory, as shown in Figure 6-65, and click **OK**.

Adding the Buttons

29 Click **Edit Panel** to open the **Panel Editor** window, as shown in Figure 6-66.

30 Select the **Push Button** widget from the list of widgets, as shown in Figure 6-67.

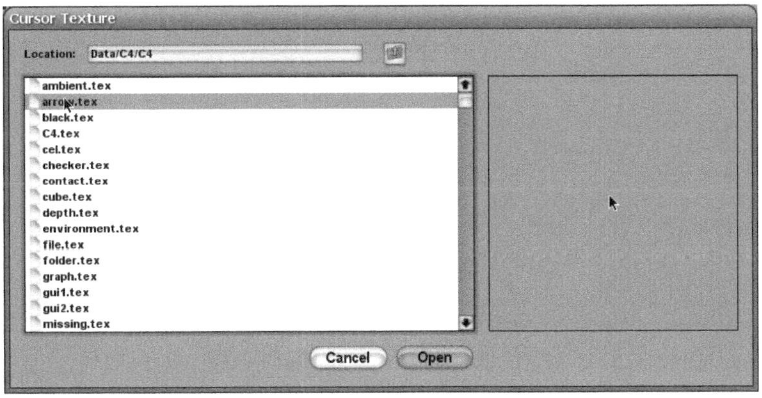

Figure 6-65. Selecting the `arrow.tex` cursor texture.

31 Drag out two buttons below the camera panel item, and label them ON and OFF. Using the **Move** and **Resize** tools, adjust the position and size of the ON and OFF buttons to match the appearance shown in Figure 6-68.

32 Using the **Select Tool**, select the ON button, as shown in Figure 6-69.

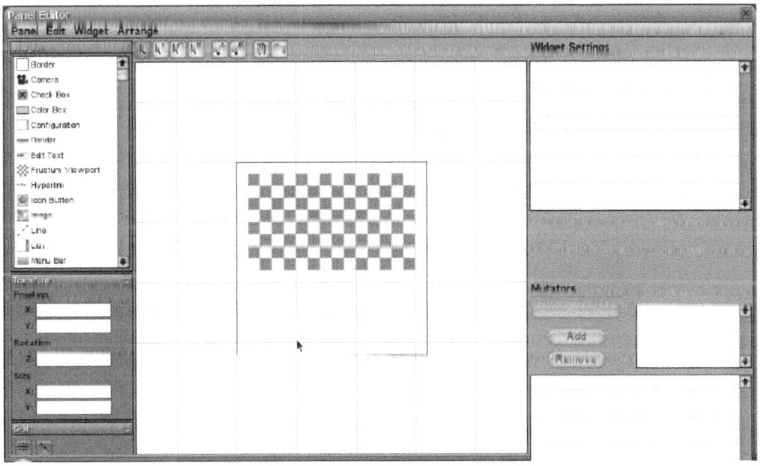

Figure 6-66. The panel effect with a camera widget.

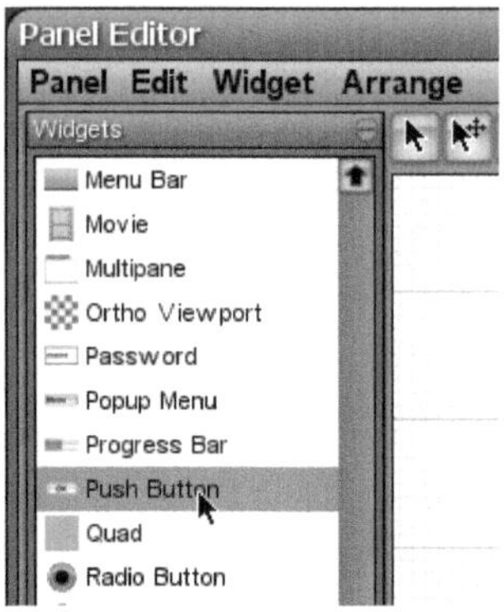

Figure 6-67. Selecting the **Push Button** widget.

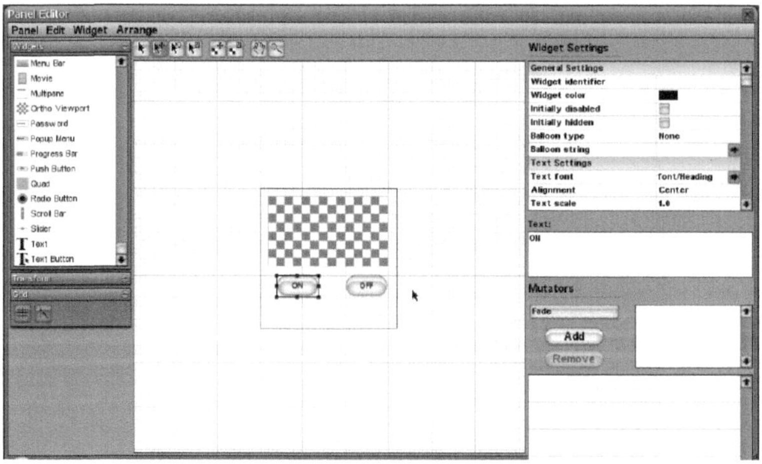

Figure 6-68. Adding two buttons, ON and OFF.

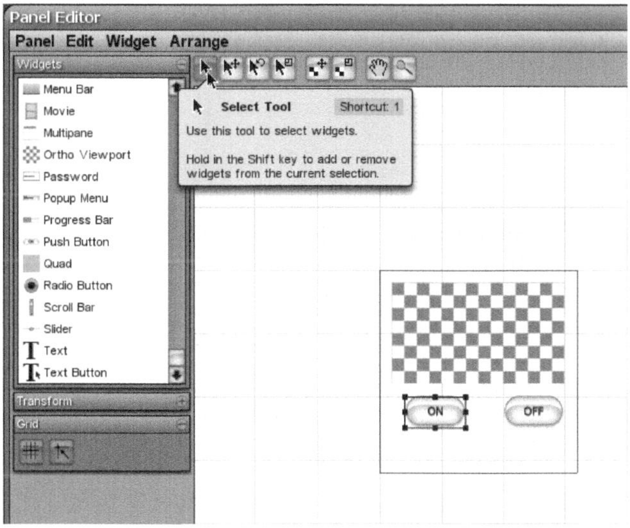

Figure 6-69. Selecting the ON button.

Setting up the Scripts

33 From the **Panel Editor** menu, select **Widget > Edit Script (Ctrl-E)**. The **Script Editor** dialog opens, as shown in Figure 6-70.

34 Select the **Standard** methods tab panel.

35 Select the **Play Source** method, and then click in the center of the **Script Editor** work area to create a new **Play Source** method, as shown in Figure 6-71.

36 Choose **Script > Get Info (Ctrl-I)** to open the **Method Info** dialog, as shown in Figure 6-72. Alternatively, you can double-click the new method using the **Select / Move Tool**.

37 Select **Connector SON0** in the Target node list, as shown in Figure 6-73.

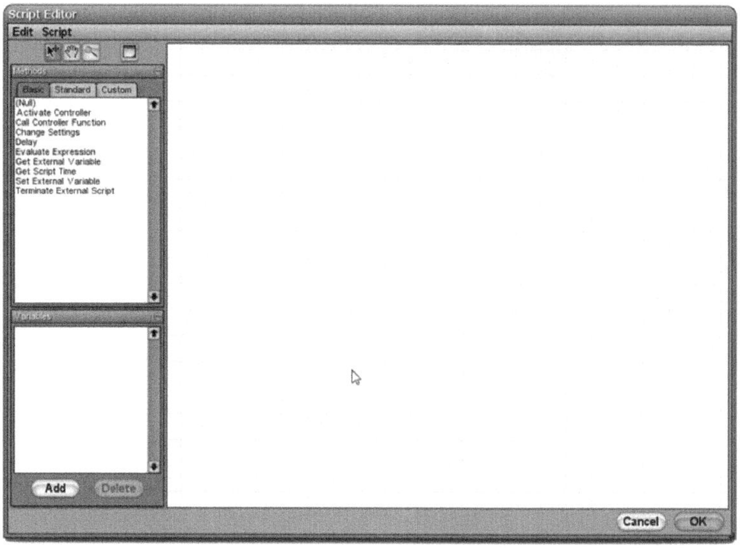

Figure 6-70. The **Script Editor** dialog.

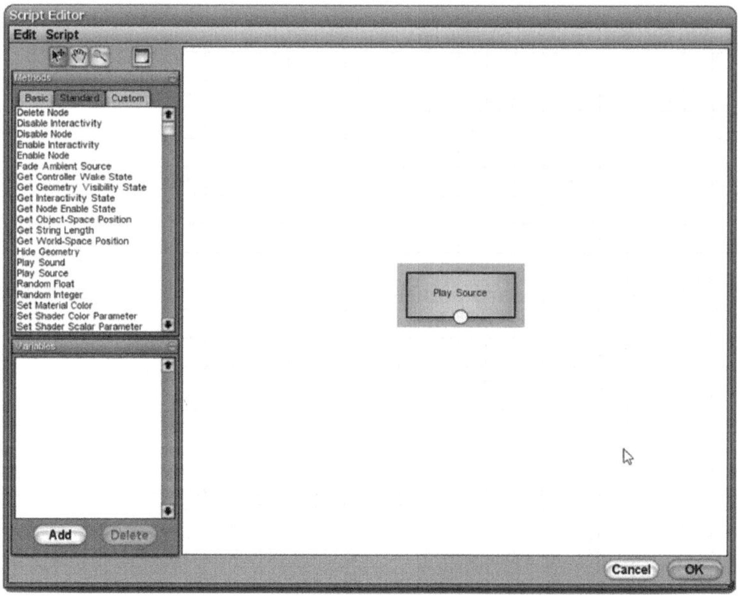

Figure 6-71. Creating a new **Play Source** method.

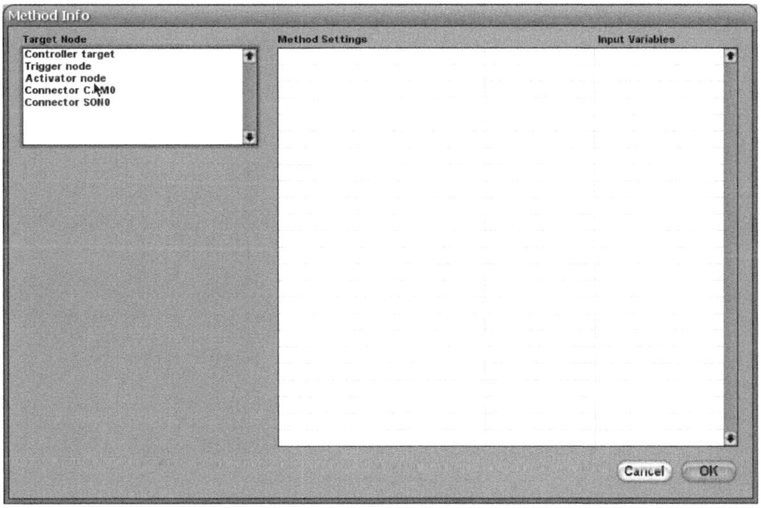

Figure 6-72. The **Play Source** method settings in the **Method Info** dialog.

38 Click **OK** twice to confirm your changes, once for the **Method Info** dialog, and again for the **Script Editor** dialog.

39 In the **Panel Editor** dialog, select the OFF button image panel item, as shown in Figure 6-74.

40 From the **Panel Editor** menu, select **Widget > Edit Script (Ctrl-E)**. The **Script Editor** dialog opens, as shown in Figure 6-75.

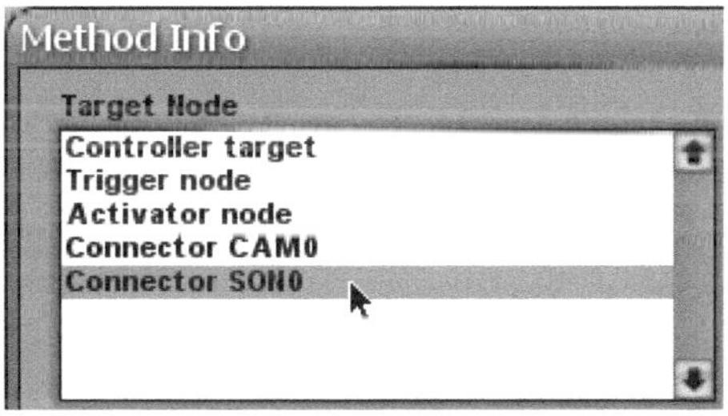

Figure 6-73. Selecting the target node named **Connector SON0**.

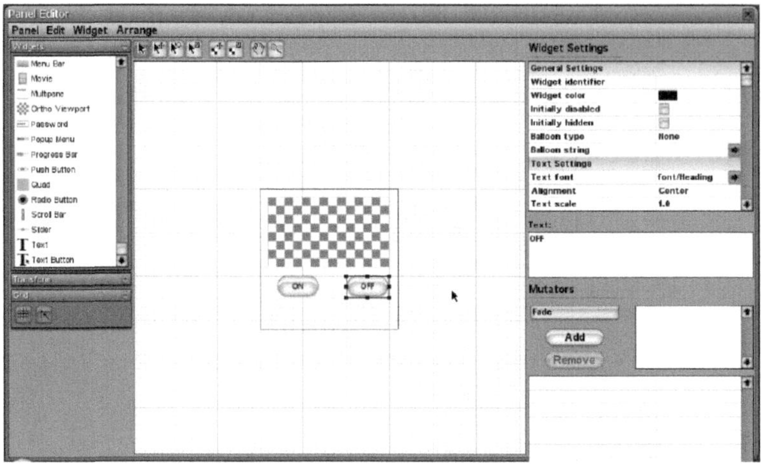

Figure 6-74. Selecting the OFF image panel item.

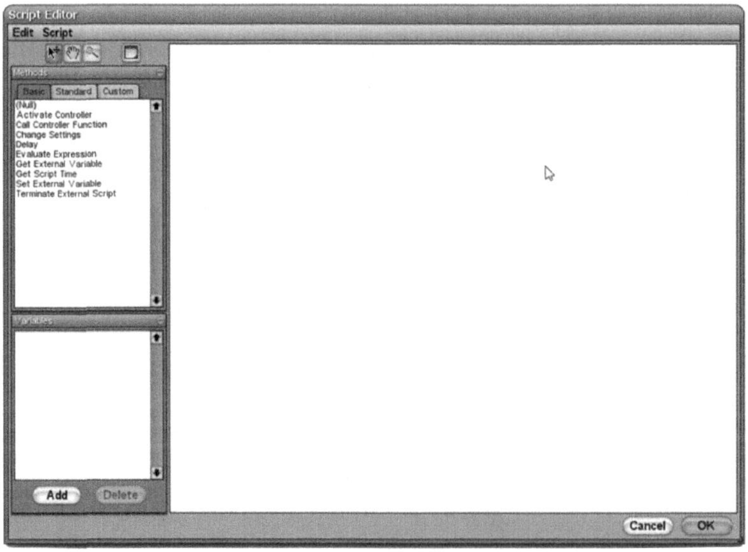

Figure 6-75. The **Script Editor** dialog.

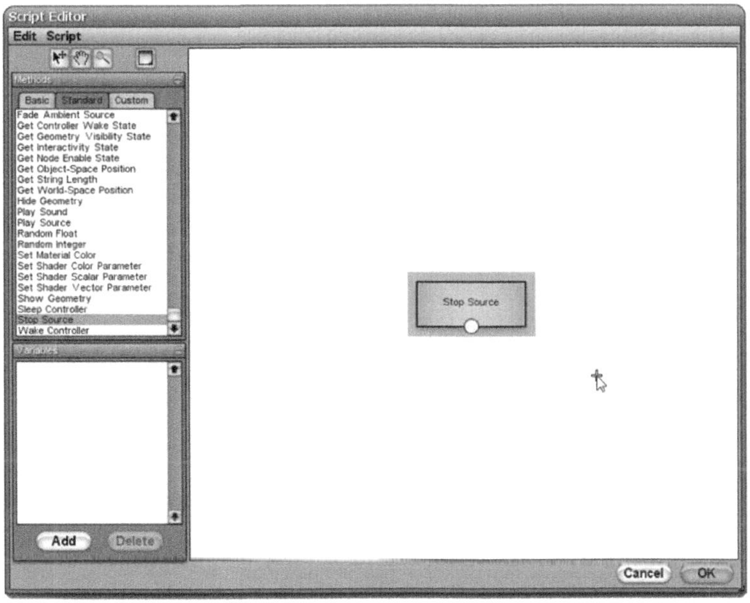

Figure 6-76. Creating the **Stop Sound Source** method.

41 Select the **Standard** methods tab panel.

42 Select the **Stop Source** method, and then click in the center of the **Script Editor** work area to create a new **Stop Source** method, as shown in Figure 6-76.

43 Choose **Script > Get Info (Ctrl-I)** to open the **Method Info** dialog, as shown in Figure 6-77. Alternatively, you can double-click the new method using the **Select** or **Move Methods** tool.

44 Select **Connector SON0** in the **Target Node** list, as shown in Figure 6-78.

45 Click **OK** twice to confirm your changes, once for the **Method Info** dialog, and again for the **Script Editor** dialog.

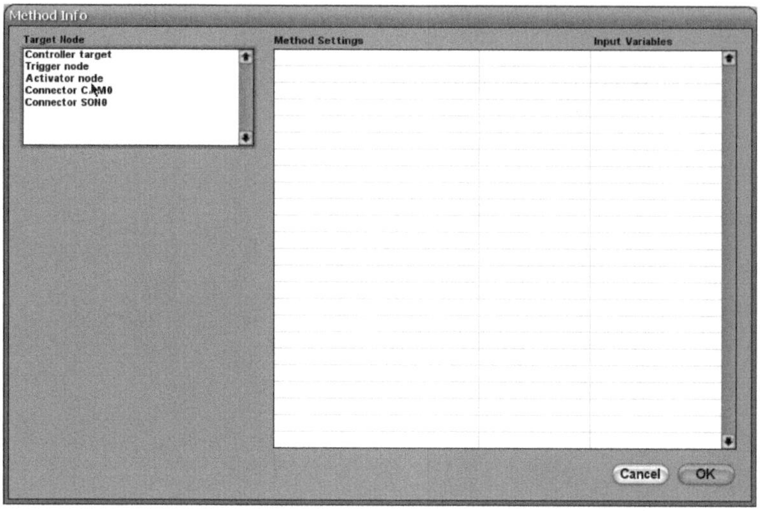

Figure 6-77. The **Stop Source** method settings in the **Method Info** dialog.

Adding a Grid Background

To make the buttons easier to see, let's add a translucent grid to the background of our panel.

46 Select the **Image** widget from the list of widgets, and drag out the image panel item to enclose the entire extent of the panel effect, as shown in Figure 6-79.

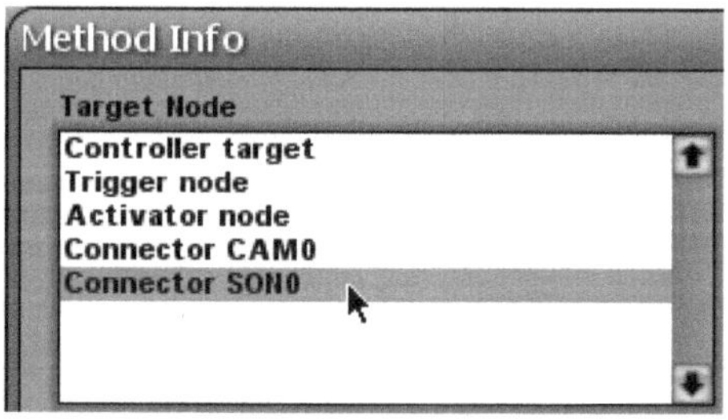

Figure 6-78. Selecting the target node named **Connector SON0**.

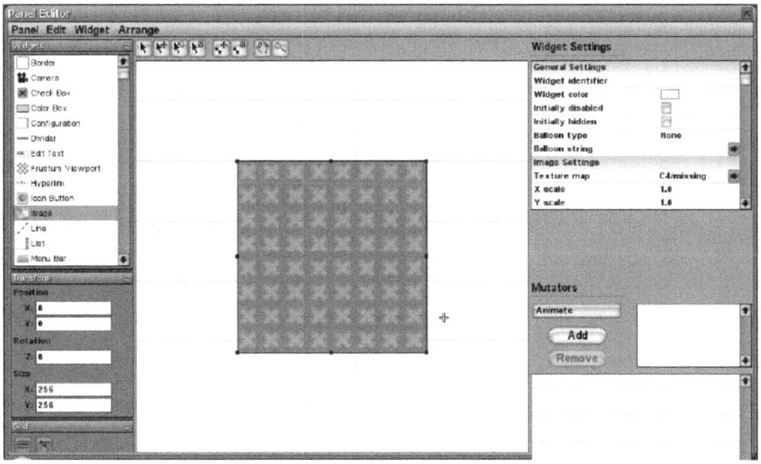

Figure 6-79. Adding a grid background texture.

47 In the **Image Settings** subgroup under the **Widget Settings** group, set the **Primary Texture map** to `panel/Grid`. The location of this file is Data/Demo/panel.

48 Also in the **Image Settings** subgroup under the **Widget Settings** group, set the **X scale** and **Y scale** to both have the value 8.0.

49 In the **General Settings** subgroup, click the color swatch to the right of the **Widget color** setting, to open the widget color dialog. Set the **Alpha** component setting to a value of 128, as shown in Figure 6-80. Click **OK** to confirm the change.

50 Choose **Widget > Send to Back (Ctrl-Shift-[)** to send the grid texture to the background of the panel. The panel effect should now appear as shown in Figure 6-81.

Testing Your Changes

51 Select **Panel > Save Panel (Ctrl S)** to save your changes and then select **Panel > Close Panel (Ctrl-W)** to return to the **Node Info** dialog. Click **OK** to confirm your **Node Info** dialog changes.

52 Choose **World > Save and Play World (Ctrl-P)**. The panel effect should appear as shown in Figure 6-82.

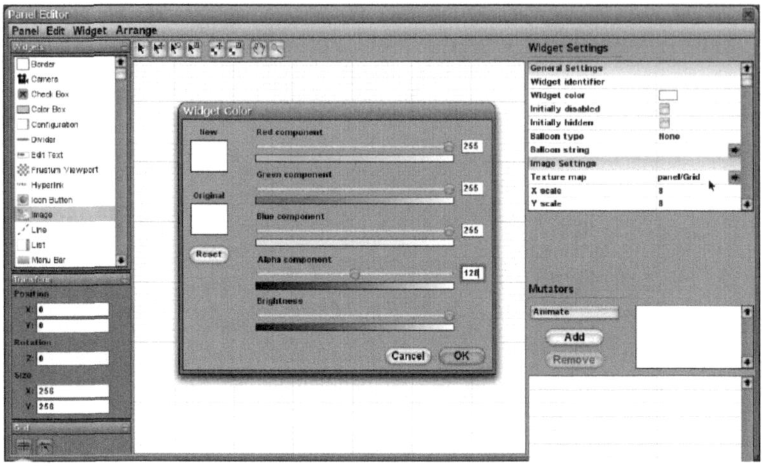

Figure 6-80. Setting the widget color.

To use the ON and OFF buttons on the panel to switch the sound on and off, move up close enough to the panel such that the arrow cursor appears, as shown in Figure 6-83.

Camera Switching

Let's add another camera and use the buttons to switch between the different views. We'll also add another button which when pressed, causes the cameras to be cycled automatically.

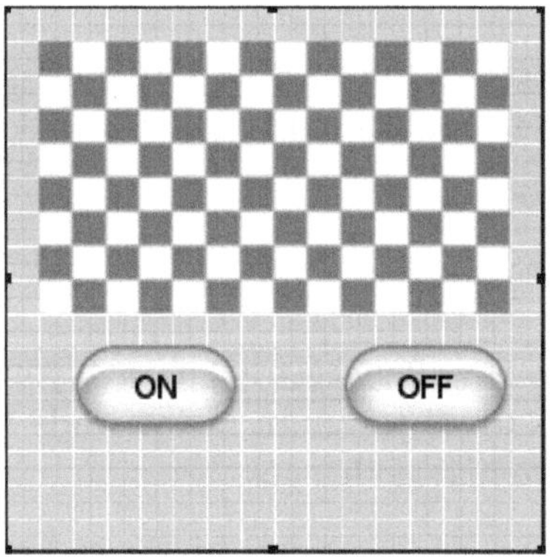

Figure 6-81. The panel effect with a grid texture background.

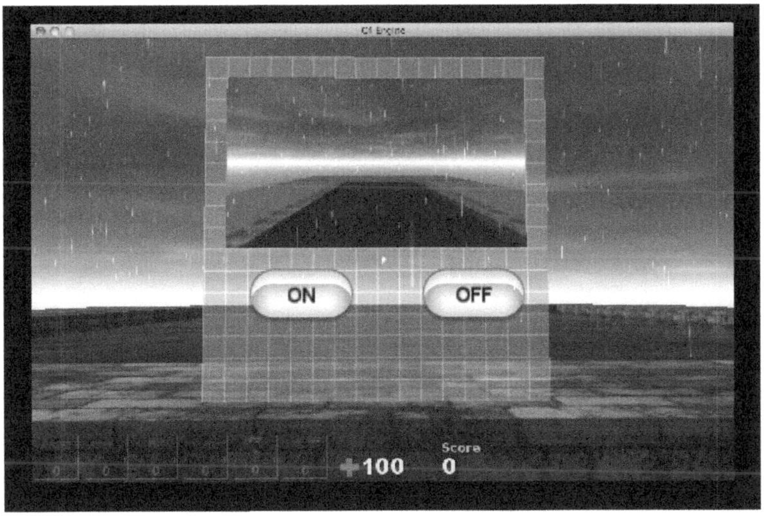

Figure 6-82. The panel effect with the buttons in-game.

1 To add another frustum camera, copy and paste the existing one using the scene graph.

2 Use the **Transform** page to give the new camera a position of (0, 40, 10) and a rotation of (90, 0, 180). Set the **X size** to 5 and the **Y size** to 1

3 Select the panel effect.

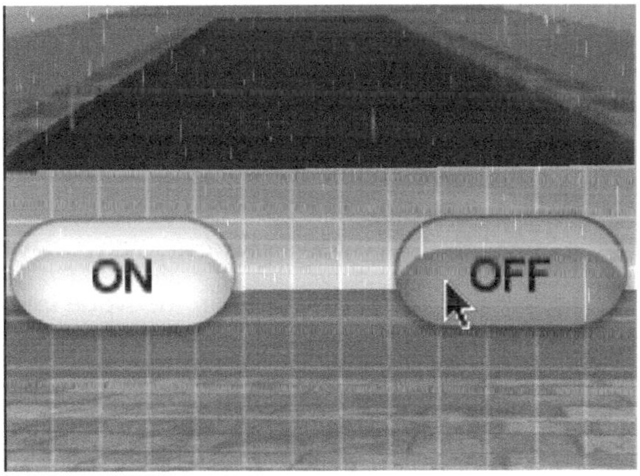

Figure 6-83. Moving up close to interact with the buttons.

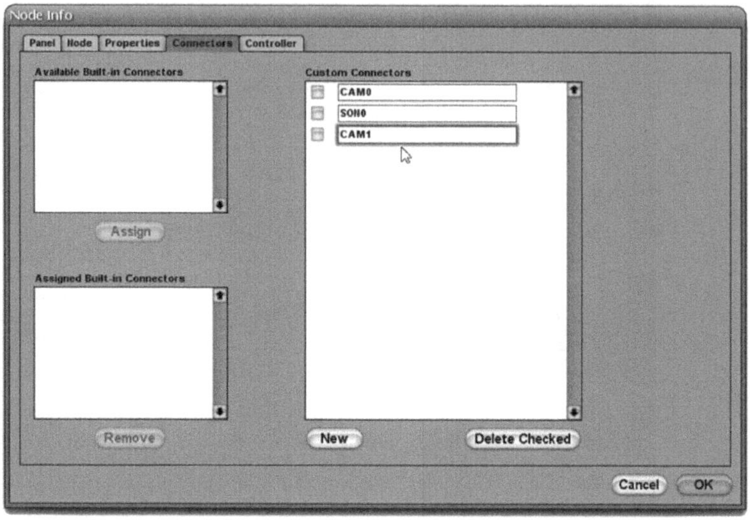

Figure 6-84. Adding the `CAM1` connector.

4 Choose **Node > Get Info (Ctrl-I)** to open the **Node Info** dialog.

5 Select the **Connectors** tab panel.

6 Add a new connector with the **Key** value of `CAM1`, as shown in Figure 6-84.

7 Click **OK** to save your changes.

8 Select the **Connect Node (5)** tool, and select the panel effect.

9 Select the `CAM1` connector and then select the second frustum camera in the scene graph viewport.

10 Connect the panel effect to the second camera by choosing **Node > Connect Node (Ctrl-L)**. The selection should appear similar to that shown in Figure 6-85.

11 Using the **Select Nodes (1)** tool, select the panel effect.

12 Choose **Node > Get Info (Ctrl-I)** to open the **Node Info** dialog.

13 Select the **Controller** tab panel.

14 Click **Edit Panel** to open the **Panel Editor** dialog.

15 Next, we'll edit the script for each of the panel buttons. Select the ON button, and select **Widget > Edit Script (Ctrl-E)**.

Figure 6-85. The panel effect connected to the second frustum camera.

16 Select the **Call Controller Function** method in the **Basic** methods list, and place it on the canvas of the script window, to the left of the existing **Play Source** method, as shown in Figure 6-86.

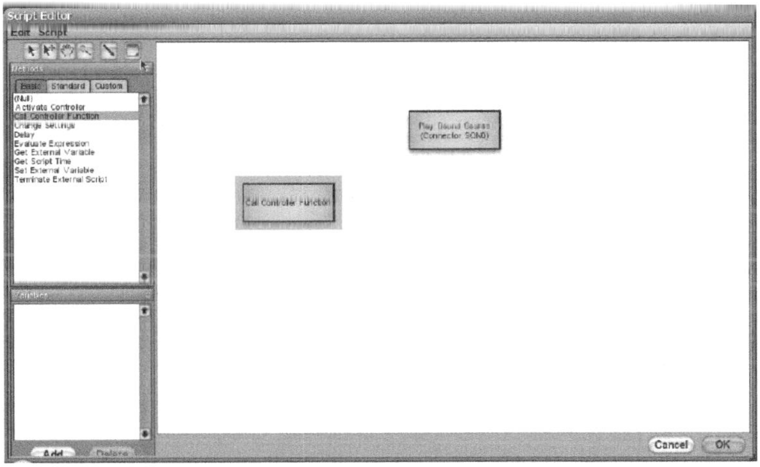

Figure 6-86. Creating a **Call Controller Function** method.

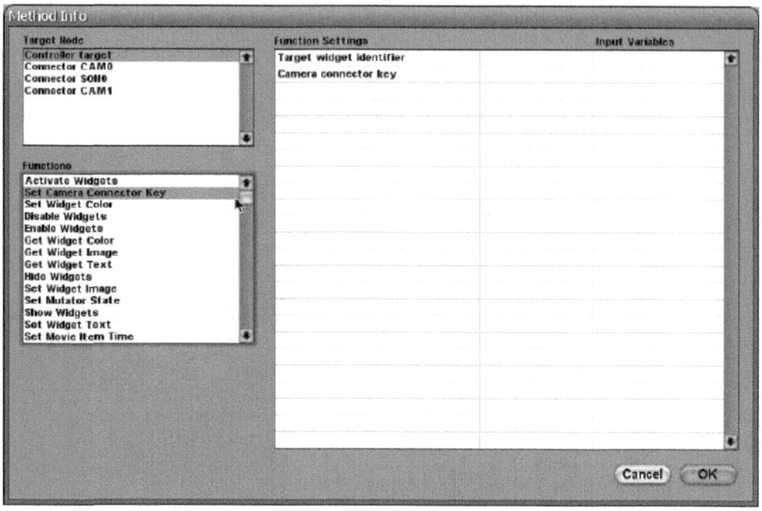

Figure 6-87. Selecting **Set Camera Connector Key** in the **Functions** list.

17 Choose **Script > Get Info (Ctrl-I)** to edit the new method's settings in the **Method Info** dialog. Alternatively, you can double-click the new method using the **Select / Move Tool**.

18 Select **Controller target** in the **Target Node** list.

19 Select **Set Camera Connector Key** in the **Functions** list, as shown in Figure 6-87.

20 Set the key value for the **Target widget identifier** setting to `CAMM`.

21 Set the **Camera connector key** value to `CAM0`. The **Method Info** dialog should now appear as shown in Figure 6-88.

22 Click **OK** twice to confirm your changes in the **Method Info** and **Script Editor** dialogs.

23 Next, we'll follow a similar set of steps for the OFF button. Select the OFF button.

24 Select **Widget > Edit Script (Ctrl-E)**.

25 Select the **Call Controller Function** method in the **Basic** methods list, and place it on the canvas of the script window, to the left of the existing **Stop Source** method, as shown in Figure 6-89.

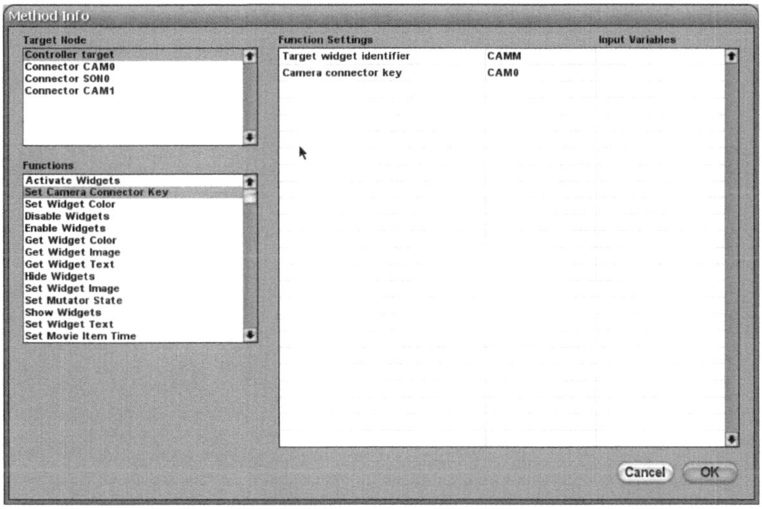

Figure 6-88. The **Function Settings** for the **Set Camera Connector Key**, as used by the ON button.

26 Choose **Script > Get Info (Ctrl-I)** to edit the new method's settings in the **Method Info** dialog. Alternatively, you can double-click the new method using the **Select / Move Tool.**

27 Select **Controller** target in the **Target Node** list.

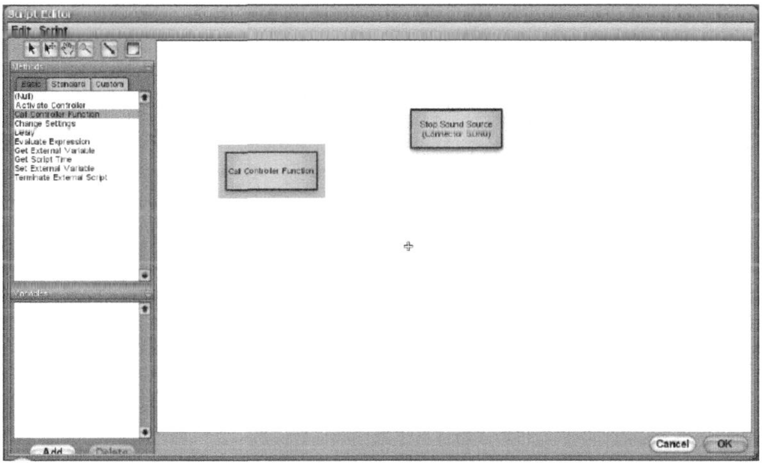

Figure 6-89. Creating a **Call Controller Function** method.

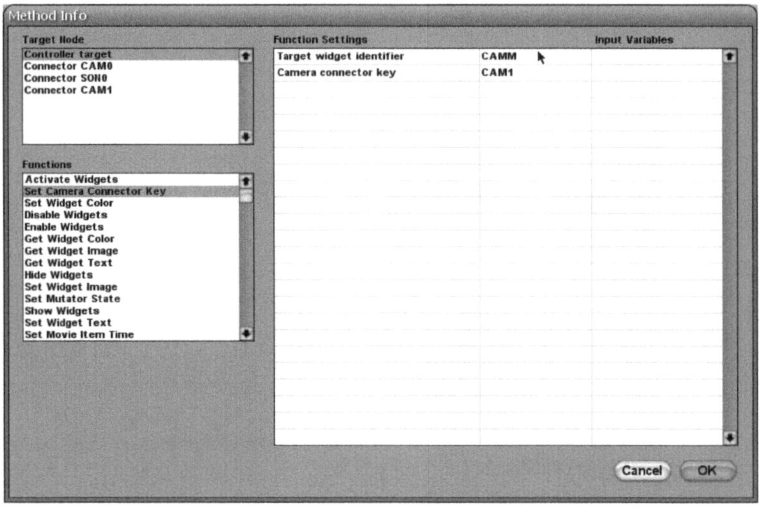

Figure 6-90. The **Function Settings** for the **Set Camera Connector Key**, as used by the OFF button.

28 Select **Set Camera Connector Key** in the **Functions** list.

29 Set the value of the **Target widget identifier** to `CAMM`, to match the ON button.

30 Set the value of the **Camera connector key** to `CAM1`, as shown in Figure 6-90.

31 Click **OK** twice to save your changes in the **Method Info** and **Script Editor** dialogs. Now save and close the **Panel Editor** as before. Click **OK** to save your **Node Info** changes.

32 Back in the **World Editor**, choose **World > Save and Play World (Ctrl-P)** to test your changes. You can now switch between the two cameras using the ON and OFF buttons. The sound will also be switched on and off as before.

Controlling the Rain with Button Scripts

Let's set up the buttons to turn the rain on and off.

1 Back in the **World Editor**, select the panel effect node.

2 Choose **Node > Get Info (Ctrl-I)** to open the **Node Info** dialog.

3 Select the **Connectors** tab panel.

4 Click **New** to create a new connector.

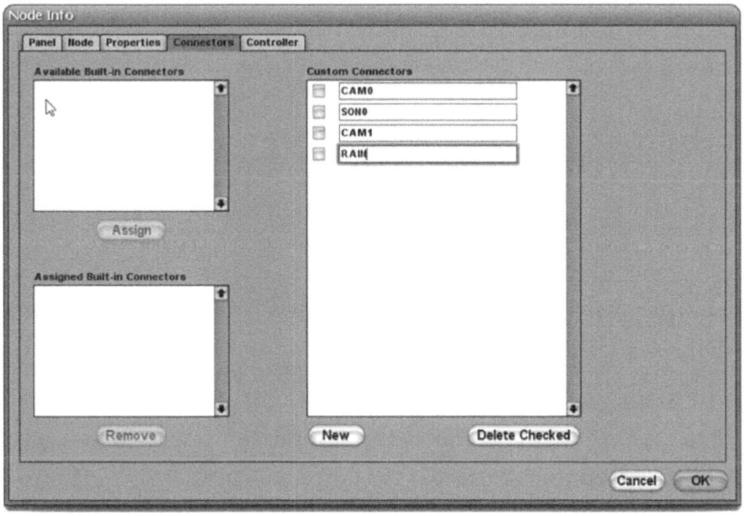

Figure 6-91. Adding the `RAIN` connector.

5 Set the connector **Key** value to `RAIN`, as shown in Figure 6-91.

6 Click **OK** to save your changes.

7 Select the **Connect Node (5)** tool.

8 Select the panel effect node in the scene graph viewport.

9 Select the `RAIN` connector in one of the orthographic viewports.

10 Select the rain particle system node in the scene graph viewport.

11 Link the `RAIN` connector with the rain particle system, by choosing **Node > Connect Node (Ctrl-L)**. The selection should now appear as shown in Figure 6-92.

12 Using the **Select Nodes (1)** tool, select the panel effect node.

13 Choose **Node > Get Info (Ctrl-I)** to open the **Node Info** dialog.

14 Select the **Controller** tab panel.

15 Click **Edit Panel.**

16 We'll now edit the scripts for the ON and OFF buttons. Select the ON button and select **Widget > Edit Script (Ctrl-E).**

Figure 6-92. The panel effect's `RAIN` connector connected to the rain particle system.

17 From the list of **Standard** methods, select the **Enable Node** method and add it to the script canvas, as shown in Figure 6-93.

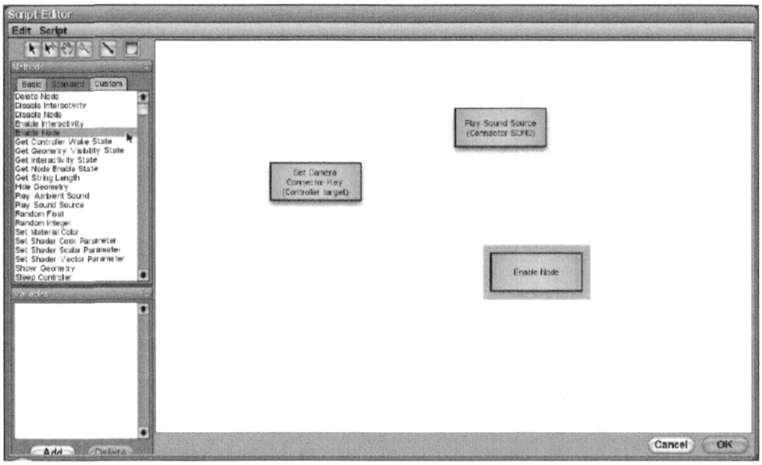

Figure 6-93. Adding an **Enable Node** method to the ON button.

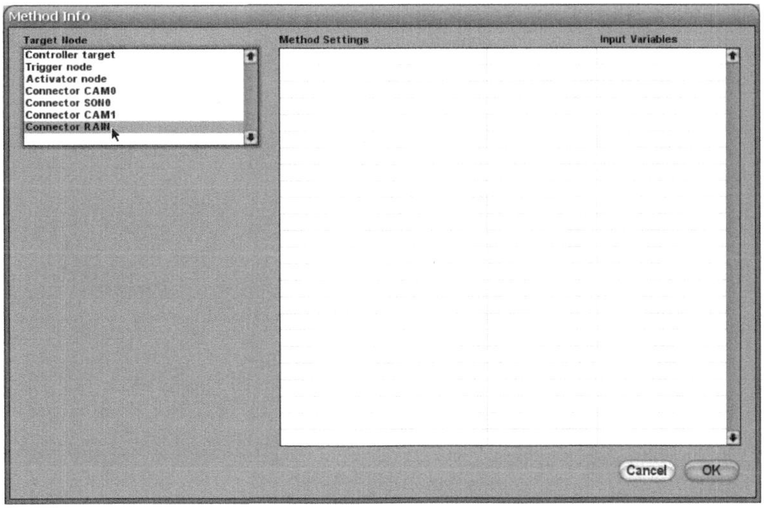

Figure 6-94. Setting the **Target Node** for the **Enable Node** method used by the ON button.

18 Choose **Script > Get Info (Ctrl-I)** to edit the new method's settings in the **Method Info** dialog. Alternatively, you can double-click the new method using the **Select** or **Move Methods** tool.

19 Select **Connector RAIN** in the **Target Node** list, as shown in Figure 6-94.

20 Click **OK** two times to confirm your changes in the **Method Info** and **Script Editor** dialogs.

21 Next, we'll edit the script for the OFF button. Select the OFF button, and select **Widget > Edit Script (Ctrl-E)**.

22 From the **Standard** methods list, add a **Disable Node** method to the script canvas, as shown in Figure 6-95.

23 Choose **Script > Get Info (Ctrl-I)** to edit the new method's settings in the **Method Info** dialog. Alternatively, you can double-click the new method using the **Select / Move Tool**.

24 Select **Connector RAIN** in the **Target Node** list, as shown in Figure 6-96.

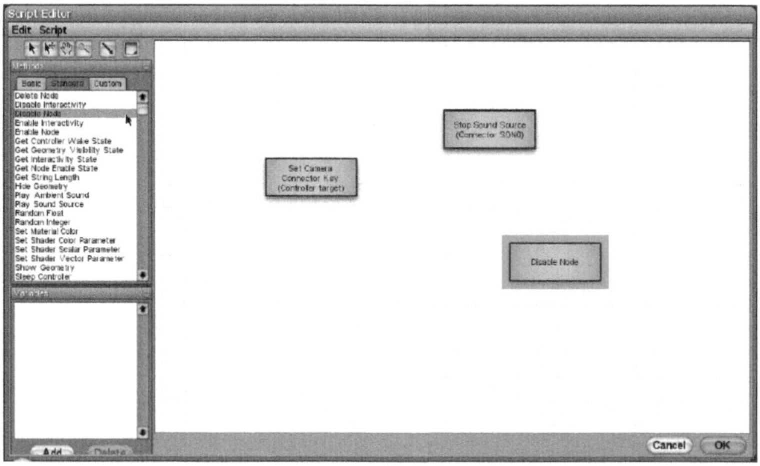

Figure 6-95. Adding a **Disable Node** method to the OFF button.

25 Save and confirm all your changes in the **Method Info**, **Script Editor**, **Panel Editor**, and **Node Info** dialogs.

26 Choose **World > Save and Play World (Ctrl-P)**. You can now turn the rain on and off with the panel buttons.

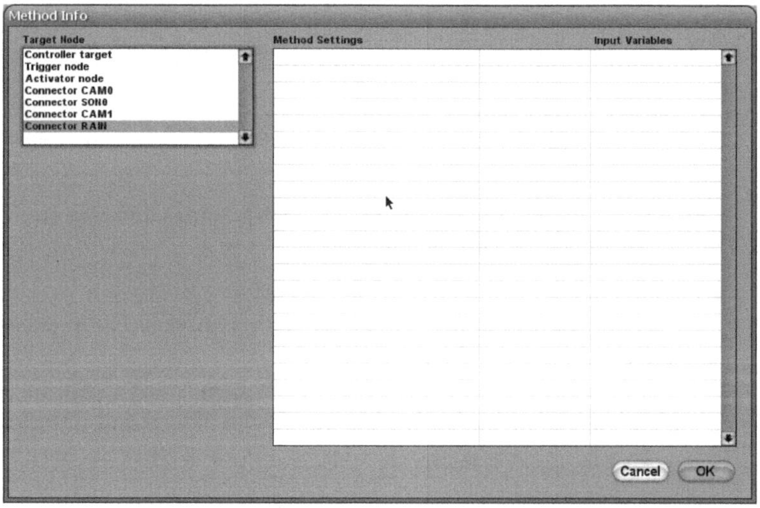

Figure 6-96. Setting the **Target Node** for the **Enable Node** method used by the ON button.

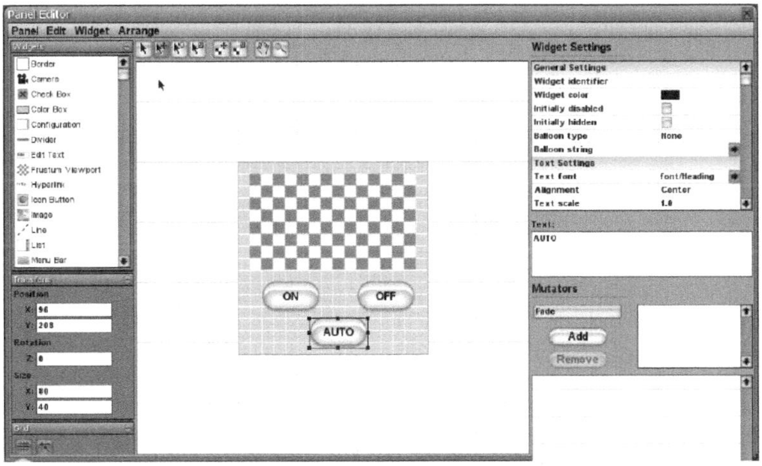

Figure 6-97. Adding the AUTO button to the panel effect.

Automatic Camera Switching

Let's add a third button which, when pressed, will cause the cameras to switch automatically, after a small delay.

1. Select the panel effect and choose **Node > Edit Script or Panel (Ctrl-E)** to open the **Panel Editor** dialog directly.
2. In the **Panel Editor** dialog, add a new push button and label it AUTO, as shorthand for automatic. The panel should now appear as shown in Figure 6-97.
3. Now select and edit the widget script for the AUTO button with **Widget > Edit Script (Ctrl-E)**.
4. In the **Basic** methods list, select the **Null** method.
5. Place the **Null** method near the top of the script canvas.
6. Below the **Null** method, add two **Call Controller Function** methods and two **Delay** methods in the **Script Editor** dialog.
7. Line up the new methods from top to bottom as shown in Figure 6-98, with the **Delay** methods in the third and fifth positions.
8. Double-click each of the **Delay** methods and set the **Delay time** setting to a value of three seconds, as shown in Figure 6-99.

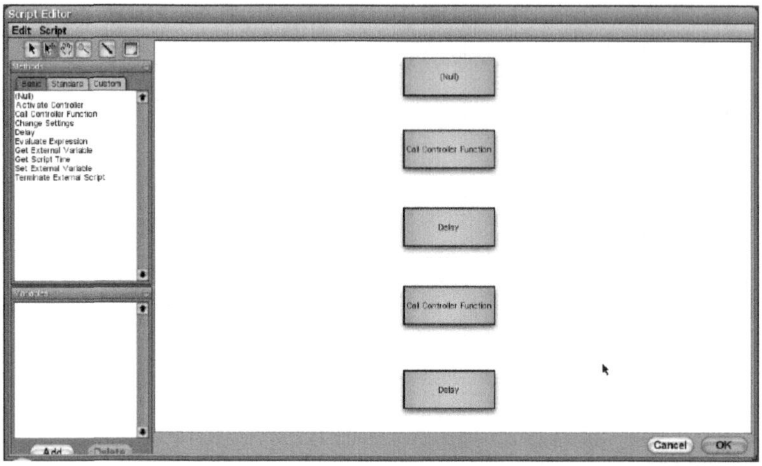

Figure 6-98. Adding **Call Controller Function** and **Delay** methods.

9 Double-click the topmost **Call Controller Function** method to open the **Method Info** dialog.

10 Set the **Target Node** to **Controller target**.

11 Select **Set Camera Connector Key** from the **Functions** list.

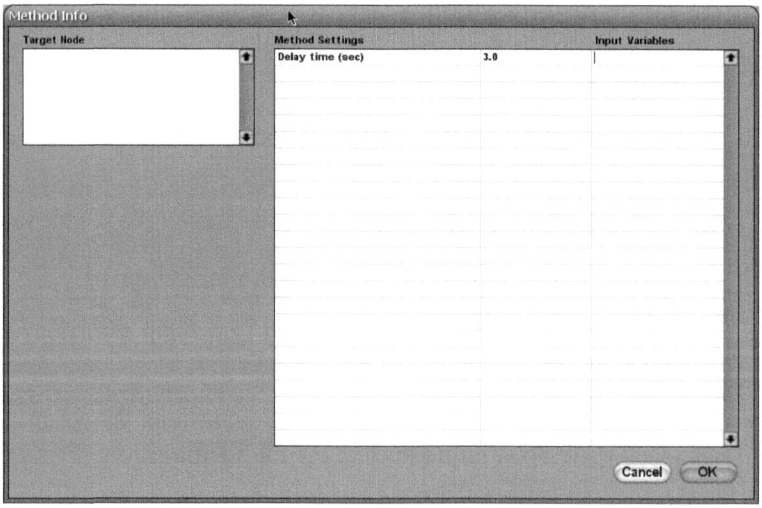

Figure 6-99. Setting the **Delay time** value.

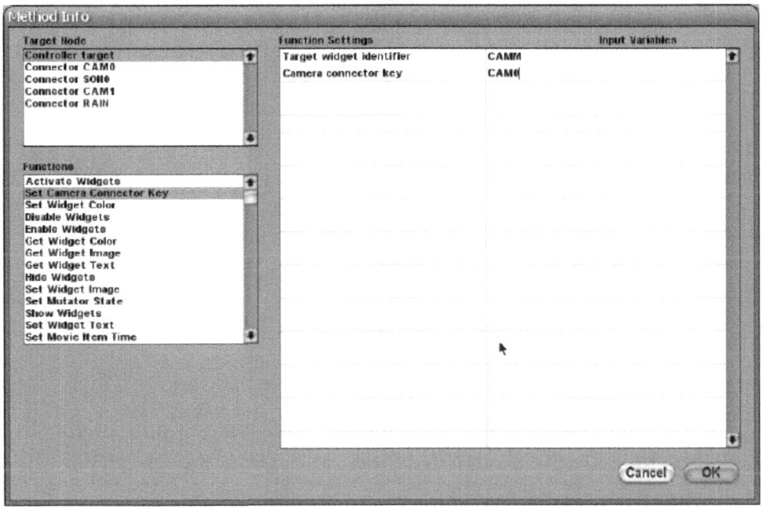

Figure 6-100. Settings for the first **Call Controller Function**.

12 Set the **Target widget identifier** to `CAMM`, and the **Camera connector key** to `CAM0`. The **Method Info** dialog should now appear as shown in Figure 6-100.

13 Click **OK** to save your changes in the **Method Info** dialog. The title of the **Call Controller Function** method changes to **Set Camera Connector Key (Controller target)**.

14 For the second **Call Controller Function** method, use the same setting values, except for the **Camera connector key** setting—set its value `CAM1` instead of `CAM0`, as shown in Figure 6-101.

15 Click **OK** to save your changes in the **Method Info** dialog.

16 Connect the **Null** method to the **Set Camera Connector Key** method, by left clicking the little white circle of the null method, and dragging the arrow until the mouse is over the **Set Camera Connector Key** method, as shown in Figure 6-102.

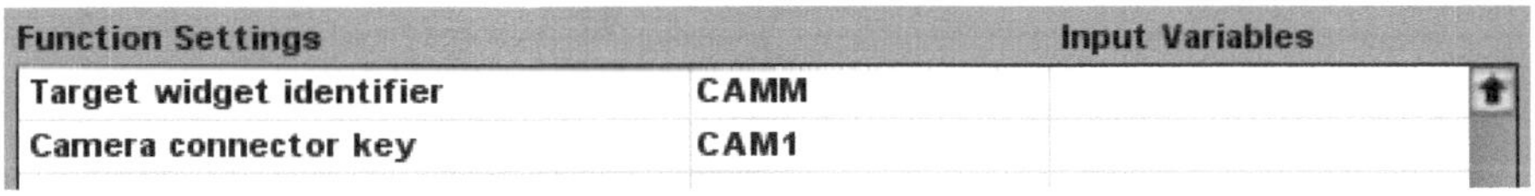

Figure 6-101. Setting the second **Call Controller Function** method settings.

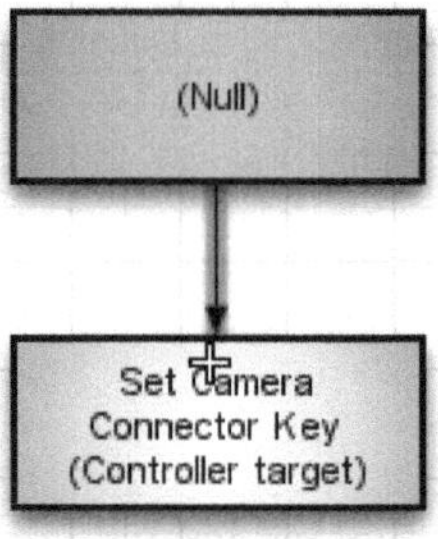

Figure 6-102. Connecting the first two methods.

17 Drag out additional connections from the second to the third method, from the third to the fourth method, and from the fourth to the fifth method, as shown in Figure 6-103.

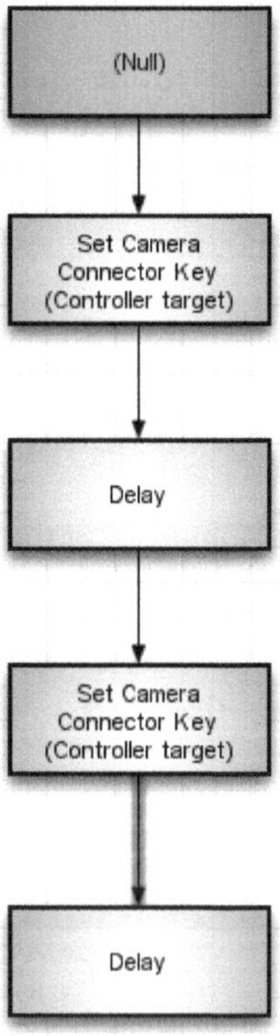

Figure 6-103. Connecting all five methods with fibers.

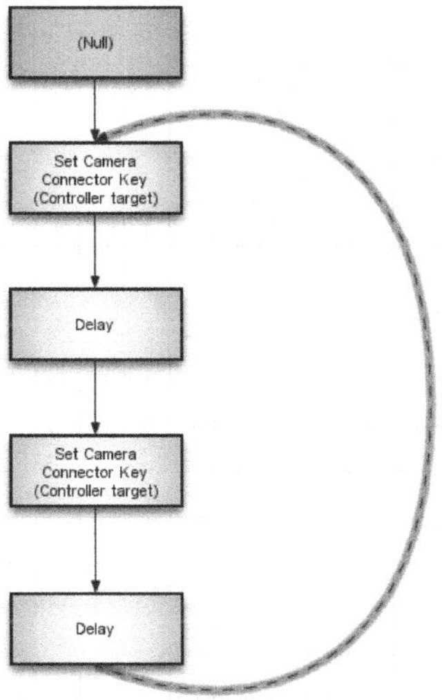

Figure 6-104. Creating a fiber loop.

18 Drag out a connection from the fifth method at the bottom back up to the second method, as shown in Figure 6-104. The **Script Editor** will recognize the loop, and will display the connection using a dashed style to indicate the new control flow.

19 Click **OK** to save your changes, then save your changes in the **Panel Editor**.

20 Choose **World > Save and Play World (Ctrl-P)** to run the world, which should appear as shown in Figure 6-105.

21 Walk up close enough to the panel effect such that the interaction arrow cursor appears. Clicking the AUTO button on the panel effect causes the camera panel item to start switching back-and-forth between the two frustum cameras automatically, every three seconds. Stand back to see the changes better.

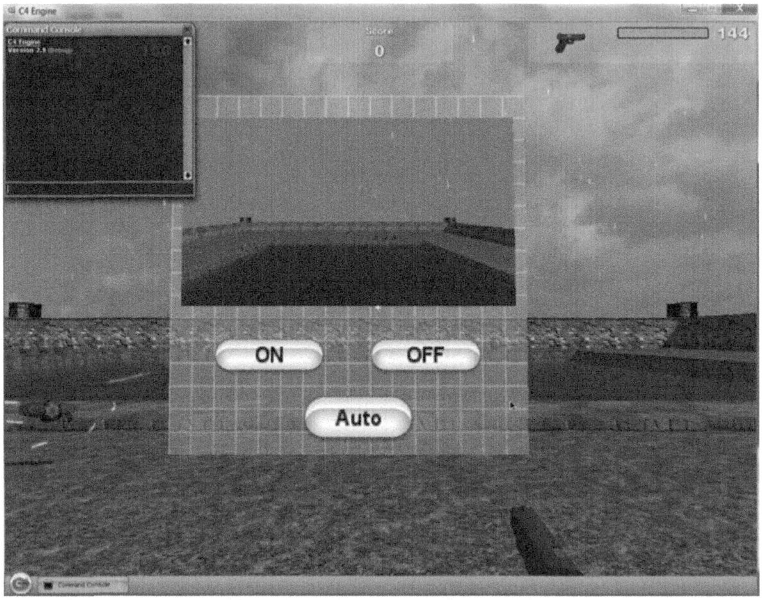

Figure 6-105. The panel effect with the AUTO button in-game.

Variables and Conditions

Let's make things a little more interesting. When we click the AUTO button, we would like either the rain to stop or the camera to switch, depending on whether a random number is above or below a threshold we define. Let's do it.

1. Open your world in the **World Editor**.
2. Select the panel effect node.
3. Choose **Node > Edit Script or Panel (Ctrl-E)** to open the Panel Editor.
4. To the right of the AUTO button, add a text widget.
5. In the **Widget Settings**, set the **Widget identifier** value to `RNUM`.
6. Set the widget color of the new text item to blue, the font to `Block`, and the alignment to **Center**.
7. Set the initial text to "Num = 0".

Move the AUTO button over to the left to make enough room, so that the panel effect appears as shown in Figure 6-106.

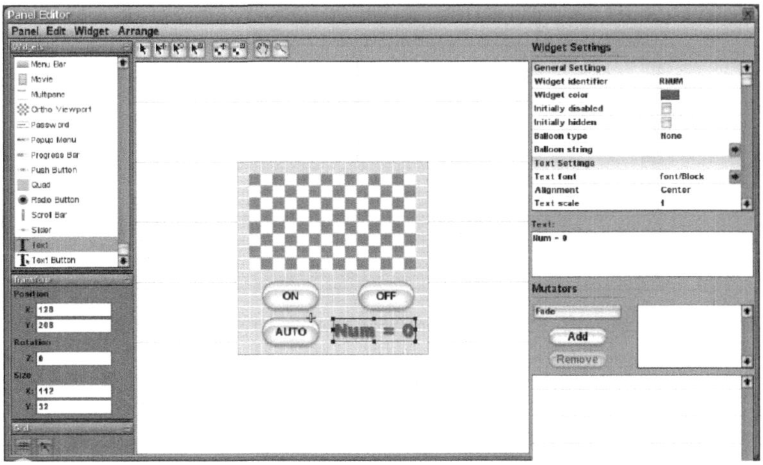

Figure 6-106. Adding a text widget for a random number.

8 Select the AUTO button and edit the script by selecting **Widget > Edit Script (Ctrl-E)**.

9 Using the **Select** tool, delete all of the old connections from the earlier version of the AUTO button script.

10 Add a new variable by clicking **Add**, which opens the **Variable Info** dialog.

11 Set the **Variable name** value to `random`.

12 Set the **Variable type** to **Integer**.

The **Variable scope** and **Initial value** settings don't need to be changed. The **Variable Info** dialog should now appear as shown in Figure 6-107.

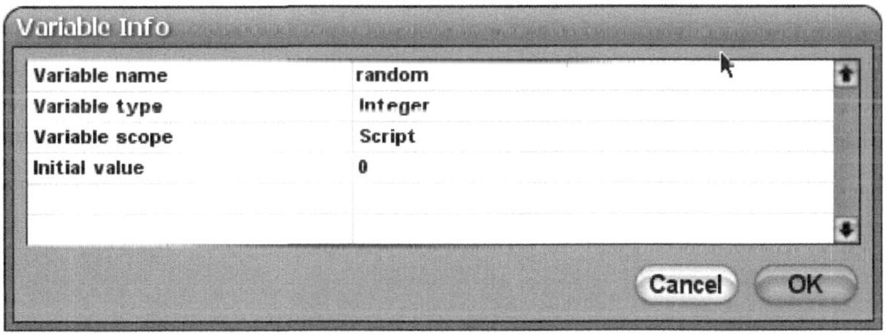

Figure 6-107. Setting the **Variable Info** values for the `random` integer variable.

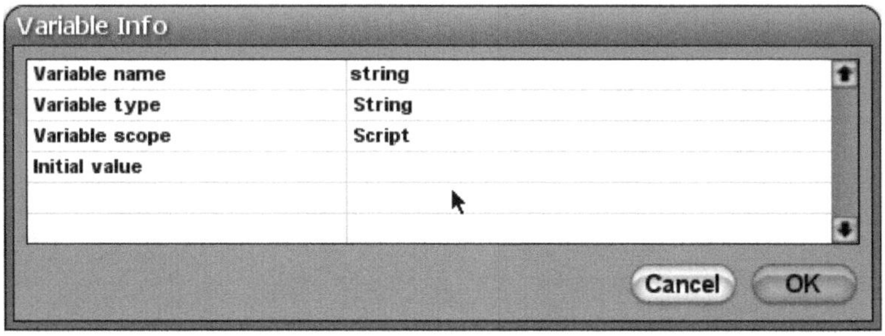

Figure 6-108. Setting the **Variable Info** values for the string variable.

13 Click **OK** to save your changes.

14 Create a second variable by clicking **Add**, which opens the **Variable Info** dialog.

15 Set the **Variable name** value to `string`.

16 Set the **Variable type** to **String**.

The **Variable scope** and **Initial value** settings don't need to be changed. The **Variable Info** dialog should now appear as shown in Figure 6-108.

17 Click **OK** to save your changes.

18 From the **Standard** methods list, select the **Disable Node** method and then click around the middle of the left side of the script canvas to add it.

19 Choose **Script** > **Get Info** to open the **Method Info** dialog, and set the **Target Node** setting to **Connector RAIN**. Click **OK**.

20 From the **Standard** methods list, select the **Enable Node** method and then click below the **Disable Node** method on the script canvas to add it.

21 Choose **Script** > **Get Info** to open the **Method Info** dialog, and set the **Target Node** setting to **Connector RAIN**. Click **OK**.

22 From the **Basic** methods list, add two **Evaluate Expression** methods to the script canvas.

23 From the **Standard** methods list, add one **Random Integer** method to the script canvas.

24 From the **Basic** methods list, add one **Call Controller Function** method to the script canvas.

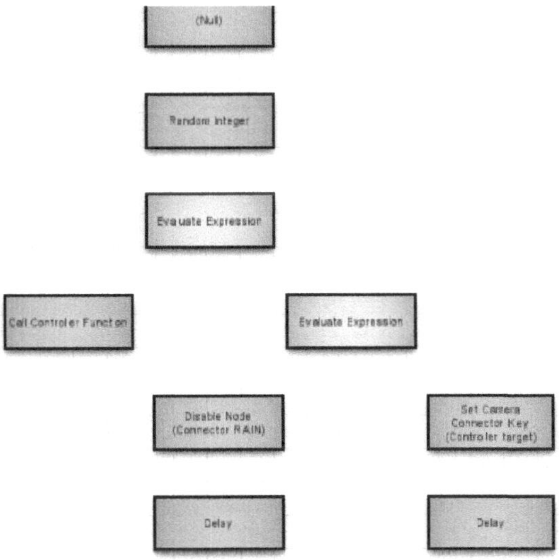

Figure 6-109. Organizing the method layout.

25 From the **Basic** method list, add two more **Delay methods** to the script canvas.

26 Open the **Method Info** dialog for each of the new **Delay** methods, and set each method's **Delay** time setting to a value of 3.0 seconds.

27 Move the methods around until they match the organization shown in Figure 6-109. See also Figure 6-114 for the full layout.

28 Double-click the **Call Controller Function** method to open the **Method Info** dialog.

29 In the **Target Node** list, select **Controller target**.

30 In the **Functions** list, select **Set Widget Text**.

31 Set the **Target widget identifier** value to `RNUM`.

32 Set the **Input variables** value for the **Widget text** setting to string. The **Method Info** dialog should now appear as shown in Figure 6-110.

This method is now configured to set the value of the text in the text widget to the value of the string variable.

33 Click **OK** to save your changes. The title of the **Call Controller Function** method changes to **Set Widget Text (Controller target)**.

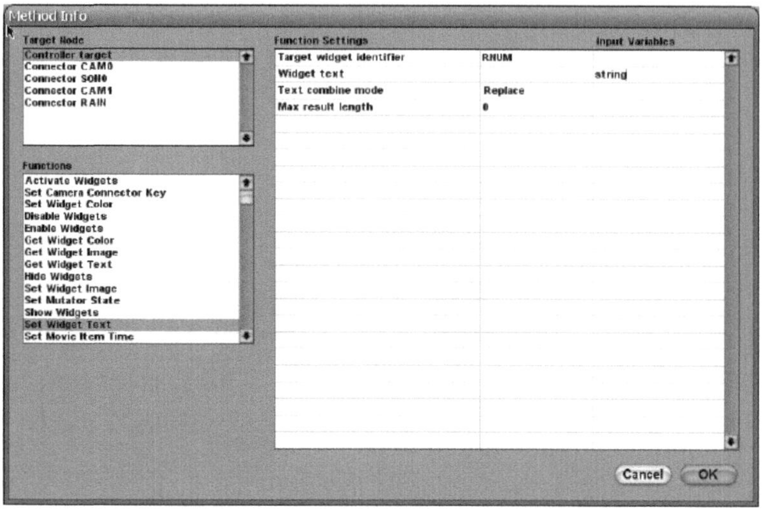

Figure 6-110. Calling the **Set Widget Text** function.

34 Double-click the **Random Integer** method to open the **Method Info** dialog.

35 Set the **Minimum value** to 0.

36 Set the **Maximum value** to 10.

37 Set the **Output Variable** to `random`. `random` is the same name you used for the integer variable earlier. The **Method Info** dialog should appear as shown in Figure 6-111.

38 Click **OK** to save your changes in the **Method Info** dialog.

39 Select the **Evaluate Expression** method just below the **Random Integer** method, and choose **Script > Get Info (Ctrl-I)** to open the **Method Info** dialog.

40 Set the **Expression** to `"Num = " + random`.

41 Set the **Output Variable** to `string`. The **Method Info** dialog should now appear as shown in Figure 6-112.

42 Click **OK** to save your changes in the **Method Info** dialog. The title of the **Evaluate Expression** method changes to display the custom expression value.

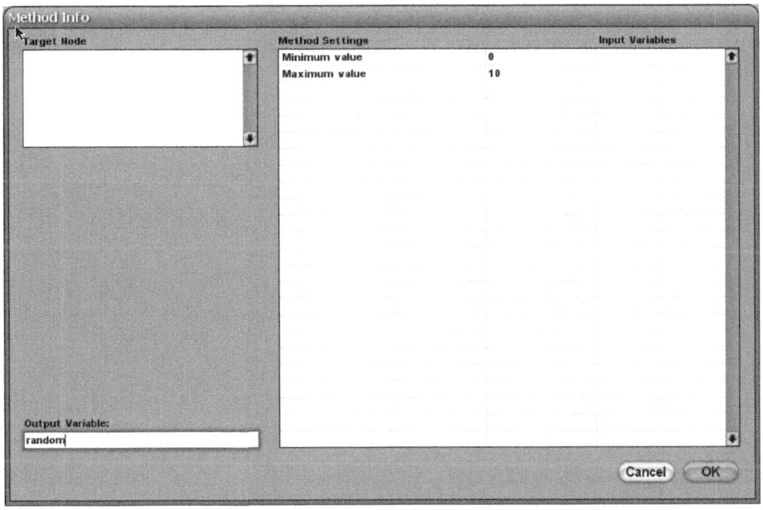

Figure 6-111. The **Random Integer** method settings.

43 Select the other **Evaluate Expression** method on the right side of the script canvas, and choose **Script > Get Info (Ctrl-I)** to open the **Method Info** dialog.

44 Set the **Expression** value to `random < 5`, as shown in Figure 6-113.

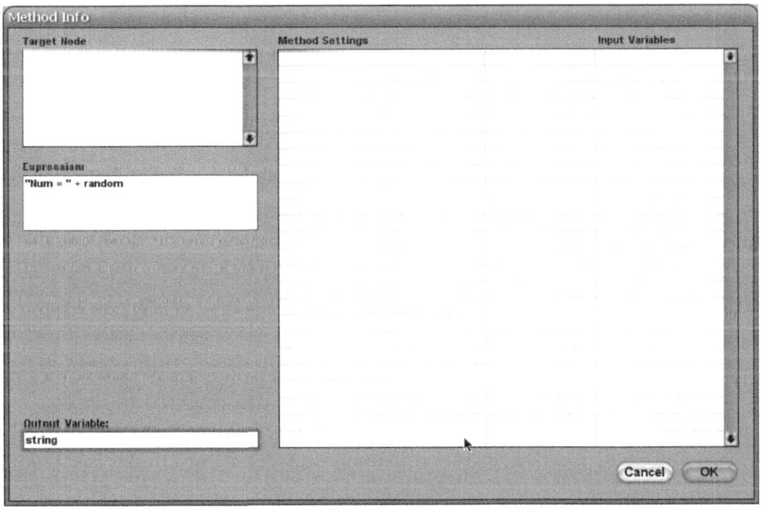

Figure 6-112. Setting the **Evaluate Expression** method settings.

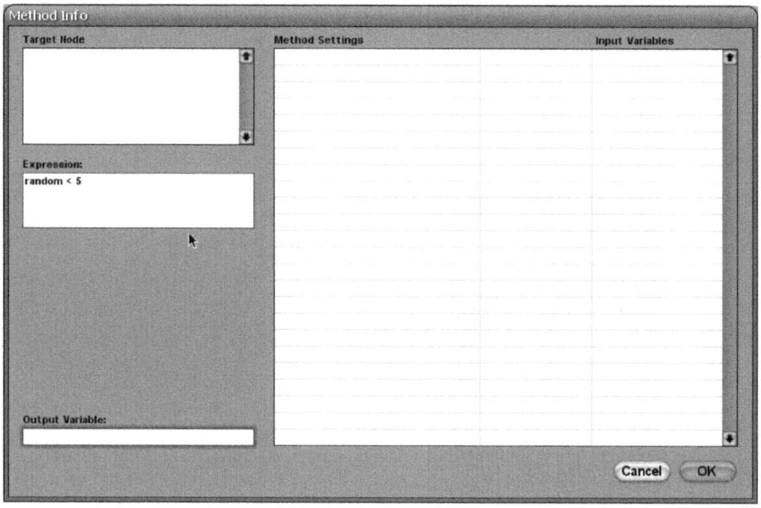

Figure 6-113. Settings for the second **Evaluate Expression** method.

This expression will evaluate to true or false, so there is no need to set the **Output Variable** value.

45 Click **OK** to save your changes in the **Method Info** dialog.

46 The methods should appear as shown in Figure 6-114. You can zoom in and out with the middle mouse button.

47 Join the methods together by dragging from one method box to the next, as shown in Figure 6-114, Figure 6-115, and Figure 6-116.

You can move the methods around until the loops route themselves along a visually clean path. Loops are recognized automatically and are drawn with a dashed style.

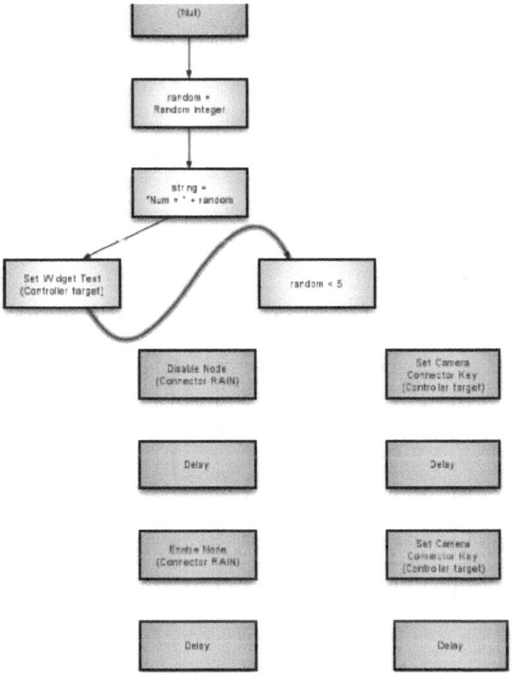

Figure 6-114. Connecting the methods in the AUTO script.

48 Set the control flow resulting from the `random < 5` expression by selecting the leftmost output fiber, and choosing **Script > Cycle Fiber Condition (Ctrl-F)** to cycle through the available colors until it is displayed in green (for true), and then select the rightmost fiber and cycle its color until it is red (for false).

49 Click **OK** to save your changes in the **Script Editor**, then save and close the **Panel Editor**.

50 Choose **World > Save and Play World (Ctrl-P)** to test your changes.

That's all the scripting we're going to cover for now, but we hope you'll explore the **Script Editor** in more depth on your own.

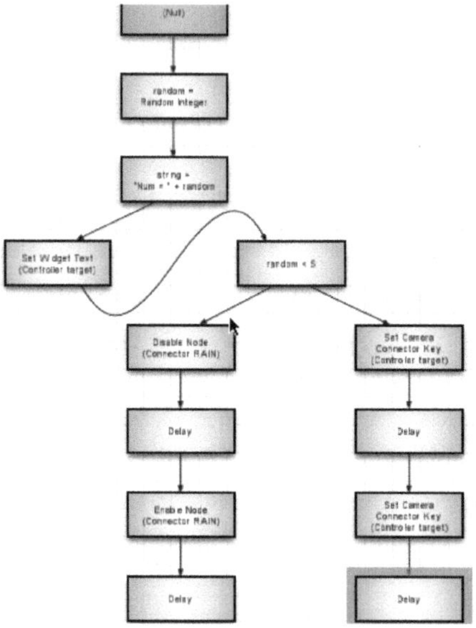

Figure 6-115. Connecting more fibers in the AUTO script.

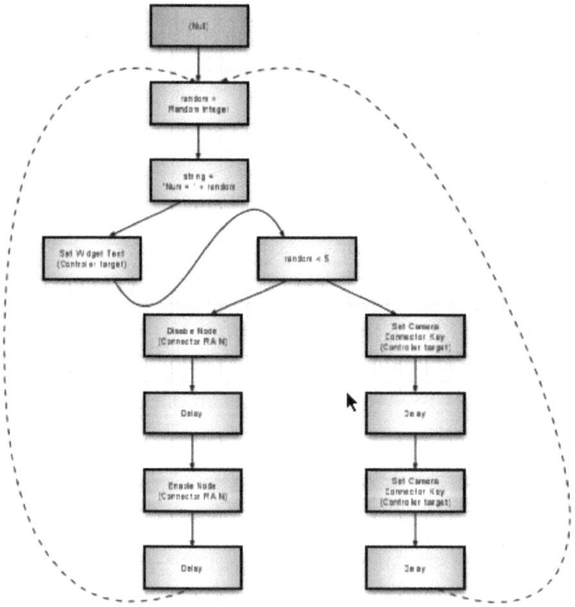

Figure 6-116. Connecting the loop fibers in the AUTO script.

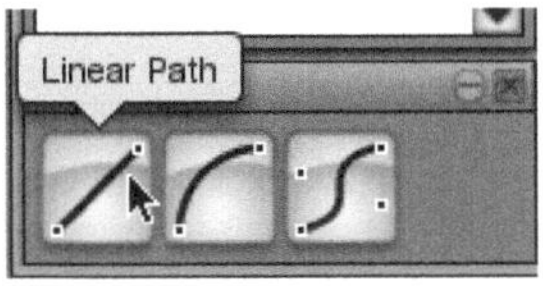

Figure 6-117. Selecting the **Linear Path** tool on the **Paths** page.

Path Tubes for Tunnels

Let's make a tunnel using paths.

1. Choose **Tools > Open World (Ctrl-O)** and open your EditorFeatures world in the **World Editor**.
2. Choose **Page > Paths** to open the **Paths** page panel.
3. Select the **Linear Path** tool, as shown in Figure 6-117.
4. Drag a linear path from top-to-bottom, in a viewport showing the *x*-*y* plane, such that the path is about the same length as your world, as shown in Figure 6-118.

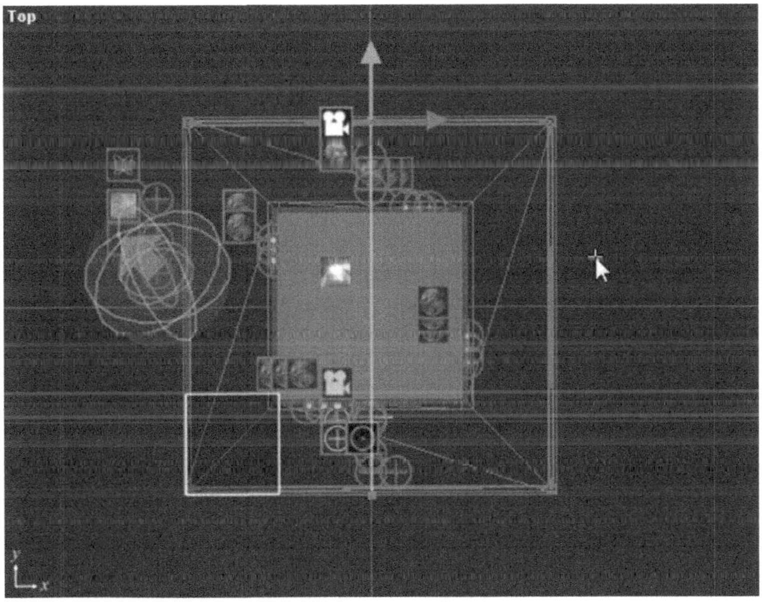

Figure 6-118. Creating a linear path.

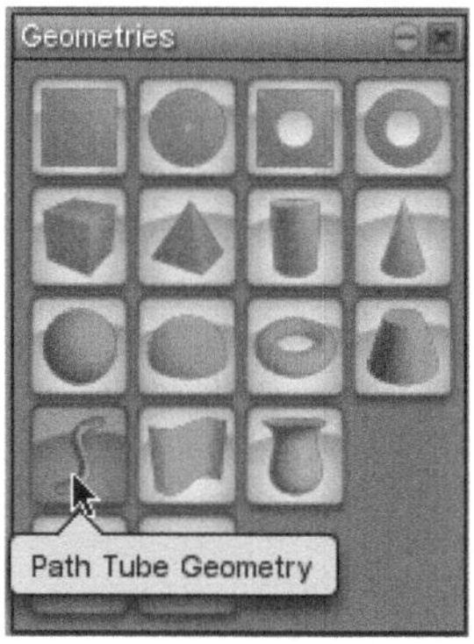

Figure 6-119. Selecting the **Path Tube** tool in the **Geometries** page.

5 Select the **Path Tube** tool in the **Geometries** page panel, as shown in Figure 6-119.

6 In the *x-y* **Top (+z)** viewport, drag out a tunnel shape that will cover the world completely, starting at the origin of the linear path node.

Keep an eye on the *x-z* **Left (+y)** viewport to ensure that the cross-section is approximately circular, as shown in Figure 6-120.

7 Move the tunnel as needed using the **Move Nodes (2)** tool. Half of the tunnel should be above ground, and the other half should be below ground level.

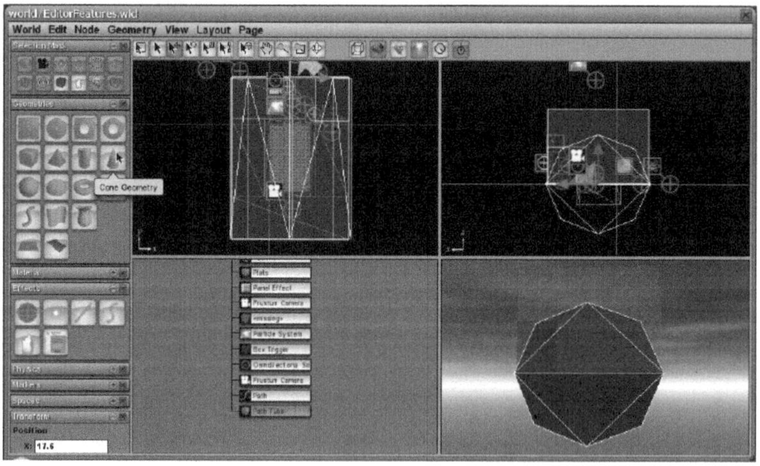

Figure 6-120. Creating a path tube geometry.

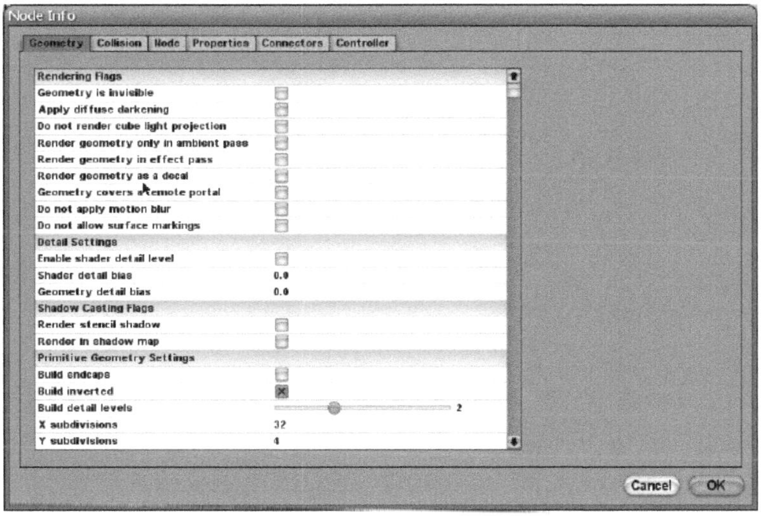

Figure 6-121. The **Geometry** settings for the path tube geometry.

8 Apply a material of your choice, such as cinder block.

9 Choose **Node > Get Info (Ctrl-I)** to open the **Node Info** dialog.

10 In the **Geometry** tab panel, deselect the **Build endcaps** option, and select the **Build Inverted** option. These options will allow us to see the texture on the inside wall of the tunnel.

11 Because the endcaps are not being built, the tube geometry will be open, and cannot cast stencil shadows, so deselect the **Render stencil shadow** option.

12 To smooth the appearance of the tube, increase the **X subdivisions** value to 32 and reduce the **Y subdivisions** value to 4. The **Node Info** dialog should now appear as shown in Figure 6-121. Click **OK**.

13 Choose **World > Save and Play World (Ctrl-P)**. The world should appear similar to the world shown in Figure 6-122.

14 To create a different type of tunnel, use the **Box Geometry** on the **Geometry** page panel to draw a large box shape right over the water, as shown in Figure 6-123.

Figure 6-122. Using a tube extruded along a path to build a tunnel.

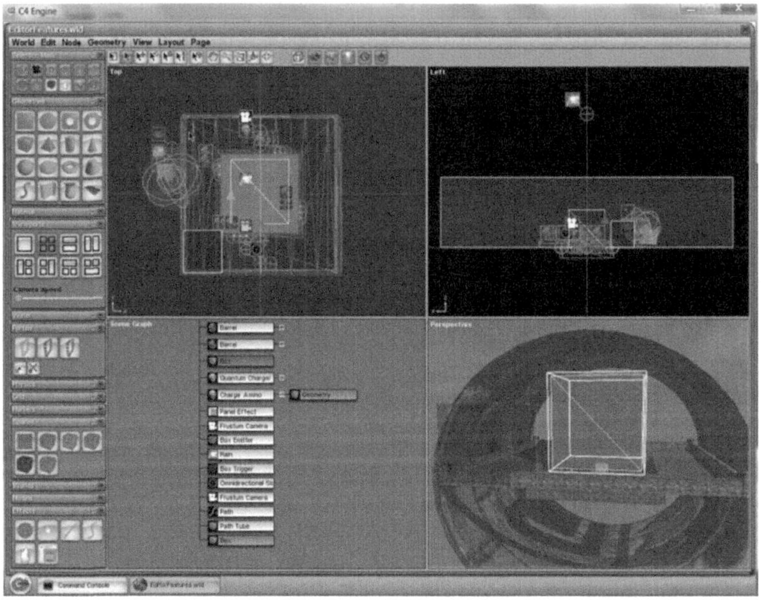

Figure 6-123. Adding a box shape to construct a different kind of tunnel.

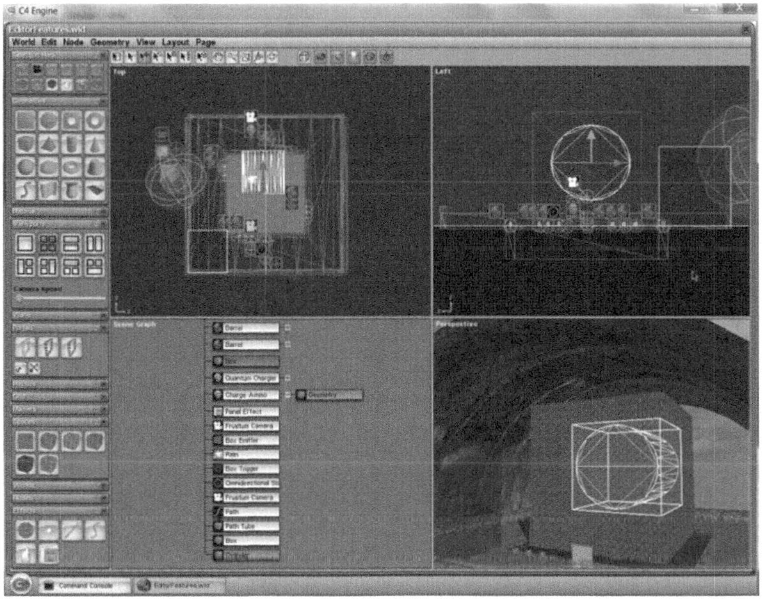

Figure 6-124. Adding a cylinder that will be subtracted from the box.

15 In the *x-z* **Left (+y)** viewport, use the **Cylinder Geometry** from the **Geometries** page panel to draw out a cylinder in the middle of the box, as shown in Figure 6-124.

16 In the *x-y* **Top (+z)** viewport, use the **Resize Tool (4)** to stretch the cylinder so that it extends through the middle of the box on both sides, parallel to the *y* axis, as shown in Figure 6-125.

17 With just the cylinder still selected, choose **Geometry > Invert geometry (Ctrl-Shift I)**.

18 Shift-select the box to add it to the selection, as shown in Figure 6-126.

19 With both the cylinder and the box selected, choose **Geometry > Intersect Geometry (Ctrl-Shift-J)** to cut a hole out of the middle of the box.

20 With just the box geometry selected, choose **Node > Get Info (Ctrl-I)** to open the **Node Info** dialog.

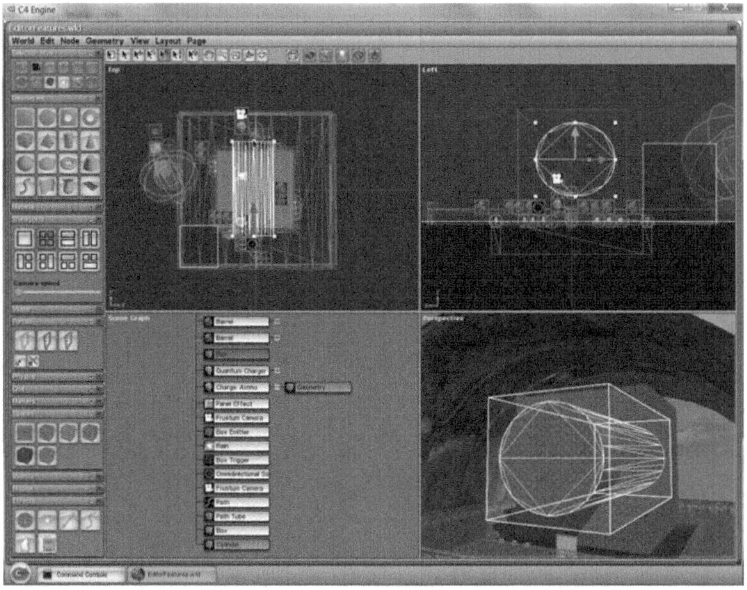

Figure 6-125. Setting the size of the cylinder that will be subtracted from the box.

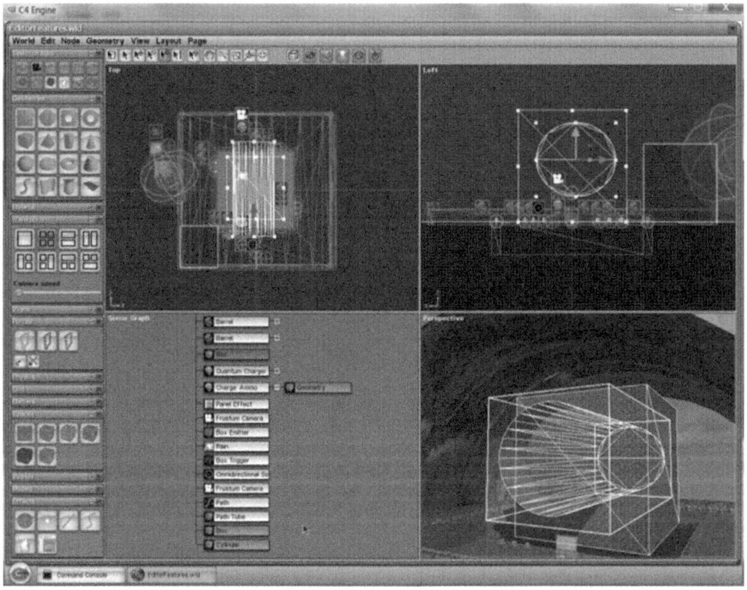

Figure 6-126. The cylinder and the box selected, ready for the geometry intersection operation.

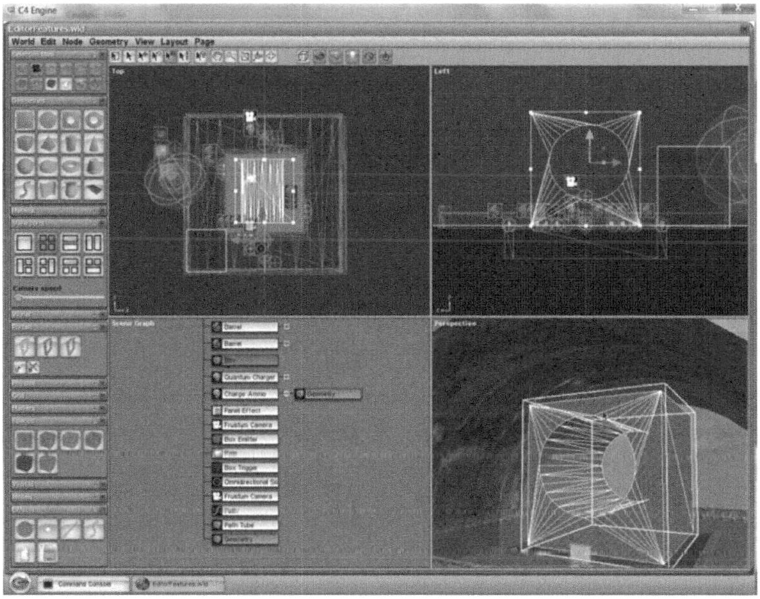

Figure 6-127. A different kind of tunnel.

21 In the **Geometry** tab, deselect the **Render stencil shadow** option. The results should appear as shown in Figure 6-127.

22 Choose **World > Save and Play World (Ctrl-P)** to test your changes.

Your Turn

We encourage you to experiment with the **World Editor** in a world like the Water world or any of the other tutorial worlds:

- Add effects such as glow and tube.
- Play around with the various items within panels.
- Use scripts to vary panel items depending on which buttons are pressed. Try out each of the animation types for the various panel items.
- You can also add effects, such as a flare effect to simulate the sun, and you can easily add fire using the fire effect. You can turn the fire on and off using your ON / OFF buttons, by using the **Enable Node** and **Disable Node** methods in the **Script Editor**.

- Try out the particle emitters.
- Familiarize yourself with the **Grid** page panel. It's quite intuitive, so it's best to just play with the various options to see their effect on the grid in the various viewports.
- The **Visibility** page panel allows you to hide or show various node types. Toggling visibility is useful if you only wish to work with say effects or sound sources, for example, hiding everything else.
- The **Viewports** page allows you to select from eight different ways to divide up the **World Editor** window using viewports.
- Make a semi-transparent tunnel with bends in it. Adjust the alpha value to about 100 in the material, and use the **Render in effect pass** option on the tunnel geometry, to make it semi-transparent.

The **World Editor** offers you almost infinite possibilities, and the only limitation is your own creativity!

Next Steps

We only touched on a few of the material features provide by the World Editor up until now. Chapter 7, "Material Manager", introduces the world of possibilities provided by the material features in the C4 Engine.

7

Material Manager

This chapter explains how to create new materials, shows each of the material attributes, and provides pointers to help you organize your materials. We'll start by showing you how to create a material and change how it is previewed. Next, we'll show each of the material attributes one at a time, and also show a number of attribute combinations that can be used to create complex, multi-faceted material appearances.

After we explain each of the material attributes, you'll be ready to design a collection of materials, which can be organized within a world using the Material Manager window. Materials can also be re-used in other worlds by exporting them to a .mat file. For more details about organizing materials, see the section Managing Materials.

Show and Tell

The C4 Engine provides designers with a rich set of attributes for creating custom materials that can be applied to objects, to control their visual appearance. Material designers can adjust a number of settings that control various types of color channels, and can also refer to images stored in texture files, for per-pixel control of various texture map attributes for lighting and shadow effects.

To experiment with the materials presented in this chapter, download the *Guide* version of the Material Showroom from the "Resources" section of the "My Account" section of the C4 Engine download page here:

https://www.terathon.com/c4engine/reg/index.php

Figure 7-1. Starting the Material Showroom world.

Extract the `GuideMaterialShowroom.zip` archive to a convenient directory, and then run the application, which is named `Material Showroom.exe` on Windows. The main window for the Material Showroom appears as shown in Figure 7-1. Click **Enter Showroom** to enter the world and begin your tour, as shown in Figure 7-2.

Creating a New Material

Before we explore the Material Showroom, let's create a new material in the **Material Manager** window, set its name, and adjust the preview of its appearance.

1. Start up C4 and show the main menu bar.
2. Choose **C4 > New World (Ctrl-N)**, as shown in Figure 7-3.
3. C4 creates a new **World Editor** window, as shown in Figure 7-4.

Figure 7-2. Making your entrance into the Material Showroom world.

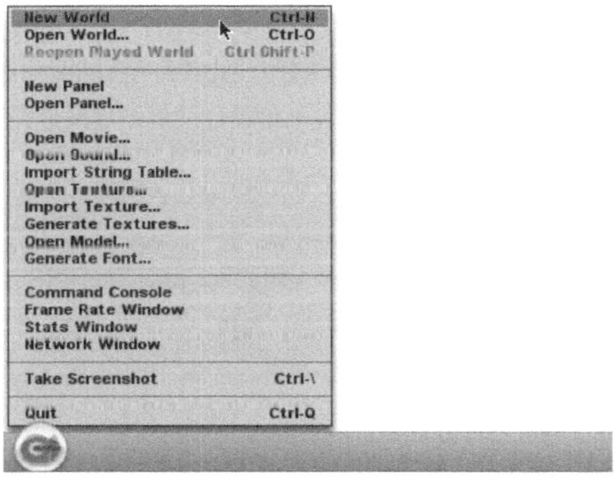

Figure 7-3. Choosing the **New World** command.

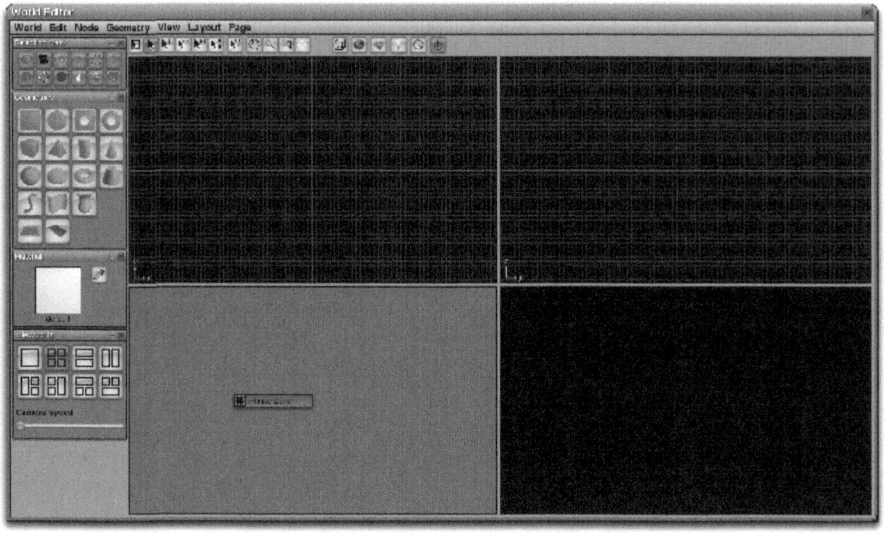

Figure 7-4. A new **World Editor** window.

4 Choose **Page** > **Material** to show the **Material** page panel, as shown in Figure 7-5.

5 Next, open the **Material Manager** window by double-clicking the material thumbnail in the **Material** page panel. The **Material Manager** window should appear as shown in Figure 7-6.

6 Create a fresh material with the default settings by clicking the **New** button in the lower left-hand corner of the **Material Manager** window.

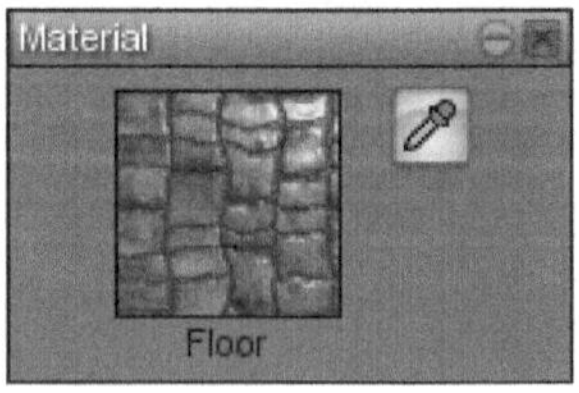

Figure 7-5. The **Material** page.

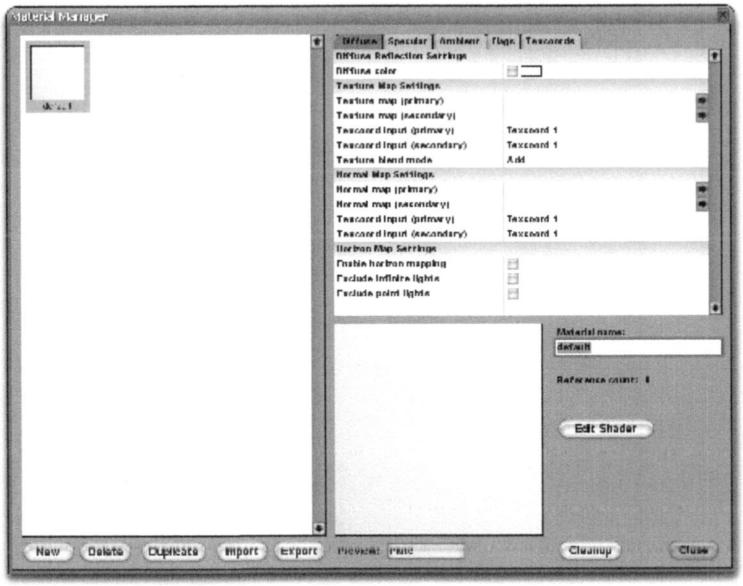

Figure 7-6. The **Material Manager** window.

Material Name

7 We recommend that you make a practice of entering descriptive names in the **Material** name text box, to make it easier to find and select materials. In Figure 7-7 we have named our material MyFirstMaterial.

Material Preview Geometry

The **Preview** option allows you to choose the type of geometry that is used to render the large material preview, as shown in Figure 7-8. The default material preview geometry type is **Plate**, which is useful for viewing a flat representation of a material.

8 Change the material preview display type by clicking the pop-up menu underneath the **Preview** text label. Figures 7-9, 7-10, 7-11, and 7-12 show each of the four additional types that are available—the **Box**, **Sphere**, **Torus**, and **Cylinder**.

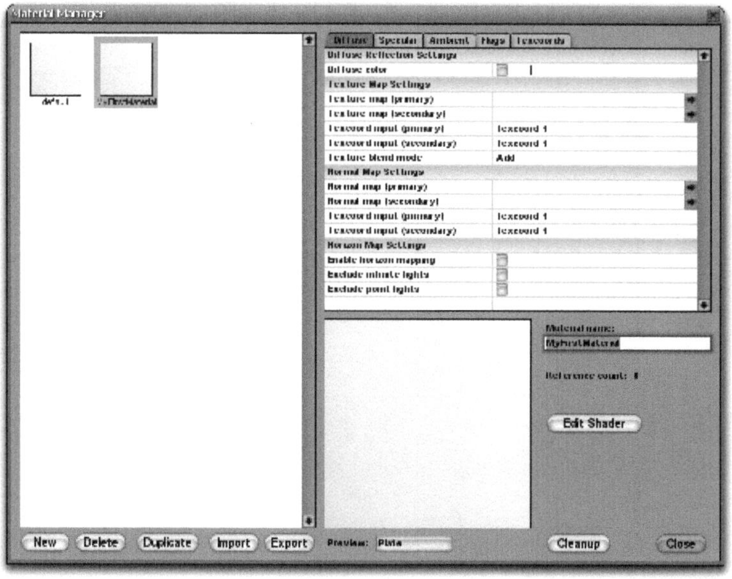

Figure 7-7. Entering a descriptive material name.

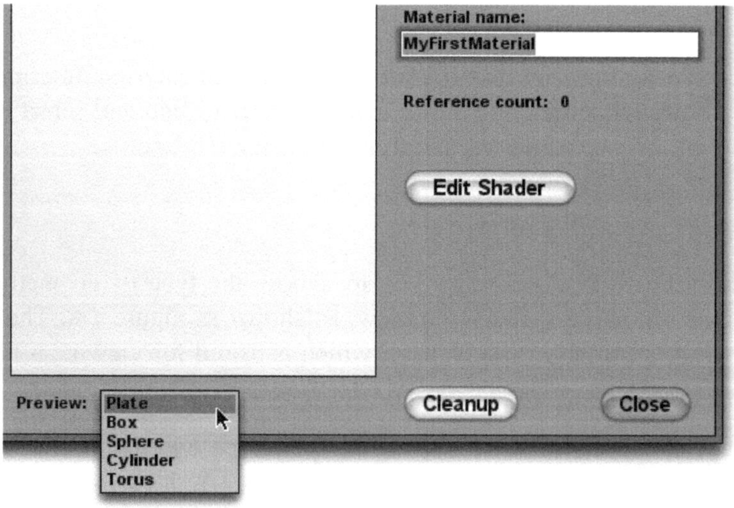

Figure 7-8. The material preview geometry type.

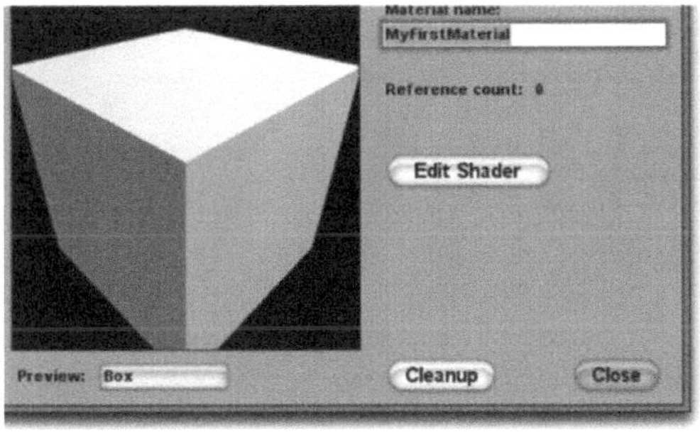

Figure 7-9. Material preview set to use the box geometry.

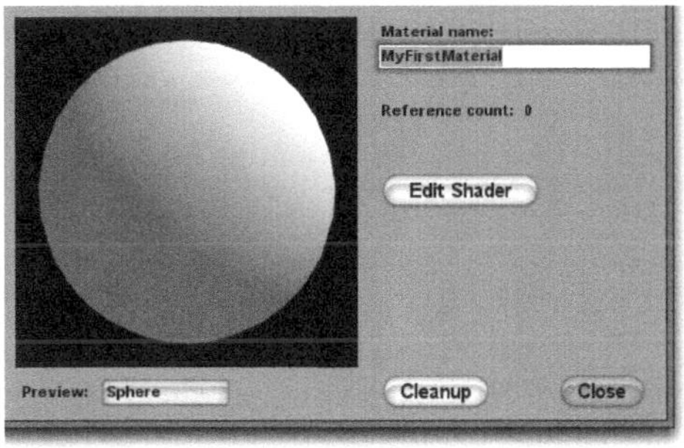

Figure 7-10. Material Preview set to use the sphere geometry.

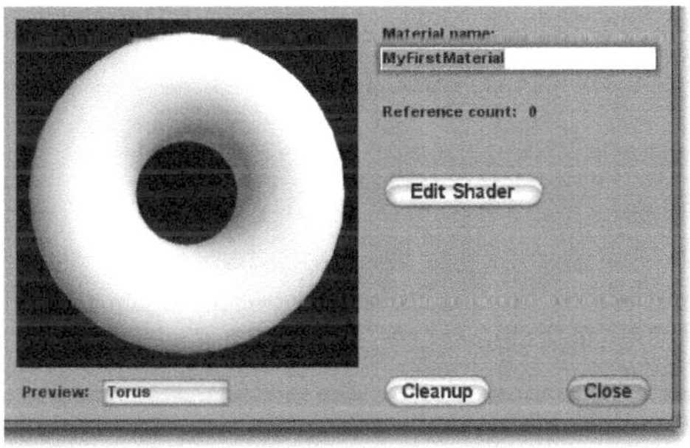

Figure 7-11. Material Preview set to use the torus geometry.

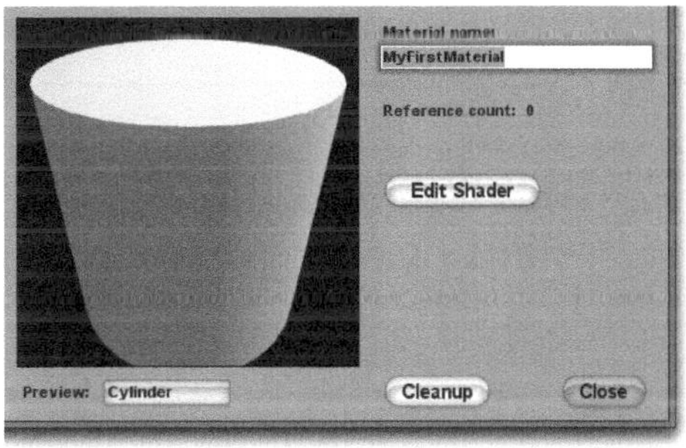

Figure 7-12. Material Preview set to use the cylinder geometry.

Material Settings

The material attributes are presented in five tabbed panels in the upper-right area of the **Material Manager** window. These panels are named **Diffuse**, **Specular**, **Ambient**, **Flags**, and **Texcoords**, as shown in Figure 7-13. Click each of the tab names to familiarize yourself with the contents of each tab panel.

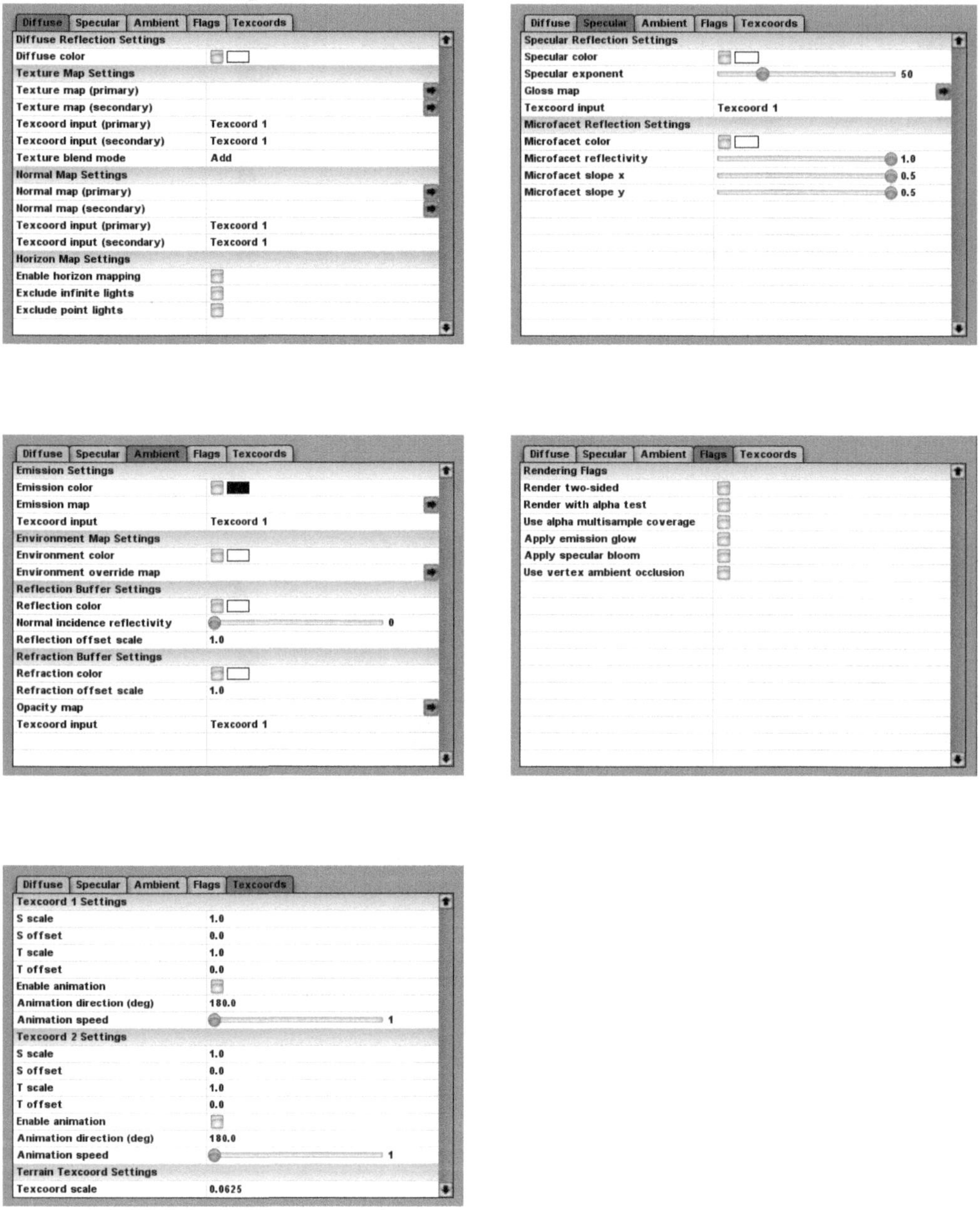

Figure 7-13. The five **Material Manager** tab panels.

Figure 7-14. The **Diffuse Attributes** material demo stations.

Diffuse Attributes

The diffuse attribute settings include options for diffuse reflection, texture maps, normal maps, horizon maps, and other specialized settings. To follow along with the examples in this next section, close the **World Editor** and run the Material Showroom world. Look for the sign announcing **Diffuse Attributes**, as shown in Figure 7-14.

Walk over to the first material demo station on your left, which contains two panels labeled **Diffuse Reflection Settings** and **Diffuse Map Settings**, as shown in Figure 7-15.

The **Diffuse Reflection Settings** group has a single attribute called **Diffuse Color**, which controls the color of diffuse light reflected by a surface—the natural color of a given object, without regard to lighting or shadow. A comparison of various **Diffuse Color** settings is shown in Figure 7-16.

Experiment with various settings for the **Red**, **Green**, **Blue**, and **Brightness** sliders, and then leave the sliders set to a full white setting (255, 255, 255, 255) for the next demonstration.

Figure 7-15. The **Diffuse Reflection Settings** and **Diffuse Map Settings**.

Texture map (primary)

The primary texture map serves as a base texture that controls the diffuse reflection color. On the **Diffuse Map Settings** panel, select the **Texture Map (Primary)** check box to enable the primary texture map, as shown in Figure 7-17.

Texture map (secondary)

The optional secondary texture map is combined with the primary texture map using the blending function specified by the **Texture blend mode** setting, described later in this chapter. On the **Diffuse Map Settings** panel, select the **Texture Map (Secondary)** check box to enable the secondary texture map, as shown in Figure 7-18. Note the two smaller samples above the main sample geometry, which show the primary and secondary texture maps as separate materials.

Figure 7-16. Various settings for the **Diffuse Color** attribute.

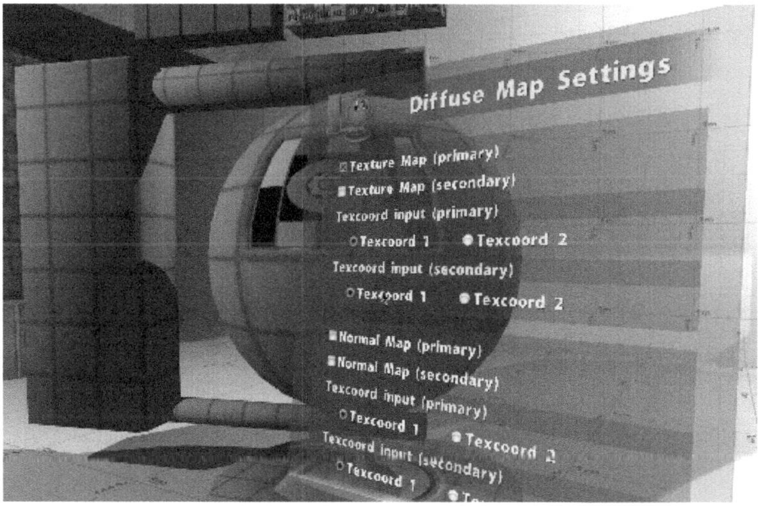

Figure 7-17. The **Texture Map (primary)** attribute.

Texcoord input (primary)

The primary texcoord input setting controls which set of scale, offset, and animation settings are applied to the primary texture map.

Texcoord input (secondary)

The secondary texcoord input setting controls which set of scale, offset, and animation settings are applied to the secondary texture map. You can create layered patterns, which have a more random appearance as they are repeated, by using scale, offset, and animation settings for the secondary texcoord that are different from the primary scale, offset, and animation texcoord settings.

Click the **Texcoord 2** radio buttons under the primary and secondary **Texcoord input** headings to see the effect of switching to the secondary texcoord set, as shown in Figure 7-19. See the Texcoords Attributes section later in this chapter for a description of the texcoord settings.

> **PICKING A TEXTURE MAP**
> Back in the **Material Manager** window, you can choose a texture map by clicking the right arrow button along the right edge of the setting to open the texture selection dialog, or type the name of a texture name (along with its path starting from the root Data directory if it isn't local to the world file) directly into the texture map field. All types of texture maps throughout the material settings are set in the same manner.

Figure 7-18. The **Texture Map (secondary)** attribute.

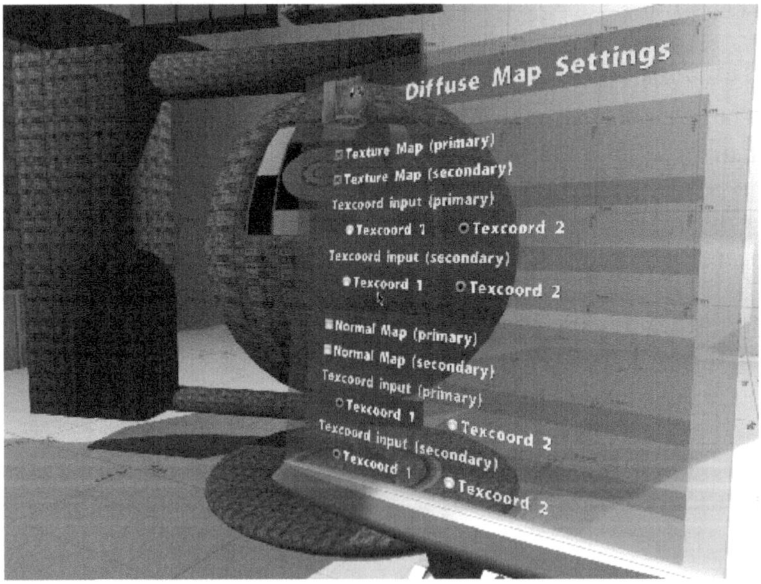

Figure 7-19. Using the second texcoord input for the primary and secondary texture map attributes.

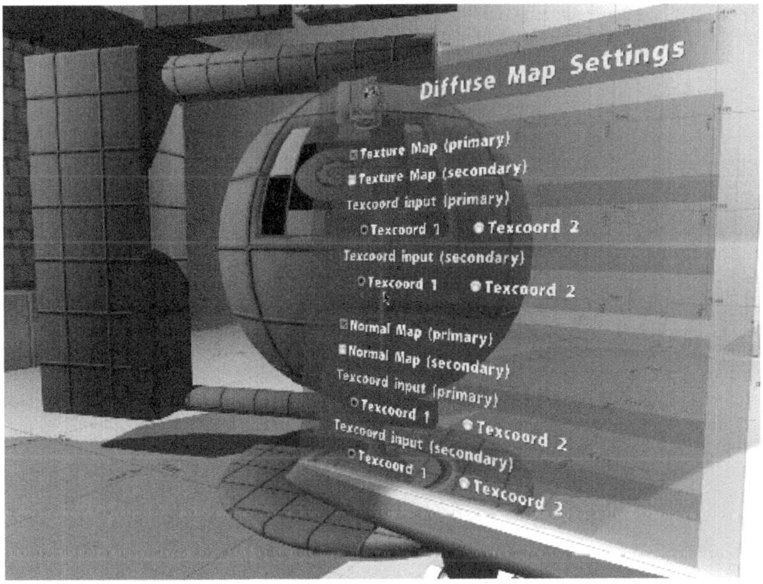

Figure 7-20. A normal map controls the bumpiness of a surface.

Normal map (primary)

The primary normal map controls the bumpiness of a surface. If the secondary texture map attribute is still selected, first deselect it for this example. Also, make sure that the **Texcoord 1** input is selected for the primary texture map. Now, select the **Normal Map (primary)** attribute, as shown in Figure 7-20.

The alpha channel of a normal map texture may contain extra information that affects different aspects of the material:

- If the alpha channel contains a gloss map, then it modulates the specular reflection and the environment map. This modulation works in the same manner as when a gloss map is stored in the alpha channel of a diffuse texture map, as shown later in this chapter in the Specular Reflection Settings section.

- If the alpha channel contains parallax data, then the parallax mapping calculation is applied in all rendering passes. The parallax mapping effect simulates a displacement effect.

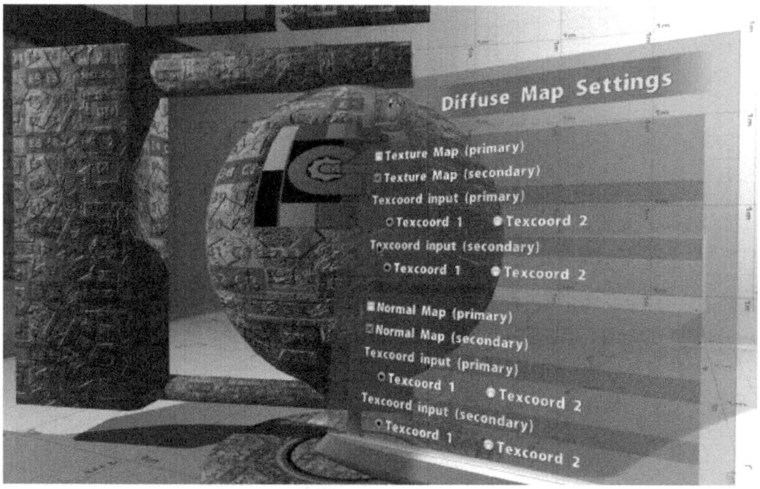

Figure 7-21. A secondary normal map.

Normal map (secondary)

The secondary normal map also controls the bumpiness of a surface, and can be layered with the primary normal map to create a layered appearance. This feature is useful for combining a large-scale normal map with a finely-detailed normal map that offers more detail when viewed up close.

First, let's take a look at the sample secondary normal map by itself. Deselect the **Texture Map (primary)** and **Normal Map (primary)** attributes, and then select the **Texture Map (secondary)** and **Normal Map (secondary)** attributes, as shown in Figure 7-21.

Now let's see what the primary and secondary texture and normal maps look like when they are layered together. Select the **Texture Map (primary)** and **Normal Map (primary)** attributes, as shown in Figure 7-22.

The color in the texture maps partially obscures what's going on with the normal maps, so you can isolate the effect of the normal maps by turning off the primary and secondary texture maps, as shown in Figure 7-23.

When a texture map is used by a material, at each mapping of a texture map pixel to the object, the diffuse color color is multiplied by the corresponding pixel color in the texture map, resulting in a colorization effect. Leave the **Texture Map** check boxes selected, and then on the **Diffuse Reflection Settings** panel, move the **Red** and **Green** sliders down to zero, creating a fully saturated blue diffuse color, as shown in Figure 7-24.

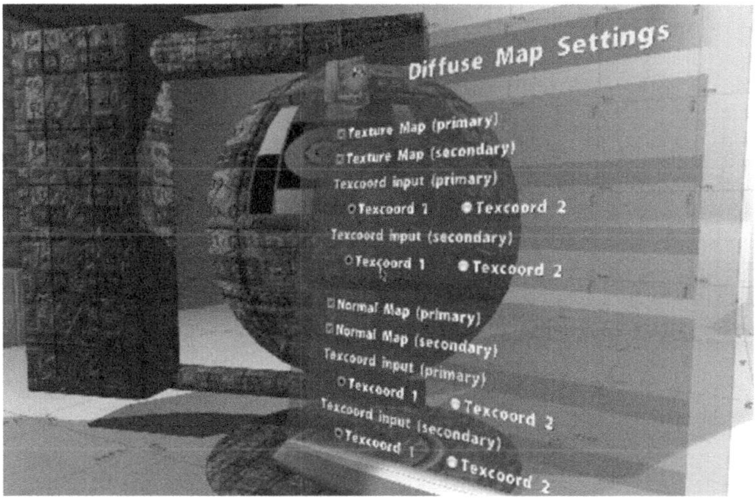

Figure 7-22. Layering the primary and secondary normal map together.

Figure 7-23. The normal maps without their corresponding texture maps.

Figure 7-24. The diffuse color attribute applied in combination with the texture map attributes.

> **DISABLING A MATERIAL COLOR**
> When the **Diffuse color** check box is not selected, the visual appearance is the same as if the diffuse color was set to a pure white color, with the values (255, 255, 255) for the red, green, and blue color channels. The other material color attributes work a bit differently when they are disabled, as we'll see later on in this chapter.

Texture blend mode

If two diffuse textures are used by a material, then the **Texture blend mode** setting determines how they are combined. In the **Material Manager** window, all of the possible blend mode settings appear in a popup menu when the **Texture blend mode** value is left-clicked, as shown in Figure 7-25.

The preset texture blend mode setting is **Add**, which simply adds the RGB color values together at each pixel where the textures overlap, as shown in Figure 7-26.

The other blend modes produce the following effects:

- **Average** renders an evenly-weighted average of the primary and secondary texture map colors, which creates a cross-dissolved effect as shown in Figure 7-27.

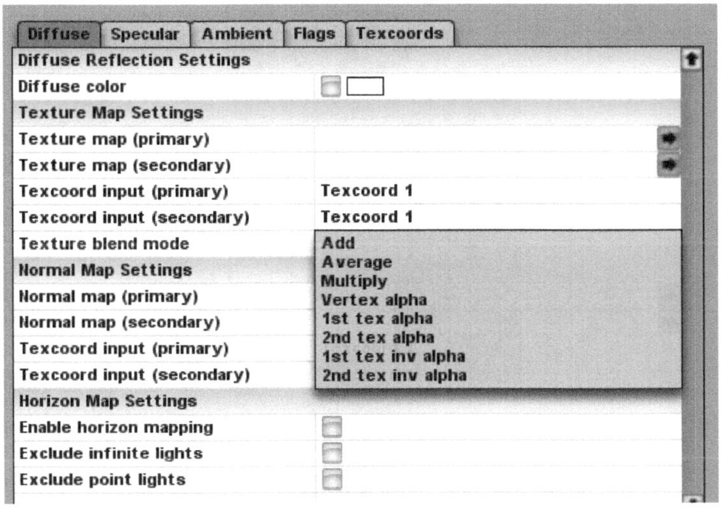

Figure 7-25. The **Texture blend mode** options.

Figure 7-26. The **Add** texture blend mode.

Figure 7-27. The **Average** texture blend mode.

- **Multiply** causes the primary and secondary texture map colors to darken each other, as shown in Figure 7-28.
- **Vertex alpha** is a blending mode that blends the secondary texture with the primary texture map, using alpha values that are calculated by interpolating between the alpha channel values of the RGBA color assigned to each vertex of the polygon containing a given pixel. This effect is useful for creating a

Figure 7-28. The **Multiply** texture blend mode.

Figure 7-29. The **Vertex Alpha** texture blend mode.

geometry-space alpha channel gradient that is decoupled from the alpha values of the primary and secondary texture maps. The per-vertex ambient occlusion is stored in the vertex alpha (if it has been generated for a particular geometry), and per-vertex colors can be imported with a mesh. The **Vertex alpha** texture blend mode produces an effect as shown in Figure 7-29.

- **1st tex alpha** combines the secondary texture map with the primary texture map, using the alpha channel values of the primary texture map, as shown in Figure 7-30.

- **2nd tex alpha** combines the secondary texture map with the primary texture map, using the alpha channel values of the secondary texture map, as shown in Figure 7-31.

- **1st tex inv alpha** combines the secondary texture map with the primary texture map, using the inverted alpha channel values of the primary texture map, as shown in Figure 7-32.

Figure 7-30. The **1st tex alpha** texture blend mode.

Figure 7-31. The **2nd tex alpha** texture blend mode.

Figure 7-32. The **1st tex inv alpha** texture blend mode.

- **2nd tex inv alpha** combines the secondary texture map with the primary texture map, using the inverted alpha channel values of the secondary texture map, as shown in Figure 7-33.

Figure 7-33. The **2nd tex inv alpha** texture blend mode.

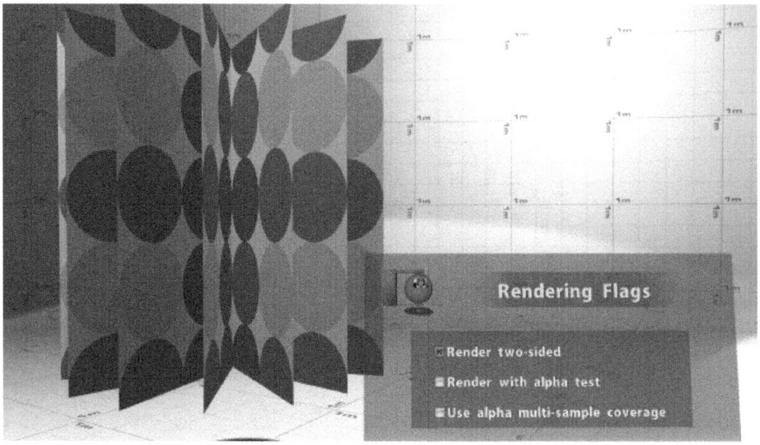

Figure 7-34. A material rendered with the **Render two-sided** option.

Flags

The **Flags** group provides flags for double-sided materials, materials which render with holes, and alpha multisample coverage.

Render two-sided

This option indicates that geometry to which the material is applied should be rendered two-sided, such that faces can be seen from their front or back side. The front side is determined by evaluating the angle between the vertex normals on each face and the camera, as shown in Figure 7-34.

Turning off the **Render two-sided** option causes the material to render on just one side, as shown in Figure 7-35.

Render with alpha test

This option allows designers to use the alpha channel of the diffuse texture to cut holes in the geometry to which the material is applied. Pixels for which the alpha value is less than 0.5 are not rendered. (Each pixel is either fully opaque or not rendered at all—alpha testing does not provide partial transparency. This option was shown disabled in the two previous figures, and is shown enabled in Figure 7-34, which results in an transparent background.

For finer control over the edges of textures that use alpha, designers can select the **Use alpha multisample coverage** option, as shown in Figure 7-37.

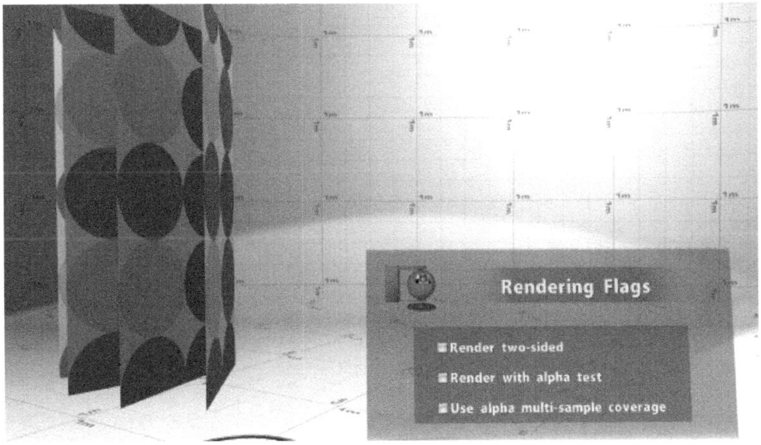

Figure 7-35. A material rendered with the **Render two-sided** option turned off.

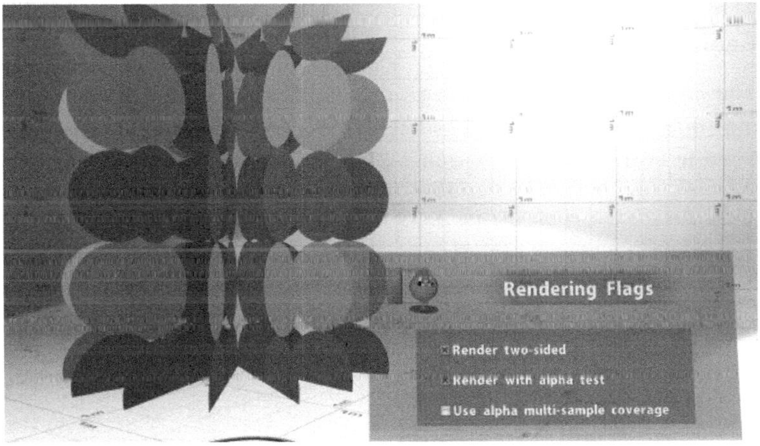

Figure 7-36. A material rendered with the **Render with alpha test** option turned on.

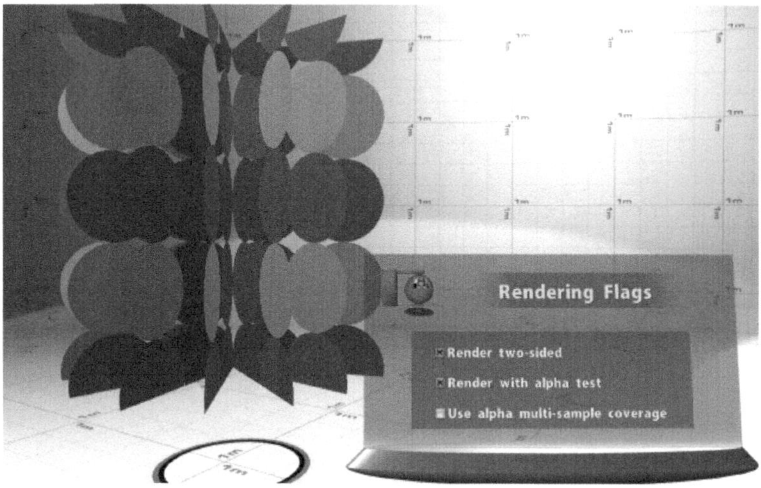

Figure 7-37. The **Use alpha multisample coverage** option.

Horizon Map settings

The **Horizon Map Settings** allow you to enable horizon mapping, and to exclude certain types of light from the shadows created by any linked horizon maps. To view the horizon map material demo station, proceed clockwise through the Material Showroom until you come upon a portal, and walk on through, as shown in Figure 7-38.

Enable horizon mapping

The **Enable horizon mapping** option indicates that a material using a single normal map should be rendered with horizon mapping. Figure 7-39 shows a side-by-side comparison of a material with horizon mapping turned on and off. The

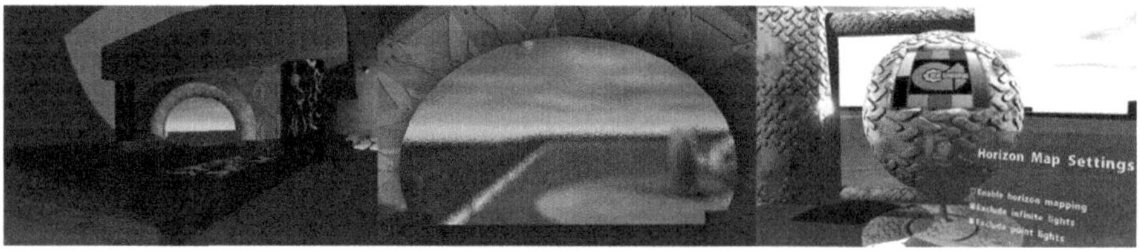

Figure 7-38. Finding the horizon map material demo station.

Figure 7-39. A side- by-side comparison of a material with horizon mapping turned on and off.

normal map must have been imported with horizon map generation enabled. For details about generating horizon maps with the **Texture Tool**, see Chapter 8, "Texture Tools".

The horizon mapping setting can be globally enabled or disabled using the Enable horizon mapping option in the **Graphics Settings** window, as shown in Figure 7-40.

Exclude infinite lights

This setting tells the renderer to leave out any infinite lights when rendering the result of the horizon map.

Exclude point lights

This setting tells the renderer to leave out any point lights when rendering the result of the horizon map.

Figure 7-41 shows a material with a horizon map that excludes both infinite lights and point lights.

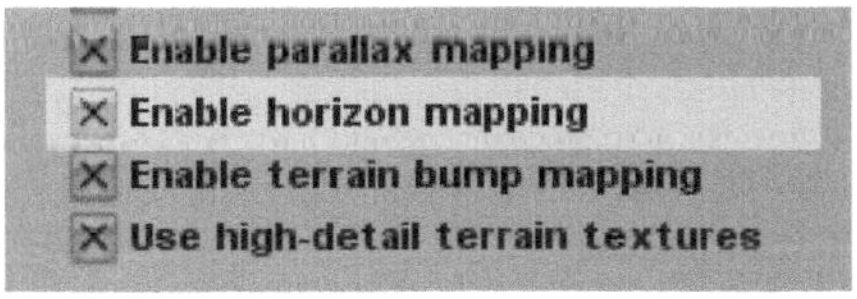

Figure 7-40. The **Enable horizon mapping** option in the **Graphics Settings** window.

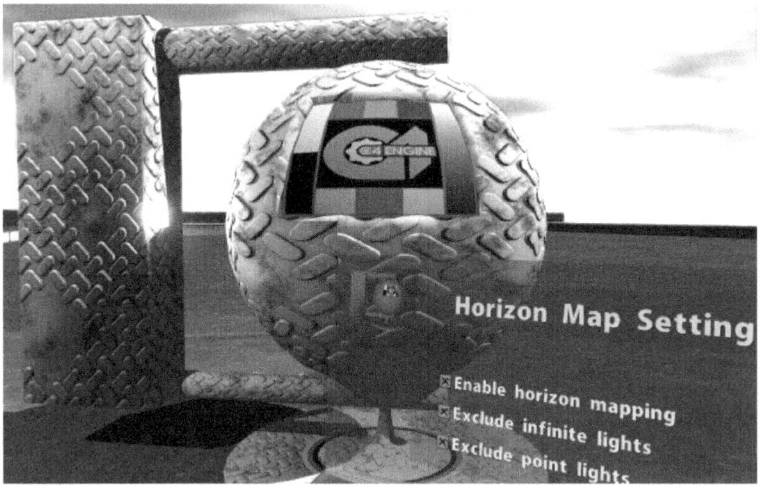

Figure 7-41. Excluding infinite lights and point lights from a horizon map.

Specular Attributes

The **Specular Attributes** includes settings for specular and microfacet reflection. Proceed clockwise in the Material Showroom, looking for the sign announcing Specular Attributes, as shown in Figure 7-42. The **Specular Reflection Settings** group includes options for specular color, exponent, gloss, texture coordinate input, and bloom.

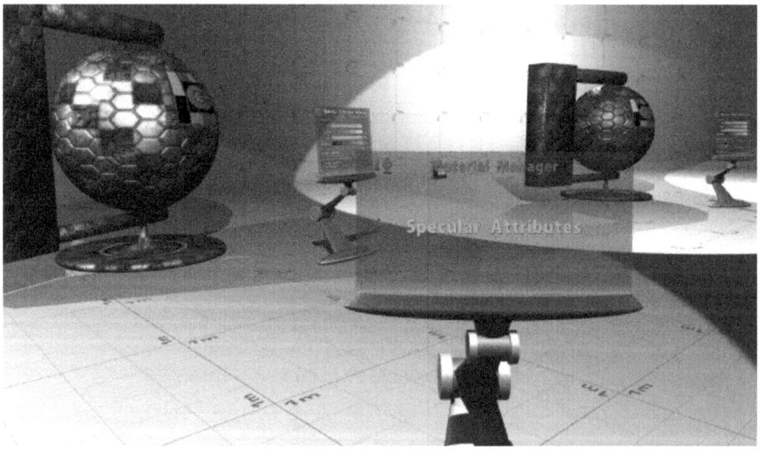

Figure 7-42. The **Specular Attributes** material demo stations.

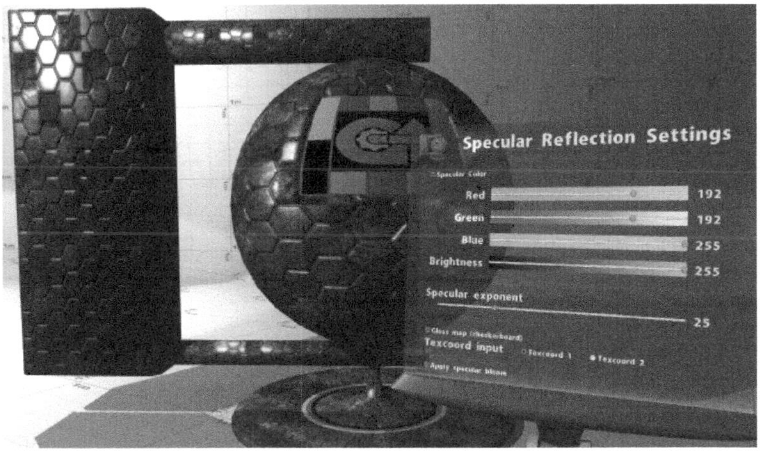

Figure 7-43. Specular color interacting with a gloss map.

Specular color

This setting controls the color of the specular reflection. This color is multiplied by the color read from the gloss map. which we have preset to a checkerboard pattern for our demo, as shown in Figure 7-43.

Try varying the **Red**, **Green**, and **Blue** color sliders to see the effect of changing the specular color. Figure 7-44 shows a side-by-side comparison of moving the **Blue** slider to vary the color between light blue and yellow.

Specular exponent

This value controls the sharpness of the specular reflection. Smaller values are sharper, as shown in Figure 7-45.

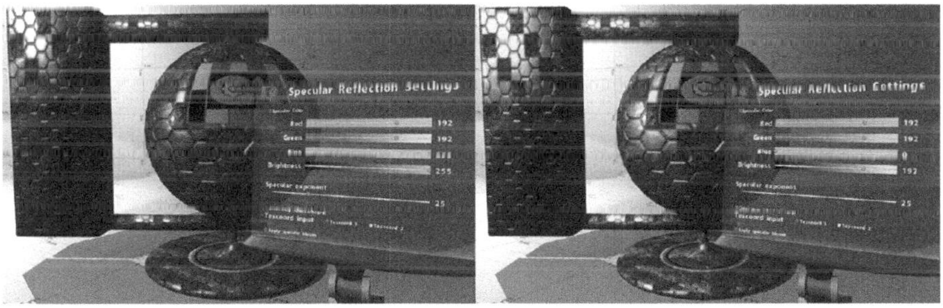

Figure 7-44. Varying the **Blue** component of the **Specular color** attribute.

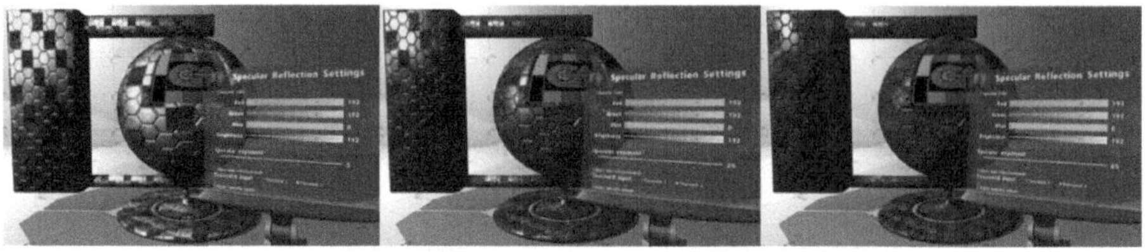

Figure 7-45. A range of specular exponent values.

Gloss map

This texture controls the specular reflection color, and modulates the specular reflection, the environment map, and/or the ambient reflection term. If the **Gloss map** texture is used, then any gloss map existing in the alpha channel of another texture is ignored. Figure 7-46 shows a side-by-side comparison of a material with a gloss map turned off and on.

Texcoord input

The specular **Texcoord input** setting controls which set of scale, offset, and animation settings will be used to transform the texture coordinates of the gloss map. See the Texcoords Attributes section later in this chapter for a description of the texcoord settings. Figure 7-47 shows a side-by-side comparison of a material with the gloss map set to two different texcoord inputs.

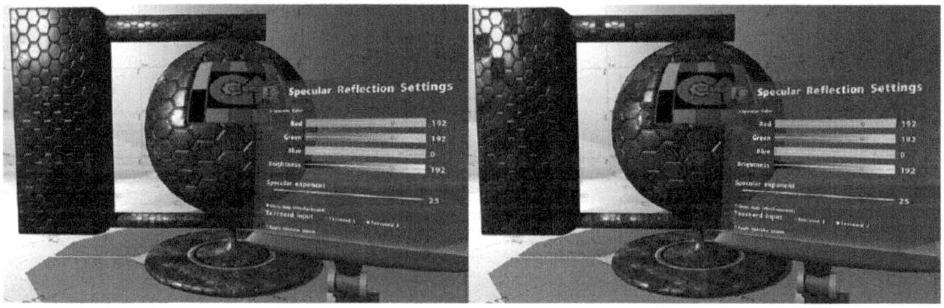

Figure 7-46. A side- by-side comparison of a material with a gloss map turned off and on.

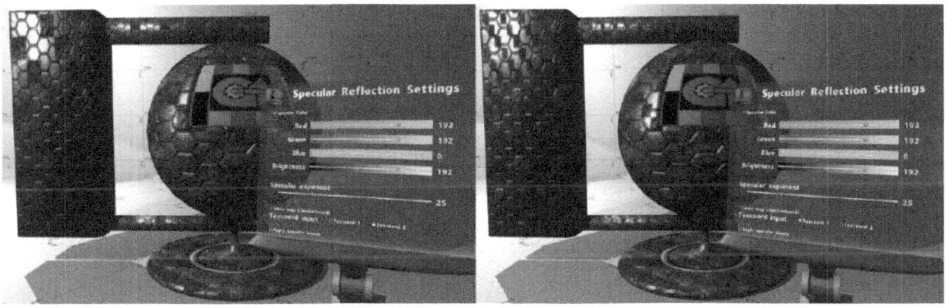

Figure 7-47. A side-by-side comparison of a material with the gloss map set to two different texcoord inputs.

Apply specular bloom

This option applies the bloom post-processing effect to bright specularities (highlights), as shown in Figure 7-48.

Bloom can be enabled or disabled globally in the **Graphics Settings** dialog, using the **Enable glow and bloom effects** option, as shown in Figure 7-49.

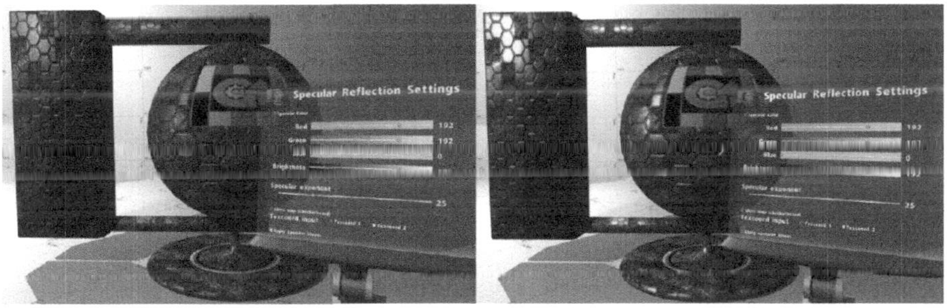

Figure 7-48. The specular bloom post-processing effect.

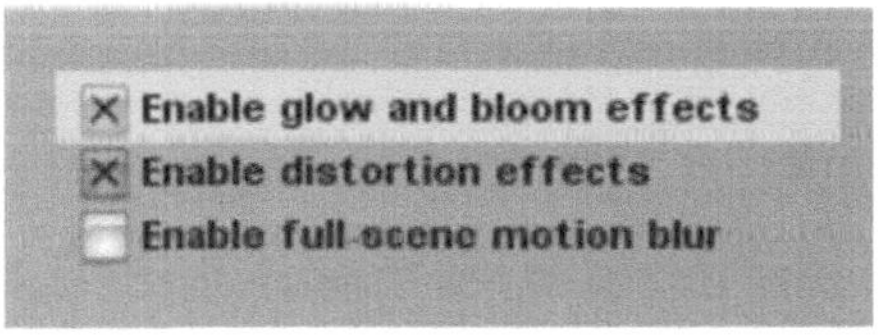

Figure 7-49. The **Enable glow and bloom effects** option in the **Graphics Settings** dialog globally enables or disables the specular bloom effect.

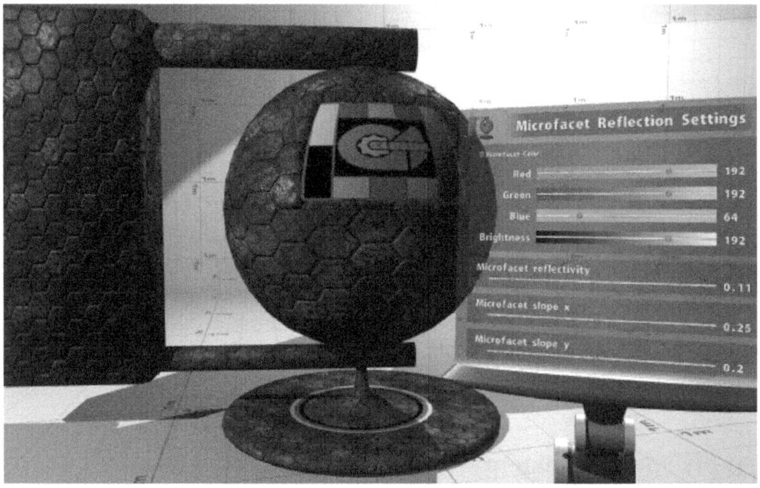

Figure 7-50. The microfacet color attribute.

Microfacet Reflection Settings

The **Microfacet Reflection Settings** group includes options for microfacet color, reflectivity, and slope.

Microfacet color

The normal-incidence color of a microfacet reflection. The microfacet color option provides a higher quality simulation of specular highlights than the basic specular color setting described earlier, as shown in Figure 7-50.

Microfacet reflectivity

This value controls the degree of reflectivity for the microfacet color. Several values are shown for comparison in Figure 7-51.

Microfacet slope

The *x* and *y* values for the microfacet slope setting adjust the horizontal and vertical spread of the microfacet reflection color. This setting is useful for materials with directional surface characteristics that are aligned along the horizontal or vertical axis of the material, as shown in Figure 7-52.

Figure 7-51. A range of microfacet reflectivity values: 0.11 (upper-left); 0.24 (upper-right); 0.51 (lower-left); and 0.83 (lower-right).

Figure 7-52. A comparison of various microfacet slope settings: 0.45, 0.11 (upper-left); 0.11, 0.11 (upper-right); 0.11, 0.45 (lower-left); and 0.45, 0.45 (lower-right).

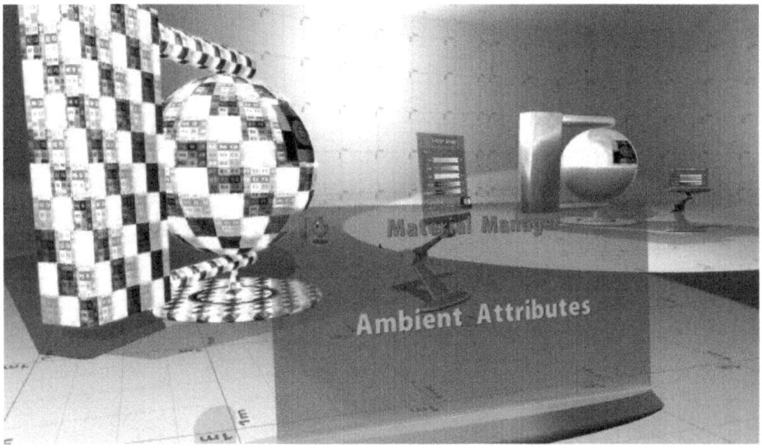

Figure 7-53. The **Ambient Attributes** material demo stations.

Ambient Attributes

The **Ambient Attributes** include settings for emission, environment maps, reflection buffers, and refraction buffers. Look for the sign announcing **Ambient Attributes** as you continue to walk clockwise in the Material Showroom world, as shown in Figure 7-53.

The **Emission Settings** attributes includes options for emission color, an emission map and emission texture coordinate mapping.

Emission color

Emission color is the color of light that the surface appears to emit by itself. The emission color is added to the ambient light that the surface reflects. Figure 7-54 shows a side-by-side comparison of various **Emission color** values. Adjust the **Red**, **Green**, or **Blue** sliders to vary the color.

Figure 7-54. A side-by-side comparison of various **Emission color** values.

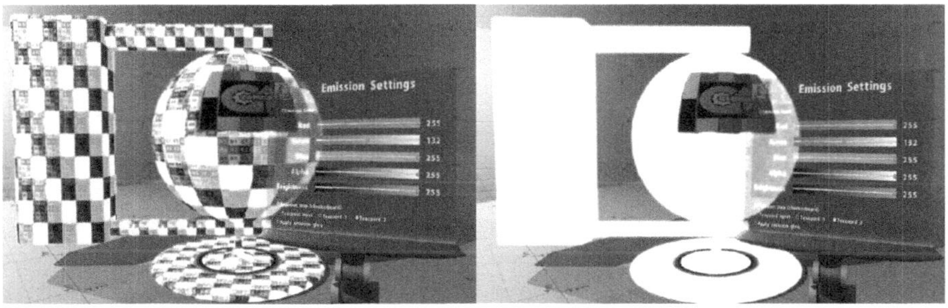

Figure 7-55. A material that uses an emission map.

Emission map

The emission color can be multiplied by the color read from the **Emission map**, which in our example material, is preset to a checkerboard pattern. This texture controls the emission color, as shown in Figure 7-55.

Texcoord input

The **Texcoord input** setting in the **Emission Settings** group controls which set of scale, offset, and animation settings will be used to transform the texture coordinates of the emission map. See the Texcoords Attributes section later in this chapter for a description of the texcoord settings. Figure 7-56 shows a side-by-side comparison of a material using two different texcoord inputs for the emission map.

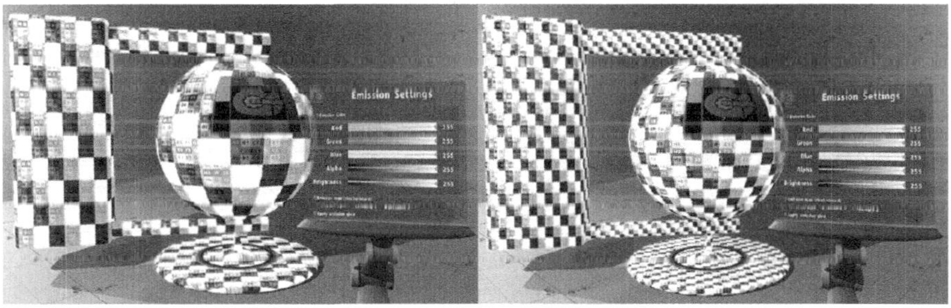

Figure 7-56. A side-by-side comparison of a material using two different texcoord inputs for the emission map.

Figure 7-57. A close- up of a material with emission glow turned on (left) and off (right).

Apply emission glow

This option enables emission glow locally for a given material. Figure 7-57 shows a close-up of a material with emission glow turned off (left) and on (right).

Glow can also be enabled or disabled globally in the **Graphics Settings** dialog, using the **Enable glow and bloom effects** option, as shown in Figure 7-58.

Environment Map Settings

The **Environment Map Settings** controls the environment color and the environment map texture. These attributes can be used to efficiently simulate a highly-polished, reflective surface.

Environment color

The environment color is multiplied by the local environment map in the ambient rendering pass, if this option is selected, as shown in Figure 7-59.

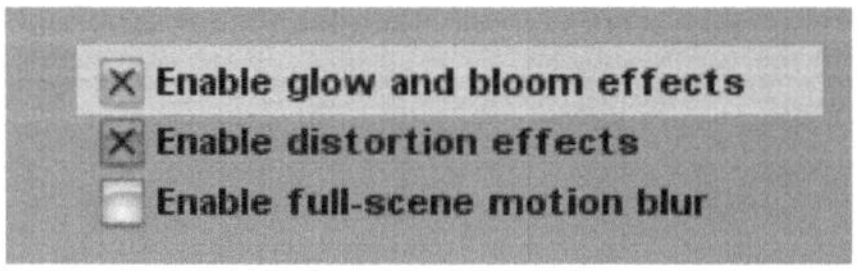

Figure 7-58. The **Enable glow and bloom effects** option in the **Graphics Settings** dialog globally enables or disables the emission glow attribute.

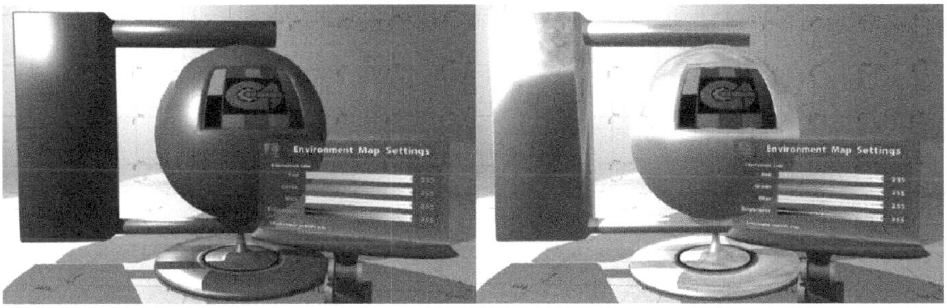

Figure 7-59. The **Environment color** attribute turned off (left) and on (right).

Figure 7-60. Varying the values for the environment color.

You can experiment with different values for the environment color, as shown in Figure 7-60.

Environment override map

The **Environment override map** texture can be used to override any environment map specified in a zone, as shown in Figure 7-61. The **Environment override map** texture must be imported as a cube map. The environment map is only used during rendering when the environment color is also specified in the **Environment Map Settings** attributes. See the section Cube Maps, in Chapter 8, "Texture Tools", for more information about preparing and importing cube map textures with the **Texture Tool**.

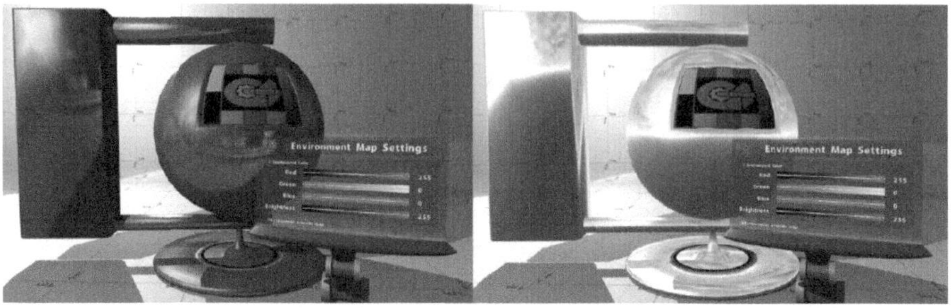

Figure 7-61. Using an Environment override map texture.

Reflection and Refraction Buffer Settings

The material demo stations for the **Reflection and Refraction Buffer Settings** are located side-by-side in the lot in front of the Material Showroom. These attribute settings are typically combined for a water effect, as shown in Figure 7-62.

The **Reflection Buffer Settings** attributes control the reflection color, normal incidence reflectivity, and reflection offset scale.

Reflection color

The **Reflection color** attribute specifies the color of the contribution from the reflection buffer, as shown in Figure 7-63. The reflection color is modulated by the color read from the gloss map.

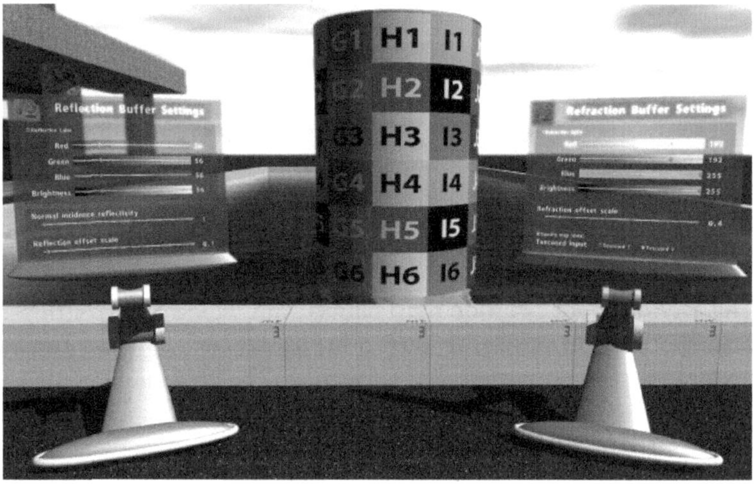

Figure 7-62. The **Reflection and Refraction Buffer Settings**.

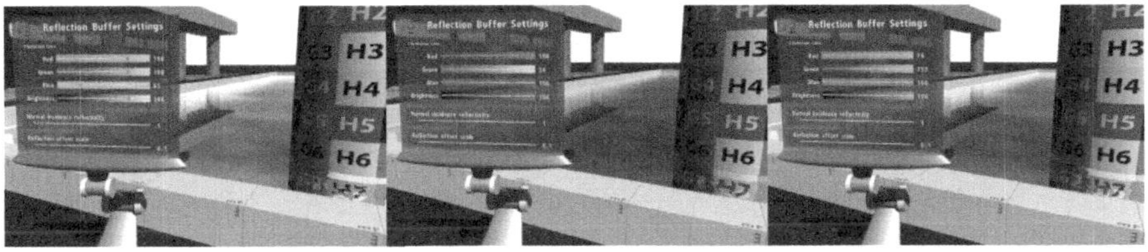

Figure 7-63. Varying the **Reflection color** attribute value.

Normal incidence reflectivity

The **Normal incidence reflectivity** changes the strength of the reflective highlights within a material, as shown in Figure 7-64.

Reflection offset scale

The **Reflection offset scale** controls the strength of the reflection turbulence, as shown in Figure 7-65.

The **Refraction Buffer Settings** attributes provide settings for a refraction color, an offset scale, and an opacity map with a corresponding texcoord option.

Refraction color

The **Refraction color** specifies the color of the contribution from the refraction buffer, as shown in Figure 7-66.

Figure 7-64. A comparison of various normal incidence reflectivity values.

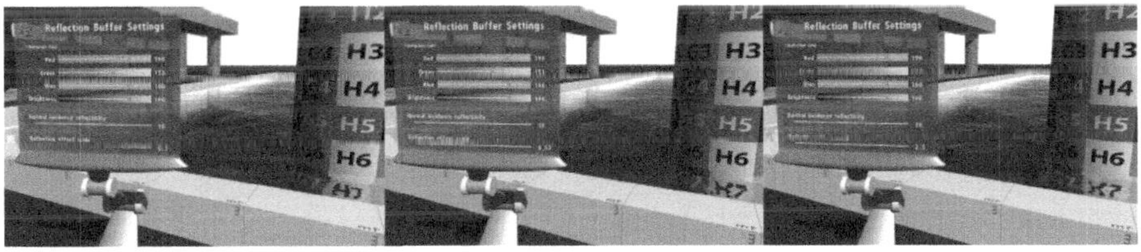

Figure 7-65. A comparison of various reflection offset scale values.

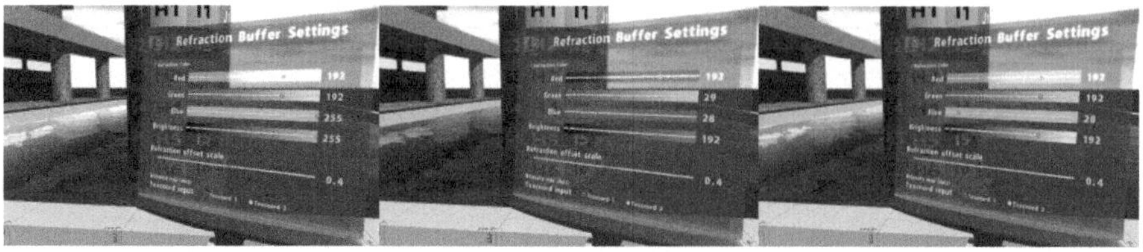

Figure 7-66. Varying the refraction color attribute value.

Figure 7-67. Varying the refraction offset scale value.

Refraction offset scale

The **Refraction offset scale** controls the strength of the refraction turbulence, as shown in Figure 7-67.

Opacity map

The **Opacity map** texture controls the surface opacity when there's a refraction term, as shown in Figure 7-68. The opacity texture values are used to linearly interpolate between the diffuse reflection term and the refraction term in the ambient pass. If this texture is present, then any opacity map existing in the alpha channel of another texture is ignored.

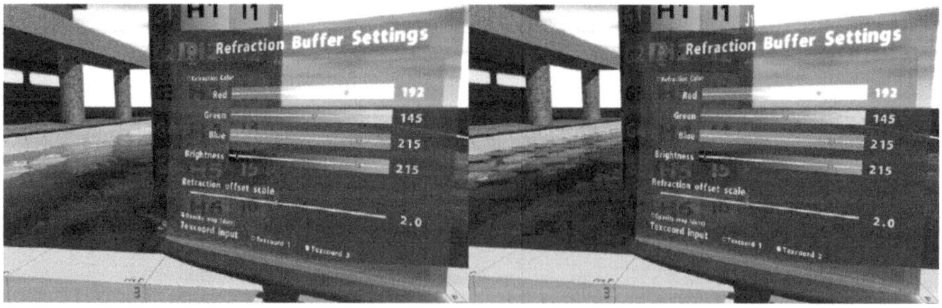

Figure 7-68. A material with an opacity map.

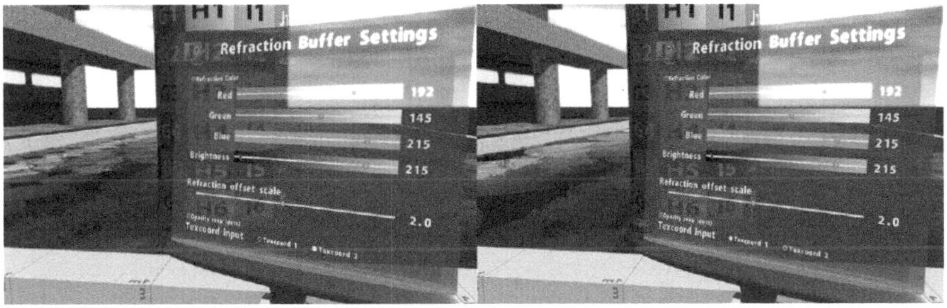

Figure 7-69. Using the second set of texcoords for an opacity map.

Texcoord input

This option selects which set of scale, offset, and animation settings are used to transform the texture coordinates of the associated opacity map, as shown in Figure 7-69. See the next section, Texcoords Attributes, for a description of the texcoord settings.

Texcoords Attributes

Navigate back inside the Material Showroom floor, to the last demo station found when walking clockwise through the room. The **Texcoords Attributes** includes settings to control two sets of scale, offset, and animation properties for texture coordinates applied to a given texture map, as shown in Figure 7-70.

Figure 7-70. The **Texcoords** attributes.

S and T scale

These two settings increase or decrease the tile size at which a given texture is stamped onto an object. Varying the scale of the first and second set of texcoord attributes is shown in Figure 7-71 and Figure 7-72.

The remaining texcoord settings, **S** and **T offset**, **Animation direction**, and **Animation speed**, are best shown using a live example, so go ahead and adjust the corresponding values on the demo material station to follow along with the descriptions of those settings in the next three sections.

S and T offset

This setting offsets or translates the projection of a given texture map along the animation direction angle.

Figure 7-71. Varying the **S** and **T scale** values for the first set of texcoord attributes.

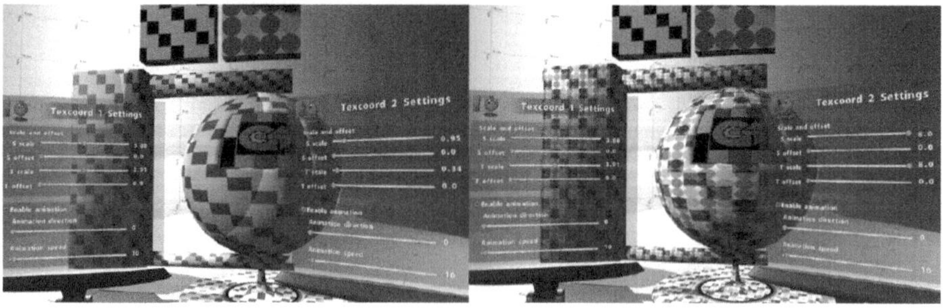

Figure 7-72. Varying the **S** and **T scale** values for the second set of texcoord attributes.

Animation direction

The value for the Animation direction setting is an angle specified in degrees, that determines the direction in which the offset value is applied for each animation cycle.

Animation speed

Animation is based on a 120 second period, so individual coordinate velocities must be set so that an integer number of complete cycles have occurred every 120 seconds. (The setting in the **Material Manager** window enforces this.) Since the coordinate velocities are quantized, not all animation directions are available at slow speeds. At the slowest possible speed (making one cycle every 120 seconds), the available directions are multiples of 45 degrees.

Managing Materials

As you create new materials back in the **World Editor**, they will appear in the catalog view in the left half of the **Material Manager** window. Let's see how we can organize and manage a collection of materials.

Duplicating Materials

Sometimes it is convenient to create a new material by starting from a copy of an existing material, instead of starting from the default material settings.

1 Select any material in the material catalog view.

2 Click **Duplicate** a few times to create some copies, as shown in Figure 7-73.

It's good practice to give a unique name to a duplicated material to avoid confusing it with the original. You can safely edit a duplicated material without affecting the original material.

When the catalog view does not have enough room to display all of the material swatches, the scroll bar along its right edge is enabled.

Deleting Materials

3 Click New a few times to create a few unused materials.

4 Delete the unused materials by select each one in the catalog view, and then clicking the **Delete** button.

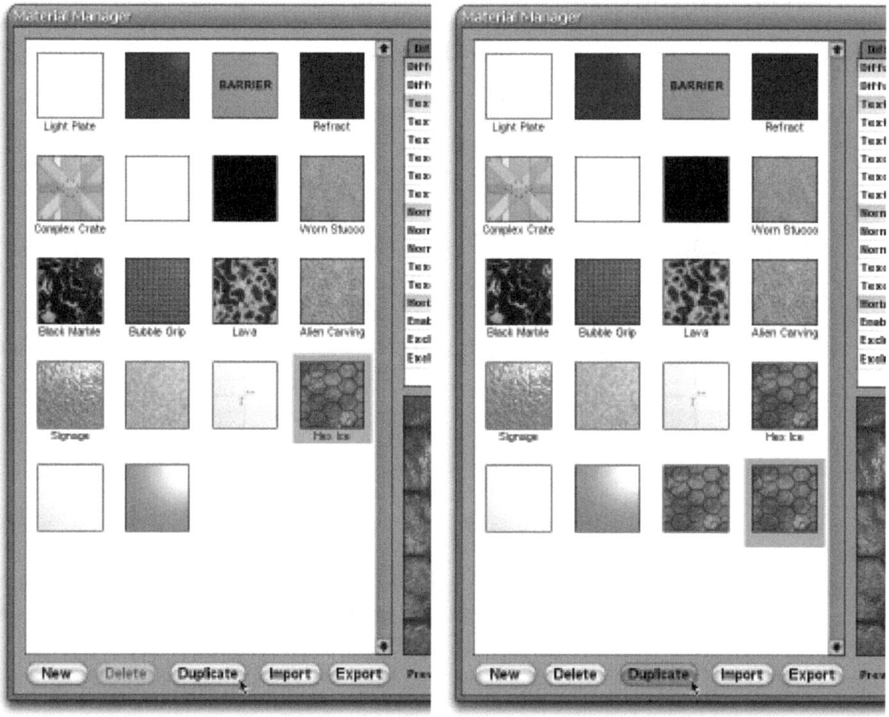

Figure 7-73. Duplicating a material in the **Material Manager** window.

If the selected material is still in use somewhere in the world, the **Delete** button is disabled.

Cleaning Materials

To delete unused materials, click **Cleanup**.

Exporting Materials

Materials can be shared with other designers, or used in another world, by exporting the material to a .mat material file.

5 Select the material named MyFirstMaterial in the material catalog view.

6 Click **Export**.

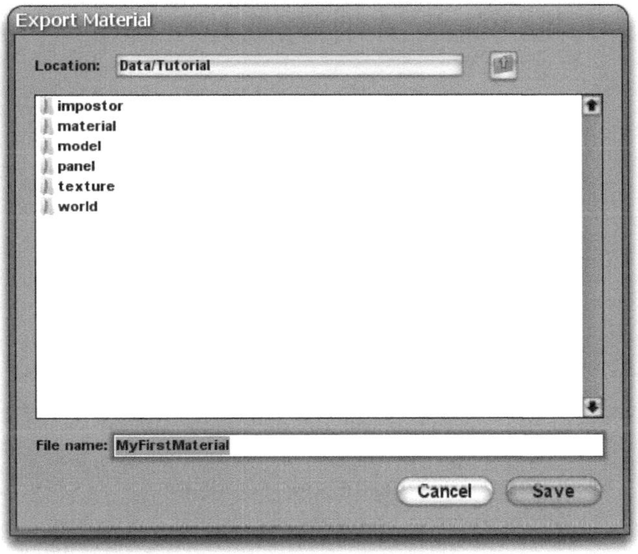

Figure 7-74. The **Export Material** dialog.

The **Export Material** dialog will open, as shown in Figure 7-74. By default, the name of the material file is set to the name provided in the **Material name** text box in the **Material Manager** window.

The C4 Engine requires that material files are exported to a subdirectory of the Data directory. (The **Save** button is disabled at the root of the Data directory. If you were to export or move the material file directly into the Data directory, the **Material Manager** would not be able to import the material again until it was moved to a nested directory.)

7 Save the material as MyFirstMaterial.

Importing Materials

Material can be shared between worlds using .mat material files.

8 Import a material by clicking **Import**. The **Import Material** dialog opens, as shown in Figure 7-75.

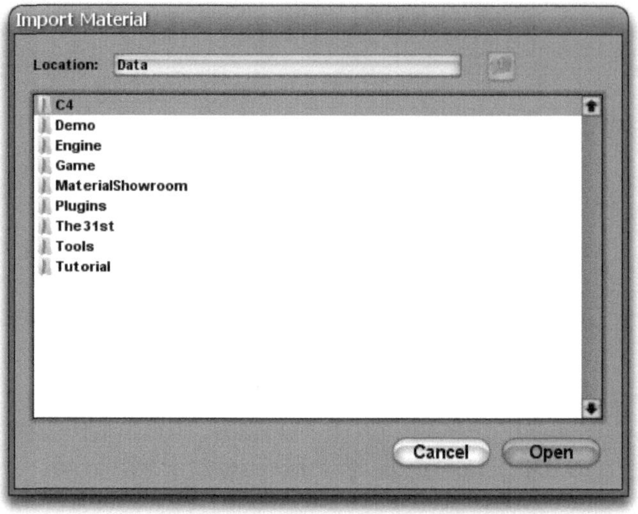

Figure 7-75. The **Import Material** dialog.

Next Steps

Now that we understand how to create, edit, and organize materials, let's take a look at how to import source images from third-party tools into the C4 Engine, in Chapter 8, "Texture Tools".

8

Texture Tools

This chapter shows how to import texture files and adjust settings using the **Texture Tool**. We'll also show how to customize the GUI skin used by the C4 Engine.

Importing and Configuring Textures

In this section, we'll cover each of the texture import options, and show the import option combinations that are used to create texture maps with various types of channel data.

Texture File Storage

You can create custom texture maps in third-party applications, and then import them into the C4 Engine using the **Texture Tool**. These texture maps are stored in files in a subdirectory of the Data directory, with a `.tex` extension.

Importing Textures

Image files should be placed in a subdirectory of the Import directory. During the import operation, the texture tool outputs the texture to a corresponding subdirectory under the Data directory in the C4 Engine directory structure. To change the output directory, use the **Output file name** option, which is described later in this chapter in the options settings section.

To import a texture, either choose **Tools > Import Texture**, or invoke the `itexture` [*name*] command in the **Command Console** window.

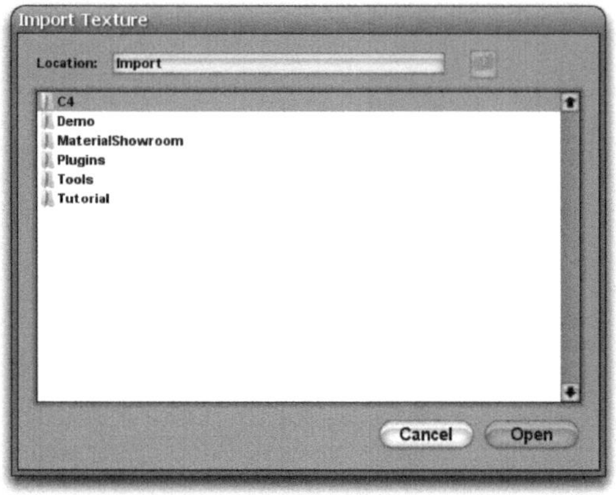

Figure 8-1. The **Import Texture** dialog.

Import Texture Dialog

If the menu command is chosen, or the name is omitted from the console command, then the **Texture Tool** will open an **Import Texture** dialog, as shown in Figure 8-1. You can use this dialog to navigate to a subdirectory of the Import/ directory to select a `.tga` file to import.

Import Settings Dialog

After selecting an image file to import, the **Import Texture Settings** dialog is opened with the default settings, as shown in Figure 8-2. The default settings are usually appropriate for ordinary color texture maps.

Texture Format Settings

The **Texture Format** settings control the basic type, alpha usage, wrap mode, and compression settings for the imported texture.

Texture type

The **Texture type** menu selects the OpenGL texture target for this texture map. It can be one of the following values:

- **2D** An ordinary 2D texture whose coordinates lie in the range $[0,1]$ in both dimensions. The texture must have a width and height that is a power of two (64, 128, 256, 512, etc.), as shown in Figure 8-3. The width and height can

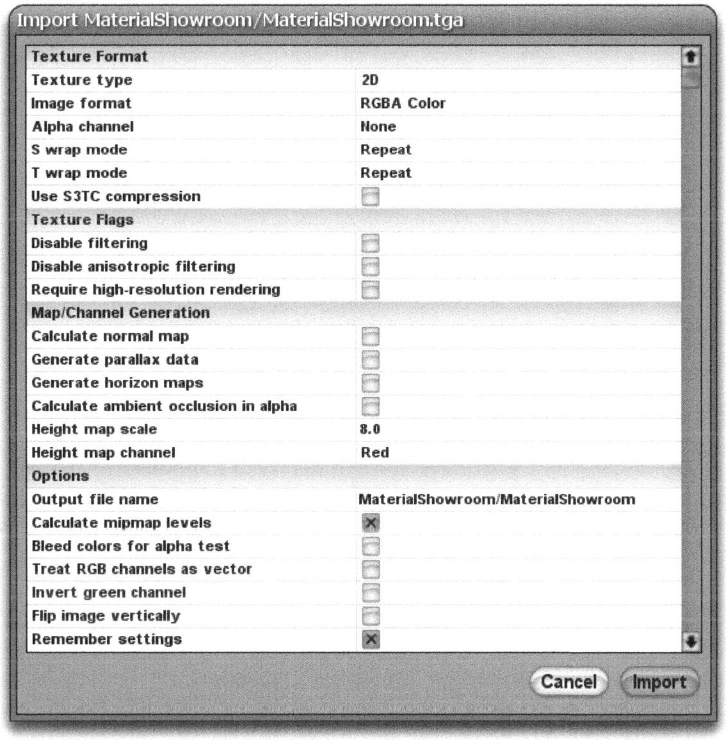

Figure 8-2. The **Import Texture Settings** dialog.

be set to different power-of-two values, so the texture does not need to be square.

- RECT A rectangle texture whose coordinates lie in the range $[0, width]$ and $[0, height]$. This setting uses the `GL_ARB_texture_rectangle` extension. This type of texture is useful for decals or other textures that are created at custom sizes that do not need to be powers of two.
- CUBE A cube map texture. For more details about cube maps, see the section "Cube Maps" later in this chapter.

Image format

The Image format setting sets the output format, as shown in Figure 8-4. The C4 Engine supports the following output formats:

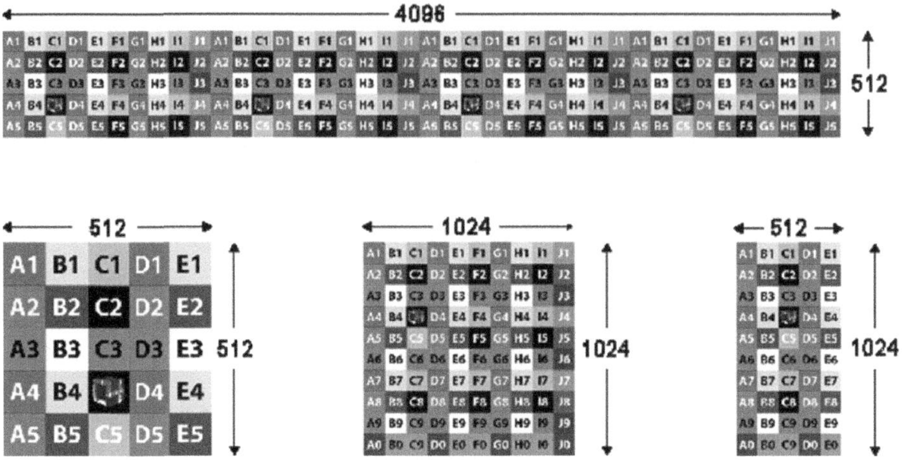

Figure 8-3. Textures sized to powers-of-two.

- **RGBA Color** The standard, four-channel RGBA format.
- **Luminance Alpha** A specialty format most commonly used for fonts, where the luminance specifies the brightness of the font color, and the alpha specifies the transparency. Use a low luminance value for drop shadows that should appear darker than the font color.
- **Luminance** This format contains one component that maps to RGBA as $(L, L, L, 1.0)$.
- **Intensity** This format contains one component that maps to RGBA as (I, I, I, I).

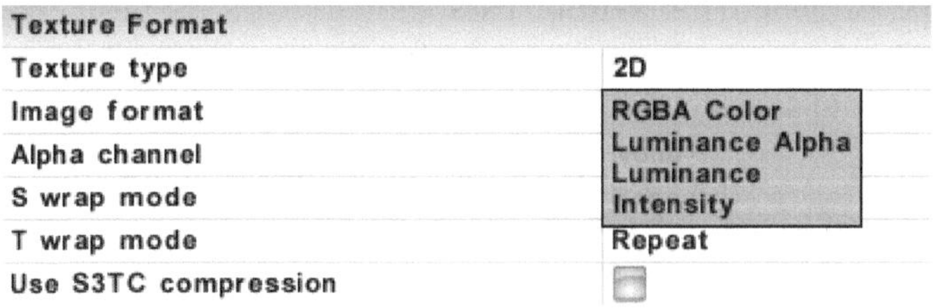

Figure 8-4. The **Image format** setting.

Figure 8-5. The **Texture Tools** demonstration stations.

Texture Tools Demonstrations

A number of the texture import settings are demonstrated interactively in the *Guide* version of the Material Showroom world. Using the steps given in the "Show and Tell" section of Chapter 7, "Material Manager", open and run the Material Showroom world. Navigate to the **Texture Tools** area along the left side of the main showroom floor, where a sign announces four groups of texture tool demonstration stations, as shown in Figure 8-5.

Alpha channel

The **Alpha channel** setting specifies what kind of information is stored in the alpha channel of the texture, as shown in Figure 8-6. When alpha channel information is specified, then the `.tga` file being imported must be stored in a 32-bit format. The C4 Engine supports the following types of alpha channels:

- **None** There is no information stored in the alpha channel, as shown in Figure 8-7.
- **Transparency** The alpha channel contains transparency information, as shown in Figure 8-8.

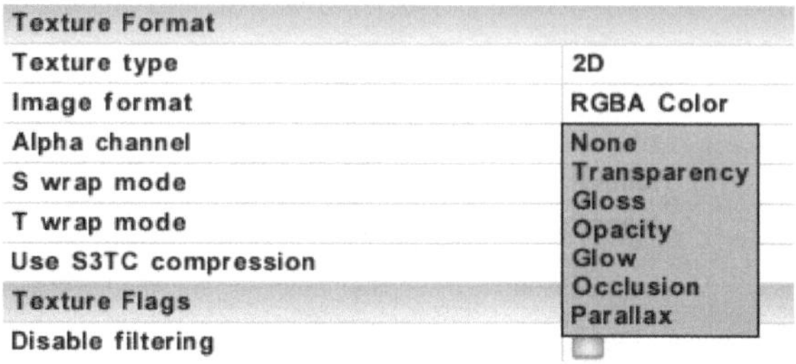

Figure 8-6. The Alpha channel setting.

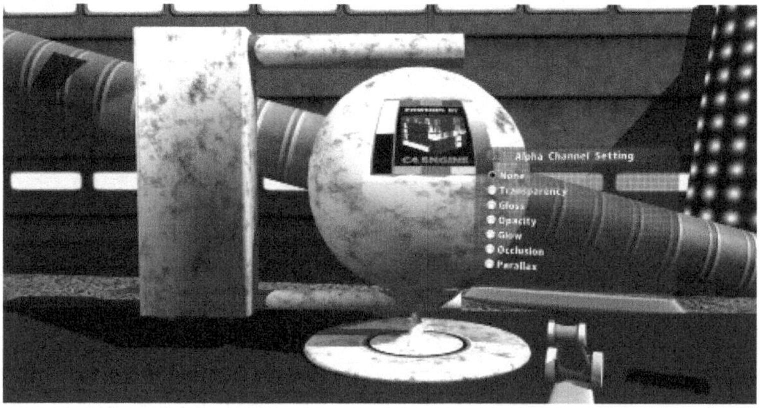

Figure 8-7. The **None** alpha channel setting.

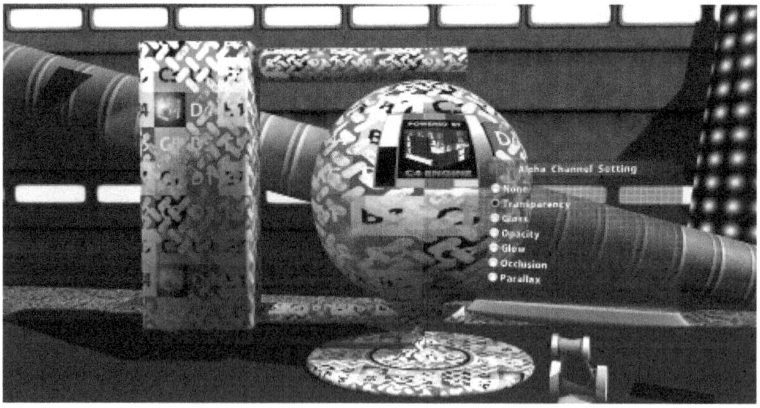

Figure 8-8. The **Transparency** alpha channel setting.

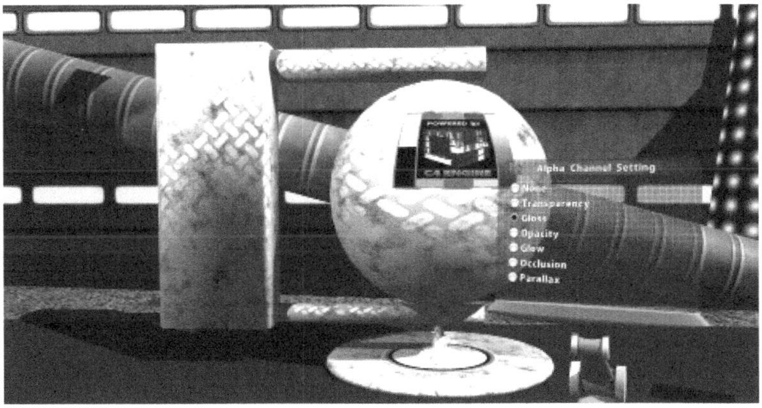

Figure 8-9. The **Gloss** alpha channel setting.

- **Gloss** The alpha channel contains a gloss map. Whenever a texture containing a gloss map in the alpha channel is used in a material, any specularity, environment map, or reflection term is modulated by the gloss map, as shown in Figure 8-9.
- **Opacity** The alpha channel contains an opacity map. Whenever a texture containing an opacity map in the alpha channel is used in a material, the opacity is used to linearly interpolate between the diffuse term and the refraction term, as shown in Figure 8-10.

Figure 8-10. The **Opacity** alpha channel setting.

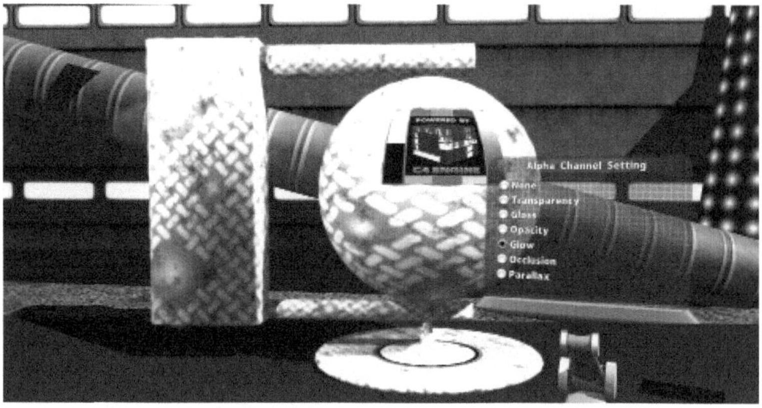

Figure 8-11. The **Glow** alpha channel setting.

- **Glow** The alpha channel contains glow intensity values that are used by the glow post-processing effect, as shown in Figure 8-11. The glow option should only be used for emission maps.
- **Occlusion** The alpha channel will contain ambient occlusion information, as shown in Figure 8-12. Occlusion can be a supplied as a precomputed channel, or it can be generated when the texture is imported. See the description of the **Calculate ambient occlusion in alpha** option later in this chapter for more details.

Figure 8-12. The **Occlusion** alpha channel setting.

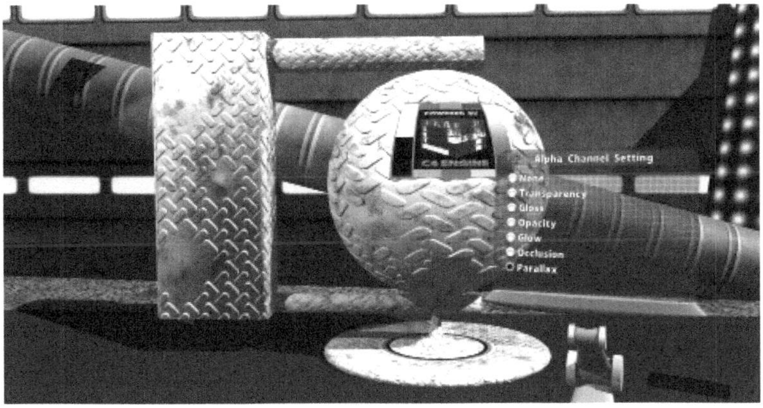

Figure 8-13. The **Parallax** alpha channel setting.

- **Parallax** The alpha channel of the import texture contains a height map from which parallax mapping information should be calculated, as shown in Figure 8-13. The parallax option only takes effect when the **Generate parallax data** option is also selected, and in this case, all four channels of the import texture should contain the same values. If the alpha channel of a normal map in a material contains parallax information, the parallax mapping is applied during all rendering passes.

Wrap Modes

The **S wrap mode** and **T wrap mode** settings specify what wrap modes to apply to the texture map. They can each be one of the following values:

- **Repeat** The texture is addressed using the `GL_REPEAT` wrap mode. This mode renders the texture as a tile which repeats side-by-side in both the horizontal and vertical directions, as shown in Figure 8-14.
- **Clamp** The texture is addressed using the `GL_CLAMP_TO_EDGE` wrap mode. If this mode is not available, the `GL_CLAMP` is used instead. This mode causes the texture to tile only once within the texture coordinate space, and to then repeat the edge pixels in the remaining *s* and *t* space, as shown in Figure 8-15.

Figure 8-14. The **Repeat** texture wrap mode.

Figure 8-15. The **Clamp** texture wrap mode.

- **Clamp to Border** The texture is addressed using the `GL_CLAMP_TO_BORDER` wrap mode. This mode causes the texture to tile only once within the texture coordinate space, as shown in Figure 8-16.
- **Mirror Repeat** The texture is addressed using the `GL_MIRRORED_REPEAT` wrap mode. This mode causes the texture to alternately tile with and without a flip across the horizontal and vertical axis, as shown in Figure 8-17.

Figure 8-16. The **Clamp to Border** texture wrap mode.

Figure 8-17. The **Mirror Repeat** wrap mode.

- **Mirror Clamp** The texture is addressed using the `GL_MIRROR_CLAMP_TO_EDGE` wrap mode. This mode causes the texture to mirror once across the *s* and *t* origin, and to then repeat the edge pixels in the remaining *s* and *t* space, as shown in Figure 8-18.
- **Mirror Clamp to Border** The texture is addressed using the `GL_MIRROR_CLAMP_TO_BORDER` wrap mode. This mode causes the texture to mirror once across the *s* and *t* origin with clamping at the edges, as shown in Figure 8-19.

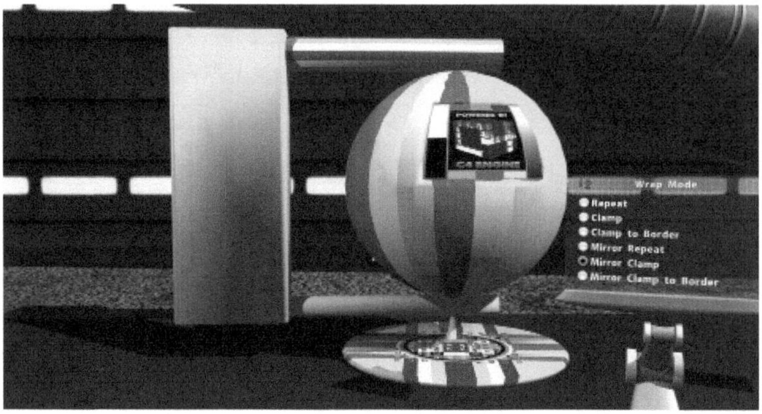

Figure 8-18. The **Mirror Clamp** wrap mode.

Figure 8-19. The **Mirror Clamp to Border** wrap mode.

The effects that the various wrapping modes have on the *s* and *t* texture coordinates are illustrated in Figure 8-20. Note that texture coordinates in the range [0,1] are never changed by any wrapping mode—it is only outside this range that texture coordinates have different mappings in different modes.

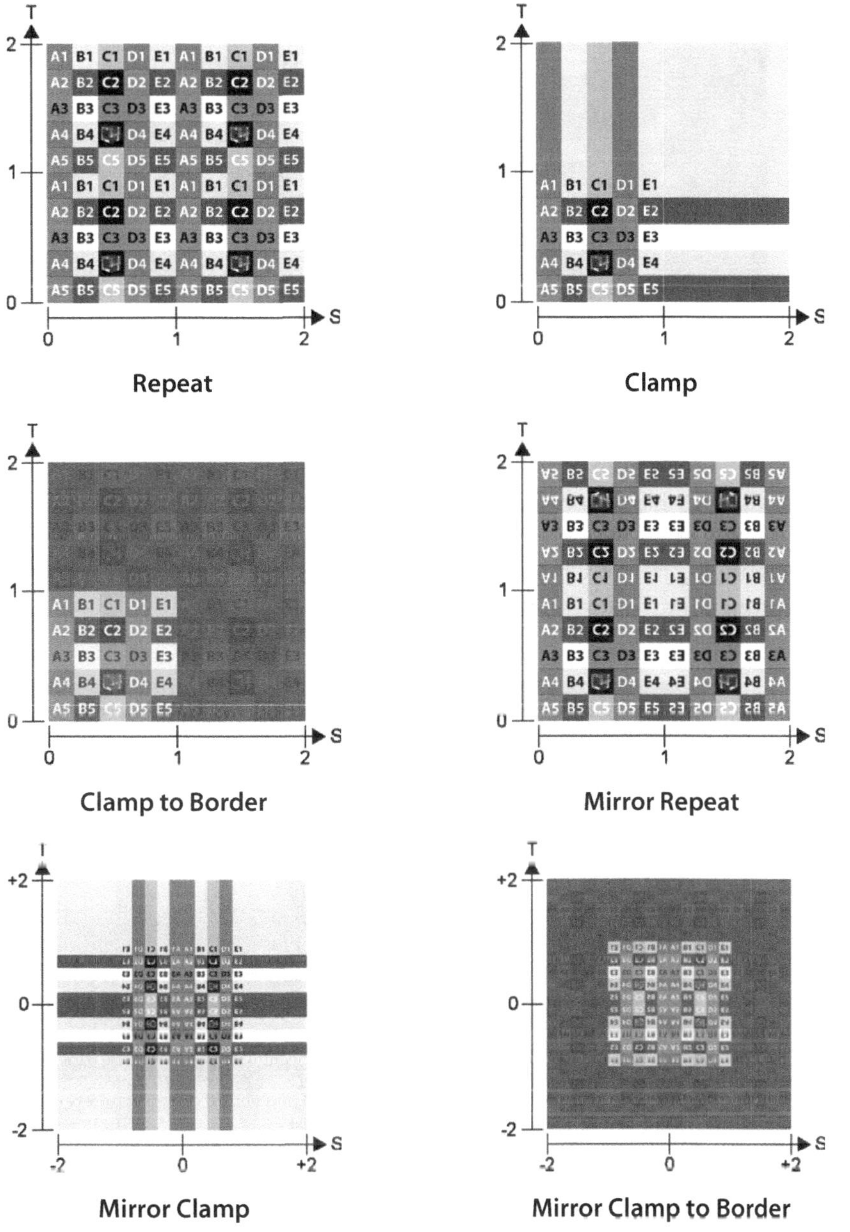

Figure 8-20. The *s* and *t* coordinate mapping for the various texture wrap modes.

Figure 8-21. A comparison of uncompressed (left) and compressed (right) versions of a texture.

Texture Compression

If the **Use block compression** option is selected, then the output texture is compressed. A comparison of a texture with this setting turned off and on is shown in Figure 8-21. The C4 Engine will select the best compression after evaluating the settings for the texture to be imported.

Figure 8-22. A comparison of S3TC compressed (top) and uncompressed (bottom) versions of a texture, at 2x image magnification.

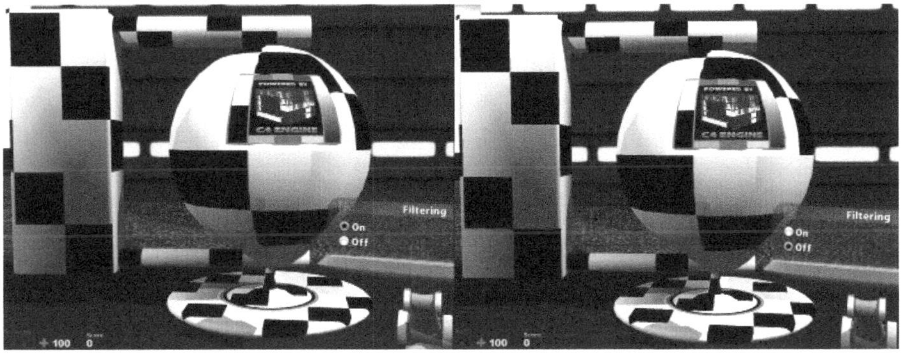

Figure 8-23. A comparison of texture filtering (left) and point sampling (right).

Texture Flags Settings

If the **Disable filtering** option is selected, then no filtering is applied to the imported texture map, and point sampling is used instead. A comparison is shown in Figure 8-23. Figure 8-24 shows a magnified comparison of texture filtering turned on or off.

If the **Disable anisotropic filtering** option is selected, then anisotropic filtering is disabled for the imported texture map, but ordinary bilinear or trilinear filtering is still applied.

The **Require high-resolution rendering** option indicates that the texture map should always be rendered using the highest resolution available, even if the user has selected a lower-quality option in the **Graphics Settings** dialog.

Figure 8-24. A comparison of texture filtering (top) and point sampling (bottom), at 2× image magnification.

Map/Channel Generation Settings

If the **Calculate normal map** option is selected, then the imported texture is treated as a height map from which a normal map should be calculated. Each height is multiplied by the value specified in the **Height map scale** field and then used to determine the normal vector at each pixel.

If the **Generate parallax data** option is selected, then the same height map must be stored in all four channels of the import texture. The height in the alpha channel is converted into special parallax data used by the C4 Engine.

If the **Generate horizon maps** option is selected, then two additional textures are generated that contain horizon map data. These textures have the same name as the normal map, but with the suffixes `-h1` and `-h2`. Horizon maps are applied to a material when the **Enable horizon mapping** option is selected in the **Material Manager** window.

If the **Calculate ambient occlusion in alpha** option is selected, then the alpha channel of the import texture should contain a height map. The heights in this map are scaled by the value specified in the Height map scale field and used to calculate an ambient occlusion factor that is applied in the ambient rendering pass.

The **Height map scale** specifies a scale that is applied to all height values. A scale factor of 1.0 corresponds to the width of a single texel in the import texture.

The **Height map channel** menu lets you select a channel to be used as the source of the height map for all calculations. The supported channels include red, green, blue, and alpha.

Options Settings

The **Output file name** setting contains the name of the texture file that will be created. Do not include the `.tex` file extension.

If the **Calculate mipmap levels** option is selected, then all mipmap levels for this texture are calculated and stored in the texture resource. Turning this option off for textures that are used in a 3D environment can have a negative effect on performance.

The **Bleed colors for alpha test** option causes texels that would fail the alpha test to pick up the color of the nearest texel that passes the alpha test. This process helps remove borders that can appear when alpha-tested textures are rendered. When this setting is checked, the alpha values in lower-resolution mipmaps are also boosted to prevent fade-out of alpha-tested geometries.

If the **Treat RGB channels as vector** option is selected, then mipmaps are calculated for vector data instead of color data. This is useful if you're importing a precomputed normal map that was rendered by a third-party tool, as opposed to calculating a normal map from a height field.

If the **Invert green channel** option is selected, then the green channel is inverted. This option is useful for changing handedness in normal maps.

If the **Scale texture to half resolution** option is selected, the import texture image is reduced to half size in each direction before being processed.

If the **Scale horizon maps to half resolution** option is selected, horizon maps are generated from an import texture image that has been reduced to half size in each direction. Using this option can usually save a significant amount of memory without a noticeable reduction in rendering quality. (If "Scale texture to half resolution" is also checked, then both scales are applied, so horizon maps are only one-quarter the size in each direction.)

If the **Flip image vertically** option is selected, then the texture image is flipped in the vertical direction before being stored in the texture resource. This option is useful when creating textures for the preview images shown by the demo game's **Start Game** dialog.

The **Remember settings** option causes the import settings to be saved for future imports of the same texture, which can speed up the import process when making revisions to textures that have already been imported.

Skybox Haze Settings

When checked, the **haze color** is applied at the bottom of the texture image with the appropriate warping for use as a skybox texture. The **Haze elevation** specifies the relative height to which the haze extends above the horizon. This setting is ignored if "Haze color" is not checked.

Cursor Data Settings

The cursor data settings specify the center point of the texture when it is used as a cursor. The values are given as **Image center X** and **Image center Y** for the x and y coordinates.

Cube Maps

A cube map can be imported by creating a `.tga` file that is six times as tall as it is wide. Each sixth of the image represents one face of the cube. As shown in Figure 8-25, the order of faces is positive x, negative x, positive y, negative y, positive z, and finally negative z. Each face must have the correct orientation in order for the cube map to work properly. The z axis always represents the up direction, and the direction specified in the center of each face represents the axis that points into the image.

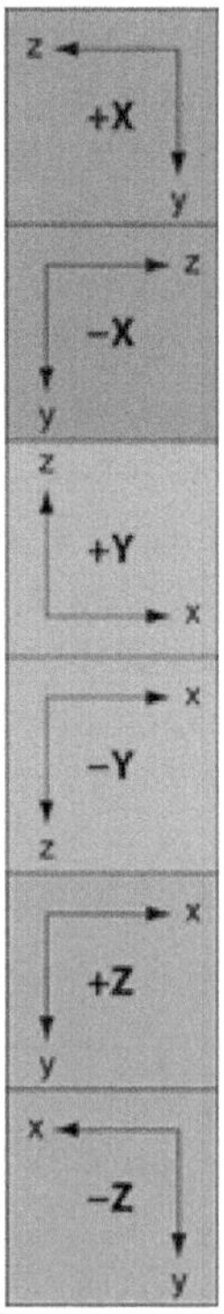

Figure 8-25. Face layout for a cube map.

Batch Texture Importing

All of the texture import options can be set for batch texture import using a `.cfg` file that lists a series of `itexture` command lines.

The `itexture` command can take parameters corresponding to all of the settings in the texture import dialog. The general form of this command is as follows:

`itexture` *name params*

If any parameters are specified on the command line, then the import dialog is not displayed. Command line operation enables batch texture importing by allowing `itexture` commands to be executed from a `.cfg` file.

The parameters accepted by the `itexture` command are listed in Table 8-1. Multiple parameters should be separated by a space. Any unrecognized parameters are ignored.

Table 8-1. The `itexture` command line parameters.

Parameter	Description
`-o` *name*	The name of the output file is given by name. (The extension should not be included in the file name.)
`-type` *id*	The texture type is given by *id*. The value of *id* must be `2D`, `RECT`, or `CUBE`.
`-format` *id*	The image format is given by *id*. The value of *id* must be `RGBA`, `LMAL`, `LUMI`, or `INTS`.
`-alpha` *id*	The alpha channel data type is given by *id*. Accepted values are `ALFA`, `GLOS`, `OPAC`, `GLOW`, and `OCCL`.
`-swrap` *id*	The *s* wrap mode is given by *id*. Accepted values are `REPT`, `CLMP`, `CBDR`, `MRPT`, `MCLP`, and `MCBD`.
`-twrap` *id*	The *t* wrap mode is given by *id*. Accepted values are the same as for the *s* wrap mode.
`-compress`	Applies S3TC compression.
`-nofilter`	Disable filtering.
`-noaniso`	Disable anisotropic filtering.
`-highres`	Require high-resolution rendering.
`-normal`	Calculates a normal map.
`-parallax`	Generates parallax data.
`-horizon`	Generates horizon maps.
`-occlusion`	Calculates ambient occlusion in alpha.
`-scale` *value*	Sets the height map scale to value.
`-height` *channel*	Gets the height map from channel, which must be 0–3, representing (in order) red, green, blue, or alpha.
`-nomipmaps`	Suppresses the calculation of mipmap levels.
`-bleed`	Bleed colors for alpha test.
`vector`	Treats the RGB channels as vector values.
`-half`	Scale texture to half resolution.
`-halfhorizon`	Scale horizon maps to half resolution.

`-invgreen`	Inverts the green channel.
`-flip`	Flips the image vertically.
`-haze` *elevation red green blue*	Apply skybox haze using the color given by the floating-point values *red*, *green*, and *blue* and the elevation given by *elevation* (in the range [1,255]).

Sample Batch Import Command Lines

Here are some examples of commonly used batch texture import command lines:

- Importing a simple, diffuse colored texture of type 2D, with "Repeat" mode UVs, named "DiffuseColor" (note that `swrap` and `twrap` can normally be omitted when using the `REPT` value):

```
itexture DiffuseColor -type 2D -swrap REPT -twrap REPT;
```

- Importing a diffuse colored texture with ambient occlusion in the alpha channel:

```
itexture DiffuseWithAO -type 2D -alpha OCCL -occlusion
-scale 20.0
```

- Importing a gray-scale height map to generate a normal map with parallax and horizon mapping with a scale of 20:

```
itexture MyHeightMap -type 2D -normal -parallax -horizon
-scale 20.0
```

- Importing a texture with a gloss map in the alpha channel:

```
itexture TextureWithAlphGloss -type 2D -alpha GLOS
```

Creating a Custom GUI Appearance

The standard UI control appearance supplied by Terathon Software for use with the C4 Engine can be replaced with a custom UI control appearance.

The appearance of the graphical user interface (GUI) is controlled by two texture maps and a small set of colors. The information contained in those items is called a skin, and can be customized by the user. We'll discuss some of the internal workings of the GUI system, and then describe how you can change the appearance of windows and controls by customizing the skins and colors.

Rendering Process

There are two texture maps that the Interface Manager loads when the engine starts up, and they are stored in the resources Data/C4/C4/gui1.tex and Data/C4/C4/gui2.tex. The texture `gui1.tex` contains the base color and transparency information for the GUI, and the texture `gui2.tex` contains information about highlights. When a control is rendered by the Interface Manager, it multiplies the pixel data from `gui1.tex` by a constant color and adds the pixel data from `gui2.tex`.

For example, to render a green round button, the Interface Manager takes pixel data from the appropriate rectangle in both textures and performs the calculation shown in Figure 8-26.

The pixel data in `gui1.tex` is normally grayscale so that arbitrary colors can be used by the Interface Manager. The highlights from `gui2.tex` are not affected by the color multiplying the base texture. Note that the drop shadow comes from the alpha channel in the base texture (and the red color in the base texture comes from transparency shown in Photoshop when you select all four channels).

Texture Layout

The textures `gui1.tex` and `gui2.tex` are both 512 × 512 pixels in size. The Interface Manager expects certain graphics to be in predefined locations inside the textures, and these locations are the same for both textures. Figure 8-27 shows the base texture map `gui1.tex` for the default skin that ships with the C4 Engine. The red background shows transparency as displayed in Photoshop when all four channels are selected. The RGB color at these points is black.

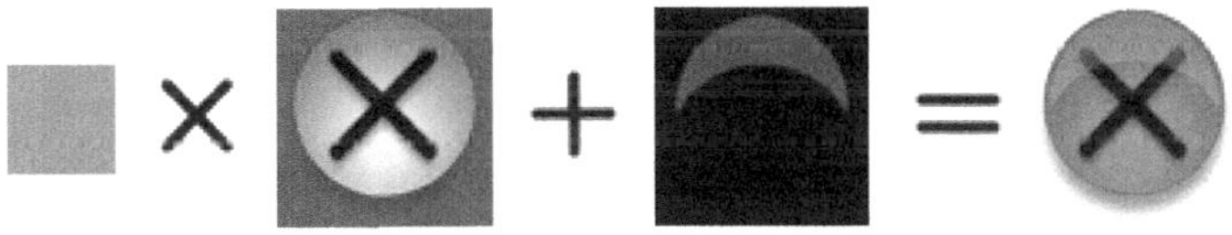

Figure 8-26. The calculation for the Interface Manager rendering process.

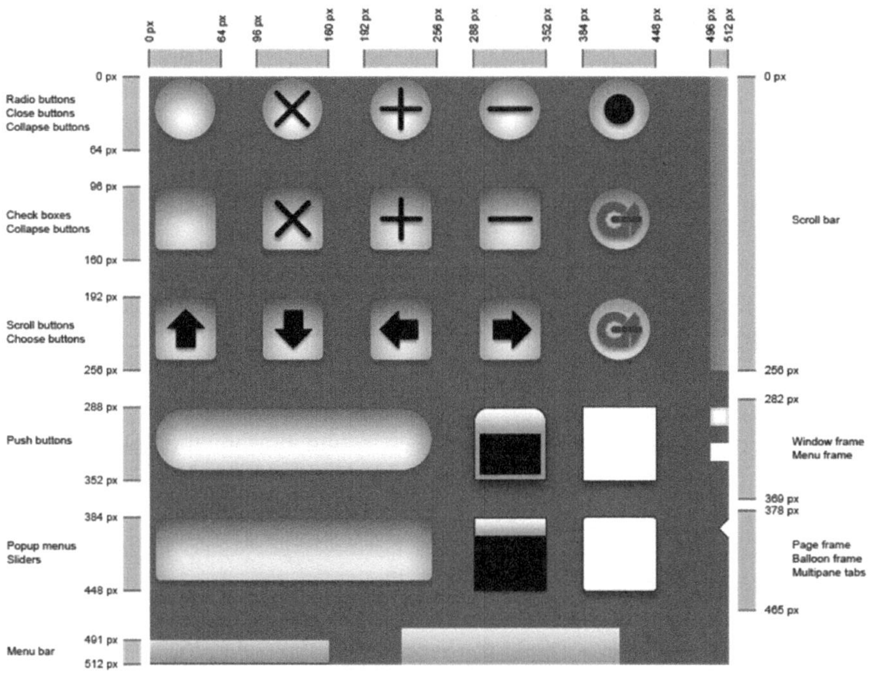

Figure 8-27. The texture layout expected by the Interface Manager.

Each graphical element has a size that is generally a multiple of 64 pixels in both width and height. There are 32 pixels of padding between adjacent elements so that bleeding doesn't occur during mipmap generation. This is important because interface controls are normally rendered from lower-resolution mipmaps. Figure 8-27 identifies the 64-pixel ranges for all of the buttons used in the interface.

Push buttons and popup menus use the elongated graphics near the bottom of the texture map. Since these kinds of buttons can vary in size, the Interface Manager always uses the 32 pixels on the left and right ends of the buttons, and then uses as many pixels as necessary from the center region of the button. If such a button is more than four times as wide as it is high, then the pixels in the central region are stretched.

Window frames are rendered using the template shown near the lower-right corner of the texture map. The actual frame of a window is rendered using the pixels inside the 64×64 rectangle ranging from 352px to 416px horizontally, and from 384px to 448px vertically. The remainder of the larger region shown in the diagram contains the drop shadow. The Interface Manager renders exactly 16 pixels from both the left and right sides of the 84 × 87 rectangle, exactly 30 pixels from the top side, and exactly 23 pixels from the bottom side. The pixels in the center of the window frame are not used.

The menu bar is rendered using the bottom 21 rows of the texture map, and the entire 512-pixel width of the texture is stretched to fit the display size.

Importing New GUI Skin Textures

The source images for the two default skin textures can be found in the Import/C4/C4/ directory. These images can be used as a template for designing a custom skin using a third-party image editing tool.

Once the source images are ready to be used, they can be imported using the Texture tool. When importing the textures `gui1.tga` and `gui2.tga`, the following settings should be made in the texture import dialog:

- Set the **Alpha channel** to **Transparency**.
- Set the **S wrap mode** and **T wrap mode** to **Clamp**.
- Select the **Disable anisotropic filtering** option.
- Select the **Require high-resolution rendering** option.

The last setting is particularly important so that the GUI continues to be rendered at high quality even if the user has selected low-quality textures in the **Graphics Settings** dialog.

Both of the textures `gui1.tga` and `gui2.tga` must have an alpha channel. The final alpha channel used for blending by the Interface Manager is determined in the same manner as the color channels. Ordinarily, the alpha channel of the base texture, `gui1.tga`, determines the transparency of a graphical element, and the alpha channel of the highlight texture is filled with zeros (black).

Once the textures have been imported, the C4 Engine must be restarted to see the changes.

Interface Colors

There are several constant colors used by the Interface Manager to control the appearance of various graphical elements of the GUI. Each color is stored in a system variable that can be set in a `.cfg` file or changed in the **Command Console** window. These colors are described in Table 8-2. Their values are represented using two hexadecimal digits for each of the red, green, and blue color component values.

Table 8-2. Interface colors used by the Interface Manager for GUI skins.

Variable	Default	Description
$desktopColor	404040	The color of the desktop when no game is running.
$windowColor	A0B0C0	The color of a window frame.
$backgroundColor	A0A0A0	The background color of a window's interior.
$hiliteColor	00C080	The color used to highlight various elements, such as selected text.
$buttonColor	40D0FF	The color applied to various buttons used in the GUI, such as the default push button or a checked check box.
$pageColor	BFA587	The background color of a tool page in the World Editor.
$windowTitleColor	FFFFFF	The text color for window titles.
$buttonTitleColor	000000	The text color for button titles.
$menuTitleColor	000000	The text color for menu titles.

Previewing a GUI Skin in Photoshop

To speed up the iterative design process while you are creating a custom GUI skin, you can configure layers in Photoshop to simulate the normal and highlighted appearance as follows:

1. Layer your gui1, gui2, and $buttonColor layers as shown in Figure 8-28.
2. Set the $buttonColor colorization layer to **Multiply** mode, as shown here. We have filled the layer with the factory default color of 40D0FF, as shown in Figure 8-29.
3. Set your gui2 highlight layer to **Screen** blending mode, as shown in Figure 8-30.
4. Hide the $buttonColor layer to display the buttons with the normal highlighted appearance, as shown in Figure 8-31.

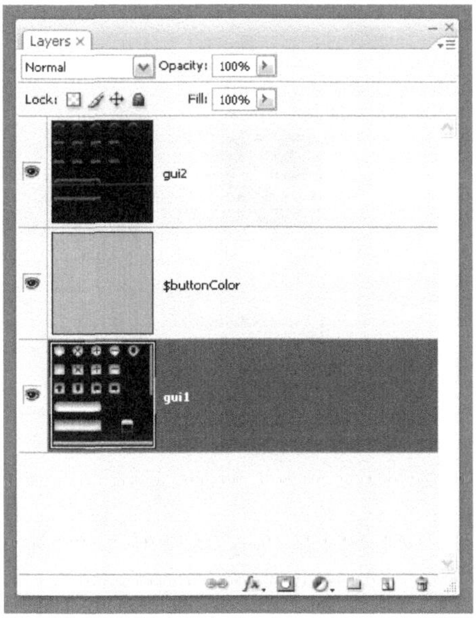

Figure 8-28. The GUI layer preview stack.

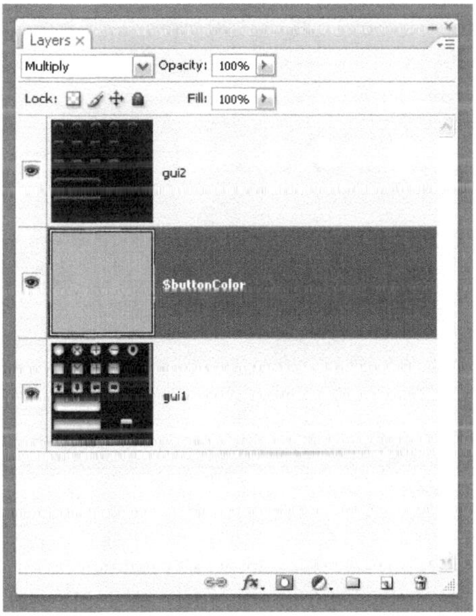

Figure 8-29. Setting the button colorization layer to Multiply mode.

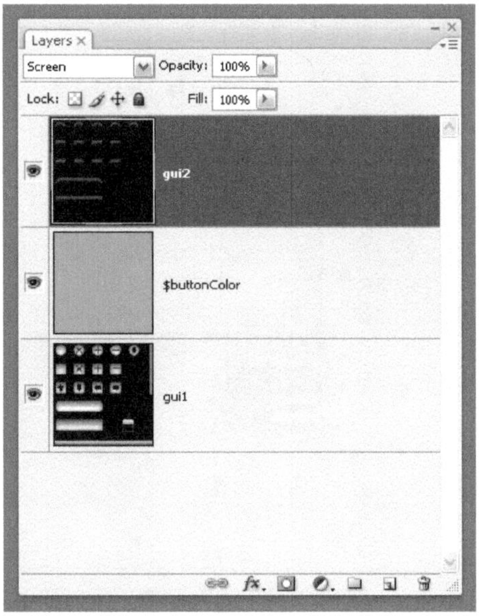

Figure 8-30. Setting the highlight layer to **Screen** blending mode.

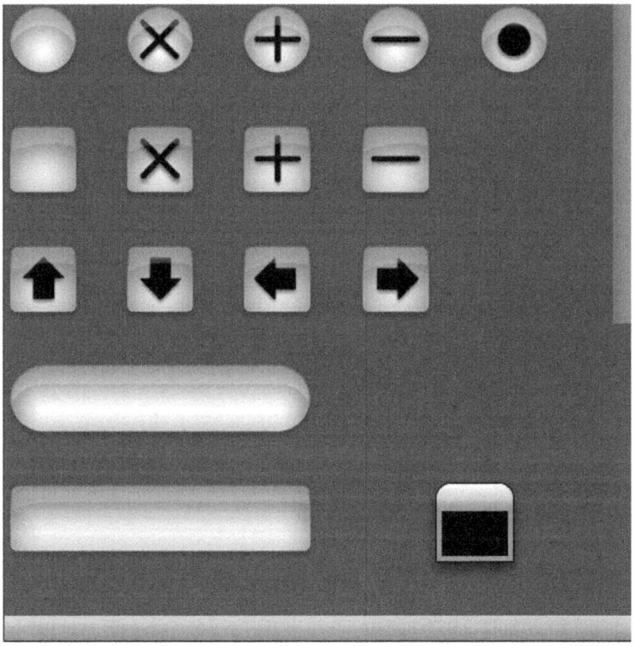

Figure 8-31. Displaying the buttons with the normal highlighted appearance.

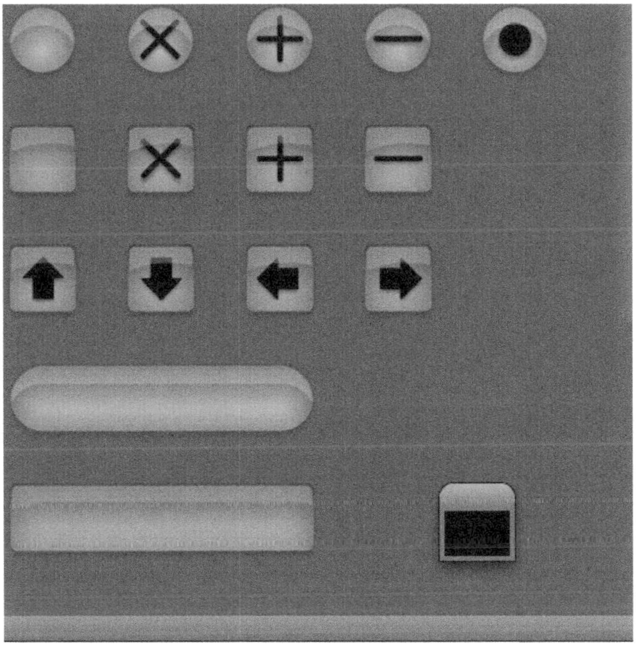

Figure 8-32. Displaying the buttons with the default push button or checked appearance.

5 Show the $buttonColor layer to display the buttons with the default push button or checked appearance, as shown in Figure 8-32.

With this layer stack setup in Photoshop, you can modify your GUI skin and see what it will look like interactively, without having to constantly restart C4 Engine.

A Dark GUI Skin

The `gui1.tex` texture for a dark GUI skin is shown in Figure 8-33. Figure 8-34 shows the dark GUI used in the **World Editor** window and the **Graphics Settings** dialog.

Our example dark GUI uses the following color variable settings in the `variables.cfg` file. To experiment with other values, you'll need to quit and restart the C4 executable to see the results of your changes.

```
$backgroundColor = "505050";
$buttonColor = "606060";
$buttonTitleColor = "F0F0F0";
```

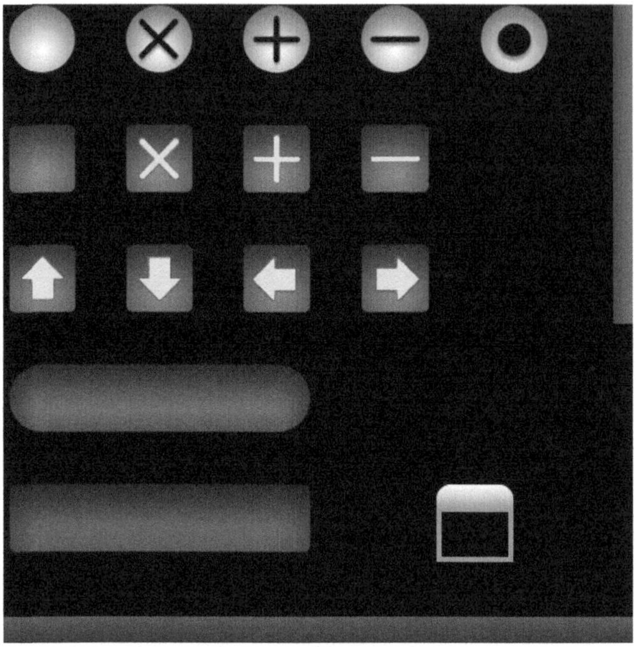

Figure 8-33. A dark GUI skin texture.

```
$desktopColor = "200060";
$editorGridColor = "7070D0";
$hiliteColor = "1010A0";
$menuTitleColor = "F0F0F0";
$panelGridColor = "8080FF";
$surfaceColor = "A06000";
$windowColor = "404040";
$windowTitleColor = "F0F0F0";
```

Next Steps

We've covered enough ground in Part II • Designing Worlds, that you should be ready to create your own worlds and explore quite a few design possibilities on your own. Once you have a world set up, you'll need a technical foundation to help you implement your game play. Part III • Under the Hood starts that learning process.

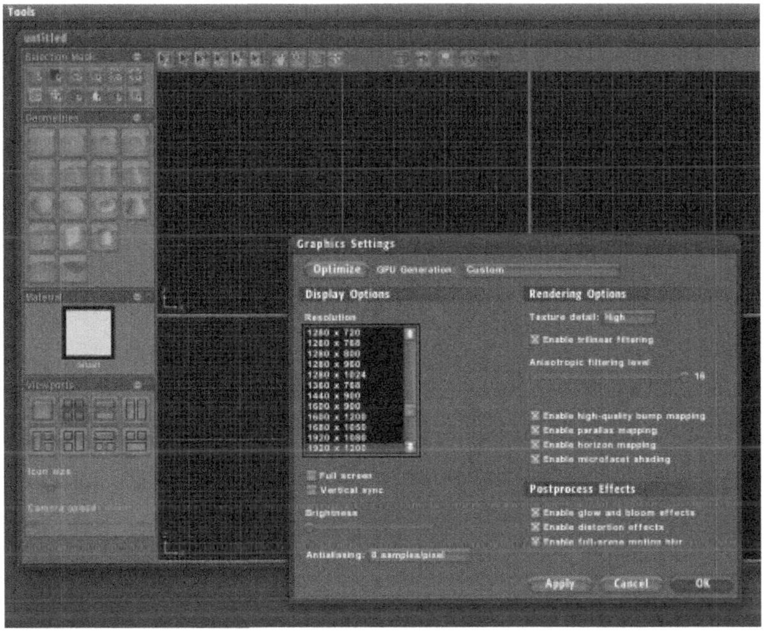

Figure 8-34. The dark GUI skin in the **World Editor** and **Graphics Settings** dialogs.

Part III

Under the Hood

9

Powered by the C4 Engine

This chapter looks at the underpinnings of the C4 Engine, such as the game loop, initialization, user input, world updating, and rendering.

The Big Picture

Before we get into detailed explanations about what the C4 Engine is doing for you, let's take a step back and consider what any game engine [EBER05] must do when running your games and applications.

Animate and Inanimate Game Objects

Consider the game play elements in the C4 demo game. The player spawns into the world as a soldier, and you are immersed in a rich, visually appealing environment, with sounds to enhance the experience. Roughly speaking the world contains objects with behaviors and objects with- out behaviors. You might call them animate and inanimate game objects.

As an example of animate objects in this context, there is a flag swaying in the wind and there is a waterfall with water gushing down to a stream below. Use the left mouse button to fire a bullet from your weapon, and a projectile comes into life and is launched in the direction you are aiming. That projectile is moving, so it too is an example of a game object with a behavior, an animate game object.

On the other hand, the satellite dish doesn't do anything at all. It's just sitting there, looking pretty, along with the rocks and trees, and the bridge, which are all examples of inanimate game objects. They have no associated behaviors.

So as a basic design requirement, we need a mechanism to handle a world made up of inanimate objects that only need to be rendered, and animate objects that need to be animated, in some cases taking user input into account, and otherwise interacting with the game environment. This mechanism is called the game loop.

The Game Loop

Just about any game engine, including the C4 Engine, which renders a game world with animate objects, uses some form of a game loop to run the world. At a very high level, the game goes through an initialization process, followed by a game loop designed like this:

```
InitializeObjects();

while (gameNotFinished)
{
    // Handle User Input (mouse, keyboard, gamepad etc.)
    // Update Objects in the World
    // Render the World
}
```

Let's look at each step inside the game loop, and explain what the C4 Engine does, but more importantly, what the C4 Engine expects you, the application writer, to do in relation to each step.

Initializing World Objects

The initialization step is very important in that this is where the game can collect all information from the world file so that it can be used more effectively in game code. Objects managed by the C4 Engine are initialized via the `Preprocess()` function. Each node, controller, and property, as well as the `World` class, has a virtual `Preprocess()` function that can be overridden. Here is an example of the type of initialization that is done in the `Preprocess()` function:

```
ResourceResult GameWorld::Preprocess(void)
{
   ResourceResult result = World::Preprocess();
   if (result != kResourceOkay) return (result);

   SetCamera(&spectatorCamera);
   playerCamera = &firstPersonCamera;

   spawnLocatorCount = 0;
   CollectZoneMarkers(GetRootZone());

   const Marker *marker = GetFirstSpectatorLocator();
   if (marker)
   {
      // Initialize spectatorCamera to the marker's
      // position and direction.
   }
   else
   {
      spectatorCamera.SetNodePosition(Point3D(0.0F, 0.0F, 1.0F));
   }

   return (kResourceOkay);
}
```

This is the processing step for the `GameWorld` class, which is part of the demo game supplied with builds of the C4 Engine. The first thing this function does is call the `Preprocess()` function of the base class, and it immediately returns with an error code if something went wrong. `Preprocess()` then initializes some camera values, after which we get to the interesting part—the `CollectZoneMarkers()` function searches the entire world for all markers, so that it can be used to initialize the camera's position. If `CollectZoneMarkers()` can't find any markers at all, the camera is set to a default position.

What's important about the `CollectZoneMarkers()` function is that it illustrates a method for searching through all of the objects in the world, and storing them in logical structures that you can use for your game. Some examples include lists of cameras, lists of players, or lists of object states. Those logical structures are completely defined by you, and should serve as a quick way to get information about your world in other parts of your code.

Handling User Input

The C4 Engine has a `Singleton` class (a class for which there is always only one instance) called `InputMgr`, generally known as the Input Manager, and you can access the single instance of that class in your own code, through a global pointer called `TheInputMgr`. The Input Manager handles all the low-level details needed to pick up and interpret various signals and messages from the operating system, when various input devices are being used. The Input Manager makes sure to inform any subclass of the `Action` class about what is happening with user input.

In your application code, you need to subclass the `Action` class and implement the `Begin()` and `End()` functions. When a key (or mouse or other device button) is pressed, and if that key has been correctly "bound", say in a configuration file, then the code inside your `Begin()` function will be called. And when the key has been released, then the code inside your `End()` function will be called.

So, the steps for you to route user input, as an application developer using the C4 Engine, are simple:

1. Find the configuration file `input.cfg` in the <User>/AppData/Roaming/C4 Engine/ directory, and make sure to bind the key to a four-character identifier.

Here is an example of how to bind the W key to a four-character identifier, that your code will in turn associate, through an enumeration, with a more meaningful name, such as `kActionForward`, which would be interpreted in your code to mean "move forward".

In the configuration file, you'll have a bind command like this:

```
bind "W" %frwd;
```

and in your code, an enumeration value such as:

```
enum
{
    kActionForward = 'frwd'
    // etc. for other action types
};
```

About Four-Character Identifiers

The four-character identifier is actually a 32-bit code that is meant to uniquely distinguish items in an enumeration, whether they are action IDs, model IDs, controller IDs, etc., 32 bits allows for billions of unique identifiers for any enumeration.

And remember, different enumerations can share IDs, as long as they are not intended for the same type (i.e., controllers can have a `'frwd'` code, while actions can also have a `'frwd'` code, since they're not used in the same context). So, instead of having to type out "1718777700" for an identifier, you can type its ASCII equivalent, `'frwd'`, which is far easier to understand and remember.

The Custom Action Class

2 Create a subclass of `Action`. For example, in the *SimpleChar* project there is a class called `MovementAction`, which derives directly from `Action` like this:

```
class MovementAction : public Action
```

3 Implement the `Begin()` and `End()` functions in your subclass, indicating what should happen on key press, and key release respectively.

The simplest thing to do in your first prototype programs is to set some global boolean variables from within these functions. The `Move()` function of your various controllers can then check on each cycle, if the value of those globals has changed or not, and can update node transforms accordingly. You can also use a variable to capture user input by setting bits within the variable which act as movement flags. This is exactly what we will be doing in our *SimpleBat* game tutorial, which you can read more about in Part IV • The Games.

In the game application that is delivered with builds of the C4 Engine, here are some examples of classes that subclass the Action class:

```
MGInput.h class ChatAction : public Action
MGInput.h class FireAction : public Action
MGInput.h class MovementAction : public Action
MGInput.h class LookAction : public Action
MGInput.h class SwitchAction : public Action
MGInput.h class WeaponAction : public Action
```

And in the tutorial game applications, the only subclass of `Action` is `MovementAction`:

```
SimpleBall.h class MovementAction : public Action
SimpleChar.h class MovementAction : public Action
```

Updating the World

First of all, it's important to understand some concepts about how the C4 Engine organizes the information that corresponds to the world objects in the game world.

The Scene Graph

A world managed by the C4 Engine contains what is called a scene graph, which is a tree structure made up of nodes. You can view the scene graph of your game world directly within the **World Editor** window, by right-clicking on a viewport and choosing **Scene Graph**. Figure 9-1 shows part of the scene graph used to organize and manage the nodes contained in the demo game application.

In this scene graph you can see various nodes connected together in a structure that resembles a family tree, except that in this picture, the parent-child relationships go from left-to-right, instead of from top-to-bottom. Each node in the tree has a parent node and zero to many child nodes. The exception is the root node, which is called the "Infinite Zone", which itself has no parent.

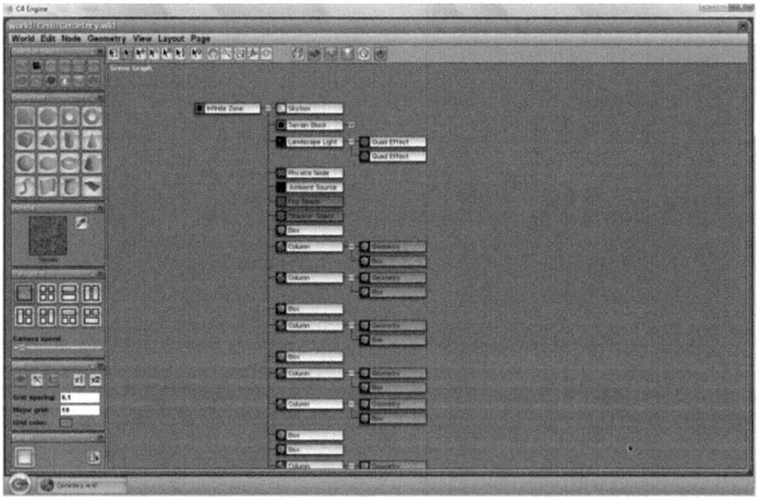

Figure 9-1. A portion of the scene graph in the Cemetery world that ships with the C4 Engine.

A viewport displaying the scene graph in the **World Editor** is providing a visual representation of the node hierarchy that is constructed and manipulated in code. It's worth noting that a scene graph view only represents the initial state of the scene graph. Being able to manipulate nodes during game play is an entirely different thing. The C4 Engine API provides functions that allow you to dynamically alter the structure and contents of the scene graph as needed during game play.

In code, the `World::GetRootNode()` function returns the root of the scene graph. The scene graph can easily be manipulated while the application is running, using functions such as `AddSubnode()`, `AddSubnodeBefore()`, and `AddSubnodeAfter()`, and can easily be traversed by using one of the many traversal functions, such as `GetFirstSubnode()`, `GetNextNode()`, `GetPreviousNode()`, etc. Check out the `Tree` class in the C4 Engine API documentation for a full list of the tree traversal and editing functionality that can be used with the scene graph. We also cover the scene graph and scene graph traversal again in more detail in Chapter 11, "Scene Graph Traversal".

Nodes

Let's look more deeply into what makes up a node. In the **World Editor**, you can get more information on any node, by selecting the node in the tree using a left mouse click, and then choosing **Node > Get Info (Ctrl-I)** to open the **Node Info** dialog. If you change the node's name in the **Node Info** dialog, then the new node name will be visible in the box representing the node in the scene graph.

The small icons to the left of each node name indicate the node type. A green cube icon represents a "Geometry" node, which contains geometry mesh data, and a "target" icon represents a so-called "Locator" node, which can be used, for example, to define the position in the world at which a player should spawn. If you browse the C4 Engine API documentation, and search using the word "hierarchy", you will see that the documentation includes diagrams representing the various class hierarchies for many of the key C4 Engine classes. Figure 9-2 shows a portion of the node class hierarchy.

As you can see from this class hierarchy, there are node subclasses for geometries, lights, cameras, zones, portals, effects, sounds, etc. And since they are derived from the `Node` class, they can be directly attached to the scene graph.

The **Node Info** dialog contains all information associated with a node that has been exposed to the **World Editor** from the underlying code. The contents of the **Node Info** dialog varies depending on the type of node that you have selected, but generally speaking, most types of nodes are configured using four common tab panels: **Node**, **Properties**, **Connectors**, and **Controller**. Some node types don't use

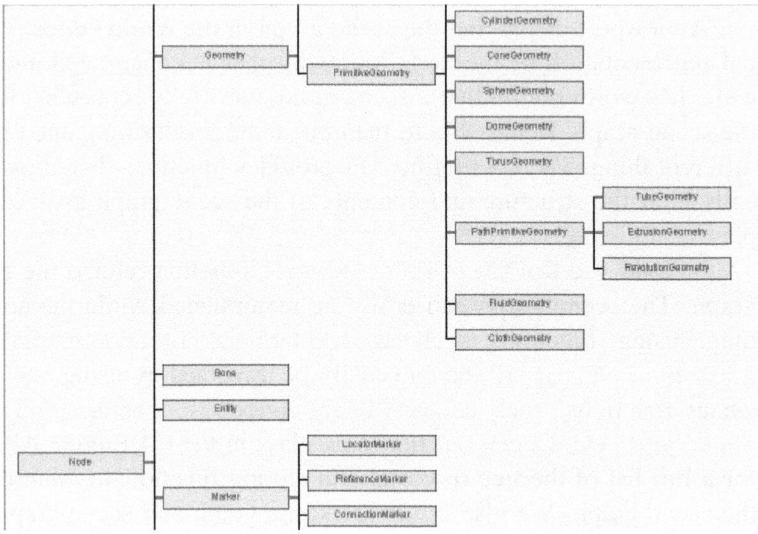

Figure 9-2. A portion of the `Node` class hierarchy.

all of these tabs (as an example, an infinite zone node only uses the **Properties** tab panel), but it is common that each type of node has a tab panel that is specific to its type.

Let's take a look at the settings for a geometry node in the **Node Info** dialog, to familiarize ourselves with the various tab panels.

In Figure 9-3, you can see that there are six tabs in the dialog. The **Geometry** and **Collision** tabs are specific to a geometry node, but the remaining four tabs are available for most types of nodes.

As shown in Figure 9-4, the **Node** tab panel has a list of settings available to the node. The first section, **Node Settings**, is typically available to most node types, while the remaining sections are specific to geometry nodes. This section allows you to set a custom name for your node. and to optionally disable the node on startup.

As shown in Figure 9-5, the **Properties** tab panel gives you access to any of the properties that are valid for the selected node type. The **Available Properties** list in the upper-left of the panel displays the properties available to the node. To assign one of these properties, select it from the list and click **Assign**. The new property then appears in the **Assigned Properties** list in the lower-left of the panel, indicating that the property is now attached to this node. The **Property Settings** list on the right side of the panel shows the settings of the currently selected property. Properties may or may not have settings associated with them.

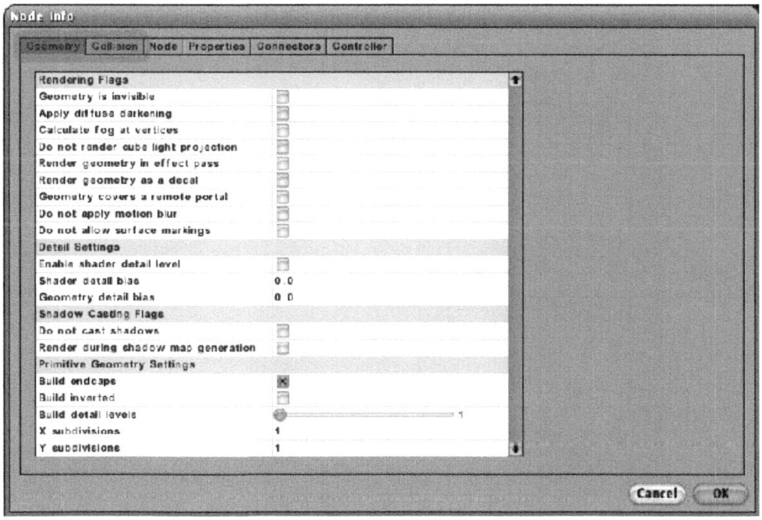

Figure 9-3. Settings for a geometry node in the **Node Info** dialog.

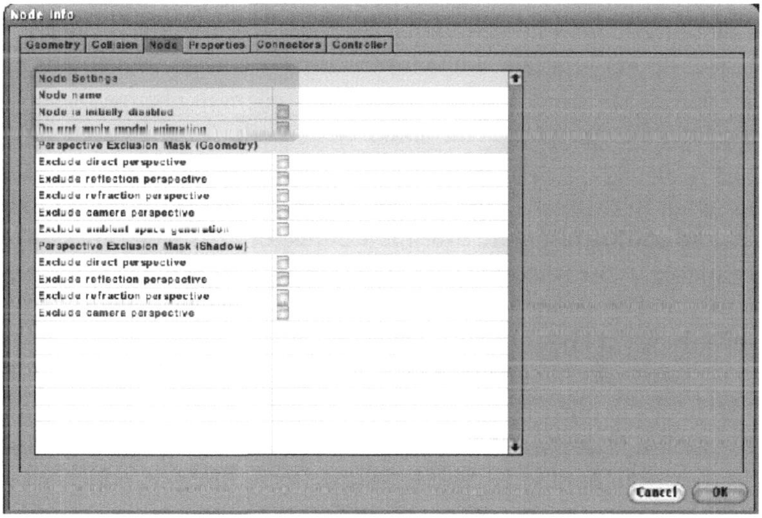

Figure 9-4. The **Node** tab panel for a selected geometry in the **Node Info** dialog.

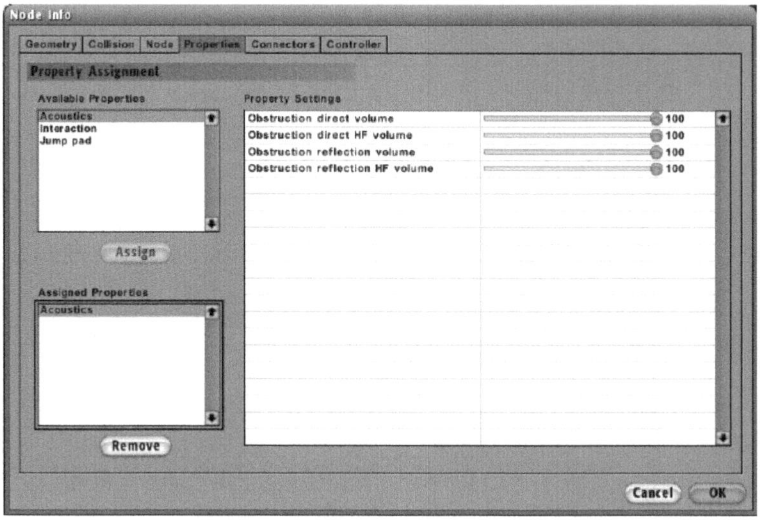

Figure 9-5. The **Properties** tab panel.

It's possible to add your own custom properties to the **Properties** tab panel by writing code for a new property. See the C4 Engine Wiki article "Defining a Custom Property" [WIKI08.09] for details on how to implement custom properties. Properties are a quick way for level designers to change the behavior of nodes in a game. For instance, you could write code for a custom property called "Armor", that has a slider setting for the value of the armor, which would enable a designer to easily add the "Armor" property and set a default value for the armor.

As shown in Figure 9-6, the **Connectors** tab panel lists all of the connectors available to the selected node. We already touched upon the use of connectors in Part II • Designing Worlds, when we connected a camera, a sound source and other types of nodes to a panel effect.

Connectors have user-definable identifiers that allow level designers to easily link nodes to other nodes. In Figure 9-7, the ABCD connector that was defined in Figure 9-6 is displayed when the **Connect Nodes (5)** tool is selected.

It would be just as easy to simply store link IDs between nodes in code, but this does not allow anyone who uses the **World Editor** to modify the links. Using connectors is more of a preference rather than a necessity, but it definitely makes visualizing and editing the connections between nodes much easier than having to maintain them in code.

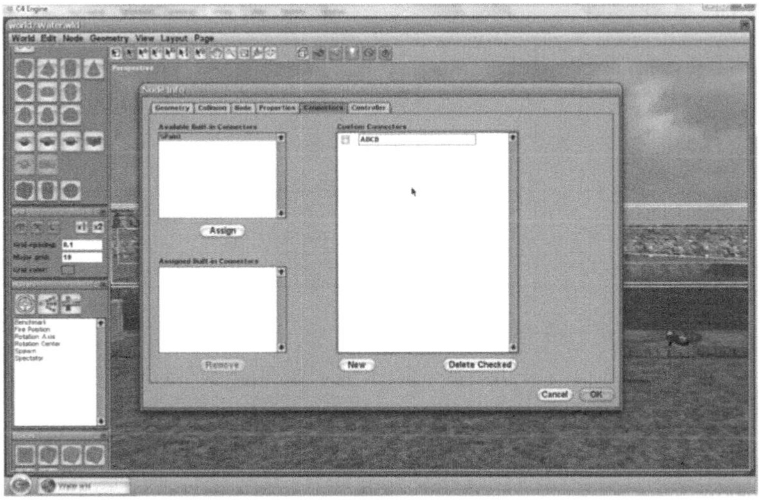

Figure 9 6. The **Connectors** tab panel.

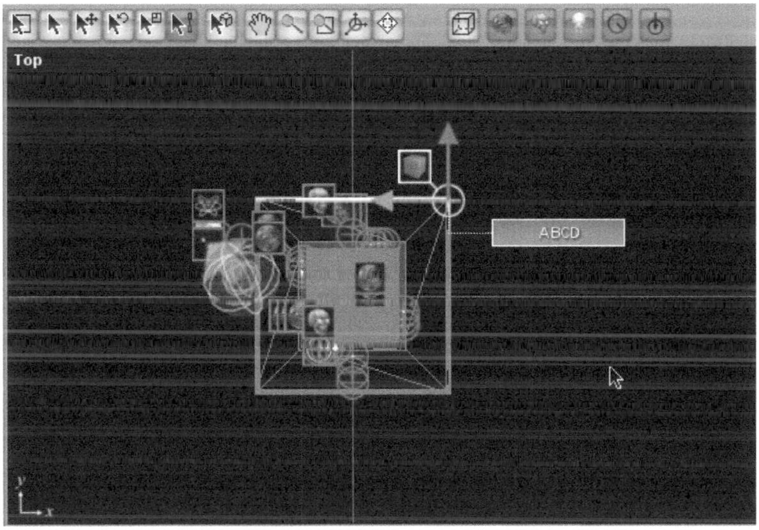

Figure 9-7. The connector ABCD, which was defined in the **Connectors** tab panel.

Table 9-1. Built-in connector key values.

Node Type	Connector Key	Connection
Zone	`%Fog`	Fog space
Zone	`%Ambient`	Ambient space
Zone	`%Acoustics`	Acoustic space
Portal	`%Zone`	Destination zone
Light	`%Shadow`	Shadow space
Joint	`%Body1`, `%Body2`	Physics joint node
Particle system	`%Emitter`	Emitter volume
Cloth geometry	`%Wind`	Field with a wind force
Geometry	`%Paint`	Paint space
Path primitive, Tube effect	`%Path`	Path that defines the shape of the geometry or effect

There are a few special connectors that are built into specific types of nodes. These connector keys are automatically provided by the C4 Engine, as shown in Table 9-1.

We briefly covered a few of the built-in connector types, when we assigned an emitter volume to the `EMIT` connector of a particle system, in Chapter 6, "More World Editor Features". See also the article "Using Connectors" on the C4 Engine Wiki, for more details.

As shown in Figure 9-8, the **Controller** tab panel allows you to assign a controller to the selected node. Select one of the entries in the controller type list to set the specific type of controller that should be associated with the selected node. As with the **Properties** tab panel, a number of settings may or may not appear on the right hand side. The particular options shown in the **Controller Settings** list on the right side of the panel are specific to the selected controller.

Like properties, you can define your own custom controllers. Considering that most of a node's behavior is handled in a controller, it is very common to associate custom controllers with the nodes in your game. We'll provide more information about controllers in the Controllers section later in this chapter, as well as in Chapter 15, "The Controller". The *Guide* also provides examples of

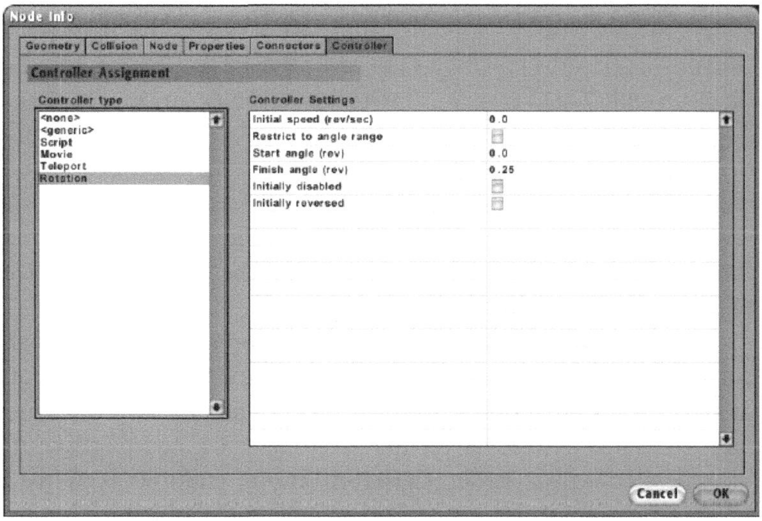

Figure 9-8. The **Controller** tab panel.

how to create your own custom controllers as we build several game prototypes in Part IV • The Games.

Transforms

For your applications, one of the key things to remember is that the `Node` class contains the information needed to locate, rotate, and scale the node in the game world. In this context, position, rotation, and scale of a node are referred to as the *transform* of the node.

A node stores two key transforms. There is a so-called local transform—or in the C4 Engine terminology, a *node transform*—which contains the position, rotation, and scale of a node relative to its immediate parent in the scene graph. And a node also stores a *world transform*, which contains what one might call the absolute position, rotation, and scale of a node, directly in world coordinates.

For nodes whose parent is the root node, the node and world transforms will be identical. See the Matrices and Transforms section, in Chapter 10, "Essential Mathematics", for more of the mathematical details relating to transforms, and how they are implemented and used in the C4 game engine.

Objects

It's also important to realize that nodes do not store the geometry mesh for a model. Mesh information is stored in a so-called *geometry object*, which the node—in this case, a geometry node—refers to. The `Node` class has a function called `SetObject()`, which is used to assign an `Object` to a `Node`. It also has a function called `GetObject()`, which will return any object currently assigned.

Mesh data, which can use up a significant amount of memory, only needs to be stored once in a single geometry object. If you have several instances of a model in your game, you can have more than one geometry node pointing to the same geometry object. Each geometry node will have its own separate transforms, so each can move independently of the others. Figure 9-9 shows a portion of the `Object` class hierarchy.

OK, so now we know that the scene graph is used to organize the nodes that comprise your game world, and that each node has a local node transform and a global world transform. A transform is a mathematical object—a 4×4 matrix in fact—which is used to define the position, scale, and rotation of the object which is associated with a node. Therefore, in the game loop, if we want to move or rotate a model, all we have to do is update the transform stored with the corresponding node.

It follows that in each cycle of the game loop we can further break down the step we previously referred to as "Update Objects in the World" as follows:

- Starting at the root node of the scene graph, traverse from parent to child node recursively
- For each node, if certain conditions are met, call some function to up- date the transform of that node

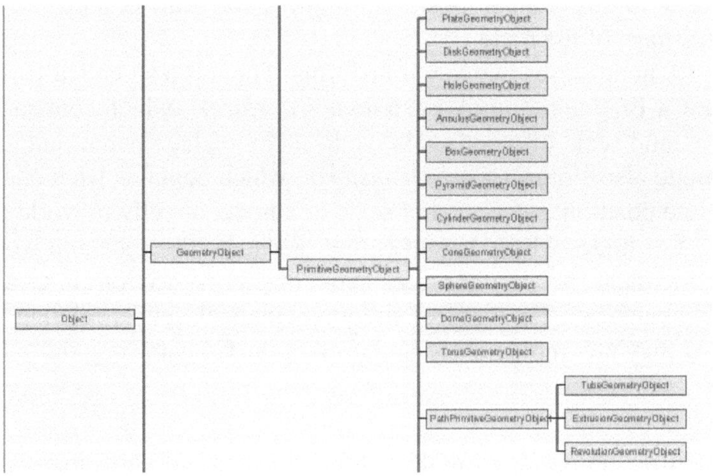

Figure 9-9. A portion of the C4 Engine `Object` class hierarchy.

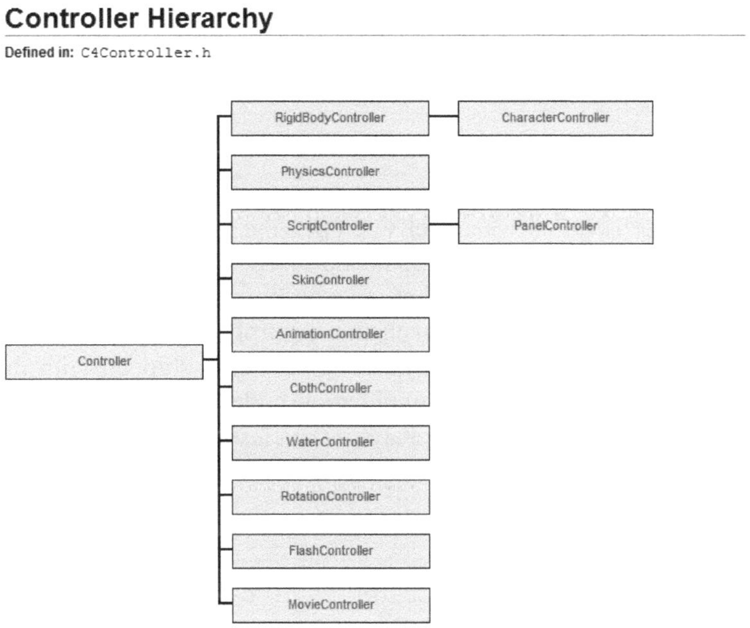

Figure 9-10. The C4 Engine class hierarchy for the `Controller` class.

Controllers

One way to achieve the second step—to update a node's transform on each frame—is to assign a controller to the node. Note that the `Node` class contains a function called `SetController()` for this purpose. It also has a function called `GetController()` that returns a pointer to the controller already assigned to that node, if any.

The `Controller` class itself contains a function called `Move()`, and it is exactly that function which is called in the second step above. It is there that you update a node's transform, depending on user input and other game state information. Note that a controller can also be used to update the transform of other nodes, not just its own transform. Figure 9-10 shows the `Controller` class hierarchy.

You can define the node types to which a `Controller` class may be assigned in its `ValidNode()` function. Here is an example of the code you would use to specify that a controller can only be attached to nodes of type model or geometry:

```
bool PathController::ValidNode(const Node *node)
{
   return ((node->GetNodeType() == kNodeModel) ||
      (node->GetNodeType() == kNodeGeometry));
}
```

This code is called whenever you open the **Node Info** dialog in the **World Editor**, to check if the controller should be listed in the **Controller** tab for the selected node type. You can check that yourself by setting a breakpoint in this code when you are debugging your own custom controllers.

If you scan through the game code that is shipped with the C4 engine, you will find that much of the application code is concerned with the `Controller` class and its subclasses. Here are of the classes in the file `MGControllers.h` that are direct subclasses of the `Controller` class:

```
class CollectableController : public Controller
class DoorController : public Controller
class FlickerController : public Controller
class LightningController : public Controller
class RotationController : public Controller
class TeleportController : public Controller
class TorchController : public Controller
class WindController : public Controller
```

And here are some of the indirect subclasses of `Controller` in some additional files:

```
class GameCharacterController : public CharacterController
class MonsterController : public GameCharacterController
class FighterController : public GameCharacterController
class FireballController : public ProjectileController
class GrenadeController : public ProjectileController
class RocketController : public ProjectileController
```

Everything that has some kind of behavior has some type of controller assigned to it. The rockets you fire? `RocketController`. The moving doors? `DoorController`. The items you can collect? You guessed it, `Collectable-Controller`.

Notice that all the bullets and rockets and other types of projectile in the demo game are subclasses of `ProjectileController`. Notice also that the players and NPC controllers are subclasses of the C4 Engine class `Charac-`

`terController`. Besides the `Controller` class, the other key base classes used for making the demo application include `Action`, `Animator`, `Message` (for multi-player games), `Camera`, `ParticleSystem` (for explosions and effects like rain, etc.), and `World` for the game world itself.

To summarize, if you want to animate any of your game objects, make sure that the associated node has a controller assigned to it, and add code to the `Move()` function of the controller to update the node's transform.

Rendering the World

In this section, we outline a general rendering pipeline and how transforms are used to calculate the 2D screen coordinates, given the camera frustum and the transforms of the 3D game objects. Whole volumes have been written on this topic alone. See the references at the back for our personal recommendations. For this book, we'll be very brief! We will cover no more than the bare essentials here.

Let's start with an analogy. Look out the nearest window to you, or if you're stuck in a windowless room, or if its night time and the curtains are closed, then instead, just imagine you are looking out of a window! In this analogy, the window corresponds to the 2D screen of your computer, where your 3D game world will get rendered by the engine. Your eyes represent the eye of the camera in the game world. If you move your head, then the positions, sizes, and orientations of the various 3D objects "out there in the world" will change on the 2D window in front of you. And so too in your game world.

As the camera in the game world is moved and rotated, say by pressing keys or moving the mouse, so too are the projections of the various 3D games objects altered and the image on your 2D screen changes to reflect that. Now imagine that your head remains still, and that a bird flies past the window of the room you are sitting in. The coordinates of the projection of the bird on the 2D screen will also change with time, even though this time you didn't move your eyes, "the camera". Similarly, without moving the game camera, game objects like planes and tanks and even virtual birds will move in virtual 3D and the projection of those objects on your 2D screen will change over time. And notice that if the bird flies behind a tree, then for that short time the bird is invisible, there is no projection of the bird onto the window of your room. And any virtual bird, passing behind a virtual tree in your game world, will similarly not get projected onto the 2D game window of your computer screen.

The previous analogy isn't perfect, because the game camera is represented by a frustum, whose eye-point moves together with the "window" of the camera, which is also called the "near-plane". We will learn more about the camera frustum in the next chapter.

The 3D rendering pipeline concerns itself with the calculations the engine uses to project the appearance of your 3D game objects onto the game window on your computer screen. In the real world outside of the computer, light from the sun and other sources in the environment is reflected from objects according to the laws of physics, traveling along a line connecting each object with your eye. And physics ensures that you cannot see objects which are blocked by other objects that are in the way, such as walls and trees. Although this behavior of light all seems perfectly natural, the 3D rendering pipeline performs quite a few calculations to simulate this behavior.

Transforms

But how does all that work inside the game engine? The answer is that, among other things, the model data representing your 3D game objects undergoes several transforms, from model space to world space, then from world space to camera space, and finally through what is called a perspective projection, from camera space to screen space. These transforms are explained in Chapter 10, "Essential Mathematics".

The C4 Engine also takes care of lighting, culling, clipping, special effects, and a whole host of other operations that you, as a game programmer and user of the C4 Engine, do not need to worry too much about.

10

Essential Mathematics

This chapter introduces the essential mathematics a 3D game programmer will need to use the C4 Engine, including a short overview of vectors, matrices, and transforms.

The Bare Essentials

As we mentioned at the start of the Guide, you will need to understand and apply the mathematics of basic linear algebra, and in particular that of vectors, matrices, and transforms. That will suffice for beginners, but as you become more proficient as a user of the C4 Engine, you will begin to use parts of the API which will probably inspire you to delve deeper into the mathematics, and we would encourage you to do so.

Instead of first describing the mathematical theory and then showing how it's used, let's first look at things from the C4 Engine's point of view. The 3D models which you want the engine to display, are stored as lists of vertices. Each vertex is described by three values, one each for the x, y, and z coordinates. The mathematical objects used to represent these coordinates are called vectors, in this case 3D vectors. We describe them in more detail later in this chapter.

Let's say that you created a simple square (or plane) in a modeling package, and that the square is positioned at the origin in that package, as shown in Figure 10-1.

The coordinates of the object in the modeling package are called the model-space coordinates. The four model coordinates of the square in this example might be $(0,0,0)$, $(1,0,0)$, $(1,1,0)$, and $(0,1,0)$. The engine knows the model coordinates, since those are the coordinates, (`x_model`, `y_model`, `z_model`) of each

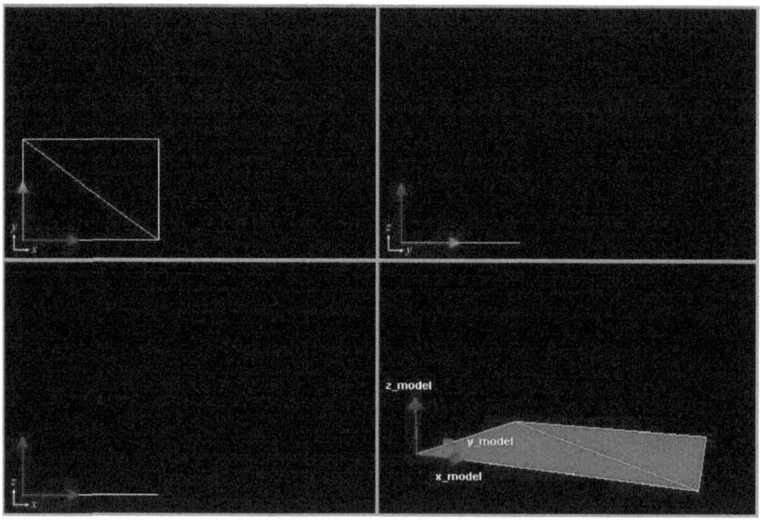

Figure 10-1. A square at the origin in model space.

of the model's vertices, which were imported from the Collada file which represented the model. And that vertex data for the model is saved in a .mdl file, which the C4 Engine loads and uses when your game is running.

Now in your game world, you may have a controller which wants to rotate the square counter-clockwise, and perhaps to position the model away from the world's origin, as shown in Figure 10-2. And this rotation and repositioning of each of your models when the game is running is carried out using 4×4 matrices, which are also explained in detail later on.

Not all objects in the game world actually get rendered to the screen of course. A frustum camera is used to view the world, and objects outside the camera's frustum are either ignored if they are completely outside, or "clipped" if they are partially outside. In Figure 10-3, the green objects are inside the view frustum and they will be rendered to the screen. The red cube is completely outside the frustum, and so it will not be rendered.

As you can see in Figure 10-3, the view frustum has six clipping planes labeled near, far, top, bottom, left, and right. These clipping planes define the boundary between what will be rendered and what will not be rendered to the final screen image, every frame. Note that, under normal circumstances, the C4 Engine uses an infinite far plane, so nothing gets clipped because it's too far away.

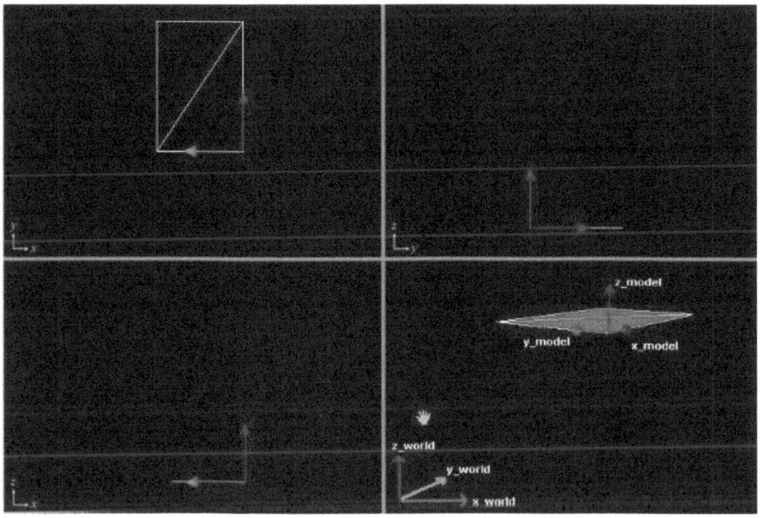

Figure 10-2. A square in world space, i.e., inside in your game world–rotated and "translated" away from the world origin.

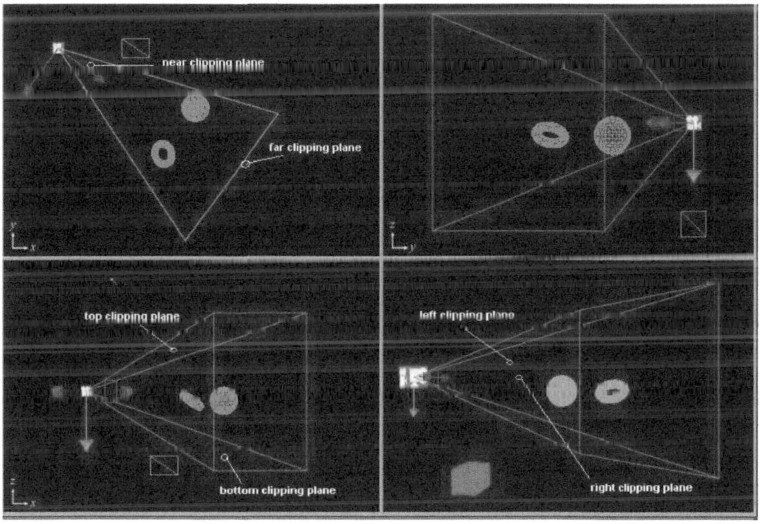

Figure 10-3. The *view frustum* has six clipping planes.

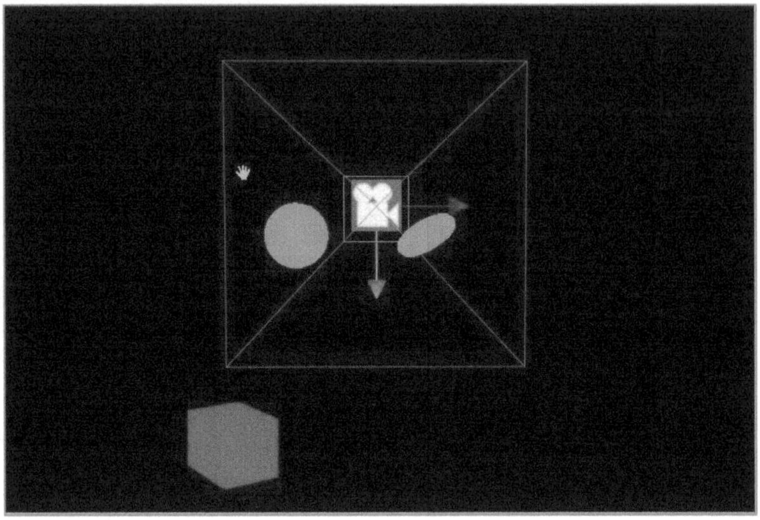

Figure 10-4. In *camera space*, the view frustum is positioned at the origin and is facing down the negative z axis.

Having transformed the vertex data from model to world space, the world-space data is in turn then transformed to camera space. This transform is the same as would be required to rotate the camera frustum so that the eye of the camera is placed at the world origin, so that it is looking down the negative z axis as shown in Figure 10-4.

The camera is then also scaled so that the near, far, right, left, top, and bottom clipping planes of the frustum end up in the shape of a cube made from the intersection of the planes $x = \pm 1$, $y = \pm 1$, $z = \pm 1$. Using a cube like this for camera space makes the clipping calculations much simpler. The z value is stored in a so-called z-buffer and is used to determine which pixels are closer to the viewer and are rendered, and which do not. Note that this transform is also called the perspective projection. Objects which were far from the camera's eye now appear smaller than objects which were near to the camera's eye.

Let's recap what we have covered so far. We explained in Chapter 9, "Powered by the C4 Engine", that the C4 Engine uses a so-called scene graph to organize the data used to describe your game world. And we explained that the scene graph is made up of nodes. You use the **World Editor** to build up the scene graph, by creating and positioning the various nodes the way you want them. Some nodes (e.g., lights, primitive geometries, markers, etc.) are created using the tools of the **World Editor** itself.

Now, we also noted in Chapter 9, "Powered by the C4 Engine", that associated with every scene graph node, is a so-called world transform. This transform contains all of the values needed to tell the C4 Engine the position, rotation, and scale to render the nodes—including your models—in the game world. It turns out that the world transform is a 4×4 matrix—which, when multiplied by the model-space coordinate vectors, results in world-space coordinate vectors, which represent the correct position, rotation, and scale of the object in your game world.

Besides the world transform, we noted earlier that each node also stores another 4×4 matrix known as the node transform. This transform contains all of the values needed to position, rotate, and scale a node relative to its parent node. When you open up the **Transform** page panel in the **World Editor**, what you see is the node transform—not the world transform.

Recapping somewhat from Chapter 9, "Powered by the C4 Engine", but with slightly more detail, the C4 Engine does the following on each game cycle:

Starting at the root node, traverse the scene graph from each parent, to each of its children recursively. For each node do the following:

1. Using the node transform, update the world transform for the node in the Scene Graph—but only if there has been a change, e.g., a movement or rotation
2. Multiply the world transform stored at that node by the model- space coordinates (a vector) to get the world-space coordinates (also a vector) for that node
3. Render the node based on these updated world-space coordinates

Note that in Step 1, the world transform is actually calculated from the node transform, only if a flag has been set for that node (using the `node->Invalidate()` function). And again, rendering in Step 3 involves a series of transforms from world to camera to screen space.

We clearly need to understand vectors—which are used to represent model coordinates—and matrices—which are used to move, rotate, and scale (or "transform") vectors. If you are unsure about either of these mathematical concepts, then the next section is for you. If you know all of this stuff already, you can safely skip to the section Matrices and Transforms, where the application of these mathematical concepts to game programming with the C4 Engine will be discussed.

Points and Vectors

A point in space is exactly what you would imagine it to be—a location, which is represented by the coordinates of that location as a list of numbers. In 2D, we have two numbers which we will write as (x, y), representing the x and y coordinates of the point, and in 3D, we have three numbers, which we will write as (x, y, z). We will represent points with lowercase letters taken from the middle of the alphabet, such as **p** and **q**.

Now a vector is defined to be a line segment which has magnitude and direction and you can best think of a vector as simply an arrow. A vector doesn't have a location however, so parallel arrows which all point in the same direction and have the same length, each represent the same vector. Vectors also have components just as points do. For example, the 3D vector **v** would be written as the list of values (x, y, z).

Operations on Vectors

Here we talk about some of the operations which any vector class will need to implement.

Addition and subtraction of vectors are intuitive—you simply add or subtract the component numbers

$$\mathbf{u}+\mathbf{v}=\begin{bmatrix}u_1\\u_2\\u_3\end{bmatrix}+\begin{bmatrix}v_1\\v_2\\v_3\end{bmatrix}=\begin{bmatrix}u_1+v_1\\u_2+v_2\\u_3+v_3\end{bmatrix}$$

and

$$\mathbf{u}-\mathbf{v}=\begin{bmatrix}u_1\\u_2\\u_3\end{bmatrix}-\begin{bmatrix}v_1\\v_2\\v_3\end{bmatrix}=\begin{bmatrix}u_1-v_1\\u_2-v_2\\u_3-v_3\end{bmatrix}.$$

If you subtract two points, you get a vector, and that vector is the arrow pointing from one point to the other point.

$\mathbf{v}=\mathbf{q}-\mathbf{p}$ represents a vector (arrow) pointing from **p** to **q**.

So if **p** is the point $(1,0,0)$, and **q** is the point $(1,1,0)$, then $\mathbf{v} = \mathbf{q} - \mathbf{p}$ is the vector $(0,1,0)$, which is a vector from **p** to **q**, pointing up along the y axis. The coordinates of a vector are the same as the coordinates of the point at the head of the vector, if you place the tail of the vector at the origin.

Multiplication by a scalar (i.e., by a number) is also intuitive—you simply multiply each of the components by that scalar:

$$a\mathbf{v} = a\begin{bmatrix} v_1 \\ v_2 \\ v_3 \end{bmatrix} = \begin{bmatrix} av_1 \\ av_2 \\ av_3 \end{bmatrix}.$$

For example,

$$4\mathbf{v} = 4\begin{bmatrix} v_1 \\ v_2 \\ v_3 \end{bmatrix} = \begin{bmatrix} 4v_1 \\ 4v_2 \\ 4v_3 \end{bmatrix}.$$

The magnitude of a vector **v**, written $\|\mathbf{v}\|$ and often called the norm of **v** or $\text{norm}(\mathbf{v})$, is the length of the arrow or line segment representing that vector and is given by the formula from Pythagoras' Theorem

$$\|\mathbf{v}\| = \left\|\begin{bmatrix} v_1 \\ v_2 \\ v_3 \end{bmatrix}\right\| = \sqrt{v_1^2 + v_2^2 + v_3^2}.$$

Two other key operations on vectors are the dot product and the cross product, and we will see their use later in the section on orientation.

Dot Product

The dot product of two vectors is a scalar which is defined to be the sum of the products of the individual components. So

$$\mathbf{u} \cdot \mathbf{v} = \begin{bmatrix} u_1 \\ u_2 \\ u_3 \end{bmatrix} \cdot \begin{bmatrix} v_1 \\ v_2 \\ v_3 \end{bmatrix} = u_1v_1 + u_2v_2 + u_3v_3.$$

As you can see, this result is scalar, and not a vector. It turns out that this is also equal to the product of the magnitude of the vectors with the cosine of the angle between them

$$\mathbf{u}\cdot\mathbf{v} = \|\mathbf{u}\|\|\mathbf{v}\|\cos\theta,$$

where θ is the angle between the two vectors.

The projection of a vector **u** onto another vector **v**, or the amount of **u** which is along the direction **v**, is given by

$$\|\mathbf{u}\|\cos\theta = \frac{\mathbf{u}\cdot\mathbf{v}}{\|\mathbf{v}\|}.$$

Cross Product

The cross product of two vectors **u** and **v** is written $\mathbf{u}\times\mathbf{v}$, and you say "**u** cross **v**". Unlike the dot product, which results in a scalar, the result of the cross product is another vector, and it is defined as

$$\mathbf{u}\times\mathbf{v} = \begin{bmatrix} u_1 \\ u_2 \\ u_3 \end{bmatrix} \times \begin{bmatrix} v_1 \\ v_2 \\ v_3 \end{bmatrix} = \begin{bmatrix} u_2v_3 - u_3v_2 \\ u_3v_1 - u_1v_3 \\ u_1v_2 - u_2v_1 \end{bmatrix}.$$

Like the dot product, the cross product satisfies a trigonometric relationship

$$\|\mathbf{u}\times\mathbf{v}\| = \|\mathbf{u}\|\|\mathbf{v}\|\sin\theta,$$

where θ is the angle between **u** and **v**.

Note that the vector which results from the cross product of two other vectors, is a vector which points in a direction which is perpendicular to the plane defined by the two original vectors.

It turns out that $\mathbf{u}\times\mathbf{v} = -\mathbf{v}\times\mathbf{u}$ and that $\mathbf{u}\times(\mathbf{v}\times\mathbf{w})$ is not generally equal to $(\mathbf{u}\times\mathbf{v})\times\mathbf{w}$.

Matrices

What is a Matrix?

You can think of a matrix as a two-dimensional array of numbers, with a certain number of rows and columns. The number of rows and columns defines the so-called dimension of the matrix. Here is an example of a 3×4 matrix:

$$\mathbf{M} = \begin{bmatrix} m_{11} & m_{12} & m_{13} & m_{14} \\ m_{21} & m_{22} & m_{23} & m_{24} \\ m_{31} & m_{32} & m_{33} & m_{34} \end{bmatrix}$$

This matrix has three rows and four columns. Each element of the matrix is a number represented by M_{ij}, where i is the row number and j is the column number.

Note that a vector is also in fact a matrix. For example, in 3D space there are row vectors, which have one row and three columns, and there are column vectors, with three rows and one column. Just to save space, we will be (and have so far been) writing column vectors like this (x, y, z). We won't be using row vectors in the *Guide*.

Operations on Matrices

Multiplication of a matrix by a scalar is intuitive—each component gets multiplied by the scalar. So $a\mathbf{M}$ has the components aM_{ij}.

In order to multiply two matrices, you need to be sure that the rows and columns of the matrices match up. So if **M** has i rows and j columns, then to multiply by another matrix **N**, **N** must also have j rows (but can have any number of columns, say k). The components of the resulting matrix **L** are defined by multiplying the rows of **M** into the columns of **N** as

$$\mathbf{L} = \mathbf{MN} \Rightarrow L_{ij} = \sum_k m_{ik} n_{kj},$$

which is row i of **M** multiplied into column j of **N**.

For example, if **M** is a 2×3 matrix—i.e., it has two rows and three columns— and **N** is a 3×2 matrix—i.e., it has three rows and two columns, then the result $\mathbf{L} = \mathbf{MN}$ is a 2×2 matrix:

$$\mathbf{L} = \mathbf{MN} = \begin{bmatrix} m_{11} & m_{12} & m_{13} \\ m_{21} & m_{22} & m_{23} \end{bmatrix} \begin{bmatrix} n_{11} & n_{12} \\ n_{21} & n_{22} \\ n_{31} & n_{32} \end{bmatrix}$$

$$\mathbf{L} = \begin{bmatrix} m_{11}n_{11} + m_{12}n_{21} + m_{13}n_{31} & m_{11}n_{12} + m_{12}n_{22} + m_{13}n_{32} \\ m_{21}n_{11} + m_{22}n_{21} + m_{23}n_{31} & m_{21}n_{12} + m_{22}n_{22} + m_{23}n_{32} \end{bmatrix}.$$

Similarly, a 4×7 matrix that multiplies a 7×2 matrix will result in a 4×2 matrix. You multiply the rows into the columns.

Now, since a vector is just an $n \times 1$ column matrix, where n is the dimension of the space (e.g., three for 3D space), we can pre-multiply a vector $\mathbf{v}$ ($n \times 1$) by another matrix **M**, as long as **M** has n columns. The result is another vector. For example, if **M** is a 3×3 matrix and **v** is a vector (i.e., a 3×1 column matrix), then the results of multiplying **v** by **M** is another vector $\mathbf{u} = \mathbf{Mv}$:

$$\begin{bmatrix} u_1 \\ u_2 \\ u_3 \end{bmatrix} = \begin{bmatrix} m_{11} & m_{12} & m_{13} \\ m_{21} & m_{22} & m_{23} \\ m_{31} & m_{32} & m_{33} \end{bmatrix} \begin{bmatrix} v_1 \\ v_2 \\ v_3 \end{bmatrix} = \begin{bmatrix} m_{11}v_1 + m_{12}v_2 + m_{13}v_3 \\ m_{21}v_1 + m_{22}v_2 + m_{23}v_3 \\ m_{31}v_1 + m_{32}v_2 + m_{33}v_3 \end{bmatrix}.$$

Identity matrix

The *identity matrix* has ones along the diagonal and zeros everywhere else. It is only defined for so-called square matrices, which have the same number of rows and columns. It has the property that when it is multiplied by another matrix of the appropriate dimension, the result is the same matrix:

$$\mathbf{M} = \mathbf{MI} = \mathbf{M} \begin{bmatrix} 1 & 0 & 0 \\ 0 & 1 & 0 \\ 0 & 0 & 1 \end{bmatrix} = \mathbf{IM} = \begin{bmatrix} 1 & 0 & 0 \\ 0 & 1 & 0 \\ 0 & 0 & 1 \end{bmatrix} \mathbf{M} = \mathbf{M}.$$

The inverse and identity matrices

The inverse of a matrix **M**, which is written $\mathbf{M}^{-1}$, is defined by the fact that when it is multiplied by the original matrix itself, the result is the identity matrix.

Matrices and Transforms

It turns out that the information needed to represent a rotation or a scaling can be contained within a simple 3×3 matrix. To carry out that rotation and/or scaling operation (or "transform") on a 3D model, whose vertices are represented by vectors, you simply pre-multiply those vectors by the matrix.

In general, you will also want to move (or "translate") vertices of models, and not just rotate and scale them. The way to do this is to add a vector (represented as a 3×1 column matrix). So for example, let's say you have a model vertex at $(1,0,0)$ and you want to translate it by seven units in the y direction. Then you would add the vector $(0,7,0)$, producing the resulting vector of $(1,7,0)$.

So a single transform with rotation, scaling, and translation is then

$$\mathbf{u} = [\mathbf{RS}]\mathbf{v} + \mathbf{t} \Rightarrow \begin{bmatrix} u_1 \\ u_2 \\ u_3 \end{bmatrix} = \begin{bmatrix} rs_{11} & rs_{12} & rs_{13} \\ rs_{21} & rs_{22} & rs_{23} \\ rs_{31} & rs_{32} & rs_{33} \end{bmatrix} \begin{bmatrix} v_1 \\ v_2 \\ v_3 \end{bmatrix} + \begin{bmatrix} t_1 \\ t_2 \\ t_3 \end{bmatrix},$$

where $[\mathbf{RS}]$ is a 3×3 matrix representing the rotation and scaling transform, and $\mathbf{t}$ is a column vector representing the displacement or translation.

If you wanted to apply two transforms, one after the other, you would have

$$\mathbf{u}' = [\mathbf{R}'\mathbf{S}']\mathbf{u} + \mathbf{t}'$$

$$\Rightarrow \mathbf{u}' = [\mathbf{R}'\mathbf{S}']([\mathbf{RS}]\mathbf{u} + \mathbf{t}) + \mathbf{t}'$$

$$\Rightarrow \begin{bmatrix} u'_1 \\ u'_2 \\ u'_3 \end{bmatrix} = \begin{bmatrix} r's'_{11} & r's'_{12} & r's'_{13} \\ r's'_{21} & r's'_{22} & r's'_{23} \\ r's'_{31} & r's'_{32} & r's'_{33} \end{bmatrix} \left(\begin{bmatrix} rs_{11} & rs_{12} & rs_{13} \\ rs_{21} & rs_{22} & rs_{23} \\ rs_{31} & rs_{32} & rs_{33} \end{bmatrix} \begin{bmatrix} v_1 \\ v_2 \\ v_3 \end{bmatrix} + \begin{bmatrix} t_1 \\ t_2 \\ t_3 \end{bmatrix} \right) + \begin{bmatrix} t'_1 \\ t'_2 \\ t'_3 \end{bmatrix},$$

where $[\mathbf{R}'\mathbf{S}']$ is another 3×3 matrix that represents the second rotation and scaling transform, and $\mathbf{t}'$ is a column vector representing the second translation.

You can see that even the composition of just two transforms looks complicated—and it is indeed computationally inefficient. It would be very helpful if we could represent each transform—including rotation, scaling, and translation—by a single matrix. And thankfully, we can! The trick is to use a 4×4 matrix and what are called homogeneous coordinates.

Homogeneous coordinates

It turns out that a single 4×4 matrix can be used to represent not only rotations and scaling, but also translations at the same time. The structure of this matrix is

$$\mathbf{M} = \begin{bmatrix} \mathbf{RS} & \mathbf{t} \\ \mathbf{0} & 1 \end{bmatrix} = \begin{bmatrix} rs_{11} & rs_{12} & rs_{13} & t_1 \\ rs_{21} & rs_{22} & rs_{23} & t_2 \\ rs_{31} & rs_{32} & rs_{33} & t_3 \\ 0 & 0 & 0 & 1 \end{bmatrix},$$

where **RS** is the 3×3 matrix for rotation and scaling as above, **t** is the 3×1 translation column vector, and **0** represent a row of three zeros.

In order to be able to use this 4×4 matrix on 3D points, we need to add a fourth value to the 3D points, to convert them to a 4D representation. This fourth coordinate, labeled w, is called the homogeneous coordinate and it always has the value one for points. For vectors in the 4D representation, the value of w is zero.

> **Vectors and Points in the C4 Engine API**
> From the C4 Engine API documentation for the class `Point3D`: "The difference between a point and a vector is that a point is assumed to have a w coordinate of one whenever it needs to be converted to a four-dimensional representation, whereas a vector is assumed to have a w coordinate of zero. Such a conversion occurs when a vector or point is assigned to a `Vector4D` object or is multiplied by a `Transform4D` object."
>
> And for `Vector4D`: "If the `Vector4D` object is constructed using a `Vector3D` object, then the w coordinate is set to zero. If the `Vector4D` object is constructed using a `Point3D` object, then the w coordinate is set to one."

So to rotate, scale, and translate the point with coordinates (x, y, z), we first make it 4D, with $w = 1$, i.e., $(x, y, z, 1)$. We then premultiply it by the 4×4 matrix

$$\mathbf{u} = \begin{bmatrix} \mathbf{RS} & \mathbf{t} \\ \mathbf{0} & 1 \end{bmatrix} \mathbf{v} = \begin{bmatrix} \mathbf{RS} & \mathbf{t} \\ \mathbf{0} & 1 \end{bmatrix} \begin{bmatrix} x \\ y \\ z \\ 1 \end{bmatrix} = \begin{bmatrix} rs_{11} & rs_{12} & rs_{13} & t_1 \\ rs_{21} & rs_{22} & rs_{23} & t_2 \\ rs_{31} & rs_{32} & rs_{33} & t_3 \\ 0 & 0 & 0 & 1 \end{bmatrix} \begin{bmatrix} x \\ y \\ z \\ 1 \end{bmatrix},$$

and the result is

$$\mathbf{u} = \begin{bmatrix} (\mathbf{RS})\mathbf{v} + \mathbf{t} \\ 1 \end{bmatrix} = \begin{bmatrix} \mathbf{u} \\ 1 \end{bmatrix}.$$

This result **u** is the same result we got above, except this time in homogeneous coordinates (with $w = 1$).

Because the composition of transforms is much more efficient when the individual transforms are represented by single 4×4 matrices, these 4×4 matrices are used by the C4 Engine to store both the node and world transforms for all nodes.

Using Vectors and Points for Projectiles

In Chapter 19, "*SimpleEnemies*", we will have a turret on a battleship and the turret will face and fire at the player. Let's take a look at how vectors and points are used for projectiles in this scenario.

The initial direction of the velocity vector of the projectile is the difference between the locations (i.e., the positions) of the player and the turret. Here it is important to use the world positions of the two objects, since the local turret position is only relative to the ship, and not relative to the world origin. Subtracting the turret's local position from the player's local position (which is also the player's world position) would result in a vector pointing in the wrong direction. See Figure 10-5 for an illustration of this concept.

The resulting velocity vector for the projectile would provide us the correct trajectory in a world where there is no gravity. But for worlds like our own which do have gravity, we will need to adjust the z component of the velocity vector in such a way that the projectile reaches the player. It's an interesting problem.

Remember that a vector (in this case the projectile velocity) has a magnitude (in this case the "speed" of the projectile) and a direction (the arrow going from turret to player). It's not enough to specify a speed, because the direction is also needed. And similarly, it's not enough to know the direction; the speed is needed too. For the velocity of the projectile, we need both magnitude and direction, i.e., we need a vector.

We know the distance "as the bird flies", almost directly along the surface of the ocean from turret on the ship, to the player. The question is: Can we calculate the angle of fire and the speed of fire based on that alone? Yes, we can.

Along the x-y plane (i.e., basically along the water), we have

$$distance = speed_{xy} \times time.$$

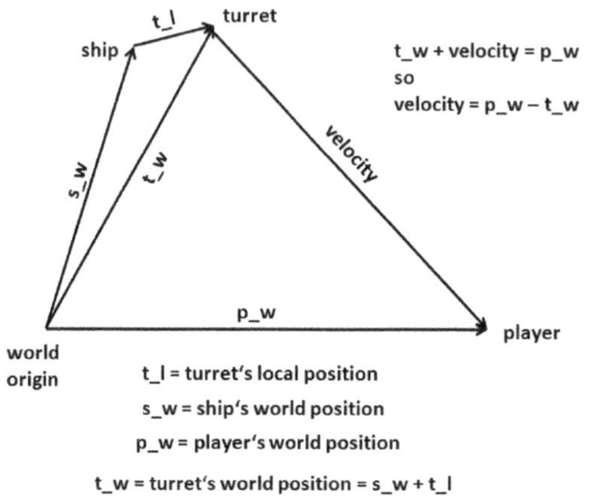

Figure 10-5. The direction of the velocity vector results from the difference of the player and turret world positions, and not their respective local positions.

So

$$time = \frac{distance}{speed_{xy}},$$

where *time* is the time that the projectile will take to get from turret to player. In the *z* direction (i.e., up-down), we have

$$height = speed_z \times time - \frac{1}{2} \times gravity \times time^2$$

Any physics book will explain that formula for you in case you're not familiar with it—you may have seen it written in this notation:

$$d = vt + \frac{1}{2}at^2,$$

where d is distance, t is time, and a is the acceleration of gravity. In our case, the acceleration is due to gravity, and it has a value of approximately (negative) 9.8 meters per second squared.

The projectile will go up and come down again. By the time the projectile comes back down to earth (or in this case down to water!), the height is zero, so we have

$$speed_z = \frac{1}{2} \times gravity \times time,$$

and so

$$speed_z = \frac{gravity \times distance}{2 \times speed_{xy}}.$$

Now, $speed_{xy}$ is the length of the velocity vector in the *x-y* plane, which is

$$speed_{xy} = \sqrt{velocity_x^2 + velocity_y^2},$$

and therefore we have

$$speed_z = \frac{gravity \times distance}{2 \times \sqrt{velocity_x^2 + velocity_y^2}}.$$

As you would expect, the upward speed we need to fire at (which we have called $speed_z$) increases if the distance from turret to player increases, but decreases if the *x-y* plane velocity increases. So you could scale the *x-y* plane velocity by any factor, and work out what the *z* velocity needs to be based on that. And that's exactly what you can do in your code:

```
objectVelocity.z = (distance +
   Math::RandomFloat(100.0F) - 50.0F) /
   Sqrt(objectVelocity.x * objectVelocity.x
      + objectVelocity.y * objectVelocity.y);
```

The `Math::RandomFloat()` function call ensures that the turret doesn't hit the player on every shot. The shots should land just right beside the player most of the time, to scare him or her instead!

Transforms in the C4 Engine

SetNodeTransform() vs SetWorldTransform()

You may run into a case where you know exactly where a node should be in the world, and not in respect to its parent node. If you need this, instead of setting the world transform of a node directly by calling the `SetWorldTransform()` function, call the `SetNodeTransform()` function like this:

```
node->SetNodeTransform(
    node->GetSuperNode()->GetInverseWorldTransform() *
        targetWorldTransform);
```

This looks a bit complicated, so let's see what's going on here.

Let's say we have nodes in our scene graph with the following parent-child relationships:

$$A \to B \to C \to D$$

Here, C is D's parent, B is C's parent and A, the root, is B's parent. The root itself has no parent. D has a node transform, which is the transform—think position, rotation, and scale—of D in C's coordinate system. Let's call it $\mathbf{L}_D$, for local transform.

D also has a world transform, which is the transform of D in the world coordinate system. You might call it D's "absolute" transform. Call it $\mathbf{W}_D$. Now to calculate the world transform of a node, you premultiply the node transform by the world transform of its parent. So for example,

$$\mathbf{W}_D = \mathbf{W}_C \mathbf{L}_D,$$

and that is the key to all of this. This means that to get the world transform of D, you multiply the node transform of D by the world transform of its parent, C. Similarly, $\mathbf{W}_C = \mathbf{W}_B \mathbf{L}_C$, and $\mathbf{W}_B = \mathbf{W}_A \mathbf{L}_B$.

Now, premultiplying both sides by the inverse of $\mathbf{W}_C$—call it $\mathbf{W}_C^{-1}$—gives

$$\mathbf{W}_C^{-1} \mathbf{W}_D = \mathbf{W}_C^{-1} \mathbf{W}_C \mathbf{L}_D = \mathbf{I} \mathbf{L}_D = \mathbf{L}_D,$$

where $\mathbf{I}$ is the 4×4 identity matrix. And that result—$\mathbf{L}_D$, the node transform of D—is what we need to supply to the `SetNodeTransform()` function: $\mathbf{L}_D = \mathbf{W}_C^{-1} \mathbf{W}_D$. This corresponds to

```
node->SetNodeTransform(node->GetSuperNode()
   ->GetInverseWorldTransform() * targetWorldTransform);
```

since

$\mathbf{W}_C$ = `node->GetSuperNode()`

$\mathbf{W}_C^{-1}$ = `node->GetSuperNode()->GetInverseWorldTransform()`

$\mathbf{W}_D$ = `targetWorldTransform`

So just remember that $\mathbf{W}_D = \mathbf{W}_C\mathbf{L}_D$, and premultiply both sides by the inverse of $\mathbf{W}_C$.

You may still be asking, why do I not just simply set the world transform directly? The answer is that the engine calculates the world transforms for us, based on node transforms. If we just set the world transform and didn't correctly set the node transform, then the engine would overwrite our world transform based on the node transform which would no longer be valid. By using this code:

```
node->Invalidate();
```

we tell the engine to do exactly that—i.e., to calculate the new world transform based on the new node transform, in the next traversal of the scene graph.

Orientation

In the Code Snippets [WIKI08.03] section on the C4 Engine Wiki, you can find the following code to orient a node in a particular direction:

```
void OrientToDirection(Node *node, const Point3D& position,
   const Vector3D& direction, const Vector3D& up)
{
   Vector3D front = direction * InverseMag(direction);
   Vector3D left = Cross(up, direction).Normalize();
   Vector3D top = Cross(front, left);

   node->SetNodeTransform(Transform4D(front, left,
      top, position));
}
```

There are often questions on the forums about this code, so let's look at it in some detail.

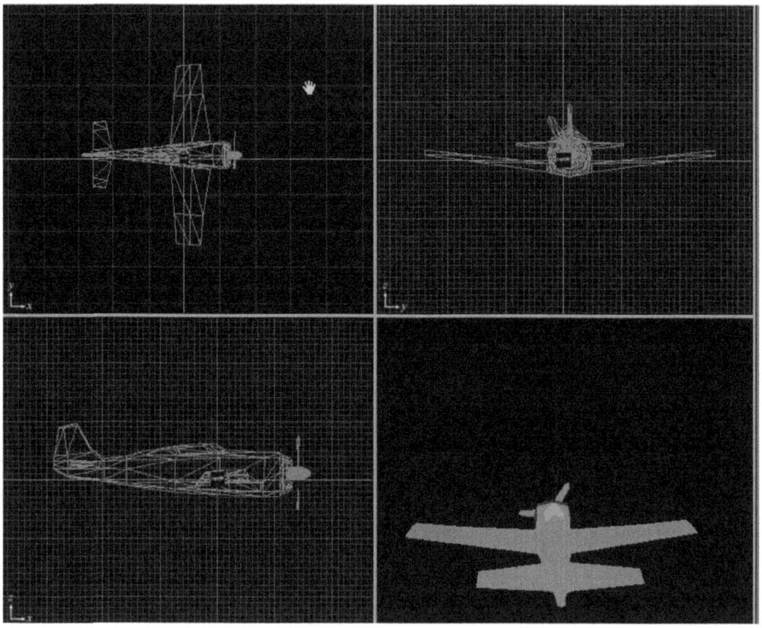

Figure 10-6. An airplane flying along the x axis.

The `OrientToDirection()` function takes node, position, direction, and up parameters. The method then calculates what the node transform of the node needs to be in order to meet your request. Picture a coordinate system, where your model—say an airplane—is placed at the origin $(0,0,0)$ and is flying down along the x axis, as shown in Figure 10-6. Then its "left" wing is along the y axis of this coordinate system. The tail "fin" is pointing along its local z axis—i.e., up for the airplane. So to "dive" the airplane at say 45 degrees, so that the nose of the airplane goes down, you tell the function that the "general up direction" is $(0,0,1)$, but you would pass in a "direction" vector of $(1,0,-1)$, to point the nose 45 degrees down.

So the function first uses the cross product of "direction" $(1,0,-1)$, normalized, and "up" $(0,0,1)$ to find out "left"—which is perpendicular to the up and direction vectors. That result is along the local y axis $(0,1,0)$. It then uses the cross product of "direction" and "left" to calculate the correct local z axis for the plane. And that result is $(1,0,1)$, which is not the same as the general up direction $(0,0,1)$ when the airplane is diving.

Note that position—which is the fourth column of the transform—just offsets (or translates) the result to the point "position". Note also that the `SetNode-`

`Transform()` function is used here, which will result in setting the world position and orientation only if the node is a direct child of the root. Again, to set the world transform if the node is not a direct child of root, you will again need to use

```
node->SetNodeTransform(node->GetSuperNode()
   ->GetInverseWorldTransform() * targetWorldTransform);
```

Why does this work?

We might ask the question: why is it that the correct transform matrix results from using normalized (mutually perpendicular) vectors in the order (front, left, top), for the columns of the 3×3 part of the matrix? Imagine a 3×3 matrix $\mathbf{T}$ that represents a rotation and/or scale. Say $\mathbf{T}$ is the matrix with columns

$$\mathbf{T} = \begin{bmatrix} t_{11} & t_{12} & t_{13} \\ t_{21} & t_{22} & t_{23} \\ t_{31} & t_{32} & t_{33} \end{bmatrix}.$$

Then the effect of $\mathbf{T}$ on a unit column vector along the x axis is:

$$\mathbf{T}\begin{bmatrix} 1 \\ 0 \\ 0 \end{bmatrix} = \begin{bmatrix} t_{11} & t_{12} & t_{13} \\ t_{21} & t_{22} & t_{23} \\ t_{31} & t_{32} & t_{33} \end{bmatrix}\begin{bmatrix} 1 \\ 0 \\ 0 \end{bmatrix} = \begin{bmatrix} t_{11} \\ t_{21} \\ t_{31} \end{bmatrix},$$

which is the same as the first column of the transform matrix $\mathbf{T}$.

Similarly, multiplying by $(0,1,0)$ and $(0,0,1)$ results in the second and third columns of the matrix $\mathbf{T}$ respectively:

$$\mathbf{T}\begin{bmatrix} 0 \\ 1 \\ 0 \end{bmatrix} = \begin{bmatrix} t_{11} & t_{12} & t_{13} \\ t_{21} & t_{22} & t_{23} \\ t_{31} & t_{32} & t_{33} \end{bmatrix}\begin{bmatrix} 0 \\ 1 \\ 0 \end{bmatrix} = \begin{bmatrix} t_{12} \\ t_{22} \\ t_{32} \end{bmatrix}$$

$$\mathbf{T}\begin{bmatrix} 0 \\ 0 \\ 1 \end{bmatrix} = \begin{bmatrix} t_{11} & t_{12} & t_{13} \\ t_{21} & t_{22} & t_{23} \\ t_{31} & t_{32} & t_{33} \end{bmatrix}\begin{bmatrix} 0 \\ 0 \\ 1 \end{bmatrix} = \begin{bmatrix} t_{13} \\ t_{23} \\ t_{33} \end{bmatrix}.$$

Basis Vectors

Before we move on, we'll note that these unit vectors—i.e., $(1,0,0)$, $(0,1,0)$, and $(0,0,1)$—are called *basis vectors*, since all other vectors in the 3D space can be made by a linear combination of the basis vectors. They are often called, **i**, **j**, and **k**, respectively.

As an arbitrary example, the vector $(3,-4,19)$ is

$$3(1,0,0)-4(0,1,0)+19(0,0,1)=3\mathbf{i}-4\mathbf{j}+19\mathbf{k},$$

which is a linear combination of **i**, **j**, and **k**. Front, left, and top from the examples in this section also "form a basis" for the space.

Generally speaking, if you can find three mutually perpendicular (orthogonal) vectors, then they will form a basis for 3D space. If the elements of a basis are mutually orthogonal and are of unit length, as in these examples, then the basis is said to be an orthonormal basis.

When You Know What You Need

If you know in advance the effect the matrix should have on these *x*, *y*, and *z* unit vectors, then you can simply place those results into the columns of the transform matrix.

Let's assume our model faces along the *x* direction, and we want to dive by 45 degrees to $(1,0,-1)$, which when normalized, is approximately $(0.707,0,-0.707)$. So with a sheet of paper, you can easily see that the effect on $(1,0,0)$ should be to produce $(0.707,0,-0.707)$, forming the first column. The effect on $(0,1,0)$ is to leave it unchanged at $(0,1,0)$, forming the second column and the effect on $(0,0,1)$ is to make $(1,0,1)$, which normalized is approximately $(0.707,0,0.707)$, forming the third column.

So without doing all the cross products, the resulting 4×4 transform matrix should turn out to be

$$\begin{bmatrix} 0.707 & 0.0 & 0.707 & P_x \\ 0.0 & 1.0 & 0.0 & P_y \\ -0.707 & 0.0 & 0.707 & P_z \\ 0.0 & 0.0 & 0.0 & 1.0 \end{bmatrix}.$$

Now double-check this, using the code above. Diving down 45 degrees from the *x* axis, the direction is $(1,0,-1)$ and so the front vector is calculated as:

```
// results in front = (0.707, 0, -0.707)
Vector3D front = direction * InverseMag(direction);
```

since $1/\sqrt{2} \approx 0.707$. The `InverseMag(direction)` call simply calculates one divided by the magnitude, or norm, of the `direction` vector. The left vector is calculated as:

```
// results in left = (0, 1, 0)
Vector3D left = Cross(up, direction).Normalize();
```

since $(0,0,1)\times(1,0,-1)=(0,1,0)$, which has length one and is the unit vector along the y axis. And the top vector is calculated as:

```
// results in (0.707, 0, 0.707)
Vector3D top = Cross(front, left);
```

since $(0.707,0,-0.707)\times(0,1,0)=(0.707,0,0.707)$, which is $(1,0,1)$ normalized.

The 4×4 transform is then made up of the columns (front, left, top, position):

$$\begin{bmatrix} 0.707 & 0.0 & 0.707 & P_x \\ 0.0 & 1.0 & 0.0 & P_y \\ -0.707 & 0.0 & 0.707 & P_z \\ 0.0 & 0.0 & 0.0 & 1.0 \end{bmatrix}.$$

And voila! This is the same result we obtained by creating the matrix "manually", by checking the effects of the transform on basis vectors.

The take-away is that if you can figure out the effect of your transform on the basis vectors—**i**, **j**, and **k**—then you immediately have the columns of your transform matrix. That's exactly what this code is doing.

Code Example of a C4 Engine Transform

If you still have doubts about this, it might help to rotate objects in the **World Editor**, and see the numbers in the transform for yourself. Add these lines to the method `TransformPage::HandleRotationTextEvent()`, which is in the file `C4EditorPages.cpp`, just after the following line:

```
node->SetNodeMatrix3D(Matrix3D().SetEulerAngles(x, y, z));
```

Add the following code:

```
Vector3D firstColumn = node->GetNodeTransform()[0];
Vector3D secondColumn = node->GetNodeTransform()[1];
Vector3D thirdColumn = node->GetNodeTransform()[2];

String<100> outputString = "";
Engine::Report(outputString);

outputString.Append(Text::FloatToString(firstColumn.x), 6);
outputString.Append(" | ", 3);
outputString.Append(Text::FloatToString(secondColumn.x), 6);
outputString.Append(" | ", 3);
outputString.Append(Text::FloatToString(thirdColumn.x), 6);
Engine::Report(outputString);

outputString = "";
outputString.Append(Text::FloatToString(firstColumn.y), 6);
outputString.Append(" | ", 3);
outputString.Append(Text::FloatToString(secondColumn.y), 6);
outputString.Append(" | ", 3);
outputString.Append(Text::FloatToString(thirdColumn.y), 6);
Engine::Report(outputString);

outputString = "";
outputString.Append(Text::FloatToString(firstColumn.z), 6);
outputString.Append(" | ", 3);
outputString.Append(Text::FloatToString(secondColumn.z), 6);
outputString.Append(" | ", 3);
outputString.Append(Text::FloatToString(thirdColumn.z), 6);
Engine::Report(outputString);
```

About GetNodeTransform()

If you check the C4 Engine API, you will see that the `Node::GetNodeTransform()` function returns a reference to a `Transform4D` object:

```
http://www.terathon.com/c4engine/doco/WorldMgr/Node_GetNode
Transform.html
```

The C4 Engine API also specifies that `node->GetNodeTransform()[i]` returns the *i*-th column of the 3×3 portion of the 4×4 node transform matrix.

We encourage you to check it out here—scroll down to the first of the "Overloaded Operators":

```
http://www.terathon.com/c4engine/doco/Math/Transform4D.html
```

This code will display the 3×3 portion of the node transform in the **Command Console** window, whenever you use the **Transform** page of the **World Editor** to rotate an object. To test this code, open up the Water world, located in the Data/Tutorial/world/ directory, and save the world under a different name, such as Transform. Remove all page panels on the left side of the **World Editor** window, except for the **Geometry** and **Transform** panels, by clicking the close button of each one.

Move the **World Editor** window slightly to the right to make room for the **Command Console** window. If it's not already visible, open the **Command Console** window by choosing **Tools > Command Console** (or by pressing the tilde/grave key). Now click back on the **World Editor** window to make it active, and use the **Geometry** panel to draw a cylinder (or post) in the top (x-y) viewport. Use the scale tool to stretch it to be about the height of the other geometries of the world in the right (x-z) viewport. Use the **Transform** page panel to rotate the post by 45 degrees around the y axis, as shown in Figure 10-7. Note that the 3×3 matrix, which is written to the **Command Console** window, has the same values you calculated above.

Application of Orientation Code

One good application of all this is when trying to create the correct transform for a node (say for an airplane) which is following a parameterized 3D curved path. Let's call the path **X**. For a given value of the parameter t (with t between 0 and 1), $\mathbf{X}(t)$ defines a 3D point on the curve:

$$\mathbf{X}(t) = (x(t), y(t), z(t))$$

Now the tangent for any value of t along the path is the rate of change with respect to the parameter t, i.e., $d\mathbf{X}/dt$. And this corresponds to the direction vector, which when normalized, we will call "front". So

$$tangent = \frac{d\mathbf{X}}{dt},$$

and

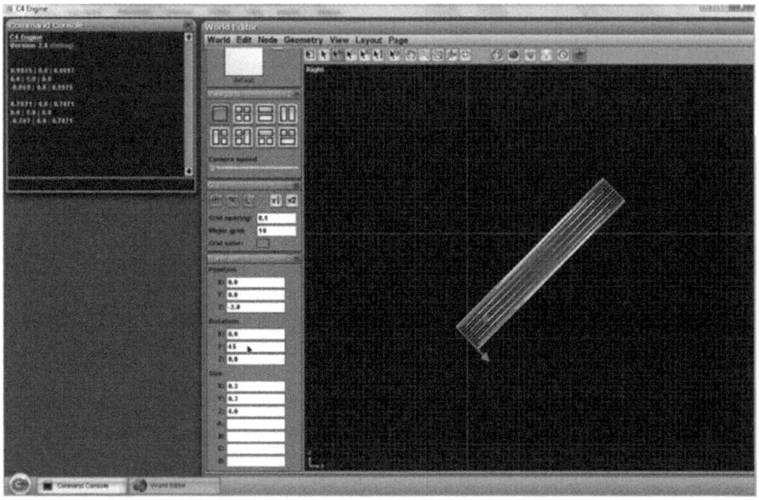

Figure 10-7. Writing the 3×3 part of a transform matrix to the **Command Console** window.

```
front = tangent.normalize();
```

If you didn't want to have the plane bank while it was turning, you would choose the "up" vector to be $(0,0,1)$, i.e., the same as the up direction in the world space. And the left vector would be `Cross(up, front)`, i.e., a vector perpendicular to both front and up. To be sure that "up" for the airplane, (or its "top"), is orthogonal to the other two basis vectors, use

```
top = Cross(front, left);
```

You will probably have discretely sampled your curve, so the calculation of the tangent can use those precalculated points

$$tangent(n) = \frac{curvepoint(n+1) - curvepoint(n)}{stepDistance}$$

Note that this dividing factor, *stepDistance*, is not really needed, as we would normalize the result of the division anyway.

Another use of this orientation code is for calculating the 3×3 matrix portion of the transform for a node which represents a turret gun that needs to continuously track and aim at the player. The direction vector is the player's position minus the turret's position, and since up will be the general up direction for the world, $(0,0,1)$, that is all you need to calculate the orientation matrix.

Next Steps

We'll use some code that is similar to this orientation code later on, when we change a turret's transform to track a player which is moving, in the game tutorial described in Chapter 19, "SimpleEnemies".

11

Scene Graph Traversal

The C4 Engine scene graph describes the relationships between all of the nodes that are contained in your world. The scene graph changes as nodes in your world do things. And for nodes to do things, you have to describe what they do in code. But first, you have to find the node, as explained in this chapter.

Why Do I Need to Traverse the scene graph?

In Part II • Designing Worlds, we touched on the scene graph when it is viewed in a viewport in the **World Editor**. When writing the code for your C4 Engine-based application, you will commonly need to gain access to the nodes in your scene graph. This access is useful for changing node hierarchies, by reparenting nodes to different super nodes or simply shifting their order. Accessing the scene graph also allows you to add and remove nodes to your scene. Most importantly, being able to navigate the scene graph in code allows you to find a node and edit its behaviors by accessing its properties, connectors, controllers, and other custom public attributes.

Where to Make the Calls

Scene graph traversal functions have to be called after the scene graph has already been initialized. The most common place to reliably start doing any calls on the scene graph is in the `Preprocess()` and `Move()` functions in your `World` subclass as well as those in your custom controllers. This is where you would typically reparent nodes, add or remove nodes, or edit nodes.

Node Types

Since the C4 Engine provides so many node types (not to mention all of the custom nodes that you may create), you will frequently have to find out what type of node you are dealing with, and then cast that node to the specific subclass based on its type. Here are some snippets of code that you will commonly see for casting a node to its specific subclass:

```
if (node->GetNodeType() == kNodeGeometry)
{
   Geometry *geometry = static_cast<Geometry *>(node);
}

if (node->GetNodeType() == kNodeModel)
{
   Model *model = static_cast<Model *>(node);
}
```

After casting a node to its subclass, you have the freedom to call any public functions and access any public variables available to that subclass.

Full Scene Traversal

The code snippet on the C4 Engine Wiki called "Iterating over World Nodes"[1] illustrates how to do a full traversal on the scene graph:

```
// Start at the root.
Node *root = TheWorldMgr->GetWorld()->GetRootNode();
Node *node = root;
do
{
    if (node->GetNodeType() == kNodeGeometry)
    {
        // Do something with a geometry node.
    }
```

[1] http://www.terathon.com/wiki/index.php/Iterating_over_World_Nodes

```
    node = root->GetNextNode(node);
} while (node);
```

You can get the root node of the world, and initialize an "iterator" node, as shown in the code snippet. Notice the use of the function `GetNextNode()`, which is a function of the `Node` class. This usage is reassigning node to the next node. But what determines the "next Node?"

Remember from the first section of this chapter, we mentioned that the scene graph is logically structured like a tree, where each node has any number of subnodes beneath it. The `GetNextNode()` function does a depth-first search which means this function will attempt to traverse to the first subnode and its siblings, if any subnodes exist. The search will attempt to go as deep into the tree as possible, until the search reaches any node that has no subnodes. Otherwise, the function traverses to the next sibling node and its subnodes if it has any. If there are no more sibling nodes, the function traverses to the next supernode and its subnodes, and so on, as shown in the node containment hierarchy in Figure 11-1.

It may not look exactly like the scene graph that you know from the **World Editor** scene graph viewport (this graph is laid out in the more traditional "tree" sense), but as we mentioned in the first chapter of the section, hierarchal tree data like this can be represented in many ways, including as source code which we are now discussing! The numbers above each representation of a node in the figure indicate the run order in a depth-first search traversal of the scene graph.

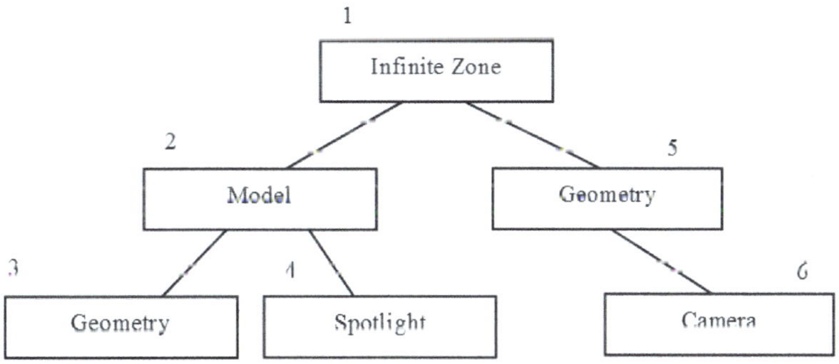

Figure 11-1. The `GetNextNode()` traversal does a depth-first search into the subtree whose root is the node that calls this function.

So, that was a long detour of an explanation on what's going on behind the scenes with the `GetNextNode()` function. The function will return `nullptr` if it cannot find any more nodes that belong to the root node. This is how the above code visits all nodes in the scene graph.

Typically, iterating through the entire scene graph is done in the `Preprocess()` function of your `World` subclass to perform any necessary initialization of the world or of the nodes. It would not be practical to run a traversal on the entire scene graph in the `Move()` function of a controller or world, simply because the `Move()` function is called on each cycle of the main game loop. It could potentially be doing a lot more work than is necessary during a time-critical section of code.

Accessing the World during Preprocess()

When calling the `Preprocess()` function in your custom controllers, you may have a need to access the world that the controller's target node is a part of. If you use `TheWorldMgr` singleton instance, it is likely that it will return `nullptr` instead of the world that you need. This is because this pointer is not set yet. To get a pointer to the world that you are working with, call `GetTargetNode()` from your controller, and once you have a pointer to the node, you can call `GetWorld()`.

We already know from the previous few chapters, that the root node is the infinite zone of the world. We can verify this by putting the following code in the do...while loop of the full scene traversal code above:

```
bool isInfiniteZone = false;
if (node->GetNodeType() == kNodeZone)
{
    Zone *zone = static_cast<Zone *>(node);
    if ((zone) && (zone->GetZoneType() == kZoneInfinite))
    {
        isInfiniteZone = true;
    }
}
```

If you run this code, you will find that `isInfiniteZone` would be set to true in the first pass of the do...while loop. The C4 Engine `Node` subclasses often contain subtypes of their own as seen by this example. In the code just shown, notice that after casting node to its `Zone` subclass, the zone has its own zone type, which is `kZoneInfinite`. This is the typical technique for "drilling down" to the specific subclass of a node type.

Partial Traversals

As your world gets more complex, your scene graph will obviously get larger. As you start to work with a larger scene graph, you will have to find ways of more efficiently iterating through your node hierarchy to get the exact node that you want.

In the previous example, we grabbed the root node of the world and traversed the entire scene graph. It is also possible (and more practical) to just traverse parts of the scene graph, as illustrated in Figure 11-2, and you already used one of the functions that can do this! Since `GetNextNode()` is a member function of the `Node` class, the call to this function is in relation to this node. That means the node for which the `GetNextNode()` function is called is actually the root node of the subtree in the scene graph. This function returns the node that follows the one that you pass into the function as a parameter, based on the depth-first search explained above.

A common use case for traversing down a subtree of the scene graph is modifying all `Geometry` nodes that are parented to a `Model` node.

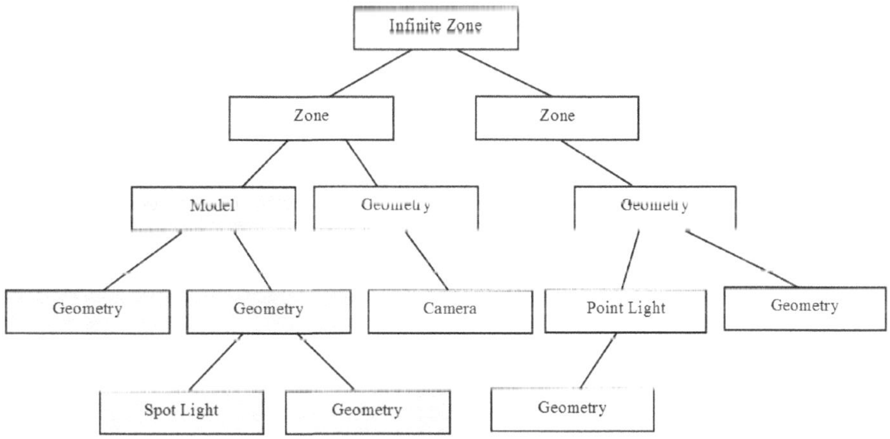

Figure 11-2. Calling `GetNextNode()` on a subnode of the scene graph will allow you to traverse just a part of the scene graph.

```
// myModel is a pre-existing node in the scene graph.
Model *rootModel = myModel;
Node *traversalNode = rootModel;

while (traversalNode)
{
   if (traversalNode->GetNodeType() == kNodeGeometry)
   {
      // Do something with the geometry node.
   }

   traversalNode = rootModel->GetNextNode(traversalNode);
}
```

Of course, this requires you to have already had access to the `myModel` node. You can simply save a pointer to that model during the `Preprocess()` function of your `World` subclass.

Drilling Down Further

We've seen that with the node traversal functions and node types, we are able to find a node of a specific type in the scene graph. There is a chance that you may need something more granular than that. Perhaps one of the nodes in a model needs special attention, such as being able to change the emission value or rotation independently of the other nodes.

A quick way of distinguishing a specific node from others with that same node type is checking the node's name. You can do this by calling the function `GetNodeName()` from any node. It returns a `const char *` that you can use to check against another string. In the scene graph subtree shown in Figure 11-3, a model has four spot light nodes and one geometry node as immediate subnodes. One of the spot lights has the name "rotatorspot."

```
// myModel is a pre-existing node in the scene graph.
Model *model = myModel;
Node *iteratorNode = model->GetFirstSubnode();

while (iteratorNode)
{
```

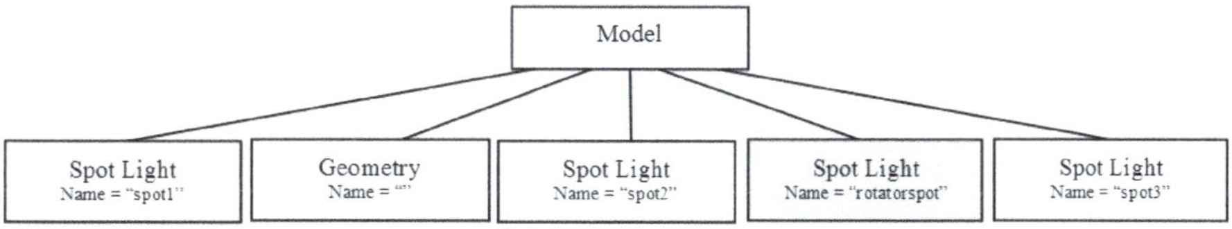

Figure 11-3. Subtree of a model node that has five subnodes, one of which has the name "rotatorspot."

```
    if (iteratorNode->GetNodeType() == kNodeLight)
    {
        // This is definitely a light.

        const char *name = iteratorNode->GetNodeName();
        if ((name) && (Text::CompareText(name, "rotatorspot")))
        {
            // Do something with this light.
        }
    }

    iteratorNode = iteratorNode->Next();
    // Next()? What does that do? Keep reading...
}
```

Upon entering the while loop, we check if the node has the `kNodeLight` type. If it does, we can go ahead and check if the node name matches "rotator-spot". We could have easily skipped the node type check and just searched the node name, but it would generally be faster to check the unsigned long node type as opposed to the character string of indeterminate length. It's not a big deal for small subtrees like this, but for larger scenes, it is best to narrow down your choices as soon as possible to prevent unnecessary node traversals.

You may notice that the `Next()` function is used to go to the next node instead of the `GetNextNode()` function. This is a function of the `Tree` class from which nodes are derived. The `Next()` function will simply go to the next sibling node of the common supernode, whereas `GetNextNode()` is used to traverse an entire tree or subtree.

A more complex method for distinguishing specific types of nodes is creating settings or public attributes that contain information specific to the node that you really want. We discuss how to add settings and other public attributes to your controllers and other configurable objects in Chapter 14, "Configurable Settings" and Chapter 15, "The Controller". Instead of checking the node name, you can check if one of the settings or public attributes holds a particular value.

Adding and Removing Nodes

You will more than likely need to add, remove, and move nodes from one supernode (parent) to another during the run of your application. Here are some common examples in which this may be needed:

- A character picks up a weapon and the weapon is now in the hand of the character.
- A bullet is shot out of a gun and hits a wall or character.
- Tentacles from a large octopus pick up and flail around your teammates.
- A track runner passes a baton to the next track runner.

Each of these examples will require you to add a node to the scene graph. Let's take the track runner example and look at some code to get a baton passed on to a second runner.

```
// modelNode1 is a pre-existing node in the scene graph.
Model *runner1 = modelNode1;
Model *baton = Model::Get(kModelBaton);
runner1->AddNewSubnode(baton);
```

For this example, we are assuming we already have a `modelNode1` model in the scene, which was probably placed in the world using the **World Editor**, and that we have `kModelBaton` defined and registered somewhere. The code above can be placed in the `Preprocess()` function of your `World` subclass to initialize baton in code. You can see that we are creating a new instance of the baton model, and that it is also not part of the scene graph at this point. We add it to the scene graph by calling `runner1->AddNewSubnode(baton)`.

There is a function called `AddSubnode()`, but we are using the `AddNewSubnode()` function here because it performs the `Preprocess()` step for the new node, baton, since it is a newly created node. Conversely, the `AddSubnode()` function is used for nodes that do not need to be initialized, as in the following code which may be contained in the `Move()` function of a world or controller:

```
// modelNode1 is the same node referred to earlier.
Model *runner1 = modelNode1;

// modelNode2 is a pre-existing node in the scene graph.
Model *runner2 = modelNode2;

runner1->RemoveSubnode(baton);
runner2->AddSubnode(baton);
```

The baton has already been initialized and in fact, it was already part of the scene graph. In this code, we assume that `modelNode2` is already in the scene graph as `modelNode1` was.

Before we add the node to `runner2`, we remove baton from its supernode, `runner1`. It is not necessary to remove a node from its supernode before reparenting it to a different supernode in the scene graph because `AddSubnode()` does this automatically for you, but we are explicitly removing the node here to illustrate the usage of the `RemoveSubnode()` function.

Other Traversal Functions

An important aspect of the scene graph is that every node in it is (indirectly) derived from the `Tree` class. This means that the `Node` class has more than just the functions that we've discussed in this chapter regarding scene traversal. You can refer to the API documentation for the `Tree` class[2] to see the full list of functions that can be used by a `Node` to traverse the scene graph (and it is a rather exhaustive list). You will find functions such as `GetSuperNode()`, `GetRootNode()`, `GetLastSubnode()`, `MoveSubtree()`, and many more.

Conclusion

You will find that in order to write any of your game code that actually "does stuff" in the game, you will have to find the nodes to "do the stuff" on. Traversing the scene graph can quickly get monotonous and at times confusing if you are not fully familiar with what is going on with your scene graph, but ultimately, it is rewarding to be able to identify the nodes that you want, so that you can finally perform the game functionality that you want with them.

[2] http://www.terathon.com/c4engine/doco/Utilities/Tree.html

12

Serialization

The C4 Engine serialization system is used for saving and loading data by a number of classes, such as nodes, properties, controllers, methods, and functions. You can also use the serialization system to save and load data for your own custom classes.

Packing and Unpacking

In the next few chapters we will be visiting some of the key areas of C4 Engine development and we will need an example to work towards. We will be developing an example controller called `MyShotController`. The next three chapters cover the various concepts of the class and finally we will create the controller. We will also be working with the **SimpleChar** project and selecting the controller from the **Node Info** dialog in the **World Editor**.

Serialization data is usually stored in `.wld` (world) or `.mdl` (model) files in your project. For example, when a world file is saved in the **World Editor**, the data is serialized and saved in the `.wld` file, and when the `.wld` file is loaded back in again, the saved data is deserialized back into the **World Editor**.

The C4 Engine manages serialization through the `Packable` class. This class contains two key virtual functions: `Pack()` and `Unpack()`. There are also a couple of other functions that can be used, although not key, they are required to reset variables that are set but undone after a save, they are `BeginSettingsUnpack()` and `EndSettingsUnpack()`, called before the settings are iterated through and afterwards respectively.

Some of the main classes in the C4 Engine, such as the `Controller` class, inherit from the `Packable` class, and utilize the `Pack()` and `Unpack()` functions.

- `Pack()` is used for storing data, in preparation for it to be saved out to the hard drive. This process is called *serialization.*
- `Unpack()` is used for retrieving data that was stored with the `Pack()` function. This process is called *deserialization.*
- `BeginSettingsUnpack()` is used for initializing variables prior to unpacking them.

Naturally, the data you store via the `Pack()` function matches the data loaded via the `Unpack()` function, for every class that implements `Packable`. (If this matching is not maintained, be prepared for undefined behavior.)

Let's work with the example `Controller` subclass called `MyShotController` that implements the `Packable` class functions. (We can do this because the `Controller` class itself already derives from the `Packable` class). We will be building on the `MyShotController` class throughout the next few chapters.

To use the serialization capabilities in a class that inherits from `Packable`, it is first necessary to declare the two public functions mentioned earlier, `Pack()` and `Unpack()`:

```
void Pack(Packer& data, unsigned_int32 packFlags) const;
void Unpack(Unpacker& data, unsigned_int32 unpackFlags);
```

For this example we declare six private attributes:

```
float           gravity;
int32           noOfShots;
ResourceName    shotSound;
bool            playSound;
ColorRGBA       shotColor;
AttributeType   shotType;
```

Next, within the two functions in the main body of code it is necessary to call the same function from the super class, so that all data from the super classes is serialized correctly. At the very least, this will get you the same result as if you added nothing else to serialize. Then, the custom serialization code can be written afterward.

```
void MyShotController::Pack(Packer& data,
   unsigned int32 packFlags) const
{
   Controller::Pack(data, packFlags);

   // Custom serialization code goes here.
}

void MyShotController::Unpack(Unpacker& data,
   unsigned_int32 unpackFlags)
{
   Controller::Unpack(data, unpackFlags);

   // Custom deserialization code goes here.
}
```

At the simplest level, using the C4 Engine serialization support involves outputting each attribute one at a time, as shown in this excerpt from a `Pack()` function:

```
data << gravity;
data << noOfShots;
data << shotSound;
data << playSound;
data << shotColor;
data << shotType;
```

As shown above, we output the contents of all of the variables into a serial data stream named data.

The opposite process happens in the `Unpack()` function:

```
data >> gravity;
data >> noOfShots;
data >> shotSound;
data >> playSound;
data >> shotColor;
data >> shotType;
```

Here, we take the serial data and read it back into the variables. (The streaming operator knows the expected size of each variable, so the deserialization process knows how much data to read from the data stream.)

When you serialize and deserialize data like we did above, the syntax looks very straightforward, and most of the time, keeping track of the sizes of each variable is taken for granted.

Problems can arise though when you need to add more attributes to the class at a later stage, for example, adding a new attribute to the `Pack()` and `Unpack()` functions will throw an error loading worlds previously saved without this attribute. This happens because the data being deserialized does not contain the new attribute. Unpacking the data stream moves through the data one attribute at a time (based upon the size of each attribute). When it gets to the end of the previously saved stream, there is still the new attribute to populate and no data to retrieve—the C4 Engine will throw an error at this point.

There is an easier way to deal with adding new attributes to existing controllers, through the use of chunks.

Chunks

In the previous scenario, the contents of the serialized data were different from the data the code was expecting to deserialize. We can prevent this problem by making the packing system more robust with chunks. A chunk is simply a section of data that has a chunk header, containing a chunk type and the length of the data in the chunk.

When using chunks, the deserialization function iterates through the chunk headers and checks if the chunk type matches the type we are looking for, skipping over any types that we do not want to use. This approach gives far more flexibility to add and remove attributes from the serialization process.

Prior to version 2.8, the sizes of the variables that are being serialized needed to be added to the `ChunkHeader`. Follow these general guidelines for basic data types. First, it is essential to align the sizes of the data types to multiples of four bytes. Generally, you can find the size of a data type using `sizeof(datatype)`, which works with most of data types apart from `bool`, because the C4 Engine serializes the `bool` data type using four bytes.

For some data types however, you needed to use other ways of returning the size. For example, the size of a `ResourceName` can be ascertained using `Packer::GetStringSize(resourceName)`. (`GetStringSize()` has been deprecated as of version 2.8)

In version 2.8 this has now changed and sizes do not need to be calculated beforehand. The functions `BeginChunk()` and `EndChunk()` can be used for each chunk and size is automatically calculated. In the example below and the included code, both methods, version 2.8 and pre version 2.8 are being used if possible so that you can see how to transition your code to version 2.8. As noted earlier anywhere you used `GetStringSize()` you will have to use the new `BeginChunk()` and `EndChunk()` functions.

First, we'll look at modifying the `Pack()` function to write out chunks. We'll put some of the previous data into a chunk called `'defa'` for default attributes and will use the pre version 2.8 method of calculating the `ChuckHeader` size. This is where the sizes of the variables come into play. For the first chunk notice that we pass in the size of the chunk, which is the size of one float, one long, one `ColorRGBA`, and one `AttributeType`.

We will also add a second chunk labeled `'soun'`, which contains the sound attributes, a `ResourceName` and a `bool`. This chunk must use the new version 2.8 `BeginChunk()` and `EndChunk()` functions to automatically calculate size.

```
void MyShotController::Pack(Packer& data,
   unsigned int32 packFlags) const
{
   Controller::Pack(data, packFlags);

   data << ChunkHeader('defa', 4 + 4 + sizeof(ColorRGBA)
      + sizeof(AttributeType));
   data << gravity;
   data << noOfShots;
   data << shotColor;
   data << shotType;

   if (shotSound[0] != 0)
   {
      PackHandle handle = data.BeginChunk('soun');
      data << shotSound;
      data << playSound;
      data.EndChunk(handle);
   }

   data << TerminatorChunk;
}
```

Now we can look at how to deserialize the data using the Unpack() function. We will need to set up a couple of new functions to help with this; BeginSettingsUnpack() and UnpackChunk().

Declare a new public function called `BeginSettingsUnpack()` that will initialize the `ResourceName` variable if undo is called to revert any settings.

```
void *MyShotController::BeginSettingsUnpack(void)
{
   shotSound[0] = 0;

   return (Controller::BeginSettingsUnpack());
}
```

Declare a new public function called `UnpackChunk()`:

```
bool UnpackChunk(const ChunkHeader *chunkHeader, Unpacker& data,
   unsigned_int32 unpackFlags);
```

Now, the `Unpack()` function will look a little different. Instead of simply reading in the data per variable, we call the template function `UnpackChunkList()`, passing in the data and `unpackFlags`, as we did in the `Unpack()` function, but also passing in a function pointer to a new function defined in our `Controller` subclass. Here, it is called `UnpackChunk()`:

```
void MyShotController::Unpack(Unpacker& data,
   unsigned int32 unpackFlags)
{
   Controller::Unpack(data, unpackFlags);
   UnpackChunkList<MyShotController>(data, unpackFlags);
}
```

Here is the definition of the `UnpackChunk()` function:

```
bool WeaponController::UnpackChunk(const ChunkHeader *chunkHeader,
   Unpacker &data, unsigned int32 unpackFlags)
{
   switch (chunkHeader->chunkType)
```

```
    {
        case 'defa':

            data >> gravity;
            data >> noOfShots;
            data >> shotColor;
            data >> shotType;
            return (true);

        case 'soun':

            data >> shotSound;
            data >> playSound;
            return (true);
    }

    return (false);
}
```

You can see that we've changed the `Unpack()` functionality and moved it into `UnpackChunk()`, which contains a switch statement that checks the chunk type before deserializing the data inside the chunk. This structure prevents any problems if you need to add any more chunk types to the serialization code for your controllers, because the deserialization process simply skips over any chunks for which the chunk type is not recognized. What you cannot do easily though is create another attribute inside an existing chunk.

FAQs

I want to add another attribute to an existing chunk but don't want to create a new chunk, what can I do?

The easiest way to do this is to comment out the whole switch statement in the `UnpackChunk()` function where the new attribute will reside and add the new attribute to the Pack function.

Next, open all of the world and model files that contain the controller in question and save them. They will now contain the new attribute, and all of the other attributes in that chunk will have been reset to their default values.

Finally, uncomment the case statement and add the new attribute. The world and model files will now open successfully.

I have a world file that crashes on Unpack every time I open it but am unsure what Controller is causing this, what can I do?

The only way to do this is through a process of elimination. Start by locating all of your custom controller code, and comment out the code in each `Unpack()` function.

Next, load the world to see if your custom controller caused the crash. It is labor-intensive, but at least you can save most of the work in the world file. Once the world is opened, save the file and uncomment the commented code, after which the world should open successfully.

You could set breakpoints on every controller, but if you have hundreds of controllers active, it could take a long time to find the offending one.

13

Using String Tables

The C4 Engine provides support for string tables, which you can use to store visible user interface strings separately from your code. String tables enable you to easily localize a game for different markets, by reducing the amount of time needed to change visible UI strings and test the results. By using string tables, you will no longer need to rebuild projects when text needs to be changed.

Text vs Binary

String tables allow you to store all of your UI strings in a separate file and load them when they are needed. Whenever the string text needs to be changed, you can then update the text file instead of your source code.

Reading text files during runtime can be slow, and so the C4 Engine provides a **String Importer** tool that converts text files into a binary format, which the C4 Engine `StringTable` class can load more quickly.

Throughout this chapter, we will incrementally setup a string table for use in the controller called `MyShotController`, which we first looked at in Chapter 12, "Serialization". We'll complete the implementation of the `MyShotController` class in Chapter 14, "Configurable Settings", and Chapter 15, "The Controller".

Declaring the String Table

For this example, we will add a new string table member variable declaration to the Game class.

1 Open up `SimpleChar.h` and locate the `Game` class.

2 Add the following code after the access specifier keyword `private`.

```
private:
   const StringTable myStringTable;
```

We have named the new string table `myStringTable`.

3 Add the public accessor for the string table, as shown in the following code after the public `Game` constructor and destructor.

```
Game();
~Game();

const StringTable *GetMyStringTable(void) const
{
   return (&myStringTable);
}
```

`myStringTable` needs to be initialized upon class construction, which will happen in the `Game` class constructor.

4 Open `SimpleChar.cpp` for editing, and add the following code to the constructor underneath the existing string table initialization. The `Singleton` code has been left in for reference. `myStringTable` is initialized with the location of the file that is going to be used, the path name uses the virtual file system naming convention, so the Data/<Subdirectory>/ has been removed for the path.

```
Singleton<Game>(TheGame), myStringTable("game/MyStrings"),
```

The extension used for string table files is `.str`. We will be using the directory Data/Demo/game/ to store our string table file. But there is a problem straight away, as we have referenced a binary file in the Data directory that does not yet exist. If you compile and run C4, the engine will throw an exception when it cannot find the referenced string table `myStringTable`.

5 Set a breakpoint in the constructor and step through the code to watch this happen, as shown in Figure 13-1. The stack trace will look something like Figure 13-2.

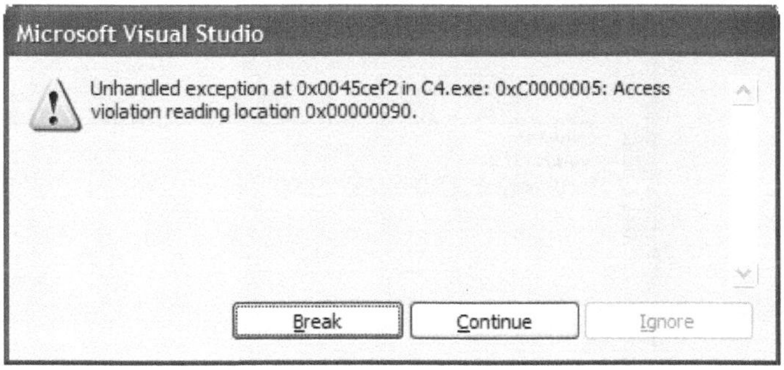

Figure 13-1. Error running C4 without the string table file available in the Data directory. Note that we are running in debug mode.

6 Until we can rectify this situation, comment out the `myStringTable` declaration, the `GetMyStringTable()` accessor function, and the initialization code, and recompile the project. When you run C4 again, it will not throw an exception.

Basic String Table Usage

At a minimum, a string table consists of a single identifier and the text associated with that identifier. Let's work through a basic example, building up the text through a number of incremental steps so it can be used by the `myShotController` class.

1 Create and save a blank text file named `myStrings.txt`, in the Import/Demo/game/ directory.

```
C4.exe!C4::StringTable::StringTable(const char * name=0x0678ce00)  Line 60 + 0x5 bytes  C++
PhysXDemoGame.dll!C4::Game::Game()  Line 388 + 0x76 bytes       C++
PhysXDemoGame.dll!ConstructApplication()  Line 22 + 0x2e bytes  C++
C4.exe!C4::ApplicationModule::Load(const char * name=0x0012fdec)  Line 1995 + 0x9 bytes C++
C4.exe!C4::Engine::LoadApplicationModule()  Line 750 + 0x14 bytes       C++
C4.exe!C4::Engine::Initialize(const char * name=0x006865a4, HINSTANCE__ * instance=0x00400000, c
C4.exe!WinMain(HINSTANCE__ * instance=0x00400000, HINSTANCE__ * prevInstance=0x00000000, char *
C4.exe!__tmainCRTStartup()  Line 263 + 0x2c bytes       C
C4.exe!WinMainCRTStartup()  Line 182    C
kernel32.dll!7c817067()
[Frames below may be incorrect and/or missing, no symbols loaded for kernel32.dll]
C4.exe!raise(int signum=-268435456)  Line 492 + 0x10 bytes      C
```

Figure 13-2. The stack trace, again running in debug mode.

Figure 13-3. The Import String Table dialog.

2 Open the text file and add the following line:

```
'CTRL' "Controller"
```

This is the basic format of the string table. The text is split into two parts, an identifier and a textual description. The identifier is delimited by single quotes, and the textual description is delimited by double quotes.

3 To use this file in-game you will have to import the text file to convert it into a binary file. There are two ways to achieve this—either open a command prompt and type `istring`, or choose **Tools > Import String Table**. The Import String Table dialog appears as shown in Figure 13-3.

4 Navigate to the `MyStrings.txt` text file and click OK to import it. A new binary file named `MyStrings.str` is created in a similar directory structure within the Data directory, in this case Data/Demo/game/.

5 Uncomment the `myStringTable` declaration, the `GetMyStringTable()` accessor function, and the initialization code that we earlier commented out in the `Game` class constructor.

6 Compile and run C4, and it should now run without the exception being thrown.

If you find yourself in a similar situation, when you have added the initialization code or accidentally deleted the `.str` file, and don't want to comment out the code and recompile your project, you can switch to another project (by changing the `$gameModuleName` variable value) that you know works, such as the stock demo game, and import the string table while running that project. Then switch back to your current project (again changing the `$gameModuleName` variable value).

To access the text description from the identifier `'CTRL'`, use the following code:

```
TheGame->GetMyStringTable()->GetString( StringID('CTRL'));
```

This is all very well for a similar textual setup, but sometimes you will want to create a list of textual descriptions grouped by the `'CTRL'` identifier. In this next example we have added another level down from the name of the controller, so that the `'CTRL'` identifier is just being used as an identifier for all of the controllers in our project:

```
'CTRL' ""
{
   'cmsh' "My Shot"
}
```

Note that we have removed the description from the first identifier and left it blank (unless we wanted to use it later then we would add a description), and the introduction of the braces denotes a level of hierarchy one down from the first example.

To access the new `'cmsh'` description, we will use the following code.

```
TheGame->GetMyStringTable()->GetString(StringID('CTRL', 'cmsh'));
```

Now note that we have used a lowercase identifier to describe the name of the controller. The reason for this is that we already have an identifier for the `MyShotController` declared in `MyShotController.h`:

```
enum
{
   kControllerMyShot = 'cmsh'
};
```

This identifier can be used for retrieving the description text, as shown in the following code:

```
TheGame->GetMyStringTable()->GetString(StringID('CTRL',
   kControllerMyShot));
```

To use this in game you would have to re-import `MyStrings.txt`, and as long as there is a file in the **Data** directory, you will not have to comment/uncomment the `MyStringTable` initialization. If the text is not found, a null value is returned.

Adding an additional level to our string table, the text appears as follows:

```
'CTRL' ""
{
   'cmsh' "My Shot"
   {
      'HEAD' "Shot Settings"
      'GRAV' "Gravity"
      'NOSH' "Maximum No of Shots"
      'SSOU' "Shot Sound"
      'PICK' "Details"
      'PSOU' "Play Sound"
      'SCOL' "Shot Color"
      'SHOT' "Shot Type"
   }
}
```

To access the text for the identifier `'GRAV'`, use the following code:

```
TheGame->GetMyStringTable()->GetString(StringID('CTRL',
   kControllerMyShot, 'GRAV'));
```

As you can see, there is a pattern starting to emerge. Adding the final level of text, the complete text file appears as follows:

```
'CTRL' ""
{
    'cmsh' "My Shot"
    {
        'HEAD' "Shot Settings"
        'GRAV' "Gravity"
        'NOSH' "Maximum No of Shots"
        'SSOU' "Shot Sound"
        'PICK' "Details"
        'PSOU' "Play Sound"
        'SCOL' "Shot Color"
        'SHOT' "Shot Type"
        {
            'SPHE' "Sphere Projectile"
            'SCON' "General Convex Projectile"
            'SCAP' "Capsule Projectile"
        }
    }
}
```

Access the text for the `'SPHE'` identifier using the following code:

```
TheGame->GetMyStringTable()->GetString(StringID('CTRL',
    kControllerMyShot, 'SHOT', 'SPHE'));
```

(A string table supports a maximum of five levels.) Finally, import the completed text file into the C4 Engine.

Next Steps

The `MyShotController` string table is used extensively throughout Chapter 14, "Configurable Settings".

14

Configurable Settings

All of the dialogs in the C4 Engine are user configurable and can display a number of attributes, called *settings* through a set of interface controls. Supported controls include check boxes, text boxes, sliders, file pickers, color box pickers, and drop-down list boxes.

Displaying and Retrieving Data

The C4 Engine manages user configurable dialogs through the `Configurable` class. This class contains three key virtual functions; `GetSettingCount()`, `GetSetting()` and `SetSetting()`.

As discussed in Chapter 12, "Serialization", most of the main classes that you will use are also derived from the `Configurable` class; for example, `Node`, `Controller`, and `Property`.

The *Guide* contains many examples of configurable classes being used to display and manipulate private attributes. Also have a look through the C4 Engine source code. One of the easiest ways to find relevant code for your configurable setting is to open the C4 Engine API documentation and browse to the Interface Manager, all of the user controls are listed there. Find the control you would like more information on and search for it in the **Engine**, **MGGame**, and **World Editor** code.

Throughout this chapter, we will build part of a fictitious controller called `MyShotController`, continuing on from the initial version created in Chapter 13, "Using String Tables", and Chapter 12, "Serialization". The `MyShotController` class will be completed in Chapter 15, "The Controller".

The Main Configurable Functions

Let's now concentrate on understanding the main `Configurable` functions.

- The `GetSettingCount()` function is used to inform the class how many settings will be displayed. Returning less than the actual number settings will only display the returned value.
- The `GetSetting()` function is used to retrieve a particular setting value and for example, populate a private variable with it.
- The `SetSetting()` function is used to display data on the dialog using a specific interface control.

It is now time to work through the relevant part of the example `MyShotController` class that will display and retrieve the following data using some well known types of interface controls. Table 14-1 shows a list of private attributes and how we would like to display them in a dialog. The Control column is a more familiar general term for the interface control followed by the actual setting type that it maps to in the Control column.

To use the configuration capabilities in a class that inherits from the `Configurable` class, declare three new public functions:

```
int32 GetSettingCount(void) const;
Setting *GetSetting(int32 index) const;
void SetSetting(const Setting *setting);
```

Table 14-1. Attribute-to-C4 Engine interface control mappings.

Attribute	Data type	Control	Setting
"Show Details" heading	`char *`	Heading	`HeadingSetting`
`gravity`	`float`	Editable text box	`TextSetting`
`noOfShots`	`int32`	Slider	`IntegerSetting`
`shotSound`	`ResourceName`	File pick box	`ResourceSetting`
`playSound`	`bool`	Check box	`BooleanSetting`
`shotColor`	`ColoRGBA`	Color pick box	`ColorSetting`
`shotType`	`AttributeType`	Drop-down list	`MenuSetting`

Also for this example, declare six new private member variables:

```
float           gravity;
int32           noOfShots;
ResourceName    shotSound;
bool            playSound;
ColorRGBA       shotColor;
AttributeType   shotType;
```

The `AttributeType` data type is an unsigned long, so we can define our values for the popup menu. Outside of the class, we define some shot types, using text defined in the string table.

```
enum
{
   kAttributeShotSphere      = 'assp',
   kAttributeShotConvex      = 'asco',
   kAttributeShotCapsule     = 'asca'
};
```

GetSettingCount()

In Table 14-1, we listed seven data values that we want to display on the **Controller** tab panel. This equates to seven settings items that need to be created. To let the class know how many settings there will be, use the following code:

```
int32 MyShotController::GetSettingCount(void) const
{
   return (7);
}
```

GetSetting()

When the settings for one or more nodes are about to be displayed by the **World Editor**, it acquires the node's configurable values from the following:

- The node's category tabs.
- The node's `Controller` class, if present.
- The node's `Property` classes, if present.

As previously mentioned in this chapter, we are primarily focusing on a `Controller` example, but the basics are exactly the same for a `Property` class and almost the same for a `Node` class.

Once the C4 Engine has reached the controller it will retrieve the number of settings by calling the `GetSettingCount()` function, and then iterate through each setting, calling `GetSetting()` with the respective index. Returning a `GetSettingCount()` value less than the number of attributes will not return a `Setting` outside of the index, likewise for a higher value, null values will need to be returned.

We will now set up the attribute data that is displayed in the node's **Controller** tab panel using the public `GetSetting()` function we declared earlier. Write the following code:

```
Setting *MyShotController::GetSetting(int32 index) const
{
   // The rest of the example code will go here.

   return (nullptr);
}
```

If an index value is not found then a null pointer is returned.

String Table

The purpose of the string table is described in Chapter 13, "Using String Tables", and the text values were defined for the `MyShotController` class we are building. The strings were defined as shown in Table 14-2.

To access the text values for each setting, we need a reference to the string table:

```
const StringTable *table = TheGame->GetMyStringTable();
```

In each of the following if statements, the textual title is retrieved from the string table using:

```
const char *title = table->GetString(StringID('CTRL',
      kControllerMyShot, 'FBAN'));
```

Table 14-2. Identifiers and their text.

Identifier	Text
`HEAD`	Shot Settings
`GRAV`	Gravity
`NOSH`	Maximum No of Shots
`SSOU`	Shot Sound
`PICK`	Details
`PSOU`	Play Sound
`SCOL`	Shot Color
`SHOT`	Shot Type
`SPHE`	Sphere Projectile
`SCON`	General Convex Projectile
`SCAP`	Capsule Projectile

Heading

The first setting we want to create is a heading that describes the attributes underneath it. We start at index 0 and create a new `HeadingSetting` with the unique identifier that was used to return the title. The `HeadingSetting` constructor takes two parameters, as shown in Table 14-3.

```
if (index == 0)
{
    const char *title = table->GetString(StringID('CTRL',
            kControllerMyShot, 'HEAD'));
    return (new HeadingSetting('HEAD', title));
}
```

This will display the text "Shot Settings" as the header, as shown in Figure 14-1.

Figure 14-1. A heading displayed in the controller settings.

Table 14-3. Parameter descriptions taken from the C4 Engine API documentation.

Parameter	Description
`identifier`	The setting's unique identifier.
`text`	The initial text for the setting.

Text Box

We need to create a free entry text box to enable the entry of the gravity value for the shot, using the `TextSetting` class. The `TextSetting` constructor takes five parameters, as shown in Table 14-4.

- The identifier is `'GRAV'`.
- The text value has to be displayed as a string but is currently a float data type, so the `Text` utility class is used for the conversion.
- The title is retrieved from the string table using the identifier.

```
else if (index == 1)
{
    const char *title = table->GetString(StringID('CTRL',
        kControllerMyShot, 'GRAV'));
    return (new TextSetting('GRAV', gravity, title);
}
```

Table 14-4. Parameter descriptions taken from the C4 Engine API documentation.

Parameter	Description
`identifier`	The setting's unique identifier.
`text`	The initial text for the setting.
`title`	The title of the setting.
`maxLen`	The maximum number of characters that can be entered in the text box.
`filterProc`	A character filter function. If this parameter is `nullptr`, then all characters are allowed.

This code will display the following text box, defaulting to `0.0F`. The value can be typed directly into the box.

Figure 14-2. A text box displayed in the controller settings.

Slider

A slider in C4 is called the `IntegerSetting` class for displaying integer values. Similarly, if you wanted to display float values and increment by an amount less than one, you could use the `FloatSetting` class. The `IntegerSetting` constructor takes six parameters, as shown in Table 14-5.

- The identifier is `'NOSH'`.
- The initial value is the value of `noOfShots`.
- The title is retrieved from the string table using the identifier.
- The minimum value for the slider is 0.
- We will make the maximum value for the slider 20.
- The increments in this case will be 1, as the data type for `noOfShots` is a long, for float data types, you can use values such as `0.1F`.

Table 14-5. Parameter descriptions taken from the C4 Engine API documentation.

Parameter	Description
`identifier`	The setting's unique identifier
`value`	The initial value of the setting.
`title`	The title of the setting.
`min`	The minimum value allowed for the setting.
`max`	The maximum value allowed for the setting.
`step`	The smallest increment allowed between the minimum and maximum values.

```
else if (index == 2)
{
    const char *title = table->GetString(StringID('CTRL',
        kControllerMyShot, 'NOSH'));
    return (new IntegerSetting('NOSH', noOfShots, title, 0, 20, 1));
}
```

The slider can be operated by either slider the control or entering the value directly into the text box to the right of the slider:

Figure 14-3. Slider displayed in the controller settings.

File Pick Box

The file picker provided with the C4 Engine is accessible through the `ResourceSetting` class. It is a control made up of a free entry text box and an image button—in this case an arrow. The resource descriptor being used is from the `SoundResource` class, meaning it will only display files in the dialog with extensions of `.wav`. The `ResourceSetting` constructor takes seven parameters, as shown in Table 14-6.

Table 14-6. Parameter descriptions taken from the C4 Engine API documentation.

Parameter	Description
`identifier`	The setting's unique identifier.
`name`	The initial resource name for the setting.
`title`	The title of the setting.
`picker`	The title of the file picker dialog.
`descriptor`	A pointer to the resource descriptor for the type of resource that can be chosen with the setting.
`subdir`	A subdirectory within the main resource directory to which the resource selection should be restricted.
`flags`	Flags that affect the behavior of the setting.

- The identifier is `'NOSH'`.
- The resource name is the private attribute `shotSound`.
- The title is retrieved from the string table using the identifier.
- The picker relates to the title on the *picker* dialog box. You may remember from Chapter 13, "Using String Tables", that the text for `'PICK'` is "Details", as shown in Figure 14-5.
- As mentioned earlier the descriptor used here is from the `SoundResource` class and will only display files with the .wav extension. Custom descriptors can be easily programmed in order to select your own file types.
- The subdirectory that we will use is the default used by the C4 Engine, so leave this value empty.
- Finally we do not want to add any flags, but use the default behavior.

```
else if (index == 3)
{
   const char *title = table->GetString(StringID('CTRL',
      kControllerMyShot, 'SSOU'));
   const char *picker = table->GetString(StringID('CTRL',
      kControllerMyShot, 'PICK'));
   return (new ResourceSetting('SSOU', shotSound, title, picker,
      SoundResource::GetDescriptor()));
}
```

Figure 14-4. The empty file pick box displayed in the controller settings.

Clicking on the arrow opens up the dialog with the text Details displayed and will only show `.wav` files. Click OK to accept the sound file name and it will be displayed in the text box part of the resource setting. The full path is truncated and Data/<First Subdirectory>/ is removed.

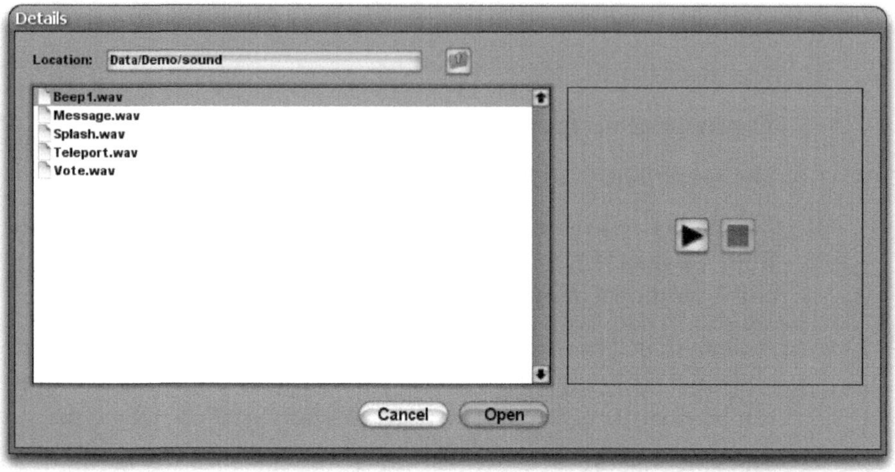

Figure 14-5. The file picker dialog.

Check Box

The check box represents the `BooleanSetting` class based around boolean operation, true for checked with an X, false for unchecked and left blank. The `BooleanSetting` constructor takes three parameters, as shown in Table 14-7.

- The identifier is `'PSOU'`.
- The initial value is the value of `playSound`, defaulted to true, so the check box will be shown for the first time checked.
- The title is retrieved from the string table using the identifier.

Figure 14-6. A checked check box.

Table 14-7. Parameter descriptions taken from the C4 Engine API documentation.

Parameter	Description
`identifier`	The setting's unique identifier.
`value`	The initial value of the setting.
`title`	The title of the setting.

```
else if (index == 4)
{
   const char *title = table->GetString(StringID('CTRL',
      kControllerMyShot, 'PSOU'));
   return (new BooleanSetting('PSOU', playSound, title));
}
```

Color Pick Box

The color pick box represents the `ColorSetting` class showing the selected color in a box that displays a dialog to enable a new color to be selected when it is clicked. The `ColorSetting` constructor takes five parameters, as shown in Table 14-8.

- The identifier is `'SCOL'`.
- The color is the private attribute `shotColor`.
- The title is retrieved from the string table using the identifier.
- The picker relates to the title on the *picker* dialog box. As shown in Chapter 13, "Using String Tables", the text for `'PICK'` is "Details", as shown in Figure 14-5.
- Finally we do not want to add any flags, but use the `kColorPickBoxAlpha` flag to allow the alpha to be modified.

Table 14-8. Parameter descriptions taken from the C4 Engine API documentation.

Parameter	Description
`identifier`	The setting's unique identifier.
`color`	The initial color for the setting.
`title`	The title of the setting.
`picker`	The title of the color picker dialog.
`flags`	The flags passed to the color picker dialog.

```
else if (index == 5)
{
   const char *title = table->GetString(StringID('CTRL',
      kControllerMyShot, 'SCOL'));
   const char *picker = table->GetString(StringID('CTRL',
      kControllerMyShot, 'PICK'));
   return (new ColorSetting('SCOL', shotColor, title, picker,
      kColorPickBoxAlpha));
}
```

In this example, the default `shotColor`, black (`0.0F`, `0.0F`, `0.0F`) is displayed in a rectangular box.

Figure 14-7. The default color is displayed.

Clicking on the box will display the color picker dialog, shown in Figure 14-8. Modify the textual values or move the sliders to create a new color.

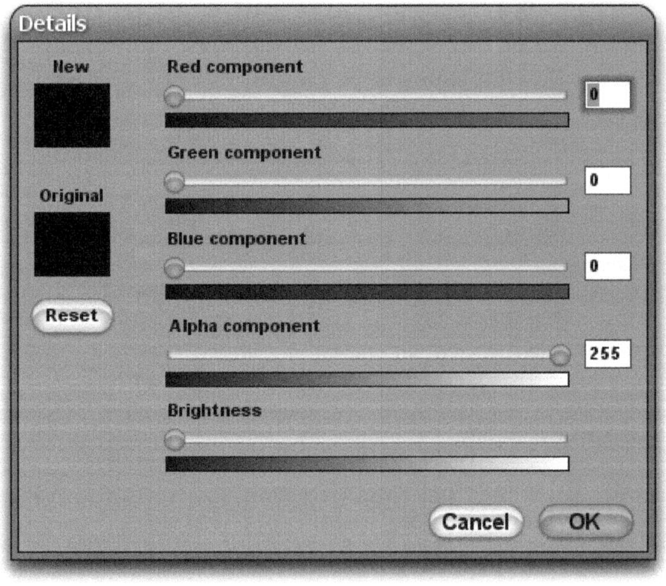

Figure 14-8. The color picker dialog.

Finally, when OK is pressed, the new color is displayed in the color setting.

Figure 14-9. The new color is displayed.

Popup Menu

The popup menu in the C4 Engine represents the `MenuSetting` class, and it is a control made up of a text box to display the selection and a popup menu to display the menu items. The `MenuSetting` constructor takes four parameters, as shown in Table 14-9.

- The identifier is `'SHOT'`.
- The selection is a long data type that represents the selected item. The selection value is aligned to the `shotType`.
- The title is retrieved from the string table using the identifier.
- Finally the `itemCount` in this example will be 3.

Table 14-9. Parameter descriptions taken from the C4 Engine API documentation.

Parameter	Description
`identifier`	The setting's unique identifier.
`selection`	The initial selection for the setting.
`title`	The title of the setting.
`itemCount`	The number of items that will appear in the menu.

Added to the menu setting will be menu item strings, each one containing the text values from the string table underneath the `'SHOT'` identifier, in the My-Strings file.

```
'SHOT' "Shot Type"
{
   'SPHE' "Sphere Projectile"
   'SCON' "General Convex Projectile"
   'SCAP' "Capsule Projectile"
}
```

Let's look at the code:

```
else if (index == 6)
{
    int32 selection = 0;
    if (shotType == kAttributeShotSphere) selection = 0;
    else if (shotType == kAttributeShotConvex) selection = 1;
    else if (shotType == kAttributeShotCapsule) selection = 2;

    const char *title = table->GetString(StringID('CTRL',
        kControllerMyShot, 'STYP'));
    MenuSetting *menu = new MenuSetting('SHOT', selection,
        title, 3);
    menu->SetMenuItemString(0, table->GetString(StringID('CTRL',
        kControllerMyShot, 'SHOT', 'SPHE')));
    menu->SetMenuItemString(1, table->GetString(StringID('CTRL',
        kControllerMyShot, 'SHOT', 'SCON')));
    menu->SetMenuItemString(2, table->GetString(StringID('CTRL',
        kControllerMyShot, 'SHOT', 'SCAP')));
    return (menu);
}
```

The default selection is 0, and returns `kAttributeShotSphere`.

Figure 14-10. A popup menu.

Clicking on the text in the popup menu control will display the menu.

Figure 14-11. Making a selection in a popup menu.

Selecting the second value, `kAttributeShotConvex`.

Figure 14-12. A new selection is made.

SetSetting()

When new configurable settings are confirmed in the **World Editor**, each setting is passed to the `SetSetting()` function one at a time. The identifier is returned from the base `Setting` class and used to populate each of the attributes.

```
void MyShotController::SetSetting(const Setting *setting)
{
   Type identifier = setting->GetSettingIdentifier();

   // Rest of code goes here.
}
```

As we know the data type of each identifier, it is straightforward to return the correct value from the setting. The text box data is returned as a float using the utility `Text` class.

```
if (identifier == 'GRAV')
{
   gravity = Text::StringToFloat(static_cast<const TextSetting *>
      (setting)->GetText());
}
```

The next few identifiers are quite straightforward:

```
else if (identifier == 'NOSH')
{
   noOfShots = static_cast<const IntegerSetting *>(setting)
      ->GetIntegerValue();
}
else if (identifier == 'SSOU')
{
   shotSound = static_cast<const ResourceSetting *>(setting)
      ->GetResourceName();
}
```

```
else if (identifier == 'PSOU')
{
    playSound = static cast<const BooleanSetting *>(setting)
        ->GetBooleanValue();
}
else if (identifier == 'SCOL')
{
    shotColor = static cast<const ColorSetting *>(setting)
        ->GetColor();
}
```

The only one that is a little different is the menu setting, as it returns the selection value, which we use to determine which value is selected.

```
else if (identifier == 'SHOT')
{
    int32 selection = static cast<const MenuSetting *>(setting)
        ->GetMenuSelection();
    if (selection == 0)
        shotType = kAttributeShotSphere;
    else if (selection == 1)
        shotType = kAttributeShotConvex;
    else if (selection == 2)
        shotType = kAttributeShotCapsule;
}
```

Next Steps

Now it's time to move on to one of the most central classes that application developers will use when working with the C4 Engine, in Chapter 15, "The Controller".

15

The Controller

The `Controller` class is one of the most important classes in the C4 Engine. It is used to give dynamic behavior to the node to which it is attached. Controllers are used everywhere in the C4 Engine. Have a look through the main EngineCode, GameCode, and PluginCode directories to get an idea of the current controllers and their behavior.

The Finished Controller Class

Over the past few chapters, we have been working through different parts of a custom controller class called `MyShotController`, focusing on serialization and configurable settings. These two topics are brought together here as part of the `MyShotController` class. This chapter will cover the remaining functions, but will not delve into adding functional logic to the class with respect to what the controller can actually do, but it will give you a skeleton framework to base your own classes on.

Rather than list both the contents of the `MyShotController.h` and `MyShotController.cpp` source code files, we'll look at the complete `MyShotController.h` file, and focus on the parts of the class that we have not yet covered. The source for the remaining parts of the class is documented in the previous chapters. If you want to see the code and use it as a reference as we work through the chapter, the source code for the `MyShotController` class is included as part of the *Guide* resources. See the end of the chapter on how to set up the source code and supporting files for the Controller class.

Let's start by looking at the `MyShotController.h` file. Create two new files in your current project, `MyShotController.h` and `MyShotController.cpp`. Open the `MyShotController.h` file for editing and add the following code.

```
#ifndef MyShotController h
#define MyShotController h

#include "C4Controller.h"
```

Add the `C4` namespace declaration, the attribute values for the popup menu control, and the type identifier for the class, `kControllerMyShot`.

```
namespace C4
{
    enum
    {
        kAttributeShotSphere        = 'assp',
        kAttributeShotConvex        = 'asco',
        kAttributeShotCapsule       = 'asca'
    };

    enum
    {
        kControllerMyShot           = 'cmsh'
    };
```

The class inherits from the main `C4::Controller` class.

```
class MyShotController : public Controller
{
```

Add the six private member variables that we used in Chapter 12, "Serialization" and Chapter 14, "Configurable Settings".

```
    private:

        float           gravity;
        int32           noOfShots;
        ResourceName    shotSound;
        bool            playSound;
        ColorRGBA       shotColor;
        AttributeType   shotType;
```

Add the copy `Controller` constructor and the `Replicate()` function (we shall discuss these both later on).

```
MyShotController(const MyShotController& myShotController);
Controller *Replicate(void) const;
```

And add the constructor and destructor as well as the public accessors for the private member variables.

```
public:

   MyShotController(void);
   ~MyShotController(void);

   float GetGravity(void) const
   {
      return (gravity);
   }

   void SetGravity(float shotGravity)
   {
      gravity = shotGravity;
   }

   int32 GetNoOfShots(void) const
   {
      return (noOfShots);
   }

   void SetNoOfShots(int32 count)
   {
      noOfShots = count;
   }

   const ResourceName& GetShotSound(void) const
   {
      return (shotSound);
   }
```

```
void SetShotSound(const char *name)
{
   shotSound = name;
}

bool GetPlaySound(void) const
{
   return (playSound);
}

void SetPlaySound(bool play)
{
   playSound = play;
}

const ColorRGBA& GetShotColor(void) const
{
   return (shotColor);
}

void SetShotColor(const ColorRGBA& color)
{
   shotColor = color;
}

const AttributeType& GetShotType(void) const
{
   return (shotType);
}

void SetShotType(AttributeType type)
{
   shotType = type;
}
```

The next three functions are new and will also be covered later on.

```
static bool ValidNode(const Node *node);
void Preprocess(void);
void Move(void);
```

Add the remainder of the public serialization functions.

```
        void Pack(Packer& data, unsigned int32 packFlags) const;
        void Unpack(Unpacker& data, unsigned int32 unpackFlags);
        bool UnpackChunk(const ChunkHeader *chunkHeader,
           Unpacker& data, unsigned int32 unpackFlags);
        void *BeginSettingsUnpack(void);
```

And the configurable settings functions.

```
        int32 GetSettingCount(void) const;
        Setting *GetSetting(int32 index) const;
        void SetSetting(const Setting *setting);
    };
}

#endif
```

Now it's time to move onto the main class body covering parts we have not yet looked at. Open the `MyShotController.cpp` file for editing and add the code to include the correct header files.

```
#include "MyShotController.h"
#include "MGGame.h"

using namespace C4;
```

The constructor code inherits from the `Controller` class and also initializes the private member variables to their default settings. At first glance, this looks a little like the `Preprocess()` function, but there are quite a few differences in functionality. See the `Preprocess()` function later on for a more in-depth discussion of these differences.

Also note how the `ResourceName` member variable `shotSound` is initialized.

```
MyShotController::MyShotController() :
      Controller(kControllerMyShot),
```

```
        gravity(0.0F),
        noOfShots(0),
        playSound(true),
        shotColor(0.0F, 0.0F, 0.0F),
        shotType(kAttributeShotSphere)
{
    shotSound[0] = 0;
}
```

The copy constructor and the `Replicate()` function are used by the **World Editor** and only need to be added if you want your controller to be accessible in the **World Editor**.

```
MyShotController::MyShotController(const MyShotController&
    myShotController) :
        Controller(myShotController),
        gravity(myShotController.gravity),
        noOfShots(myShotController.noOfShots),
        playSound(myShotController.playSound),
        shotColor(myShotController.shotColor),
        shotType(myShotController.shotType),
        shotSound(myShotController.shotSound)
{
}

MyShotController::~MyShotController()
{
}
```

The `Replicate()` function is used internally by the C4 Engine to create a new version of the controller.

```
Controller *MyShotController::Replicate(void) const
{
    return (new MyShotController(*this));
}
```

The `ValidNode()` function is used to determine which node type the controller will be displayed in the respective **Controllers** tab. Return `true` for the controller to appear in the list or `false` for it not to be displayed. In the example code, the controller will appear on nodes of type `kNodeGroup` and `kNodeGeometry`. If the `ValidNode()` function is left out from the code, then the controller will be displayed for all node types.

```
bool MyShotController::ValidNode(const Node *node)
{
   if (node->GetNodeType() == kNodeGeometry)
      return (node->GetNodeType() == kNodeGeometry);
   else if (node->GetNodeType() == kNodeGroup)
      return (node->GetNodeType() == kNodeGroup);

   return (false);
}
```

On paper, it looks like the `Preprocess()` function and the constructor are pretty similar, so, why have a `Preprocess()` function? `Preprocess()` is called after the class has been instantiated and when the scene graph is being loaded. When the controller is instantiated, it is created with the default values, but as the scene graph is loaded, the controller is unpacked and the saved attributes are restored.

This means that you will be able to reference the restored attributes for the node to which the controller is attached, in your `Preprocess()` function. You will also be able to reference the root node—the first node loaded in the scene graph.

```
void MyShotController::Preprocess(void)
{
   Controller::Preprocess();
   // ...
}
```

A controller's `Move()` function is called once per frame provided that it is awake, which makes controllers ideal for use with dynamic nodes, i.e., nodes that need to be updated as they interact with the environment.

```
void MyShotController::Move(void)
{
   Controller::Move();
   // ...
}
```

That's it for creating the skeleton class code for a simple controller in the C4 Engine. Obviously, it is not all required—the serialization and configurable settings functions can be left out if not needed. But it is a good practice to include those functions if you will be saving data and want to display it in the **Node Info** dialog.

Registering the Controller

For the controller to be visible in the node's **Controller** tab panel, and be used in the world, it needs to be registered with the Game class. First, open `SimpleChar.h` and add the controller header underneath all of the other header files.

```
#include "MyShotController.h"
```

Also add the `C4Configuration.h` header file so that we can use the `StringTable` class.

```
#include "C4Configuration.h"
```

Find the `SoldierController` declaration and add the following code underneath it, the first line of the existing code has been included.

```
SoldierController                   *soldierController;
ControllerReg<MyShotController>     myShotControllerReg;
```

Now open the `SimpleChar.cpp` file, find the `soldierModelReg` initialization and add the following code underneath it to initialize our controller. Note that the string table is used to return the name of the controller that will be displayed in the **Controllers** tab panel.

```
myShotControllerReg(kControllerMyShot,
   myStringTable.GetString(StringID('CTRL', kControllerMyShot))),
```

Finally, when you compile and run the project, open the **World Editor**, add a geometry node to the world, open the **Node Info** dialog, and click the **Controllers** tab, you can see our controller listed.

FAQ

Here are some commonly asked questions that might come up while you are working with controllers.

How do I find out which Node a controller is attached to?

Use the `GetTargetNode()` function declared in the base controller class to return a pointer to the node.

```
Node *node = GetTargetNode();
```

How do I know if the Controller Preprocess is being executed in the Game or World Editor, or how do I stop it being executed in the World Editor?

The `Preprocess()` function is always called when a world is loaded, even if it is loaded in the **World Editor**. Sometimes, this functionality is not desired in the **World Editor**, and in this case we do not want the code to be executed, so we need to determine if we are running in the **World Editor**.

Every node in the **World Editor** has a manipulator assigned to it, so if we successfully test for the presence of a manipulator, then we are currently running in the **World Editor**; otherwise, we are running in the game.

The following example tests if we are running in a game.

```
if (!GetTargetNode()->GetManipulator())
{
   // ...
}
```

How do I find the Scene Graph's root node?

Using the `GetTargetNode()` code above to return the controller's node, you can easily return the root node using `GetRootNode()`:

```
Node *node = GetTargetNode();
Node *rootNode = node->GetRootNode();
```

I know the node and want to set its myShotController Z Gravity value to 0.0F?

If you are in a custom function that already has a node reference and you want to change a value on its controller, there are a couple of steps to go through. First, make sure that the node has a controller attached to it, and then make sure that the controller type is of type (for this example) `kControllerMyShot`. This can be done in a single `if` statement, testing for the presence of the controller first.

```
Node *node = <the node that I have a reference to>
if ((node->GetController()) &&
    (node->GetController()->GetControllerType() ==
        kControllerMyShot))
{
    // ...
}
```

By looking at the above code you would think that it would be easier to just type the following.

```
if (node->GetController()->GetControllerType() ==
    kControllerMyShot)
```

This can cause the code to throw an exception if the node does not have a controller attached to it because the controller will return a null pointer, so make sure you always check for the presence of a controller before testing for its type.

Finally, we want to change the value of the *z* axis gravity attribute to `0.0F`. Inside the `if` statement, we need to declare a new variable and point to the `MyShotController`, then change its *z* gravity value.

```
MyShotController *myController =
    static_cast<MyShotController *>(node->GetController());
Vector3D gravity = myController->GetGravity();
myController->SetGravity(Vector3D(gravity.x, gravity.y, 0.0F));
```

When casting the controller type, always use `static_cast`.

How do I find all of the instances of myShotController in the scene graph and set their Gravity z values to 0.0F?

The code for this is very similar to the previous snippet, the difference here is that we do not know which nodes need to be changed, so we will need to iterate through all of nodes in the scene graph, testing to see if they have a controller and what type of controller it is.

To iterate through the scene graph, we first need to find the root node. If you already have a controller reference then you can find the root node as specified in the second example. Otherwise, you can use the world reference, and this can only be used when the world has been loaded using the following code:

```
GameWorld *world = static cast<GameWorld *>(GetWorld());
Node *rootNode = world->GetRootNode();
```

Then to iterate through the scene graph, use the following code.

```
Node *node = rootNode;
while (node)
[
    // ...
    node = rootNode->GetNextNode(node);
}
```

Then, putting together all of the code examples so far, we can iterate through the scene graph, test for the controller, and change the gravity *z* values. The final code is:

```
GameWorld *world = static cast<GameWorld *>(GetWorld());
Node *rootNode = world->GetRootNode();
Node *node = rootNode;
while (node)
{
    if (node >GetController() &&
        node->GetController()->GetControllerType() ==
            kControllerMyShot)
    {
        MyShotController *myController =
```

```
        static cast<MyShotController *>(node->GetController());
    Vector3D gravity = myController->GetGravity();
    myController->SetGravity(Vector3D(gravity.x, gravity.y,
        0.0F));
  }

  node = rootNode->GetNextNode(node);
}
```

How do I make a node dynamic?

To make a node dynamic involves letting the engine know that any shadow volumes that it has are not cached. This is achieved by adding the `kGeometryDynamic` flag to the geometry object that makes up the node.

First, find the node's `GeometryObject`, remembering that the `Geometry` class is also derived from the `Node` base class.

```
Node *node = GetTargetNode();
Geometry *geometry = static cast<Geometry *>(node);
GeometryObject *object = geometry->GetObject();
```

Then add the flag to the `GeometryObject`.

```
object->SetGeometryFlags(object->GetGeometryFlags() |
    kGeometryDynamic);
```

To make sure that the geometry is updated, the following code needs to be called that invalidates it and updates with its new position and orientation.

```
geometry->Invalidate();
```

As the node is now dynamic, how do I make sure the node will be visible if it moves zones?

If you can recall, a node is visible only in the zone that it is currently a child of. If a node is dynamic, then it has the ability to move between zones and so it needs to be removed from its current zone and added to the new one.

The first thing to do is find out the current position of the geometry based on the center of the bounding sphere, this is used to determine the new zone.

```
Geometry *geometry = static cast<Geometry*>(node);
const Point3D& position = geometry->GetBoundingSphere()
   ->GetCenter();
```

Make sure that the world is currently loaded, i.e., you don't want to be doing this in the **World Editor**.

```
World *world = TheWorldMgr->GetWorld();
```

Then we need to test to see if the node has moved into a new zone. Because the geometry's final position is not calculated until the `Invalidate()` function is called, the geometry can be used to find the current zone and its position used to find the new zone. If the zones are different then the geometry needs to be added to the new zone.

```
if (world)
{
   Zone *newZone = world->FindZone(position);
   Zone *oldZone = geometry->GetOwningZone();

   if (newZone != oldZone)
   {
```

When adding the geometry to a new zone as a subnode, it is automatically removed from its current zone, a node can only exist in one zone at any one time.

```
      newZone->AddSubnode(geometry);
```

The node transform for the new zone needs to be calculated as well.

```
      Transform4D transform = newZone->GetInverseWorldTransform()
         * geometry->GetWorldTransform()

      geometry->SetNodeTransform(transform);
   }
```

And finally, the geometry is invalidated to update its position and orientation.

```
    geometry->Invalidate();
}
```

Setting up the Guide's Controller Code

Look for the supplied Code folder that contains four subfolders

- BookCode
- Data
- Import
- VisualStudio2010

Just drop this folder into the root C4 folder. Open C4 in Visual Studio 2010 and from the file menu select **Add > Exisitng Project**. Navigate to VisualStudio2010 > C4 > MySimpleChar and select `MySimpleChar.vcxproj`, Compile the project and then change your `$gameModuleName` to

```
$gameModuleName = "MySimpleChar";
```

The string file called `MyStrings.txt` resides in Import/Book/game/ and the binary `MyStrings.str` resides in Data/Book/game/.

Part IV

The Games

16

SimpleBat

This chapter presents the first of five tutorials that show how to create simple games with the C4 Engine. We start by showing how to extend the *SimpleBall* application to create a *Breakout*-style game, which we have called *SimpleBat*.

Introduction

When first starting to learn about the C4 Engine, you may be one of many who struggles for a while, trying to understand how to use the keyboard to control a piece of geometry. You might begin by trying to create a very simple game, similar to "Breakout", starting with a "bat" that you create with simple geometry in the **World Editor**. (See Chapter 4, "Creating a Simple World" to learn more about the **World Editor** tool.)

Once your bat and the playing field are designed, the next question is, "How do I control the movement of that bat with the keyboard?" This first game tutorial provides you with the know-how to start making games of that sort. There are no fancy graphics here, no animated characters, and no special effects, beyond what is already provided by the *SimpleBall* application.

The game we will create in this chapter is called *SimpleBat*, and a preview is shown in Figure 16-1. It allows the player to use a semi-transparent "bat" to hit a ball against a wall, which also bounces off other geometries, such as the blocks in the game world. If the ball moves past the player, a life is lost. The ball speeds up on each collision by a small percentage, which increases the difficulty of the game as play continues.

This game is an extension of the code used for the *SimpleBall* tutorial on the C4 Engine Wiki. While it is helpful if you have tried that tutorial first, it is not absolutely essential.

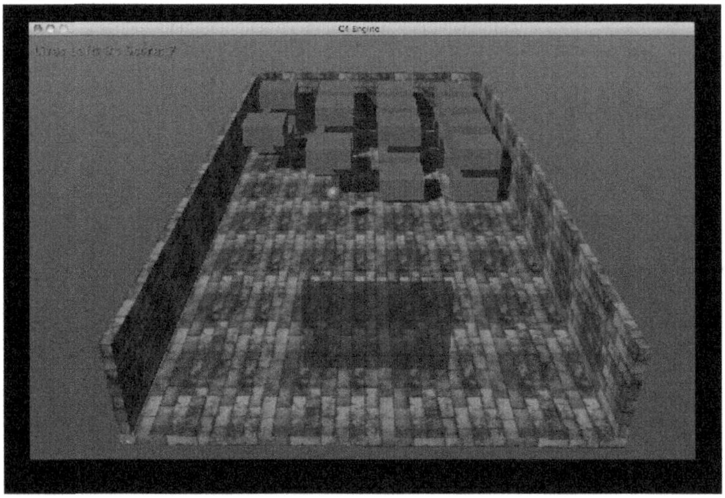

Figure 16-1. A preview of the *SimpleBat* game. Sparks fly when the ball hits a block and the block disappears.

Moving a piece of Geometry in the C4 Engine

As we discussed in Part III • Under the Hood, if we want a game object to have a behavior, then we have to create a controller—or reuse an already existing one—and then assign the controller to the node representing the game object.

The `RotationController` is one of the example controllers that comes with the C4 Engine. To use it, follow the Using the Rotation Controller tutorial on the C4 Engine Wiki.

Note that *you do not need to follow that tutorial for the SimpleBat game*, since we'll create a custom controller of our own that will move the object it is assigned to, depending on whether certain keyboard keys are pressed or not.

Let's start writing some code.

Moving the Bat with a Custom Controller

In this section, we will add a custom `BatController` to the *SimpleBall* code, and assign our controller to a piece of geometry, representing a rectangular-shaped bat. That way, we will have converted the *SimpleBall* demonstration into the makings of a *Breakout*-style game, where the player uses the keyboard to control a bat to "hit" the ball, which in turn destroys blocks within in the game arena.

If you want to check out the results first, you can skip these step-by-step directions for now, and simply overwrite your existing *SimpleBall* files with the code provided with this chapter and recompile. (Make a copy of the original `SimpleBall.h` and `SimpleBall.cpp` files before you overwrite them.) You can then just study the changes marked in the new code, if that's your preferred way of learning. You will need to skip down to the section below, The *SimpleBat* world, in order to create the world to test your code in. Otherwise, read on.

You'll remember that we want to provide behavior for our "Bat" geometry. So at this stage, we need to add a controller, which we will call "BatController". The changes you'll see here basically involve copying the *SimpleBall* controller code and adjusting it as needed. We'll derive our custom controller class directly from the `Controller` class, instead of inheriting behavior from the `RigidBody-Controller`, since our bat doesn't need to behave like a rigid body. In the next Chapter, *SimpleSnake*, we will provide an example of a controller which derives from `RigidBodyController`.

If you look at the code for this chapter in the files `SimpleBat.cpp` and `Sim-pleBat.h`, you will find numbered comments marked "Change 1", "Change 2", etc. These are the additions or changes to the *SimpleBall* code, and the numbers represent the order that the changes were made in.

Before you make your changes, save a copy of the original *SimpleBall* `.cpp` and `.h` files. To do that in Visual C++, double-click on each of the `Simple-Ball.cpp` and `SimpleBall.h` files in the Solution Explorer list view, to open them in the Visual C++ editor. Then choose **File > Save As** to save a copy of the files, for example as "SimpleBall_original" (`.cpp` and `.h` respectively).

Next, reopen your *SimpleBall* (`.cpp` and `.h`) files in Visual Studio by again double-clicking on them in the Solution Explorer list view and make the changes in the order we've marked them.

1 Add the following code to declare our new controller in the `SimpleBall.h` header file, just after the closing curly bracket of the `MovementAction` class declaration, and just before the start of the `BallController` class declaration:

```
// Change 1: This is the controller for the bat.

class BatController : public Controller
{
   private:
```

```
    Transform4D       originalTransform;
    Transform4D       translation;
    Point3D           myTranslation;
    unsigned int32  movementFlags;

  public:

    BatController();
    ~BatController();

    static bool ValidNode(const Node *node);

    void Preprocess(void);
    void Move(void);

    unsigned int32 GetMovementFlags(void) const
    {
      return (movementFlags);
    }

    void SetMovementFlags(unsigned int32 flags)
    {
      movementFlags = flags;
    }
};

// End Change 1
```

2 Add the constructor, destructor, `ValidNode()`, and `Preprocess()` functions for our new controller to the `SimpleBall.cpp` source file, just after the `MovementAction::End()` function implementation:

```
// Change 2: Add constructor, destructor, ValidNode(),
// and Preprocess() functions for our new controller in
// the source file.

BatController::BatController() : Controller(kControllerBat)
{
  movementFlags = 0;
```

```
    TheGame->SetBatController(this);
}

BatController::~BatController()
{
}

bool BatController::ValidNode(const Node *node)
{
    // This function is called by the engine to determine whether
    // this particular type of controller can control the particular
    // node passed in through the node parameter. This function
    // should return true if it can control the node, and otherwise
    // it should return false. In this case, the controller can only
    // be applied to geometry nodes.
    // Our bat will be a geometry made within the World Editor.

    return (node->GetNodeType() == kNodeGeometry);
}

void BatController::Preprocess(void)
{
    // This function is called once before the target node is ever
    // rendered or moved. The base class Preprocess() function
    // should always be called first, and then the subclass can do
    // whatever preprocessing it needs to do.

    Controller::Preprocess();

    // Add preprocessor code to record the initial
    // bat transform and other data members.

    const Node *target = GetTargetNode();
    originalTransform = target->GetNodeTransform();
    myTranslation = target->GetWorldPosition().GetVector3D();
    translation.SetIdentity();
}

// End Change 2
```

3 Staying in `SimpleBall.cpp`, add the `Move()` function to your bat controller:

```
// Change 3: Add the Move() function for the bat controller.

void BatController::Move(void)
{
    // This function is called once per frame to allow the
    // controller to move its target node.

    Node *target = GetTargetNode();

    if (movementFlags & 1)    // Forward
    {
        originalTransform[3].x -= speed;
    }

    if (movementFlags & 2)    // Backward
    {
        originalTransform[3].x += speed;
    }

    if (movementFlags & 4)    // Left
    {
        originalTransform[3].y -= speed;
    }

    if (movementFlags & 8)    // Right
    {
        originalTransform[3].y += speed;
    }

    target->SetNodeTransform(originalTransform);
    target->Invalidate();
}

// End Change 3
```

4 In the header file , add a private pointer to a `BatController` object in the Game Class, and declare the `batControllerReg` object just after the line "`ControllerReg<BallController> controllerReg;`" as follows:

```
// Change 4: Add a pointer to an instance of the bat
// controller and then register it.

BatController                   *batController;
ControllerReg<BatController>    batControllerReg;
```

Now add this line to `SimpleBall.h`, just after the line "`kControllerBall = 'ball'`". Be sure to add a comma to the end of that line. Note that if you copy and paste code from an electronic document, some characters may not copy correctly so you may need to edit them in the source file after copying:

```
kControllerBat = 'pbat'   // Change 4
```

5 In `SimpleBall.cpp`, register the `BatController` class in the `Game` constructor, just after the line that registers the `BallController` class, as "`controllerReg(kControllerBall, "Bouncing Ball"),`":

```
// Change 5: Register our new bat controller with the editor.
batControllerReg(kControllerBat, "Moving Bat"),
```

and remaining in the `Game` constructor, add this line just before the line "`TheMessageMgr->BeginSinglePlayerGame();`" at the end of the constructor implementation:

```
batController = nullptr;     // Change 5
```

6 Now, back in the header file, add public getter and setter functions to the `Game` class to obtain and set the `batController` variable we just declared.

```
// Change 6

BatController *GetBatController(void) const
{
   return (batController);
}

void SetBatController(BatController *controller)
```

```
{
    batController = controller;
}

// End Change 6
```

7 Add the following global variables at the top of the `.cpp` file, just after the line "`Game *C4::TheGame = nullptr;`":

```
// Change 7

float speed = 0.05F;        // Speed at which the bat will move.
int lifeCount = 5;          // Number of lives the player has.
int score = 0;              // Player's score.
int numBlocks = 16;         // Number of blocks in the game.
```

At this point, your new bat controller has been added and your code should compile without errors. Try it. If there are problems with the compilation, recheck the steps to this point. Again, there may also be errors if you are copying and pasting code directly from an electronic version of the book. Some characters may not copy correctly to your editor. The compilation errors in this case should help you locate any such issues quite easily.

8 Let's move on to capturing key presses and using them to update the `movementFlags` variable of the `BatController` class. Those flags are used in the `Move()` function of our bat controller to update the position of the bat. First, in the `Begin()` function for the `MovementAction` class, comment out the existing code, to prevent key presses from updating the position of the camera. We will want to move the bat instead with the following code:

```
void MovementAction::Begin(void)
{
    // This function is called when the input control
    // associated with this particular action is activated
    // (e.g., a key was pressed).

    /* Change 8: Comment out the next lines to avoid moving the
       camera when the WASD keys are pressed.
    GameWorld *world = static_cast<GameWorld *>
```

```
        (TheWorldMgr->GetWorld());
    if (world)
    {
        SpectatorCamera *camera = world->GetSpectatorCamera();
        camera->SetSpectatorFlags(camera->GetSpectatorFlags()
            | movementFlag);
    }
    */

    // We want to move the bat now instead, so we update the
    // movementFlags variable of the BatController class here.
    // We will check the value of the movementFlags later
    // in the Move() function of the BatController and will
    // update the position of the bat accordingly.

    BatController *controller = TheGame->GetBatController();
    if (controller) controller->SetMovementFlags
        (controller->GetMovementFlags() | movementFlag);
}

// End Change 8
```

Here, we obtain a pointer to our bat controller object from the `TheGame` instance, and we use this pointer to set the `movementFlags` variable.

9 In the `End()` function of the `MovementAction` class we now remove the flag associated with any key which was just released by the player, and again remove the code related to moving the camera:

```
void MovementAction::End(void)
{
    /* Change 9 - commenting out the following section:
    GameWorld *world = static_cast<GameWorld *>
        (TheWorldMgr->GetWorld());
    if (world)
    {
        // If a world is loaded, remove the movement from
        // the spectator camera.
        SpectatorCamera *camera = world->GetSpectatorCamera();
        camera->SetSpectatorFlags(camera->GetSpectatorFlags()
```

```
            & ~movementFlag);
    }
    */

    // Here, we remove the flag associated with any key that was
    // just released by the player.

    BatController *controller = TheGame->GetBatController();
    if (controller) controller->SetMovementFlags
        (controller->GetMovementFlags() & ~movementFlag);
}

// End Change 9
```

If you compile and run your code at this point you can already check that you can add the bat controller to any geometry inside the **World Editor** and that you can move that geometry using the WASD keys at runtime. In fact, if you copy the Bat world from the resources for this chapter into the <C4>/Data/Tutorial/World/ folder, and then open and run that world, you will already be able to play the game. Go ahead and test that if you wish. You will notice that the ball bounces around, but that the blocks it interacts with do not disappear when hit. There is also no score on the screen to inform the player about progress. Lets make some more changes to include these features next.

10 OK, now that we have the bat working, let's make changes to the `BallController` class to improve the interactions with the other objects in the game world. Start by adding some private data members as in `SimpleBall.h` as follows:

```
// Change 10: Add private data members.

Point3D       startingPosition;

TextWidget    *displayScoreText;
TextWidget    *displayGameOverText;
String<25>    scoreText;
String<25>    lifeText;
String<25>    winText;
String<40>    loseText;
```

```
// See chapter in Part III called "Using String tables".
const StringTable myStringTable;

// End Change 10
```

And then add the following public functions to the `BallController` class:

```
// Change 10: Add new public functions.

const StringTable *GetMyStringTable(void) const
{
   return (&myStringTable);
}

RigidBodyStatus HandleNewGeometryContact(const GeometryContact
   *contact);

TextWidget *DisplayText(char *pText, const float x, const float y);

// End Change 10
```

11 Back in the source file, replace the constructor and destructor functions as follows:

```
// Change 11

BallController::BallController() :
      RigidBodyController(kControllerBall),
      myStringTable("game/MyStrings")
{
}

BallController::BallController(const BallController&
   ballController) :
      RigidBodyController(ballController),
      myStringTable("game/MyStrings")
{
   // This constructor is called when a ball controller is cloned.
}
```

```
BallController::~BallController()
{
    delete displayGameOverText;
    delete displayScoreText;
}

// End Change 11
```

12 Now replace the `Preprocess()` function with the following:

```
// Change 12

void BallController::Preprocess(void)
{
    // This function is called once before the target node is ever
    // rendered or moved. The base class Preprocess() function
    // should always be called first, and then the subclass can do
    // whatever preprocessing it needs to do.

    RigidBodyController::Preprocess();

    // Make sure the ball will bounce sufficiently.
    SetRestitutionCoefficient(0.9F);

    // The number of lives is reset to 5 at the start of each game.
    lifeCount = 5;
    score = 0;

    // We use a string table for static game text instead
    // of hard-coded strings stored directly in the code.

    scoreText = GetMyStringTable()->GetString(StringID('SCOR'));
    lifeText = GetMyStringTable()->GetString(StringID('LIFE'));
    winText = GetMyStringTable()->GetString(StringID('WINT'));
    loseText = GetMyStringTable()->GetString(StringID('LOSE'));

    displayGameOverText = nullptr;
    displayScoreText = DisplayText(lifeText +
        Text::IntegerToString(lifeCount) + " : " + scoreText +
```

```
        Text::IntegerToString(score), 10.0F, 10.0F);

    // Record ball's initial position.
    startingPosition = GetTargetNode()->GetWorldPosition();

    // Give the ball a definite x and y direction velocity
    // initially. Change this to say -2.5F for a more
    // challenging game!

    Vector3D      ballInitialVelocity;

    ballInitialVelocity.x = ballInitialVelocity.y = -1.5F;
    ballInitialVelocity.z = 0.0F;

    // Set the ball off towards the blocks at the start of the game.
    SetLinearVelocity(ballInitialVelocity);
}

// End Change 12
```

13 Still in `SimpleBall.cpp`, replace the `HandleNewRigidBodyContact()` function with `HandleNewGeometryContact()`, since we want to react to interactions of the ball with geometries such as the blocks. Be sure to also comment out the declaration of `HandleNewRigidBodyContact()` in `SimpleBall.h`:

```
// Change 13   Replace HandleNewRigidBodyContact() with
// HandleNewGeometryContact().

// We want to react to interactions of the ball with geometries,
// such as the blocks.

RigidBodyStatus BallController::HandleNewGeometryContact(
    const GeometryContact *contact)
{
    Node *node = GetTargetNode();
    String<30> nodeName = "NoName";
    Geometry *geometry = contact->GetContactGeometry();
```

```
if (geometry->GetNodeName())
{
    // Get name of node that was hit, if any.
    nodeName = geometry->GetNodeName();
}

// Add a sound effect and some sparks.

Zone *zone = node->GetOwningZone();
Point3D zonePosition = zone->GetInverseWorldTransform()
    * contact->GetGeometryContactPosition();
OmniSource *source = nullptr;

// Play a different sound depending on what was hit.

if (Text::CompareText(nodeName, "OutOfBounds"))
{
    lifeCount--;    // Lose a life!

    source = new OmniSource("model/Teleport", 50.0F);

    delete displayScoreText;
    displayScoreText = DisplayText(lifeText
        + Text::IntegerToString(lifeCount) + " : " + scoreText
        + Text::IntegerToString(score), 10.0F, 10.0F);

    if (lifeCount == 0)
    {
        // If no lives left.
        delete displayGameOverText;
        displayGameOverText = DisplayText(loseText,
            450.0F, 10.0F);

        // Let ball bounce simply on the spot - game over!
        SetLinearVelocity(Vector3D(0.0F, 0.0F, 0.0F));
        return (kRigidBodyDestroyed);
    }
}
else if (Text::CompareText(nodeName, "Bat"))
{
```

```
        source = new OmniSource("model/Beep1", 50.0F);

        // Increase speed of ball on each hit of the bat.
        SetLinearVelocity(GetLinearVelocity() * 1.2F);
    }
    else if (Text::CompareText(nodeName, "Block"))
    {
        source = new OmniSource("model/Ball", 50.0F);
    }

    if (source)
    {
        source->SetNodePosition(zonePosition);
        zone->AddNewSubnode(source);
    }

    // This code adds sparks when a block is hit.

    if (Text::CompareText(nodeName, "Block"))
    {
        score++;
        delete geometry;

        SparkParticleSystem *sparks = new SparkParticleSystem (20);
        sparks->SetNodePosition(zonePosition);
        zone->AddNewSubnode(sparks);

        delete displayScoreText;
        displayScoreText = DisplayText(lifeText
            + Text::IntegerToString(lifeCount) + " : " + scoreText
            + Text::IntegerToString(score), 10.0F, 10.0F);

        if (score >= numBlocks)
        {
            // You won, so end the game by deleting the ball.
            delete displayGameOverText;
            displayGameOverText = DisplayText(winText, 450.0f, 10.0f);
            SetLinearVelocity(Vector3D(0.0F, 0.0F, 0.0F));
            return (kRigidBodyDestroyed);
        }
```

```
    }

    return (kRigidBodyUnchanged);
}

// End Change 13
```

14 At the end of the `SimpleBall.cpp` file, add a new `DisplayText()` function to display text on screen:

```
// Change 14: Function to display score, etc., on the screen.

TextWidget *BallController::DisplayText(char *pText, const float x,
    const float y)
{
    TextWidget *pTextWidget = new TextWidget(pText);
    pTextWidget->SetFont("font/Sword");
    pTextWidget->SetWidgetColor(ColorRGBA(1.0F, 0.0F, 0.0F));
    pTextWidget->SetWidgetPosition(Point3D(x, y, 0.0F));
    pTextWidget->SetWidgetSize(Vector2D(250.0F, 10.0F));
    TheInterfaceMgr->AddWidget(pTextWidget);
    return (pTextWidget);
}

// End Change 14
```

You should be able to compile your code now without errors. And now that we have the bat controller and ball controller behavior coded and ready to go, let's build a world to test it in.

The SimpleBat World

Before we get started in the **World Editor**, make sure to copy the file named `myStrings.str` into the directory <C4>/Data/Demo/game/. This file contains the string tables for the user interface text that is shown in the game. If you later want to change the text in those strings, place the file named myStrings.txt into the directory <C4>/Import/Demo/game/. Then choose **Tools > Import String Table** to import that file. For more details about string tables, see Chapter 13, "Using String Tables".

A completed SimpleBat world is shown in Figure 16-2 and is supplied with the resources for this chapter. It is called `BatWorld.wld`. To try out the game right away, you can copy `BatWorld.wld` into the directory <C4>/Data/Tutorial/World/ and then run C4 code using that world to test it.

To create the SimpleBat world in the **World Editor** yourself, do the following:

1. Open the Water world that is located in the Data/Tutorial/world/ directory.
2. Save the world as "BatWorld".
3. Open the scene graph in one of the viewports by right-clicking and choosing **Scene Graph** from the contextual menu.
4. Use the middle-mouse button to move the scene graph until it is in view.

You can also scroll with the middle-mouse button to zoom in and out if needed.

5. Delete all nodes except for the spectator camera, (which is the first node in the scene graph by default), the infinite light, the physics node, and the skybox.
6. Select the Cinder Block material in the **Material Manager** window.

Figure 16-2. The completed SimpleBat world in the **World Editor**.

7 Select the **Box** tool on the **Geometry** page panel.

8 In a top, front or side viewport, drag out seven cubes of any size, anywhere in the world.

Six of these cubes will be used for the geometry of the playing area and one of the cubes will be the bat. We will update their sizes and positions in a few steps.

9 For each of the six of these cubes we just created, choose **Node > Get Info (Ctrl-I)** to open the **Node Info** dialog, and set the node names to the values (e.g., "far wall", "near wall", and "floor") that are indicated in the following list:

- "Far Wall"
- "Floor"
- "Right Side Wall"
- "Left Side Wall"
- "Roof " (which will be invisible)
- "OutOfBounds" (which will be the nearest wall to the player)

10 Choose **Page > Transform** to open the **Transform** page panel, if its not already open. Minimize or close some of the other pages if you can't see the **Transform** page panel at the bottom left of the screen.

11 Assign the following position, rotation and size details to the each of these six cubes, so that they become the walls, the floor and the roof of the game world.

- near wall called "OutOfBounds": Position (5.9, -2.0, 0.0), Rotation (0,0,0), Size (0.1, 4.0, 1.0)
- far wall: Position (-2, -2, 0.0), Rotation (0,0,0), Size (0.3, 4.3, 1.0)
- floor: Position (-2.0, -2.0, 0.0), Rotation (0,0,0), Size (8.0, 4.3, 0.3)
- right side wall: Position (-2.0, 2.0, 0.0), Rotation (0,0,0), Size (8.0, 0.3, 1.0)
- left side wall: Position (-2.0, -2.0, 0.0), Rotation (0,0,0), Size (8.0, 0.3, 1.0)
- roof: Position (-2.0, -2.0, 1.0), Rotation (0,0,0), Size (8.0, 4.0, 0.3)

The seventh cube will be our bat, so give that cube the following position and size using the Transform page:

- bat: Position (5.0, -0.5, 0.2), Rotation (0,0,0), Size (0.2, 1.3, 0.7)

12 To make the bat semi-transparent, click on it and choose **Node > Get Info (Ctrl-I)** to open the **Node Info** dialog.

13 In the **Geometry** tab of the **Node Info** dialog, select the "Render geometry in effects pass" option.

14 Turn off shadows for the bat by deselecting the "Render stencil shadow" option.

15 In the **Node** tab, set the node name to "Bat". The code will look for that name and will use it to decide which sound to play when the ball is hit by the bat.

16 In the **Controller** tab, make sure to set the controller to "Moving Bat", for the bat geometry. Set the restitution coefficient to 0.9 to make sure the ball bounces when it hits other geometries. Set the friction coefficient to 0.0 so that the ball keeps moving and doesn't slow down. The controller will enable the bat to respond to keyboard presses.

17 Click OK to save your changes.

18 In the **Material Manager**, create a new material for the bat and set the diffuse color to red and the diffuse alpha value to about 150.

19 Name the new material "Bat".

20 Click Close to exit the **Material Manager**, and then choose **Geometry > Set Material (Ctrl-M)** to assign it to the bat geometry.

21 Assign the following values to the spectator camera so that the camera is at the right position and facing the right way when you start the game:

- Locator (spec): Position (10.0, 0.0, 4.0), Rotation (0,-20,180)

22 With the spectator camera still selected, choose **Node > Get Info (Ctrl-I)** to open the **Node Info** dialog and select the **Locator** tab panel.

23 Type "spec" for spectator as the locator type in the **Locator** tab, if it isn't already set to that value.

24 For each of the near ("OutOfBounds") and roof geometries, open the **Node Info** dialog once again. Select the "Geometry is invisible" option. Turn off shadows for these invisible geometries by deselecting the "Render stencil shadow" option.

25 Assign any material you like to the visible walls and the floor. We used the Cinder Block material.

26 Turn off shadows for the visible walls and floor too.

27 If you haven't done so already, make sure to name the near wall node "OutOfBounds". The code will look for this node to see if the ball has passed the player.

28 Add in a ball model from the **Models** page.

29 If it isn't open, choose **Page > Models** to open the **Models** page panel.

30 Place the ball model anywhere in the world by first left-clicking on the model named Bouncing Balls in the **Models** page panel and then clicking on one of the directional viewports, or by clicking on the Infinite Zone node of the scene graph viewport.

31 Use the **Transform** page panel to position the ball at (4.0, 0.0, 1.0).

32 Set the rotation of the ball model to zero using the **Transform** page panel. You may have also noticed that the code looks for nodes named "Block" when a ball hits a geometry.

33 Use the **Geometries** panel of the **World Editor** to add box geometries (or any other shape). Place these geometries inside the playing area. The player will try to destroy these geometries by hitting them with the ball.

34 Name each of the box nodes "Block" by selecting the geometry, choosing **Node > Get Info (Ctrl-I)** to open the **Node Info** dialog, and setting the name in the **Node** tab panel.

It's best to create size, position, material and name for a single block node first, and then copy-and-paste to create the others. This will eliminate the step of naming and resizing each block individually. The named geometry nodes will disappear when hit by the ball.

Now try it out. You win if you can eliminate all of the blocks before losing all of your lives. Have fun!

Your Turn

The best way to continue your learning experience with the C4 Engine is to start making games like *SimpleBat* yourself. You might want to begin by changing the game world, perhaps by copying the room we used above and connecting the original room to the new room via a glass tube. The ball will then sometimes escape from one room and move into another to wipe out the blocks there. You may or may not have a bat in that other room to hit the ball with, your choice.

> **GLASS MATERIAL**
> To make a glass (transparent) material for any geometry, assign a diffuse alpha value of about 100 using the **Material Manager**. Then choose **Node > Get Info (Ctrl-I)** to open the **Node Info** dialog, and select the "Render in effects pass" option.

You might want to make a whole series of rooms, each with different features and connect them all together in interesting ways with glass tubes. Then see if you can use what you've learned here to start making a 3D version of a game like *Pac-Man*. Instead of controlling a bat, you will be controlling a spherical shape that "eats" items in it's path. That's easy. Just use the **World Editor** to change the geometry that you call "Bat" from cuboid to spherical. You could create a 3D maze of transparent tubes.

You might change the rules so that if you (the player) are hit by the bouncing ball, then you loose a life. The goal of the game would be to eat all the "edible" items in the game world before losing all your lives. Edible here means that the item disappears when "hit" by the player.

The next Chapter, *SimpleSnake*, provides code to implement some of these ideas. Note that unlike the controller used for our bat, the controller used in *SimpleSnake* derives from `RigidBodyController`, providing additional functions which are useful for checking collisions with objects in the environment.

Extra Credit

If your spherical "hero" is an animated model, you would choose to activate certain animations depending on which keys were pressed. You can study the code in the *SimpleChar* tutorial, which has an animated soldier character, for an example of how to control model animations from code. "Ghost" enemy models might chase the hero along predefined paths. Our game tutorial *SimpleEnemies* in Chapter 19 shows you how to program your enemies to follow predefined paths.

You might also want to use artificial intelligence (AI) to make your enemy objects chase the hero intelligently (i.e., *not* along fixed predefined paths). AI is not within the scope of the *Guide*, but see the article "Pathfinding with C4" on the C4 wiki[1] for an example of such a navigation system. You can also search for

---

[1] http://www.terathon.com/wiki/index.php/Main_Page

the keyword "Pathfinding" on the C4 Forums to see how others have approached the topic. And importantly, the demo game shipped with C4 provides the source code for monsters which chase after and attack the player. As you become more proficient with C4, you should study those examples to see how to provide interesting behaviors for your game characters.

17

SimpleSnake

In this chapter, we will look at how to create a 3D version of the well-known 2D game called *Snake*.

Introduction

The *SimpleSnake* game builds on the game in Chapter 16, "*SimpleBat*", but this time, instead of controlling a geometry with the keyboard, we will allow the user to control a rigid body and will be utilizing C4's native physics. Some additional C4 Engine features are introduced in this tutorial game, such as adding models to the game world at run time from within the *SimpleSnake* code.

In the *SimpleSnake* game, shown in Figure 17-1, the main character is a snake whose head and body are made up of spheres created using the **World Editor** tool. The snake will eat "food", which we will place in the game world using a simple shape created within the **World Editor** tool.

Getting the Game Up and Running with the C4 Engine

To get the SimpleSnake game up and running with the C4 Engine, follow these steps:

1. Open up Visual C++.
2. Open your C4 solution file.
3. Right-click the C4 solution at the top of the Solution Explorer pane, and choose **Add > New Project** from the contextual menu.

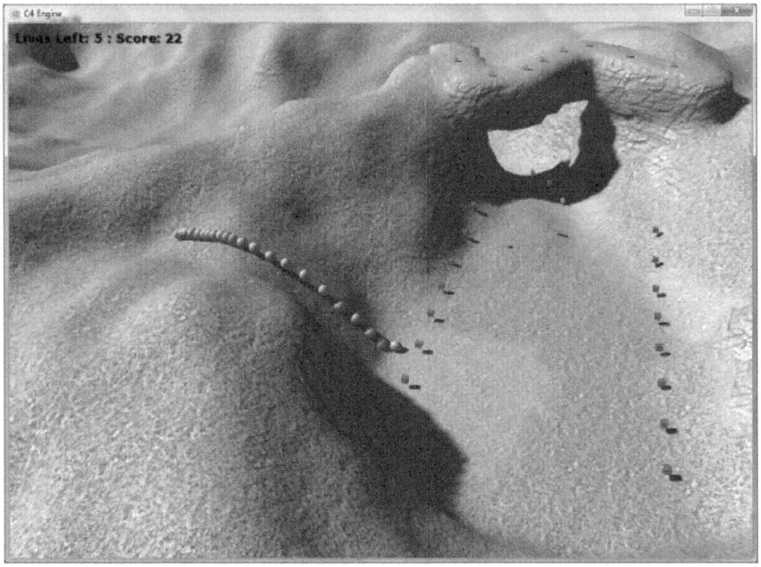

Figure 17-1. A preview of the *SimpleSnake* game.

4. Choose a Win32 Console Application and name it *SimpleSnake*.
5. Click OK.
6. When the application wizard appears, click Next.
7. Choose DLL and Empty Project.
8. Click Finish.
9. Copy the files `SimpleSnake.cpp` and `SimpleSnake.h` that come with the resources for this chapter into the <C4>/GameCode/ directory.
10. In the new *SimpleSnake* project group in the Solution Explorer, right-click on the Source folder, and choose **Add > Existing Item**.
11. Choose the source file named `SimpleSnake.cpp`, located in the <C4>/GameCode/ directory.
12. In the same way, add the header file named `SimpleSnake.h` to the Header folder of your *SimpleSnake* project.
13. Press F7 to compile the your solution.

At this point, you'll encounter compiler errors, which will be fixed in the next section.

Setting the Project Properties

14 Right-click on your *SimpleSnake* project and choose **Properties**.

15 Select the **C++ > General** panel.

16 Add the directory <C4>/EngineCode/ to the Additional Include Directories field.

17 Select the **Preprocessor** panel and add the following entries to the list of preprocessor definitions:

```
C4WINDOWS
C4DEBUG
```

18 Click OK and then click Apply.

Next, we need to tell the linker where it can find `C4.lib`.

19 In the **Linker > General** panel group, select Additional Library Directories, and browse to <C4>/VisualStudio2010/C4/Engine/Debug/.

20 Click OK, and then click Apply.

21 In the **Input** panel, just below the General section for the linker, add `C4Engine.lib` to the Additional Dependencies setting.

22 Click Apply.

Finally, let's make sure that the compiled `SimpleSnake.dll` file gets copied to the same directory as your C4 executable.

23 In the **Custom Build Setup > General** panel group, set the value of Command Line to this command:

```
xcopy $(Outdir)$(TargetFileName) ..\..\.. /Y
```

Note that you can also copy and paste these values from the properties of one of the existing C4 projects, say *SimpleChar*.

24 Also in the **Custom Build Setup > General** panel group, set the value of Description to this value:

```
Copying Executable
```

25 And finally, staying in the **Custom Build Setup > General** panel group, set the value of Outputs to this value:

```
..\..\..\$(TargetFileName)
```

26 Click Apply and then click OK, and you're done.

To recap, using the project properties you told the compiler

- about some C4 specific preprocessor definitions,
- to place the compiled DLL in the same directory as `C4.exe`,
- that the header (include) files are located in <C4>/EngineCode/, and
- you told the linker that the `C4.lib` file is located in <C4>/VisualStudio/C4/Engine/Debug/.

27 Go ahead and compile again—this time you should get no errors.

Check that the `SimpleSnake.dll` file has been copied to the same directory as your C4 executable.

28 Browse to Data/Game/ and edit the file named `game.cfg`.

29 Change the `$gameModuleName` variable to the value "SimpleSnake".

In this game, as in the previous chapter with *SimpleBat*, we will use the WASD keys to move the snake. We will use an additional key (e.g., the U key) to move upwards. The camera will continue to be controlled by the mouse, but will not be moved. So we will need to place the spectator camera in the world so that the user has a good view of the playing field. We will do that later.

In `SimpleSnake.h`, you will see lines like this:

```
kActionForward     = 'frwd',
kActionBackward    = 'bkwd',
kActionLeft        = 'left',
kActionRight       = 'rght',
kActionUp          = 'jump'
```

These show the four-character codes that we need to bind to keys for movement. In our `input.cfg` file, located in the <WindowsUser>/AppData/Roaming/C4 Engine/ directory (on Windows), we bind keys to those four-character codes.

30 Check that the file contains bindings for each of these codes, e.g.:

```
bind "D" %rght;
bind "A" %left;
bind "W" %frwd;
bind "S" %bkwd;
bind "SPACE" %jump;
```

Depending on your keyboard language ssettings, the jump key may or may not be linked to the „SPACE“ key. For example, for a German keyboard, the default binding is to the "LEER" key.

31 Since we are again using C4 string tables, copy the file named `SnakeStrings.str` into the directory <C4>/Data/Demo/game/.

If you later want to change the strings, place the file named `Snake-Strings.txt` into the directory <C4>/Import/Demo/game/, and choose **Tools > Import String Table** to import that file. For more details about string tables, see Chapter 13, "Using String Tables".

Note that two sample worlds have been provided as part of the resources for this chapter. One is called SnakeWaterWorld, and it results from following the tutorial steps below. Another uses a terrain and is called SnakeTerrain. When playing in this world, you will notice how C4's physics system calculates the trajectory of the rigid body for us, as our snake follows the contours of the landscape.

We suggest you try out the game using the SnakeTerrain world first, before building your own world using the steps below.

To build a world to test the new `SnakeController` code, carry out the following steps in the **World Editor**.

32 Start C4 and choose **World > New World (Ctrl-N)** to create a new world to create a model for our snake body parts. We'll use simple geometries for the food.

33 Create a simple sphere geometry for the snake piece, by selecting the sphere geometry in the **Geometries** page panel and then dragging out a sphere in the top (x-y) viewport.

34 Open the **Transform** page panel.

35 Set all rotations and x, y, and z position coordinates to a value of 0.0.

36 Set the size values to 1.0 for x, y, and z.

37 Choose **Node > Get Info (Ctrl-I)** to open up the **Node Info** dialog for the Snake model. Select the **Collision** tab and deselect all checkboxes. Click OK to save your changes.

38 Apply the default material for the snake piece. You can of course apply any material you choose.

39 Now open the **Physics** page panel and drag out a sphere shape. In the **Transform** page set the position, rotation and size values to be the same as for the spherical geometry.

40 Select **World > Save to Model Resource** to save the the snake piece as `SnakeHead.mdl` and place it models in the Data/Tutorial/model/ directory. This step is important—the code will look for the model there.

41 Close the world and discard any changes. We only used this world temporarily, to create our simple model for the snake.

42 Choose **World > Open World (Ctrl-O)**.

43 Select the `Water.wld` file, which is located in the Data/Tutorial/world/ directory.

44 Save the world under a new file name, such as SnakeWaterWorld.

45 Choose **Page > Models** to open the **Models** page panel.

46 Left-click to select the Snake Head model.

47 Click in any viewport to place the model in the world. Click on the "Toggle Models" button in the **World Editor** button panel if your model is not visible in the perspective viewport.

48 Choose **Node > Get Info (Ctrl-I)** to open up the **Node Info** dialog for the snake-head node.

49 Select the **Controller** tab panel, and select the Snake Head controller if it's not already selected.

50 Use the **Transform** page panel to set the *z* value of the snake head so that it is located above the ground when the game starts.

You should place the snake model at the location of the head of the snake when the game starts. We placed the snake model in our copy of the Water world at $(-20, -30, 5)$. The x, y, and z rotations are all set to 0.0.

51 For the food, create a simple sphere geometry by selecting the sphere geometry in the **Geometries** page panel and then dragging out a sphere in the top (*x-y*) viewport.

We are using a geometry for the food to illustrate the use of `RigidBodyController` function `HandleNewGeometryContact()`. As described later in this Chapter, this function is called whenever our snake hits a geometry and provides automatic collision detection for your game, so that you don't need to code collision detection functionality yourself.

52 Open the **Transform** page panel.

53 Set all rotations to a value of 0.0. and position the food at the location you want it to be when the game starts up. We placed ours at $(10,-30,1)$.

54 Set the size values to 1.0 for x and y. Flatten the geometry somewhat by setting the z size value to 0.5.

55 Apply a different colored material for the food piece. We used yellow.

56 Choose **Node > Get Info (Ctrl-I)** to open up the **Node Info** dialog for the food node, and in the **Node** tab, set the node name to "Food".

57 Still in the **Node Info** dialog for the food node, select the **Controller** tab and check that the food node has no controller set for it, since the food itself doesn't move. Click OK.

58 Copy and paste this food geometry as many times as you wish and place the copies around the world.

59 Next, use the **Geometries** page panel to create additional geometries of your choosing and place them as obstacles for the snake. Give them a different color, say red. Use **Node > Get Info (Ctrl-I)** to open up the **Node Info** and in the **Node** tab, set the node name to "Enemy".

When the snake hits one of these "Enemy" nodes, the player loses a life. This is also handled in the `HandleNewGeometryContact()` function, as described later in the chapter.

60 Finally, place the spectator camera in your world so that you have a good view of the playing field.

We placed the camera in our copy of the **Water** world at $(-50,-25,30)$. The x and z rotations are both zero, and we gave the y rotation a value of 45.0.

61 Choose **World > Save and Play World (Ctrl-P)** to try out the game.

Game Design and Implementation

When it comes to making simple games, there is a tendency to get straight down to coding. Resist that temptation. Your best tool at this point is a piece of paper and a pencil. Before you begin any coding at all, make sure to make an outline design for your game. For this game, the main designing activity revolved around figuring out

- how to update the snakes position each frame,
- how to add a new body piece when food was eaten, and
- how to ensure that all body parts follow along the same path as the head of the snake.

That all sounds relatively simple, but it is full of devious surprises. The only way to make sure the code will have a chance of working, is to sit down first of all and at the very least, sketch out a design on a piece of paper. A little time invested in design work up front, will guarantee to save you hours of corrections and bug fixing in the end.

Here is an overview of the steps this game goes through along with the corresponding code.

1 Initialize some game variables in the `Preprocess()` function of our controller:

```
// Change this (say to 0.2F) to give the snake more bounce
SetRestitutionCoefficient(0.0F);

// We use a string table for static game text
// instead of hard-coded strings stored directly in the code.
scoreText = GetMyStringTable()->GetString(StringID('SCOR'));
lifeText = GetMyStringTable()->GetString(StringID('LIFE'));
winText = GetMyStringTable()->GetString(StringID('WINT'));
loseText = GetMyStringTable()->GetString(StringID('LOSE'));

displayGameOverText = displayScoreText = nullptr;

// Reset Game Variables
speed = 30.0F;       // Factor to multiply external forces
lifeCount = 5;       // Number of lives the player has
score = 0;           // Player's score
```

```
myCount = 0.0F;      // Counter for time passed
bodyCount = 0;       // Length of the Snake's body.
```

2 When the game is running, keyboard presses are processed in the `Begin()` function of the `MovementAction` class. Depending on which key was pressed, we update movement flags, which are then used to determine how the head of the snake moves—forward, backward, left, right, up, or down.

Here is the code which is executed when a key is pressed:

```
void MovementAction::Begin(void)
{
   // ...

   SnakeController *controller = TheGame->GetSnakeController();
   if (controller)
   {
      controller->SetMovementFlags(controller->GetMovementFlags()
         | movementFlag);
   }

   // ...
}
```

If the forward key is pressed, the `movementFlag` variable is set to the value for forward, which is 1. And then later in the `Move()` function, we update the force variable (`snakeForce`), which will be used to apply external force on the snake, as follows:

```
void SnakeController::Move(void)
{
   // ...
   if (movementFlags & 1)     // Forward
   {
      snakeForce.x += 1.0F;
   }
   // ...
}
```

3 Staying in the `Move()` function, we use the function `SetExternalForce()` to translate the request to move forward into a change in external force upon the snake. We also dampen the acceleration using `SetExternalLinearResistance()`. The speed variable is a factor used to scale the force. It increases as more food is eaten by the snake.

```
SetExternalForce(speed * snakeForce);
SetExternalLinearResistance(Vector2D(5.0F, 5.0F));
```

4 Because our snake controller is a subclass of `RigidBodyController`, the head of the snake is moved automatically by C4's physics system. If you study the code in `C4Physics.cpp`, you will see that as part of the processing the following functions are called:

- `CalculateAppliedForces()` – adds the external forces to gravity, as well as any impulses applied to the rigid body.
- `DetectGeometryCollisions()` – detects if there is a collision with another geometry. This in turn calls several functions, which calculate how the rigid body should react to the collision.

5 Then the functions `Constrain()`, `Integrate()`, and `Finalize()` are called. Within `Finalize()`, there is a call to our `HandleNewGeometryCollision()` function, which is where we code the application specific response to collisions. We will come back to the `HandleNewGeometryCollision()` function again below.

6 Note that within the `Move()` function, we do not move the body parts of the snake each cycle—a counter (called `myCount`) is used to ensure that at least 250 ms pass before the body parts of the snake are moved again. You can raise or lower that value and check how it changes the rate of update of the body parts.

```
myCount += TheTimeMgr->GetFloatDeltaTime();

if (myCount > 250.0F)
{
   // minimum of 250 ms per movement
   myCount = 0.0F;
   if (bodyCount > 0)
```

```
    {
        MoveLastToFront();
    }
}
```

7 The function `MoveLastToFront()` works as follows. The body pieces of the snake are models which are stored in an array called `bodyModel`. The last body part in the chain is updated to the location of the head, while the head in the meantime has moved on due to the forces acting on it. All other body parts remain where they are. This gives the illusion that the whole snake is moving:

```
void SnakeController::MoveLastToFront(void)
{
    Transform4D startTransform = GetTargetNode()->
        GetNodeTransform();    // Transform of snake's head
    Point3D startPos = startTransform.GetTranslation();
    bodyModel[Index[bodyCount - 1]]->SetNodePosition(startPos);
    bodyModel[Index[bodyCount - 1]]->Invalidate();
    int tmp = Index[bodyCount - 1];
    for (int i = 1; i < bodyCount; i++)
        Index[bodyCount - i] = Index[bodyCount - (i + 1)];
    Index[0] = tmp;
}
```

8 As mentioned above, when the snake's head collides with a geometry, C4's physics calls the function `HandleNewGeometryContact()` for us. So there we can implement checks to see what geometry was "eaten" by the snake. We simply use the node's name, which can easily be set within the **World Editor** as described earlier in this chapter. We used the name "Food" for food and "Enemy" for obstacles. If the head of the snake "eats food", i.e., if the head of the snake collides with a food node, then we create a new body part. The new body part goes to the position of the head node, while the head node continues to be moved automatically by the physics system, because of the forces acting on it. All other body parts, this time including the last body part, remain where they are. This is the code to create a new body part, which is a new instance of the snake model.

```
if (Text::CompareText(nodeName, "Food"))     // Hit food
{
    // ...

    Model *model = nullptr;
    Transform4D startTransform = GetTargetNode()->
        GetNodeTransform();    // leader's transform
    Point3D startPos = startTransform.GetTranslation();
    model = Model::Get(kModelSnake);
    bodyModel[bodyCount++] = model;
    if (model)
    {
        Zone *zone = world->FindZone(startPos);

        for (int i = 1; i < bodyCount; i++)
            Index[bodyCount - i] = Index[bodyCount - (i + 1)];

        Index[0] = bodyCount - 1;
        Point3D zonePosition = zone->GetInverseWorldTransform()
            * startPos;
        model->SetNodePosition(zonePosition);
        zone->AddNewSubnode(model);
        model->Update();
    }

    // ...
}
```

Note that we do not assign a controller to body parts. Only the head has been assigned the `SnakeController` and it determines how the body parts "move".

9 When the snake collides with the food, the first thing we did was to call `Set-LinearVelocity()`. The reason is that we want the snake to "eat" the food but not be recoiled by it.

```
SetLinearVelocity(GetOriginalLinearVelocity());
```

10 When the snake collides with and "Enemy" node, we decrease the number of lives by one. If you hit an enemy too often you lose the game. Note that we do not call `SetLinearVelocity()` in this case, and you will notice that the

snake "bumps" into enemy nodes, whereas it glides through the food it eats, as explained above.

```
else if (Text::CompareText(nodeName, "Enemy"))
{
   delete geometry;    // remove the obstacle
   lifeCount--;        // lose a life!

   // ...

   if (lifeCount == 0)    // if no lives left
   {
      // ...

      Sleep();      // Put the Snake to sleep!
      return (kRigidBodyDestroyed);
   }
}
```

11 You win the game if you manage to make a snake which is `MAX_BODY_PARTS` body parts long. Don't forget to use the "up" key to eat some of the harder to reach food pieces!

```
else
{
   // The snake is MAX_BODY_PARTS long now,
   // so GAME OVER, you WON!!
   delete displayGameOverText;
   displayGameOverText = DisplayText(winText, 250.0F, 10.0F);
}
```

Your Turn

Here are a number of enhancements you could make to the *SimpleSnake* game:

- Use the world editor to create additional levels in your game with collidable walls, and other obstacles, which would make for a more challenging game. Each game level could involve ever more complex obstacle courses to be managed. Perhaps the snake does not have enough energy initially to reach all the food items. Perhaps there are "keys" in the world which open doors to otherwise unreachable parts of the world.

- Make the required changes to detect collisions with other rigid bodies. Use the C4 callback `HandleNewRigidBodyContact()`.
- Replace the simple geometries with more snake-like or food-like 3D models from your modeling package.
- See if you can go back and change the code in the *SimpleBat* tutorial, so that the `BatController` class derives from `RigidBodyController` instead of deriving from `Controller`.

18

SimpleCar

This chapter presents some simple changes you can make to the *SimpleChar* tutorial code, to control a vehicle such as a tank or a sports car, instead of the soldier model.

About *SimpleCar*

Before we begin this chapter, it is important to be aware that the changes we will be making here to *SimpleChar*, to transform it into *SimpleCar*, are less about a how to make a realistic vehicle controller, and more about understanding the code that's there already. Our intention is to show where and how you can tweak the available *SimpleChar* tutorial code, and then check the effects of those changes by running the updated application with the C4 Engine.

The *SimpleChar* tutorial is an example of the minimal code required to get an animated character up and running in a game world running with the C4 Engine. The *SimpleChar* tutorial doesn't include weapons, nor enemies, nor sound, nor special effects. It's purpose is to demonstrate how to work with the C4 Engine APIs to get an FPS-type game off the ground. In this chapter, we will make changes to control a simple vehicle, like a car or a tank. We will add code to create a spring camera, which will trail behind the vehicle and we will make additional changes to swing the camera as the vehicle is turned. We will also make use of a small subset of the new C4 physics API, specifically to set the linear velocity of the vehicle when certain keys are pressed by the user.

Driving a Vehicle Instead of Walking Around

A question sometimes arises on the forums along the lines of, "How do I replace the human-like character of *SimpleChar*, with a vehicle, such as a tank or a car?"

The first attempt most people make is to simply replace or rename the soldier model, but they quickly learn that this is not sufficient. They may notice that the vehicle model they use is shaking from side to side when they start up the game. The reason for this is that the soldier's animations are still being played for the new character model. And since the new character is a vehicle, the animation files don't match at all.

Besides simply swapping out the model, the next thing to do is to switch off those soldier animations, which would otherwise cause your vehicle to move like the soldier does.

Here are the basic steps.

1 Save a copy of the original `SimpleChar.cpp` tutorial file, which you will find under the folder **C4/GameCode/**, then open up `SimpleChar.cpp` in your IDE. In the `SoldierController::Preprocess()` function, comment out these lines:

```
// Model *soldier = GetTargetNode();
// frameAnimator = new FrameAnimator(soldier);
// soldier->SetRootAnimator(frameAnimator);
// ...
// soldier->GetWorld()->AddInteractor(&soldierInteractor);
```

2 At the end of `SoldierController::Move()`, comment out these lines:

```
// if (motion != soldierMotion) SetSoldierMotion(motion);
// ...
// GetTargetNode()->Animate();
```

Now you may want to position the camera differently depending on the size and shape and type of vehicle character you are using.

3 In the `ChaseCamera::Move()` function, you can adjust the height and trail distance of the camera, by adjusting the values in these two lines:

```
// was 1.5F, now (say) 3.5F, so a bit higher up
Point3D p1(position.x, position.y, position.z + 3.5F);

// was 4.0F, now (say) 20.0F, a bit further back
Point3D p2 = p1 - view * 20.0F;
```

4. After you compile these changes (press F7), to test them, change the application name in `Data/Game/game.cfg` file to "SimpleChar":

   ```
   $gameModuleName = "SimpleChar";
   ```

   This change lets the C4 Engine knows that it needs to locate and use the application in `SimpleChar.dll`, which you just changed and recompiled.

5. Start up C4, press Escape and then the tilde/grave key to display the main menu bar.
6. Choose **Tools > Open World (Ctrl-O)**.
7. Navigate to the Tutorial/world/ directory and select the world named `Water.wld`.
8. Choose **World > Save World As**, and save the world as CarWorld.
9. Choose **World > Save and Play World**.

Now you can use the mouse and keyboard to start driving your "soldier", as if it were a vehicle. Kind of weird, eh? This was just a quick test to check if we successfully turned off the soldier animations.

Tanks!

Let's insert a tank model to replace the soldier. If you don't have a tank model, see Appendix C, "Using Blender with the C4 Engine", which shows how you can import free models from Turbosquid to use with the C4 Engine, via Blender (which is also free).

If you want to obtain a more realistic model later on, you can create a simple tank model yourself, using geometry created in the **World Editor**, such as cubes and cylinders. Make sure to completely enclose your model with a physics box shape (see Figure 18-1). An example is provided with the resources for this chapter.

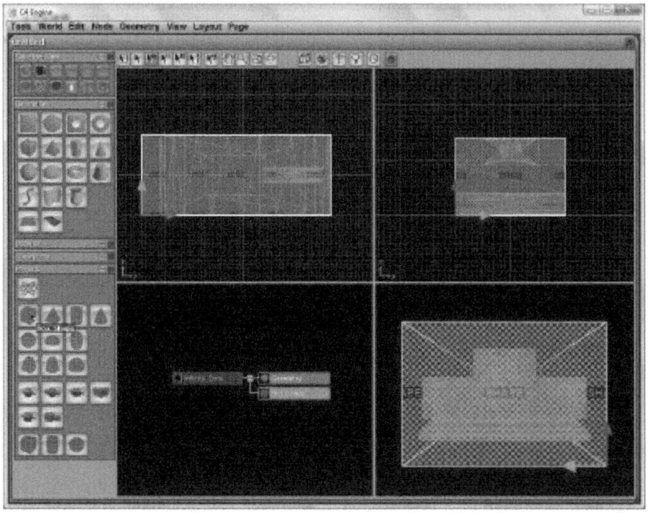

Figure 18-1. The tank shape model in the **World Editor**.

1 Name your tank model TankShapeModel.

2 The code will look in the <C4>/Data/Tutorial/model/ directory, so place the tank model in that location.

3 Select the geometry node of your model and then choose **Node > Get Info (Ctrl-I)** to open up the **Node Info** dialog. Select the **Collision** tab panel.

4 Deselect all checkboxes on the **Collision** tab panel and press OK to save those changes.5 In your code, register your tank model in the `Game::Game()` constructor by changing the following line to use your model instead of the soldier model:

```
soldierModelReg(kModelSoldier, "Tank", "model/TankShapeModel",
    kModelPrecache, kControllerSoldier),
```

Note that your model name does not contain the ending `.mdl` file extension. For this example, it is simply `TankShapeModel`.

6 Compile your code and start up C4 again. Now we are ready to test with the tank model.

7 Choose **Tools > Open World (Ctrl-O)**, and then browse to Tutorial/world/ and again choose your CarWorld.

8 Choose **World -> Save and Play World (Ctrl-P)**.

Now you can start driving your tank around with the mouse and keyboard. Note that if you find your model is still not facing the right way, you can change that by adding a rotation in the code at this line:

```
SetCharacterOrientation(modelAzimuth + K::pi_over_2);
```

In this example, we have added 90 degrees, which may or may not work for you. It depends on the model you are using, so you may have to try subtracting `K::pi_over_2`, or perhaps adding `K::pi` instead. You shouldn't have these problems if you face your model along the *x* axis in the C4 World Editor, and set the *z* axis as the up direction for the model. If you make adjustments to your model, save it using **World > Save to Model Resources**.

Controlling the Model's Altitude and Azimuth Using the Keyboard

When test driving your model, you will notice that the left and right movement keys cause the tank model to slide unrealistically to the left or to the right. The model doesn't turn as you would want it to. Let's change that next.

To use the keyboard instead of the mouse to control the model's orientation (in this case the pitch and yaw, or "altitude" and "azimuth" as it's called in the tutorial code), modify the `SoldierController::Move()` function, in `SimpleChar.cpp`, as follows. The inline comments explain each change:

```
void SoldierController::Move(void)
{
    // This function is called once per frame to
    // allow the controller to move its target node.
    //
    // The movementIndexTable is a 16-entry table that
    // maps all combinations of the forward, backward,
    // left, and right movement flags to one of eight
    // directions.
    //
    // The direction codes are as follows:
    //
```

```
// 0-forward
// 1-backward
// 2-left
// 3-right
// 4-forward and left
// 5-forward and right
// 6-backward and left
// 7-backward and right
//
// The number 8 in the table means no movement,
// and it appears where either no movement buttons
// are being pressed or two opposing buttons are
// the only ones pressed.
// (e.g., left and right pressed simultaneously
// cancel each other out)
static const unsigned char movementIndexTable[16] =
{
    8, 0, 1, 8,
    2, 4, 6, 2,
    3, 5, 7, 3,
    8, 0, 1, 8
};

// First, we grab the mouse deltas from the
// Input Manager.
//
// We use these to change the angles representing
// the direction in which the player is
// looking or moving.

float azm = modelAzimuth;

// Remove mouse control of the azimuth (i.e.,
// "yaw", or rotation around the local z-axis)
// + TheInputMgr->GetMouseDeltaX();

// These next lines update the azimuth based on
// movement of the left and right keyboard controls.

if (movementFlags & 4)        // left
```

```
   azm += 0.005f;
else if (movementFlags & 8)  // right
   azm -= 0.005f;

// Be sure to comment out these next lines:
// if (azm < -K::pi)
// azm += K::two pi;
// else if (azm > K::pi)
// azm -= K::two pi;

// Remove the altitude (or pitch) motion completely.
float alt = 0.0f;

// the line above was:
// float alt = modelAltitude + TheInputMgr->GetVerticalDelta();

// and comment out the next two lines:
// if (alt < -1.45F) alt = -1.45F;
// else if (alt > 1.45F) alt = 1.45F;

modelAzimuth = azm;
modelAltitude = alt;  // this is always zero!

// We have no model animation so comment this line
// int32 motion = kMotionStand;
Vector2D propel(0.0F, 0.0F);

int32 index = movementIndexTable[movementFlags
   & kMovementPlanarMask];
if (index < 8)
{
   // The movementDirectionTable maps each
   // direction code looked up in the
   // movementIndexTable to an angle measured
   // counterclockwise from the straight ahead
   // direction in units of pi/4.

   // Set the 5th and 6th values to zero to prevent
   // movement in those directions.
```

```
static const float movementDirectionTable[8] =
{
   0.0F, 4.0F, 2.0F, -2.0F,
   0.0F, 0.0F, 4.0F, -4.0F
};

float direction = movementDirectionTable[index]
   * K::pi over 4 + modelAzimuth;

/*
If motion is forward, i.e. movementFlags = 1, then index =
movementIndexTable[1] = 0. So, movementDirectionTable[index]
is also 0.0F, and direction = 0.0F * K::pi over 4 +
modelAzimuth, which is simply modelAzimuth, and the model
doesn't turn.

If the motion is backwards, then index = 1 and
movementDirectionTable[index] = 4.0F, so direction = 4.0F *
K::pi over 4 + modelAzimuth = K::pi + modelAzimuth, as you
would expect for backward motion, since K::pi is 180 degrees,
which is facing directly backwards.
*/

// Set propulsive force based on the direction of movement.
// propel = CosSin(direction) * 100.0F;

if (movementFlags & 1)    // forward
{
   if (movementFlags & 4 || movementFlags & 8) // left/right
   {
      // Reduce multiplier to slow on corners
      propel.x = Cos(direction) * 18.0F;
      propel.y = Sin(direction) * 18.0F;
   }
   else  // just forward, straight ahead
   {
      propel.x = Cos(direction) * 20.0F;
      propel.y = Sin(direction) * 20.0F;
   }
}
```

```
        else if (movementFlags & 2) // backward
        {
            propel.x = Cos(direction) * 10.0F;
            propel.y = Sin(direction) * 10.0F;
        }
        // Comment out animation code.
        // motion = ((index == 1) || (index >= 6)) ?
        // kMotionBackward : kMotionForward;
    }

    // Update the external force for the rigid body representing
    // the character. The GetGroundContact() function is a member
    // of the CharacterController base class.

    if (GetGroundContact())
    {
        SetExternalLinearResistance(Vector2D(10.0F, 10.0F));
        SetExternalForce(propel);
    }
    else
    {
        // If the soldier is not on the ground, reduce the
        // propulsive force down to 2%. This controls how well
        // the player is able to control his movement while
        // falling through the air.

        SetExternalLinearResistance(Vector2D(0.0F, 0.0F));
        SetExternalForce(propel * 0.02F);
    }

    // Change the model's orientation.
    // The SetCharacterOrientation() function is a
    // member of the CharacterController base class.
    SetCharacterOrientation(modelAzimuth);

    // The velocity of the model is set now based on the
    // the value of propel, which in turn was set based
    // on which keys were pressed by the user.
    SetLinearVelocity(Vector3D(propel.x, propel.y, 0.0F));
}
```

Now test your new Move() function by building (press F7 in VC++), then starting C4 and running your CarWorld. You'll notice that the turning motion is still very jerky, which just happens to lend itself quite well to controlling a vehicle like a tank or other tracked vehicle.

Sports Car Motion

For smooth motion of other vehicle types, such as a sports car, the values in the code above will need to be adjusted differently. Let's look at the places in the code that will smooth out the movement, and provide some other camera effects that might be useful for a car simulation, or indeed for any other game.

In the ChaseCamera::Move() function, you can use the following change to make the camera look down slightly on the vehicle.

```
// Look down a bit.
Vector2D u = CosSin(controller->GetModelAltitude() - 0.2F);
```

And to have the camera slowly swing after the vehicle has turned, you should replace the line beginning with Vector2D t with the following code instead:

```
// Change 50.0F to slow or speed up the "spring" angular motion.

float azm = controller->GetModelAzimuth();
float updatedAzm = playerAzm + (azm - playerAzm) / 50.0F;
playerAzm = updatedAzm;
// Note use of updatedAzm in next line.
Vector2D t = CosSin(updatedAzm);
```

Note that you could provide a side view by adding K::pi_over_4 to updatedAzm as follows:

```
updatedAzm += K::pi_over_4;
```

You could do so for example, depending on certain keys being pressed or not, to change the view while in game.

For a "spring camera" you can add this code:

```
if (accelerating)
{
   // Forward key is pressed.
   delta += 0.003F;
   if (delta >= 1.0F)
      delta = 1.0F;
   // accelerating = false;
}
else
{
   // Forward key is not pressed.
   delta -= 0.003F;
   if (delta <= 0.5F)
      delta = 0.5F;
}

p2 = p1 * (1.0F - delta) + p2 * delta;
```

just before the line

```
if (DetectCollision(p1, p2, 0.3F, kCollisionCamera, &data))
```

Note that you need to set the boolean "accelerating" in the `SoldierController::Move()` function:

```
// Forward key is pressed.
if (movementFlags & 1) accelerating = true;
else accelerating = false;
```

just before the line:

```
modelAzimuth = azm;
```

You will also want to prevent the car from turning unless it is moving. To do so, change the following in the `SoldierController::Move()` function from:

```
if (movementFlags & 4)        // left
   azm += 0.005f;
else if (movementFlags & 8)  // right
   azm -= 0.005f;
```

to

```
if (movementFlags & 1 || movementFlags & 2)
{
   // Only turn car if moving forward or backward.
   if (movementFlags & 4)        // left
      azm += 0.005F;
   else if (movementFlags & 8)  // right
      azm -= 0.005F;
}
```

To get this to compile, you should add the following global declarations at the top of your `SimpleChar.cpp` file:

```
Game *C4::TheGame = nullptr;
float delta = 0.3F;    // used for "spring" camera
bool accelerating = false;
float playerAzm = 0.0F;
```

Compile and try out your new code now using either the TankModel model or the Sports Car model that comes with the resources for this chapter. If you are using the Sports Car model, you'll again need to register your sports car model in the `Game::Game()` constructor by changing the following line:

```
soldierModelReg(kModelSoldier, nullptr, "model/SportsCarRB",
   kModelPrecache, kControllerSoldier),
```

While the vehicle control is now better than in the tank version above, I'm sure you'll agree that the turns just don't seem to be right. We want the sports car to slide around corners. The trick is to make it go forward and right when you press the left key and to make it go forward and left, when you press the right key. That's what happens when a car skids around a corner at high speed. This can be achieved by adding values like the following to the `movementDirectionTable`:

```
static const float movementDirectionTable[8] =
{
   // sliding
   0.0F, 4.0F, 0.0F, 0.0F, -0.5F, 0.5F, 4.0F, -4.0F
};
```

If you increase the 0.5 values to say 0.8, 0.9, or even 1.0, then there will be more sliding when moving forward and turning. There is no sliding when reversing. You could add a variable for the sliding on corners. The value would be 0.0 if the car was moving slowly (or if there was good grip to the road surface) and would increase to ±1.0 as the car speed increased (or as the surface became slipperier, for example on ice or on snow).

Now compile again and take the sports car for another spin. This time the motion around corners feels much better. Our test drive is shown in Figure 18-2.

Figure 18-2. Driving around the corners.

You can tweak all of these values to get the effects similar to what you would expect from a vehicle controller. You could also use keyboard keys to control the various constants in game, for example to provide a camera change from behind to side view to front view.

The beauty of the C4 Engine is that the code provided is so clean and easy to understand that even beginner and intermediate C++ programmers can produce nice results relatively quickly. Many other engines that we have experimented with, do not lend themselves so simply and elegantly to tuning of this nature.

Your Turn

Instead of using `SetLinearVelocity()` in order to move the model in response to the user's key presses, experiment with other native physics functions like `SetExternalForce()` and `SetFrictionCoefficient()` instead. You can use friction to slow the model if no longer being accelerated and you can also increase the friction coefficient to slow the model on corners and to prevent too much unrealistic sliding. There is a `RigidBodyController` function called `CalculateAppliedForces()`, which is defined within `C4Physics.cpp`. It calculates the linear velocity of a rigid body based on external forces, including gravity and friction.

Next, try to add code to make the car accelerate from zero to a maximum speed given by a `maxSpeed` parameter. Then add a "sliding" variable that causes the car to skid depending on the car speed (or on the surface conditions). You will need to ensure that the sliding variable influences the values in the `movementDirectionTable` array, as mentioned above.

See if you can also make the changes needed to make the car rebound if it hits a wall or other obstacle. Hint: use the `SetRestitutionCoefficient()` function. If you are feeling confident and ambitious, why not go ahead and make the required changes for a simple flight controller? Or a helicopter controller?

The spring camera can be reused, but this time you will want to bank the model when you turn left or right. You can turn off gravity for your model by using the function `SetGravityMultiplier(float multiplier)`. As stated in the API documentation, "The gravity multiplier scales the force exerted on a rigid body by the global gravity set in the `PhysicsController` object. A multiplier of 1.0 means that the ordinary gravity force is applied, while values higher or lower than 1.0 mean that proportionately more or less gravity is applied. If the gravity multiplier is 0.0, then no gravity is applied to the rigid body at all."

It's probably best to start with a fresh copy of the *SimpleChar* tutorial and then make the changes yourself bit-by-bit, until you produce the effects you are looking for.

Next Steps

At the end of the next chapter, Chapter 19, "*SimpleEnemies*", we'll add a very basic helicopter simulation, so that you can fly around and shoot at enemies, which in turn are shooting back at you.

19

SimpleEnemies

This chapter presents a game in which enemies follow predefined paths. We will explain how the path-following code works and we will also explain how to make a turret gun that can track and fire at the player.

Path Following Enemies

If you want to try out the code for this chapter right away, you can skip down to the section Getting the Game Up and Running with the C4 Engine.

First, let's talk about how to get your enemies to follow along paths you have made yourself using the **World Editor**. Most of this functionality is implemented within functions which we call from within the Move function of the our custom controller class, which we have named `PathController`.

Here is an overview of the steps this game goes through.

1 We first search through all of the nodes in the scene graph, and find the path node whose name is the same as the name stored in the variable `pathName`. The default name is "EnemyPath":

```
if (!lookedForEnemyPath)
{
   Node *root = TheWorldMgr->GetWorld()->GetRootNode();
   Node *thisNode = root;
   PathMarker *pathMarker = nullptr;

   do
```

```
    {
        stringOutput = " ";

        // First check that the node has a name,
        // because not all nodes do.

        if (thisNode->GetNodeName())
            stringOutput = thisnode->GetNodeName();

        // At this point, stringOutput has the
        // node's name (if any), so compare that
        // with the value stored in pathName, which
        // is "EnemyPath" by default.

        if (Text::CompareText(pathName, stringOutput))
        {
            // OK, now we have found the path node.
            // Here we will break the path up into
            // equidistant pieces.
        }

        thisNode = root->GetNextNode(thisNode);

    } while ((thisNode) && (!lookedForEnemyPath));
    lookedForEnemyPath = true;
}
```

2 Now that we have found the path node, we chop it up into equidistant pieces, and store those 3D points in a C4 Array for later use:

```
// We can cast the node to a marker,
// since we know this is a path
// and a path is a marker.
Marker *marker = static_cast<Marker *>(thisnode);

// Now cast to a PathMarker and get the
// path object using GetPath()
if (marker->GetMarkerType() == kMarkerPath)
{
```

```
    pathMarker = static_cast<PathMarker *>(marker);
}

const Path *path = pathMarker->GetPath();

// Paths are made up of components.
//
// Each component can be linear, elliptical, or
// Bezier, in any order. Here we run through each
// component one by one, starting at the first.

const PathComponent *component = path->GetFirstPathComponent();
while (component)
{
    // Here we start to fill our C4 array called pathPoint.
    //
    // The points in pathPoint will be equidistant from
    // each other. The first point corresponds to the
    // first point in the component.

    pathPoint.AddElement(component->GetPosition(0));
    pointCount++;

    // Each component is parametrized by a number, t,
    // that varies from 0 to 1.
    //
    // Our goal is to find the values of t that
    // correspond to equidistant segments of the
    // component.
    //
    // The method we use is called Newton's Method.
    //
    // It starts with a guess for the value of t.
    //
    // It then calculates the distance from that point
    // to the previous point, and adjusts the value of t
    // depending on how close we are to the target
    // distance.
    //
    // Newton's method doesn't always converge on a
```

```
// solution, so we use a best guess if a certain
// number of iterations (MAX ITERATIONS) have
// passed.

float t = 0.5F, t_old = 0.0F, speed = 0.0F;
while (t < 1.0F)
{
    float diff = 0.0F;
    bool found = false;
    int iterations = 0;
    float bestDiff = 100.0F;
    pathPoint.AddElement(component->GetPosition(t));

    do
    {
        pathPoint[pointCount] = component->GetPosition(t);
        Vector3D tangent = (pathPoint[pointCount]
            - pathPoint[pointCount-1]);
        x = tangent.x; y = tangent.y; z = tangent.z;
        distance = Sqrt(x * x + y * y + z * z);

        speed = distance / (t - t old);
        diff = distance - pathRate;

        // Using Newton's method to converge on
        // t for target distance along path
        if (Fabs(diff) > EPSILON && iterations++ < MAX ITERATIONS)
        {
            t -= diff / speed;
            if (Fabs(t) >= 1.0F)
                t = t old + 0.05F;
        }
        else
        {
            // if didn't converge
            if (iterations >= MAX ITERATIONS)
            {
                t = t old + t old / (float) pointCount;
                if (Fabs(t) > 1.0F)
                    t = 1.0F;
```

```
                pathPoint[pointCount] = component->GetPosition(t);
            }

            iterations = 0;
            found = true;
            t old = t;
            t += t / (float) pointCount; // 2.0F;
            length += distance;
            pointCount++;
        }
    } while (!found);
}

// Move on to the next component of
// the path if there is one.
component = component->Next();

// Avoid looking for path each cycle
lookedForEnemyPath = true;
}
```

At this point, the C4 array called `pathPoint` contains data corresponding to the 3D points which are equally spaced along the path.

3 Start the model where it was placed in the editor. On each cycle, update the model's position by a distance determined by one of the path pieces, and in a direction determined by the corresponding piece of the path for that cycle:

```
Node *target = GetTargetNode();
Transform4D translation;
Point3D myTranslation;

// pathPointCount is initially zero, so in the
// first cycle, the variable myTranslation gets
// the position of the first point on the path.

myTranslation.x = pathPoint[pathPointCount].x;
myTranslation.y = pathPoint[pathPointCount].y;
myTranslation.z = pathPoint[pathPointCount].z;
```

```
// Increment pathPointCount each cycle so that the
// translation follows the path, one point at a time.
pathPointCount++;

// Translation is a 4x4 Matrix, whose 4th
// column gets the next position on the Path.
// Remember that the 4th column corresponds
// to the translation.

translation.SetIdentity();
translation.SetTranslation(myTranslation);

// If we are at the end of the Path,
// start back at the beginning again.

if (pathPointCount > pointCount)
    pathPointCount = 0;

// Update the node (i.e. local) transform of the model.
target->SetNodeTransform(originalTransform * translation);
```

Orientation

The direction of the view vector is simply the next position minus the current position. We store that in a `Vector3D` called view, and use that to calculate a 3×3 portion of the local transform, which corresponds to the model's orientation.

```
if (pathPointCount > 0)
{
    Vector3D view = pathPoint[pathPointCount]
        - pathPoint[pathPointCount-1];

    view = view.Normalize();
    float x = view.x;
    float y = view.y;
    float f = InverseSqrt(x * x + y * y);

    Vector3D right(y * f, -x * f, 0.0F);
    Vector3D down = view % right;
```

```
    target->SetNodeMatrix3D(view, -right, -down);

    // Make sure the engine knows that this node's
    // local transform has changed.
    //
    // Then the engine will update the node's world
    // transform.

    target->Invalidate();
}
```

Note that you can bank the plane model using code like this:

```
// Try e.g., 0.3F, or vary with path curvature.
float bankAngle = 0.0F;
right = right.RotateAboutAxis(bankAngle, view);
down = down.RotateAboutAxis(bankAngle, view);
```

Later, we will also be adding a value called `crashCount` to several of these variables, to simulate a crash-dive, when the plane has been damaged by too many hits.

Getting the Game Up and Running with the C4 Engine

Our custom game is relatively easy to set up, since the Visual C++ project for the Game application, which you are extending, already exists.

1 Copy the two files which declare and define the path controller, namely `CustomControllers.h` and `CustomControllers.cpp`—into the directory which contains the game code that shipped with the engine.

2 In Visual C++, open the `C4.sln` file, and browse to the directory named General, which is underneath the Game Project in the Solution Explorer.

3 Add the two new "CustomControllers" files into the Game project, by right-clicking the General folder and then choosing **Add > Existing Item**, and then browsing to <C4>/GameCode/ to select them.

Before compiling with your new code, we need to make some minor changes to the `MGGame` and `MGControllers` demo game files.

4 Add the following line to `MGControllers.h`, just after the other includes:

```
#include "CustomControllers.h"
```

and in the same file, add this to the end of the enumeration for controller types:

```
kControllerPath = 'path'
```

Be sure to put a comma at the end of the preceding line.

5 In the `Game` class declaration in `MGGame.h`, add this line just before "`ControllerReg<DoorController>`":

```
ControllerReg<PathController>   pathControllerReg;
```

6 In `MGGame.cpp`, add the following code, just before the line which starts with "`doorControllerReg(kControllerDoor,`":

```
// Register the new path controller with the World Editor
pathControllerReg(kControllerPath, "Path"),
```

OK, you're done with the coding! Now compile the solution (press F7 in Visual Studio), and if you made the changes correctly, the `Game.dll` file should be generated and placed in the same directory as your `C4.exe` file.

Testing the new PathController Code

You can already test the new code as follows.

1 Navigate to <C4>/Data/Game/ and edit the `game.cfg` file.

2 Set the `$gameModuleName` variable value to "Game". It is set to that value by default, but you may have changed it if you have already run through some of the other tutorials.

3 Launch C4, and select **Open World (Ctrl-O)** from the Tools Menu to open the tutorial world `Water.wld`, which is located in the Tutorials/world/ directory.

4 Save the Water world immediately as PathWorld, or some other name of your choice, to leave the original tutorial world unchanged.

5 In the **World Editor**, choose **Page > Models** to open the **Models** page panel. Minimize some of the other pages if necessary so that you can see the **Models** page at the bottom.

6 Click Ctrl-4 to minimize the perspective viewport and to show the 4 default viewports.

7 Select any model, such as the Pumpkinhead model and place it anywhere in the world, by clicking on the model name in the **Models** page, and then clicking anywhere in the top viewport. The top viewport is marked with a *y* and an *x* axis and is the top left of the four default viewports.

8 Open the **Transform** page panel from the page menu if it is not already open. To position the model, set all rotation values to 0.0, the *x* and *y* position values to 45 and 0.0 respectively, and then make sure the z value is above zero. 2.0 will do fine. That way you know the model will start above ground.

9 With the model still selected, choose **Node > Get Info (Ctrl-I)** to open the **Node Info** dialog and select the **Controllers** tab panel.

10 Change the controller for this model from "Pumpkinhead" to "Path".

11 Set the speed to 0.2, which is five times slower than the default value.

12 Click OK to save those changes.

Next, we will create a path for the model to follow along.

13 Open up the **Paths** page from the **Page** menu, and select the **Linear Path** for starters.

14 Drag out a path from right to left in the top viewport so that the path is about as wide as the ground used in the Water world. You may need to first use the scroll wheel on your mouse to zoom out of the top viewport, in order to see the ground and not just the water. Also note that if you drag from right to left, the models attached to that path will also move in that direction. If you drag out the path from left to right, then the models will also move left to right. So if you are going to place you models initially on the right, then you will want to drag out the path from right to left, because otherwise the models will just move further away from the player and not towards it.

15 Choose **Node > Get Info (Ctrl-I)** to open the **Node Info** dialog, and select the **Node** tab panel.

16 Set the node name to "EnemyPath". The controller code will look for a path with this name, so if you don't label the path correctly, then the model won't know which path to follow, and won't move at all.

17 Choose **World > Save and Play World (Ctrl-P)** to test your changes.

If all went well, you should now see the Pumpkinhead model moving along the path you created in the **World Editor**. Note that the model will not be playing the animation that you may be used to seeing for that model. That's simply because we changed its controller to be our new controller. And our new controller is all about moving along paths, and does not include code for otherwise animating models.

If you want both animation and path following, you'll need to merge the path following controller code with the Pumpkinhead (or other model) controller code that handles the animation. We'll leave that exercise for another day.

Adding Other Types of Enemies

Now that we have basic paths working, let's add our own enemy models to the game.

First of all, we want a plane to come at us from over the horizon. In fact, we want a whole squadron of them! If you don't already have a model of an airplane, see Appendix C, "Using Blender with the C4 Engine", to learn how to find a 3D model plane on the web and how to import it for use with the C4 Engine.

You can also make a simple plane using geometry created in the **World Editor** tool, and choose **World > Save to Model Resources** to create a temporary "plane" model for testing purposes. You could use a cylinder for the body of the plane, and boxes for the wings and tail. Once you have the created and positioned the parts of your basic airplane, choose **Geometry > Union Geometry** to join the various meshes together.

We provide an example prototype plane, made using the **World Editor**, in the resources for this chapter. However you obtain your airplane model, follow these steps to add it to your game:

1 Set the name of the model to "PlaneModel".

2 Place the model file in the directory <C4>/Data/Tutorial/model/.

3 Register your airplane model with the **World Editor** tool, by adding the following code to `MGGame.cpp`, just before the line starting with `appleModelReg`:

```
planeModelReg(kModelPlane, "Plane", "model/PlaneModel",
    kModelPrecache, kControllerPath),
```

4 Add this line to `MGGame.h`, just before "`ModelRegistration appleModelReg;`":

```
ModelRegistration  planeModelReg;
```

5 We also need to define `kModelPlane`, so note that we added this code at the top of `CustomController.h`, just after the line containing "`namespace C4 {`":

```
enum
{
    kModelPlane = 'plne'
};
```

6 Recompile your code (press F7 in Visual C++), then restart C4 and open up your PathWorld again.

7 Select the Plane model on the **Models** page panel, and position it in the world by clicking anywhere in the top viewport.

8 With the Plane model still selected, choose **Node > Get Info (Ctrl-I)** to open the **Node Info** dialog.

9 Check that the controller is set to "EnemyPath", and then set the speed you want the plane to fly at.

10 Use the **Transform** page panel to place the model at $x = 50.0$, $y = 15.0$, $z = 5.0$.

11 Choose **World > Save and Play World (Ctrl-P)** to test the world. You should now see your plane model flying along the path you assigned to it.

12 Back in the **World Editor**, copy and paste the plane model several times to a slightly different location each time, using the **Transform** page panel to arrange the copies into an aerial formation. Each copy automatically contains the reference to the path controller and the same speed value.

13 Move the aerial formation quite a distance from the player (e.g., you could use coordinates in the following ranges $x = 100 \pm 25$, $y = 20 \pm 5$, $z = 5 \pm 2$).

• Keep the planes fairly close together, perhaps giving one group of planes one speed and another group a different speed.

• If your path is simply a straight line, make your path long enough so that your planes will disappear over the opposite horizon before reappearing again from the starting location.

We included an example PathWorld with the resources for this chapter.

Figure 19-1. A squadron of World War II planes using the `PathController` code to follow a path set up in the **World Editor** tool.

Getting the Enemies to Shoot at the Player

Let's add some turret guns that will fire projectiles at the player. Since we are focused on learning how to program intelligent turrets, and not how to model them in an external package, let's use the C4 **World Editor** to make a prototype turret gun which we can use for testing. When you are happy with your code, you can later swap out the model for a better one.

1 Fire up C4, and create a new world by choosing **World > New World (Ctrl-N)**.

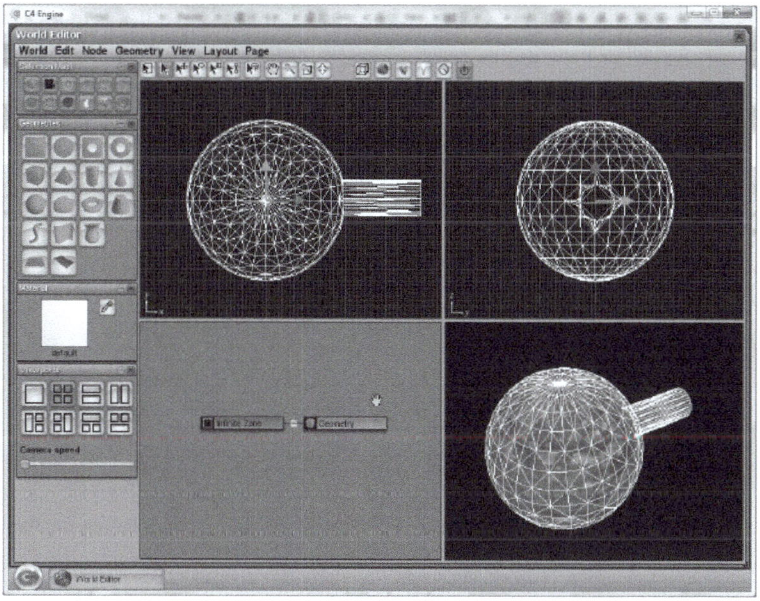

Figure 19-2. The turret model in the **World Editor** window.

2 Select the sphere tool on the **Geometries** page panel, and drag out a sphere of any size.

3 Use the **Transform** page panel to zero all positions and rotations and set the *x*, *y*, and *z* sizes to 2.0 each.

4 Create a cylinder in the top-right viewport and then change its size and position so that it resembles the barrel of a turret gun.

5 For a texture, double-click the **Materials** swatch, and in the **Material Manager** window, create a new material named "Turret". We decided to use the AgedMetal texture that comes with the demo game.

6 To set the texture, browse to and select that texture as your **Texture Map (primary)**. The texture is located in the Data/Demo/texture/ directory. Figure 19-2 shows the model in the **World Editor**.

7 Click on the barrel and shift-left-click on the sphere to select both geometries and choose **Geometry > Set Material (Ctrl-M)** to assign the new material to your geometry.

8 Select both of the geometries again, and then choose **Geometry > Union Geometry** to join them.

9 Choose **World > Save as Model** to save the model as TurretModel in the directory Data/Tutorial/model/.

10 Close and discard changes to the open world, and quit C4.

It's time to add some more code. We'll need a new controller for the turret motion.

11 Copy the files `TurretController.cpp` and `TurretController.h` into <C4>/GameCode/.

12 Open up your C4 solution in Visual C++, and now drag the new files from the GameCode folder into the Game project, under the General folder. You can also right-click on General and choose **Add > Existing Item**, and browse to the location of the files if you'd prefer.

Skip ahead to the section called Integrating the Turret Code into Your Project if you are eager to integrate this new code straight away. If you want to learn first how that code works, then read on.

Here's what's going on inside the turret controller code. In the `Preprocess()` function, we store the original transform of the node in a variable called `originalDirection`. We also use a variable called `originalView`, to store the direction the turret is pointing in initially:

```
originalTransform = target->GetWorldTransform();
Point3D originalDirection = Point3D(originalTransform[0].x,
      originalTransform[0].y, originalTransform[0].z);
(originalView = originalDirection).Normalize();
```

The interesting code is in the `Move()` function of the controller. We get the player's position with this code:

```
const GamePlayer *player = static_cast<const GamePlayer*>(
      TheMessageMgr->GetLocalPlayer());
FighterController *controller = player->GetPlayerController();
Point3D point = controller->GetTargetNode()->GetWorldPosition();
```

Then we calculate the vector pointing from the turret to the player. Remember that a vector, which has a magnitude and a direction, is the difference between to points (or locations). We call this vector view.

```
Vector3D view = (point - target->GetWorldPosition());
```

We then calculate the distance from the turret to the player, which is simply the length of the view vector. We then normalize view, i.e., make its length equal to one.

```
float x = view.x;
float y = view.y;
float z = view.z;
float distance = Sqrt(x * x + y * y + z * z);
view = view.Normalize();
```

Now, if we are close enough to the turret then the turret should become "active"—it should rotate to follow the player and should shoot at the player periodically.

```
if (distance < 5000.0F)
{
```

Next, we calculate a direction for the turret to face, stored in `updatedView`, which is somewhere between the initial viewing direction stored in `originalView`, and the target viewing direction, stored in view. The number we divide by will determine how quickly the target direction is reached—how quickly the turret will turn to follow the player.

```
// Interpolate between the current viewing direction and
// the target viewing direction.
//
// If you use say 10.0F instead of 20.0F then it will
// rotate twice as fast.
Vector3D updatedView = Vector3D(originalView.x
   + (view.x - originalView.x) / 20.0F, originalView.y
   + (view.y - originalView.y) / 20.0F, originalView.z
   + (view.z - originalView.z) / 20.0F);

originalView = updatedView;
```

Next we update the transform for the turret. We use the projection of the direction vector onto the *x-y* plane, and create a right vector which is the original just rotated by 90 degrees. Remember, the orientation 3×3 matrix is made up of direction, left, and up—that's why we use the values `updatedView`, `-right`, and `-down`. The line beginning with "`target->setNodeTransform()`" was explained in Part III • Under the Hood:

```
x = updatedView.x;
y = updatedView.y;

float f = InverseSqrt(x * x + y * y);

// The next line rotates by 90 degrees to get
// the right vector. Multiply by f to normalize.
Vector3D right(y * f, -x * f, 0.0F);
Vector3D down = updatedView % right;
Target->SetNodeMatrix3D(updatedView, -right, -down);
Point3D startPos = target->GetWorldPosition();
```

The next section of code is used to fire a projectile from the turret to the player. We use the starting position which we stored in `startPos` above. You don't want the ammo to start inside the enemy—we want a position just in front of the enemy. You can vary the value `10.0F` depending on your model. Better still would be to use a marker on the model to specify the point where the projectile exits.

```
startPos.x += 10.0F * updatedView.x;
startPos.y += 10.0F * updatedView.y;
startPos.z += 10.0F * updatedView.z;
```

The projectile velocity, `objectVelocity`, is multiplied by a factor of your choice to increase or decrease the difficulty for the player. This factor could also be a setting of your Controller.

```
Vector3D objectVelocity = Vector3D(100.0F * updatedView.x,
   100.0F * updatedView.y, 100.0F * updatedView.z);
```

This next code can be used if you want the projectiles to follow a parabolic path (up and down under gravity's influence), like when fired from a gun on a battleship. Leave it commented out for now, and uncomment it later when you place your turrets on a battleship.

```
objectVelocity.z = 4.9F * (distance +
    (Math::RandomFloat(40.0F) - 20.0F)) *
    InverseSqrt(objectVelocity.x * objectVelocity.x +
    objectVelocity.y * objectVelocity.y);
```

Finally, we reach the code used to fire the projectiles. We create a new instance of a `FireBallController` and attach that to a FireBall model. The `FireBallController` gets the starting position and velocity which was calculated in the preceding code:

```
if (world)
{
    Controller *controller;
    Model *model = nullptr;

    // Fire on some condition, such as
    // after a certain time has passed.
    if ((myCount++ % 300) == 0)
    {
        // create fireball!!
        controller = new FireballController(objectVelocity);
        model = Model::Get(kModelFireball);
        if (model)
        {
            model->SetController(controller);
            Zone *zone = world->FindZone(startPos);
            Point3D zonePosition = zone->GetInverseWorldTransform()
                * startPos;
            model->SetNodePosition(zonePosition);
            zone->AddNewSubnode(model);
            model->Update();
        }
    }
}
```

Integrating the Turret Code into Your Project

Your project will compile now—try it with F7 in Visual Studio—but the **Game** application hasn't been told to register the new controller yet, so the **World Editor** won't be aware of it. To fix that, we again make a few minor changes to `MGGame` and `MGController`, just as we did earlier for the path controller. Double-click the source code and header files for `MGGame` and `MGController` to open them in the editor window of Visual C++.

1. Add the following line to `MGControllers.h`, just after the other includes:

```
#include "TurretController.h"
```

2. In the `Game` class declaration in `MGGame.h`, add this line just before "`ControllerReg<DoorController>`":

```
ControllerReg<TurretController>    turretControllerReg;
```

3. In `MGGame.cpp`, add the following code, just before the line which starts with "`doorControllerReg(kControllerDoor,`":

```
// Register the new Turret Controller with the
// World Editor
turretControllerReg(kControllerTurret, "Turret"),
```

4. Let's register our turret model. As we did above for the **Plane** model, add the following code to `MGGame.cpp`, just before the line starting with `appleModelReg`:

```
turretModelReg(kModelTurret, "Turret",
    "model/TurretModel", kModelPrecache,
    kControllerTurret),
```

5. Add this line to `MGGame.h`, just before the line containing "`ModelRegistration appleModelReg;`":

```
ModelRegistration  turretModelReg;
```

The coding is finished for now. Compile the solution (press F7), and again, if you made the changes correctly, the `Game.dll` file should be generated and placed in the same directory as your `C4Engine.exe` file.

Testing the Turret Controller

Let's test our new turret controller code. (See Figure 19-3.)

1 Start C4 and open the Water world and click Ctrl-4 to minimize the perspective viewport and to show the 4 default viewports.

2 Save the world as TurretWorld, or a similar name of your choice.

3 Open the **Models** page panel, and select the Turret model.

4 In the top (*x*-*y*) viewport, use the middle mouse button to zoom out somewhat. Then place four of these turret models on the four corners of the pool by simply left clicking at those locations in the top view.

5 Open the **Transform** page panel in the **World Editor**, if it isn't already open, using **Page > Transform**.

6 Use the **Transform** page to set the z position value for each turret to 2.5, so that the turrets are not stuck in the ground.

7 Choose **World > Save and Play World (Ctrl-P)** to save and play your new world.

You should find that the turrets rotate and track the player. They then shoot every few seconds as determined by the code in the `TurretController::Move()` function. Don't just stand there, run!

These are not the prettiest turrets in the world, but then again, turret guns aren't normally that pretty anyway. If you find that the barrel of the gun is facing in the wrong direction, just open up the model again in a new world, and use the **Transform** page panel to rotate it by 90 degrees around *x*, *y*, or most probably, *z*, probably save the model and test it again.

Exposing other variables to the World Editor

We might also want to have a battleship, or other enemy type, but we will probably want that enemy to follow a different path. So you may ask, how do we do that? Well, we could make a new controller, and call it `BattleShipPathController`, and perhaps it would subclass a generic `PathController` class. Instead, we exposed another variable to the **World Editor**, one that allows us to name the path we want the model to follow. That way we can have several paths, each with a different label, and we can set up the association between paths and entities using the information panel directly in the editor.

Figure 19-3. Testing the turret controller code using turrets created in the **World Editor** tool.

Here are the steps we used to expose a new variable in the **World Editor**. In `CustomControllers.cpp`, in the `PathController::Pack()` function, we added this line:

```
// Write the path name.
data << pathName;
```

just after "`data << pathRate;`". And in the `PathController::Unpack()` function, we added

```
// Read the path name.
data >> pathName;
```

just after "`data >> pathRate;`". Next, we changed the `PathController::GetSettingCount()` function as follows:

```
int32 PathController::GetSettingCount(void) const
{
   // There are two settings, so changed the
   // return value from 1 to 2.
   return (2);
}
```

And we added this code to the `PathController::GetSetting()` function:

```
else if (index == 1)
{
   // Yes, return a new text setting and set its value.
   return (new TextSetting('pnme', pathName, "Path Name", 20));
}
```

The final change in `CustomControllers.cpp` is to add this code to the `PathController::SetSetting()` function:

```
// Check for path name.
else if (setting->GetSettingIdentifier() == 'pnme')
{
   // Yes, grab the value from the setting.
   const char *text = static_cast<const TextSetting *>(setting)->
      GetText();
   pathName = text;
}
```

You can try this out by adding a new path to the world which you have been using to test your paths. After you add a new path, perhaps using the elliptical or Bézier path types—or indeed using a mixture of any of the three path types—name the new path “FlightPath” say, and then add another model from the **Models** page.

Choose **Node > Get Info (Ctrl-I)** to open the **Node Info** dialog, and assign the path controller to it. You can assign the path name “FlightPath” to this model, as shown in Figure 19-4.

Check that your previous models have the correct path name assigned to them as well. Go ahead and choose **World > Save and Play World (Ctrl-P)** to try out your new paths!

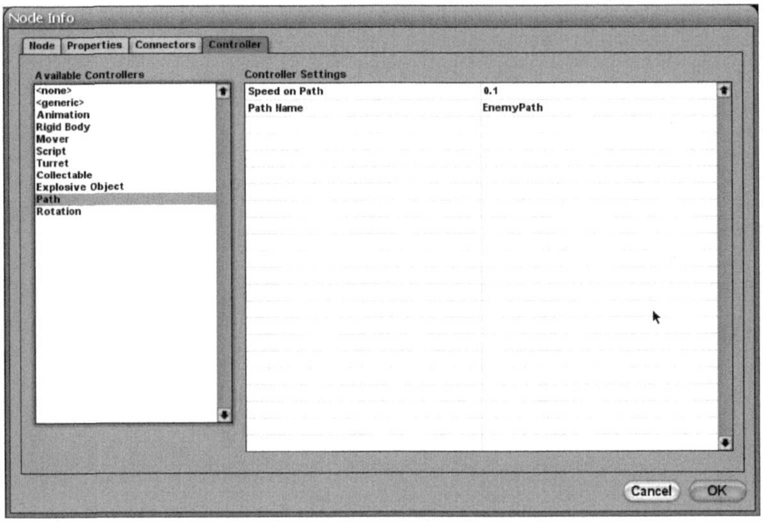

Figure 19-4. The controller settings showing that the speed and path name can be assigned on a model-by-model basis.

Adding a "Health Bar" on top of Each Enemy to Show Its Level of Health

Here we describe the code we used to add a health bar to our enemies so that we can see how badly they have been damaged. And while we are at it, we made sure that they do get some damage when we hit them! We did so by making minor changes to the file MGPistol.cpp, which is in the Weapons folder of the Game project in Visual Studio. Open up that file now and add the following code to the PistolController::UpdateWeapon() function, just after the line "if (state == kCollisionStateGeometry) {":

```
Controller *entityController = collisionData.geometry->
   GetController();
Controller *entityParentController = collisionData.geometry->
   GetSuperNode()->GetController();

if (entityController && entityController->GetControllerType()
   == kControllerPath)
{
   static_cast<PathController *>(entityController)->damage += 10;
```

```
}
else if (entityParentController && entityParentController->
   GetControllerType() == kControllerPath)
{
   static_cast<PathController *>(entityParentController)->
      damage += 10;
}
```

To add the health bar in our `PathController` code, we added the variable damage and a `QuadWidget`—which we will called "planeHealth"—in `CustomControllers.h`:

```
QuadWidget *planeHealth;
```

The C4 Engine `QuadWidget` class provides a rectangle primitive that can be displayed directly on the screen.

HUDs

Before we move on, you might have noticed that in the demo game there is a HUD which contains images used to display how much ammunition each weapon still has. The HUD itself is a panel (`.pan`) file, and it is loaded within the `DisplayBoard()` constructor in the file MGInterface.cpp as follows:

```
healthGroup.Load("hud/Health");
```

If you want to try and load a panel file which you made yourself using the **Panel Editor**, first save your file under Data/Tutorials/world/, say. If you called your HUD say `myTestHUD.pan`, then add this line after the one above in the `DisplayBoard()` constructor:

```
healthGroup.Load("hud/Health");
Load("world/myTestHUD");
```

When you try out any of the demo games delivered with C4, with `$gameModuleName = "Game"`, you should now see your HUD appear on the lower left of the screen. You can load your panels onto any subclass of `Widget`. For example, the following code will create a transparent `QuadWidget` and load a test panel onto it:

```
if (TheInterfaceMgr)
{
   QuadWidget *myWidget = new QuadWidget(Vector2D(TheDisplayMgr->
      GetDisplayWidth(), TheDisplayMgr->GetDisplayHeight()),
      K::white);
   myWidget->SetWidgetPosition(Point3D(0.0F, 0.0F, 0.0F));
   myWidget->SetWidgetAlpha(0.0F);     // Transparent widget
   myWidget->Load("world/myTestHUD");
   TheInterfaceMgr->AddWidget(myWidget);
}
```

To test that code, you could add that to say the *SimpleBall* tutorial code, at the end of the `GameWorld::Preprocess()` function, just before the line "`return (kWorldOkay);`". If you then run any world with `$gameModuleName = "SimpleBall"`, you will see your test panel on a transparent widget. Note that we included a panel called `myTestHUD.pan` with the resources for this chapter.

If you want to use some transparent images for your panels or HUDs, use an image editing package—such as Gimp, which is free—to create an alpha channel. Save the image as a 256 by 256, 512 by 512, or 1024 by 1024 TGA image, then import it into C4 as a `.tex` file using **Tools > Import Texture**. Place the resulting `.tex` files in a directory where the **Panel Editor** can locate them.

Setting up the Damage Display

You can initialize damage to the value 0.0 in the `Preprocess()` function of your `PathController` class:

```
damage = 0.0F;
```

The meat is in the `ShowHealthBar()` function for the `PathController` class, which is called from within the `Move()` function. Activate this code by uncommenting the line used to call the `ShowHealthBar()` function:

```
if (TheDisplayInterface && !planeHealthAdded)
{
   planeHealth = new QuadWidget(Vector2D(25.0F, 55.0F), K::white);
```

```
    TheInterfaceMgr->AddWidget(planeHealth);
    planeHealthAdded = true;
}

World *myWorld = TheWorldMgr->GetWorld();
const FrustumCamera *myCamera = myWorld->GetCamera();
Node *thisNode = GetTargetNode();
const Point3D thisNodesPosition = thisNode->GetWorldPosition();

// Project world point to display.
Point3D myPoint = myCamera->GetInverseWorldTransform()
    * thisNodesPosition;

const FrustumCameraObject *object = myCamera->GetObject();
float focalLength = object->GetFocalLength();
myPoint.x *= focalLength / myPoint.z;
myPoint.y *= focalLength / myPoint.z;

float width = (myPoint.z > 50.0F) ? 10.0F :
    10.0F + 2.0F * (50.0F - myPoint.z);
float red = Fmin((damage / 100.0F), 1.0F);
float green = Fmin(((100.0F - damage) / 100.0F), 1.0F);
float alpha = 1.0F;

// Rescale to the width and height of the display.
float w = (float) (TheDisplayMgr->GetDisplayWidth() / 2);
float h = (float) (TheDisplayMgr->GetDisplayHeight() / 2);
myPoint.x = w * myPoint.x + w;
myPoint.y = (h * myPoint.y / object->GetAspectRatio()
    + h + 2.0F);

planeHealth->SetWidgetSize(Vector2D(width, 5.0F));
planeHealth->SetWidgetColor(ColorRGBA(red, green, 0.0F, alpha));
if (myPoint.z > 1.0F) // in front of camera
{
    myPoint.z = 0.0F;
    planeHealth->SetWidgetPosition(myPoint);
    planeHealth->Invalidate();
}
else  // behind camera
```

```
{
   planeHealth->SetWidgetSize(Vector2D(0.0F, 0.0F));
}
```

To test the health bar, recompile and restart C4. Open your PathWorld. You might want to slow the planes right down for this test, perhaps with a speed value of about 0.2.

OK, now choose **World > Save and Play World (Ctrl-P)** to test your health bar code. Figure 19-5 shows a plane with a health bar on top. The color changes from green to red with more damage, and the damage bar gets smaller as you get further from the plane.

Figure 19-5. A squadron of planes following along a path with a health bar to show how badly it has been damaged.

Explosions!

Here is how we simulated explosions and made the plane crash to the ground if the damage goes above a certain level. The demo game comes with fireballs that explode, so they will do nicely. The trick is to create fireballs at the plane if the damage value goes above, say 100, give them the same position as the plane, and don't give them an initial velocity.

```
// If there is too much damage,
// the plane explodes and crashes down.
if (damage >= 100)
{
   crashCount += 0.15F;
   if (world)
   {
      Controller *controller; Model *model = nullptr;

      // Create explosion on some condition -
      // here is just an example

      // explosion every x seconds
      if (((int) crashCount) % 5 == 0)
      {
         // Create a fireball which will not
         // move, so it will simulate an
         // explosion at the plane!
         Point3D startPos = GetTargetNode()->GetNodePosition();
         controller = new FireballController(startPos,
            Vector3D(0.1F, 0.0F, 0.1F));
         model = Model::Get(kModelFireball);
         if (model)
         {
            model->SetController(controller);
            Zone *zone = world->FindZone(startPos);
            Point3D zonePosition = zone->GetInverseWorldTransform()
               * startPos;
            model->SetNodePosition(zonePosition);
            zone->AddNewSubnode(model);
            model->Update();
         }
      }
   }
}

// End Explosions
```

And later, we subtracted the value of `crashCount` from the plane's height:

```
myTranslation.z = pathPoint[pathPointCount].z - crashCount;
```

and we then let the plane twist as it falls to the ground:

```
float bankAngle = 0.0F; // can use path curvature here

// spins if crashing
right = right.RotateAboutAxis(bankAngle + crashCount * 2.0F, view);

// spins if crashing
down = down.RotateAboutAxis(bankAngle + crashCount * 2.0F, view);

target->SetNodeMatrix3D(view, -right, -down);
```

Then at the end of the `Move()` function, to definitively remove the node from the scene when it "hits" the ground, we used `delete target` as follows:

```
if (GetTargetNode()->GetNodePosition().z <= 0.0F)
   delete target;
else
   target->Invalidate();
```

To activate this code, uncomment the following lines in the `PathController::Move()` function, which are used to call the `CreateExplosion()` function:

```
if (damage >= 100) CreateExplosion();
```

Now recompile (press F7 in Visual Studio) and try it out.

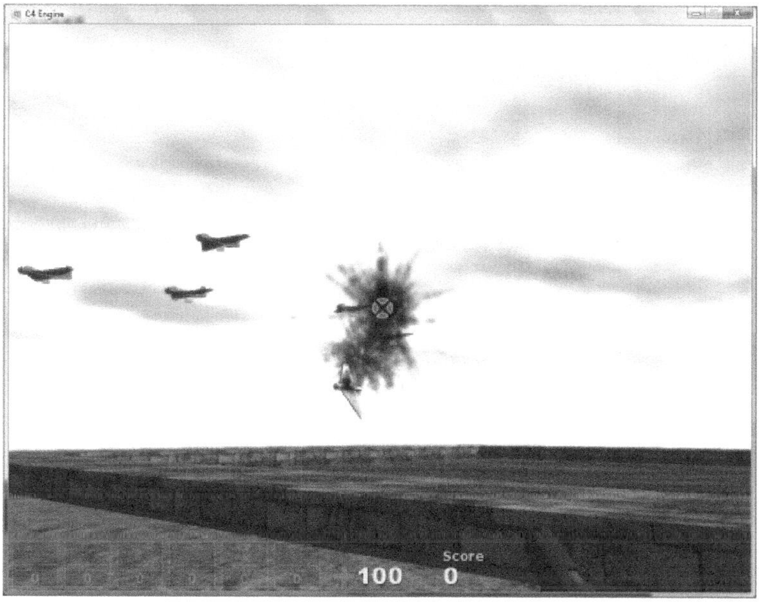

Figure 19-6. A plane explodes as it crashes to the ground after sustaining too much damage.

Battleships

To add a battleship, either add a model of a battleship to your scene or simply add a piece of geometry using the **World Editor**. If you use a geometry, you will need to change your `ValidNode()` function to allow geometry nodes when using the path controller, as follows:

```
bool PathController::ValidNode(const Node *node)
{
    return (node->GetNodeType() == kNodeModel ||
        node->GetNodeType() == kNodeGeometry);
}
```

Create a path for the ship, choose **Node > Get Info (Ctrl-I)** to open the **Node Info** dialog, and set the path node name to "ShipPath". Add a controller to your ship (again in the **World Editor**, using the **Node Info** dialog) and give it a slow speed, say 0.2.

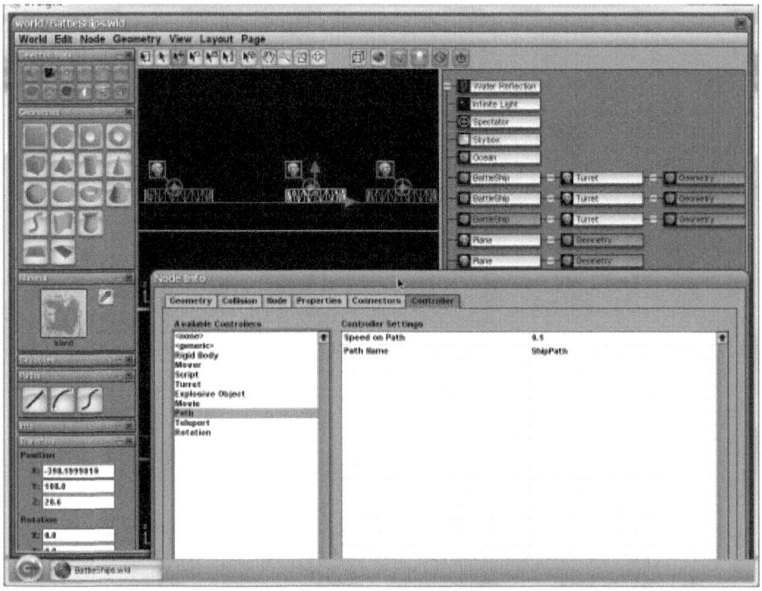

Figure 19-7. Turret guns are placed on Battleships. They are made child nodes using the scene graph.

Next, add a piece of geometry or a model for the turret gun on the ship. Assign the turret controller to that turret (using the **Node Info** dialog), and you are now almost ready to go.

The last thing we need to do is to make the turret a child of the ship, so that as the ship follows the ShipPath, the turret will follow along. The turret will still rotate to face the player and shoot. To do that, click on the move button in the World Editor and drag the turret on top of the BattleShip node in the scene graph. Figure 19-7 shows the resulting scene graph.

We have provided an example world named `Battleships.wld`, which you can find in the resources that come with this chapter. It contains an ocean, some path-following planes and some rudimentary "battleships" (made of elongated C4 cylinders!). The turret model is placed on each ship, and the ships themselves follow a C4 Path called "ShipPath". Note again that the C4 Engine will look for the PlaneModel and the TurretModel in the Tutorial/model/ directory, so be sure to place you models there when trying out the Battleships world.

As mentioned above, don't forget to uncomment the code in the `TurretController::Move()` function which is used for projectiles fired from a battleship:

```
objectVelocity.z = 4.9F * (distance +
   (Math::RandomFloat(40.0F) - 20.0F)) *
   InverseSqrt(objectVelocity.x * objectVelocity.x +
   objectVelocity.y * objectVelocity.y);
```

This line is used to determine the *z* component of the projectile's velocity. The random number in there is used to ensure that the battleships don't hit you every time! That wouldn't be very fair to the player. The projectile's velocity is simply the vector calculated as the difference between the 3D points representing the world positions of the player and the turret gun. And some simple math shows that, given the *x* and *y* components of the velocity, and the horizontal distance the projectile should travel, the *z* component of the projectile's velocity is:

```
objectVelocity.z = (4.9F * distance) /
   Sqrt(velocity_x * velocity_x + velocity_y * velocity_y);
```

So it is proportional to the distance and inversely proportional to the norm of the velocity along the *x-y* plane (i.e., along the water).

Helicopter Simulation

We thought you might like to see how a simple helicopter simulation could be implemented, with some very minor changes. With this code, you will actually enter as a spectator—and not spawn as a player—and you can "fly" around as if you were piloting a helicopter. The changes to the code presented here allow you to fire rockets from your "helicopter" at the enemies. The turrets on the battleships will also aim at the camera this time, instead of at the player.

The purpose is simply to expose some more parts of the game code to you, and by changing those areas, you will begin to see why the game code works the way it does. By trying to make a player out of a spectator, you will begin to see how both the player and the spectator work. And besides, its fun to fly around and shoot at Battleships!

OK, first comment out these lines in the `TurretController::Move()` function:

```
/*
To aim and fire at player, use these lines.
```

```
const GamePlayer *player = nullptr;

player = static cast<const GamePlayer *>(TheMessageMgr->
   GetLocalPlayer());
if (!player) return;
FighterController *controller = nullptr;
controller = player->GetPlayerController();
if (!controller) return;

// We do not want to use GetColliderPosition here.
Point3D point = controller->GetTargetNode()->GetWorldPosition();

end to aim and fire at player
*/
```

and immediately below that, uncomment these lines:

```
// To fire at camera, do this instead.
World *myWorld = TheWorldMgr->GetWorld();
const FrustumCamera *myCamera = myWorld->GetCamera();
Point3D point = myCamera->GetWorldPosition();
// end to fire at camera
```

Now recompile and then restart C4. Open your Battleships world in the **World Editor**. Change all locators to be of type `spec`. For each locator, select its node and choose **Node > Get Info (Ctrl-I)** to open the **Node Info** dialog. Select the **Locator** tab panel, and change the value `spwn` to `spec` and click OK. Choose **Save and Play World (Ctrl-P)** to check that you can fly around the world, and verify that the turrets on the ships track you as you do so.

Next, let's add code to allow us to fire from the camera position, to simulate firing rockets at our enemies as we fly around. Add the following code to the `MovementAction::Begin()` function in `MGInput.cpp`, immediately after the line containing `GameWorld *world = static_cast<GameWorld *>(TheWorldMgr->GetWorld());`:

```
if (world)
{
   Controller *controller1;
```

```
Model *model1 = nullptr;

Controller *controller2;
Model *model2 = nullptr;

Point3D zonePosition;

// Increase or decrease to change the speed.
float speed = 1000.0F;
// Look up [2] for front.
Vector3D direction = world->GetSpectatorCamera()->
   GetWorldTransform()[2];
// Look up [0] for right.
Vector3D right = world->GetSpectatorCamera()->
   GetWorldTransform()[0];
Point3D startPos = world->GetSpectatorCamera()->
   GetWorldPosition();
Zone *zone = world->FindZone(startPos);

if (GetActionType() == kActionUp)
{
   controller1 = new RocketController(speed * direction, 0);
   controller2 = new RocketController(speed * direction, 0);
   model1 = Model::Get(kModelRocket);
   model2 = Model::Get(kModelRocket);

   if (model1)
   {
      model1->SetController(controller1);

      zonePosition = zone->GetInverseWorldTransform()
         * (startPos + 3.0F * right);
      model1->SetNodePosition(zonePosition);
      zone->AddNewSubnode(model1);
      model1->Update();
   }

   if (model2)
   {
      model2->SetController(controller2);
```

```
            zonePosition = zone->GetInverseWorldTransform()
                * (startPos - 3.0F * right);
            model2->SetNodePosition(zonePosition);
            zone->AddNewSubnode(model2);
            model2->Update();
        }
    }
}
```

In order to use the RocketController, you will need to add the following include at the top of MGInput.cpp

```
#include "MGRocketLauncher.h"
```

You will notice that we are abusing kActionUp, which is typically bound to the "SPACE" key in your input.cfg configuration file through the code %jump. To bind this action to your left mouse button, you can use the Control Settings user interface, which you see each time you launch C4 with the **Game** application. Just change the setting for up to be the left mouse click. Equivalently, you can change the following line in your input.cfg file from

```
bind "Button 0" %fire;
```

to

```
bind "Button 0" %jump;
```

and change

```
bind "SPACE" %jump;
```

to

```
bind "SPACE" %fire;
```

Next, comment out the following line in C4Cameras.cpp, which is in the **World** folder of the engine code. It will prevent the camera from moving up when you press the fire button:

```
// if (flags & kSpectatorMoveUp) delta.z += t;
```

To deactivate backwards movement, comment out this line, just above the line you just commented out.

```
// if (flags & kSpectatorMoveBackward) delta -= view * t;
```

If you want to make it so that the helicopter is flying forward by default, add this to the line just after "`t *= spectatorSpeed;`":

```
// Always move forward a bit by default.
delta += view * t * 2.0;
```

To make sure that is called even if the forward key isn't pressed, you will need to change the if statement above that from

```
if ((flags & kSpectatorMoveMask) != 0)
```

to

```
// Always move by default.
if (true)    // (flags & kSpectatorMoveMask) != 0)
```

See if you can make the helicopter go up and down when the left and right keys are pressed respectively. That way the movements will be restricted to forward, up and down, which is what you might expect for a simple simulation of a helicopter.

OK, compile your code and try it out. You'll notice that the ships don't sink, and the planes don't crash when you hit them. Why is that? Well, now you are using rockets instead of bullets, so you will need to make changes like the ones we made to `MGPistol.cpp` above—this time however to the `RocketController::HandleNewGeometryContact()` function, which is in the file `MGRocketLauncher.cpp`.

. Add the following code to that function, just after the line "`const Controller *controller = geometry->GetController();`":

```
Controller *entityController = geometry->GetController();
Controller *entityParentController = geometry->GetSuperNode()->
   GetController();
if (entityController && entityController->GetControllerType()
   == kControllerPath)
{
   static cast<PathController *>(entityController)->damage += 20;
}

if (entityParentController && entityParentController->
   GetControllerType() == kControllerPath)
{
   static cast<PathController *>(entityParentController)->damage
      += 20;
}
```

Rockets from a helicopter will cause more damage than simple bullets from a gun, so we changed the damage increment accordingly. Have fun!

Your Turn

Add sound effects including a helicopter sound that loops continuously and the rocket launch sound when you fire a rocket from the helicopter. See if you can also add an image (a HUD) with plenty of transparent areas to simulate the cockpit of a helicopter. Or disable player motion altogether to simulate firing long range projectiles out to sea from a motionless turret gun on shore. See if you can get the planes to also fire at you (or drop bombs on you!) when the pass overhead.

We look forward to seeing screen shots from your games up on the C4 Engine Wiki. Enjoy!

20

RTS—Creating a Game from Scratch

In the previous game tutorials, we started from the demo applications that are available with each build of the C4 Engine. The RTS game described in this chapter will show you how to approach building a game project from the ground up. After completing this tutorial, you should have a better understanding of some of the systems that go into making things move around in a world powered by the C4 Engine.

Step-by-Step

This chapter is by no means an example of how to structure a complex game, and is only intended to familiarize you with writing code that directly interacts with some of the basic C4 Engine API features. Some of the topics that are covered in this example include: Scene Graph traversal, making use of the engine's `Node::Move()` function, creating your own camera in code, importing your own hierarchical models, and other simple features provided by the C4 Engine. You may notice some of the material in this chapter overlaps with some of the material you've learned in the previous examples, as we construct the game in a step-by step fashion.

A Man Has to Know His Limitations

This tutorial does not cover the following topics: zone and portal setup, multiplayer networking, importing sounds or textures, creating geometry in the Collada format, and special effects.

Creating an Application and a World

The first step is to create a new Visual Studio project. If you're not familiar with how to set up a new project in Visual Studio, you can revisit some of the other game examples earlier in the book. We'll be using RTS as the project name and the name for our base `Application` class. Type out (or copy) the following code into two new files called `RTS.h` and `RTS.cpp`:

RTS.h

```
#ifndef RTS_H
#define RTS_H

#include "C4Application.h"
#include "C4Engine.h"

using namespace C4;

class RTS : public Singleton <RTS>, public Application
{
   private:

   public:

      RTS(void);
      ~RTS(void);
};

extern "C"
{
   C4MODULEEXPORT Application *ConstructApplication(void);
}

#endif
```

RTS.cpp

```
#include "C4Engine.h"
#include "C4Interface.h"
```

```
#include "RTS.h"

using namespace C4;

// Global pointer to our game object.
RTS *TheGame = nullptr;

Application *ConstructApplication(void)
{
   return (new RTS);
}

// Called when our game is started.
RTS::RTS(void) : Singleton<RTS>(TheGame)
{
}

// Called when our game is closed down.
RTS::~RTS(void)
{
}
```

In Windows Explorer, create a subdirectory named **RTS** in the **Data** directory, and also in the **Import** directory where the C4 executable and `RTS.dll` reside. These directories will be used for all of your game data, including your world file and model files later on in this chapter.

Start up C4 with the RTS game DLL, display the menu bar by pressing tilde/grave, and choose **C4 Button > New World (Ctrl-N)** to create a new world.

Create a large enough box primitive to serve as the ground plane for the units ($10 \times 10 \times 1$ is fine). Make sure the box surface is positioned so that it is somewhat flush to the *x*-*y* plane.

In the scene graph panel (the lower left panel by default), double click on the Infinite Zone to bring up the Node Info window. Under the Zone tab, double click on the color swatch next to Ambient light color and select a low brightness. Something around 64 will do.

Also add a point light in the center of the playing field, slightly above it, and give it a decent radius. It may be easiest if you click and drag away from the center of the light in the viewport while you are creating the point light. If you just click and release in the viewport, the point light will look small, and could be hard to find later on. Turn on **Toggle Lighting** to see the effect of the point light.

Save your new world as `RTS/rts.wld`. This saves the new world asset into the Data directory. The RTS subdirectory is where your game project will find all of the assets for this tutorial.

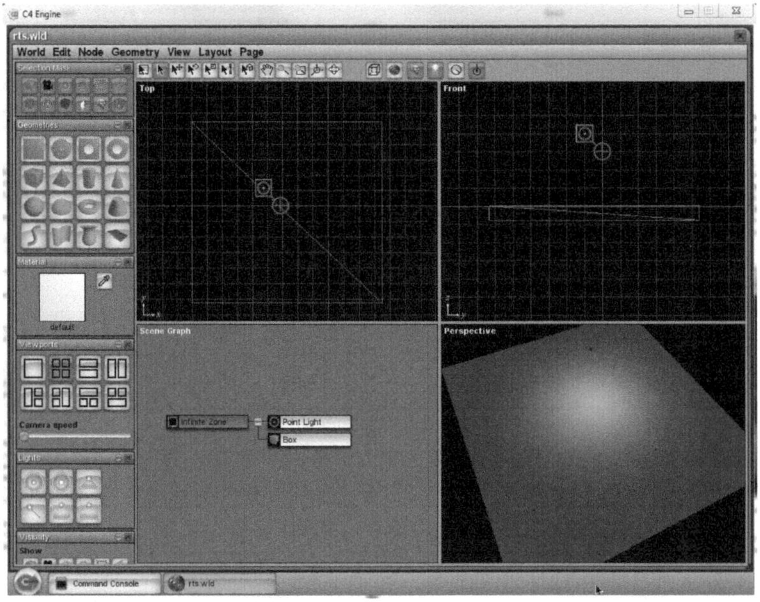

Figure 20-1. Simple playing field with a box geometry and a point light.

Now that we have our base application created and a world to work with, let's put in some world code and a camera so that we can run our game and check out the world in-game. Before creating the camera, we'll create a class to represent our world or level in the game. We'll call it CombatWorld. All it contains right now is a constructor, destructor, and overridden `Preprocess()` and `Render()` functions to which we'll be adding more code later on.

Create two new source files: `CombatWorld.h` and `CombatWorld.cpp`:

CombatWorld.h

```
#ifndef COMBAT_WORLD_H
#define COMBAT_WORLD_H
```

```
#include "C4Engine.h"
#include "C4World.h"

namespace C4
{
   class CombatWorld : public World
   {
      public:

         CombatWorld(const char *name);
         ~CombatWorld();

         WorldResult Preprocess(void);
         void Render(void);
   };
}

#endif
```

CombatWorld.cpp

```
#include "CombatWorld.h"

using namespace C4;

CombatWorld::CombatWorld(const char *name) : World(name)
{
}

CombatWorld::~CombatWorld()
{
}

WorldResult CombatWorld::Preprocess(void)
{
   WorldResult result = World::Preprocess();
   if (result != kWorldOkay) return (result);

   return (kWorldOkay);
```

```
}

void CombatWorld::Render(void)
{
   World::Render();
}
```

The application now needs a way to create the world that we made above. Does that make sense? We made a world, so why do we have to create it again? Well, we created a level, but it's not loaded into our application. That is what this code will do. We add a static `ConstructWorld()` function here. (The majority of this code is copied directly from the *SimpleBall* demo game.)

RTS.h

```
#ifndef RTS H
#define RTS H

#include "C4Application.h"
#include "C4Engine.h"
#include "C4World.h"          // Add
#include "CombatWorld.h"      // Add

using namespace C4;

class RTS : public Singleton<RTS>, public Application
{
   private:

   public:

      RTS();
      ~RTS();

      // Add
      static World *ConstructWorld(const char *name, void *cookie);
};

extern "C"
```

```
{
   C4MODULEEXPORT Application *ConstructApplication(void);
}

#endif
```

RTS.cpp

```
RTS::RTS() : Singleton<RTS>(TheGame)
{
   // Add
   TheWorldMgr->SetWorldConstructor(&ConstructWorld);
}

RTS::~RTS()
{
   TheWorldMgr->UnloadWorld();                   // Add
   TheWorldMgr->SetWorldConstructor(nullptr);   // Add
}

// New function
World *RTS::ConstructWorld(const char *name, void *cookie)
{
   return (new CombatWorld(name));
}
```

The `ConstructWorld()` function simply creates a new instance of a `CombatWorld` in our application.

At this point, you can try loading your world by typing `load rts` in the **Command Console** window, but there is actually nothing to see at this point because we do not have any cameras set up in the world. You'll end up seeing something like Figure 20-2.

Creating a Basic Navigation Camera

Let's create the camera code next. We'll call our camera class `RTSCamera`, so create the header and source files, `RTSCamera.h` and `RTSCamera.cpp`:

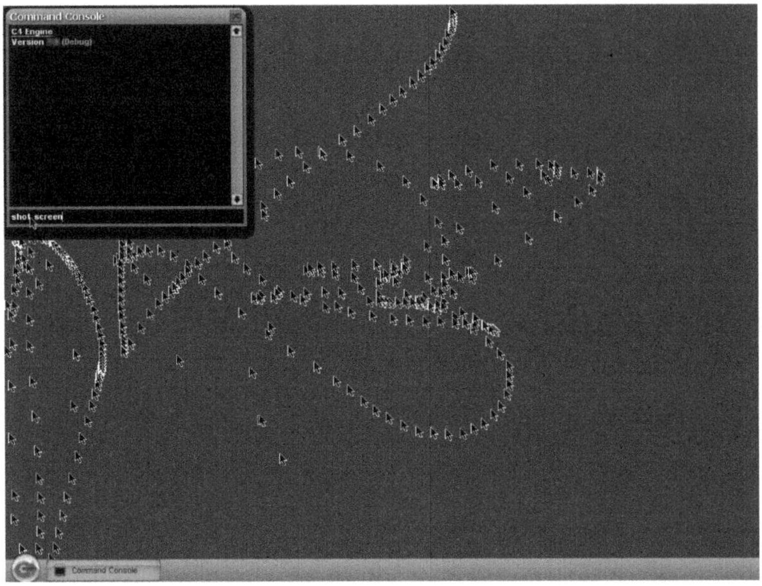

Figure 20-2. The world is not visible without a camera.

RTSCamera.h

```
#ifndef RTS_CAMERA_H
#define RTS_CAMERA_H

#include "C4Cameras.h"

namespace C4
{
   class RTSCamera : public FrustumCamera
   {
      public:

         RTSCamera();
         ~RTSCamera();

         void Preprocess(void);
         void Move(void);
   };
```

```
}

#endif
```

RTSCamera.cpp

```
#include "RTSCamera.h"
#include "RTS.h"

using namespace C4;

RTSCamera::RTSCamera() : FrustumCamera(2.0F, 1.0F)
{
}

RTSCamera::~RTSCamera()
{
}

void RTSCamera::Preprocess(void)
{
    FrustumCamera::Preprocess();
}

void RTSCamera::Move(void)
{
    SetNodePosition(Point3D(4.0F, 4.0F, 3.0F));
    LookAtPoint(Point3D(0.0F, 0.0F, 0.0F));
}
```

The `Move()` function simply contains some test code to make sure it points at the playing field. For now, define constants for camera node position and direction, just to make sure we have the world and camera working correctly.

Now that the camera code is implemented, the hooks to use the camera can be added in the `CombatWorld` class.

CombatWorld.h

```
#ifndef COMBAT WORLD H
#define COMBAT WORLD H

#include "C4Engine.h"
#include "C4World.h"
#include "RTSCamera.h"    // Add

namespace C4
{
   class CombatWorld : public World
   {
      private:

         RTSCamera    navCamera;   // Add

      public:

         CombatWorld(const char *name);
         ~CombatWorld();

         WorldResult Preprocess(void);
         void Render(void);
   };
}

#endif
```

CombatWorld.cpp

```
WorldResult CombatWorld::Preprocess(void)
{
   WorldResult result = World::Preprocess();
   if (result != kWorldOkay) return (result);

   SetCamera(&navCamera);    // Add

   return (kWorldOkay);
}
```

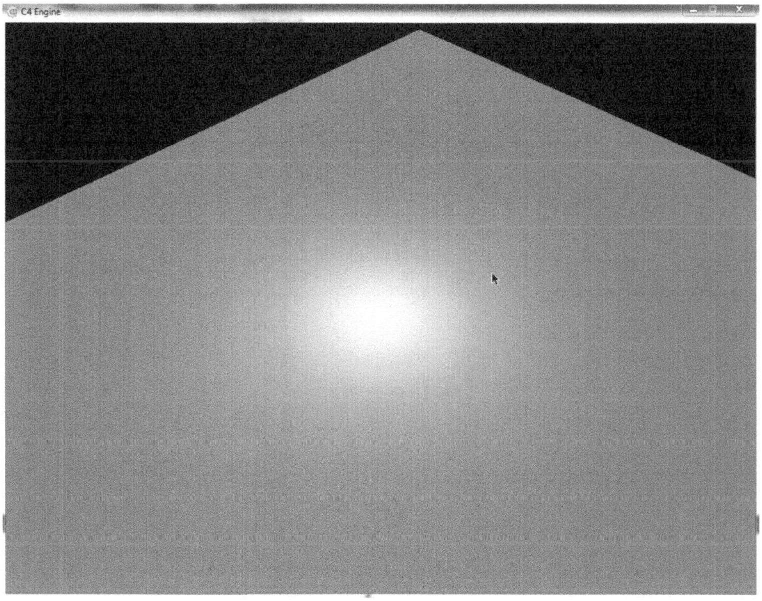

Figure 20-3. The world renders now that a camera exists.

That's it for now. Run C4, type `load rts` into the **Command Console** window, and you should get something like Figure 20-3.

Congratulations on loading your first game world from scratch in C4! Next step is to get some keyboard actions into the game. And then with keyboard actions, we'll be able to pan and rotate the camera.

The Navigation Action

Create a new `Action` class named `NavAction`. As you'll notice, the enumeration lists all of the constants that map to the appropriate four-character keywords listed in the `input.cfg` file in the <C4>/Data/Engine/ directory (except for `'rotl'` and `'rotr'`, which will need to be added).

NavAction.h

```
#ifndef MOVEMENT_ACTION_H
#define MOVEMENT_ACTION_H
```

```
#include "C4Input.h"

namespace C4
{
    enum
    {
        kActionForward      = 'frwd',
        kActionBackward     = 'bkwd',
        kActionRotLeft      = 'rotl',
        kActionRotRight     = 'rotr',
        kActionLeft         = 'left',
        kActionRight        = 'rght'
    };

    class NavAction : public Action
    {
        private:

            unsigned long movementFlag;

        public:

            NavAction(unsigned long type, unsigned long flag);
            ~NavAction();

            void Begin(void);
            void End(void);
    };
}

#endif
```

NavAction.cpp

```
#include "NavAction.h"
#include "RTS.h"

using namespace C4;
```

```
NavAction::NavAction(unsigned long type, unsigned long flag) :
      Action(type)
{
   movementFlag = flag;
}

NavAction::~NavAction()
{
}

void NavAction::Begin(void)
{
   CombatWorld *world = static cast<CombatWorld *>(TheWorldMgr
      ->GetWorld());
   RTSCamera *camera = world->GetNavCamera();
   camera->SetNavFlags(camera->GetNavFlags() | movementFlag);
}

void NavAction::End(void)
{
   CombatWorld *world = static cast<CombatWorld *>(TheWorldMgr
      ->GetWorld());
   RTSCamera *camera = world->GetNavCamera();
   camera->SetNavFlags(camera->GetNavFlags() & ~movementFlag);
}
```

Okay, what's `type` and what's `flag`? `type` will be one of the items in the enumeration above that lets the engine know what key to map to this action, and `flag` is the movement flag that we will define in our camera class that maps the type to the actual movement of the camera. Got it? Onward then!

You'll notice that we also need to add a few accessor functions. The `RTSCamera` class now uses `SetNavFlags()` and `GetNavFlags()` functions, and the `CombatWorld` uses an accessor to the `RTSCamera` class.

Add the following public function to `CombatWorld.h`:

CombatWorld.h

```
RTSCamera *GetNavCamera(void)
{
```

```
    return (&navCamera);
}
```

You really don't need to create this accessor since the `World` class already has a `GetCamera()` function, but this saves us some casting.

Next, we'll add the `movementFlags` variable and the accessor functions for this in `RTSCamera.h`:

RTSCamera.h

```
    private:
        ...
        unsigned long movementFlags;

    public:

        void SetNavFlags(unsigned long flags)
        {
            movementFlags = flags;
        }

        unsigned long GetNavFlags()
        {
            return movementFlags;
        }
```

Don't forget to initialize `movementFlags` in the constructor, too.

RTSCamera.cpp

```
RTSCamera::RTSCamera() :
        FrustumCamera(2.0F, 1.0F), movementFlags(0)
{
}
```

All right, now let's define the list of possible values for the `movementFlags` variable. In `RTSCamera.h`, add the following code right outside the class definition:

RTSCamera.h

```
enum
{
    kNavMoveForward     = 1 << 0,
    kNavMoveBackward    = 1 << 1,
    kNavMoveLeft        = 1 << 2,
    kNavMoveRight       = 1 << 3,
    kNavMoveRotLeft     = 1 << 4,
    kNavMoveRotRight    = 1 << 5,
    kNavMoveZoomIn      = 1 << 6,
    kNavMoveZoomOut     = 1 << 7,
    kNavMoveMask = kNavMoveForward | kNavMoveBackward |
        kNavMoveLeft | kNavMoveRight | kNavMoveRotLeft |
        kNavMoveRotRight | kNavMoveZoomIn | kNavMoveZoomOut
};
```

With these changes, we can finally register the actions that map to the specific navigation commands. Create six private `NavAction` member variables in the `RTS` class (remember to include the header files):

RTS.h

```
#include "C4Input.h"
#include "NavAction.h"

...

      NavAction *moveForwardAction;
      NavAction *moveBackwardAction;
      NavAction *moveLeftAction;
      NavAction *moveRightAction;
      NavAction *rotLeftAction;
      NavAction *rotRightAction;
```

And then initialize and register them in the constructor:

RTS.cpp

```
moveLeftAction = new NavAction(kActionLeft, kNavMoveLeft);
moveRightAction = new NavAction(kActionRight, kNavMoveRight);
moveForwardAction = new NavAction(kActionForward, kNavMoveForward);
moveBackwardAction = new NavAction(kActionBackward,
      kNavMoveBackward);
rotLeftAction = new NavAction(kActionRotLeft, kNavMoveRotLeft);
rotRightAction = new NavAction(kActionRotRight, kNavMoveRotRight);

TheInputMgr->AddAction(moveLeftAction);
TheInputMgr->AddAction(moveRightAction);
TheInputMgr->AddAction(moveForwardAction);
TheInputMgr->AddAction(moveBackwardAction);
TheInputMgr->AddAction(rotLeftAction);
TheInputMgr->AddAction(rotRightAction);
```

And delete them in the destructor:

RTS.cpp

```
delete moveLeftAction;
delete moveRightAction;
delete moveForwardAction;
delete moveBackwardAction;
delete rotLeftAction;
delete rotRightAction;
```

This finally compiles, but no movement is going to happen until we finish hooking up the camera movement flag to some actual code in the camera's `Move()` function.

We'll rip out our previous `RTSCamera::Move()` code and put in something a little more interesting this time. But first, create some private variables and initialize them:

RTSCamera.h

```
float    curDirAngle;
```

```
Point3D   curFocus;
float     curDistance;
float     curTiltAngle;
```

RTSCamera.cpp

```
RTSCamera::RTSCamera() :
      FrustumCamera(2.0F, 1.0F),
      movementFlags(0),
      curDirAngle(0.25f * K::pi),
      curFocus(0.0f, 0.0f, 0.0f),
      curDistance(10.0f),
      curTiltAngle(0.25f * K::pi)
{
}
```

Then add the math to make it happen:

```
void RTSCamera::Move(void)
{
   float dt = TheTimeMgr->GetFloatDeltaTime() * 0.001f;
   float deltaFwd = 0.0f;
   float deltaRight = 0.0f;
   float deltaRot = 0.0f;

   // Position
   if ((movementFlags & kNavMoveLeft) != 0)
   {
      deltaRight -= 1.0f * dt;
   }
   if ((movementFlags & kNavMoveRight) != 0)
   {
      deltaRight += 1.0f * dt;
   }
   if ((movementFlags & kNavMoveForward) != 0)
   {
      deltaFwd += 1.0f * dt;
   }
   if ((movementFlags & kNavMoveBackward) != 0)
```

```
{
    deltaFwd -= 1.0f * dt;
}
// Rotation
if ((movementFlags & kNavMoveRotLeft) != 0)
{
    deltaRot -= 1.0f * dt;
}
if ((movementFlags & kNavMoveRotRight) != 0)
{
    deltaRot += 1.0f * dt;
}

curDirAngle += deltaRot;

// Update Focus Point
Vector3D dirVector(deltaRight, deltaFwd, 0.0f);
Matrix3D dirMatrix;
dirMatrix.SetRotationAboutZ(curDirAngle);
dirVector = dirVector * dirMatrix;
curFocus += dirVector;

// Update Camera position
Point3D camPosition(0.0f, -curDistance, 0.0f);

Matrix3D tiltMatrix;
tiltMatrix.SetRotationAboutX(curTiltAngle);

Transform4D tiltTransform;
tiltTransform.SetMatrix3D(tiltMatrix);
camPosition = camPosition * tiltTransform;

Matrix3D orbitMatrix;
orbitMatrix.SetRotationAboutZ(curDirAngle);

Transform4D orbitTransform;
orbitTransform.SetMatrix3D(orbitMatrix);

camPosition = camPosition * orbitTransform;
camPosition += curFocus;
```

```
    SetNodePosition(camPosition);
    LookAtPoint(curFocus);
}
```

The first part of this is simply grabbing the application's elapsed time and using it to calculate the delta for the actual movement from the keyboard input. The second part is the math behind rotating and positioning the camera. `dirVector` holds the forward/backward and left/right incremental movement, and then this is multiplied by the `dirMatrix` to account for the rotation.

This final change is then added to `curFocus`. After we have the focus point locked down, the camera is positioned around it. First, `camPosition` is offset by the given `curDistance` on the *y* axis. Then, a `tiltTransform` is created from the `tiltMatrix` that contains the tilt rotation angle. This transform is then multiplied into the `camPosition` to tilt it up. Lastly, an `orbitTransform` is created from the `orbitMatrix` that contains the orbit rotation angle, and now this transform is multiplied into the `camPosition` to rotate it around the focus point. After the rotations are completed, simply add the `curFocus` as the camera offset.

Notice that we are calling `SetNodePosition()` and `LookAtPoint()` as before, but now we use `camPosition` as the node's position and `curFocus` as the look-at point. Keep in mind, there are several ways of actually doing this math, but it was done this way for the purposes of instruction.

One more thing we need to do is enable the engine's input mode to accept in-game mouse input. Enable this in the application's constructor.

RTS.cpp

```
RTS::RTS(void) : Singleton<RTS>(TheGame)...
{
    ...
    TheInterfaceMgr->
        SetInputManagementMode(kInputManagementAutomatic);
    ...
}
```

You can finally compile this and run it. The W, S, A, and D keys are already mapped to the forward, backward, left, and right movement actions, but you'll have to add `'rotl'` and `'rotr'` to the `input.cfg` file to get rotation to work. We hooked rotation up to the Q and E keys.

Figure 20-4. The screen is not being refreshed, so the image is "smearing".

You may also notice that when you pan around the world, it looks something like Figure 20-4. This smearing effect happens because we never set a clear color. To set the clear color, follow these steps:

1. Open our world in the **World Editor**.
2. Switch one of the viewports to the scene graph.
3. Find and select the infinite zone node.
4. Choose **Node > Get Info (Ctrl-I).**
5. Select the **Properties** tab panel.
6. Select the **Clear Color** property and click **Assign**.
7. Click OK to close the **Node Info** dialog.
8. Choose **World > Save (Ctrl-S).**

Now the background will be cleared before any rendering is done.

Great! Now we have a working view, and our first movement commands.

Implementing the Mouse Cursor and AutoScroll

This tutorial will implement the mouse cursor in a way that may not be the most ideal way to implement in C4. A border widget is used for the cursor, instead of creating a full-blown interface and interface task handler. There are other, more correct ways to do the mouse cursor, but this will suit our purposes.

The cursor is declared in `CombatWorld`, and since we're using user interface widgets, `#include "C4Interface.h"` and `"C4Widgets.h"` need to be added.

CombatWorld.h

```
private:

    BorderWidget     *mouseCursor;
    Point2D          mousePosition;

public:

    void ChangeCursorPosition(float deltaX, float deltaY);
    Point2D GetCursorPosition();
```

In the constructor, initialize the cursor widget, its position, and add it to the Interface Manager:

CombatWorld.cpp

```
float halfDisplayWidth = 0.5F * TheDisplayMgr->GetDisplayWidth();
float halfDisplayHeight = 0.5F * TheDisplayMgr->GetDisplayHeight();

mousePosition.Set(halfDisplayWidth, halfDisplayHeight);

mouseCursor = new BorderWidget(Vector2D(10.0f, 10.0f),
   kLineSolid, K::white);
mouseCursor->SetWidgetPosition(Point3D(mousePosition.x,
   mousePosition.y, 0.0f));
TheInterfaceMgr->AddWidget(mouseCursor);
```

And cleanup code in the destructor:

CombatWorld.cpp

```
delete mouseCursor;
```

Now the two new functions:

CombatWorld.cpp

```
void CombatWorld::ChangeCursorPosition(float deltaX, float deltaY)
{
    mousePosition.x += deltaX;
    mousePosition.y += deltaY;

    float displayWidth = TheDisplayMgr->GetDisplayWidth();
    float displayHeight = TheDisplayMgr->GetDisplayHeight();

    mousePosition.x = C4::FmaxZero(mousePosition.x);
    mousePosition.y = C4::FmaxZero(mousePosition.y);


    mousePosition.x = C4::Fmin(displayWidth - 1, mousePosition.x);
    mousePosition.y = C4::Fmin(displayHeight - 1, mousePosition.y);

    if (mouseCursor)
    {
        Vector2D cursorSize = mouseCursor->GetWidgetSize();
        float posX = mousePosition.x - 0.5 * cursorSize.x;
        float posY = mousePosition.y - 0.5 * cursorSize.y;

        mouseCursor->SetWidgetPosition(Point3D(posX, posY, 0.0f));
        mouseCursor->Invalidate();
    }
}

Point2D CombatWorld::GetCursorPosition()
{
    return (mousePosition);
}
```

The `ChangeCursorPosition()` function accepts a change in position, and also takes responsibility in clamping the mouse position to the extents of the application's display dimensions.

Update the cursor position in the `RTSCamera::Move()` function by adding the following code before the keyboard input checks:

RTSCamera.cpp

```
float sensitivity = 300.0f;

float deltaX = -sensitivity * TheInputMgr->GetMouseDeltaX();
float deltaY = -sensitivity * TheInputMgr->GetMouseDeltaY();
Point2D cursorPos(0.0f, 0.0f);
CombatWorld *world = static_cast<CombatWorld *>
    (TheWorldMgr->GetWorld());
if (world)
{
    world->ChangeCursorPosition(deltaX, deltaY);
    cursorPos = world->GetCursorPosition();
}
```

Sensitivity is just a constant so that the camera movement is noticeable. The delta is returned as the negative of what you would expect, so it's handled by flipping the sign. Running this code will result in a moving mouse cursor.

Notice that the `cursorPos` variable is set. Add the following code right after setting `cursorPos`:

```
float autoScrollThreshold = 0.1f;

float displayWidth = TheDisplayMgr->GetDisplayWidth();
float displayHeight = TheDisplayMgr->GetDisplayHeight();

if (cursorPos.x < autoScrollThreshold * displayWidth)
    deltaRight -= 1.0f * dt;

if (cursorPos.x >= (1.0f - autoScrollThreshold) * displayWidth)
    deltaRight += 1.0f * dt;

if (cursorPos.y < autoScrollThreshold * displayHeight)
```

```
    deltaFwd += 1.0f * dt;

if (cursorPos.y >= (1.0f - autoScrollThreshold) * displayHeight)
    deltaFwd -= 1.0f * dt;
```

This is the autoscroll code. `autoScrollThreshold` is the percentage of the edge of the screen that qualifies as the region that is auto-scrollable. The variables `deltaRight` and `deltaFwd` are the same variables used earlier for the keyboard input code.

That should be it for the autoscroll. Pretty simple. Although it's not the most ideal place to put the cursor update code, it works and gets the idea across.

Creating a Unit Model

It's time to add a model to the game. For this tutorial, the unit model will be a tank. Generally, there are two parts to setting up a model to be used in the game world: The world editor part and the code part. We'll do the World Editor part first since it's straightforward.

Find the Collada file `tank.dae` in the TBGC4_Resources/Chapter_RTS/Import/ directory, and place it in the <C4>/Import/RTS/ directory. Now launch C4, and create a new world by choosing **C4 Button > New World (Ctrl-N)**. Next, choose **World > Import Scene**. Navigate to the RTS subdirectory, and select the `tank.dae` file. Click OK to accept the default "Merge materials" option, and the tank geometry should appear in the **World Editor** window, as shown in Figure 20-5.

The tank was created at a small scale, so that's why it's so small in the **World Editor**. Save the world as a model by choosing **World > Save to Model Resource**. Navigate to the RTS subdirectory, and save the model as `tank.mdl`.

You can now open up this model in the **Model Viewer** by choosing **C4 Button > Open Model**, and selecting `tank.mdl` from the RTS subdirectory. The tank is untextured to keep it simple, and it's fairly small, so you may have to move the camera a little lower to see it, as shown in Figure 20-6.

If you open up this model in the **World Editor** (by creating a new world, choosing **World > Load from Model Resource**, and selecting `tank.mdl`) you have the ability to edit the model in the **World Editor**. Switching over to the scene graph view (right-click on a viewport and choose **Scene Graph** if it is not already visible), you'll see the hierarchy in Figure 20-7.

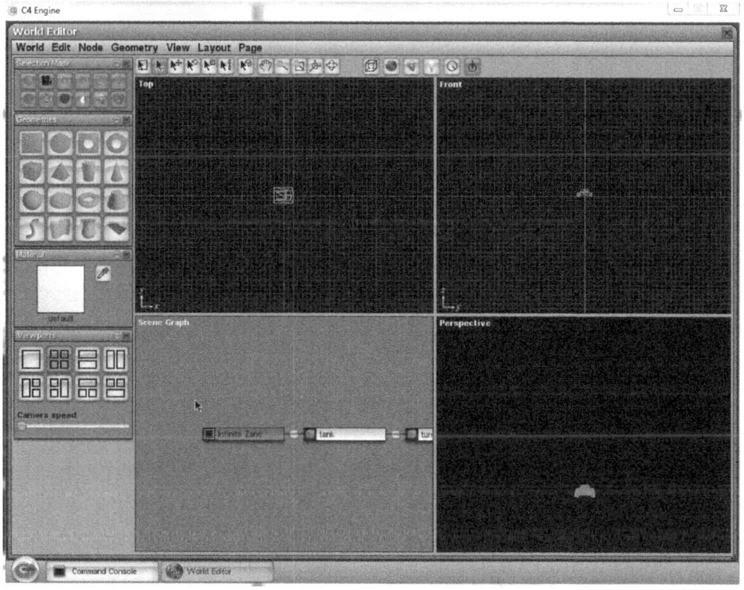

Figure 20-5. Importing the tank geometry into the **World Editor**.

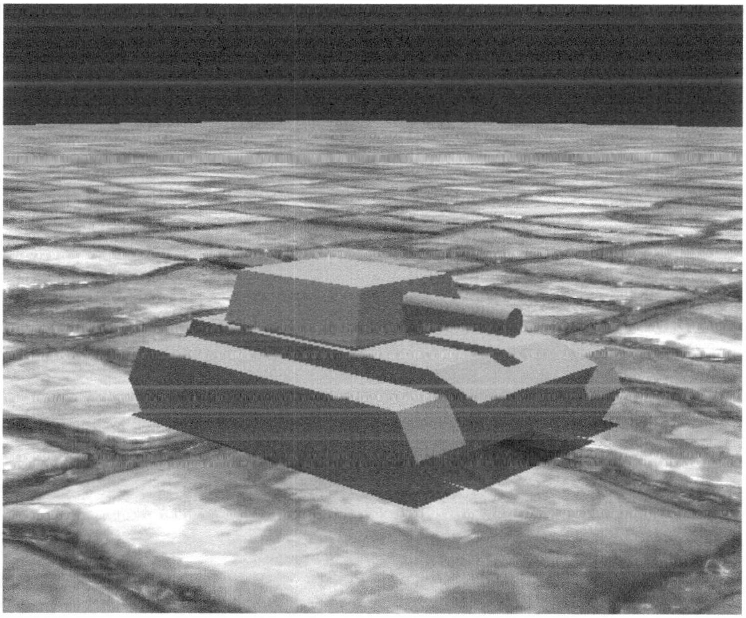

Figure 20-6. The tank in the **Model Viewer**.

Figure 20-7. Hierarchy of the tank model.

The tank and turret nodes represent the geometries that we imported. The turret node was automatically made a subnode of the tank node because that is how it was parented in the 3D modeling program before it was exported to a Collada file. The tank node is made a sub-node of the model node. The infinite zone node is not a part of the model, only the world, and it represents the root zone in the world.

Knowing the hierarchy of these nodes will help in understanding the programming part. The code will register the tank in a list of models that can be placed in your world via the **World Editor**. (Where it may seem that we're already done, because we can import a model into the world, the **Load from Model Resource** command is only used for editing model files, and not for adding models to the world).

Start off by creating two new files in your project for the tank-related code: `Tank.h` and `Tank.cpp`. These files will contain the `TankController` class along with a few constants that are used for model and controller registration. Most of the functions are stubs, that we'll add to later, but this makes up the essential function overrides for creating a new `Controller` subclass. For the basics of creating a controller class, see Chapter 15, "The Controller".

Tank.h

```
#ifndef TANK_H
#define TANK_H

#include "C4Controller.h"
#include "C4World.h"

namespace C4
{
    enum
    {
        kControllerTank = 'tank'
    };
```

```
    enum
    {
        kModelTank = 'tank'
    };

    class TankController : public Controller
    {
        private:

            TankController(const TankController& tankController);

            Controller *Replicate(void) const;

        public:

            TankController();
            ~TankController();

            static bool ValidNode(const Node *node);

            void Pack(Packer& data, unsigned long packFlags) const;
            void Unpack(Unpacker& data, unsigned long unpackFlags);

            void Preprocess(void);
            void Move(void);
    };
}

#endif
```

The `kModelTank` constant is added to the tank header file. We don't have to put it in `Tank.h`, but it will remind us that this model type belongs to the `TankController` class, especially since we've implemented the `ValidNode()` function to attach to only model node types.

Tank.cpp

```
#include "Tank.h"
#include "RTS.h"
```

```
using namespace C4;

TankController::TankController() : Controller(kControllerTank)
{
}

TankController::TankController(const TankController&
   tankController) : Controller(tankController)
{
}

Controller *TankController::Replicate(void) const
{
   return (new TankController(*this));
}

TankController::~TankController()
{
}

bool TankController::ValidNode(const Node *node)
{
   return ((node) && (node->GetNodeType() == kNodeModel));
}

void TankController::Pack(Packer& data,
   unsigned long packFlags) const
{
   Controller::Pack(data, packFlags);
}

void TankController::Unpack(Unpacker& data,
   unsigned long unpackFlags)
{
   Controller::Unpack(data, unpackFlags);
}

void TankController::Preprocess(void)
{
   Controller::Preprocess();
```

```
}

void TankController::Move(void)
{
}
```

Now for the actual registration. In the `RTS` class, we will register both the tank model and the tank controller. (Don't forget to add `#include "Tank.h"` in `RTS.h`). Add the following private member variables:

RTS.h

```
        private:

            ModelRegistration                    tankModelReg;
            ControllerReg<TankController>   tankControllerReg;
```

Construct the tank controller and the tank model registration. In the initialization list of the constructor of the `RTS` class:

```
RTS::RTS(void)  :
        Singleton<RTS>(TheGame),
        tankControllerReg(kControllerTank, "Tank"),  // Add
        tankModelReg(kModelTank, "Tank", "tank", kModelPrecache,
            kControllerTank)    // Add
```

The constructor for `tankControllerReg` specifies the type to be `kControllerTank` and attaches the name "Tank" to it, which will appear in the list of controllers when the **Node Info** dialog is shown.

The constructor for `tankModelReg` specifies the type to be `kModelTank`. The second parameter `"Tank"` is the text that will appear in the models list in the **World Editor** tool. The third parameter is also `"tank"`, but this is actually the path and resource name of the `.mdl` file. The model is set to be precached, and `kControllerTank` is the default controller assigned to the model when it's placed in the **World Editor**.

At this point, the project should compile and run. Launch C4 and open up the RTS world by typing `world rts` into the **Command Console** window. If the

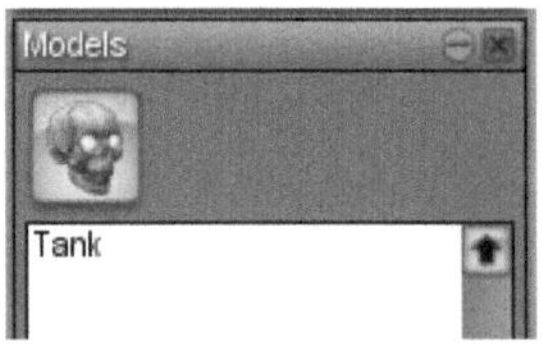

Figure 20-8. The **Models** page panel in the **World Editor**.

Models page panel is not showing in the page column (you may have to scroll down to see if it's there or not), choose **Page > Models**.

The **Models** page panel should now have tank listed, as shown in Figure 20-8. Click "tank" and then click in any of the viewports to place a tank model into the world. Next, choose **Node > Reset Transform to Identity**. This will snap the model to the center of the playing field. You may not actually see the tank geometry appear in the world when you place the model. If not, click on the **Toggle Models** button on the main tool bar, and the tank geometry will appear in the viewports. Choose **World > Save and Play World (Ctrl-P)** to see the tank in the game, shown in Figure 20-9.

Figure 20-9. The tank model in the game.

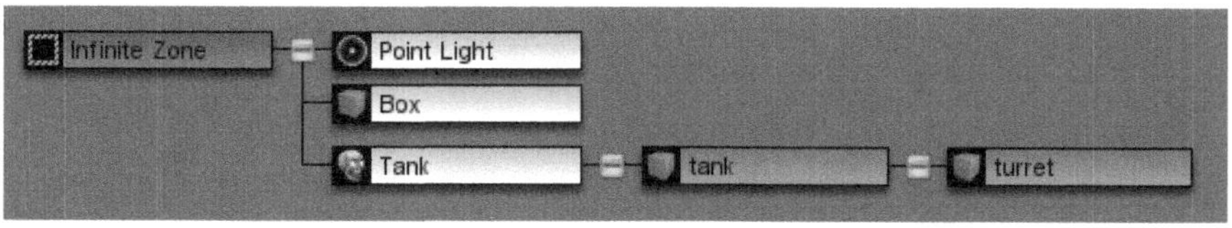

Figure 20-10. The tank model in the game.

If all goes well, the new tank model is in your world. Figure 20-10 shows another look at the scene graph now that the tank model has been dragged into the world.

Notice that there is now a "tank" node with an icon of a skull in it. This is the model node, and it is the parent node of the tank geometry node. The model node shows up here because it is now part of the game world. The **World > Load from Model Resource** command is only intended for editing models rather than adding models to the game world.

We now have a model that we can select, so the next step will be to handle the actual mouse selection.

Mouse Input—Unit Selection

Now to get some mouse input going. The first thing we'll do is to implement unit selection and de-selection. As a visual selection indicator, we'll add some color to the tank. We'll make the friendly tank blue, and later on, we can make the enemy tank red. When it is clicked, the tank will illuminate to show that it is selected. When the user clicks on anything but the tank, the tank will be de-selected.

To implement these features, we'll be modifying the `TankController` class, adding a new `RTSCommandAction` class, and making some minor modifications to the `CombatWorld` and `RTSCamera` classes, as well as the `RTS` application class.

Starting with the `TankController` class, add these variables and functions:

Tank.h

```
class TankController : public Controller
{
   private:
      ...
      DiffuseAttribute        *diffuse;
      EmissionAttribute       *emission;
```

```
    MaterialObject          *matObject;

    bool selected;

  public:
    ...
    void SetSelected(bool select);
    bool IsSelected(void) const;
};
```

Tank.cpp

```
void TankController::SetSelected(bool select)
{
  if (selected != select)
  {
    selected = select;

    if (emission)
    {
      if (selected)
      {
        emission->SetEmissionColor(ColorRGB(0.1f, 0.1f, 0.1f));
      }
      else
      {
        emission->SetEmissionColor(ColorRGB(0.0f, 0.0f, 0.0f));
      }
    }
  }
}

bool TankController::IsSelected(void) const
{
  return (selected);
}
```

And also add this initialization code to the constructor and `Preprocess()` function:

Tank.cpp

```
TankController::TankController() :
        ...
        selected(false),
        matObject(nullptr),
        ...
{
    ...
}

void TankController::Preprocess(void)
{
    Controller::Preprocess();

    Node *node = GetTargetNode();
    Model *model = static_cast<Model *>(node);

    if (model)
    {
        matObject = new MaterialObject();
        diffuse = new DiffuseAttribute();
        emission = new EmissionAttribute();
        diffuse->SetAttributeColor(ColorRGB(0.5f, 0.5f, 1.0f));

        emission->SetEmissionColor(ColorRGB(0.0f, 0.0f, 0.0f));
        matObject->AddAttribute(diffuse);
        matObject->AddAttribute(emission);

        Geometry *tankGeo = static_cast<Geometry *>
            (model->GetFirstSubnode());

        if (tankGeo)
        {
            Geometry *turret = static_cast<Geometry *>
                (tankGeo->GetFirstSubnode());

            tankGeo->SetMaterialObject(0, matObject);

            if (turret)
```

```
            {
               turret->SetMaterialObject(0, matObject);
            }
         }
      }
}
```

And the cleanup code in the destructor:

Tank.cpp

```
TankController::~TankController()
{
   if (matObject) matObject->Release();
}
```

That `Preprocess()` code looks a little unruly, so let's look at how it's broken down. Essentially, we're creating a new `MaterialObject`, assigning a new diffuse and emission attribute to the `MaterialObject`, and then setting this new material object to the tank's geometry as well as the turret's geometry.

In the `TankController` destructor, the material object is released. Since a material object can potentially contain numerous references to it, the material object cannot be explicitly deleted. Instead, `Release()` is called to clean up the material object and its references.

Next, let's focus on allowing the user to click on the tank to select it. We'll start by extending the `RTSCamera` class with a new `GetWorldRayFromPoint()` function, that is nearly identical to the `GetWorldRayFromClick()` function described in the wiki article "Creating a Ray for a Click Location"[1]. Our version of the function has a different parameter list, since it's a member of the camera class, so the camera does not need to be passed in as a parameter.

RTSCamera.h

```
class RTSCamera : public FrustumCamera
{
   public:
```

[1] http://www.terathon.com/wiki/index.php/Creating_a_Ray_for_a_Click_Location

```
        ...
        void GetWorldRayFromPoint(const Integer2D& p, Ray *ray);
};
```

RTSCamera.cpp

```
void RTSCamera::GetWorldRayFromPoint(const Integer2D& p, Ray *ray)
{
    const Rect& viewRect = GetObject()->GetViewRect();

    float x = p.x / (float) viewRect.Width();
    float y = p.y / (float) viewRect.Height();

    this->CastRay(x, y, ray);

    const Transform4D& cameraTransform = GetNodeTransform();
    ray->origin = cameraTransform * ray->origin;
    ray->direction = (cameraTransform * ray->direction).Normalize();

    ray->radius = 0.0f;
    ray->tmin = 0.0f;
    ray->tmax = 500.0f;
}
```

Also in `RTSCamera.h`, add an accessor for the `curFocus` variable that we added in Creating a Basic Navigation Camera:

RTSCamera.h

```
class RTSCamera : public FrustumCamera
{
    public:
        ...
        Point3D GetCurrentFocus(void) const
        {
            return (curFocus);
        }
        ...
};
```

Next, let's add a new action to the project. We'll call the class `RTSComman-dAction`. (We can't use `CommandAction`, because the C4 Engine already uses this function name internally). For now, this class will handle selection of the tank unit, but will be expanded further to issue commands to the tank for moving and attacking.

CommandAction.h

```
#ifndef COMMAND_ACTION_H
#define COMMAND_ACTION_H

#include "C4Input.h"
#include "C4Cameras.h"
#include "C4Models.h"

namespace C4
{
   enum
   {
      kActionSelect = 'fire'
   };

   class RTSCommandAction : public Action
   {
      private:

         bool      clicked;

         void ModelSelect(void);
         Model *IsOverTank(void) const;

      public:

         RTSCommandAction(unsigned long type);
         ~RTSCommandAction();

         void Begin(void);
         void End(void);
   };
}
```

```
#endif
```

Notice that `kActionSelect` was assigned the constant `'fire'`. This was only because the key bindings configuration file has the left-click mouse button already assigned to `'fire'`. Naturally, you may want to use another constant like `'slct'` for "select" but just remember to change your key binding configuration file to reflect that change.

CommandAction.cpp

```
#include "CommandAction.h"
#include "C4Engine.h"
#include "RTS.h"
#include "Tank.h"

using namespace C4;

RTSCommandAction::RTSCommandAction(unsigned long type) :
      Action(type),
      clicked(false)
{
}

RTSCommandAction::~RTSCommandAction()
{
}

void RTSCommandAction::Begin(void)
{
   if (!clicked)
   {
      if (this->GetActionType() == kActionSelect)
      {
         ModelSelect();
      }

      clicked = true;
   }
```

```
}

void RTSCommandAction::End(void)
{
   clicked = false;
}
```

The implementations for `IsOverTank()` and `ModelSelect()` are longer than usual, so we'll separate the breakdown here. The function `IsOverTank()` is the workhorse of the selection process. Its responsibility is to construct a ray that is used to attempt any collision with any nodes in the world. If the ray has collided with a model node, the code checks to see if it is of type `kModelTank`. If the ray has collided with a geometry node, the code then looks up its super node to find the attached model node. If it finds one, and the type is of `kModelTank`, we return that model. Otherwise, we return a null pointer.

CommandAction.cpp

```
Model *RTSCommandAction::IsOverTank(void) const
{
   CombatWorld *world = static_cast<CombatWorld *>
      (TheWorldMgr->GetWorld());
   if (world)
   {
      RTSCamera *cam = world->GetNavCamera();
      Point3D camPosition = cam->GetNodePosition();
      Point3D curFocus = cam->GetCurrentFocus();

      CollisionData data;
      CollisionState state = kCollisionStateNone;

      Ray ray;
      Point2D cursorPoint = world->GetCursorPosition();
      cam->GetWorldRayFromPoint(Integer2D(cursorPoint.x,
         cursorPoint.y), &ray);

      float distance = Magnitude(camPosition - curFocus);
      Point3D p1 = ray.origin;
      Point3D p2 = ray.origin + ray.direction * ray.tmax;
```

```
        // Test against all geometry.
        state = world->QueryCollision(p1, p2, 0.0f, 0, &data);

        if (state != kCollisionStateNone)
        {
            Geometry *geo = data.geometry;
            Node *node = geo->GetSuperNode();
            bool overTank = false;

            while (node)
            {
                if (node->GetNodeType() == kNodeModel)
                {
                    Model *model = static_cast<Model *>(node);
                    if ((model) &&
                        (model->GetModelType() == kModelTank))
                            return (model);
                    else
                        return (nullptr);
                }

                // Not a model, so keep looking to the super node.
                node = node->GetSuperNode();
            }
        }
    }

    return (nullptr);
}
```

The `ModelSelect()` function uses the `IsOverTank()` function to select a tank model. However, before determining if the mouse is over a tank, the function de-selects all tank model selections via their respective `TankController` objects. If the function has found a tank model, we go ahead and select the tank.

CommandAction.cpp

```
void RTSCommandAction::ModelSelect(void)
{
```

```
    // Reset all tanks.
    CombatWorld *world = static_cast<CombatWorld *>
        (TheWorldMgr->GetWorld());
    Array<Model *> tanks;
    world->GetModelTanks(tanks);

    TankController *tankController = nullptr;
    Model *tankModel = nullptr;
    for (long i = 0; i < tanks.GetElementCount(); i++)
    {
        tankModel = static_cast<Model *>(tanks[i]);
        if (tankModel)
        {
            tankController = static_cast<TankController *>
                (tankModel->GetController());
            if (tankController)
            {
                tankController->SetSelected(false);
            }
        }
    }

    // Now see if any of them is clicked on.
    tankModel = IsOverTank();

    if (tankModel)
    {
        tankController = static_cast<TankController *>
            (tankModel->GetController());
        if (!tankController->IsSelected())
            tankController->SetSelected(true);
    }
}
```

Notice the usage of the `GetModelTanks()` function, which is part of the `CombatWorld` class. Generally, we'll want a quick way to retrieve all tank models in the world, so the `CombatWorld` class implements this function to do just that. Also remember to include `Tank.h`, since the `GetModelTanks()` function references `kModelTank`. The function implementation is as follows:

CombatWorld.h

```
class CombatWorld : public World
{
   public:
      ...
      void GetModelTanks(Array<Model *>& modelTanks);
};
```

> **A Note About Practicality**
> Please note that the `GetModelTanks()` function traverses the entire scene graph, looking for all tank models. Although this is acceptable for this tutorial, a large-scale project with numerous nodes in the scene graph would make this function impractical. Instead, the step to validate the `modelTanks` array can be performed during preprocessing of the world, and the array can be modified during run-time as needed.

CombatWorld.cpp

```
void CombatWorld::GetModelTanks(Array<Model*>& modelTanks)
{
   modelTanks.Purge();

   Node *root = GetRootNode();
   Node *node = root;
   unsigned int nodeType = 0;
   do
   {
      nodeType = node->GetNodeType();
      if (nodeType == kNodeModel)
      {
         Model *model = static_cast<Model *>(node);
         if (model)
         {
            if (model->GetModelType() == kModelTank)
            {
               modelTanks.AddElement(model);
            }
         }
```

```
        }

        node = root->GetNextNode(node);
    } while (node);
}
```

As with `NavAction`, let's register the `RTSCommandAction` with the main application (remember to add `CommandAction.h` to `RTS.h`):

RTS.h

```
class RTS : public Singleton <RTS>, public Application
{
    private:
        ...
        RTSCommandAction *selectAction;
        ...
};
```

RTS.cpp

```
RTS::RTS(void) :
        Singleton<RTS>(TheGame),
        tankControllerReg(kControllerTank, "Tank"),
        tankModelReg(kModelTank, "tank", kModelPrecache,
            kControllerTank)
{
    ...
    selectAction = new RTSCommandAction(kActionSelect);
    ...
    TheInputMgr->AddAction(selectAction);
    ...
}
```

Don't forget to delete the select action in the destructor!

RTS.cpp

```
RTS::~RTS(void)
{
    ...
    delete selectAction;
    ...
}
```

Now you're ready to run the app! Just click the mouse cursor on and around the tank, and the tank should light up or turn off. Figure 20-11 shows an example of what it should look like.

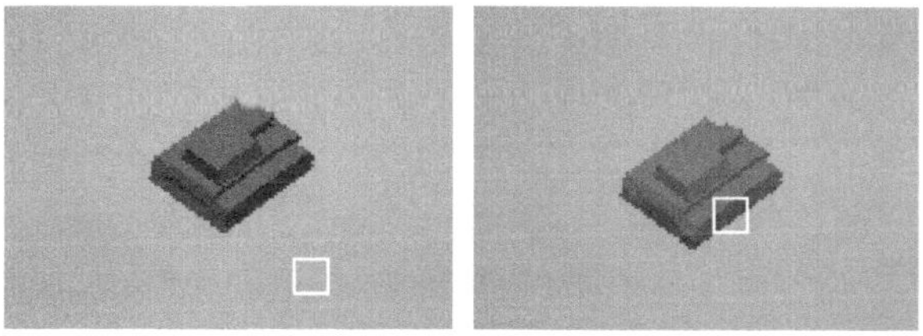

Figure 20 11. Tank in deselected (left) and selected (right) states.

Whew! Looks like a lot of work just to get something selected! However, this implementation was designed to make ownership of member variables and functions as clear as possible, to avoid any spaghetti logic and to be easier to build upon later on. Also, the principles of how to navigate a C4 Engine scene graph is something that will be done over and over again when implementing more complex nodes, actions, controllers, and properties, so this implementation serves as good practice.

With unit selection, we can now start moving the unit tank around with the click of the right mouse button.

Mouse Input—Unit Movement

We'll allow the player to start the selected tank model's movement by right-clicking an area of the playing field. It's not too fancy. The tank simply rotates in the direction of the clicked waypoint, and travels to that waypoint. (Turret rotation will come in later.) The majority of our edits will be in `Tank.h` and

Tank.cpp. We'll be focusing on the implementation of the Move() function. Start by adding the following members and member functions to the TankController class:

Tank.h

```
class TankController : public Controller
{
   private:
      ...
      Point3D   waypoint;

      float     curRotation;
      float     reqRotation;

      void MoveTank(Model *model, float dt);
      ...

   public:
      ...
      void SetWaypoint(const Point3D& point)
      {
         waypoint = point;
      }
      ...
};
```

The waypoint will be the point where the tank wants to be. Setting the waypoint will make the Move() function rotate and then move the tank towards the waypoint until it has arrived at the waypoint. curRotation will be used as the current rotation, and reqRotation will be the required or requested rotation that the current rotation should attempt to achieve. The MoveTank() function will contain all of the work we'll be doing to modify the rotation and position of the tank, and it is called by the TankController::Move() function.

Next, add initialization code for these variables in the constructor's initialization list:

Tank.cpp

```
TankController::TankController() :
        ...
        curRotation(0),
        reqRotation(0),
        waypoint(0.0f, 0.0f, 0.0f)
{
}
```

Although `waypoint` is initialized to the origin, let's set the waypoint's initial location to the tank's position in the `Preprocess()` function, so that when the application starts up, the tank will already be at the waypoint. We will also initialize `curRotation` based on the tank's initial transform:

Tank.cpp

```
void TankController::Preprocess(void)
{
    Controller::Preprocess();

    Node *node = GetTargetNode();
    Model *model = static_cast<Model *>(node);
    if (model)
    {
        // BEGIN: Initializing rotation and waypoint
        float x, y;
        model->GetNodeTransform().GetEulerAngles(&x, &y,
            &curRotation);

        waypoint = model->GetNodePosition();
        // END: Initializing rotation and waypoint
        ...
    }
}
```

In the `Move()` function, we'll simply get the current delta time, get the target model node of the controller, and pass these into `MoveTank()`, and then invalidate the model:

Tank.cpp

```
void TankController::Move(void)
{
   float dt = TheTimeMgr->GetFloatDeltaTime() * 0.001f;

   Model *model = static_cast<Model *>(GetTargetNode());
   MoveTank(model, dt);
   model->Invalidate();
}
```

The following `MoveTank()` function contains all of the logic to get the tank to move toward the waypoint:

Tank.cpp

```
void TankController::MoveTank(Model *model, float dt)
{
   if ((!model) || (model->GetModelType() != kModelTank)) return;

   // Get the direction that the tank should be facing.
   Vector3D reqDirVector = waypoint - model->GetNodePosition();

   // Get the distance to the waypoint.
   float travelDistance = C4::Magnitude(reqDirVector);

   reqDirVector.Normalize();

   reqRotation = Atan(reqDirVector.y, reqDirVector.x);

   float deltaRotation = reqRotation - curRotation;

   while (deltaRotation < -K::pi) deltaRotation += K::two_pi;
   while (deltaRotation > K::pi) deltaRotation -= K::two_pi;

   bool rotationArrived = true;

   // Check if delta rotation is larger than threshold.
   if (Fabs(deltaRotation) > 0.1f)
```

```
    {
        rotationArrived = false;

        if (deltaRotation < 0)
        {
            curRotation -= 1.0f * dt;
        }
        else if (deltaRotation > 0)
        {
            curRotation += 1.0f * dt;
        }
    }

    // Start with the current position.
    Point3D newPosition = model->GetNodePosition();
    if ((travelDistance > 0.1f) && (rotationArrived))
    {
        // Advance the position.
        newPosition += reqDirVector * 0.5f * dt;
    }

    // Start with a transform about the pivot.
    Transform4D transform;
    transform.SetRotationAboutZ(curRotation);
    model->SetNodeTransform(transform);

    // Then move the node to the new position.
    model->SetNodePosition(newPosition);
}
```

`reqDirVector` represents the difference vector between the current location and the desired location. `travelDistance` saves the length of this vector, so that `reqDirVector` can be normalized afterward. This vector is normalized so that we can use the resulting unit vector to generate the required rotation from an arc tangent calculation. `deltaRotation` stores the amount of rotation needed to get to the required rotation.

A couple of while loops bring `deltaRotation` within $-\pi$ to π, the range of the arctangent calculation. An absolute value check is then done to see if the tank is rotated enough. If it isn't, `curRotation` is modified to get closer to `reqRota-`

tion. The new position is then changed only if the desired rotation is met with the rotationArrived flag. The last few steps generate an appropriate visual transformation for the tank model.

Expanding on the RTS Command Action

If you trudge through all of the math in the MoveTank() function, you'll notice that the tank movement is ultimately controlled by the waypoint variable. If the waypoint doesn't differ from the tank model's current position, no movement takes place. That being said, the waypoint variable is controlled through the RTSCommandAction class, which was also the class used for selecting a tank.

To start off, add a new action type:

CommandAction.h

```
enum
{
    kActionSelect    = 'fire',
    kActionCommand   = 'trig'      // New action type
};
```

The kActionCommand action type is issued when the key bound to 'trig' is pressed, which defaults to the right mouse button in the input.cfg file. Modify the Begin() function to account for this change. In this function, you'll find the action type is checked by calling the GetActionType() function:

CommandAction.cpp

```
if (GetActionType() == kActionSelect)
{
    ModelSelect();
}
```

Remove this, and replace it with the switch statement below:

```
void RTSCommandAction::Begin(void)
{
```

```
    if (!clicked)
    {
        // BEGIN: New switch statement.
        switch (this->GetActionType())
        {
            case kActionSelect:
                ModelSelect();
                break;

            case kActionCommand:
                ModelCommand();
                break;
        }
        // END: New switch statement.

        clicked = true;
    }
}
```

That's much cleaner now!

And finally, add the implementation of `ModelCommand()` as follows:

CommandAction.h

```
class RTSCommandAction : public Action
{
    private:
        ...
        void ModelCommand(void);
        ...
};
```

CommandAction.cpp

```
void RTSCommandAction::ModelCommand(void)
{
    CombatWorld *world = static_cast<CombatWorld *>
        (TheWorldMgr->GetWorld());
```

```
if (world)
{
    RTSCamera *cam = world->GetNavCamera();
    Point3D camPosition = cam->GetNodePosition();
    Point3D curFocus = cam->GetCurrentFocus();

    CollisionData data;
    CollisionState state = kCollisionStateNone;

    Ray ray;

    Point2D cursorPoint = world->GetCursorPosition();
    cam->GetWorldRayFromPoint(Integer2D(cursorPoint.x,
        cursorPoint.y), &ray);
    float distance = Magnitude(camPosition - curFocus);

    Point3D p1 = ray.origin;
    Point3D p2 = ray.origin + ray.direction * ray.tmax;

    state = world->QueryCollision(p1, p2, 0.0f, 0, &data);
    if (state != kCollisionStateNone)
    {
        Geometry *geo = data.geometry;
        Node *node = geo->GetSuperNode();
        if (node)
        {
            Array<Model *> tanks;

            world->GetModelTanks(tanks);
            for (long i = 0; i < tanks.GetElementCount(); i++)
            {
                Model *tank = tanks[i];
                if (tank)
                {
                    TankController *tankController =
                        static_cast<TankController *>
                            (tank->GetController());
                    if ((tankController) &&
                        (tankController->IsSelected()) && (cam))
                    {
```

```
                        tankController->SetWaypoint(data.position);
                    }
                }
            }
        }
    }
  }
}
```

The first half of the function is largely similar to the `IsOverTank()` function's first half, in that the function constructs a ray from the camera into the world to act as a collision "probe" The second half of the function then takes the collision information and iterates through all the model tanks, compares its geometry with that of the collided geometry, and sets the waypoint to that `TankController`.

And now, register the new command action as we did with the select action:

RTS.h

```
class RTS : public Singleton <RTS>, public Application
{
  private:
      ...
      RTSCommandAction *commandAction;
      ...
};
```

In the constructor:

RTS.cpp

```
RTS::RTS(void) : ...
{
   ...
   commandAction = new RTSCommandAction(kActionCommand);
   ...
   TheInputMgr->AddAction(commandAction);
   ...
}
```

And in the destructor:

RTS.cpp

```
RTS::~RTS(void)
{
   ...
   delete commandAction;
   ...
}
```

At this point, the project compiles and you can click and move the tank around. We're done, right? Well, not quite...

Support Code

As it is right now, there's a small problem with how we determine the click location in 3D space. The problem is that the collision check from the mouse click queries all geometry in the scene for a position to set the waypoint to. That means that the user can potentially click on, say, a wall or another vehicle in the scene, and the waypoint will be set somewhere above or below the intended ground plane.

Figure 20-12 shows an example of what could happen with bad collision detection when clicking. Notice that the tank is on top of the wall because the user clicked on top of the wall surface, and that's where the collision with the mouse cursor occurred. How do we fix this? Well, the key line of code is the call to `QueryCollision()`, more specifically, the fourth parameter in that function. To fix this, we'll have to utilize exclusion masks for the geometry in the world. What the heck is an exclusion mask? Read on!

The Collision Exclusion Mask

The collision exclusion mask is a value you can set to any geometry or rigid body to prevent it from being processed by collision detection via the `QueryCollision()` or `DetectCollision()` functions. This value is set by calling the `SetCollisionExclusionMask()` function of the geometry or rigid body. See the API documentation details for this function.

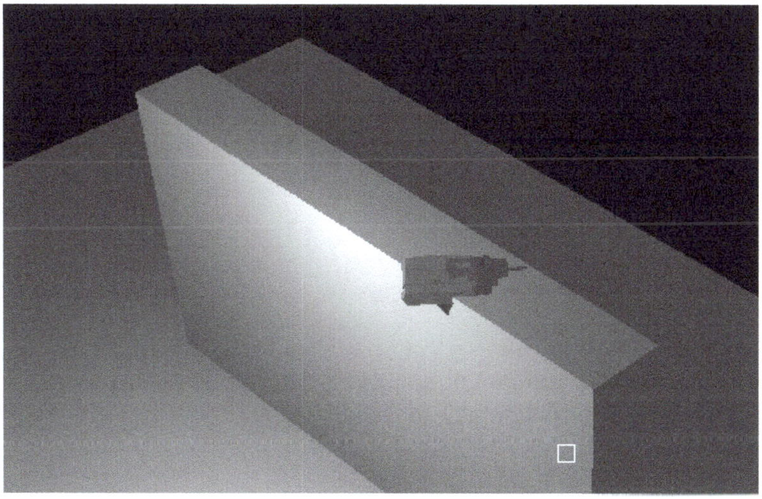

Figure 20-12. An example of bad collision detection when clicking.

For this tutorial, we will pass in the `kCollisionSightPath` bit flag to all objects that will ignore the click command. This will be done below, but before we do that, let's handle the receiving end.

In the `QueryCollision()` function (and the `DetectCollision()` function), the fourth parameter is an unsigned long called `kind`. The API documentation states the following:

> The `kind` parameter can be used to invalidate certain types of collisions. When a candidate geometry or rigid body is encountered in the collision detection process, its collision exclusion mask is logically ANDed with the value of the `kind` parameter. A collision can only occur if the result of this operation is zero.

This means that if any of the valid flags for this value matches those assigned to any geometry's collision exclusion mask, the collision for that geometry is ignored.

Change the `QueryCollision()` call in the `ModelCommand()` function to exclude geometry and colliders with the `kCollisionSightPath` flag set:

CommandAction.cpp

```
void RTSCommandAction::ModelCommand()
{
    ...
    state = world->QueryCollision(p1, p2, 0.0f,
        kCollisionSightPath, &data);
    ...
}
```

It's a little unclear at this point as to what this flag is actually supposed to do, but don't worry. It will all make sense later on.

Identifying the Ground

For the unit movement to be complete, we again have to implement some support code. What we need to do is identify the ground geometry and then mark all other geometries as non-collidable for click commands. This is needed so that when the user clicks the mouse on a location, the click is processed only for the ground geometry and no other geometry. If the click is processed for any other geometry, another tank for instance, the click location could potentially end up on top of the tank!

There are several ways that the ground geometry can be marked separately from all other geometry, but the method we'll use here is to create a new property class called `GroundProperty`, and assign it to the ground geometry in the **World Editor**. It's rather simple, and contains the absolute bare bones required for implementing a `Property` subclass. All it is used for at this time is so that during the `Preprocess()` function, the world can get a pointer to the ground. (Some other future applications for this property could be settings for things like friction coefficient, damage over time, heal over time, safety zone, hostile territory, etc.).

Let's create the new header and source files for the `GroundProperty` class.

GroundProperty.h

```
#ifndef GROUND PROPERTY H
#define GROUND PROPERTY H

#include "C4World.h"
```

```
namespace C4
{
   enum
   {
      kPropertyGround = 'grnd'
   };

   class GroundProperty : public Property
   {
      private:

      public:

         GroundProperty();
         ~GroundProperty();

         static bool ValidNode(const Node *node);

         void Pack(Packer& data,unsigned long packFlags) const;
         void Unpack(Unpacker& data, unsigned long unpackFlags);
   };
}

#endif
```

GroundProperty.cpp

```
#include "GroundProperty.h"

using namespace C4;

GroundProperty::GroundProperty() : Property(kPropertyGround)
{
}

GroundProperty::~GroundProperty()
{
}
```

```
bool GroundProperty::ValidNode(const Node *node)
{
   return (node->GetNodeType() == kNodeGeometry);
}

void GroundProperty::Pack(Packer& data,
   unsigned long packFlags) const
{
   Property::Pack(data, packFlags);
}

void GroundProperty::Unpack(Unpacker& data,
   unsigned long unpackFlags)
{
   Property::Unpack(data, unpackFlags);
}
```

As with models and controllers, properties also have to be registered with the application so that they can be used in the **World Editor** tool:

RTS.h

```
#include "GroundProperty.h"
...

class RTS : public Singleton <RTS>, public Application
{
   private:
        ...
        PropertyReg<GroundProperty> groundPropertyReg;
        ...
};
```

And in the initialization list of the `RTS` constructor, initialize the new property:

RTS.cpp

```
RTS::RTS(void) :
        ...
```

```
        groundPropertyReg(kPropertyGround, "Ground Type")
        ...
{
    ...
}
```

Now that we have the ability to label which geometry the ground will be, the rest of the code part traverses the scene graph in `CombatWorld::Preprocess()`, finds all geometry that does not have the ground property, and marks them as excluded from collision detection with the `kCollisionSightPath` flag. Here's the code block for that function:

CombatWorld.cpp

```
#include "GroundProperty.h"
...

WorldResult CombatWorld::Preprocess(void)
{
    WorldResult result = World::Preprocess();
    if (result != kWorldOkay) return (result);

    // BEGIN: NEW CODE

    Node *root = GetRootNode();
    Node *node = root;
    unsigned int nodeType = 0;

    do
    {
        nodeType = node->GetNodeType();
        if (nodeType == kNodeGeometry)
        {
            Geometry *geo = static_cast<Geometry *>(node);
            if (geo)
            {
                Property *prop = geo->GetProperty(kPropertyGround);
                if (!prop)
                {
```

```
                GeometryObject *geoObj =
                    static_cast<GeometryObject*>(geo->GetObject());
                if (geoObj)
                {
                    geoObj->SetCollisionExclusionMask
                        (kCollisionSightPath);
                }
            }
        }
    }

    node = root->GetNextNode(node);
} while (node);

// END: NEW CODE

SetCamera(&navCamera);
return (kWorldOkay);
}
```

This is a useful scene graph tree traversal for any sort of preprocessing that needs to be done on nodes during initialization. For now, all it does is set the collision exclusion mask for all geometry objects except for the ground object, but expect several modifications to be done to this traversal in future sections.

Fire up C4, open up `RTS.wld` in the **World Editor** tool, select the ground geometry, and choose **Node > Get Info (Ctrl-I)**. Select the **Properties** tab panel, click on **Ground Type**, click **Assign**, and then click OK. Save the world and it's all good to go!

Conclusion

Most of this section focused on preventing the user from clicking on anything other than the ground. Although there are many ways to accomplish this, a property was introduced to denote that we're dealing with a special node, and we introduced some initialization code when preprocessing the world. Ultimately, what we got out of this is that we can finally command our tank to move around by right clicking anywhere on the ground plane!

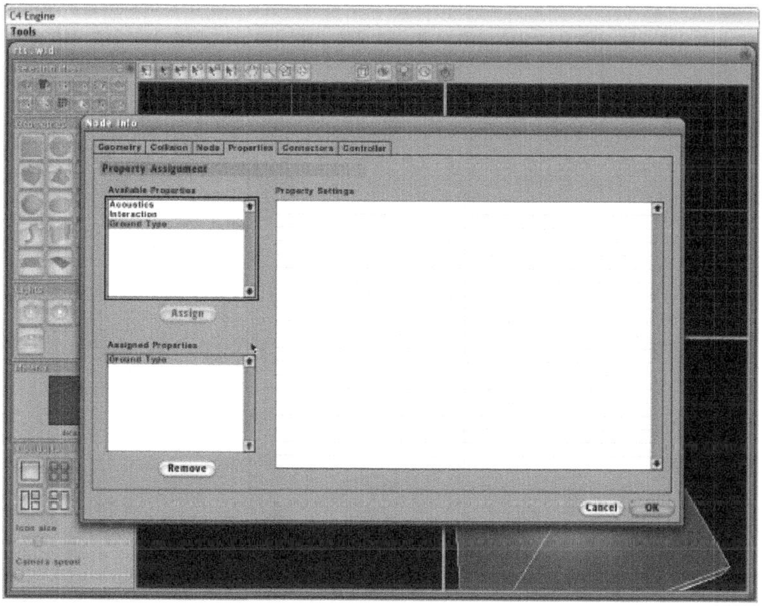

Figure 20-13. Adding a **Ground Type** property to the ground geometry.

Creating an Enemy Unit

In this section, we'll add an enemy tank unit, and we'll also add turret rotation so that the tanks can aim at a target.

The "Player-Controlled" Flag and Setting

Our first step is adding a flag to the `TankController` class to mark it as either a player-controlled tank or an enemy-controlled tank.

Tank.h

```
class TankController : public Controller
{
   private:
      ...
      bool       playerControlled;
      ...
```

```
    public:
        ...
        bool IsPlayerControlled(void) const
        {
            return (playerControlled);
        }
        ...
};
```

Initialize the flag in the `TankController` constructor's initialization list:

Tank.cpp

```
TankController::TankController() :
        ...
        playerControlled(false)
        ...
{
    ...
}
```

After creating a flag for this setting, we can allow a level designer to mark the tank as player-controlled by adding a setting to the `TankController` class. (See the C4 Engine Wiki article, "Defining a Custom Controller,"[2] if you are unfamiliar with settings in a controller.)

Add the following function declarations and definitions for adding controller settings (note that `C4Configuration.h` is included for all settings-related types):

Tank.h

```
...
#include "C4Configuration.h"
...
class TankController : public Controller
{
```

[2] http://www.terathon.com/wiki/index.php/Defining_a_Custom_Controller

```
    private:
        ...
    public:
        ...
        long GetSettingCount(void) const;
        Setting *GetSetting(long index) const;
        void SetSetting(const Setting *setting);
        ...
};
```

Tank.cpp

```
long TankController::GetSettingCount(void) const
{
    return (1);
}

Setting *TankController::GetSetting(long index) const
{
    if (index == 0)
    {
        return (new BooleanSetting('pctl', playerControlled,
            "Player Controlled"));
    }

    return (nullptr);
}

void TankController::SetSetting(const Setting *setting)
{
    if (setting->GetSettingIdentifier() == 'pctl')
    {
        playerControlled = static_cast<const BooleanSetting *>
            (setting)->GetBooleanValue();
    }
}
```

With this support for settings, a level designer can open a world in the **World Editor** and select the **Player Controlled** option to mark a tank as a player tank or an enemy tank.

You can try this now if you'd like. Fire up C4, open up the world by typing `world rts` in the **Command Console** window, select the tank model, and then choose **Node > Get Info (Ctrl-I)**. Select the **Controllers** tab panel, and you will see that the new **Player Controlled** setting is now associated with the `TankController` class, as shown in Figure 20-14.

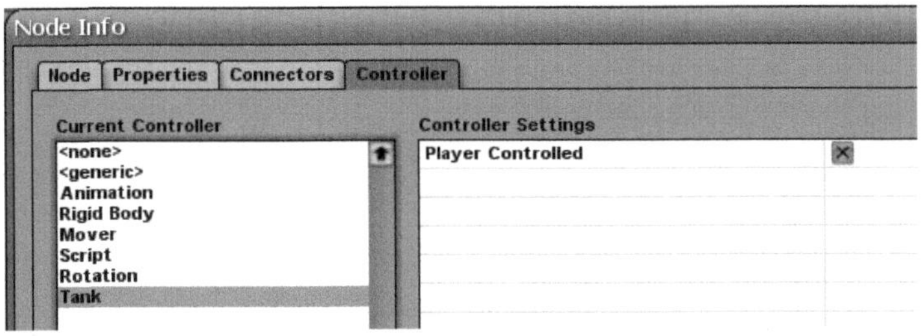

Figure 20-14. Adding a **Player Controlled** `TankController` setting.

You can click on it, but that's about all it does at this point, because we haven't hooked up the **Player Controlled** flag to do anything yet.

Why Isn't the Setting Saved?

Before we add any functionality to support the **Player Controlled** flag, there is one more thing that needs to be done. As it is right now, when you quit out of C4, the **Player Controlled** flag does not stick, and your setting is lost. Let's finish up the support code by adding serialization for this new setting by modifying the `Pack()` and `Unpack()` functions, and then adding a new private function called `UnpackChunk()`.

Tank.h

```
class TankController : public Controller
{
   public:
      ...
      // These functions already exist,
      // but we will be editing their definitions.
```

```
        void Pack(Packer& data, unsigned long packFlags) const;
        void Unpack(Unpacker& data, unsigned long unpackFlags);

        // Add this line.
        bool UnpackChunk(const ChunkHeader *chunkHeader,
           Unpacker& data, unsigned long unpackFlags);
};
```

Serialization can sometimes be a delicate situation to deal with. For instance, if this next part is not done carefully, we can very well end up with a game world that can be difficult to recover. We want the data to be read in properly, but if the new serialization code attempts to read old data that expects to be new data, it has a potential for crashing.

Modify the `Pack()` function as follows:

Tank.cpp

```
void TankController::Pack(Packer& data,
   unsigned long packFlags) const
{
   Controller::Pack(data, packFlags);

   data << TerminatorChunk; // Add this line
}
```

Now, open up the RTS world in the **World Editor**, and save it, so that the updated `TankController` class writes the terminator chunk to the world file. After that's done, the format of the `TankController` settings in your world file has changed, so the `Unpack()` function has to handle this:

Tank.cpp

```
void TankController::Unpack(Unpacker& data,
   unsigned long unpackFlags)
{
   Controller::Unpack(data, unpackFlags);

   // Add this line.
```

```
    UnpackChunkList<TankController>(data, unpackFlags);
}
```

You will notice that this is a little different from how the C4 Engine Wiki article, "Defining a Custom Controller",[3] packs and unpacks serialized data. The Unpack function internally calls the `UnpackChunk()` function to handle chunk-specific data. Here is what `UnpackChunk()` looks like:

Tank.cpp

```
bool TankController::UnpackChunk(const ChunkHeader *chunkHeader,
    Unpacker &data, unsigned long unpackFlags)
{
    switch(chunkHeader->chunkType)
    {
        case 'pctl':
            data >> playerControlled;
            return (true);
    }

    return (false);
}
```

In `UnpackChunk()`, the chunk type is checked, and if it matches a specific chunk type, it processes data specific to that chunk (This reminds us of the FLI format. We miss that format). Now that we can read in the `'pctl'` chunk type, let's write out the `'pctl'` chunk type to the file:

Tank.cpp

```
void TankController::Pack(Packer& data,
    unsigned long packFlags) const
{
    Controller::Pack(data, packFlags);

    data << ChunkHeader('pctl', 4);     // Add this line.
```

[3] http://www.terathon.com/wiki/index.php/Defining_a_Custom_Controller

```
    data << playerControlled;            // Add this line.

    data << TerminatorChunk;
}
```

With the `Pack()` function, we write out the `'pctl'` chunk type, which contains the value of the `playerControlled` flag, and then we read that value back in with the `Unpack()` function via the `'pctl'` chunk type. When you save and load the world, the value of `playerControlled` is maintained for each tank model in the world.

Now we're set up to use the `playerControlled` flag. Look for this line in the `TankController::Preprocess()` function:

```
diffuse->SetAttributeColor(ColorRGB(0.5f, 0.5f, 1.0f));
```

We'll change this line so that the enemy tank will be red instead of blue:

Tank.cpp

```
if (playerControlled)
    diffuse->SetAttributeColor(ColorRGB(0.5f, 0.5f, 1.0f));
else
    diffuse->SetAttributeColor(ColorRGB(1.0f, 0.5f, 0.5f));
```

One other place that we'll check for player control at this time is in the `RTSCommandAction` class. In the `ModelSelect()` function, we check if the tank is currently selected before actually selecting it:

CommandAction.cpp

```
void RTSCommandAction::ModelSelect(void)
{
    ...
    if (tankModel)
    {
        tankController = static_cast<TankController*>
            (tankModel->GetController());
        if (!tankController->IsSelected())
```

```
            tankController->SetSelected(true);
    }
}
```

Add the `playerControlled` flag to this check so that the user is only allowed to select player tanks:

CommandAction.cpp

```
void RTSCommandAction::ModelSelect()
{
    ...
    if (tankModel)
    {
        tankController = static_cast<TankController *>
            (tankModel->GetController());
        if ((!tankController->IsSelected()) &&
            (tankController->IsPlayerControlled()))
                tankController->SetSelected(true);
    }
}
```

Drop in a Red Enemy Tank

Now let's see what an enemy tank looks like. Start up C4, and load up the world by typing `world rts` in the **Command Console** window. Scroll to the **Models** page panel (again, you may have to open it by choosing **Page > Models**). Select the model named "Tank", and then click somewhere on top of the playing field in the upper-left viewport to create a new tank model. Again, you may have to choose **Reset Transform** to orient the tank correctly. At this point, feel free to move the tanks around to whatever starting position you would like:

If you haven't done so after we changed the `Pack()` and `Unpack()` functions, select the **Player Controlled** flag for the first tank. Select the first tank model (you can select it by either clicking on the first tank model in a viewport or by switching to the scene graph viewport and select the model node), choose **Node > Get Info (Ctrl-I)**, select the **Controllers** tab, and select the **Player Controlled** setting.

Save the world (because the world is always in trouble), fire up C4, and the game should appear as shown in Figure 20-16.

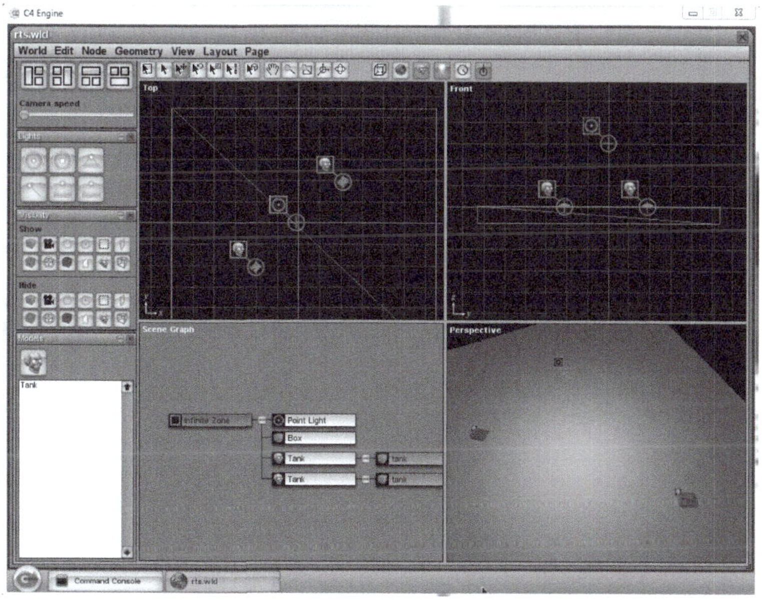

Figure 20-15. Adding the enemy tank in the world.

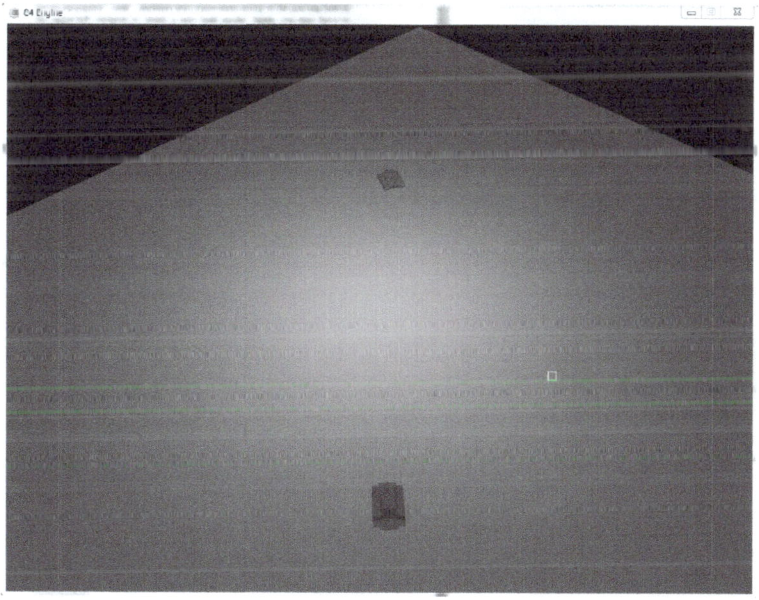

Figure 20-16. The enemy tank in-game.

Nice. We now have a red enemy tank in the game, but otherwise, it's not that much fun. Check out the next part for adding some turret rotation to the tanks.

Turret Rotation

Turret rotation is not related to adding an enemy tank in any way, but it's completely related to being able to fire a projectile at it! This part is mainly an exercise in applying transformations on a sub-node (turret) of a transformed node (tank).

Let's start off with adding variables and function declarations as usual:

Tank.h

```
class TankController : public Controller
{
   private:
      ...
      float curTurretRotation;
      float reqTurretRotation;

      Transform4D initialTurretTransform;

      bool moving;

      void MoveTurret(Model *model, float dt);
      ...
   public:
      ...
};
```

And then initialize the variables in the constructor:

Tank.cpp

```
TankController::TankController() :
      ...
      curTurretRotation(0),
      reqTurretRotation(0),
      initialTurretTransform(K::identity_4D),
```

```
        moving(false)
        ...
{
}
```

The variable `initialTurretTransform` keeps track of the initial position of the turret in relation to the tank. It is initialized in the constructor merely to give it some stable values, but the real initialization occurs in the `Preprocess()` function. Look for the last block of code in the `Preprocess()` function that searches for the turret geometry:

Tank.cpp

```
Geometry *turret = static cast<Geometry *>
    (tankGeo->GetFirstSubnode());
if (turret)
{
    turret->SetMaterialObject(0, matObject);
}
```

Since we have a pointer to the turret here, add a line to correctly initialize `initialTurretTransform`:

Tank.cpp

```
Geometry *turret = static cast<Geometry *>
    (tankGeo->GetFirstSubnode());
if (turret)
{
    turret->SetMaterialObject(0, matObject);

    // Add this line.
    initialTurretTransform = turret->GetNodeTransform();
}
```

And then in `TankController::Move()`, call the `MoveTurret()` function:

Tank.cpp

```
void TankController::Move(void)
{
    float dt = TheTimeMgr->GetFloatDeltaTime() * 0.001f;

    Model *model = static_cast<Model *>(GetTargetNode());
    MoveTank(model, dt);
    MoveTurret(model, dt);    // Add this line.

    model->Invalidate();
}
```

Then, set the `moving` flag at the end of the `MoveTank()` function. The `moving` flag is used in the `MoveTurret()` function to determine how to rotate the turret while the tank is moving and while it is not moving.

Tank.cpp

```
void TankController::MoveTank(Model *model, float dt)
{
    ...
    moving = ((travelDistance > 0.1f) || (!rotationArrived));
}
```

`travelDistance` and `rotationArrived` are variables that were previously defined in the Unit Movement section. The tank's moving flag is true if the `travelDistance` to the waypoint is beyond a certain small distance or if the tank has not completely rotated toward the waypoint.

And finally, the definition of the `MoveTurret()` function:

Tank.cpp

```
void TankController::MoveTurret(Model *model, float dt)
{
    if ((!model) || (model->GetModelType() != kModelTank)) return;

    TankController *myController = static_cast<TankController *>
```

```
        (model->GetController());
    if (!myController) return;

    Geometry *tankGeo = static_cast<Geometry *>
        (model->GetFirstSubnode());
    if (tankGeo)
    {
        Geometry *turret = static_cast<Geometry *>
            (tankGeo->GetFirstSubnode());
        if (turret)
        {
            CombatWorld *world = static_cast<CombatWorld *>
                (TheWorldMgr->GetWorld());
            Array<Model *> tanks;
            if (world)
            {
                world->GetModelTanks(tanks);
            }

            Model *targetTank = nullptr;
            for (long i = 0; i < tanks.GetElementCount(); i++)
            {
                targetTank = tanks[i];
                if ((targetTank) &&
                    (targetTank->GetModelType() == kModelTank) &&
                    (targetTank != model))
                {
                    TankController *controller =
                        static_cast<TankController *>
                            (targetTank->GetController());
                    if (controller)
                    {
                        if (IsPlayerControlled() !=
                            controller->IsPlayerControlled()) break;
                    }
                }
                targetTank = nullptr;
            }

            Vector3D targetDirVector(0.0f, 0.0f,0.0f);
```

```
if (targetTank)
{
   targetDirVector = targetTank->GetNodePosition() -
      model->GetNodePosition();
   targetDirVector.Normalize();
}

if (!moving)
{
   reqTurretRotation = Atan(targetDirVector.y,
      targetDirVector.x);
}
else
{
   reqTurretRotation = curRotation;
}

float deltaRotation = reqTurretRotation -
   curTurretRotation;
while (deltaRotation < -K::pi) deltaRotation += K::two pi;
while (deltaRotation > K::pi) deltaRotation -= K::two pi;

// Check if delta rotation is
// larger than threshold.
if (Fabs(deltaRotation) > 0.1f)
{
   if (deltaRotation < 0)
   {
      curTurretRotation -= 1.0f * dt;
   }
   else if (deltaRotation > 0)
   {
      curTurretRotation += 1.0f * dt;
   }
}

Transform4D nodeTransform = initialTurretTransform;
Matrix3D turretTransform;
turretTransform.SetRotationAboutZ(curTurretRotation -
   curRotation);
```

```
            nodeTransform *= turretTransform;
            turret->SetNodeTransform(nodeTransform);
        }
    }
}
```

All right, let's run through the code. The first thing the function does is punk out if the model pointer is bad, if the model is not of type kModelTank, or if there is no controller attached to the model. Then we move on by getting the model's first sub-node's first subnode (whew!) which should be the turret geometry as defined by the node hierarchy:

Figure 20-17. Now that the tank model is part of the world, the model node appears.

Once we have a hold of the turret pointer, we loop through each model tank in the world, get a hold of its controller, and do a comparison with this controller. We break out of the loop once we've found another tank controller whose playerControlled flag does not have the same value as this tank controller's playerControlled flag. It's not the best algorithm for finding an opposing tank (you may also want to check range and closeness), but it suits our needs for this scenario, in which there is only one player tank and one enemy tank.

The value of reqTurretRotation depends on the value of the moving flag. If the tank is moving, the reqTurretRotation is set to the tank's current rotation so that the turret "resets" its rotation to match with the tank. If the tank is no longer moving, we get the angle of rotation to the target by utilizing the direction vector to the target, and reqTurretRotation is set to this angle so that the turret will rotate toward the target tank.

The last part of this function generates an appropriate transformation for the turret. We start by setting nodeTransform to the initialTurretTransform (which, remember, is the turret's position in relation to the tank when it is first initialized). Then we multiply the nodeTransform with the turretTransform, which is simply the difference in rotation between the currentTurretRotation and the tank's curRotation. After the math is done, we set the node transform to the turret geometry.

Whew! That wasn't the easiest explanation to walk through and understand what's going on, but nothing beats reading the actual code to describe what the code really does!

Conclusion

What we have now is a very simple, but functional demonstration of using the C4 Engine for making a real-time strategy game. The friendly tank can be clicked on, directed to move to another location on the map, and the enemy tank will track the friendly tank's every move. This is a great setup for doing additional experimentations into things like projectiles and more advanced pathfinding.

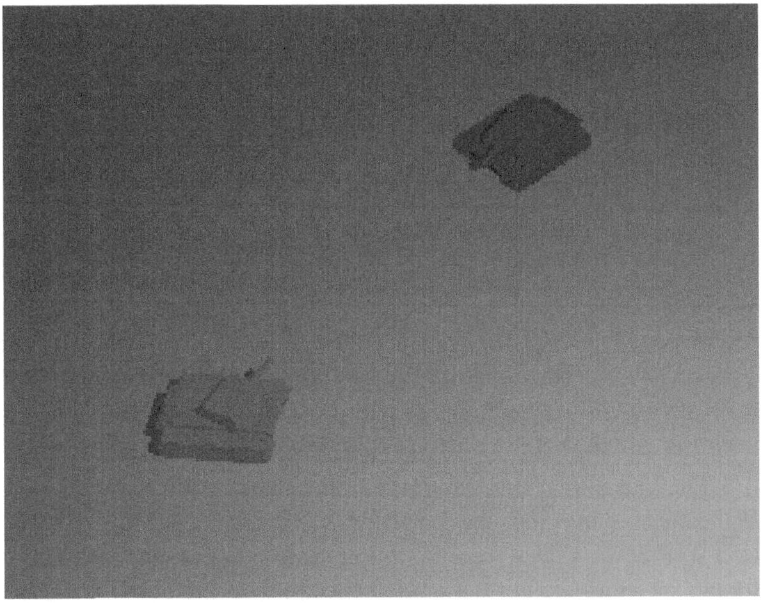

Figure 20-18. "What are YOU looking at?"

Appendices

A

Learning C++ with the C4 Engine

Learning C++ from Scratch?

There's no way you can learn C++ from scratch by reading this appendix alone. Instead, we intend to help people who are relatively new to C++, or who haven't used C++ for a long time and need a refresher.

This appendix is written for those who are confident with the basics of the language, but who are eager to move on to the next level and to understand what's going on in the tutorial, game and engine code supplied with the C4 Engine. It's for those who feel almost ready to start writing their own C4 application code, but who feel somewhat intimidated by the level of coding they see when they browse the available code examples.

> **TOTAL IMMERSION**
> As an aside, it is our own opinion that, if you want to learn (or relearn) something really quickly— foreign languages, programming languages, DIY, whatever—then the best thing to do is to totally immerse yourself in it. Get yourself motivated by a project that excites you. And when it comes to programming languages, what better project to motivate yourself if not a game project?

Crawl, Walk, and then Run

You might want to start off with a text-based version of your game. Then create a 2D version, and after you're sure that you have the basics covered, you could move on to make a 3D version of it.

> **LEARNING MORE**
> If you keep focused on, and energized by, your real goal—in this case making great games—then we are convinced that you will learn the tools you need to get there as a means to an end. You will find the information you need in books (such as [STRO00] and [MEYE05]), in online tutorials, among friends and peers, and in online video tutorials. There are countless sources of help these days. One of the most valuable skills you must learn, is how to find answers to the questions that will inevitably arise along the way.

A Simple Game in C++

Let's start off with a simple "guess a number" game, where the computer asks the player to guess a number between one and ten, and repeats the question until you guess right. Then it tells you "you've won!". Here's how quickly you can get started with C++:

1. Download Microsoft Visual C++ 2008 Express Edition, if you haven't already.
2. Start it up and then make your first project by choosing **File > New > Project**.
3. In the **Project** types list, under the **Win32** category, select **Win32 Console Application**.
4. Name the project something like "GuessingGame" and click OK.
5. In the application wizard, click **Next** and then choose **Console application**, and **empty project**.
6. In the **Solution Explorer** view on the left, right-click **Source Files** and choose **Add > New Item** from the contextual menu.
7. Choose **C++ File (.cpp)** and name it, something like "guess".
8. Click OK.
9. Copy and paste this code into the editor:

```
#include <iostream>
#include <conio.h>

using namespace std;

int main(void)
{
   int playerGuess;
   int computerGuess = 4;

   cout << "Guess a number:";

   do
   {
      cin >> playerGuess;
      if (playerGuess == computerGuess)
         cout << "Correct! You Win!";
      else
         cout << "Sorry. Guess again:";
   } while (playerGuess != computerGuess);

   getch(); // User presses any key to exit game.
   return (0);
}
```

10 Press F7 to compile your code, and then press F5 to run.

Well done! You're not a master yet, but you already know enough C++ now to start making your own simple games. See if you can work out what the individual lines of code are doing and use any online tutorial, or book, (or friend) to check if your guess was right.

Now, see if you can change that game so that the computer guesses a random number between 1 and 10, and gives the player only three chances to guess it. If the player doesn't guess correctly within three tries, then output "You lose!" and exit the program. As an exercise, try using Google if you don't know (or have forgotten) how to obtain random numbers in C++!

OK, let's move onto the next game—a text-based draw poker game. This next game will deal out five random cards, and will use arrays to store the cards which are dealt for this hand. Characters are used to represent the cards, e.g., "KH" would represent the king of hearts, or "5C" would be the five of clubs etc.

Give yourself some time to get used to the code and then extend it to allow the user to select up to five cards, which are to be re-dealt. Then add code to decide if the player has won on this hand or not.

Here is an outline "design" for the game:

1. The player begins with $1000.
2. The player places a bet, for a number of dollars between 5 and 100.
3. The computer deals five cards (here we'll learn about arrays, and use arrays to store the 52 cards).
4. The player can choose to discard up to 5 of them (we'll use "cin" to check for user input, using numbers to represent each of the cards—e.g., 0, 1, 1, 0, 1 would mean discard the first and fourth card).
5. The computer deals cards again (based on input).
6. The hand held by the player then determines how the win or loss.
7. Repeat from step 2 above (we'll use a "while" loop that check's for the win or lose condition).

Here are the winning hands together with the associated win:

- A pair of jacks or better (i.e., two jacks or two queens or two kings or two aces)—win your bet back.
- Two pair—win double your bet.
- Three of a kind—win treble your bet.
- Straight (e.g., 5, 6, 7, 8, 9 or 9, 10, J, Q, K)—win 4 times your bet.
- Flush (all five cards are of the same suit, say hearts or clubs)—win 5 times your bet.
- Full house (3 of a kind *and* 2 of a kind (e.g., three kings and two 8s or three 5s and 2 Aces, etc.)—win 8 times your bet.
- Four of a kind (e.g. four queens)—win 25 times your bet.
- Straight flush (a straight where all cards have the same suit)—win 100 times your bet.
- Royal flush (this is a straight from 10 to ace of the same suit—e.g., all hearts or all spades)—win 200 times your bet.

OK, go ahead and make a new C++ project, like you did above for the guessing game. Call it say "poker". Then add a new C++ file to the sources directory under your new project in the solution explorer and name that file `Poker.cpp`. Here is the code:

```
#include <iostream>
#include <cstdlib>

using namespace std;

int main(void)
{
   int myTotal = 1000;

   // Store up to 10 cards because you deal 5, but may
   // have to deal up to 5 more if 5 are discarded.
   int card[810], suit[10], num[10];

   // Enumerators would be even better here,
   // but I want to show the use of arrays.
   const char numName[13] = {'A', '2', '3', '4', '5', '6', '7',
      '8', '9', 'T', 'J', 'Q', 'K'};
   const char suitName[4] = {'H', 'D', 'S', 'C'};
   int bet = 5, minBet = 5, maxBet = 100, userEntry = 0;

   // Deal cards.
   while (userEntry != -1)
   {
      for (int i = 0; i < 5; i++)
      {
         // Random number between 0 and 51.
         card[i] = rand() % 52;

         // Check that card wasnt dealt already.
         int j = 0;
         while (j < i)
         {
            // If card already dealt.
            if (card[i] == card[j])
            {
```

```
                // Get a new random card.
                card[i] = rand() % 52;

                // Reset comparison card.
                j = 0;
            }
            else
            {
                // Check next card that was already dealt.
                j++;
            }
        }

        // Now you've dealt card i,
        // move on to the next card.
    }

    cout << "Here are your cards\n\n";
    for (int i = 0; i < 5; i++)
    {
        // A number from 0 to 3 representing the suit.
        suit[i] = card[i] / 13;

        // A number from 0 to 12 representing a card face number.
        num[i] = card[i] - suit[i] * 13;

        cout << numName[num[i]] << suitName[suit[i]] << " ";
    }

    cout << "\n\nEnter any number to deal next hand "
        "(or -1 to quit): ";

    // Just to pause game before finishing.
    cin >> userEntry;
  }

  return (0);
}
```

OK, go ahead and extend that code now to allow the player to discard up to five cards, and re-deal. Then decide if the player has won or not, update the player's "total" and then display that to the player. You might try coding Blackjack as your next example, and perhaps use your code to calculate the optimal strategy for the player.

What about pointers and references?

A reference is just another name for a variable. There is only one value, and the original variable name and the reference both refer to that single value in memory. There is no second copy of the value for the reference, it directly refers to the original value.

Take a look at this code:

```
int x = 10;

// Always read these from right to left - so this line reads
// "x is assigned to y, which is is a reference to an integer".
int& y = x;
```

Note that you must initiate a reference when you declare it:

```
// Changing x will also change y because x and y both refer
// to the same single value in memory.
x = 11;
cout << "x = : " << x << " and y = : " << y << "\n";
// "\n" adds a newline so the next output characters
// will start on the next line.

// Changing y will also change x because x and y both refer
// to the same single value in memory.
y = 12;
cout << "x = : " << x << " and y = : " << y << "\n";
```

Why use references?

One good use for references is to pass variables into a function, when you actually want the function to be able to change those variable in the calling code. Normally, you pass variables into a function "by value". This means that a copy is created of each variable passed in. This can be expensive if the function has whole objects, or lists of objects, as parameters. Also, the function in this case only works with copies of the variables, and so changes made by the function will not be made to variables in the calling code—with the exception being that you can use a return statement to return one object (but only one). When you pass variables into a function "by reference", then no copy is made. The reference again refers to the same single value in memory, with the result that changes to the reference value will directly change the value of the variable in the calling code.

How about pointers?

A pointer is a variable which is somewhat special, in that it holds a memory address and not just any old value. If that memory address is the address of a different variable, then we say that the pointer "points to" that other variable. The syntax is like this:

```
int x = 10;

// Always read declarations from right to left.
// "pointerToX is a pointer to an integer".
// Here, "*" is read "is a pointer to".
int *pointerToX;

// Here "&x" is to be read "the address of x". When you see an
// "&" like this you can think "address of" - but don't confuse
// this with the declaration of a reference! So here, "The address
// of x is assigned to pointerToX".
pointerToX = &x;

// The redirection operator "*" is used to access a variable
// stored at the address which the pointer holds.
cout << "x is : " << *pointerToX;
```

Here is an example of the use of references and pointers from the *SimpleChar* tutorial code:

```
if (DetectCollision(p1, p2, 0.3F, &data))
   // then do something....
```

The definition of the `DetectCollision()` function is:

```
bool Camera::DetectCollision(const Point3D& p1, const Point3D& p2,
    float radius, CollisionData *data) const
```

In this example, we pass in two `Point3D` objects, `p1` and `p2`, but copies are not made, since the parameters are passed in by reference. The `const` keyword inside the parameter list indicates that the values cannot be changed inside the function. Trying to do so would result in a compiler error like this:

```
// A line like this inside the DetectCollision() function
// will result in a compiler error like
// "'p1' : you cannot assign to a variable that is const"
p1.x = 0;
```

The radius value is passed by value, so a copy is made and the copy is used inside the function. The parameter variable data, which is a pointer to a `CollisionData` object, will point to the same object inside the function, also called data in the calling code.

The `const` at the end of that function definition means that the function is a constant member function, which in turn means that the function cannot change any member data. Note that a `const` object is only allowed (by the compiler) to call `const` member functions. Also, if you placed `const` before the function declaration and definition, then the function's return value would be `const`, but the function would be allowed to alter member data.

Of course there is a lot more to be said about references and pointers, but hopefully this will be enough to refresh the memory of those who have been away from all of this for a while. In the comments used to describe the C4 Engine tutorial code below, you will come across other examples where pointers and references are used.

Moving on to Object-Oriented Code

Up to now we've been looking at the basic syntax and fundamental built-in types of C++, but the programming itself hasn't been object-oriented. We have been using procedural, "C-like" code. If you come from a Java background, you'll know what OO programming entails. But if you haven't had any exposure to an object-oriented language, you'll still have quite a bit of learning ahead before you are ready for C4 coding. Again the references at the back will point you to some books and other resources which we have found useful.

> **C4 ENGINE API DOCUMENTATION**
> We recommend looking at the API documentation which you can access from the C4 Engine Wiki. If you browse the various classes and functions, you will come across examples of where pointers and references are used. As an example, the `Node` class has a function called `GetController()` that returns a pointer to the controller which has been assigned to the node, and returns a `nullptr` if no controller has yet been assigned. Similar `Get` and `Set` functions are used to get and set pointers to any objects to which the node points. You can read about these functions here:
>
> http://www.terathon.com/c4engine/doco/WorldMgr/Node.html

The code above does however use OO code, in that `cout` is an "object" which is ready to use if you include the library `iostream`. The `cout` object hides all the details of working with outputting data to the console and other devices, so you don't have to worry about those details. The `cout` object also "overloads" the operator <<, which, if you have a pure C background, you will recognize as being a bitwise shift operator. So, this object called `cout` knows how to handle data of various types (strings, character arrays, floats, ints, etc.) and knows how to deal with special characters such as `\n`, and with special modifiers such as hexadecimal and octal (which are used to convert the format of subsequent numbers from the default, which is decimal).

What's a Class and What's an Object?

A class is a user-defined type. In C++, as in C and other languages, there are standard types intrinsic to the language, such as `float`, `long`, `int`, and `short`. C++, as an OO language, allows you to extend the available set of types to include types which more closely map to the description of the problem you are trying to solve. In a game, you might want types to describe your game "objects", such as your enemies, your player, your terrain, your weapons etc. So a class defines each type, by specifying not only which data is associated with that type, but also which behavior that type can perform. The functions of the class define this allowed behavior. In effect they define an interface to the objects of this type because they specify in detail which messages can be sent to and processed by objects of this type. The class provides the definition of your new type. The objects, which are also called "instances" of the class, are specific, well "instances" of the class.

As an analogy, you might have a description of a person in general—with data such as age, height, weight, skills, salary, etc., and behaviors such as talk, walk, see, eat, sleep, etc.—and that general description would correspond to the class. The objects would correspond to specific people, like say you friend, your teacher, your father or mother, the president, the janitor, etc.

In the abstract, your OO games and applications can be thought of as collections of specific objects which send messages to one another.

In the next section, we discuss the C4 Engine `Controller` class as an example of what OO programming entails and why it is useful.

Moving on to the C4 Engine

As an idea for how you might progress from text based games to games developed with the C4 Engine, you could use "3D Block Numbers" for a C4 Engine version of the guessing game–you might use keys to make your choice, and then the 3D Number might rotate to display that. Or you might click on the 3D number to make your guess. You could also extend the Hello World example on the C4 Engine Wiki, to create a C4 Engine version of the poker game from above. You might then create a 3D version of it with cards that get dealt around a table of players.

For an example of object-oriented programming with the C4 Engine, let's take a closer look at the C4 Engine `Controller` class and some of its subclasses. There are posts on the forums written like "you just have to make your own controller and do this and that in the Move function". To people who are used to OO programming, and especially to those who have worked for a while with the C4 Engine, this will make sense. But to those less familiar with OO and with the C4 Engine, it may sound overly complicated. So let's see what is meant by those statements.

"Make your own controller" means that you should make a subclass of the C4 Engine class called `Controller`, or any of its subclasses. The way to do this in code is with syntax like this:

```
class MySuperController : public Controller
{
   private:
```

```
    // private data and functions

  public:

    // public data and functions
};
```

As an example, a class called `ProjectileController` controls anything which should move in a projectile trajectory under the influence of gravity. When you fire a rocket launcher, you send a rocket, and rockets are controlled by code in a special subclass of `ProjectileController` called, you guessed it, `RocketController`.

This subclassing of from a generic class to more and more specific classes provides and example of what is known as *inheritance*, with each subclass inheriting the functionality and data of the parent class, but free to add data and functionality which the parent does not provide.

The private data and functions can only be accessed by objects of the class `MySuperController`, whereas the public data and function can also be accessed by other objects of other classes. In a header file, say `MyController.h`, you will declare the class, and in a `.cpp` file, say `MyControllers.cpp`, you will define the class and its function. This particular class requires that you must define your own version of certain functions, called *virtual functions*, an example being the `Move()` function. And it is there that you write the code that the controller should do each cycle, to move the node objects associated with that controller.

Much of what you will do when working with the C4 Engine is understanding and writing your own controllers. In fact, we would say that understanding controllers is the key to understanding the C4 Engine. You can comfortably associate a controller with a node using the **World Editor**, if you use code to "register" the controller with the **World Editor**. See the comments about the *SimpleBall* application later in this chapter, for the code needed to register a controller in this way. We also highly recommend that you read the wiki tutorial Defining a Custom Controller [WIKI08.08].

And finally, here is some sample code. It is called *SimpleBall*, and it is one of two tutorial applications delivered with the engine. We have added comments to those parts of the code which we think may need additional explanation for C++ beginners. We hope that the code will appear less intimidating after you have read through these explanations.

Note that the explanations within the code are marked as follows:

```
/* C++

<code snippet explanation>
*/
#include "SimpleBall.h"

/* C++
#include is a "preprocessor directive" - the preprocessor adds the
contents of the file "SimpleBall.h" directly into this file, before
this file is actually compiled to an object file.
*/

using namespace C4;

/* C++
To understand namespaces it is important to first understand
scope, which refers to regions where a particular name or
identifier is visible and can be used. There are several types of
scope, including:

* Namespace Scope declared inside a namespace
* Block Scope declared inside a block (with curly braces {}) -
also referred to as "local" scope
* Class Scope declared within a class (and is not in block scope)
* File Scope none of the above, and if not static then it is global
and can be accessed from anywhere.

Two different programmers on the same project might use the same
variable name (say "var").

Namespaces help us distinguish between the two.

If one programmer works in namespace1 and the other in namespace2
then we can access the variables safely with namespace1::var and
namespace2::var respectively.

By saying "using namespace C4", we don't have to write "C4::" in
front of everything that follows.

Note that "::" is called the "scope operator".
```

```
*/

// This is the definition of the pointer to the Game class
// singleton. It should be initialized to nullptr, and its value
// will be set by the Game class constructor.

/* C++
"Game"  is a class  which is declared  and defined in SimpleBall.h
TheGame (or  more precisely C4::theGame) is defined here to be a
pointer to a Game object.

It is initialized with the value nullptr, the NULL pointer.
*/

Game *C4::TheGame = nullptr;

// This is the definition of the pointer to the StartWindow class
// singleton. It should be initialized to nullptr, and its value
// will be set by the StartWindow class constructor.

StartWindow *C4::TheStartWindow = nullptr;

/* C++
ConstructApplication is a function. It returns a pointer to a
C4::Application object. You may say, "No!, it returns a "Game"
object!" - but below you will see that Game is a class that
inherits (or derives) from the Application class, i.e., "Game is an
Application".
*/
C4::Application *ConstructApplication(void)
{
   // This function should simply return a pointer to a new
instance of
   // the Application class. Normally, the application/game module
will
   // define a subclass of the Application class (in this case, the
   // Game class) and return a pointer to a new instance of that
type.

   // This function is called exactly one time right after the
```

```
    // application/game module DLL is loaded by the engine. The
returned
    // class is destroyed via the virtual destructor of the
Application
    // class right before the application/game module DLL is
unloaded.

/* C++
The function returns a new Game object (Remember that "Game" is
derived from "Application").
Note that "new Game" calls the default constructor for Game. You
don't need to add brackets as in "new Game()".
*/

    return (new Game);
}

/* C++
This is a constructor for the class "MovementAction", which is
declared in SimpleBall.h. The class derives from the C4 class
"Action" - that's why the line ends with " : Action(type)". This
constructor takes two arguments, called  type and flag, both
unsigned longs. When a new object of type MovementAction is
created, this constructor is called.

Below is an example of a call to this constructor:

forwardAction = new MovementAction(kActionForward,
kSpectatorMoveForward);

Note that  ":  Action(type)" means  that  the first parameter,
"type", (which in this example is "kActionForward"), is then used
when calling the constructor in the base class, Action.

In this example, the MovementAction member variable "movementFlag",
is  set to the value of "flag", which in this case is
"kSpectatorMoveForward".
*/

MovementAction::MovementAction(unsigned long type, unsigned long
```

```
flag) : Action(type)
{
   // Each instance of the MovementAction class represents a
movement
   // in a single direction, as indicated by the flag parameter.
   // All of the MovementAction instances are constructed in the
   // Game class constructor.

   movementFlag = flag;
}

/* C++
Destructor for MovementAction - a destructor gives the programmer a
chance to clean up before an object is destroyed.

Destructors can be called explicitly by the programmer but they are
also automatically called when an object goes out of scope.

By "clean up", we mean release memory or close any open network
or file resources.
*/

MovementAction::~MovementAction()
{
}

/* C++
"Begin" is a public function of the class MovementAction.

It returns nothing (that's why it starts with the word "void") and
it takes no arguments (that's why the word "void" is in brackets).
*/

void MovementAction::Begin(void)
{
   // This function is called when the input control associated
with this
   // particular action is activated (e.g., a key was pressed).

/* C++
```

```
This next line is interesting. Let's take it in pieces.

GameWorld *world = static cast<GameWorld *>(TheWorldMgr-
>GetWorld());

First of all, "world" is defined to be a pointer to a
"C4::GameWorld" object.

Now, at the end of this line of code we have "TheWorldMgr-
>GetWorld()". "TheWorldMgr" is defined and declared - in  an engine
file called  C4World.h - to be a pointer to a "C4::WorldManager"
object. And "GetWorld()" returns a "C4::World" object - the current
world in fact.

But why the arrow (->) between TheWorldMgr and GetWorld()? That
arrow is used to access data and functions of a pointer to an
object (in this case "TheWorldMgr").

If "TheWorldMgr" was simply a "C4::WorldManager" object - and not a
pointer  to  a "C4::WorldManager" object - then you would have
"TheWorldMgr.GetWorld()" instead of "TheWorldMgr->GetWorld()" to
access the function GetWorld().

The "." and "->" are called member selection operators: the dot is
used with objects and the arrow is used with pointers to objects.

Now, because TheWorldMgr->GetWorld() returns a "C4::World" and not
a "C4::GameWorld" object, we need to use a cast to convert the type
from a pointer to a C4::World to a pointer to a C4::GameWorld. The
static cast<> keyword is used for that, with the name of the target
type inside the angle brackets.
*/
   GameWorld *world = static cast<GameWorld *>(TheWorldMgr-
>GetWorld());

/* C++
If the TheWorldMgr->GetWorld() function returned a nullptr, then
this check would be false (and camera would not  get  defined).
*/
```

```
    if (world)
    {
        // If there's currently a world loaded, apply the movement to
        // the spectator camera.

/* C++
SpectatorCamera *camera = world->GetSpectatorCamera();

Here, camera is defined to be a pointer to a SpectatorCamera
object, the one which is returned by the call to
GetSpectatorCamera().

Again the arrow is used to access the function GetSpectatorCamera()
from the object world, because  world is  a pointer to a GameWorld -
and not an actual Gameworld itself.

GetSpectatorCamera() is declared in SimpleBall.h - it returns a
reference to a SpectatorCamera - "return (&spectatorCamera);"

So, rewritten it would be:
SpectatorCamera *camera = &GameWorld::spectatorCamera;

So, you would say "camera is a pointer to a SpectatorCamera object,
the one who's address is &GameWorld::spectatorCamera.

Or, you could say, "camera contains a reference to
GameWorld::spectatorCamera, which is the spectatorCamera for this
GameWorld".

When you see an "&" sign - think "address of" or "reference to".
*/
        SpectatorCamera *camera = world->GetSpectatorCamera();

/*C++
OK, now you have the a pointer to the spectatorCamera, set some
flags - the  movementFlag and the flags returned by
GetSpectatorFlags(), which are added together using the logical OR
operation (denoted "|").

The flags are typically  bits  that  you can "AND"  or "OR"
```

```
together.

For example,

bit 0, if set, has value 1; (00000001) 2 to the power of 0 = 1
bit 1, if set, has value 1: (00000010) 2 to the power of 1 = 2
bit 2, if set, has value 4: (00000100) 2 to the power of 2 = 4
bit 3, if set, has value 8: (00001000) 2 to the power of 3 = 8

and so on to
bit 7, if set, has value 128: (10000000) 2 to the power of 7 = 128

So, bit1 OR bit3 (written bit1 | bit3) has value 1 + 8 = 9 and
looks like 00001010

You typically use an "enum" to set  the values of these flags, so
that you can associate meaningful names with these numbers. e.g.

enum
{
   kSpectatorMoveForward = 1 << 0,
   kSpectatorMoveBackward = 1 << 1,
   kSpectatorMoveLeft = 1 << 2,
   //etc.
}

Here the "<<" is the shift operator and means for example that
The number 1 corresponds to the binary 00000001

// the number 1 with no bits shifted kSpectatorMoveForward =
00000001 = 1

// 1 with bit shifted 1 place to the left using
// the shift operator "<<" kSpectatorMoveBackward = 00000010 = 2

// 1 with bit shifted 2 places to the left using
// the shift operator "<<" kSpectatorMoveLeft = 00000100 = 4

The results is that the camera object will have the flags defined
by "camera->GetSpectatorFlags() | movementFlag" after the call to
```

```
SetSpectatorFlags below.
*/
      camera->SetSpectatorFlags(camera->GetSpectatorFlags() |
movementFlag);
   }
}

/* C++
Nothing new here: pointers, casting and member selection using "->"
*/

void MovementAction::End(void)
{
   // This function is called when the input control associated
with this
   // particular action is deactivated (e.g., a key was released).

   GameWorld *world = static cast<GameWorld *>(TheWorldMgr-
>GetWorld());
   if (world)
   {
      // If there's currently a world loaded, remove the movement
from
      // the spectator camera.

      SpectatorCamera *camera = world->GetSpectatorCamera();
/* C++
Here the  flags are  "AND"ed  together-as  an example:
00101000 & 00001000 results in 00001000 - AND  operation - only
when the same bit is set in both does it appear in the result
whereas:
00100000 | 00001000 results in 00101000 - OR operation - all bits
appear in the result.

Note that the tilde before movementFlag (~movementFlag) means "not
movementFlag"-the inverse of movementFlag.

So e.g. if movementFlag = 00010000 then ~movementFlag = 11101111
*/
      camera->SetSpectatorFlags(camera->GetSpectatorFlags() &
```

```
~movementFlag);
    }
}

/* C++
This is a constructor for the class BallController.

Remember that a constructor always has the same name as the class
itself. This constructor takes no arguments.

Now the class BallController inherits from another class, called
"RigidBodyController", which is part of the engine code-see
C4Physics.h and C4Physics.cpp.

By coding

: RigidBodyController(kControllerBall)

here, we are saying that the constructor of the parent
(or  base) class-RigidBodyController-should be called
first,  and that  the value kControllerBall should be passed into
that constructor.

There may be (and there are in fact) several constructors for the
class RigidBodyController. The one that is used here will have 1
argument, of type ControllerType.
*/

BallController::BallController() :
RigidBodyController(kControllerBall)
{
    // This constructor is only called when a new ball model is
created.
}

BallController::BallController(const BallController&
ballController) : RigidBodyController(ballController)
{
    // This constructor is called when a ball controller is cloned.
}
```

```
//C++ Destructor
BallController::~BallController()
{
}

Controller *BallController::Replicate(void) const
{
   return (new BallController(*this));
}

/* C++
This is a public function of the class BallController. Its
declaration in SimpleBall.h is:
static bool ValidNode(const Node *node);

The "const Node *node" in brackets must be read
from right to left - "node is a pointer to a Node constant".

This means that the node object which is passed into this function,
cannot be changed in the function. It is "read-only". If you try to
change it, for example with node->SetNodeName("MyNode");
then you will get a compiler error.

The return type here is bool (boolean, true or false). Below in the
implementation we have:

return (node->GetNodeType() == kNodeModel);

Now "return (a == b)" returns true if a equals b and false if a is
not equal to b.

Note that "return (a = b)" is different. In the brackets, you are
assigning the value of b to a and if that is allowed and works,
then a will equal b, and the result of the operation is  true-even
if a was'nt  equal to  b
before the operation.

And  finally, the static  keyword  in the declaration means that
the function can be called EVEN IF you dont have an instance of the
```

```
(in this case BallController) object. The way to call a static
member function (if you dont have
an object of the class) is using the class name and scope
operator, ClasName::staticMemberFunction() - in this case
BallController::ValidNode(node)

Note that static member functions can only call static member
functions and can only use static data members of the class.

Finally, "kNodeModel"  is defined in  C4Node.h - it is one of
several types of node defined in an "enum" or enumeration.

An enumeration is used to give understandable and useful names to
constant integer values.

eg.

enum fruit
{
apple, orange, pear, banana, peach
};

would assign the integer 0 to apple, 1 to orange and so on, up to 4
to peach. You would access apple by fruit::apple. Note that you
don't have to name the enum.

You can also assign values inside the enum like this:

enum
{
   apple = 10;
   orange,   // orange will automatically get the value 11
   pear = 30, // you can use the same value for two separate names
   banana = 30, // just the names must be unique
   peach = 40
};

In the engine, the enum names (like node type such as kNodeModel)
are set to 4 character literals like 'abcd', which evaluate to
integers.
```

```
Enums are preferred in C++ to using "#define" preprocessor
directive, because they obey the C++ scope rules.

You could also use "const int" or "static const int", but enum is
the preferred method for assigning names to constant integers in
C++.
*/

bool BallController::ValidNode(const Node *node)
{
   // This function is called by the engine to determine whether
   // this particular type of controller can control the particular
   // node passed in through the node parameter. This function
should
   // return true if it can control the node, and otherwise it
should
   // return false. In this case, the controller can only be
applied
   // to model nodes.

   return (node->GetNodeType() == kNodeModel);
}

void BallController::Preprocess(void)
{
   // This function is called once before the target node is ever
   // rendered or moved. The base class Preprocess() function
should
   // always be called first, and then the subclass can do whatever
   // preprocessing it needs to do. In this case, we set the ball's
   // coefficient of restitution.

   RigidBodyController::Preprocess();

   SetRestitutionCoefficient(0.95F);
}

RigidBodyStatus BallController::HandleNewRigidBodyContact(const
RigidBodyContact *contact, RigidBodyController *contactBody)
```

```
{
   // This function is called when the ball makes contact with
another rigid body.

   if (contactBody->GetControllerType() == kControllerBall)
   {
      // Add a sound effect and some sparks to the zone containing
the ball.
      // Transform the contact point into the zone's local
coordinate system.

      Node *node = GetTargetNode();
      Zone *zone = node->GetOwningZone();
      Point3D zonePosition = node->GetNodeTransform() * contact-
>GetContactPosition();

      OmniSource *source = new OmniSource("model/Ball", 40.0F);
      source->SetNodePosition(zonePosition);
      zone->AddNewSubnode(source);

      SparkParticleSystem *sparks = new SparkParticleSystem(20);
      sparks->SetNodePosition(zonePosition);
      zone->AddNewSubnode(sparks);
   }

   return (kRigidBodyUnchanged);
}

// The SparkParticleSystem and StartWindow implementation goes here

/* C++
This is the constructor for the GameWorld object. Again, name is
"read-only" in here. The " : " indicates that members of the object
are to be initialized with the values given.

The base (or parent) constructor - World(const  char  *name) - is
to be called with the value "name".

The member spectatorCamera is to be constructed with the float
values, 2.0f, 1.0f and 0.3f.
```

```
That constructor can be found in the engine class C4Cameras.cpp
*/

GameWorld::GameWorld(const char *name) :
      World(name),
      spectatorCamera(2.0F, 1.0F, 0.3F)
{
   // This constructor is called when the Game::ConstructWorld()
function is
   // called to create a new world class. The world hasn't actually
been loaded
   // from disk yet when we get here.
}

GameWorld::~GameWorld()
{
}

const LocatorMarker *GameWorld::FindSpectatorLocator(const Zone
*zone)
{
   // Iterate through all of the markers in the zone.

   const Marker *marker = zone->GetFirstMarker();
   while (marker)
   {
      if (marker->Enabled())
      {
         MarkerType type = marker->GetMarkerType();
         if (type == kMarkerLocator)
         {
            const LocatorMarker *locator = static cast<const
LocatorMarker *>(marker);

/* C++
First (marker)->GetLocatorType() is evaluated.

This function returns a "C4:LocatorType" which was cast into a
pointer to a LocatorMarker.
```

```
That is compared to kLocatorSpectator, which is defined as 'spec'
in SimpleBall.h
*/

            if (locator->GetLocatorType() == kLocatorSpectator)
return (locator);
         }
      }

/* C++
marker is a pointer to a C4::Marker (in this case constant) object-
from a few lines up:

const Marker *marker = zone->GetFirstMarker();

C4::Marker is defined in  the  engine code in  C4Markers.h as
follows:

class Marker : public Node, public ListElement<Marker>

So C4:Marker inherits from Node and represents a (marker) node in
the scene graph.

But C4::Marker also inherits from ListElement<class type>, which
basically means "is a" ListElement - and that means simply that a
marker can be stored in a list - Objects of type "ListElement" can
be stored in a List.

See C4List.h for more info on the class ListElement.

Note that the angle brackets above indicate that ListElement is a
template class. This basically means that the class needs only to
be defined once, but can generate a separate class on compilation,
depending on paramters you use for the class. In this example, the
type Marker is provided so we will get a ListElement object for
Markers. See more info on ListElement class in the API:

http://www.terathon.com/c4engine/doco/Utilities/ListElement.html
```

```
"The ListElement class should be declared as a base class for
objects that need to be stored in a list."

Now, marker itself doesn't have a function called Next(). But its
parent, ListElement, does.

And Next() returns a pointer to the the next marker in the list.
*/

        // Get the next marker in the list.
        marker = marker->Next();
    }

    // Look in all of the subzones.

    const Zone *subzone = zone->GetFirstSubzone();
    while (subzone)
    {
        const LocatorMarker *locator = FindSpectatorLocator(subzone);
        if (locator) return (locator);

        subzone = subzone->Next();
    }

    return (nullptr);
}

WorldResult GameWorld::Preprocess(void)
{
    // The Preprocess() function is called after the world has been
constructed.
    // We must always call the base class Preprocess() function
first.

    WorldResult result = World::Preprocess();
    if (result != kWorldOkay) return (result);

    // The world is now completely loaded. We search for a locator
node that represents the
    // spectator camera's starting position. It has a locator type
```

```
of kLocatorSpectator.

    const LocatorMarker *marker =
FindSpectatorLocator(GetRootNode());
    if (marker)
    {
        // A spectator marker was found.
        // Set the spectator camera's initial position and
orientation.

        const Vector3D direction = marker->GetWorldTransform()[0];
        float azimuth = Atan(direction.y, direction.x);
        float altitude = Atan(direction.z, Sqrt(direction.x *
direction.x + direction.y * direction.y));

/* C++
Here are examples of using the dot to access member functions.

Since spectatorCamera is an object of type SpectatorCamera, and not
a pointer to an object of that type, the dot is used to access the
member functions here and NOT the arrow (->).
*/

        spectatorCamera.SetCameraAzimuth(azimuth);
        spectatorCamera.SetCameraAltitude(altitude);
        spectatorCamera.SetNodePosition(marker->GetWorldPosition());
    }
    else
    {
        spectatorCamera.SetNodePosition(Point3D(0.0F, 0.0F, 1.0F));
    }

    // Set the world's current camera to be our spectator camera.
    // The world will not render without a camera being set.

    SetCamera(&spectatorCamera);

    return (kWorldOkay);
}
```

```
void GameWorld::Render(void)
{
   // This function is called once per frame to render the world.
   // The subclass may do whatever it needs to before or after
rendering,
   // but at some point must call World::Render().

   World::Render();
}

/* C++

The Game constructor again has the " : " to provide a list of
initializers separated by commas. See the declaration of the Game
class in SimpleBall.h. class Game : public Singleton<Game>, public
Application Game inherits from the Singleton template which means
that there will only be max one Game object. It also inherits from
Application.

These private data members of the Game Class private:

DisplayEventHandler displayEventHandler;
ModelRegistration ballModelReg;
ControllerReg<BallController> controllerReg;
ParticleSystemReg<SparkSystem> sparkSystemReg;
LocatorRegistration locatorReg;

are all initialized here in the constructor
(behind the " : " and before the first curly brace "{".
*/

Game::Game() :

      // This is the constructor for the main application/game
module class.
      // This class is constructed by the ConstructApplication()
function,
      // which is called right after the application/game DLL is
loaded by
      // the engine. There is only one instance of this class, so
```

```
it inherits
        // from the Singleton template, which we initialize first.

        Singleton<Game>(TheGame),

        // The display event handler encapsulates a function that
gets called
        // when the Display Manager changes something like the screen
resolution.

        displayEventHandler(&HandleDisplayEvent),

        // A model registration represents a model that can be
instanced.
        // This particular declaration associates the kModelBall type
with the
        // model named "model/Ball.mdl". The fourth parameter tells
the engine
        // to pre-cache the model resource, and the last parameter
specifies
        // the default controller type to assign to models of type
kModelBall.

        ballModelReg(kModelBall, "Bouncing Ball", "model/Ball",
kModelPrecache, kControllerBall),

        // A controller registration tells the engine about an
application-defined
        // type of controller and registers its name and validation
function.
        // In this case, the name "Bouncing Ball" will appear in the
list of
        // available controllers in the World Editor for any node
that is determined
        // to be a valid target node by the
BallController::ValidNode() function.

        controllerReg(kControllerBall, "Bouncing Ball"),

        // A particle system registration tells the engine about an
```

```
application-defined
        // type of particle system and registers its name.

        sparkParticleSystemReg(kParticleSystemSpark, "Sparks"),

        // Locator markers are registered so that the World Editor
        // can display their names in the Get Info dialog box.

        locatorReg(kLocatorSpectator, "Spectator Camera")
{
    // This installs an event handler for display events. This is
only
    // necessary if we need to perform some action in response to
    // display events for some reason.

    TheDisplayMgr->InstallDisplayEventHandler(&displayEventHandler);

    // This sets the function that is called when the user hits the
    // escape key during gameplay. We save the old function so that
    // it can be restored when the game DLL is unloaded.

    prevEscapeProc = TheInputMgr->GetEscapeProc();
    prevEscapeCookie = TheInputMgr->GetEscapeCookie();
    TheInputMgr->SetEscapeProc(&EscapeProc, this);

    // This registers our world class constructor with the World
Manager.
    // We only need to do this if we have defined a subclass of the
World
    // class that holds extra information.

    TheWorldMgr->SetWorldConstructor(&ConstructWorld);

    // These create the movement actions that are used to fly the
    // spectator camera around.

    forwardAction = new MovementAction(kActionForward,
kSpectatorMoveForward);
    backwardAction = new MovementAction(kActionBackward,
kSpectatorMoveBackward);
```

```
    leftAction = new MovementAction(kActionLeft,
kSpectatorMoveLeft);
    rightAction = new MovementAction(kActionRight,
kSpectatorMoveRight);
    upAction = new MovementAction(kActionUp, kSpectatorMoveUp);
    downAction = new MovementAction(kActionDown,
kSpectatorMoveDown);

    // These register our new actions with the Input Manager.

    TheInputMgr->AddAction(forwardAction);
    TheInputMgr->AddAction(backwardAction);
    TheInputMgr->AddAction(leftAction);
    TheInputMgr->AddAction(rightAction);
    TheInputMgr->AddAction(upAction);
    TheInputMgr->AddAction(downAction);

    // Let the Interface Manager determine when to change input
devices to gameplay mode.

    TheInterfaceMgr-
>SetInputManagementMode(kInputManagementAutomatic);

    // Put the Message Manager in single-player mode.

    TheMessageMgr->BeginSinglePlayerGame();

    // Create the start window and tell the Interface Manager to
display it.

    TheInterfaceMgr->AddWidget(new StartWindow);
}

Game::~Game()
{
    // When the game DLL is about to be unloaded, this destructor is
called.

    TheWorldMgr->UnloadWorld();
    TheWorldMgr->SetWorldConstructor(nullptr);
```

```
   // If the start window exists, delete it. We need to do this
here, instead of letting the
   // Interface Manager clean it up, because the destructor code
for the window is in this DLL.

   delete TheStartWindow;

   // Tell the Message Manager to clean up.

   TheMessageMgr->EndGame();

   delete downAction;
   delete upAction;
   delete rightAction;
   delete leftAction;
   delete backwardAction;
   delete forwardAction;

   // Restore the previous escape key handling function.

   TheInputMgr->SetEscapeProc(prevEscapeProc, prevEscapeCookie);
}

World *Game::ConstructWorld(const char *name, void *cookie)
{
   // This function is called when a new world is being loaded.
   // It should return a pointer to a newly constructed subclass
   // of the World class.

   return (new GameWorld(name));
}

void Game::HandleDisplayEvent(const DisplayEventData *eventData,
void *cookie)
{
   // This function is called when a display event occurs (because
   // we registered it in the Game constructor).

   if (eventData->eventType == kEventDisplayChange)
```

```
    {
        // The screen resolution has changed. Handle accordingly.
    }
}

void Game::EscapeProc(void *cookie)
{
    // This function is called when the user hits the escape key in
    // gameplay mode because we registered it using the
    // InputMgr::SetEscapeProc() function.
}
```

B

FAQ

Frequently Asked Questions

In the World Editor, why can't I move, scale, rotate, or select a node?

Make sure you have selected the correct node manipulation tool along the top edge of the **World Editor** window, as shown in Figure B-1.

Figure B-1. Node manipulation tools in the **World Editor**.

To move nodes, select the **Move Nodes (2)** tool.

Similarly, to select, rotate, or scale nodes, select the corresponding **Select Nodes**, **Rotate Nodes**, or **Scale Nodes** tool button.

You can also choose **Page > Visibility** and **Page > Selection Mask** to open page panels to help you manage scene picking when you need to select and manipulate specific types of nodes, as shown in Figure B-2.

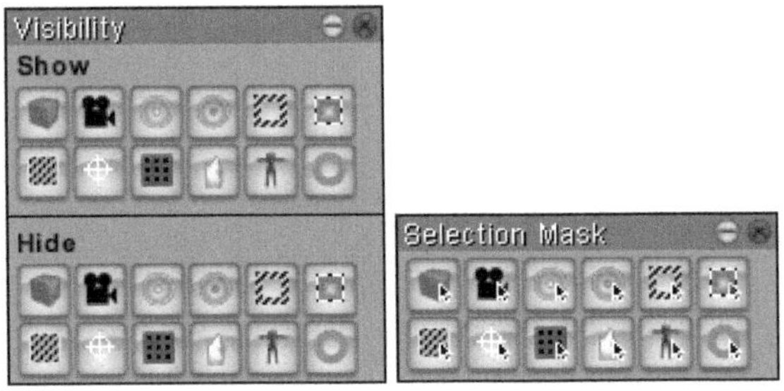

Figure B-2. The **Visibility** and **Selection Mask** page panels.

It is also helpful to open the scene graph in one of the viewports by right-clicking and choosing **Scene Graph**. In a viewport showing the scene graph, you can left-click any node to select it (unless selection of that node type has been disabled by the **Selection Mask** settings). You can also move nodes in a scene graph viewport if the **Move Nodes (2)** tool is selected.

To organize nodes into groups, to more easily manage large numbers of nodes, in the scene graph, drag a node to make it a child of another node.

How do I access forums that are only available to the C4 Engine licensees?

The e-mail that is sent to you that contains your C4 license information includes instructions for joining the Licensed Users group, which gives you access to the private forums. These forums are a place where licensees can discuss internal engine source code, ask questions about potential and existing bugs with the engine, as well as propose and promote new engine features.

How do I get access to Beta releases of new builds of the C4 Engine?

All standard licensees (and higher) have access to C4 Beta releases. Beta releases are meant to catch any last minute major bugs that may appear in normal user workflow before the final release of a C4 Engine build.

Why am I seeing a Hall of Mirrors effect in my world?

This is called "smearing." This happens when no geometry is being drawn to the frame buffer. The "smeared" image is a result of previous renderings to the frame buffer. This can be fixed by either specifying skybox textures or a clear color to do a full refresh of the frame buffer.

How do I import 3D models for use with the C4 Engine?

Your 3D model needs to be exported from your 3D modeling program into the Collada file format. It is also possible to export your model into an intermediate format, and then convert it to the Collada format. Blender for example, can read in most formats, and can then export the model to Collada. FBXConverter can also be used to convert from the FBX file format to Collada.

What is the difference between using a Model from the Models page and using the World > Insert Model command?

As a level designer, the primary method for placing models in your world is to select a model from the list in the **Models** page panel and then place it in your world by simply clicking in one of the viewports. In the C4 Engine, a model is represented by a `.mdl` file. Its contents are similar to a `.wld` file, but instead of the root node being the infinite zone, the model file's root node is a model node.

Why is my character model much larger (or smaller) than the Soldier model in the SimpleChar project?

Check the unit scale that you are working with in your 3D modeling program and in your Collada exporter. You may be working with a different unit system than the system that the C4 Engine uses. The C4 Engine uses an arbitrary unit size. 3D modeling programs may allow you to change unit size, but it really depends on which program you are using.

Why does my model have dark "rays" shooting out of it and projecting onto the ground?

The model you imported is not a closed mesh. This means that your mesh has at least one polygon that does not share an edge with another polygon. Make sure there are no holes in the geometry. 3D modeling programs achieve this in different ways, so you will have to refer to the manual for your modeling program to do this. The dark rays are the stencil shadows that cannot be calculated correctly due to an opened mesh.

Why does my model look like its vertices are scattered all over the place when I import it WITH a skeleton, but looks fine when I import it WITHOUT a skeleton?

Your model has some vertices that are not bound to the skeleton. When importing a model with a skeleton, it is assumed that all vertices are assigned to the skeleton, so that the skeleton influences each vertex of the model in some way. If by chance there are some vertices that are not attached to the skeleton, their positional data is not initialized, resulting in vertices being scattered around the world.

Why does my model disappear after I press the play button in the Model Viewer?

This commonly happens when the **Model Viewer** starts an animation that has a skeleton that is different from the skeleton that is used with the static geometry for the model. Make sure that the skeleton that is used in the animation matches exactly to the skeleton that you used with the static geometry. Things to look out for are the hierarchical relationship between the joints and the names of the joints. The best way to do this is to simply copy the static geometry file that contains the final skeleton, and start the animations from this skeleton. This guarantees that the skeletons in the static geometry file and the animation file match.

Why does my model look washed out, with super bright highlights?

It's likely that the value of the **Specular Exponent** setting is too low, as a result of the model being imported with a material that has a default value of 1.0, which results in a very wide area of specularity that washes out the diffuse color.

This problem can be corrected by either deselecting the **Specular Color** option, or by increasing the value of the **Specular Exponent** setting. Both of these settings can be found on the **Specular** tab panel in the **Material Manager** window.

How come my textures don't appear on my model after I have imported it? I only see a blue texture with green X's.

These issues can be caused by a number of reasons. We'll step through each one here:

- The C4 Engine cannot find the texture files `.tex` that are associated with your model. Make sure that you have imported the textures that your models use before importing, so that the models know where the texture files are. Another possibility that your textures aren't showing up is that the path to the texture in the Collada file may not match the same path that you have imported the textures to. Verify that the path to the texture matches the path associated in the model.

- Are your textures in a subdirectory of the Data directory? Texture files that reside at the root level Data directory will not be recognized. They have to be placed in at least a subdirectory of the Data directory. (For more details, see Understanding the C4 Virtual File System in Chapter 2, "Installation".)

- Are your textures imported? Your textures have to be in the `.tex` file format. This can be done by importing your `.tga` files into the C4 Engine using the **Texture Importer** tool. Then, the geometry must have a material assigned to it. In the **World Editor**, the **Material Manager** window can be used to create a material and assign your textures to it. (For details, see Chapter 7, "Material Manager".)

- Are your textures in a subdirectory that matches the path referenced in the material? The path to the texture may be broken or missing. The way to check this is to find the material that is being used by your geometry in the **Material Manager**. Select the **Diffuse** tab panel and verify the path to the texture file. You can either click the texture file picker control to open the texture selection dialog and reselect the texture, or you can type in the path to the texture file directly.

- Is the **Collada Importer** set up to automatically import textures? The **Collada Importer** allows you to specify if you would like the associated textures to be imported along with your geometry. Make sure this option is enabled if you would like your textures to automatically appear in the world.

Why is it a bad idea to use SetWorldTransform()?

`SetWorldTransform()` is a function used internally by the engine. Using the `SetWorldTransform()` function will directly interfere with any `Update()` calls that the engine performs when using this function. Instead, use `SetNodeTransform()`. See Part III • Under the Hood for more details on this subject.

What is the difference between a model and a geometry?

A model is a node of type `kNodeModel` and a geometry is a node of type `kNodeGeometry`. Like any other node, transformations applied to a model also affects the transformations of its subnodes. Typically, a model contains at least one geometry, but models can actually contain any number of subnodes of any type, not just geometry nodes.

You can assign controllers to both model nodes and geometry nodes, but there are some behaviors that a model has that a geometry does not. A model node can have an animator tree attached to it so that you can play and blend animation files. Also, a model will automatically reparent itself to the zone that it is currently contained in. So, while a controller can still be assigned to a geometry node, its functionality is limited in comparison to a controller assigned to a model.

Why do my animation files not show up in the animation list in the Model Viewer?

An animation shows up in the **Model Viewer** only if the `.anm` file resides in the same directory as the source `.mdl` file. Note that it is possible to import and use `.anm` files in any subdirectory in the virtual file system, but only those in the same directory as the source `.mdl` file will appear in the animation list in the **Model Viewer**.

Why do I get the following error when trying to compile my project? LINK : fatal error LNK1104: cannot open file 'C4.lib'

This error can be caused in several ways, but ultimately, this error indicates that your DLL project cannot finish linking because it could not find `C4.lib`. Here are a couple of possible reasons:

- Your project has an incorrect path to `C4.lib`. Double-check in the **Project Properties** dialog that you have specified a correct path to `C4.lib` in the **Additional Library Directories** field. One way you can check this is by looking at the build log for your project. When Visual Studio generates an error, it creates a file named `BuildLog.html` that you can access by clicking on the link in the **Output** window. You can then inspect all the paths that were used to compile your project. This is the common reason why your project cannot compile.

- The C4 Engine didn't compile correctly. If this is the case, `C4.lib` was not generated, so your project couldn't find the file because it doesn't exist. Find the reason why the engine did not compile and fix it to generate `C4.lib`.

Why am I encountering a crash when I exit from my game?

There are many reasons why your game could cause the C4 Engine can crash on exit, but it is very common that a crash occurs because memory that was previously allocated is not being deallocated. If, at one point, you used the new operator to create a UI element or some other object in your code, and then neglected use the delete operator to clean it up when shutting down, the C4 Engine can issue an error indicating that you have not cleaned up all of the memory that you have used. It's good practice to add code to free objects (usually in the destructor function of a containing class) for each use of the new operator.

Why am I encountering a crash when I start up C4?

There are a number of reasons why the C4 Engine may crash on startup. After diagnosing your code and ruling out that it wasn't any of your own changes that may have crashed C4 Engine, see if the crash is related to any of these common reasons:

- **Missing Data.** A common cause of a C4 Engine is that the engine or your application code may simply be trying to read data that is not there. Double-check that the data that you are trying to read actually exists, and that it is not corrupted.
- **Improper Initialization.** You've probably run through your code over and over again, but it doesn't hurt to try to keep running through your initialization code again. Make sure you are not doing any improper type casting, or incorrectly allocating memory. Also, make sure to check any modification you have made in the C4 Engine source code. It usually helps to retrace your steps and comment out code that you have just written, to narrow down the possibilities. There is nothing like plain-old engineering using the scientific method to track down and solve the problems you are having in your code.
- **Differing compiled library targets.** When compiling your code, there is a possibility that the DLLs for the C4 Engine and/or your project are not compiled for the same target configuration. For instance, some of the DLLs may have been compiled under the **Optimized** configuration while others have been compiled under the **Debug** configuration. It is not recommended to mix DLLs of differing output configurations. If you think this may be the case, try building all the projects that are used by your application, including the C4 engine itself. There may also be some cases in which some library files are missing. Note that the engine prevents a crash from happening this way now. You will see an error message from Windows when you start, but then the engine will run without the mismatched DLL.

Can the C4 Engine be used to create an RTS?

It is possible to create a Real-Time Strategy (RTS) game with the C4 Engine. Chapter 20, "RTS – Creating a Game from Scratch", includes a tutorial game that covers the basic concepts that are used in an RTS. However, the concepts in that chapter are geared towards illustrating the usage of the C4 Engine API rather than how to properly construct a professional-level RTS game.

One issue to consider when creating an RTS with the C4 Engine is that overhead RTS games may not be able to take advantage of the C4 Engine portal system, as do First-Person or Third-Person Action/Adventure games. From an overhead view, most of the rendering is done on a surface that is almost always visible. It's possible to use occlusion portals for larger units and possibly even UI components to prevent rendering some units underneath those areas.

How do I output debugging info?

Outputting debugging information to the screen or to a log file is one of the fundamental debugging methods available to any programmer. There are multiple methods to output debugging text in a C4 Engine application:

If you want to output text to the **Command Console** window:

```
Engine::Report("blah blah blah");
```

If you want to write data to the log file:

```
Engine::Report("blah blah blah", kReportLog);
```

If you are working in the demo game code and you would like to print text to the chat message display:

```
TheMessageInterface->AddText("blah blah blah");
```

Now we can ask the **Command Console** window to output text information from our application! But, `AddText()` only accepts text. How about printing other basic data types to the **Command Console** window? The `Text` name space in the C4 Engine contains several functions for converting non-text basic data types into text. Here are a couple of examples:

```
Text::FloatToString()
Text::IntegerToString()
```

How do I change the icon for the C4.exe application file?

It is possible to change `C4.exe` to any file name you wish, as long as it keeps the `.exe` file extension. You can also change its icon. However, these changes are usually made when you are almost done with your game, and so are considered beyond the scope of this book. There is a thread on the C4 Engine forums, "Changing C4.exe Icon", at the following address, which explains this topic in more detail.

```
http://www.terathon.com/forums/viewtopic.php?t=1730
```

C

Using Blender with the C4 Engine

Blender is sometimes criticized for being difficult to use, and for being unintuitive. It does take some getting used to. This appendix summarizes the essentials for users who are just getting started with Blender.

Download Blender for Free

We offer this crash course for people who haven't yet tried to use Blender, or who did try, but gave up immediately because it seemed too difficult to use. If you haven't done so already, you can download Blender for free from the Blender Foundation web site at:

http://www.blender.org/download/get-blender/

Online, there are hundreds of tutorials, including videos. A number of tutorials are available on the Tutorials section of the Blender web site:

http://www.blender.org/education-help/tutorials/

Essential Tips for Using Blender

- Move between object and edit modes by pressing the Tab key. Use object mode to move, rotate, and scale whole objects. Use edit mode to manipulate individual vertices, edges, and faces of objects.

- Select objects with the right and not with the left mouse button. Get into the habit of clicking with the right mouse button.
- Pressing A will select all. Press A again to deselect all. Selected objects are pink. If you do want to use the left button, then press B first, and then left-click to box select a set of objects (when in object mode) or vertices (when in edit mode).
- Move selected objects by first pressing G, rotate them by first pressing R, and scale them by first pressing the S.
- You can restrict the axes of manipulation by selecting the X, Y, or Z keys. Shift-X, Y, or Z would mean "restrict to all except for" those directions.
- Press 1, 3, or 7 on the numeric keypad to move between the front, side, and top views.
- Use the middle mouse button to rotate the view, and Shift-middle mouse button to pan.
- Press zero on the numeric keypad to show the camera view.

Getting Started

You can delete the default cube in Blender by first selecting it in object mode with a right click and then pressing the X key. Then, from the menu, choose **Add > Mesh > Cube** to add the cube again. Once created, the object is selected. Press the Tab key to enter edit mode, so you can manipulate the vertices of the object itself. Press A a few times to select or deselect all vertices.

When all are selected, for fun, choose **W > Subdivide**. Press A to deselect all vertices, then press B to select all of the vertices on any one side. Finally, press E to extrude that "region" away from the object.

Using Blender to Import Free Models from the Web into the C4 Engine

If you need a model for your games but don't have the time or money to create or buy it, have a look at sites like turbosquid.com. There are many free 3D models which you can download, then import into Blender, and then export as Collada for use with the C4 Engine.

Here is an example of how to obtain a tank model for use in the *SimpleCar* tutorial in Chapter 18, "SimpleCar".

1 Point your browser to www.turbosquid.com.

2 In the **Quick Search** box, type free tank, and then choose **3D Models** from the **Product Types** list.

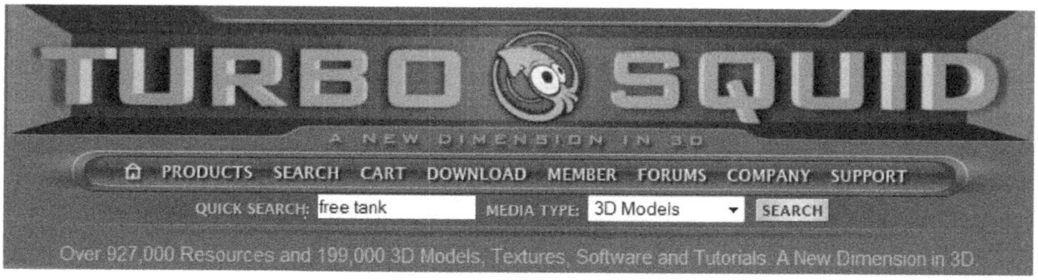

Figure C-1. The Turbosquid site is a good place to find 3D models, many of which are free of charge.

3 Look for a 3ds model, because they easily imported into Blender. We chose the A17 Light Tank Mk VII (Tetrarch) model by the author lemonsong.[1]

4 Click **Download**. You may need to log in or register if you haven't done so already.

5 Save the model to a local directory.

6 Start Blender. You can delete the default cube in Blender by pressing the X key.

7 Choose **File > Import > 3D Studio (3ds)** to import the model you just downloaded.

9 With the imported tank model still selected, export it to the Collada format using **File > Export > Collada (.dae)**.

10 Choose a location to save the exported `.dae` file, preferably directly in a subdirectory of the <C4>/Import/ directory, because that is where the C4 Engine will look for Collada files to import.

12 Click **Export and Close**. You have converted the 3ds file to Collada format, ready to import for use with the C4 Engine.

13 Copy the `.dae` file you just created into a subdirectory of the <C4>/Import/ directory, if it isn't there already.

---

[1] http://www.turbosquid.com/FullPreview/Index.cfm/ID/244264

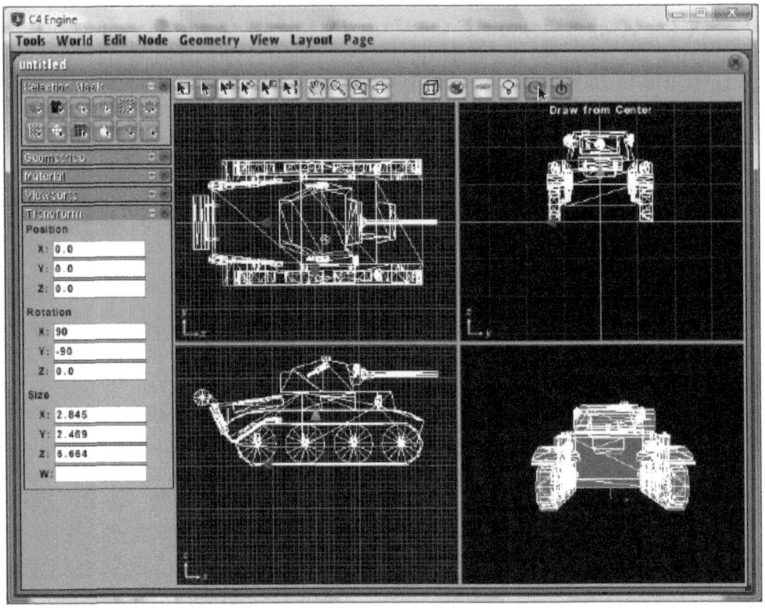

Figure C-2. The tank after being imported, rotated, and scaled in the C4 Engine **World Editor**.

14 Start up C4, then create a new world by choosing **Tools > New World (Ctrl-N)**.

15 Choose **World > Import Scene**, and select your `tank.dae` model. Select the **Import texture maps** option only, and then click OK.

16 Rotate your model so that you can see it from the top in the *x-y* viewport, and so it is facing along the *x* axis. Use the **Transform** page panel to round off numbers like 89 degrees to 90 degrees.

17 Position the model at 0.0 for X, Y, and Z. If the X, Y, and Z sizes are more than 10, then scale the model sizes down by a factor of about 10 in each direction. The tank model should appear as shown in Figure C-2.

18 Select the geometry node of the tank and then choose **Node > Get Info (Ctrl-I)** to open the **Node Info** dialog, and make sure that the settings on the **Collision** tab panel are set like those shown in Figure C-3.

19 Open the Physics page from the World Editor menu, and completely enclose the geometry of your model with a physics box shape, as shown in Figure C-4.

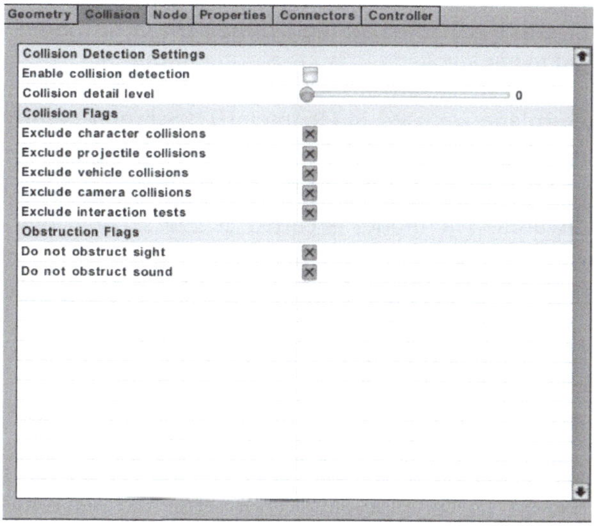

Figure C-3. The **Collision** tab panel settings for your tank model.

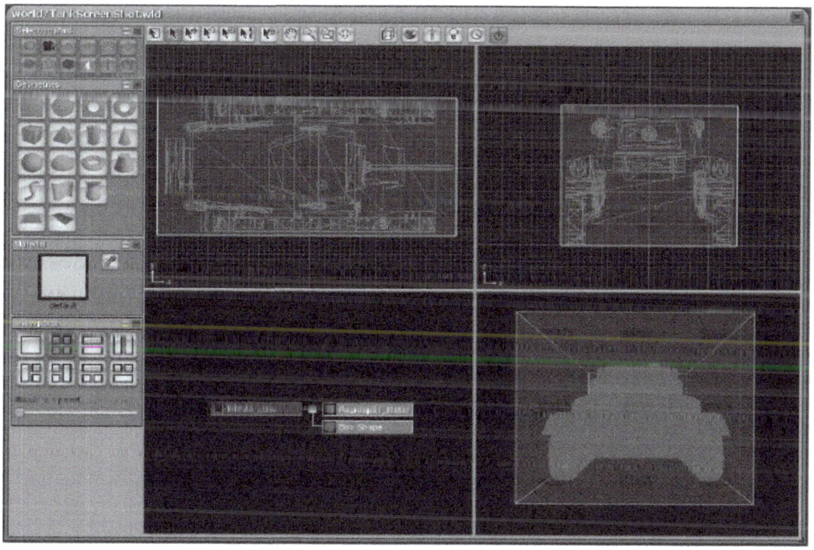

Figure C-4. Surround your model with a physics box shape.

20 After you have adjusted the settings for your model, choose **World > Save as Model** to save it as TankShapeModel, under the Tutorial/model/ directory.

The airplane we used in Chapter 19, "SimpleEnemies" was also downloaded from TurboSquid. You can find it by searching for "free plane" under the **3D Models** category. You will find this model more quickly if you search by the author eminyaren. The model is called `fw190.blend`, but strangely you'll see that the actual downloaded file is called `pirpir.blend`. Once you obtain the model, follow these steps to prepare it for use with the C4 Engine:

21 Since the file is already in the blender format, you can directly open it with blender—you don't need to import it. Right-click to select only the body of the plane for exporting. Again, selected objects in blender have a pink outline.

22 Export the file as a Collada (`.dae`) file and place the result in a subdirectory of your <C4>/Import/ directory.

23 Import the model into the **World Editor** by choosing **World > Import Scene**. Deselect all checkboxes in the dialog.

24 Scale up and rotate the model in the **World Editor** as you did for the tank model, as shown in Figure C-5.

25 Choose **World-> Save Model As**, and save the plane PlaneModel in the Tutorial/model/ directory.

Some models you get from the web might not be closed and the shadows will seem strange. If or when you become skilled with Blender, or with any other modeling tool of your choice, you can edit the vertices and patch any holes in the model.

26 If you encounter such an issue, you can switch off shadows for the model by choosing **Node > Get Info (Ctrl-I)** to open the **Node Info** dialog, and deselecting the **Render stencil shadow** option.

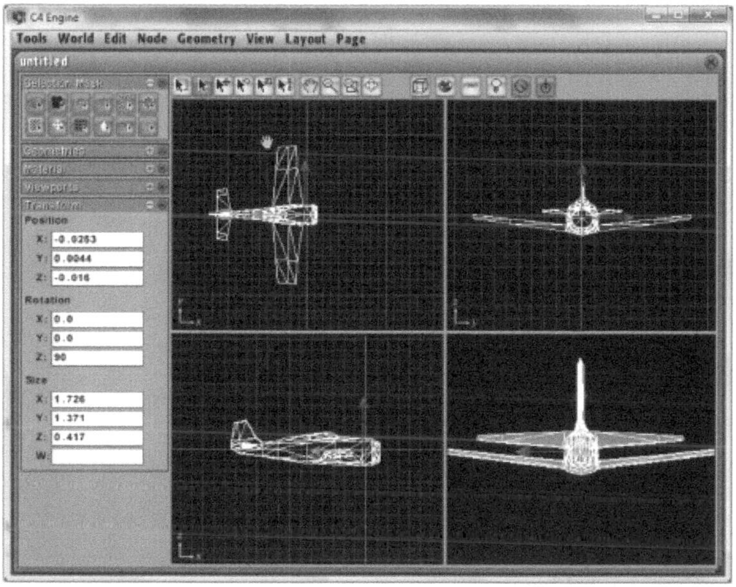

Figure C-5. Rotating and resizing the plane model in the C4 Engine **World Editor**. The position values still need to be set to zero.

D

The C4 Engine Architecture

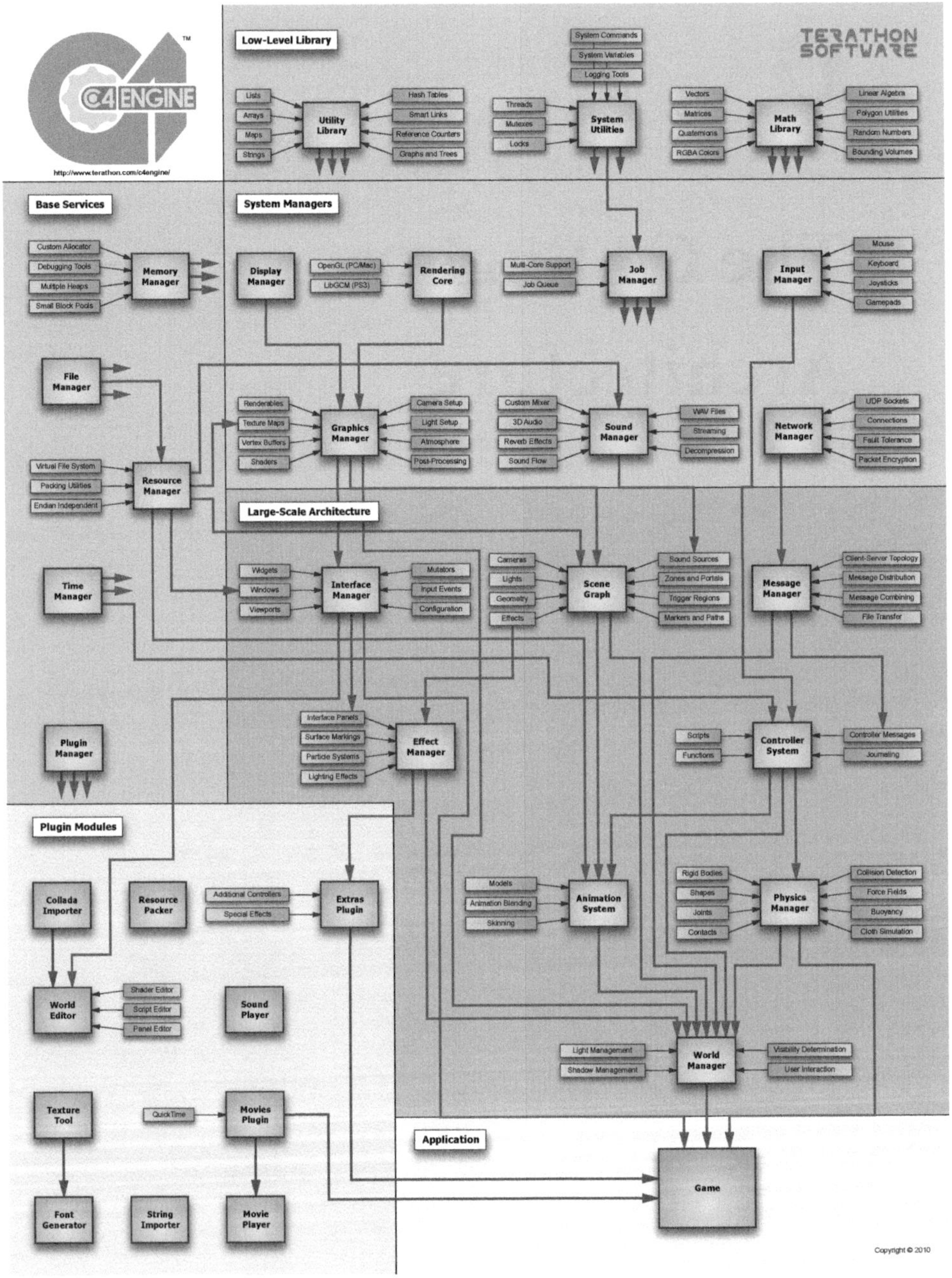
C4 ENGINE
http://www.terathon.com/c4engine/
TERATHON SOFTWARE
Low-Level Library
Lists
Arrays
Maps
Strings
Utility Library
Hash Tables
Smart Links
Reference Counters
Graphs and Trees
System Commands
System Variables
Logging Tools
Threads
Mutexes
Locks
System Utilities
Vectors
Matrices
Quaternions
RGBA Colors
Math Library
Linear Algebra
Polygon Utilities
Random Numbers
Bounding Volumes
Base Services
Custom Allocator
Debugging Tools
Multiple Heaps
Small Block Pools
Memory Manager
System Managers
Display Manager
OpenGL (PC/Mac)
LibGCM (PS3)
Rendering Core
Multi-Core Support
Job Queue
Job Manager
Input Manager
Mouse
Keyboard
Joysticks
Gamepads
File Manager
Renderables
Texture Maps
Vertex Buffers
Shaders
Graphics Manager
Camera Setup
Light Setup
Atmosphere
Post-Processing
Custom Mixer
3D Audio
Reverb Effects
Sound Flow
Sound Manager
WAV Files
Streaming
Decompression
Network Manager
UDP Sockets
Connections
Fault Tolerance
Packet Encryption
Virtual File System
Packing Utilities
Endian Independent
Resource Manager
Large-Scale Architecture
Time Manager
Widgets
Windows
Viewports
Interface Manager
Mutators
Input Events
Configuration
Cameras
Lights
Geometry
Effects
Scene Graph
Sound Sources
Zones and Portals
Trigger Regions
Markers and Paths
Message Manager
Client-Server Topology
Message Distribution
Message Combining
File Transfer
Plugin Manager
Interface Panels
Surface Markings
Particle Systems
Lighting Effects
Effect Manager
Scripts
Functions
Controller System
Controller Messages
Journaling
Plugin Modules
Collada Importer
Resource Packer
Additional Controllers
Special Effects
Extras Plugin
Models
Animation Blending
Skinning
Animation System
Rigid Bodies
Shapes
Joints
Contacts
Physics Manager
Collision Detection
Force Fields
Buoyancy
Cloth Simulation
World Editor
Shader Editor
Script Editor
Panel Editor
Sound Player
Light Management
Shadow Management
World Manager
Visibility Determination
User Interaction
Texture Tool
QuickTime
Movies Plugin
Application
Game
Font Generator
String Importer
Movie Player
Copyright © 2010

References

APPL12 "Developer Tools", Apple, 2012. https://developer.apple.com/technologies/tools/

BLEN08 "Blender", Blender Foundation, 2008. http://www.blender.org/

BUND08 "L3DT", BundySoft, 2008. http://www.bundysoft.com/L3DT/

COLL08 "Collada," The Khronos Group, 2008. http://www.collada.org/

COOK82 Robert L. Cook and Kenneth E. Torrance, "A Reflectance Model for Computer Graphics", ACM Transactions on Graphics Vol. 1, No. 1, Association of Computing Machinery, January 1982, 7–24. http://www.amazon.com/Transactions-Graphics-Vol-January-1982/dp/B001ARXKBI

DEVM12 "DevDB Engines", DevMaster.Net, 2012. http://devmaster.net/devdb/engines

EBER05 David H. Eberly, 3D Game Engine Architecture, Morgan Kaufmann Publishers, 2005. http://www.amazon.com/Game-Engine-Design-Second-Interactive/dp/0122290631/

LENG11 Eric Lengyel, Mathematics for 3D Game Programming and Computer Graphics, 3rd ed., Cengage Learning, 2011. http://www.mathfor3dgameprogramming.com/

MEYE05 Scott Meyers, Effective C++, Addison-Wesley Professional, 2005. http://www.amazon.com/Effective-Specific-Addison-Wesley-Professional-Computing/dp/0321334876

MSFT10 "Visual C++ 2010 Express Edition", Microsoft, 2010. http://www.microsoft.com/visualstudio/en-us/products/2010-editions/visual-cpp-express

MSFT12a "XAudio2", Microsoft, 2012. http://msdn.microsoft.com/en-us/library/ee415813%28v=vs.85%29.aspx

MSFT12b "XBox 360 Controller", Microsoft, 2012. http://www.microsoft.com/hardware/en-us/p/xbox-360-controller-for-windows/52A-00004

MSFT12c "XInput", Microsoft, 2008. http://msdn.microsoft.com/en-us/library/ee416996%28v=vs.85%29.aspx

PHYS08 "PhysX by NVidia," NVidia, 2008. http://www.nvidia.com/object/nvidia_physx.html

SANC03 Daniel Sanchez-Crespo, Core Techniques and Algorithms in Game Programming, New Riders, 2003. http://www.amazon.com/Techniques-Algorithms-Programming-Riders-Games/dp/0131020099

STRO00 Bjarne Stroustrup, The C++ Programming Language, Addison-Wesley Professional, 2000. http://www.amazon.com/C-Programming-Language-Special-3rd/dp/0201700735

TAPI08a "class Tree", Terathon Software, 2008. http://www.terathon.com/c4engine/doco/Utilities/Tree.html

About the Authors

James Brady (forum handle **jimbobjames**), holds a B.E. in Electronic Engineering. Since graduating in 1991, he has worked as a consultant and project manager on IT projects in Brazil, Venezuela, Peru, Colombia, the United States, Ireland, England, Iran, France, the Netherlands, Norway, Germany, Austria, Spain, and Turkey. Outside of work, his passions include physics and 3D game programming, and he has been programming computer games as a hobby for more than 20 years.

A.A. Cruz (forum handle **a2k**), has a B.S. in Computer Engineering and has been programming games and game-related applications for about eleven years. He is also a long-time game mod developer, and has experience in popular paint programs and 3D modeling and animation packages.

James Huntsman (forum handle **JamesH**), is a long-time C4 Engine licensee, who is perhaps best known for his integration of the PhysX physics library with the C4 Engine. When he's away from his computer and on holiday, James enjoys alpine snowboarding.

David Vasquez is perhaps best known for developing a Collada exporter for Luxology's modo 3D modeling and rendering tool—enabling designers to establish a pipeline between modo and the C4 Engine—as well as for building the Material Showroom, a collection of procedurally-generated materials.

Made in the USA
Middletown, DE
26 September 2026

33817763R00329